ADVANCED ADOBE® PHOTOSHOP® CS3 REVEALED

ADVANCED ADOBE® PHOTOSHOP® CS3 REVEALED

Chris Botello

COURSE TECHNOLOGY
CENGAGE Learning™

Advanced Adobe® Photoshop® CS3—Revealed
Chris Botello

Vice President, Career and Professional Editorial: David Garza

Director of Learning Solutions: Sandy Clark

Managing Editor: Larry Main

Senior Acquisitions Editor: James Gish

Product Managers: Jane Hosie-Bounar, Nicole Calisi

Editorial Assistant: Sarah Timm

Vice President, Career and Professional Marketing: Jennifer McAvey

Marketing Director: Deborah S. Yarnell

Marketing Coordinator: Jonathan Sheehan

Production Director: Carolyn Miller

Content Product Managers: Heather Furrow, Tintu Thomas

Developmental Editor: Ann Fisher

Technical Editor: Tara Botelho

Art Director: Bruce Bond

Cover Design: Lisa Kuhn, Curio Press, LLC

Cover Photo: © Jim Wehtje/Photodisc/Getty Images

Proofreader: Harold Johnson

Indexer: Kevin Broccoli

For product information and technology assistance, contact us at
Cengage Learning Customer & Sales Support, 1-800-354-9706

For permission to use material from this text or product, submit all requests online at **cengage.com/permissions**. Further permissions questions can be emailed to
permissionrequest@cengage.com

ISBN-13: 978-1-4254-1326-9

ISBN-10: 1-4354-1326-1

Course Technology
25 Thomson Place,
Boston, MA 02210
USA

Cengage Learning is a leading provider of customized learning solutions with office locations around the globe, including Singapore, the United Kingdom, Australia, Mexico, Brazil and Japan. Locate your local office at **international.cengage.com/region**

Cengage Learning products are represented in Canada by Nelson Education, Ltd.

For your lifelong learning solutions, visit **course.cengage.com**
Purchase any of our products at your local college store or at our preferred online store **www.ichapters.com**

Printed in the United States of America
1 2 3 4 5 6 7 8 9 11 10 09 08 07

Revealed Series Vision

The Revealed Series is your guide to today's hottest multimedia applications. These comprehensive books teach the skills behind the application, showing you how to apply smart design principles to multimedia products such as dynamic graphics, animation, Web sites, software authoring tools, and digital video.

A team of design professionals including multimedia instructors, students, authors, and editors worked together to create this series. We recognized the unique learning environment of the multimedia classroom and created a series that:

- Gives you comprehensive step-by-step instructions
- Offers in-depth explanation of the "Why" behind a skill
- Includes creative projects for additional practice
- Explains concepts clearly using full-color visuals

It was our goal to create a book that speaks directly to the multimedia and design community—one of the most rapidly growing computer fields today. We think we've done just that, with a sophisticated and instructive book design.

—The Revealed Series

Author's Vision

Many thanks go out to all the great people who contributed to the making of this book. Thank you to Jim Gish for your consistent and always enthusiastic support of this book. Thank you to Ann Fisher, my longtime friend and editor, for your skill and dedication to the project. Thank you to Jane Hosie-Bounar for keeping us on course, and to Christina Micek for procuring permissions. Thank you to Tara Botelho for your dedication in tech editing the manuscript on the Mac OS platform. Thank you to Bruce Bond and Lisa Kuhn for a stunning cover design, and to Heather Furrow and Tintu Thomas for their work with production.

—Chris Botello

PREFACE

Introduction to Advanced Adobe Photoshop CS3

Welcome to *Advanced Adobe Photoshop CS3—Revealed.* This book offers creative projects, concise instructions, and extensive coverage of advanced design and Photoshop skills, helping you to create polished, professional-looking graphics. Use this book both in the classroom and as your own reference guide.

This book is organized into ten chapters. In these chapters, you will explore many aspects of advanced design using Photoshop CS3. In fact, this book is sure to take your design skills as well as your Photoshop skills to the next level with its sophisticated projects. You'll work with curves, levels, blending modes, special effects, and painting and drawing tools. You'll not only be challenged as a Photoshop CS3 user, but as a designer working with real-world projects.

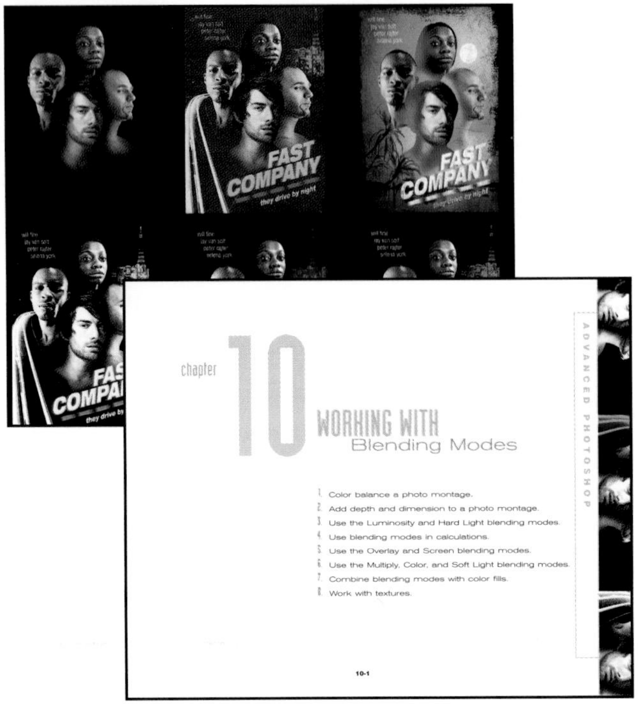

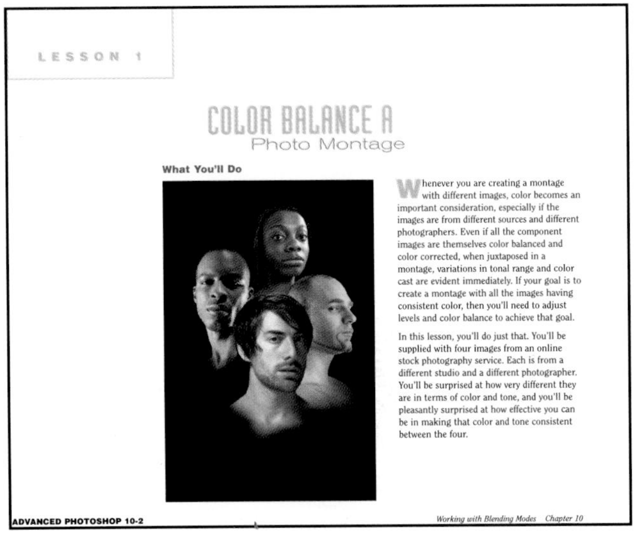

LESSON 1

COLOR BALANCE A
Photo Montage

What You'll Do

Whenever you are creating a montage with different images, color becomes an important consideration, especially if the images are from different sources and different photographers. Even if all the component images are themselves color balanced and color corrected, when juxtaposed in a montage, variations in tonal range and color cast are evident immediately. If your goal is to create a montage with all the images having consistent color, then you'll need to adjust levels and color balance to achieve that goal.

In this lesson, you'll do just that. You'll be supplied with four images from an online stock photography service. Each is from a different studio and a different photographer. You'll be surprised at how very different they are in terms of color and tone, and you'll be pleasantly surprised at how effective you can be in making that color and tone consistent between the four.

ADVANCED PHOTOSHOP 10-2 Working with Blending Modes Chapter 10

What You'll Do

A What You'll Do figure begins every lesson. This figure gives you an at-a-glance look at what you'll do in the chapter, thereby providing context and a specific goal as you work.

Lesson Narrative

In this book, you jump right into each project with a detailed explanation of its scope and challenges. Also included in the text are tips and Author's Notes to help you work more efficiently and creatively, or to teach you a bit about the history or design philosophy behind the skill you are using.

Step-by-Step Instructions

This book provides concise steps in which you create an image in Photoshop CS3. Each set of steps guides you through a lesson where you will modify or enhance the image. The step-by-step instructions refer to large, colorful figures that provide a visual representation of the project as it is being built. The Data Files for the steps are on the DVD included in the book.

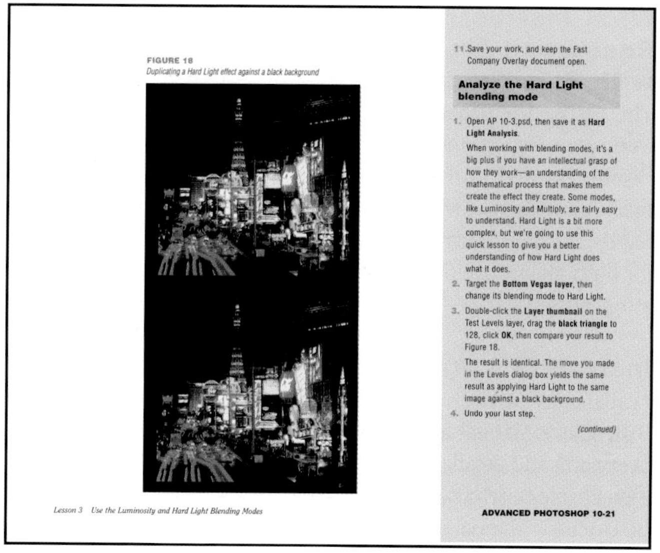

FIGURE 18
Duplicating a Hard Light effect against a black background

11. Save your work, and keep the Fast Company Overlay document open.

Analyze the Hard Light blending mode

1. Open AP 10-3.psd, then save it as **Hard Light Analysis**.
   When working with blending modes, it's a big plus if you have an intellectual grasp of how they work—an understanding of the mathematical process that makes them create the effect they create. Some modes, like Luminosity and Multiply, are fairly easy to understand. Hard Light is a bit more complex, but we're going to use this quick lesson to give you a better understanding of how Hard Light does what it does.
2. Target the **Bottom Vegas layer**, then change its blending mode to Hard Light.
3. Double-click the **Layer thumbnail** on the Test Levels layer, drag the **black triangle** to 128, click **OK**, then compare your result to Figure 18.
   The result is identical. The move you made in the Levels dialog box yields the same result as applying Hard Light to the same image against a black background.
4. Undo your last step.

(continued)

Lesson 3 Use the Luminosity and Hard Light Blending Modes

ADVANCED PHOTOSHOP 10-21

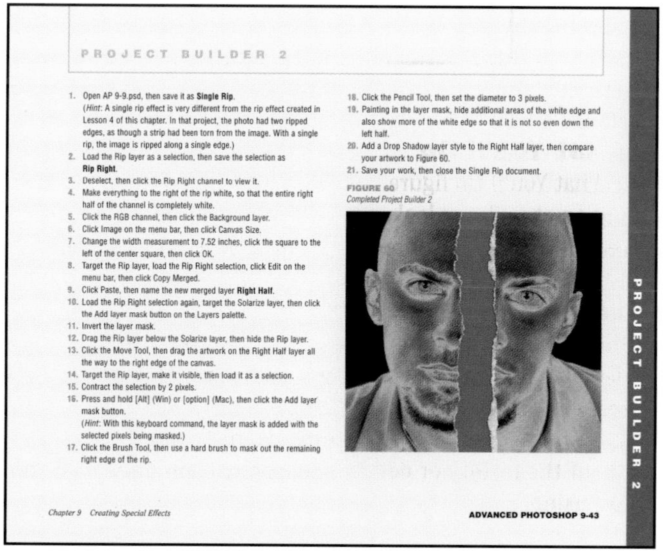

PROJECT BUILDER 2

1. Open AP 9-9.psd, then save it as **Single Rip**.
   (*Hint*: A single rip effect is very different from the rip effect created in Lesson 4 of this chapter. In that project, the photo had two ripped edges, as though a strip had been torn from the image. With a single rip, the image is ripped along a single edge.)
2. Load the Rip layer as a selection, then save the selection as **Rip Right**.
3. Deselect, then click the Rip Right channel to view it.
4. Make everything to the right of the rip white, so that the entire right half of the channel is completely white.
5. Click the RGB channel, then click the Background layer.
6. Click Image on the menu bar, then click Canvas Size.
7. Change the width measurement to 7.52 inches, click the square to the left of the center square, then click OK.
8. Target the Rip layer, load the Rip Right selection, click Edit on the menu bar, then click Copy Merged.
9. Click Paste, then name the new merged layer **Right Half**.
10. Load the Rip Right selection again, target the Solarize layer, then click the Add layer mask button on the Layers palette.
11. Invert the layer mask.
12. Drag the Rip layer below the Solarize layer, then hide the Rip layer.
13. Click the Move Tool, then drag the artwork on the Right Half layer all the way to the right edge of the canvas.
14. Target the Rip layer, make it visible, then load it as a selection.
15. Contract the selection by 2 pixels.
16. Press and hold [Alt] (Win) or [option] (Mac), then click the Add layer mask button.
    (*Hint*: With this keyboard command, the layer mask is added with the selected pixels being masked.)
17. Click the Brush Tool, then use a hard brush to mask out the remaining right edge of the rip.
18. Click the Pencil Tool, then set the diameter to 3 pixels.
19. Painting in the layer mask, hide additional areas of the white edge and also show more of the white edge so that it is not so even down the left half.
20. Add a Drop Shadow layer style to the Right Half layer, then compare your artwork to Figure 60.
21. Save your work, then close the Single Rip document.

FIGURE 60
Completed Project Builder 2

PROJECT BUILDER 2

Chapter 9 Creating Special Effects

ADVANCED PHOTOSHOP 9-43

Projects

This book contains end-of-chapter materials for additional practice and reinforcement. The Project Builders require you to apply the skills you've learned in the chapter and take them in a new direction. When you have finished the chapters in this book, you should have an impressive portfolio of the advanced work you have created using Adobe Photoshop CS3.

What Instructor Resources Are Available with This Book?

The Instructor Resources DVD is Cengage's way of putting the resources and information needed to teach and learn effectively into your hands. All the resources are available for both Macintosh and Windows operating systems.

Instructor's Manual

Available as an electronic file, the Instructor's Manual includes chapter overviews and detailed lecture topics for each chapter, with teaching tips. The Instructor's Manual is available on the Instructor Resources DVD.

PowerPoint Presentations

Each chapter has a corresponding PowerPoint presentation that you can use in lectures, distribute to your students, or customize to suit your course.

Data Files for Students

To complete most of the chapters in this book, your students will need Data Files. The Data Files are available on the DVD at the back of this book. Instruct students to use the Data Files List at the end of this book. This list gives instructions on organizing files.

Solutions to Exercises

Solution Files are Data Files completed with comprehensive sample answers. Use these files to evaluate your students' work. Or distribute them electronically so students can verify their work. Sample solutions to all lessons and end-of-chapter material are provided.

Test Bank and Test Engine

ExamView is a powerful testing software package that allows instructors to create and administer printed, computer (LAN-based), and Internet exams. ExamView includes hundreds of questions that correspond to the topics covered in this text, enabling students to generate detailed study guides that include page references for further review. The computer-based and Internet testing components allow students to take exams at their computers, and also save the instructor time by grading each exam automatically.

CONTENTS

CHAPTER 1 WORKING WITH LAYERS

CHAPTER 2 WORKING WITH LAYER STYLES

CHAPTER 5 DESIGNING WITH MULTIPLE IMAGES

CHAPTER 6 INVESTIGATING PRODUCTION TRICKS AND TECHNIQUES

CHAPTER 9 CREATING SPECIAL EFFECTS

CHAPTER 10 WORKING WITH BLENDING MODES

Intended Audience

This book is designed for the experienced Photoshop user who wants to learn advanced techniques and new features in Photoshop CS3. The book presents real world assignments and takes you through the design decisions you might be faced with as you work toward your goal. By the end of the book, you'll have gained a thorough understanding of Photoshop from an advanced perspective.

Approach

The book allows you to work at your own pace through step-by-step tutorials. A concept is presented and the process is explained, followed by the actual steps. To learn the most from the book, you should adopt the following habits:

- Make sure you understand the Photoshop skill being taught in each step before you move on to the next step.
- After finishing a set of steps, ask yourself if you could do it on your own, without referring to the steps. If the answer is no, review the steps.

Icons, Buttons, and Pointers

Symbols for icons, buttons, and pointers are shown in the steps when they are used.

Windows and Macintosh

Photoshop CS3 works virtually the same on Windows and Macintosh operating systems. When there is a significant difference, the abbreviations (Win) and (Mac) are used.

The nature of working with graphics requires detailed work. In Photoshop, this means that you will need to magnify areas of an image. Because monitor sizes and resolution preferences vary, be sure to set the magnification to the setting that allows you to work comfortably. The figures shown in this book are displayed at a monitor resolution of 1024 × 768.

Data Files

To complete the lessons in this book, you need to obtain the Data Files provided on the DVD included in this book. You can store these files on a hard drive, a network server, or a USB storage device. The instructions in the lessons will refer to "the drive and folder where your Data Files are stored" when referring to the Data Files for the book.

HAWAII
land of aloha

chapter 1

WORKING WITH Layers

1. Lock transparent pixels.
2. Apply a Hue/Saturation adjustment layer.
3. Work with a layer mask.
4. Use one layer to mask another layer.
5. Mask a layer with the Paste Into command.
6. Scale an image.
7. Use the Free Transform command.
8. Use a single layer to mask multiple layers.
9. Paint in a layer mask.
10. Add a stroke layer style.
11. Add a drop shadow layer style.
12. Apply an adjustment layer to multiple layers.
13. Edit layer styles.
14. Copy layer styles between layers.

LESSON 1

LOCK TRANSPARENT Pixels

What You'll Do

Photoshop is an application that you use to create art, and all art ultimately comes from the heart. So it's fair to say that Photoshop is an application that you use with your heart. But make no mistake: Photoshop is also an application that you use with your head. That's because Photoshop is a smart, well-designed, and powerful graphic arts application, and over the years, with each successive version, it's become a very intricate and complex application as well.

When you're designing in Photoshop, you need to keep your wits about you; you have to keep that brain active, even if you feel that you know the application through and through. There's always something new that you can learn, so you must take the time to notice.

Notice what, you ask? Everything. Not all at once, but along the way. Notice how the application works. Notice how its interface has been designed. The interface is the language that the application uses to communicate with you, and only by staying alert will you hear what it's saying to you.

So yes, of course, work with your heart—wholeheartedly, as they say. But always keep awake and alert to the Photoshop interface and everything it's telling you about itself.

FIGURE 1
Land of Aloha layer

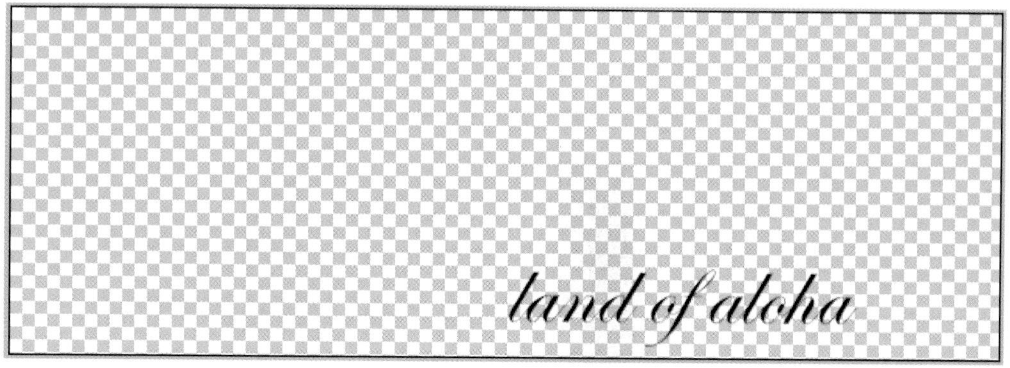

AUTHOR'S *note*

The Photoshop (*.PSD) file format is the "native" format for Photoshop—in other words, the document is simply a Photoshop document. It's not a Tiff or an EPS or a PICT or any of the common formats. All Adobe products, such as InDesign, Dreamweaver, Flash or Illustrator, can interface with Photoshop documents.

Lock transparent pixels

1. Open AP 1-1.psd, click **File** on the menu bar, then click **Save As**.
2. Type **HAWAII** in the File name text box (Win) or the Save As text box (Mac), click the **Format list arrow**, click **Photoshop (*.PSD; *.PDD)** (Win) or **Photoshop** (Mac), then click **Save**.

   TIP The Photoshop Format Options dialog box may open, asking if you want to maximize compatibility. You can program Photoshop to always maximize compatibility in the File Handling preferences dialog box. Click Edit (Win) or Photoshop (Mac) on the menu bar, point to Preferences, click File Handling, click the Maximize PSD and PSB File Compatibility list arrow, click Always, then click OK.

3. Click the **Land of Aloha layer** in the Layers palette.

   TIP Clicking a layer is called **targeting** a layer.

4. Press and hold **[Alt]** (Win) or **[option]** (Mac), click the **Indicates layer visibility button** beside the targeted layer, then compare your screen to Figure 1.

   Pressing [Alt] (Win) or [option] (Mac) while clicking the targeted layer hides all other layers. This is a quick method for viewing only that which is on a single layer. Note that the text is the only artwork on this layer. All of the other pixels on this layer are transparent, represented by the gray and white checkerboard pattern.

(continued)

5. Press **[D]** to revert to default foreground and background colors.
6. Press **[X]** to switch foreground and background colors.
7. Press and hold **[Alt]** (Win) or **[option]** (Mac), then press **[Delete]** (Win) or **[delete]** (Mac).

   Pressing [Alt][Delete] (Win) or [option][delete] (Mac) fills the entire layer with the foreground color—white in this case. Applying fills in this manner is much faster than using the Fill command on the Edit menu.

   TIP If you use the Fill command on the Edit menu to fill an object, you'll be able to choose other fill settings, including blending modes and transparency, in the Fill dialog box.
8. Click **Edit** on the menu bar, then click **Undo Fill Layer**.
9. Click the **Lock transparent pixels button**, as shown in Figure 2.

   When the Lock transparent pixels button is activated for a targeted layer, the transparent pixels on the layer—the gray and white checkerboard—cannot be modified.

(continued)

FIGURE 2
Layers palette

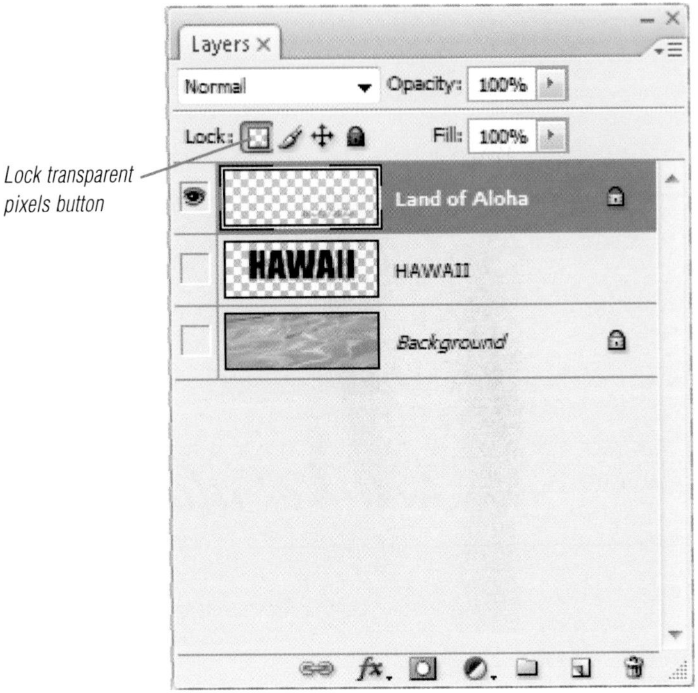

AUTHOR'S *note*

This is an opportunity to take the time to investigate how the application and the interface have been designed. At Adobe, you can be sure that much thought went into the decision to use a gray and white checkerboard to represent transparent pixels. Stay alert to these choices—that awareness will help you to build a strong, intuitive relationship with the application.

FIGURE 3
Filling only the black pixels with white on the Land of Aloha layer

10. Press and hold **[Alt]** (Win) or **[option]** (Mac), then press **[Delete]** (Win) or **[delete]** (Mac).

    Only the black pixels are filled with the foreground color. The transparent pixels are unaffected by the white fill.

11. Press and hold **[Alt]** (Win) **[option]** (Mac), then click the **Indicates layer visibility button** on the Land of Aloha layer.

    The two hidden layers become visible.

12. Compare your screen to Figure 3, then save your work.

AUTHOR'S *note*

Make a note of the lock icon on the right side of the targeted layer. If you position your cursor over it, a tool tip will appear to explain its function—Indicates layer is partially locked. If you didn't take the time to do this—if you didn't know the name of that icon—you might reasonably think the whole layer is locked. It's not—just the transparent pixels are locked. Thus the layer is partially locked.

LESSON 2

APPLY A HUE/SATURATION Adjustment Layer

What You'll Do

If you're relatively new to Photoshop, you might not fully appreciate how revolutionary the introduction of adjustment layers was to the application.

Before adjustment layers, when you made an adjustment—like a color correction with curves, levels, or hue saturation, for example—once you made it, you couldn't go back and modify it. You were stuck with it. There were ways to work around the issue, but that's all they were—work-arounds.

Adjustment layers offer you the ability to make an adjustment and then go back at any time to the same dialog box and modify the adjustment. From the designer's perspective, it's the difference between being trapped with your choices and being free to experiment.

And that's not all—adjustment layers are also a record of the adjustments you've made. For example, if you're working on a new layer and want to know what color correction you made to a previous layer, all you need to do is check the adjustment layer. In the old days, you used an old-fashioned method to keep track of this information—a pencil and paper!

Apply a Hue/Saturation adjustment layer

1. Target the **Background layer**.
2. Click **Layer** on the menu bar, point to **New Adjustment Layer**, then click **Hue/ Saturation**.

   The New Layer dialog box opens, as shown in Figure 4.
3. Type **Deep Blue Sea** in the Name text box.
4. Click **OK**.

   The Hue/Saturation dialog box opens.
5. Drag the **Hue slider** all the way to the left, then click **OK** so that your canvas resembles Figure 5.

(continued)

FIGURE 4
New Layer dialog box

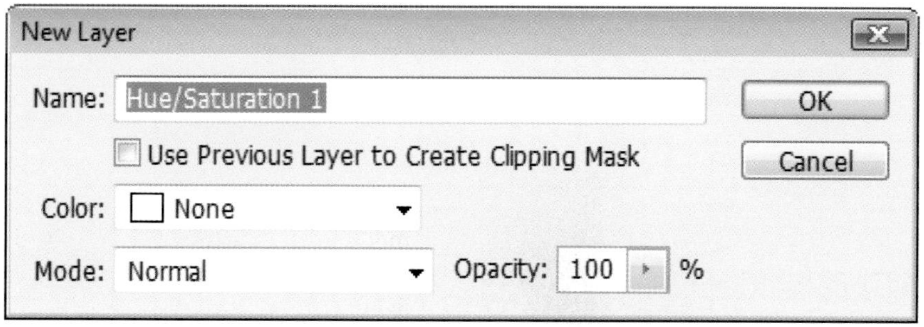

FIGURE 5
Modifying the hue of the water image

6. Click the **Indicates layer visibility icon** on  the adjustment layer to hide it, then click again to show it.

   Note that the Layer thumbnail on the Background layer hasn't changed—it's still blue even though the image on the canvas is red. That's because it is the adjustment layer that is creating the red effect—the Background layer itself has not been modified.

7. Target the **Background layer** so that you can see the adjustment layer clearly.

   As shown in Figure 6, the half-black/half-white circle is the icon for an adjustment layer. By default, the adjustment layer is created with a white layer mask.

8. Double-click the **adjustment layer icon** on the Deep Blue Sea adjustment layer.

   The Hue/Saturation dialog box opens showing the last settings chosen.

9. Drag the **Hue slider** to the right so that the Hue text box value is +155.
10. Drag the **Saturation slider** to the right so that the Saturation text box value is +28.
11. Click **OK**, then compare your screen to Figure 7.
12. Save your work.

FIGURE 6
Identifying an adjustment layer

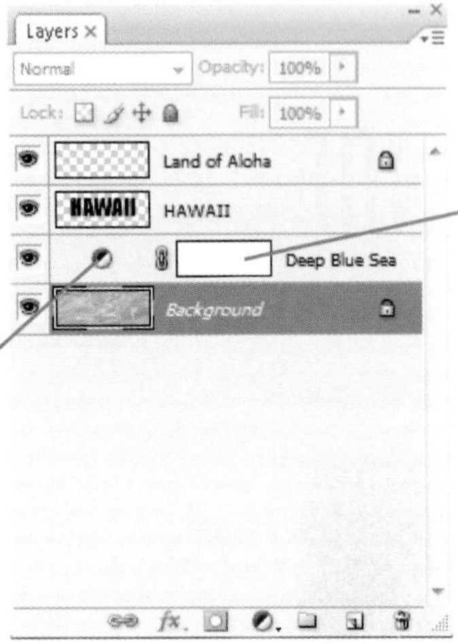

FIGURE 7
Viewing a different hue adjustment

LESSON 3

WORK WITH A Layer Mask

What You'll Do

Think about this for a moment: In the early versions of Photoshop, layers didn't exist. That's right—no layers. You had one flat canvas to work with, and if you layered one image over another, when you deselected, the two images became one.

The introduction of layers opened up a whole new realm of possibilities of what you could create with Photoshop. And with layers came layer masks. Layer masks are essential to working with layers; they allow you to choose which areas of the layer are visible and which areas are not visible.

The layer mask interface is very straightforward: Paint black over the areas that you do not want to show.

Another great thing about layer masks is that they are always available to be modified. In other words, you can paint white over the areas that you painted black, and those areas will show again.

But layer masks are not just black and white. Gray is neither white nor black; it's somewhere in between. Areas that you paint with gray in a layer mask are neither visible nor invisible—they're somewhere in between. Therein lies the power of gray in conjunction with layer masks: the ability to create semi-transparency for images on layers.

Work with a layer mask

1. Click the **Layers palette list arrow**, click **Palette Options**, click the **second largest thumbnail icon** in the Thumbnail Size section, then click **OK**.
2. Click the **layer mask** on the Deep Blue Sea adjustment layer to verify that it is targeted.
3. Press **[D]**, press **[X]**, then fill the layer mask with the black foreground color, then compare your Layers palette to Figure 8.

   The effect of the adjustment layer—the red water—disappears on the canvas. Black areas of a layer mask are completely opaque—wherever black appears in the layer mask, the adjustment layer is no longer visible.
4. Press **[Ctrl][I]** (Win) or ⌘ **[I]** (Mac) to invert the black mask to a white mask.

   The adjustment layer effect is restored. White areas of a layer mask are completely transparent—wherever white appears in the layer mask, the adjustment layer is visible

   > **TIP** The Invert command is a useful way to quickly toggle between a white and a black layer mask.
5. Press **[X]** to switch your foreground and background colors so that white is the foreground color and black is the background color.
6. Click the **Gradient Tool**, then click the **Linear Gradient button** on the Options bar at the top of the window, if necessary.

(continued)

FIGURE 8

Layer mask thumbnail on the Deep Blue Sea adjustment layer filled with black

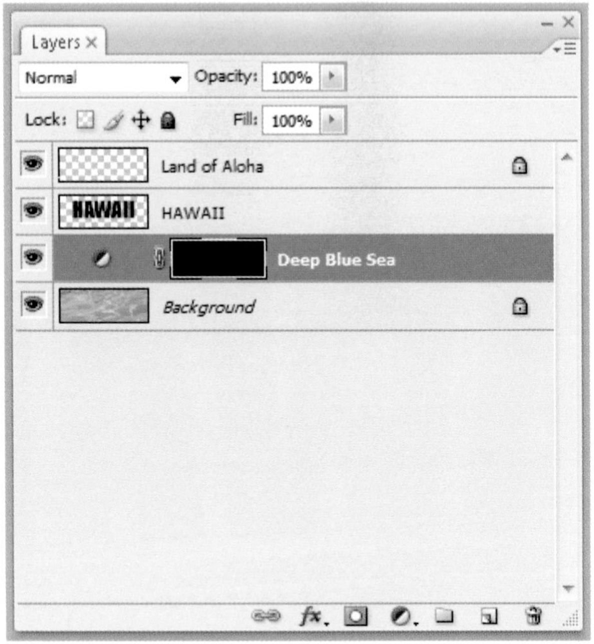

FIGURE 9

Using a layer mask to gradate the effect of an adjustment layer

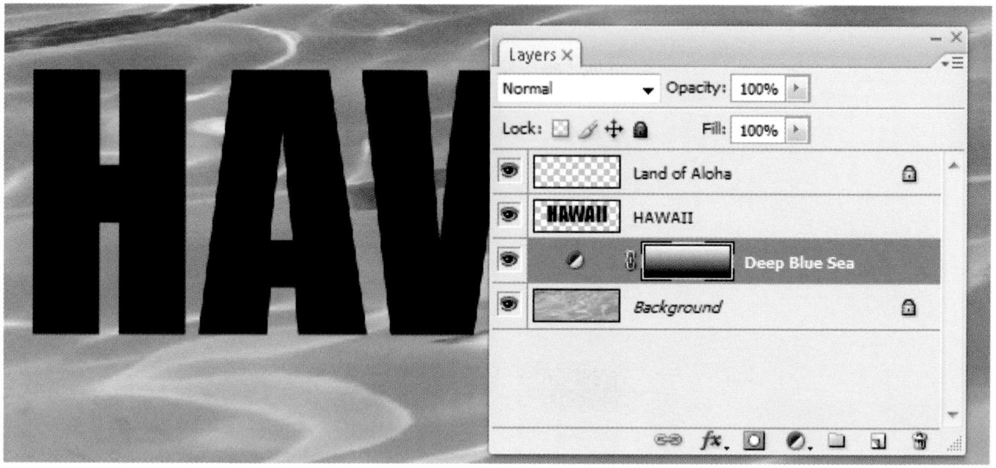

FIGURE 10

Modifying an adjustment layer

7. Position your cursor at the top center of the image, click and drag straight down, then release at the bottom of the image.

   You did not apply the gradient to the artwork on the layer—you applied the gradient to the adjustment layer's layer mask. A gradient now appears in the layer mask and the adjustment layer effect fades down the artwork as shown in Figure 9.

8. Double-click the **adjustment layer icon** in the Deep Blue Sea adjustment layer. Drag the **Hue slider** so that its setting reads +24.

9. Click **OK**, then compare your canvas to Figure 10.

   This is the real power of adjustment layers: you can always go back and tweak the adjustment. The effect is now a deep dark blue fading down to the original lighter blue.

10. Save your work.

LESSON 4

USE ONE LAYER TO
Mask Another Layer

What You'll Do

Now, of course, they can be done in Photoshop. Actually, they can be done many different ways in Photoshop, and these next few lessons are going to examine those methods closely.

Masking is a great effect for you to have in your designer's bag of tricks. Working on a project that incorporates multiple masking techniques and complex interrelationships between artwork on layers is one of the best ways to investigate the many powerful options available in the Layers palette.

Masking effects have enjoyed a long and illustrious career in the graphic arts. Long before the advent of computer graphics, masking had staked its territory as a popular and beloved design effect: think of those 50's postcards that had great beach photos inside the word FLORIDA! Come to think of it, if you can get your hands on some of those old postcards, please do. They are a great example of classic effects that were done in the days before digital.

FIGURE 11

Preparing to clip the 2 Women layer

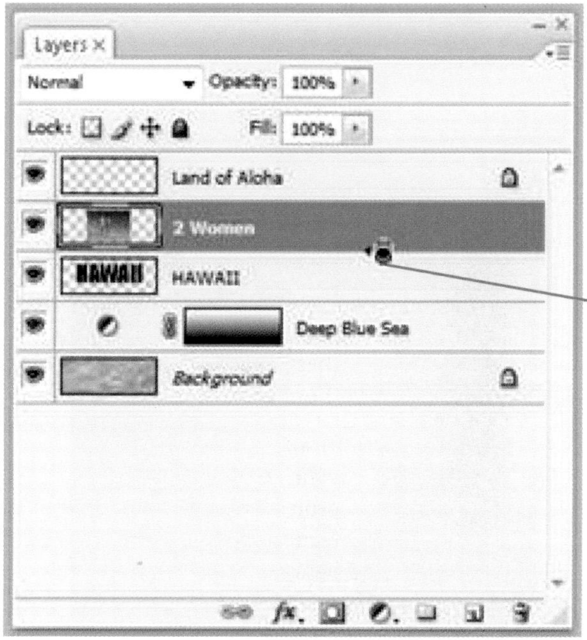

Use Previous Layer to Create Clipping Mask icon

Use one layer to mask another layer

1. Open Two Women.psd from your Data Files folder, select all, copy, then close the file.

   TIP Try doing Step 1 using four keyboard commands: [Ctrl][O], [Ctrl][A], [Ctrl][C], [Ctrl][W] (Win) or [⌘][O], [⌘][A], [⌘][C], [⌘][W] (Mac).

2. Zoom in or out so that you are viewing the canvas at 50%.

   You should be able to see the entire canvas.

3. Target the **HAWAII layer**.
4. Click **Edit** on the menu bar, then click **Paste**.

   The Two Women.psd image is pasted on its own layer immediately above the targeted layer. When you paste in Photoshop, the contents are pasted on their own layer, always above the targeted layer.

5. Name the new layer **2 Women.**
6. Press and hold **[Alt]** (Win) or **[option]** (Mac), then position the mouse pointer between the 2 Women and HAWAII layers in the Layers palette so that you see the pointer shown in Figure 11.

(continued)

AUTHOR'S *note*

When you set the view percentage for a document so that you can see the entire canvas, anything you paste into the document will be centered on the canvas. Though this doesn't sound like such a big deal, knowing this can come in very handy, especially when you are aligning pasted images or trying to center images on the canvas.

7. Click the line between the two layers.

   The 2 Women image is masked—or "clipped"—by the pixels on the layer below it—the HAWAII layer. The 2 Women image is visible only where there are pixels on the HAWAII layer. Where the HAWAII layer is transparent, the 2 Women image is not visible.

   TIP Note that the 2 Women layer now has the bent arrow icon which represents the Use Previous Layer to Create Clipping Mask option activated.

8. Click the **Move Tool** , then move the graphic so that the two women are positioned in the letter H, as shown in Figure 12.

   TIP Use the arrow keys to move the image in small increments. Each time you press an arrow, the image moves 1 pixel in that direction. Press and hold [Shift] when you press an arrow, and the image will move 10 pixels in that direction.

9. Save your work.

FIGURE 12
Positioning the 2 Women image

LESSON 5

MASK A LAYER WITH THE Paste Into Command

What You'll Do

Paste is probably one of the first commands you learned when you sat down at a computer for the first time. First copy, then paste. Paste Into is not quite so common.

Paste Into is a cool and effective way of masking a graphic—in some ways, it's more effective than some of the more popular methods that you probably use.

Paste Into is inextricably linked to layer masks, and it's this important relationship that we'll explore in this lesson.

Mask a layer with the Paste Into command

1. Open Family.psd, select all, copy, then close the file.
2. Target the **HAWAII layer**.
3. Press and hold **[Ctrl]** (Win) or [⌘] (Mac), then click the **HAWAII Layer thumbnail**.

   As shown in Figure 13, all of the pixels on the HAWAII layer are selected.

   > **TIP** Pressing and holding [Ctrl] (Win) or [⌘] (Mac), then clicking a layer thumbnail loads a selection of all the pixels on the layer. If the layer has transparent areas,as this layer does, the transparent areas will not be selected.

4. Click the **Rectangular Marquee Tool** [⬚], verify that the Style choice in the Options bar reads Normal, press and hold **[Alt]** (Win) or **[option]** (Mac), then drag a box around the letter H only.

   The letter H is deselected.

   > **TIP** Pressing and holding [Alt] (Win) or [option] (Mac) when creating a selection removes the selection from the currently selected area.

5. Click the **Polygonal Lasso Tool** [⯎], then verify that the feather value in the Options bar is set at 0 px.

(continued)

FIGURE 13
All pixels on HAWAII layer are selected

FIGURE 14
Positioning the Family graphic

AUTHOR'S *note*

You used the Polygonal Lasso Tool because it is able to make diagonal selections, which made it easy to navigate around the letter A. Using the Rectangular Marquee Tool would have made the task much more difficult—in fact, it wouldn't be possible to remove areas from the selection in just one step. This is a fine example of how knowing when to use the right tool for the right task saves you time and effort.

6. Press and hold **[Alt]** (Win) or **[option]** (Mac), then draw a box around the letters WAII.

   The letters are deselected. Only the letter A is selected.

7. Target the **2 Women layer**, click **Edit** on the menu bar, then click **Paste Into**.

   The Family.psd image is pasted on a new layer above the 2 Women layer. The new layer is created automatically with a layer mask that represents the selection that was pasted into—a white A on a black background.

8. Name the new layer **Family**, press and hold **[Alt]** (Win) or **[option]** (Mac), then click the **Layer mask thumbnail** to view the mask.

   TIP Pressing and holding [Alt] (Win) or [option] (Mac) when clicking a layer mask thumbnail displays the layer mask on the canvas.

9. Click the **Family thumbnail** to view the image again, click the **Move Tool**, then move the image so that the woman is positioned in the letter A as shown Figure 14.

   When you execute the Paste Into command, by default, the artwork is not locked to the layer mask. This means that the artwork can be moved independently from the layer mask. In this example, regardless of how you move the image, it will be visible only within the letter A, which will remain stationary.

10. Save your work.

LESSON 6

SCALE An Image

What You'll Do

Chances are, you've scaled a graphic in Photoshop before. You use the same method to scale a graphic that is part of a mask, but the mask makes it more interesting.

Use this lesson to hone your skills for scaling and repositioning a graphic within a mask *before* executing the scale. It's an important skill to have. Here's why: Any time you scale a graphic, by definition, you change the pixel structure that creates the graphic.

If you reduce the graphic, you use less pixels; that means pixels are discarded. If you enlarge the graphic, you need more pixels. Where are you going to get them from? Any guesses? You're going to get the new pixels from the pixels you already have. Using a process called interpolation, Photoshop creates new pixels based on the data of the original pixels.

In either case—but especially when enlarging—the quality of the image will be reduced as the original pixel structure is modified. What this all means is—if you have to scale a graphic—you want to scale it just once whenever possible.

FIGURE 15
Identifying the bounding box

Scale an image

1. Target the **2 Women layer**, click **Edit** on the menu bar, point to **Transform**, then click **Scale**.

   As shown in Figure 15, a bounding box appears around the entire 2 Women image—even the parts that are not visible outside the letter H.

2. Press and hold **[Shift]**, position your cursor over the top-right corner point of the bounding box, click and drag in a northeast direction, then release when the W and H values in the Options bar are 122%.

   TIP Pressing and holding [Shift] when scaling an image scales the image in proportion. The W and H text boxes in the Options bar are interactive—you can enter values in the boxes to scale a graphic.

(continued)

3. Position your cursor over the bounding box so that a black arrow appears, then click and drag to reposition the women within the letter H using Figure 16 as a guide.

   TIP The crosshair icon at the center of the bounding box represents the point of origin for a transformation. You can drag it anywhere to determine the point of origin. For example, if you want to scale or rotate a graphic from a specific point other than its center, you could move the crosshair to that point.

4. Use the arrow keys to better position the graphic, if necessary.
5. Click the **Move Tool** , then click **Apply**.

   Clicking the Move Tool offers you the choice to execute or to not execute the transformation. This is one of many ways to execute a transformation.
6. Undo and redo your last step to see the effects of scaling the image.
7. Compare your work to Figure 17, then save your work.

FIGURE 16
Positioning the 2 Women graphic precisely using the arrow keys

FIGURE 17
Scaled graphic

LESSON 7

USE THE FREE Transform Command

What You'll Do

Once upon a time, you could apply only one transformation at a time. If you wanted to scale and rotate and flip a graphic, you had to first scale it, click OK, then rotate it, click OK, then flip it.

Enter the Free Transform command. Simply put, Free Transform allows you to make all of your transformations at once. Scale, rotate, distort, flip—you can do it with one bounding box and one execution.

When you understand the quality benefits of applying multiple transformations with just one execution, that's when you appreciate the power and importance of the Free Transform command.

Use the Free Transform command

1. Target the **Family layer**, click **Edit** on the menu bar, then click **Free Transform**.

   The object here is to fit the Family image in the letter A. The choice of the photo was a good one, since the four people are positioned roughly in a triangular shape. The image will need to be scaled and rotated to fit into the letter A with all four people showing.

2. Type **50** in the W text box in the Options bar, then click the **Maintain aspect ratio icon** to automatically change the H (height) value to 50 also.

   The bounding box is now almost completely outside of the letter A and therefore, much of the image is not visible.

3. Position your cursor over the bounding box so that a black arrow appears, then click and drag to reposition the graphic as shown in Figure 18.

   TIP When transforming, you can move the bounding box any time you like. It is a good idea to reposition the bounding box as you test out different transformations. By repositioning the graphic, you can get a better sense of what you need to do to make it fit.

(continued)

FIGURE 18
Positioning the graphic

FIGURE 19
Repositioning the graphic

4. Position your cursor just outside of the bounding box.

   The Rotate icon appears.

5. Click and drag in a counterclockwise direction, then release when the Rotate value in the Options bar is –25.

6. Reposition the image, trying to fit all four faces into the letter A.

   Be sure that the bounding box covers the entire A. If it doesn't, that means that there will be no areas of the Family graphic in that area of the letter A. At this scale and rotation, the image does not fill the letter in a satisfactory way.

7. Type **44.2** in the W and H text boxes to scale the graphic to a smaller size.

   When transforming a graphic, you'll often want to zoom in and out as you work. But that poses a problem: If you click the Zoom Tool while the bounding box is still active, it's the same as clicking the Move Tool—Photoshop will ask if you want to apply the transformation. This is where you rely on your keyboard commands. Press and hold [Spacebar][Ctrl] (Win) or [Spacebar][⌘] (Mac) to access the the Zoom Plus Tool. Press and hold [Spacebar][Alt] (Win) or [Spacebar][option] (Mac) to access the Zoom Minus Tool. Make a note of these two important quick key combinations.

(continued)

8. Rotate the graphic counterclockwise to –33.4%.
9. Reposition the bounding box so that the graphic fills the letter A as shown in Figure 19.
10. Press **[Enter]** (Win) or **[return]** (Mac) to execute the transformation, then compare your canvas to Figure 20.
11. Save your work.

FIGURE 20
Results of the free transformation—both a scale and a rotation

AUTHOR'S *note*

Take a moment to remind yourself of the two methods that you've used so far to place these two images. Note that the right areas in the 2 Women graphic are visible in the W, whereas the Family image is visible only in the letter A. Each of the two images is being masked, but in different ways. Which is better? In this exercise, neither. But be sure to remember the Paste Into method we used for the Family graphic—it can be useful when you want the image to appear only in a specific area and not show anywhere else.

LESSON 8

USE A SINGLE LAYER TO
Mask Multiple Layers

What You'll Do

Things get really interesting in the Layers palette when multiple layers all "clip" themselves into a single layer that plays the role of the mask. That single layer can be used to mask multiple images placed on multiple layers; you don't need to use multiple masks to achieve the effect.

As you work through this lesson, keep in mind the complex tasks that the Layers palette handles with such ease.

Use a single layer to mask multiple layers

1. Open Beach Girls.psd, select all, copy, then close the file.
2. Target the **HAWAII layer**.
3. Click **Edit** on the menu bar, then click **Paste**.

   As shown in Figure 21, the new layer is automatically "clipped" by the HAWAII layer because it was pasted *beneath* the 2 Women layer, which was already being "clipped." Note the bent arrow icon on the new layer.
4. Name the layer **Beach Girls**.

   The Beach Girls image is obscured by the right areas of the 2 Women image, which is on the layer above it. However, no part of the Family graphic obscures the Beach Girls image. This is a great example of how the different choices you make along the way when building an illustration can yield different results and different issues you need to address.

(continued)

FIGURE 21
Viewing the new and automatically clipped layer

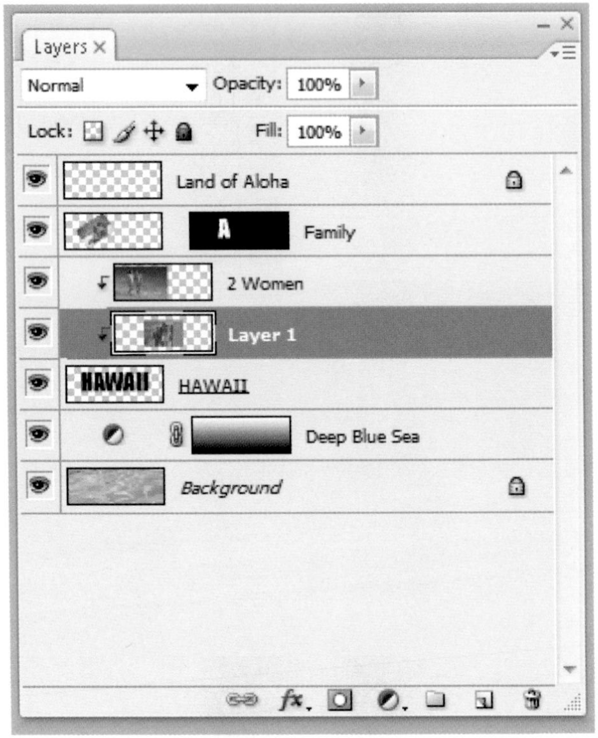

FIGURE 22
Reordering clipped layers in the Layers palette

FIGURE 23
Preparing to clip a layer

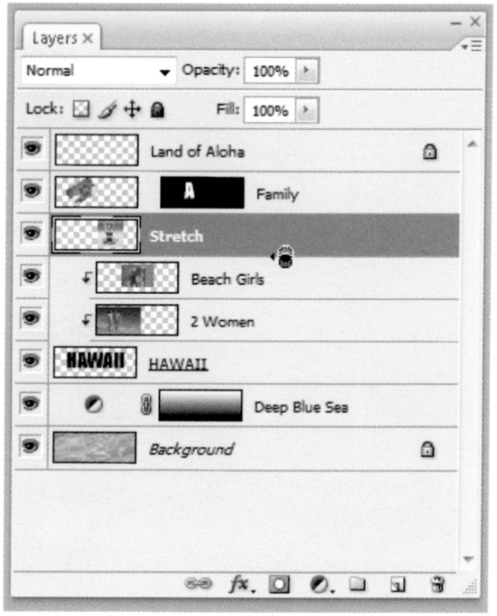

FIGURE 24
Clipped Stretch image

5. Drag the **Beach Girls layer** above the 2 Women layer.

   The Beach Girls image is no longer obscured by the 2 Women image in the letter W. Despite the move, the Beach Girls layer continues to be masked by the HAWAII layer.

6. Reposition the Beach Girls image as shown in Figure 22.
7. Open Stretch.psd, select all, copy, then close the file.
8. Verify that the Beach Girls layer is targeted, apply the Paste command, then name the layer **Stretch**.

   The Stretch image is not masked.

9. Click the **Move Tool** , then move the Stretch image over the second letter A in HAWAII.
10. Press and hold **[Alt]** (Win) or **[option]** (Mac), then position your cursor in the Layers palette over the line between the Stretch and Beach Girls layers so that you see the icon shown in Figure 23.
11. Click between the two layers.

    The Stretch image is clipped into the mask, as shown in Figure 24. There's an important distinction that you need to make here: The Stretch image is being masked by the HAWAII layer, *not* the Beach Girls layer. When you have a series of clipped layers—as you do here—it is the bottommost layer that clips the layers above it.

12. Open Oar.psd, then using the same steps that you used for the Stretch image, clip it into the first letter I and position it as shown in Figure 25.

13. Open Snorkelers.psd, clip it into the second letter I, then position it as shown in Figure 26.

14. Save your work.

FIGURE 25
Oar graphic, clipped and positioned

FIGURE 26
Snorkelers graphic, clipped and positioned

LESSON 9

PAINT IN A Layer Mask

What You'll Do

When you finish this lesson, take a moment to stop and examine the status of the Layers palette. Take a look at all the components being used to create the artwork on your canvas: transparent layers. An adjustment layer. Multiple layer masks—one with a gradient that fades the adjustment layer. Multiple layers clipped into one layer, all of them using layer masks.

The power of the Layers palette is on display when the various features are all being used and are working together in harmony.

This illustration's Layers palette is complex—and the amazing thing is, we've just scratched the surface of what layers can do.

Paint in a layer mask

1. Name the new layers **Oar** and **Snorkelers**, respectively.
2. Hide the Oar and Snorkelers layers.
3. Target the **Stretch layer**, scale the image 85%, then position it as shown in Figure 27.

   Note that part of the Stretch image still overlaps the Beach Girls image to the left.
4. Click **Layer** on the menu bar, point to **Layer Mask**, then click **Reveal All**.

   A white-filled layer mask is added to the Stretch layer.
5. Press **[D]**, then press **[X]** so that your foreground color is black, click the **Brush Tool**, then choose Hard Round 19 pixels from the Brush pull-down menu on the Options bar.

(continued)

FIGURE 27
Positioning the Stretch image

AUTHOR'S *note*

From a designer's perspective, the placement of the Stretch graphic is rather interesting. Note that the triangle in the letter A cuts into her face. It would probably be your first instinct to avoid that triangle—to try to position the graphic so that the face is on either side of the triangle, as with the Family image. However, the triangle cutting into the woman's face actually yields a more interesting effect—a playful interaction with the mask. Rather than detract from the image, it makes it more intriguing.

FIGURE 28
Repositioning the Snorkelers image

FIGURE 29
Six images positioned in six letterforms

6. With the layer mask still activated in the Layers palette, paint *on the canvas* everywhere that the Stretch image overlaps the Beach Girls image.

   The Stretch image disappears where you paint.

   > **TIP** Note that black appears in the layer mask representing where you painted in the canvas.

7. Make the Oar layer visible, target it, then click the **Add layer mask button** on the Layers palette.

   A transparent (white) layer mask is added to the layer.

8. Paint in the layer mask to remove the areas of Oar that overlap Stretch.

   > **TIP** As an alternative to painting, you can use one of the marquee tools to make a selection, then fill the selection with black.

9. Make the Snorkelers layer visible, then scale it and position it as shown in Figure 28.
10. Add a layer mask, then mask the areas of Snorkelers that overlap Oar.
11. Save your work, then compare it to Figure 29.

LESSON 10

ADD A STROKE
Layer Style

What You'll Do

At this point, we've hit a landmark point in the construction of this illustration. All six images have been placed into the mask and have been masked so that none interferes with any other. As a designer, this is the point where you'd want to take a moment to assess the art as it appears at this stage and decide how it can be improved to achieve a finished look.

The first thing to note is that the letterforms seem a bit bare. They simply butt up against the water image in the background. To remedy this, in this lesson you will apply a stroke to the letterforms.

As a designer, it is worth your time to think about and experiment with strokes. They can be very effective, or they can be trite and predictable. What makes the difference? It's hard to say. Sometimes the color makes it or breaks it. A stroke works when the art calls for it—it's that simple.

The art in this chapter is a good example. The effect is of six different images placed into six different letterforms. The key here is the word *different*—each picture and letterform should be distinct from the others. As you go through this lesson, give some thought to how a stroke makes each letterform more distinct and how the stroke lends impact to the image within the letterforms and to the illustration as a whole.

FIGURE 30
Layer Style dialog box

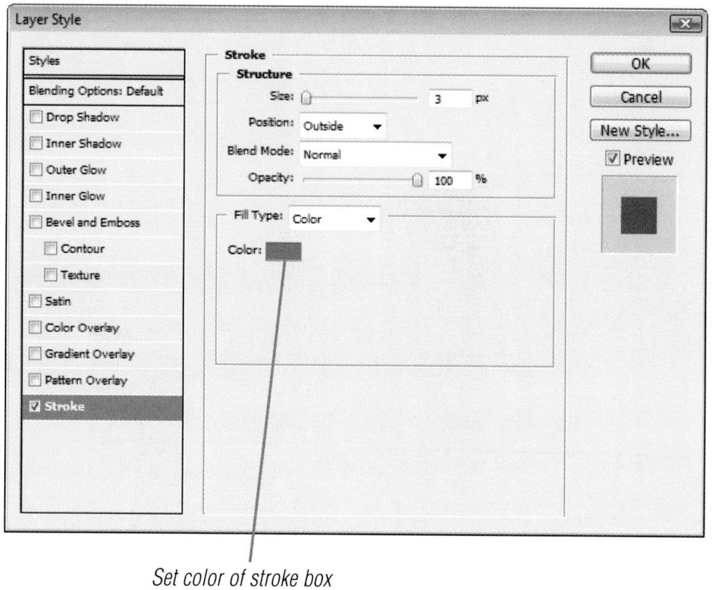

Add a stroke layer style

1. Target the **HAWAII layer**, click **Layer** on the menu bar, point to **Layer Style**, then click **Stroke**.

   The Layer Style dialog box opens, and the Stroke check box is checked, as shown in Figure 30.

2. Verify that the Preview check box is checked, then click the **Set color of stroke box** to open the Select stroke color dialog box.
3. Type **255** in the R, G, and B text boxes, then click **OK**.
4. Click the **Position list arrow**, then click **Inside**.

(continued)

5. Drag the **Size slider** to 8 px, then compare your canvas to Figure 31.

   TIP If you do not see the stroke applied to the artwork, click directly to the left of Effects in the layer below the HAWAII layer. You will see the Toggle all layer effect visibilities button appear. This button allows you to hide or show the layer effects for a particular layer.

6. Click the **Position list arrow**, then click **Outside**.

   The stroke on HAWAII is no longer obscured by the Family graphic because the stroke is positioned outside of the Family graphic.

7. Drag the **Size slider** to 3 px, click **OK**, then compare your canvas to Figure 32.

   Note that an Effects layer and a Stroke layer now appear in sublayers beneath the HAWAII layer.

   TIP Layer styles are listed in sublayers within the layer to which they are applied.

8. Save your work.

FIGURE 31

Stroke positioned inside the mask

FIGURE 32

Stroke positioned outside the mask

AUTHOR'S *note*

It is important that you understand that you are applying the stroke to the HAWAII layer. The stroke appears *over* the five images that have been "clipped" into the HAWAII layer, even though they are above the HAWAII layer. When an image is clipped into a given layer, the image takes on the layer styles applied to that given layer. However, the stroke does *not* appear in the letter A because the Family layer is above the HAWAII layer and is not clipped. Again, this is another good example of how the choices you make when building an illustration will affect choices you make later on down the line.

LESSON 11

ADD A DROP SHADOW
Layer Style

What You'll Do

As a designer, you should keep the word "flat" in the back of your mind whenever you assess your work at a given stage. Flat is usually not a good thing—not an objective you are trying to achieve.

The HAWAII art at this stage is flat. Note that even with the multiple images, the masking and the stroke, the overall effect remains stubbornly two dimensional. We want the HAWAII art to "pop"—to jump off the page.

A drop shadow is a tried and true solution for adding the illusion of depth to an illustration. In this lesson, you are going to add a drop shadow to create the effect that the word HAWAII is floating above the water in the background.

Add a drop shadow layer style

1. With the HAWAII layer still targeted, click the **Add a layer style button** *fx* on the Layers palette, then click **Drop Shadow**.

   As shown in Figure 33, the Drop Shadow check box is automatically checked because you chose Drop Shadow from the list. The Stroke check box is also checked because you previously added a stroke style, and it is still active.

2. Drag the **Distance slider** to 16 px.

   The Distance slider determines the offset of the shadow—how far it is positioned from the object.

3. Drag the **Angle slider** counterclockwise so that the text box reads 45.
4. Drag the **Size slider** to 5 px.

   Along with the size of the shadow, the Size slider determines the softness of the shadow.

5. Click the **Set color of shadow button** to open the Select shadow color dialog box.
6. Type **13R/8G/57B** to choose a dark blue color, then click **OK**.
7. Drag the **Opacity slider** to 85, click **OK**, then compare your work to Figure 34.

   Take some time to note how the drop shadow adds a sense of depth to the illustration. Note how the 16-pixel distance that you chose for the offset defines the degree of depth. Note too how the images in the letterforms appear more vibrant in contrast to the dark shadow behind them.

8. Save your work.

FIGURE 33
Drop Shadow settings in the Layer Style dialog box

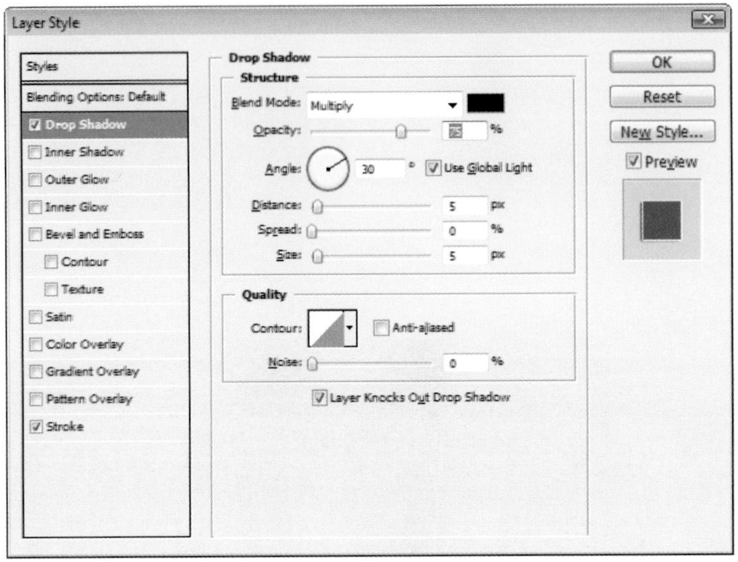

FIGURE 34
Viewing the drop shadow

LESSON 12

APPLY AN ADJUSTMENT Layer to Multiple Layers

What You'll Do

The Stretch image is perhaps the best in terms of color balance and vibrancy. The Family image lacks contrast and has an overall red cast to it. Of course, you could always adjust the color in each image. In this lesson, however, you will use an adjustment layer to modify the color in all the layers, with the goal of adding some degree of color consistency across all six letterforms.

Whenever you work with multiple images in a single piece of art, color consistency is something you need to consider.

The images that you are working with in this chapter are from a photo service and were taken in different settings, under different lighting conditions and by different photographers.

If you looked at them separately, you might not notice any distinct differences, but side by side, the inconsistency is apparent.

Apply an adjustment layer to multiple layers

1. Click the **Layer thumbnail** (not the layer mask) on the Family layer.

   When a layer has a layer mask, you can target either the image or the layer mask.

   A white frame appears around the targeted thumbnail in the Layers palette.
2. Press **[Tab]** to hide all palettes.
3. Click **Layer** on the menu bar, point to **New Adjustment Layer**, then click **Color Balance**.
4. Type **Add Red** in the Name text box, then, if necessary, remove the check mark in the Use Previous Layer to Create Clipping Mask check box.

   You would activate the Use Previous Layer to Create Clipping Mask check box if you wanted to apply the adjustment only to the Family layer. In this case, you want to apply the adjustment to all layers beneath the adjustment layer.
5. Click **OK**.
6. Drag the **top slider** to the right—toward Red—until the value in the first Color Levels text box reads +50, then compare your canvas to Figure 35.

(continued)

FIGURE 35
Color effect of the adjustment layer

AUTHOR'S *note*

When you create an adjustment layer, you have the option to click Use Previous Layer to Create Clipping Mask. This means that the adjustments made in this adjustment layer will affect only the "previous" layer—the layer that was targeted when you created the adjustment layer. If this choice is not activated, the adjustment layer will affect *all* the layers below it in the Layers palette.

FIGURE 36
Changing the Red value to +20

FIGURE 37
Color effect of the adjustment layer clipped into the mask

7. Drag the **slider** left until the value reads +20, click **OK**, then compare your canvas to Figure 36.
8. Press **[Tab]**, then hide and show the adjustment layer in the Layers palette to note the color change and which layers were affected.

   Note how the addition of red across all the images adds a sense of consistency and continuity. However, note too that the water in the background looks a bit purple, which is not what we want.
9. Press and hold **[Alt]** (Win) or **[option]** (Mac), position your cursor in the Layers palette between the adjustment layer and the Family layer, then click.

   The adjustment layer is clipped into the Family layer. If you hide and show the adjustment layer, you will see that the Family layer is now the only layer being affected by the adjustment layer.
10. Press and hold **[Alt]** (Win) or **[option]** (Mac), position your cursor in the Layers palette between the Family layer and the Snorkelers layer, then click.
11. Compare your artwork to Figure 37.

    Hide and show the adjustment layer. Because the Family layer is now part of the group that is clipped into the HAWAII layer, the adjustment layer now affects all of the clipped images. However, it does not affect the water in the background, because those two layers are not part of the clipped group.
12. Save your work.

LESSON 13

EDIT LAYER Styles

What You'll Do

As with adjustment layers, layer styles can be modified at any time. This is yet another example of how Photoshop has evolved to allow you the freedom to execute design choices knowing that you can modify them at a later time. For example, you applied a stroke as a layer style even though you could have applied it using the Stroke command. The big difference, of course, is that the stroke created with the layer style can be edited.

FIGURE 38
Three layer styles applied to the artwork

AUTHOR'S *note*

From a design perspective there's a lot to look at as the result of these three simple changes. First, note how the black stroke is so much better for the illustration than the white stroke. The black stroke delineates the letterforms, but it does so without calling attention to itself. Compare that to the white stroke, which practically screamed, "Hey, look at me! I'm a white stroke!" Note too how the black stroke is a segue to the dark drop shadow behind it. The reduction of the opacity of the shadow from 85% to 70% creates a more consistent transparency effect with the 50% opacity of the inner shadow.

Earlier, we discussed goals of adding depth to the image. Note how the drop shadow and the inner shadow conflict in such an interesting way. The drop shadow moves the masked images up off the page, as though they are floating and casting a shadow on the water. But the inner shadow pushes them back, as though they are beneath something that is casting a shadow. This is especially apparent on the first letter A. On the left edge, note how the drop shadow creates the effect that the A is above the water. On the right edge, note how the inner shadow creates the effect that the stroke is casting a shadow on the image inside the A. Interesting, yes? What's even more interesting is that the eye does not register the conflict between these effects as a problem. Instead, the varying depth effects created by the shadow layer styles serve to make the overall effect more intriguing.

Edit layer styles

1. Target the **HAWAII layer**, then double-click the **Stroke effect** listed beneath the HAWAII layer in the Layers palette.

   The Layer Style dialog box opens showing the stroke settings you applied earlier.

2. Click the **Set color of stroke box** to open the Set stroke color dialog box, type **0** in the R, G, and B text boxes, then click **OK**.
3. Click **Drop Shadow** in the list on the left side of the dialog box.

   TIP Be sure to click the Drop Shadow name itself, not the check box beside it.

   The Layer Style dialog box changes to show the drop shadow settings you applied earlier, and a check mark appears automatically beside Drop Shadow in the list.

4. Drag the **Opacity slider** to 70%.
5. Click **Inner Shadow** in the list on the left side of the dialog box.
6. Drag the **Distance slider** to 8 px, drag the **Opacity slider** to 50%, click **OK**, then compare your canvas to Figure 38.

   An Inner Shadow effect layer now appears in the Layers palette between Drop Shadow and Stroke.

   TIP Layer styles are listed in alphabetical order, regardless of the order in which they are applied.

7. Save your work.

LESSON 14

COPY LAYER STYLES
Between Layers

What You'll Do

We've spent much time up to this point discussing how adjustment layers and layer styles are so powerful because they can be modified at any time. We also have discussed how they remain in the Layers palette as a record of the adjustments and styles that you've applied to the image.

This lesson brings these two great features together. Layer styles can be copied between layers. This allows you to create a specific style only once and then use it multiple times in the document.

The ability to modify layer styles becomes very important when duplicating layer styles. Duplicating a layer style is a quick and effective method for applying the same style to multiple layers. However, the specific style settings for one layer may or may not work for the artwork on other layers. No problem. With layer styles, you can simply adjust the style to fit the new artwork.

FIGURE 39

Dragging the Effects layer to the Land of Aloha layer

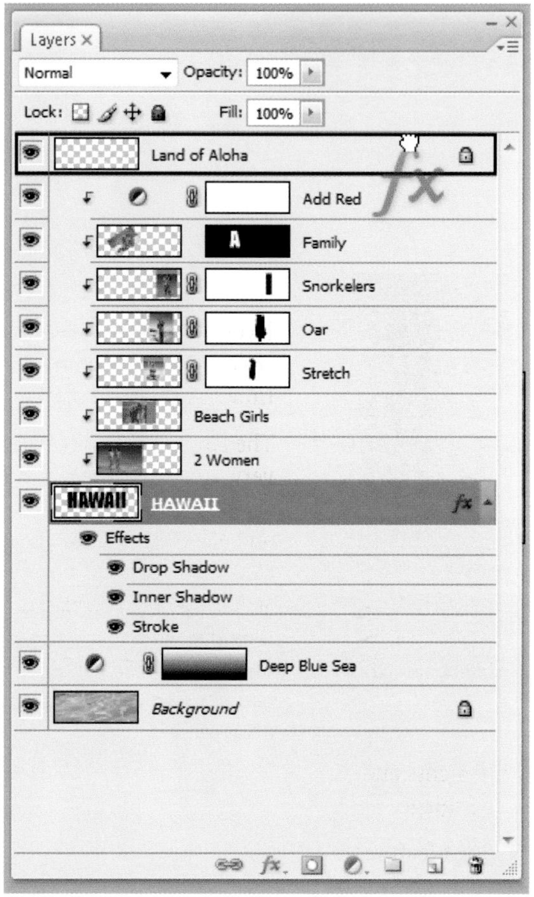

Copy styles between layers

1. Note the three layer styles listed beneath the HAWAII layer, then note the Effects layer listed above all three.

   TIP The Effects layer represents all the styles applied to the layer.

2. Verify that you can see all the layers in the Layers palette.
3. Press and hold the **Effects layer** beneath HAWAII, then drag it up to the Land of Aloha layer, releasing when you see a black rectangle around the layer, as shown in Figure 39.

(continued)

4. Compare your artwork to Figure 40.

   The three layer styles are moved—not copied—from the HAWAII layer to the Land of Aloha layer.

5. Undo the move.

6. Press and hold **[Alt]** (Win) or **[option]** (Mac), then drag only the **Drop Shadow layer style** up to the Land of Aloha layer.

   As shown in Figure 41, the Drop Shadow layer style is copied to the Land of Aloha layer.

   > **TIP** Pressing and holding [Alt] (Win) or [option] (Mac), then dragging a single layer style or the Effects layer creates a copy of the effect(s) on the destination layer.

7. If you do not see the drop shadow, click to the left of Effects to show the Toggle all layer effect visibilities button.

8. Double-click the **Drop Shadow layer style** in the Land of Aloha layer.

9. Drag the **Distance slider** to 6 px, change the Opacity to 95%, then click **OK**.

9. Press **[Tab]** to hide the palettes, hide the rulers if they are visible, then press **[F]** twice.

   Your canvas should appear alone against a black screen.

   > **TIP** Pressing [F] toggles three views of the canvas. Those views correspond with the three screen mode buttons on the toolbox.

10. Compare your canvas to Figure 42.

11. Press **[F]**, save your work, then close HAWAII.psd.

FIGURE 40
Results of moving the layer style

FIGURE 41
Copied layer style

FIGURE 42
Finished artwork

PROJECT BUILDER 1

Use layered artwork as masks

1. Open AP 1-2.psd, then save it as **On the Beach**.
2. Fill the artwork on the Outer Beach layer with white.
3. Fill the artwork on the Inner Beach layer with black.
4. Open the file named Beach Scene.psd, select all, copy, then close the file.
5. Target the Inner Beach layer, then paste.
6. Name the new layer **Beach Scene**.
7. Duplicate the Beach Scene layer, then rename the duplicate **Outer Scene**.
8. Drag the Outer Scene layer down so that it is above the Outer Beach layer.
9. Hide the Outer Scene and Outer Beach layers.
10. Clip the Beach Scene layer into the Inner Beach layer.
11. Hide the Beach Scene and the Inner Beach layers, then show the Outer Scene and Outer Beach layers.
12. Clip the Outer Scene layer into the Outer Beach layer.
13. Save your work.

Use adjustment layers and layer masks

1. Target the Outer Scene layer, then create a Hue/Saturation adjustment layer. (*Hint:* Accept the default name; Be sure to click the Use Previous Layer to Create Clipping Mask check box.)
2. Drag the Saturation to -100, then click OK.
3. Target the Outer Beach layer, then change its blending mode to Luminosity. (*Hint:* To change a blending mode, click the Normal list arrow at the top of the Layers palette, then choose a blending mode from the list.)
4. Reduce the opacity to 75%.
5. Target the Outer Scene layer, click Layer on the menu bar, point to New Adjustment Layer, then click Brightness/Contrast. (*Hint:* The top third of the Outer Scene artwork is too dark for the illustration. We will brighten all of the artwork, then use a layer mask to affect just the top third.)
6. Type **Brighten Top Third Only** in the Name dialog box, verify that the Use Previous Layer to Create Clipping Mask check box is checked, then click OK.
7. Verify that the Preview and Use Legacy check boxes are both checked.
8. Drag the Brightness slider to +35, then click OK.
9. Set your foreground color to white, then set your background color to black.
10. Click the Gradient Tool, then click the Linear Gradient button on the Options bar, if necessary. (*Hint:* You may want to verify that the Foreground to Background gradient is the active gradient in the Gradient Picker.)
11. Verify that the layer mask on the Brighten Top Third Only adjustment layer is targeted.
12. Position your cursor at the top center of the artwork, click and drag straight down, then release at the bottom of the artwork.
13. Toggle the Brighten Top Third Only adjustment layer on and off to see the change.
14. Open the Brighten Top Third Only adjustment layer, then increase the Brightness value to +50.
15. Show the Beach Scene and Inner Beach layers, then compare your artwork to Figure 43.
16. Save your work, then close On the Beach.

FIGURE 43
Completed Project Builder 1

PROJECT BUILDER 2

1. Open AP 1-3.psd, then save it as **On the Beach Styles**.
2. Target the Inner Beach layer.
3. Click Layer on the menu bar, point to Layer Style, then click Drop Shadow.
4. Verify that shadow color is set to black.
5. Verify that the blend mode is set to Multiply and the Opacity is set to 50%.
6. Check the Use Global Light check box, then set the angle to 144.
7. Verify that the Distance, Spread and Size values are set to 9, 0, and 5 respectively.
8. On the left side of the dialog box, click the words Outer Glow.
9. Verify that the blend mode is set to Multiply and the Opacity is set to 75%.
10. Set the color of the glow to black.
11. Verify that the Technique is set to Softer, the Spread is set to 5 and the Size is set to 9.
12. On the left side of the dialog box, click the word Stroke.
13. Set the size to 2 px, then set the Position to Outside.
14. Set the stroke color to black, then click OK to close the Layer Style dialog box.
15. Target the Outer Beach layer.
16. Click Layer on the menu bar, point to Layer Style, then click Inner Shadow.
17. Verify that the blend mode is set to Multiply and the Opacity is set to 75%.
18. Check the Use Global Light check box, then set the angle to 144.
19. Set the Distance, Choke and Size values to 6, 0, and 5 respectively.
20. Click OK, then compare your results to Figure 44.
21. Save your work, then close On the Beach Styles.

PROJECT BUILDER 2

FIGURE 44
Completed Project Builder 2

TOP 20

chapter 2

WORKING WITH Layer Styles

1. Copy and paste from Illustrator to Photoshop.
2. Import layers from Adobe Illustrator.
3. Create a Chisel Hard Emboss layer style.
4. Select specific areas of layer-styled artwork.
5. Create a Smooth Emboss layer style.
6. Create and apply a Gradient Overlay to a layer style.
7. Create a Pillow Emboss layer style.
8. Copy layer styles between layers.
9. Create a chrome effect without using layer styles.
10. Duplicate a chrome effect without using layer styles.

LESSON 1

COPY AND PASTE FROM
Illustrator to Photoshop

What You'll Do

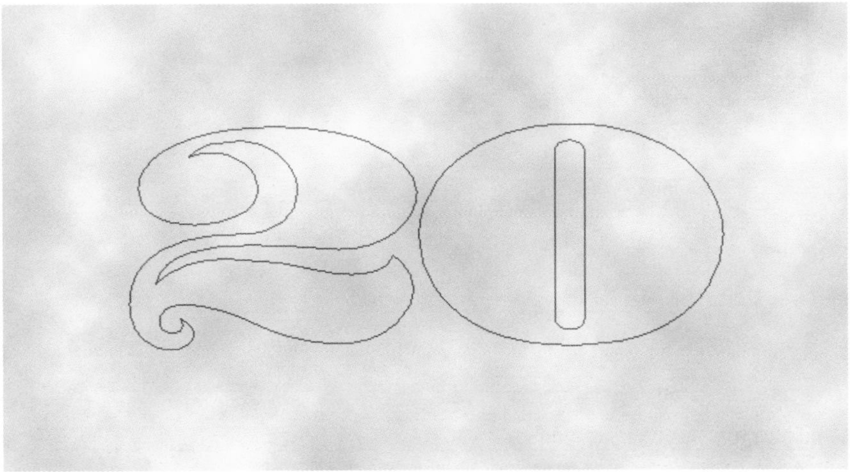

Adobe Photoshop and Adobe Illustrator have always been closely related—so much so that many users refer to them as "sister" applications. With the upgrade to the Creative Suite and now with CS3, that relationship has been highlighted. With Photoshop and Illustrator bundled together with InDesign, the relationship between the Adobe Trinity is seamless—and powerful.

Photoshop and Illustrator overlap each other in their abilities. Photoshop can do a lot of things that Illustrator can do; the Pen Tool offers the ability to draw vector graphics, and Photoshop's text-handling capabilities have been upgraded dramatically from recent versions. Illustrator, on the other hand, is exclusively a vector-based application; the bitmap world belongs to Photoshop.

Nevertheless, Illustrator is an articulate and powerful software package. But many professional designers are so Photoshop-oriented that they completely ignore Illustrator. They tell themselves that Photoshop can do everything that Illustrator can do—and that's just not true.

Illustrator offers many smart and sophisticated options for working with paths and typography. Incorporate Illustrator into your skills set, and you'll soon find that you're producing typography and graphics that are more interesting and sophisticated than what most other designers are coming up with in Photoshop. That's a sweet edge to have in the competitive world of graphic design.

The key, of course, is moving graphics from Illustrator into Photoshop—into the photographic artwork. With CS3, that transition is as seamless as Copy/Paste.

FIGURE 1
Pasting art from Illustrator into Photoshop

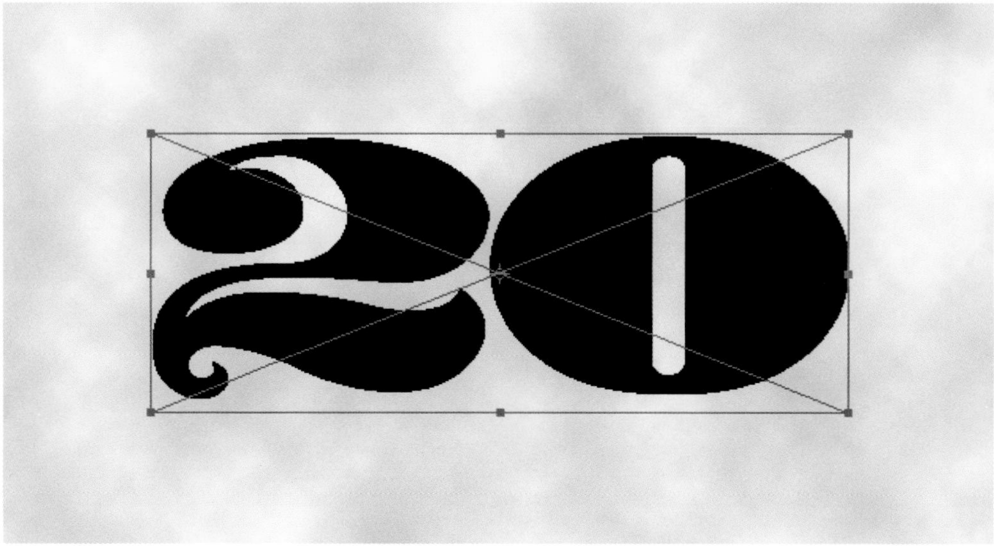

AUTHOR'S *note*

When pasting from Illustrator to Photoshop, it's a good idea to keep the File Handling & Clipboard preferences as they are set in Step 2. With these settings, you are offered the Paste dialog box when you paste Illustrator artwork into Photoshop. Without these settings, copied artwork is automatically rasterized when pasted in Photoshop.

AICB stands for Adobe Illustrator Clipboard. The phrase (no transparency support) refers to the fact that the artwork you are copying from Illustrator will be flattened when pasted—in other words, you're not copying layers. This is not a problem for most Illustrator artwork, especially artwork which, as in this case, you are using as simple base art for Photoshop.

Copy and paste from Illustrator to Photoshop

1. Open AP 2-1.ai in Illustrator, click **Edit** (Win) or **Illustrator** (Mac) on the menu bar, point to **Preferences**, then click **File Handling & Clipboard**.
2. In the Clipboard on Quit section, verify that the PDF and the AICB (no transparency support) check boxes are both checked and that the Preserve Paths option button is selected, then click **OK**.

   See the Author's note on this page.
3. Click the **Selection Tool** , select the two numbers, then copy them.
4. Switch to Photoshop, open AP 2-2.psd in Photoshop, then save it as **Paste From Illustrator**.
5. Display the Layers palette, if necessary.
6. Click **Edit** on the menu bar, then click **Paste**.

   The Paste dialog box appears, offering you four options for pasting. We will explore the Pixels, Path, and Shape Layer options in this chapter and the Smart Object option in a later chapter.
7. Click the **Pixels option button**, then click **OK**.

   As shown in Figure 1, the artwork is pasted in a bounding box, which can be resized, rotated, and so on.
8. Click the **Move Tool** , then click **Place**.

   When you paste as pixels, the result of the paste is a bitmap graphic, which is pasted as a new layer. No vector information is pasted with the graphic.

(continued)

9. Delete the new layer.

10. Click **Edit** on the menu bar, click **Paste**, click the **Path option button**, then click **OK**.

    As shown in Figure 2, the path from Illustrator is pasted; a new layer is *not* created.

11. Click **Window** on the menu bar, click **Paths**, then note that the path was pasted as a new Work Path.

12. Click below the Work Path in the Paths palette to turn the Work Path off.

    The path disappears.

13. Change the foreground color to any red swatch in the Swatches palette.

14. Paste again, click the **Shape Layer option button**, then click **OK**.

    As shown in Figure 3, the artwork is pasted as a shape layer and uses the foreground color as its fill.

    Shape layers are vector graphics positioned on layers in a Photoshop document. As vectors, they can be scaled and otherwise transformed without any loss in quality. This makes shape layers ideal for handling paths from Illustrator.

15. Save your work, close AP 2-1.ai, then close the Paste from Illustrator document.

FIGURE 2

Pasting an Illustrator path as a path in Photoshop

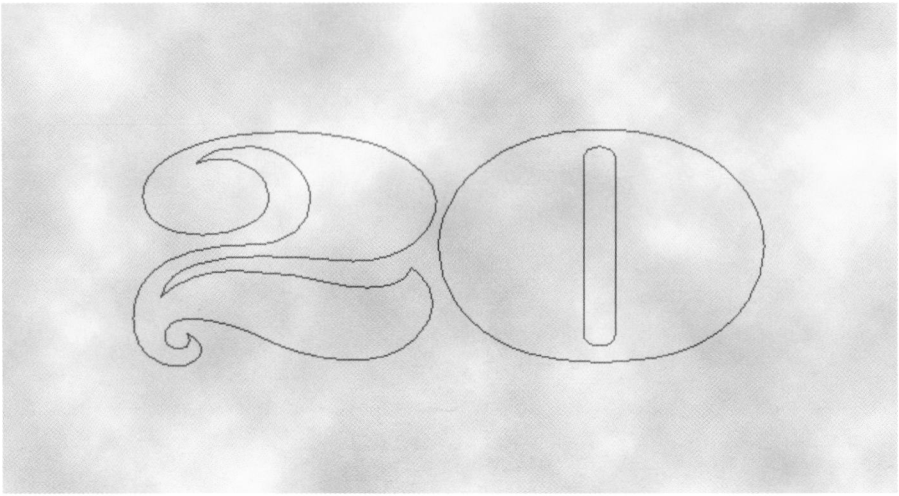

FIGURE 3

Pasting an Illustrator path as a Shape layer in Photoshop

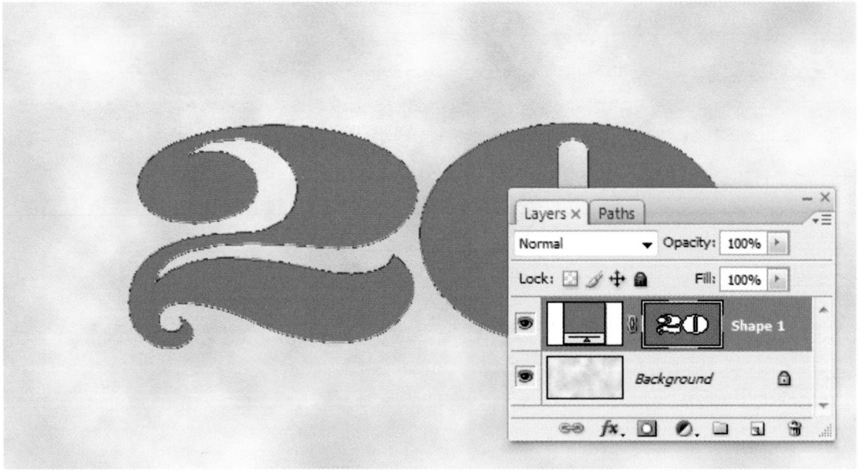

LESSON 2

IMPORT LAYERS FROM Adobe Illustrator

What You'll Do

Never forget that Photoshop and Illustrator are remarkably compatible. Incorporating the power of Illustrator into your Photoshop skills set expands your overall skills set as a designer exponentially. Indeed, when you are as fluent in Illustrator as you are in Photoshop, you'll find that much of the artwork you want to create in Photoshop is often best started in Illustrator, with all of its great drawing tools and precise typographical abilities.

With each upgrade, Adobe has strived to make Photoshop and Illustrator more and more compatible. One of the best features of that compatibility is the ability to export layered artwork from Illustrator to Photoshop while maintaining the layer structure created in Illustrator. This is an amazing feature and bravo! to Adobe for putting it in place. Once you've created layered artwork in Illustrator, this powerful option allows you to target those layers individually after the artwork has been exported to Photoshop. In other words, you maintain the same working relationship with the artwork from one application to the other.

Export layers from Illustrator to Photoshop

1. Open AP 2-3.ai in Adobe Illustrator, then save it as **Export Illustrator Layers**.

   TIP Click OK in the Illustrator Options dialog box.

2. Display the Layers palette, click the **Selection Tool** then pull the individual pieces of the illustration apart, keeping an eye on the Layers palette.
3. Click **File** on the menu bar, click **Revert,** then click **Revert** in the dialog box that follows.
4. Click **File** on the menu bar, then click **Export**.
5. Click the **Save as type list arrow** (Win) or the **Format list arrow** (Mac) in the Export dialog box, then click **Photoshop (*.PSD)** (Win) or **Photoshop (psd)** (Mac), as shown in Figure 4.

   TIP Note that the file to be exported is automatically named with the .psd extension: Export Illustrator Layers.psd.

6. Click **Save** (Win) or **Export** (Mac).

   The Photoshop Export Options dialog box opens.

7. Click the **Color Model list arrow**, click **RGB**, then click the **High (300 ppi) option button**.

   It is important to understand that, with this export, you are creating a Photoshop file. The choices you made in this step determined the color model of the file—RGB—and the resolution of the file—300 ppi.

(continued)

FIGURE 4
Export dialog box

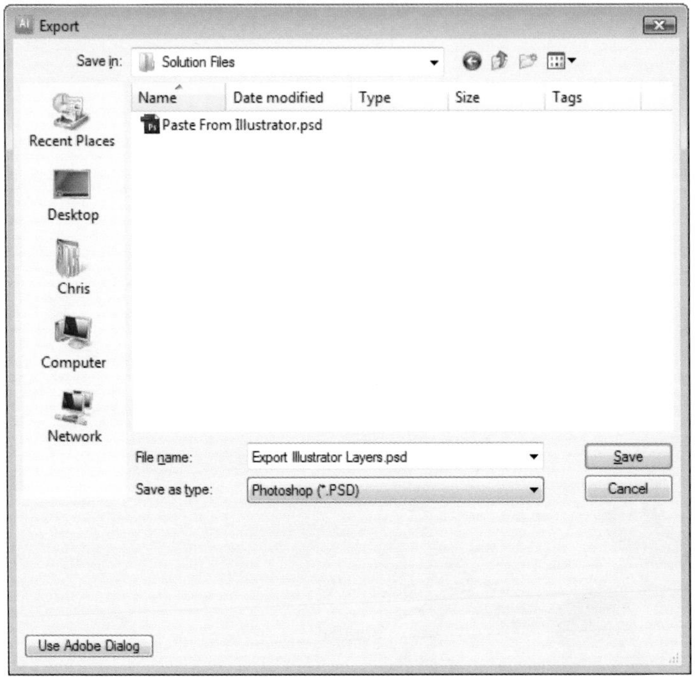

FIGURE 5
Photoshop Export Options dialog box

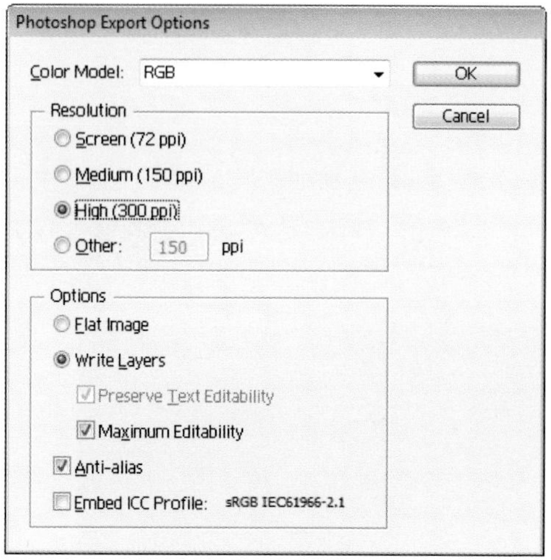

FIGURE 6
Illustrator artwork and layers exported to Photoshop

8. In the Options section, click the **Write Layers option button**, click the **Maximum Editability check box**, then click the **Anti-alias check box** so that your dialog box resembles Figure 5.

   With these choices, you have specified that you want to save or "write" the layers from the Illustrator file to the Photoshop file and that you want the artwork to be anti-aliased in the Photoshop file.

9. Click **OK**, then close the Illustrator document.
10. Open **Export Illustrator Layers.psd** in Photoshop.
11. Notice that the layers from Illustrator—including their layer names—were exported into the Photoshop Layers palette, as shown in Figure 6.
12. Close Export Illustrator Layers.

AUTHOR'S *note*

It's a good idea to always choose the highest resolution for the exported file. In Photoshop, you can always reduce the resolution if you want to. Remember the first rule of changing resolution in Photoshop: It is always better, from an image quality standpoint, to reduce the resolution of a Photoshop file than it is to increase the resolution.

LESSON 3

CREATE A CHISEL HARD
Emboss Layer Style

What You'll Do

Chisel Hard Emboss, the first of many layer styles you'll experiment and work with in this chapter, creates a dramatic, three-dimensional effect. A chisel is anything but a gentle tool, and this layer style delivers exactly what its name implies: A chiseled effect with a hard edge. Chisel Hard Emboss, a subset of the Bevel and Emboss layer style, is a very useful layer style, one that you will use often, especially when you want to create the effect of a hard metal edge.

AUTHOR'S *note*

Take a few minutes here to examine the illustration—hide and show the layers to see how it was built. It's a fairly simple illustration—just four layers—a background layer, two foreground layers, and a text layer. The number 2 is a nicely designed path, and the 0 is charmingly fat. The way the word TOP interacts with the number 20 is a fine example of the nuanced path work that makes Illustrator such a great program. With all the layers showing, note that the background gray graphic plays the role of a stroke around all five shapes—as though each shape had a gray stroke of varying weight, and those strokes overlap. Clearly, this is artwork that you would want to create in Illustrator, not in Photoshop. Even though Photoshop does have a very sophisticated Pen Tool and vector capabilities, Illustrator is far and away the best application for creating line art.

Create a Chisel Hard Emboss layer style

1. Open AP 2-4.psd, then save it as **Top 20**.
2. Verify that you are viewing the document at 25%.
3. Hide the Text layer and the 20 layer, then target the **20 Back layer**.
4. Click **Layer** on the menu bar, point to **Layer Style**, then click **Bevel and Emboss**.
5. Verify that the Preview check box is checked, then move the dialog box so that you can see as much of the artwork as possible.

   TIP If you can't see much of the art, click Cancel, reduce the view of the art to 12.5%, then return to the Layer Style dialog box.

6. Verify that Style is set to Inner Bevel in the Structure section.
7. Click the **Technique list arrow**, then click **Chisel Hard**.
8. Drag the **Size slider** to 29, then experiment by dragging the slider to different values.

   When you choose Chisel Hard, the size has an enormous impact on the final effect. Note that the more you increase the value, the greater the edge becomes. Note too that the greater the edge becomes, the less "interior" you have to the artwork.

(continued)

9. Return the **Size slider** to 29.
10. Type **42** in the Angle text box.

    The angle determines the angle that the light source strikes the artwork.
11. Experiment with various angle values, then return to **42**.
12. Click the **Gloss Contour list arrow**, then click **Ring** (the second thumbnail in the second row).

    Gloss contours are preset curves—just like the curves you use to color correct an image—that dramatically affect the contrast and the appearance of the layer effect. Explore the other contours, but be sure to return to Ring.
13. Click the **Anti-aliased check box**, and note the effect on the artwork.
14. For a dramatic effect, increase the contrast by dragging the **Highlight Mode Opacity slider** to 95%.
15. Click the **Contour check box** directly beneath the Bevel and Emboss check box in the Styles section on the left.

    Like a gloss contour, the Contour check box applies a preset curve.
16. Compare your Layer Style dialog box to Figure 7.
17. Click **OK**, then compare your canvas to Figure 8.

    Note that an aberration has occurred between the *O* and the *P* in the word *TOP*. It's that round shiny circle, and it shouldn't be there.

(continued)

FIGURE 7

Bevel and Emboss settings in the Layer Style dialog box

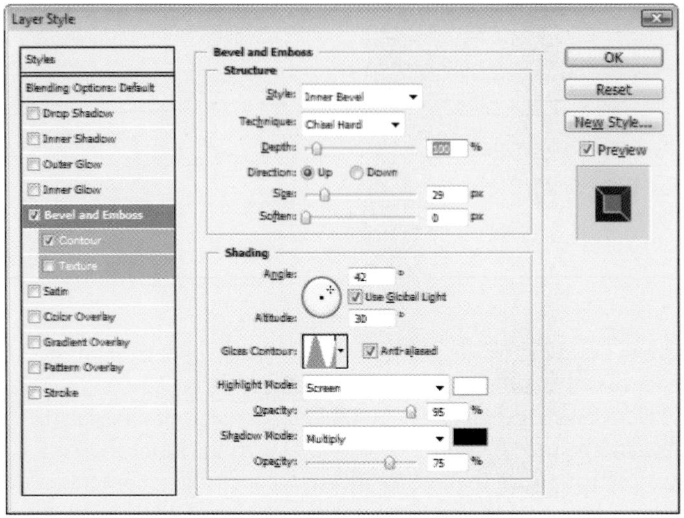

FIGURE 8

Effect of applying the Chisel Hard Inner Bevel layer style

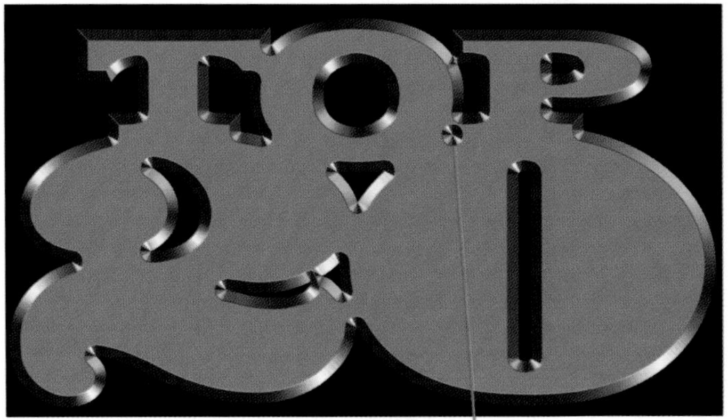

Aberration is a round shiny circle which should not be here

FIGURE 9

The effect without the aberration

FIGURE 10

Identifying other aberrations

18. Zoom in on the aberration, click the **Polygonal Lasso Tool**, draw a marquee around the circular aberration, then hide the Effects layer.

    A single pixel that is darker than the surrounding pixels caused the Bevel and Emboss layer style to create a Chisel Hard Emboss at this spot.

    TIP You'll need to really zoom in to see the pixel.

19. Use the Eyedropper Tool to sample the surrounding gray pixels, then fill the marquee with the sampled gray.

20. Return the view to 25%, make the Effects layer visible again, then deselect.

    As shown in Figure 9, the aberration has disappeared because the dark pixel is no longer there. This is a fine example of how layer styles are dynamic. Changing the artwork changes the effect that the layer style has on the artwork.

21. Save your work.

    Whenever you are working with layer styles, expect aberrations to occur. It's important that you understand that the dramatic effects that you create with layer styles are achieved by applying complex mathematical algorithms to the artwork. When artwork overlaps or when a stray pixel gets involved, strange results can occur. Figure 10 shows other, less obvious aberrations that resulted from using an Inner Bevel style with a Chisel Hard Emboss technique. Zoom in on them, and keep an eye on them as you progress through the chapter.

LESSON 4

SELECT SPECIFIC AREAS OF Layer-Styled Artwork

What You'll Do

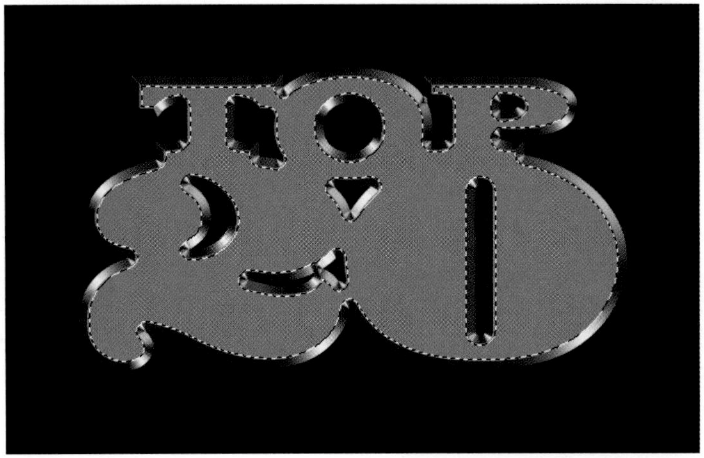

Fasten your seatbelts—we're going to hit the brakes! In this lesson we are going to select only the gray pixels that are inside the chiseled edge, as shown in the figure above. Sounds simple enough, right? As you will see, that simple goal is not so simple.

We are going to attempt to achieve the goal using various techniques, and many of them won't work. The important thing is that, along the way, you will be exposed to a number of important concepts and useful techniques that involve menu commands, layer commands, quick keys, and channels.

FIGURE 11
Magic Wand Tool selection

FIGURE 12
Selected base art

Transform a selection marquee

1. Change the name of the 20 Back layer to **Chisel Hard Emboss**.
2. Click the **Magic Wand Tool**, set the Tolerance value to **0**, make sure that both the Anti-alias and the Contiguous check boxes are checked and that Sample All Layers is not checked.
3. Verify that the Chisel Hard Emboss layer is targeted, click the **central gray area** on the artwork that is inside the chiseled edge.

   The selection that you get, shown in Figure 11, may not be what you expected. All of the artwork on the layer was selected, because all of the artwork on the layer is that same gray value.
4. Hide the Bevel and Emboss layer style in the Layers palette.

   All of the pixels were selected because they are all the same color, as shown in Figure 12. The Bevel and Emboss layer style makes it appear that there's a beveled edge, but that is just an illusion. The layer style changes the *appearance* of the base art, but it does not change the art itself. This is a very important concept for you to have in the back of your mind when you work with layer styles.
5. Show the Bevel and Emboss layer style in the Layers palette.

(continued)

6. Click **Select** on the menu bar, then click **Transform Selection**.

   A standard transform bounding box appears around the selection. Remember, the Transform Selection command allows you to transform the *selection marquee* itself. Usually, you transform the *pixels* that are selected by the selection marquee, but here you are transforming the marquee only.

7. Press and hold **[Shift]**, then drag any of the **corner handles** toward the center of the bounding box to reduce the size of the selection.

   As shown in Figure 13, you are able to reduce the selection, but no matter what you do, you won't be able to reduce it in a way that makes it select the gray areas only. Scaling the selection marquee won't work for an important reason: The outside edge of the beveled edge and the area you want to select are two different shapes.

8. Click the **Move Tool**, then click **Don't Apply**.

9. Keep the artwork selected.

Contract a selection marquee

1. Click **Select** on the menu bar, point to **Modify**, then click **Contract**.

2. Type **29**, then click **OK**.

   Because you specified the size of the chiseled edge as 29 pixels, you need to contract the selection by the same. As shown in Figure 14, this seems to have achieved the objective.

(continued)

FIGURE 13
Transforming the selection

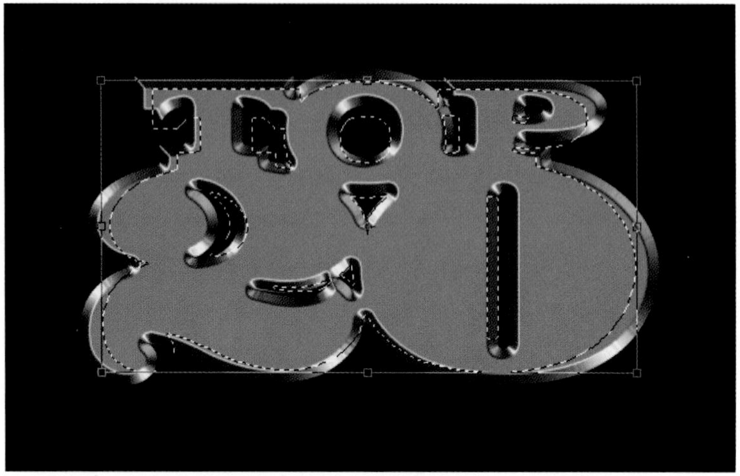

FIGURE 14
Contracted selection marquee

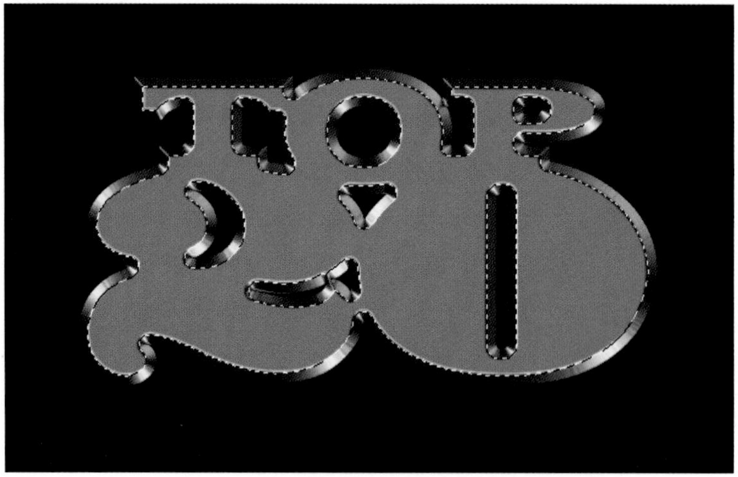

FIGURE 15
Filled selection

3. Change the foreground color to red, click the **Create a new layer button** on the Layers palette, then fill the selection.
4. Deselect, hide the other layers, then zoom in to 100%.

   On closer inspection, the edges are crudely drawn. This is especially visible on the curl at the base of the number 2, shown in Figure 15. This command was not able to contract the selection and also maintain the nuanced curves of the outer chiseled edge. The curves are poorly drawn—straight lines and pointy corners—and this will be noticeable in the final artwork.

(continued)

5. Show Layer 1, show the Chisel Hard Emboss layer, then examine how the red copy "sits" inside the gray area.

   Figure 16 proves that the relationship is not satisfactory. The unsightly gaps and crude corners will be visible when the illustration is viewed or printed at 100%.

6. Zoom down to 25%, then delete the layer with the red graphic.

Create a channel to modify a selection

1. Target the **Chisel Hard Emboss layer**, click the **Magic Wand Tool**, then select the gray area again.
2. Click **Select** on the menu bar, then click **Save Selection**.
3. Name the selection **Stroke Trick**, then click **OK**.

(continued)

FIGURE 16

Examining the relationship between the filled selection and the background art

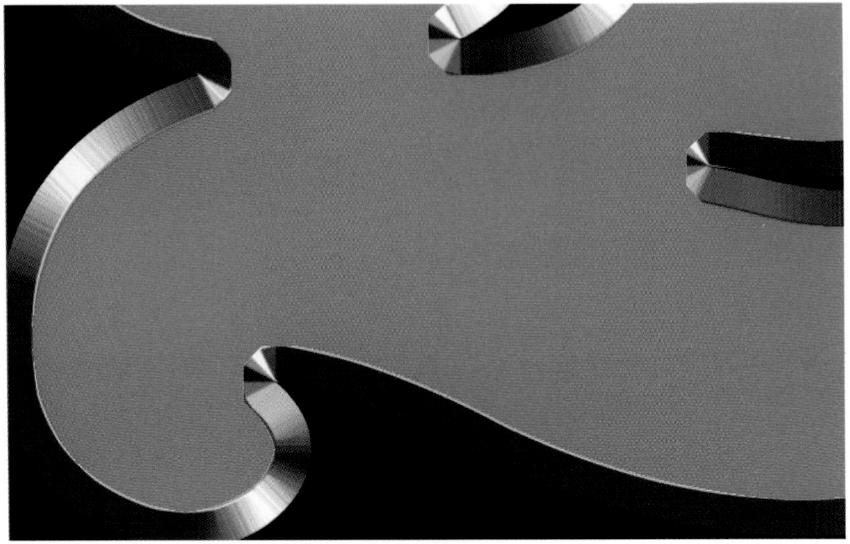

AUTHOR'S *note*

Keep in mind, you are trying to create a visually powerful illustration here—one with a big wow factor. Always remember that the bigger the wow factor, the closer it will be examined by your audience. They're going to stop and look at it, appreciate it, critique it, and *look closely* to try to guess how you did it.

FIGURE 17
Saved selection in a channel

4. Click **Window** on the menu bar, click **Channels**, then click the **Stroke Trick channel**.

   When you save a selection, you create a channel. The channel *is* the selection. As shown in Figure 17, the selected areas are represented as white, and the unselected areas are represented by black. Note that the selection is still active.

5. Change the foreground color to Black.
6. Click **Edit** on the menu bar, then click **Stroke**.

   The default location setting for the stroke is Center, which means the stroke will be positioned equally on both sides of the selection marquee.

7. Type **58** in the Width text box.

   Your goal here is to reduce the selected areas (the white pixels in the channel) by making them black. You know that you want to reduce the selected area by 29 pixels. Since the stroke will be positioned equally on both sides of the marquee, you've doubled the width of the stroke to 58.

   TIP Though we could click Inside and set the Width value to 29, I hesitate to do so because I fear it would leave a slight white or gray line at the marquee line. In other words, it might not be perfect.

(continued)

8. Click **OK**.

   With the black stroke, the white areas of channel are reduced by 29 pixels. Unfortunately, as shown in Figure 18, the result is similar if not identical to the result of contracting the selection marquee: unsightly rough corners.

9. Delete the Stroke Trick channel.

Duplicate a document

1. Verify that the Chisel Hard Emboss layer is targeted.
2. Click **Image** on the menu bar, then click **Duplicate**.
3. Type **Dupe** in the As text box, then click **OK**.
4. Click **Layer** on the menu bar, click **Flatten Image**, then click **OK** in the dialog box that follows to discard hidden layers.
5. Click the **Magic Wand Tool**, then click the **gray area**.

   Because the document is flattened, the Bevel and Emboss layer style is no longer on a layer. The Chisel Hard Emboss effect is no longer just an appearance. Thus, as shown in Figure 19, the Magic Wand Tool can make the selection that has been your goal all along.

6. Fill the selection with red.
7. Copy the selection, then close Dupe without saving changes.

(continued)

FIGURE 18
Results of stroking the selection

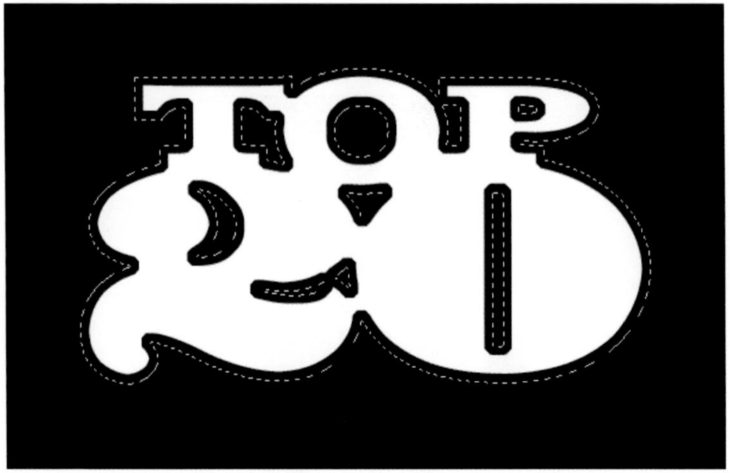

FIGURE 19
Selecting within the flattened artwork

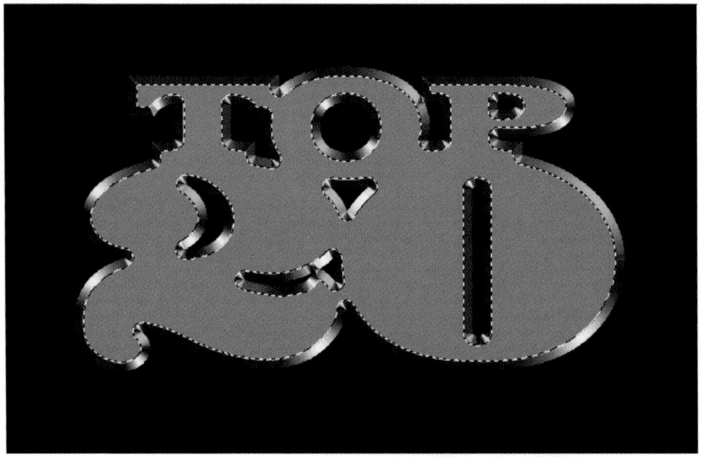

FIGURE 20
Filled selection

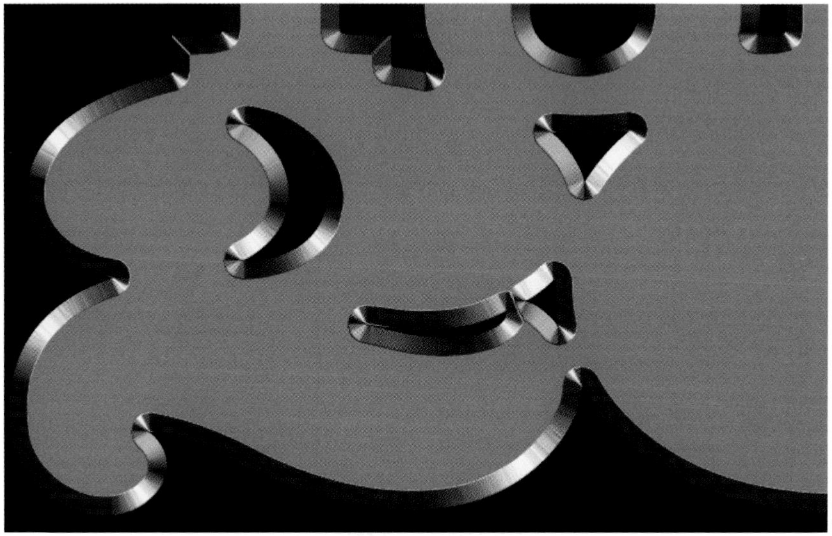

8. Paste the copied selection into the Top 20 document, then align it with the gray background area, if necessary.

   This method worked! As shown in Figure 20, the selection sits well against the embossed background without the poor edge quality that you saw with the previous methods that you tried.

9. Delete the new layer with the copied graphic.

   We will explore other methods of obtaining the selection, methods that do not require creating a duplicate file.

10. Save your work.

AUTHOR'S *note*

It turns out that our first instinct—to use the Magic Wand Tool to make the selection—was indeed the correct choice. But we needed a flattened copy to do so. Creating a flattened duplicate is an old trick for getting around obstacles that occur when working with layers—get rid of the layers, get rid of the obstacles.

Create layers from layer styles

1. Hide Layer 1 so that only the Chisel Hard Emboss graphic is visible.
2. Target the **Chisel Hard Emboss layer**.
3. Click **Layer** on the menu bar, point to **Layer Style**, then click **Create Layers**.

   The Create Layers command calculates the number of layer styles involved in the effect applied to the targeted layer, then creates layers that reproduce the effect—as many layers as necessary. In this case, two layers were created. As shown in Figure 21, both are clipped into the Chisel Hard Emboss layer.
4. Click **Window** on the menu bar, then click **History**.
5. Click the **Create new snapshot button** on the History palette.

   As shown in Figure 22, a layer named Snapshot 1 appears at the top of the History palette.

(continued)

FIGURE 21

Results of applying the Create Layers command

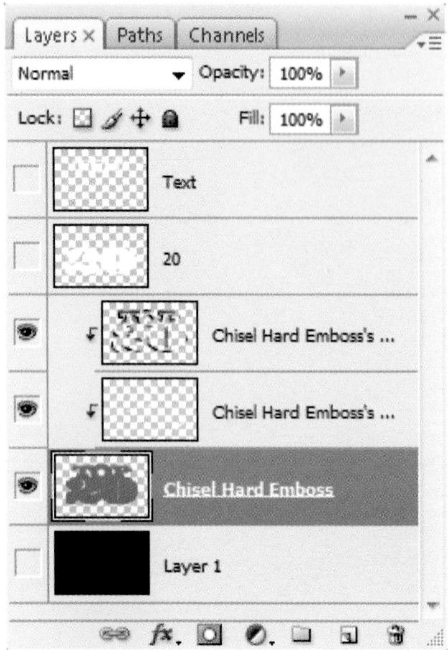

FIGURE 22

Creating a snapshot in the History palette

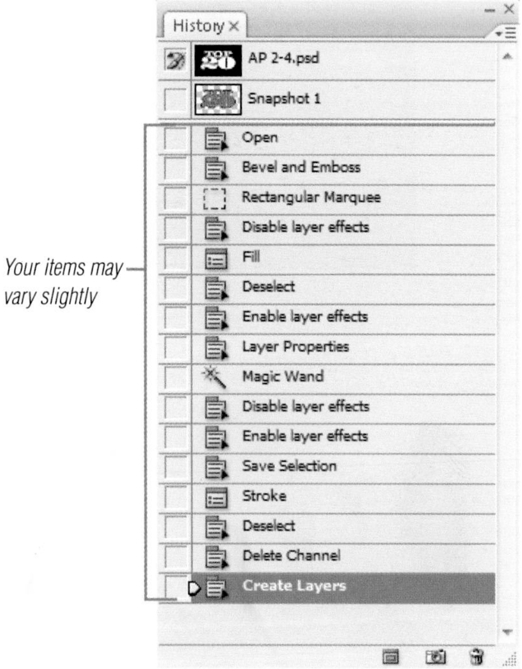

AUTHOR'S *note*

You may find this hard to believe, but in the early days of Photoshop, there was only one Undo available. That's it. If you realized too late that you made a mistake, you had to use the Revert command. And heaven help you if you hadn't saved in a while. The History palette was truly a revolutionary addition to Photoshop. Make it a point to learn everything it has to offer. As you work, it logs your moves and, at any time you can click to return to that point. The palette lists only so many previous moves, however. This is why the Snapshot utility is so useful and important. At any stage of your work, take a snapshot and it's available in the palette for you to return to at any time.

FIGURE 23
Selection on merged art

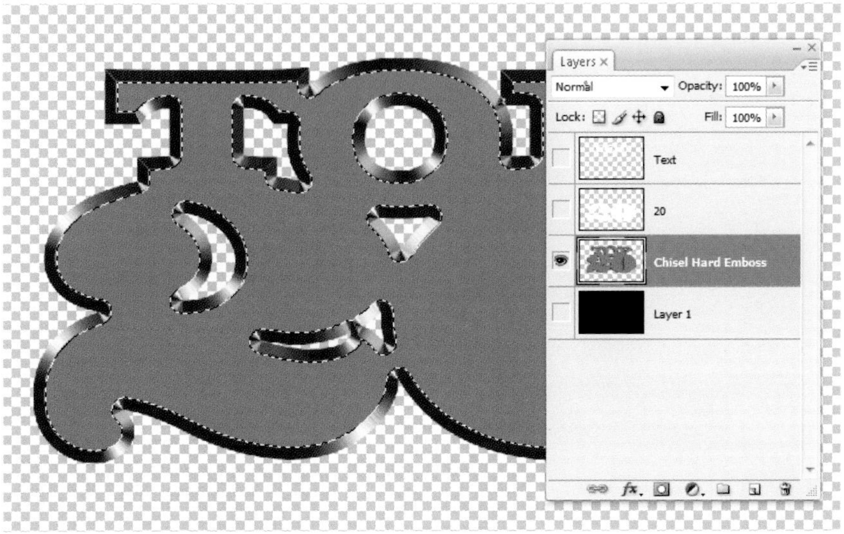

6. Examine the created layers, show the black background, then unclip the created layers to view them individually with or without the black background showing. Feel free to pull the document apart and move things around, hide show layers, and so on.
7. When you are done examining the new layers, click **Snapshot 1** in the History palette.

   The document is reverted to its status when you created Snapshot 1.
8. Click the **Layers palette list arrow**, then click **Merge Visible**.

   The visible layers are merged into a single layer.
9. Click the **Magic Wand Tool** on the gray area.

   As shown in Figure 23, the goal is achievable with this method. See the Author's note on this page.
10. Click **File** on the menu bar, then click **Revert**.

AUTHOR'S *note*

The only problem with this method is that the Chisel Hard Emboss layer style can no longer be edited. When you work in Photoshop, you always want to leave yourself with as many options as possible. Yes, you could have first created a copy of the layer then applied the Create Layers command to the copy, but that would put you back to where you started in the last lesson—making dupes to achieve a goal. The Create Layers command can be very handy; however, for this task, it's not the best choice.

Use the Stamp Visible keyboard command

1. Verify that the Chisel Hard Emboss layer is targeted in the Layers palette and that the Bevel and Emboss layer style is showing.
2. Press **[Shift][Alt][Ctrl][N]** (Win) or **[Shift][option][⌘][N]** (Mac).

   As shown in Figure 24, this keyboard sequence creates a new empty layer above the layer that was targeted. The new layer is automatically targeted.
3. Press **[Shift][Alt][Ctrl][E]** (Win) or **[Shift][option][⌘][E]** (Mac).

   This keyboard sequence is called Stamp Visible. As shown in Figure 25, it takes a picture of the document in its current visible state, then replaces what's in the targeted layer with the picture. You have created a merged copy without merging the Chisel Hard Emboss layer style.
4. Click the **Magic Wand Tool**, then click the gray area in the new layer.
5. Click **Select** on the menu bar, then click **Inverse**.
6. Delete the selected pixels.
7. Save your work.

FIGURE 24
Creating a new layer

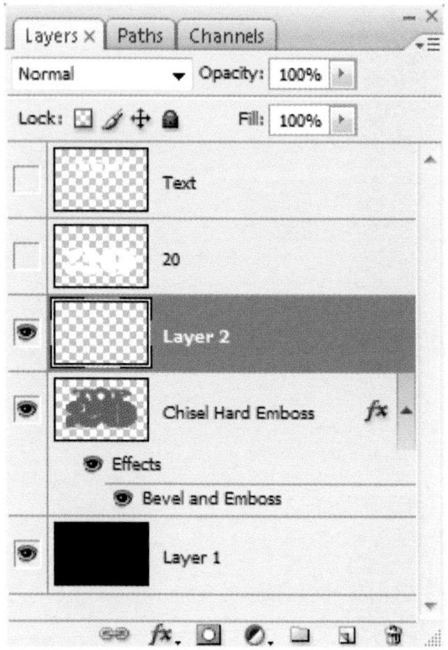

FIGURE 25
Using the Stamp Visible command

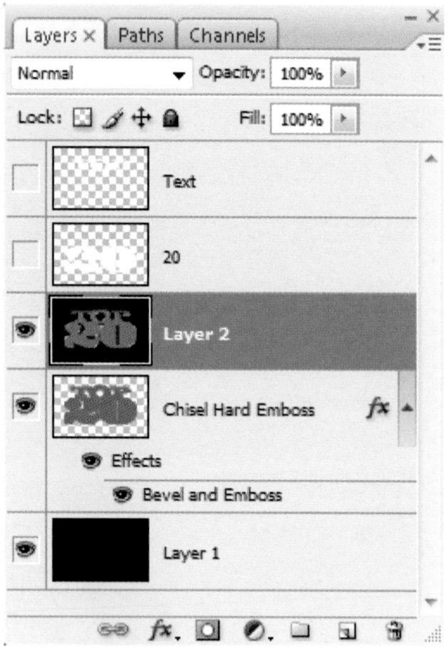

LESSON 5

CREATE A SMOOTH
Emboss Layer Style

What You'll Do

In the early days of computer graphics, naysayers dismissed computer-generated art as automated and monotonous. Their idea was that you take some artwork, run a filter, and what you get is what you get. Of course, that is an extremely limited view of computer graphics. What it overlooks is that computer graphic design is not about "running a filter"—anybody can do that. Computer graphic design is about knowing all the utilities that you have at your disposal and, even more challenging, knowing how and when to use those tools to create an image that you have in your imagination. This lesson will provide you with a great example of using two different layer styles—each from the same dialog box—and making them work together in a way that they improve upon each other.

Create a Smooth Emboss layer style

1. Rename Layer 2 **Smooth Emboss**, then verify that nothing is selected on the canvas.
2. Create a **Bevel and Emboss** layer style.
3. Set the Style to **Emboss**, set the Technique to **Smooth**, then set the Depth to **300**.
4. Drag the **Size slider** to 29.
5. Click the **Gloss Contour list arrow**, then click **Rounded Steps**, the fifth icon in the second row.
6. Compare your Layer Style dialog box to Figure 26, then click **OK**.

(continued)

FIGURE 26
Settings for the Smooth Emboss

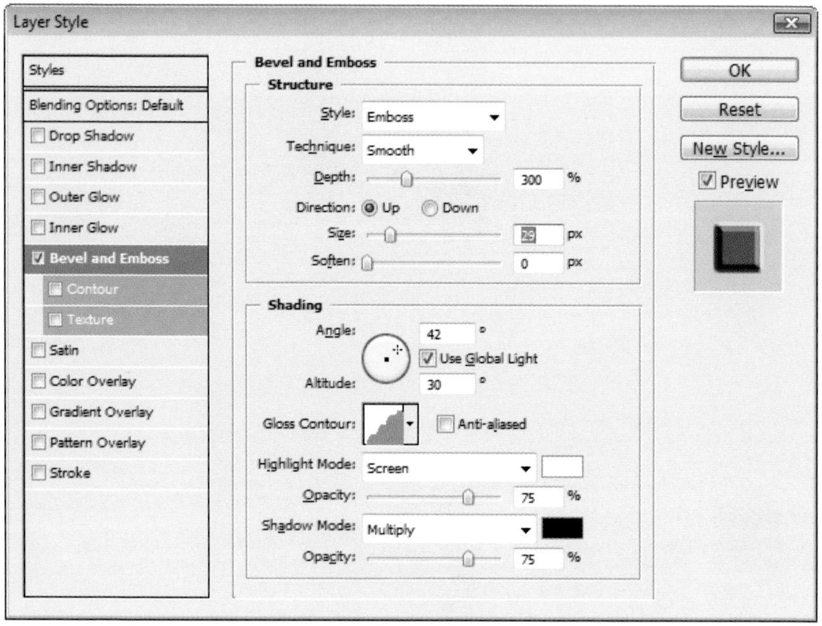

FIGURE 27
Smooth Emboss effect

7. Hide the Chisel Hard Emboss layer so that you can see the Smooth Emboss layer on its own.

   As shown in Figure 27, the Smooth Emboss effect is dramatically different than the Chisel Hard Emboss effect. Both feature a beveled edge, but where the Chisel Hard Emboss features a hard, shiny edge, the Smooth Emboss presents a much softer edge—thus the term Smooth Emboss. Note too the subtle "ghost" at the edges that adds nuance to the effect and also increases the sense of three-dimensionality.

8. Show the Chisel Hard Emboss layer, then hide and show the Smooth Emboss layer.
9. Show both embossed layers, then compare your canvas to Figure 28.

FIGURE 28
Viewing the relationship between the two layer styles

AUTHOR'S *note*

Note how the interaction of the two Bevel and Emboss layer styles work so well together. Note how they complement each other, and how the Smooth Emboss sits neatly "inside" the Chisel Hard Emboss effect. Note that all you really see of the Chisel Hard Emboss layer is its hard shiny edge. Finally, with the Smooth Emboss layer visible, note how the two layer styles work together to create a visually complex and interesting graphic.

LESSON 6

CREATE AND APPLY A Gradient Overlay to a Layer Style

What You'll Do

In most illustrations in which gradients are utilized, the gradient is often an element that calls attention to itself. By its very nature, it has movement—the shift from one color to another—and that movement is often noticeable. In this lesson, you're going to use a Gradient Overlay for a very subtle effect: to enrich the Smooth Emboss you created in the previous lesson. You'll see how the Gradient Overlay adds complexity to the layer style effect and how it contributes to the metallic effects that are the key to this illustration. But there's a little twist. As you go through the later lessons in this chapter, you'll see that the Gradient Overlay will be covered mostly by other elements. In the final version of the illustration, it will be interesting for you to note the very subtle role that this Gradient Overlay ultimately plays.

FIGURE 29
Default gradient

Create and apply a gradient overlay to a layer style

1. In the Layers palette, click the small triangle at the far right of the Smooth Emboss layer to reveal the layer effects for the Smooth Emboss layer.
2. Double-click the **Effects sublayer** in the Smooth Emboss layer group.
3. Click **Gradient Overlay** in the Styles section to highlight it.

   As shown in Figure 29, a default black-and-white gradient is applied to the Smooth Emboss layer style. Note its effect on the Smooth Emboss.
4. Click the **black-and-white gradient** in the Gradient section.
5. Double-click the **far-left color stop**, type **41** in the R, G, and B text boxes, then click **OK**.
6. Double-click the **far-right color stop**, type **140** in the R, G, and B text boxes, then click **OK**.
7. Click the **gradient ramp** anywhere between the two color stops to add a third color stop.
8. Drag the **new color stop** left until the Location text box value is 20.

(continued)

AUTHOR'S *note*

In the RGB color space, a neutral gray color is created any time the three values are the same. The lower the value, the darker the gray, with 0, 0, and 0 being black. The higher the value, the lighter the gray, with 255, 255, and 255 being white.

9. Double-click the **new color stop**, type **150** in the R, G, and B text boxes, then click **OK**.
10. Click to the right of the new color stop to add a fourth, then drag it until the Location text box value is 43.
11. Double-click the **new color stop**, type **36** in the R, G, and B text boxes, then click **OK**.
12. Click to the right of the new color stop to add a fifth, then drag it until the Location text box value is 63.
13. Double-click the **new color stop**, type **190** in the R text box, **164** in the G and B text boxes, then click **OK**.

    This color stop has a slightly pink color cast.
14. Click to the right of the new color stop to add a sixth, then drag it until the Location text box value is 81.
15. Double-click the **new color stop**, type **14** in the R, G, and B text boxes, then click **OK**.

    Your Gradient Editor dialog box should resemble Figure 30.
16. Click **New**.

    The new gradient appears as a thumbnail in the Presets section, with the name Custom.

(continued)

FIGURE 30
Specifications for the gradient

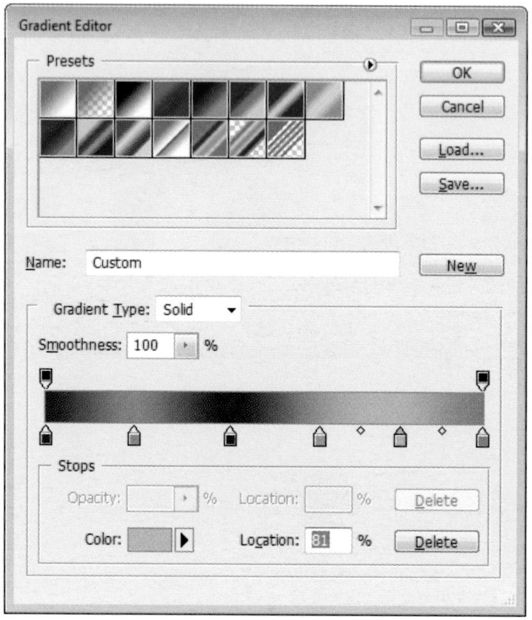

AUTHOR'S *note*

Note how you avoided making the gradient too uniform. The color stops are not evenly spaced along the gradient ramp. The darker stops are not all the same color—none are pure black; they're various dark grays. The lighter stops are not uniform in color either, and one of them has a pink color cast.

FIGURE 31
New gradient layer style

FIGURE 32
Finished gradient layer style

17. Double-click the **Custom gradient** in the Presets section, type **Smooth Emboss Overlay** in the Name section, click **OK**, then click **OK** to close the Gradient Editor dialog box.

    The new gradient appears in the Gradient section and is applied to the Smooth Emboss layer style.

18. Click **OK** to close the Layer Style dialog box, then compare your artwork to Figure 31.

    A new sublayer named Gradient Overlay appears beneath Bevel and Emboss in the Smooth Emboss layer group. The colors of the gradient are good for the illustration, and the quick transitions from light to dark enhance the metallic feel, and the slightly pink highlight is unexpected and intriguing. Note, however, that the gradient is positioned at a 90° angle—from left to right—and that makes it obvious and a bit trite.

19. Double-click the **Gradient Overlay sublayer** to edit it in the Layer Style dialog box.
20. Type **51** in the Angle text box.
21. Experiment with the Scale slider.
22. Drag the **Scale slider** to **92**, click **OK,** then compare your artwork to Figure 32.

    The often-overlooked Scale slider reduces or enlarges the Gradient Overlay within the layer style and can be useful for positioning the gradient in a way that is just right for the illustration.

LESSON 7

CREATE A PILLOW EMBOSS
Layer Style

What You'll Do

This lesson demonstrates how exporting layers from Illustrator really pays off. You're going to apply yet another layer style, but this time, you are going to apply it to a new piece of artwork. You will apply a layer style to a foreground component created for this layered illustration. Keep an eye out for how the layer style adds an entirely new dimension to the illustration, and keep in mind that the basis for the effect was the foreground and background components that were created in and exported from Illustrator.

FIGURE 33
Settings for the Pillow Emboss effect

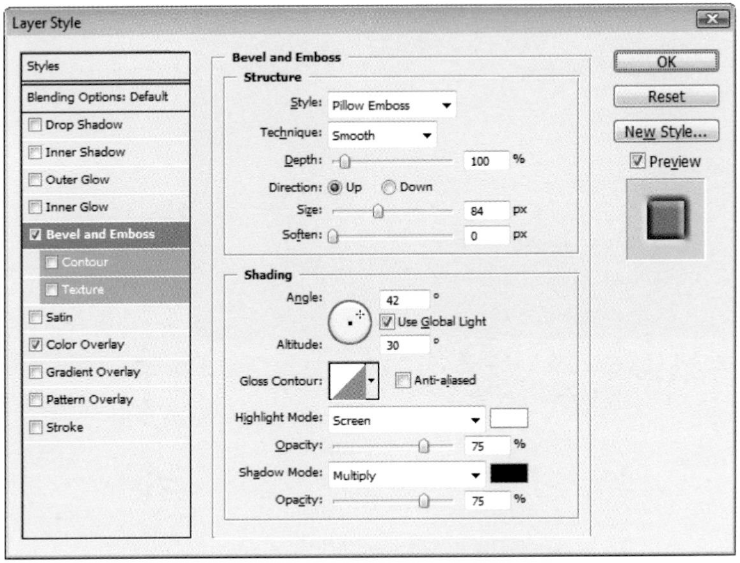

Create a Pillow Emboss layer style

1. Show the layer named **20**, then change its name to **Pillow Emboss**.
2. Create a **Color Overlay** layer style.
3. Click the **red swatch**, type **132** in the R, G, and B text boxes, then click **OK**.
4. Click **Bevel and Emboss** in the Styles section.
5. Click the **Style list arrow**, then click **Pillow Emboss**.
6. Verify that the Technique is set to Smooth and that the Depth is set to 100%.
7. Experiment with the Size slider to get a good sense of the Pillow Emboss effect.
8. Drag the **Size slider** to 84, then compare your dialog box to Figure 33.

(continued)

AUTHOR'S *note*

When using bevel and emboss effects, create your basic artwork using a midrange tone—not too dark, not too light. Bevel and emboss effects are created by applying a dramatic highlight on one edge of the artwork and a dramatic shadow on the opposite edge. If the base art is very bright, the highlight is less apparent. If it is very dark, the shadow may get lost or lose its power. So if you can choose some base art that is largely middle tones, the highlight and shadow will be very noticeable.

9. Click **OK**, then compare your artwork to Figure 34.
10. Expand the Pillow Emboss layer to reveal the layer effects, then hide and show the Bevel and Emboss layer effect to see the effect.

    Note that the Pillow Emboss layer style, in addition to embossing the basic artwork, also creates a soft highlight glow and a shadow glow. The highlight glow is immediately apparent—it is offset from the base artwork at a southwest angle. The shadow glow is more subtle; it is offset on a northeast direction, the opposite direction from the highlight glow.
11. Hide the Smooth Emboss and Chisel Hard Emboss layers to see the Pillow Emboss effect against the black background, then compare your canvas to Figure 35.
12. Show the Smooth Emboss and Chisel Hard Emboss layers, then save your work.

FIGURE 34
Results of the Pillow Emboss effect

FIGURE 35
Viewing the Pillow Emboss layer style only

AUTHOR'S *note*

Note that the glows extend *beyond* the basic artwork. Give this a few second's thought because it's an important feature of this layer style: The layer style is creating an effect that *exceeds* the boundaries of the base art. This means that the layer style is not just stylizing base art, it is creating *new* art that adds nuance and complexity to the illustration.

LESSON 8

COPY LAYER STYLES Between Layers

What You'll Do

Does this lesson title seem familiar? It should. It's the same name of a lesson from Chapter 1, the lesson when you moved the drop shadow from the HAWAII text to the Aloha text. Most of the steps in this lesson ask you to make similar moves. Why do it again, you ask? Because a fundamental part of working with layers involves duplicating layers and layer styles and duplicating layer styles and adjustment layers between layers. You are going to do it over and over and over again. In this lesson, the layer styles you're copying are more complex than a simple drop shadow.

Copy layer styles between layers

1. Show the Text layer, change its name to **Text Pillow**, then save your work.
2. Press and hold **[Alt]** (Win) or **[option]** (Mac) then drag the **Effects sublayer** in the Pillow Emboss layer group to the Text Pillow layer.

   Dragging the Effects sublayer copies all the layer styles to the new destination.
3. Double-click the **Bevel and Emboss layer style** in the Text Pillow layer.

   TIP The Size setting on the Pillow Emboss layer style that you copied is too large for the Text Pillow artwork.
4. Drag the **Size slider** to 34, click **OK**, then compare your artwork to Figure 36.
5. Hide and show the Text Pillow and the Pillow Emboss layers, then save your work.

FIGURE 36
Illustration with the top text embossed

AUTHOR'S *note*

Hiding and showing these two layers yields some interesting insights into the workings of this illustration. At this stage of construction, it is clear that the Chisel Hard and Smooth Emboss styles are the support structure for the illustration—they are in the background. The Chisel Hard Emboss remains a very important and visible element, but only at the edge of the illustration. The chiseled edge is obscured only by the white glow on the number 2. It's also interesting to note what gets hidden by the foreground art. Note how little of the Chisel Hard Emboss layer shows, yet notice how important what *does* show is to the effect. Same with the Smooth Emboss layer. Remarkably little of it shows. Turn it off and on, and note the role it plays. Note too the Gradient Overlay and its small but important effect.

LESSON 9

CREATE A CHROME EFFECT
Without Using Layer Styles

What You'll Do

They say that you can't teach an old dog new tricks. That may be true. But remember, it is often the case that the old dog remembers the old tricks that the new dog was never around to have seen in the first place. In so many ways, that is true of Photoshop. With each upgrade, Photoshop has become so much more sophisticated. It has been designed to anticipate effects that designers want, like embosses, bevels, overlays and contour effects, and it provides settings and sliders that are preset to deliver the goods. That makes for a great application, one in which you can create spectacular effects quickly and easily.

But if you've been around long enough, you remember the days when there were no layer styles. Heck, you remember when there were no layers! Back then, the effects that you wanted to create didn't come prepackaged with the software. You had to figure out how to create effects by combining such basic utilities as filters, selections, channels, and curves. The result is that you had to think harder and work longer. And some of the effects that you could create the old-fashioned way are so complex and unique that no dialog box could possibly duplicate them. That's the case with the chrome effect you will create in this lesson. It's an old recipe, handed down and traded around for years. So if you're a new dog, follow along while this old dog teaches you an old trick.

Save a selection

1. Target the **Pillow Emboss layer**, then drag it to the Create a new layer button on the Layers palette.

   The Pillow Emboss layer is duplicated.
2. Change the name of the duplicate layer to **Chrome 20**, then drag the **layer** to the top of the Layers palette.
3. Delete all the layer styles from the Chrome 20 layer, press **[D]** to access default colors in the toolbox, then click the **Lock transparent pixels button** on the Layers palette.
4. Fill the artwork with Black, then click the **Lock transparent pixels button** again to deactivate it.
5. Hide all the other layers, then compare your canvas to Figure 37.
6. Press and hold **[Ctrl]** (Win) or ⌘ (Mac), then click the **Layer thumbnail** on the Chrome 20 layer to load a selection of the artwork.

(continued)

FIGURE 37
Preparing the artwork for the Emboss filter

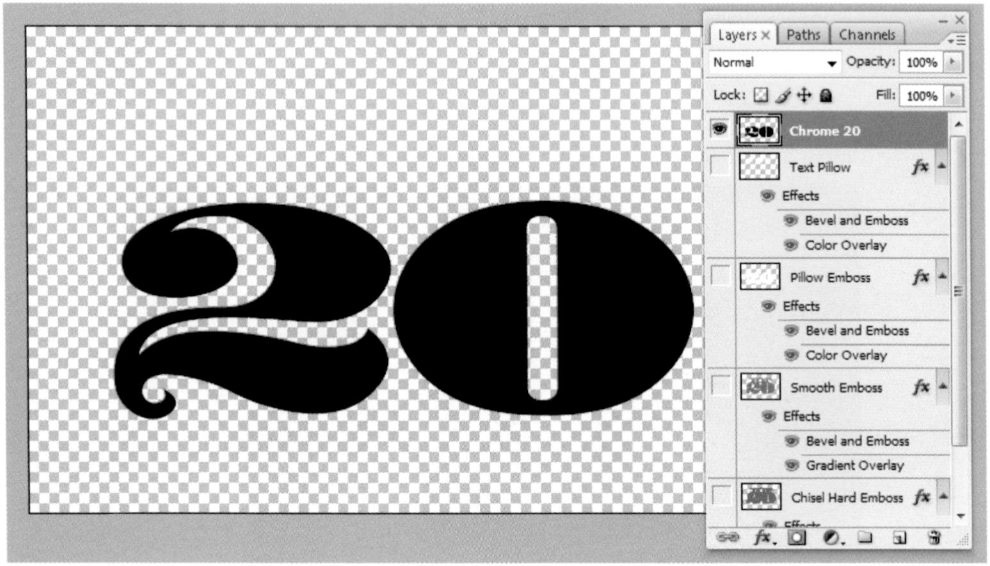

AUTHOR'S *note*

Note that the white highlights have intensified at the bottom of the number 20. This is because the Bevel and Emboss layer style was doubled. Duplicating a layer duplicates its layer styles *and the visual effects* of its layer styles. Therefore, duplicating a layer is a simple and smart way to intensify or otherwise modify the effects of a given set of layer styles.

FIGURE 38
Selection saved as a channel

FIGURE 39
Choosing a light gray swatch in the Color palette

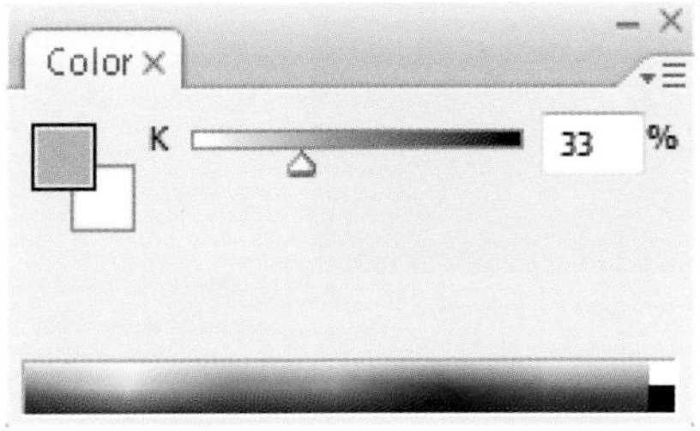

7. Click **Select** on the menu bar, click **Save Selection**, then type **Original 20** in the Name text box.
8. Click **OK**, make the Channels palette visible, then view the new channel in the Channels palette.
9. Click the **Original 20 channel** in the Channels palette, then compare your screen to Figure 38.

   The white areas of the channel represent the pixels that were selected when the selection was saved; conversely, the black areas represent those that were not selected.
10. Click the **RGB channel** in the Channels palette, then save your work.

Use the Emboss filter

1. Verify that the Chrome 20 layer is targeted and the artwork is still selected.
2. Click **Select** on the menu bar, then click **Refine Edge**.
3. Type **18** in the Feather text box, then click **OK**.
4. Display the Color palette, click the **Color palette list arrow**, then click **Grayscale Slider**.
5. Drag the **slider** to 33%, so that the foreground color is a light gray as shown in Figure 39.
6. Click **Edit** on the menu bar, then click **Stroke**.

(continued)

7. Click the **Inside option button**, type **24** in the Width text box, click **OK**, then compare your work to Figure 40.

   With this method, the stroke plays a major role in the final effect. Keep an eye on this gray stroke throughout this lesson.
8. Click **Select** on the menu bar, then click **Load Selection**.
9. Click the **Channel list arrow**, click **Original 20**, then click **OK**.

   The original selection replaces the feathered selection.
10. Click **Filter** on the menu bar, point to **Stylize**, then click **Emboss**.
11. Type **135** in the Angle text box, type **13** in the Height text box, type **160** in the Amount text box, then click **OK**.
12. Select the inverse, then delete the selection.

    You are doing this to remove the glow that was created outside the shape when you applied the stroke to the feathered edge.
13. Deselect all, make **Layer 1** visible, then compare your artwork to Figure 41.
14. Show all the layers.

Apply a Curves adjustment layer

1. Verify that the **Chrome 20 layer** is targeted.
2. Click **Layer** on the menu bar, point to **New Adjustment Layer**, then click **Curves**.
3. Type **Emboss Curves** in the Name text box, click the **Use Previous Layer to Create Clipping Mask check box**, then click **OK**.

(continued)

FIGURE 40
Viewing the stroke

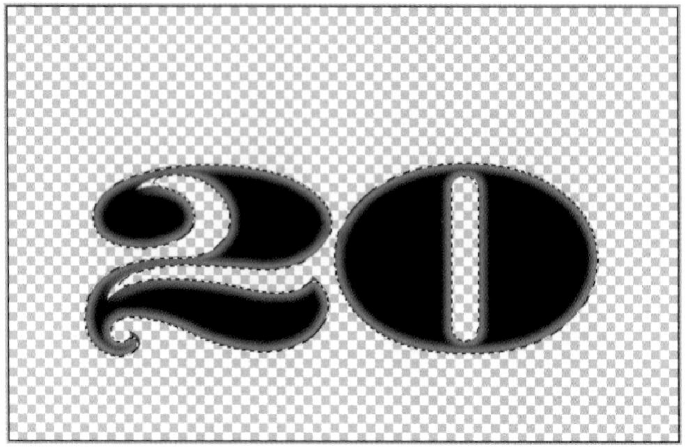

FIGURE 41
Result of the Emboss filter

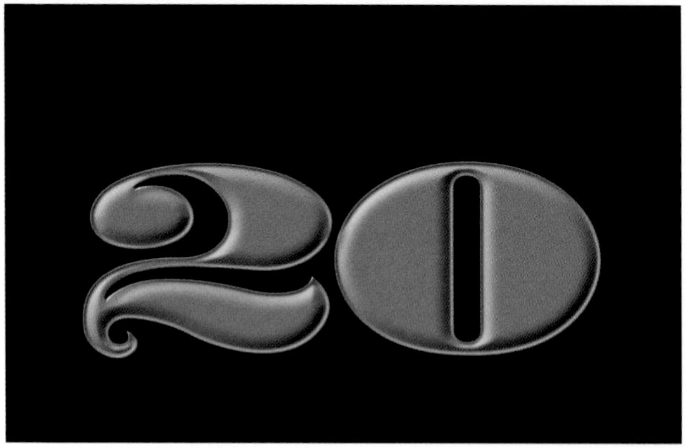

FIGURE 42
Modifying the curve to make all pixels on the layer white

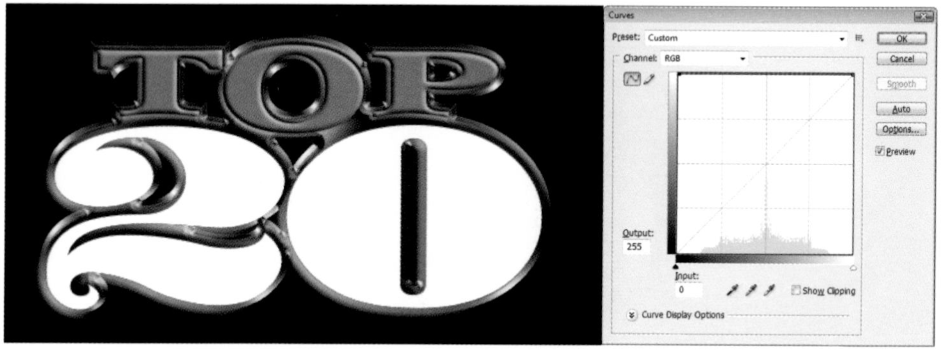

FIGURE 43
Adding points to the curve

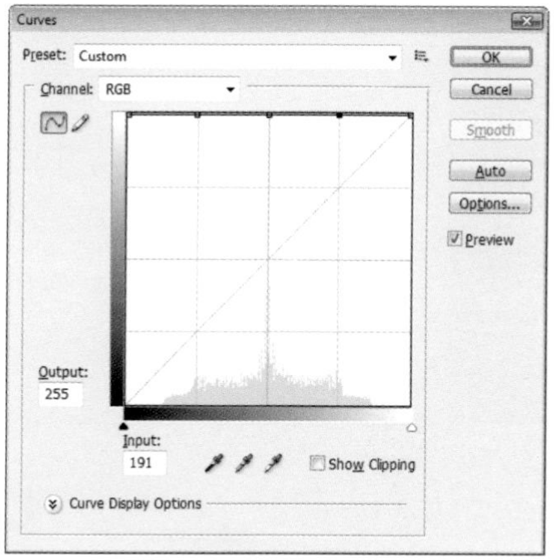

The Curves dialog box opens. Verify that the Channel menu at the top of the dialog box reads RGB.

TIP Click Preview and move your dialog box so that you can see as much of the artwork as possible.

4. Drag the **black handle** at the lower-left corner straight up to the upper-left corner, so that your dialog box resembles Figure 42.

   Note the input/output values at the bottom left area of the dialog box. The Input value of the black handle that you moved was 0 (black). Now its Output value is 255 (white). Every (imaginary) point on the horizontal line between the two points is at the top of the dialog box. This means that all the points on the line have a value of 255—they are all white.

5. Position your cursor over the horizontal line so that a + sign appears, then moving left to right, click to add three new points, as shown in Figure 43.

AUTHOR'S *note*

As an introduction, the basic concept you need to understand about the Curves dialog box is that the black handle at the lower-left corner represents all the black (0) pixels in the targeted layer. The black handle at the upper-right corner represents all the white (255) pixels in the layer. The diagonal line represents all the other pixels in the layer that fall within the range of 0–255.

Modify curves to create a chrome effect

1. Drag the **second point** down to the position shown in Figure 44.

   TIP After you select a point, you can simply enter the input/output values shown in Figure 44 to reposition it.

2. Drag the **fourth point** down to the position shown in Figure 45.
3. Relocate the far-right point to different locations and note how the chrome effect becomes more intense.

(continued)

FIGURE 44
Changing the location of the second point on the curve

FIGURE 45
Changing the location of the fourth point

FIGURE 46
Repositioning the rightmost point

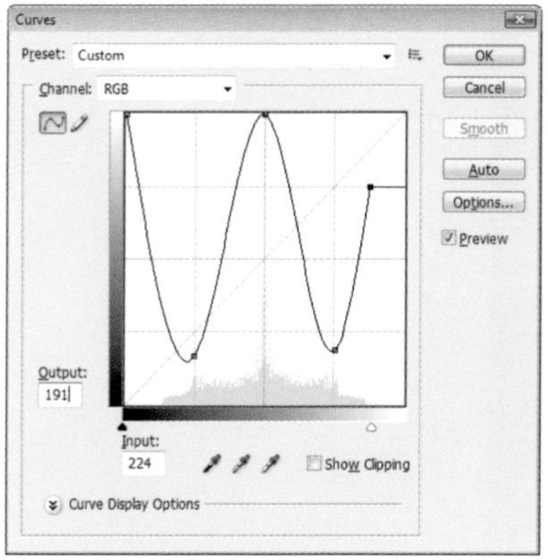

FIGURE 47
Result of the Curves modifications

4. Position the far-right point as shown in Figure 46.
5. Click the **Preset options button**, click **Save Preset**, then save the curve as **Chrome**.
6. Click **Save**, click **OK**, then compare your work to Figure 47.

   Note that the Emboss Curves adjustment layer is the targeted layer in the Layers palette.

   TIP When you apply an adjustment layer to a targeted layer, the adjustment layer is automatically targeted when you execute the adjustment.

7. Undo and redo the curves modification.

   The curves modification achieves a great effect. The only problem is that very harsh highlights can be seen at the edges of the artwork. Zoom in on them to get an idea of why they're creating an unappealing effect.

8. Target the **Chrome 20 layer** in the Layers palette, then load the Original 20 selection that you saved.
9. Click **Select** on the menu bar, point to **Modify**, then click **Contract**.
10. Type **7** in the Contract By text box, then click **OK**.
11. Click **Select** on the menu bar, click **Refine Edge**, type **3** in the Feather text box, then click **OK**.

12. Click **Select** on the menu bar, then click **Inverse**.
13. Delete the selected pixels, then deselect all.
14. Compare your artwork to Figure 48.
15. Hide and show the Chrome 20 layer to see its relationship with the Pillow Emboss effect beneath it.

    Because the Chrome 20 artwork is directly above the Pillow Emboss effect, it pretty much obscures the entire Pillow Emboss effect.
16. Click the **Move Tool**, then move the Chrome 20 artwork straight up 11 pixels.
17. Compare your artwork to Figure 49, then save your work.

FIGURE 48
Artwork after removing unwanted edge effects

FIGURE 49
Offsetting the Chrome 20 layer

AUTHOR'S *note*

Before moving on, take some time to analyze the role of the Pillow Emboss effect in the artwork. By moving the Chrome 20 artwork straight up, the Pillow Emboss artwork became visible. Turn the Pillow Emboss layer on and off to see its contribution to the illustration. Though only its edge shows, it nevertheless plays an important role in adding depth and complexity to the illustration.

LESSON 10

DUPLICATE A CHROME EFFECT
Without Using Layer Styles

What You'll Do

In the last chapter, you created a chrome effect using a Curves adjustment layer rather than the Bevel and Emboss layer style. When you created that adjustment layer, you saved the curves data as an .acv file. In this lesson, you want to apply that same curve data to the text at the top of the illustration. As with layer styles, you can duplicate adjustment layers and apply the duplicate to a different layer. In this lesson, however, you're going to use a different method—an older method, one that has been available since the earliest versions of Photoshop. Rather than duplicate the adjustment layer, you will load the curve data that you saved in the previous lesson.

Apply the Emboss filter

1. Duplicate the Text Pillow layer then change its name to **Chrome Text**.
2. Delete the effects, then fill the artwork with black.

   After filling the text with black, verify that the Lock transparent pixels button is not activated.
3. Press and hold **[Ctrl]** (Win) or [⌘] (Mac), then click the **Layer thumbnail** on the Chrome Text layer to load a selection of the artwork.
4. Save the selection as **Original Text**.
5. Click **Select** on the menu bar, then click **Refine Edge**.
6. Type **9** in the Feather text box, then click **OK**.
7. Click the **Color palette list arrow**, then verify that the Grayscale Slider is checked.
8. Drag the **slider** to 30%.
9. Click **Edit** on the menu bar, then click **Stroke**.
10. Choose the **Inside option button**, type **12** in the Width text box, then click **OK**.
11. Deselect, then compare your artwork to Figure 50.
12. Load the Original Text selection.
13. Click **Filter** on the menu bar, point to **Stylize**, then click **Emboss**.

(continued)

FIGURE 50
Applying a feathered stroke to the artwork

FIGURE 51
Applying the Emboss filter to the artwork

14. Type **135** in the Angle text box, type **6** in the Height text box, then type **160** in the Amount text box.
15. Click **OK**, then deselect all.

    Your artwork should resemble Figure 51.
16. Save your work.

Load saved curves

1. Press and hold **[Alt]** (Win) or **[option]** (Mac), click the **Create new fill or adjustment layer button**, then click **Curves**.
2. Type **Emboss Curves** in the Name text box, click the **Use Previous Layer to Create Clipping Mask check box**, then click **OK**.

   The Curves dialog box opens.
3. Click the **Preset list arrow**, then click **Chrome**.

   When you save a curve, it is automatically saved to the Preset menu.
4. Click **OK** to close the Curves dialog box.
5. Target the **Chrome Text layer** in the Layers palette, then load the Original Text selection.
6. Zoom in on the letter **T** so that you are viewing it at 100%.
7. Click **Select** on the menu bar, point to **Modify**, then click **Contract**.

(continued)

8. Type **4** in the Contract By text box, then click **OK**.
9. Click **Select** on the menu bar, click **Refine Edge**, type **3** in the Feather text box, then click **OK**.
10. Click **Select** on the menu bar, then click **Inverse**.
11. Press **[Delete]** (Win) or **[delete]** (Mac) two times.
12. Deselect, then zoom out so that you are viewing the artwork at 25%.
13. Click the **Move Tool**, then move the artwork straight up 10 pixels.

    TIP Pressing and holding [Shift] then pressing an arrow key moves a selection 10 pixels in the direction of the arrow you pressed.

14. Hide rulers, if necessary.

AUTHOR'S *note*

When you apply a feather to a selection then delete the selected pixels, remember that the pixels at the edge of the selection are not deleted entirely—because of the feather. Sometimes, as in this case, deleting twice is a good move. When working with a larger selection and a higher feather value, you might want to delete three times.

FIGURE 52
Final artwork

15. Click the **Full Screen Mode button** on the toolbox.

    Your canvas is positioned within a black screen.

    TIP Press [F] to switch between the three screen modes.

16. Press **[Tab]** to hide all palettes
17. Compare your artwork to Figure 52.
18. Save your work, then close Top 20.psd.

PROJECT BUILDER 1

1. Open AP 2-5.psd, then save it as **Pink Lady**.
2. Create a new layer above the Background layer, then name it **Back Tray**.
3. Press and hold [Ctrl] (Win) or ⌘ (Mac), then click the Layer thumbnail to load the selection of the Lady layer.
4. Press and hold [Shift] [Ctrl] (Win) or [Shift] ⌘ (Mac), then click the Layer thumbnail to load and add the selection of the Luck layer so that you have a selection of both layers.
5. Target the Back Tray layer.
6. Click Select on the menu bar, point to Modify, then click Expand.
7. Type **18** in the Expand By dialog box, then click OK.
8. Click Edit on the menu bar, then click Fill.
9. Click the Use list arrow, choose 50% Gray, verify that the Opacity is set to 100%, then click OK.
10. Deselect all.
11. Create a Bevel and Emboss layer style.
12. Set the Style to Inner Bevel, set the Technique to Chisel Hard, set the Depth to 100, then set the Size to 10 pixels.
13. Click the Use Global Light check box, then set the Angle to 120.
14. Change the Gloss Contour to Gaussian, verify that the Anti-aliased check box is not checked, then click OK.
15. Target the Lady layer, then add a Bevel and Emboss layer style.
16. Set the Style to Pillow Emboss, set the Technique to Smooth, set the Depth to 100, then set the Size to 29 pixels.
17. Verify that the Use Global Light check box is checked, that the Angle is set to 120, then click OK.
18. Target the Luck layer, then add a Bevel and Emboss layer style.
19. Set the Style to Pillow Emboss, set the Technique to Chisel Hard, set the Depth to 100, then set the Size to 10 pixels.
20. Verify that the Use Global Light check box is checked and that the Angle is set to 120.
21. Set the Gloss Contour to Cove-Deep, then click OK.
22. Compare your artwork to Figure 53, save your work, then close Pink Lady.

FIGURE 53
Completed Project Builder 1

PROJECT BUILDER 2

1. Open AP 2-6.psd, then save it as **Luck Be A Lady**. (*Hint*: The typeface is Bellevue.)
2. Target the Pink layer, then add a Bevel and Emboss layer style.
3. Set the Style to Inner Bevel, set the Technique to Chisel Hard, set the Depth to 100, then set the Size to 32 pixels.
4. Verify that the Use Global Light check box is checked and that the Angle is set to 120.
5. Set the Gloss Contour to Ring.
6. Drag the Shadow Mode Opacity slider to 50%, then click OK.
7. Target the Black layer, then add a Bevel and Emboss layer style.
8. Set the Style to Outer Bevel, set the Technique to Chisel Hard, set the Depth to 161, then set the Size to 10 pixels.
9. Verify that the Use Global Light check box is checked and that the Angle is set to 120.
10. Click OK, then compare your artwork to Figure 54.
11. Save your work, then close Luck Be A Lady.

FIGURE 54
Completed Project Builder 2

chapter 3

ADJUSTING LEVELS AND Hue/Saturation

1. Analyze a grayscale image.
2. Adjust levels.
3. Explore the Hue/Saturation dialog box.
4. Adjust hue, saturation, and lightness.

LESSON 1

ANALYZE A Grayscale Image

What You'll Do

In this chapter, we're going to look at Photoshop on its most basic level: the pixel. In Photoshop, everything you do can be reduced to two basic actions: changing the color of pixels or changing the location of pixels. It's a rather stunning statement, if you think about it: everything that this powerful piece of software does all comes down to two basic actions.

In these exercises, you're going to focus on the color of pixels and what it means to modify that color. You're also going to look at how a pixel gets its color in the first place. Understanding Photoshop at its most basic level is the best preparation for learning and executing the complex color adjustments and corrections that you will encounter throughout the remainder of this book.

Remember: It's all about the pixel.

Sample the pixels in a grayscale image

1. Open AP 3-1.psd, click **File** on the menu bar, then click **Save As**.
2. Type **Levels of Gray** in the File name text box (Win) or Save As text box (Mac), verify that Photoshop (*.PSD; *.PDD) shows in the Format text box, then click **Save**.
3. Click **Image** on the menu bar, point to **Mode**, note that Grayscale is checked, then release.

   This image is in Grayscale mode.
4. Click **Window** on the menu bar, then click **Info** to show the Info palette.
5. Minimize other palettes that may be open so that you are only using the Info palette and the toolbox.
6. Click the **Info palette list arrow**, then click **Palette Options**.
7. Click the **Mode list arrow** for the First Color Readout, then click **RGB Color**.
8. Click the **Mode list arrow** for the Second Color Readout, click **HSB Color**, then click **OK** so that your Info palette resembles Figure 1.

   TIP Clicking the eyedroppers is another way to choose the desired color mode.
9. Zoom in to 1600%, then scroll around with the **Hand Tool**.

(continued)

FIGURE 1
Info palette

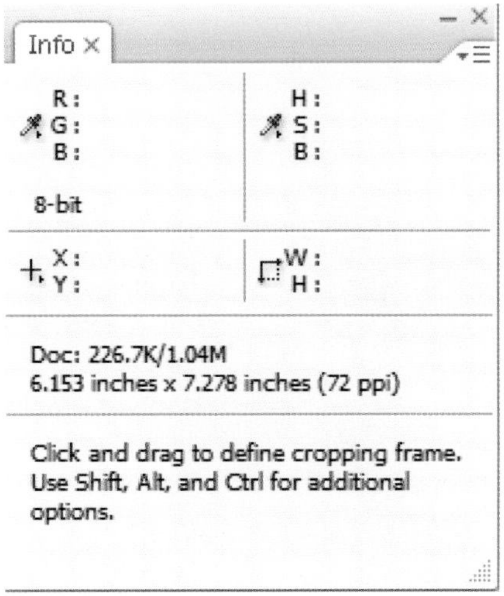

10. Click the **Eyedropper Tool** in the toolbox, then float it over the pixels.

As you move the eyedropper, the Info palette displays the values of the pixels in the RGB and HSB modes simultaneously.

11. Position the pointer over a single pixel, then note its grayscale value in the Info palette.

Terms such as grayscale and levels of gray have been bandied about for many years, and it seems that everyone uses them in a slightly different way. Here's what you need to know: In a grayscale image, a pixel can be one of 256 colors, from 0-255.

12. Zoom out so that you are viewing the image at 100%.

13. Float the eyedropper over the top black rectangle on the left, as shown in Figure 2, then note the grayscale values in the Info palette.

TIP Designers and printing professionals refer to dark areas in an image—such as the top two squares in Figure 2— as *shadows*.

14. Float the pointer over the bottom white rectangle.

TIP Designers and printing professionals refer to light areas in an image—such as the bottom two squares in Figure 2—as *highlights*.

15. Float the pointer over the middle gray rectangle.

128 is the middle value in the grayscale ramp.

TIP Designers and printing professionals refer to middle values in an image as *midtones*.

(continued)

FIGURE 2
Sampling pixels

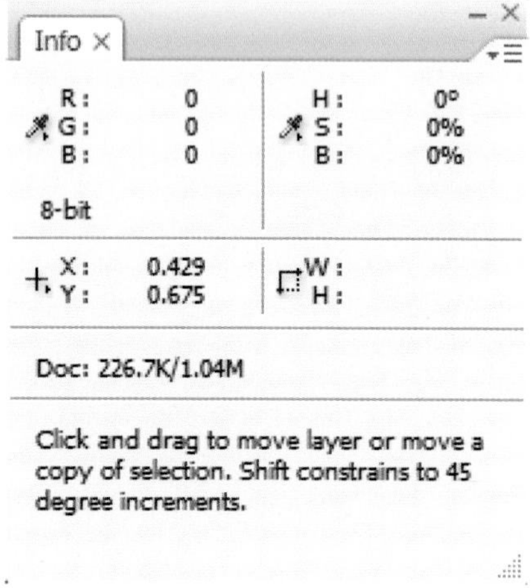

AUTHOR'S *note*

A pixel is always xone color, regardless of what color mode you are in. In the Info palette, the RGB Color mode identifies a pixel's grayscale value. In a grayscale image, a pixel can be one of 256 colors, from 0–255. Black pixels have a grayscale value of 0. White pixels have a grayscale value of 255. All other pixels fall somewhere in between.

FIGURE 3
Sampling the darkest area of the gradient

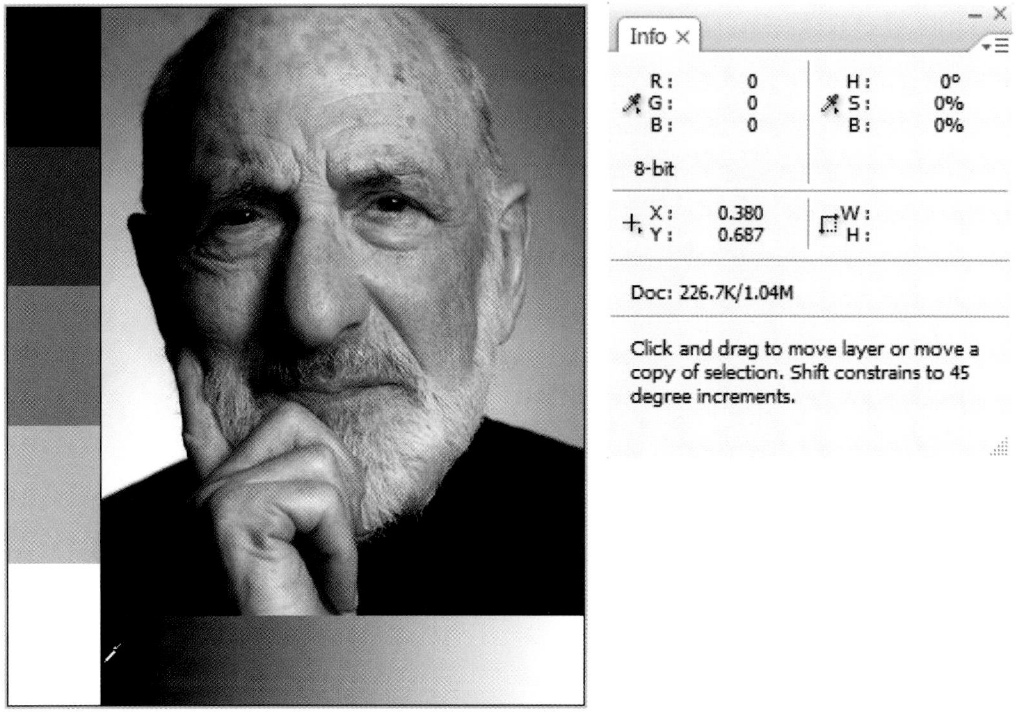

AUTHOR'S *note*

The Posterize dialog box is the best feature in Photoshop for exploring the concept of grayscale. When you set an image to Grayscale mode, by definition, each pixel can be one of 256 shades of gray. The Posterize dialog box allows you to manipulate that number.

15. Float the pointer over the light gray rectangle above the white rectangle.

    192 is the grayscale value between 128 and 255.

16. Float the pointer over the dark gray rectangle below the black rectangle.

    64 is the grayscale value between 0 and 128.

17. Position your pointer to the far left of the gradient below the image of the man, as shown in Figure 3, then note the grayscale value in the Info palette.

18. Try to find the black pixels in the gradient—the pixels with a value of 0.

19. Slowly move your pointer to the right, across the gradient, and note the grayscale values in the Info palette.

    The starting and ending colors for this gradient were black and white, respectively.

20. Explore the image to identify various grayscale values. Can you find pixels with a value of 0 in the dark sweater? Can you find pixels with a value of 255 in the man's beard? How about in the highlight area at the left side of the image? Identify which areas of the image are the midtones.

Modify the levels of gray in a grayscale image

1. Click **Select** on the menu bar, click **Load Selection**, click the **Channel list arrow**, click **Man and Gradient**, then click **OK**.
2. Click **Image** on the menu bar, point to **Adjustments,** then click **Posterize**.
3. Verify that the Preview check box is checked, type **8** in the Levels text box, then compare your artwork to Figure 4.

   Be sure you understand that the file is still in Grayscale mode and 256 shades are still *available* for every pixel. The posterization effect is forcing each pixel to be one of only eight shades of gray, despite what's available.

   With only eight shades of gray, there aren't enough grays to create the effect of a smooth transition from the shadow areas of the image to the highlight areas.
4. Float the pointer from left to right across the gradient at the bottom while noting the grayscale values in the Info palette.

   TIP The RGB section of the Info palette now shows two numbers separated by a forward slash for each value. The values to the left of the slash represent pixel values before posterizing, and the values on the right represent what the pixel values will be if you execute the posterize effect.

(continued)

FIGURE 4
Posterizing to eight levels

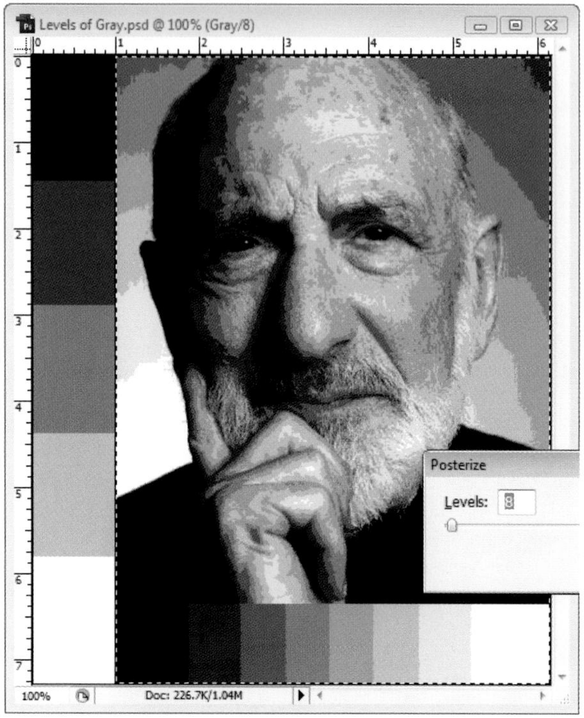

AUTHOR'S *note*

Posterizing an image is very popular—you've probably seen it many times. Now you have a better understanding of how it actually works. Does this mean you are a mathematical savant, like Dustin Hoffman in *Rain Man*? No. Absolutely not. But it does mean that some dazzling Photoshop effects are the result of relatively simple algorithms. Getting an intellectual grasp on how Photoshop is doing what it's doing is the first step to mastering this application.

FIGURE 5
Posterizing to 24 levels

AUTHOR'S *note*

Smooth gradients are the most challenging effect for Photoshop and the most challenging effect to reproduce on the Web and in a printed document. Using Figure 5 as an example, note that you would need to quadruple the number of available grays—from 64 to 255—to create a gradient that not only looks good on screen, but will also print satisfactorily.

5. Type **24** in the Levels text box, then compare your artwork to Figure 5.

   With only 24 shades of gray, the image is surprisingly normal looking. It would be difficult to notice anything amiss in the man's face or in his hands. This is because these areas do not demand the effect of a smooth and graduated transition from light to dark. However, note that the shadow areas on the side of the man's face are posterized.

   Now look at the tones in the background: the posterize effect is immediately apparent and is mirrored in the gradient at the bottom of the canvas.

6. Type **64** in the Levels text box.

   At 64 levels, the posterize effect (often called *stair-stepping* because you can see the step from one gray level to another) is hardly visible. However, note the gradient at the bottom. The stair-stepping is still visible.

(continued)

7. Type **255** in the Levels text box.

   At 255 levels, the image is realistic because enough grays are being used to transition from shadows to highlight. That concept is reflected in the gradient's smooth transition from black to white.

8. Type **4** in the Levels text box, click **OK**, then compare your artwork to Figure 6.

   See the Author's note on this page.

9. Deselect all, then save your work.

FIGURE 6
Posterizing to four levels

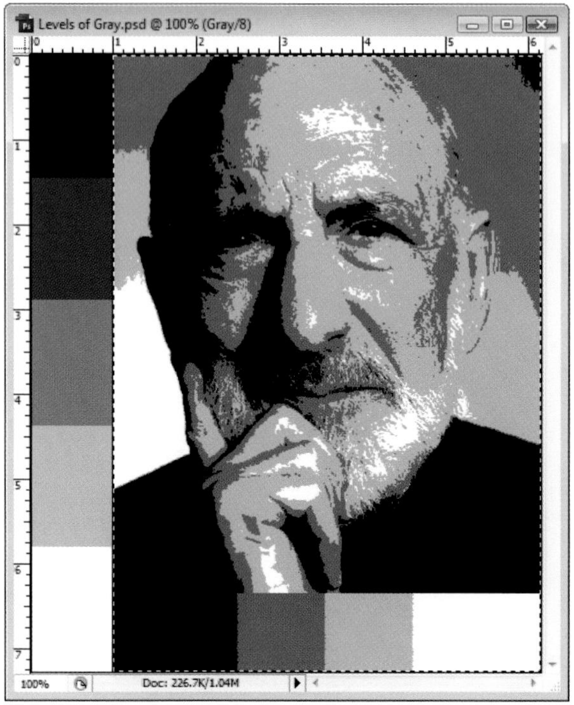

AUTHOR'S *note*

Before reading any further, try to state out loud how the posterize effect works. At 4 levels, why does this image appear the way it does?

Here's what happened: The Posterize effect identified all the pixels whose value was from 0-63 and said, "You guys are 64 different shades of dark gray, but now I only have four grays to work with. So you guys are all black, grayscale value 0. And 64-128? You're all dark gray—value 107. And 129-192? Now you're all light gray—value 187. And the rest of you, 193-255, you're all 255." Getting an intellectual grasp on how Photoshop does what it does is very empowering.

ADJUST Levels

What You'll Do

Now that you have a thorough understanding of grayscale and that every pixel in a grayscale image has a single value attached to it, you are ready to manipulate those values with the Levels dialog box.

The Levels dialog box is a great place to analyze the tonal range of your file, from shadows to highlights. Quite literally, the Levels dialog box shows every pixel in the image using a diagram based on grayscale values.

While you can use levels to adjust the color of an image, the dialog box is best used to specify the basic tonal range of the image: the shadow point, the highlight point, and the midpoint.

Explore the Levels dialog box

1. Open AP 3-2.psd, then save it as **Levels Intro**.
2. Load the selection named Man Alone.
3. Click **Image** on the menu bar, point to **Adjustments**, then click **Levels**.

   TIP Be sure to read the Author's note on this page about histograms.

(continued)

FIGURE 7
Levels dialog box showing histogram

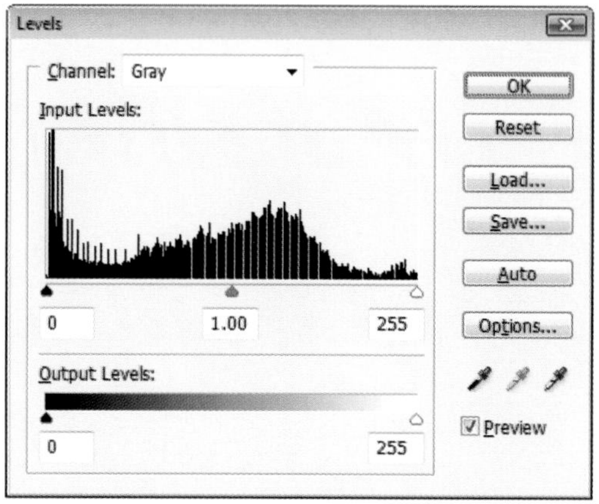

AUTHOR'S *note*

As shown in Figure 7, the most striking component of the Levels dialog box is the histogram. The *histogram* is a visual reference of every pixel in the selection—in this case, the selection of the man. Here's a good analogy for understanding the histogram: Imagine that the histogram has 256 slots, one for each of the 256 available colors in the grayscale image. The slot for the 0-value pixels is on the left, and the slot for the 255-value pixels is on the right. Imagine that there are a total of 1000 pixels in the image with a grayscale value of 64. Using a black marble to represent each pixel, imagine that you drop 1000 marbles into the 64 slot on the slider. Next, imagine that the image contains 1500 pixels with a grayscale value of 72, and you drop 1500 black marbles into the 72 slot. Imagine that you do this for each of the 256 colors in the image. Your result would be the histogram—exactly what you see in the Levels dialog box. The height of the histogram, from left to right, shows the relative number of pixels that the file—or in this case, the selected pixels—has in each of the 256 grayscale values.

FIGURE 8

Approximate representation of the histogram's relation to areas of the image

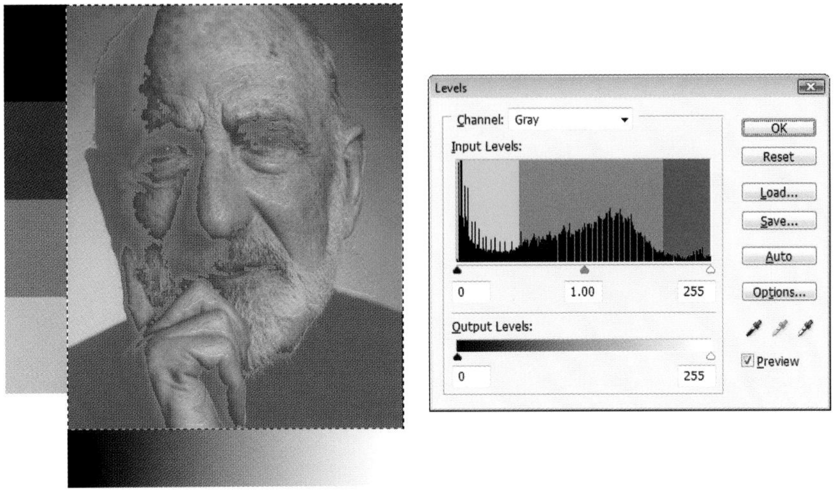

FIGURE 9

Levels dialog box showing only 4 gray values

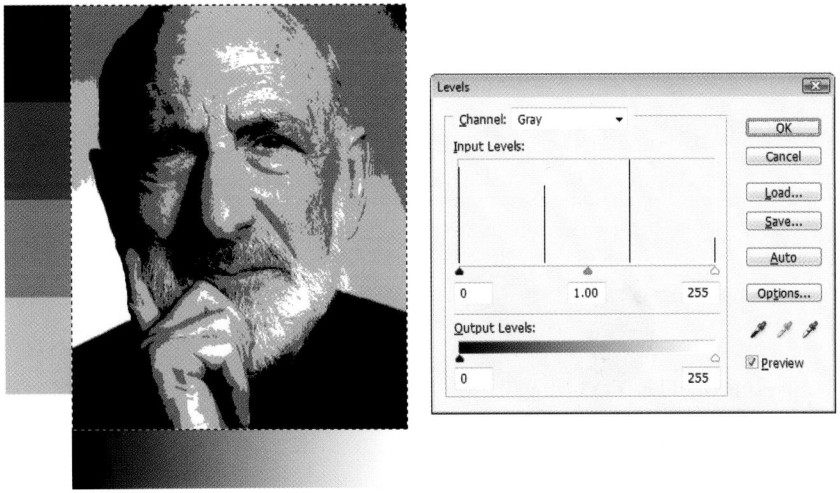

4. Verify that the Preview check box is checked, then view the Levels dialog box beside the image, as shown in Figure 8.

   Figure 8 is an approximate representation of the histogram's relation to areas of the image. The dark pixels in the image are represented by the yellow area in the histogram. The far fewer light pixels are represented by red. And the majority of the image is composed of midrange pixels, represented by blue.

5. Click **Cancel**.
6. Click **Image** on the menu bar, point to **Adjustments**, then click **Posterize**.
7. Type **4** in the Levels text box, if necessary, click **OK**, then float your pointer over the image to sample the four grayscale values that now compose the image.

   The image is composed of pixels that have grayscale values of 0, 107, 187, or 255.

8. Open the Levels dialog box, then compare it to Figure 9.

   The histogram precisely reflects the change in the image, with pixels represented only at the 0, 107, 187, and 255 points on the Levels slider. To extend the previous analogy, all of the "marbles" now fall into one of four "slots."

9. Click **OK**, then revert the file.

Analyze fundamental moves in the Levels dialog box

1. Load the saved selection named Half Gradient, then verify that your Info palette is positioned as shown in Figure 10.
2. Open the Levels dialog box, then position it as shown in Figure 11.

   The histogram describing the gradient is pretty much what you'd expect: a relatively even dispersion of pixels across the levels ramp. Note that not one area—from shadows to midtones to highlights—dominates the histogram.
3. Click **Cancel**.
4. Click **Select** on the menu bar, then click **Load Selection**.
5. Click the **Channel list arrow**, click **Man Alone**, then click **Add to Selection**.
6. Click **OK**, then press **[Ctrl][H]** (Win) or ⌘ **[H]** (Mac) to hide the selection marquee.
7. Open the Levels dialog box.

   The histogram has changed because it now represents the pixels in the two selections.
8. Note the three triangles at the base of the Levels slider.

   The black triangle on the left represents all black pixels in the selection—those with a grayscale value of 0. The white triangle on the right represents all white pixels in the image—those with a grayscale value of 255. The gray triangle in the middle represents the middle value of all the selected pixels.

(continued)

FIGURE 10
Positioning the Info palette

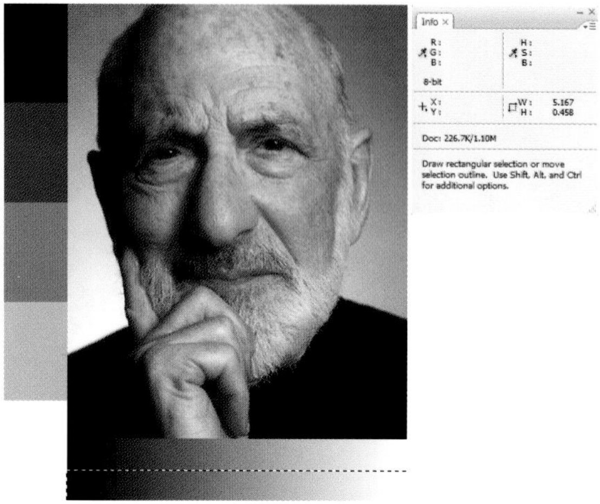

FIGURE 11
Positioning the Levels dialog box

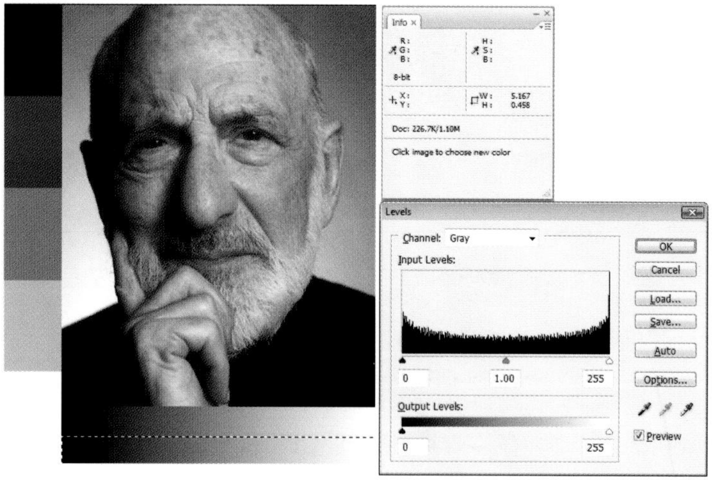

FIGURE 12
Viewing the result of moving the highlight point

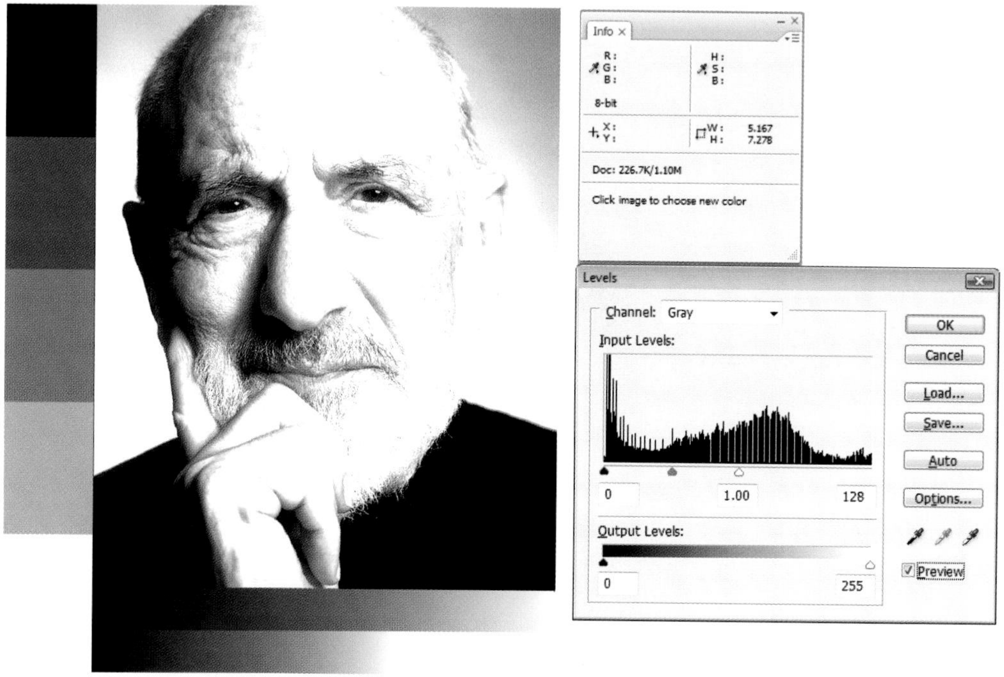

9. Drag the **white triangle** to the left until the third Input text box reads 128, then compare your screen to Figure 12.

   All of the pixels in the selection that were originally 128—middle gray—are now 255. Therefore, any pixel that was originally 128 or higher is now white. Note that the gray triangle moved with the white triangle, and the transition of black pixels to white pixels now happens in a much shortened range. Compare the bottom half of the gradient to the top half that was not affected by the move. The shortened transition from black to white then the "blow out" to white in the right half is analogous to what is happening to the image of the man above.

   TIP See the Author's note at the bottom of this page.

10. Float your pointer over the image, then note in the Info palette the before/after grayscale values.

AUTHOR'S *note*

It is important that you understand that the move affected nearly all of the pixels in the image—not just those in the "upper half" of the histogram. All of the pixels in the upper half have been changed to 255 *and* the pixels in the lower half have changed as well, because they are now used to make the transition from black to white. In terms of grayscale value, the pixels that were 0–128 in the original are now 0–255. Get it? The only pixels that didn't change are the black pixels—they were 0 in the original, and they are 0 with the adjustment.

11. Press and hold **[Alt]**(Win) or **[option]**(Mac) so that the Cancel button changes to Reset, then click **Reset**.
12. Drag the **black triangle** to the right until the first Input text box reads 128, then compare your screen to Figure 13.

    This step has the exact opposite effect on the selection. The pixels that were originally 0–128 are all now 0. The transition from black to white now occurs in the pixels that were originally 129–255. This is illustrated in the gradient: the left half is entirely black, and the right half now transitions from black to white.
13. Reset the Levels dialog box.
14. Drag the **gray triangle** left until the middle Input text box reads 1.92, then compare your screen to Figure 14.

    The effect on the image is far less drastic, but just as specific. Looking at the histogram, note how many more pixels are now positioned between the midpoint value—the gray triangle—and the white triangle. In other words, a much greater percentage of pixels now fall in the upper half of the grayscale. Note how the image of the man was substantially brightened. In the gradient, note how short the range is from shadow to midpoint, while the midpoint to highlight point has been lengthened.

> **TIP** Moving the gray midpoint triangle to the left brightens the middle range of a selection.

(continued)

FIGURE 13
Viewing the result of moving the shadow point

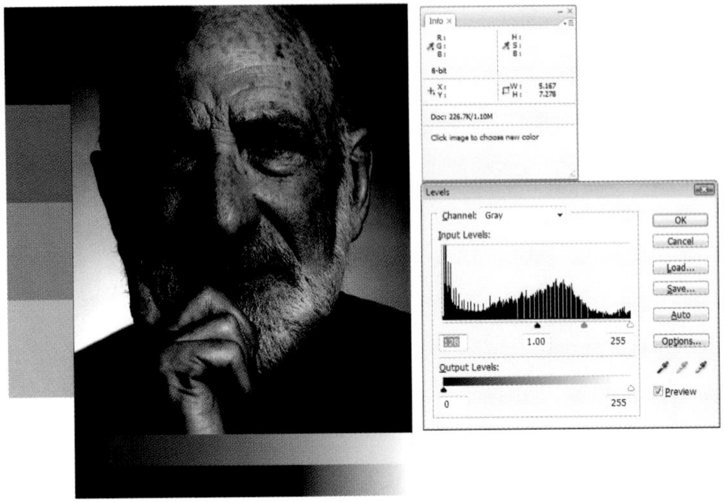

FIGURE 14
Viewing the result of moving the midpoint to the left

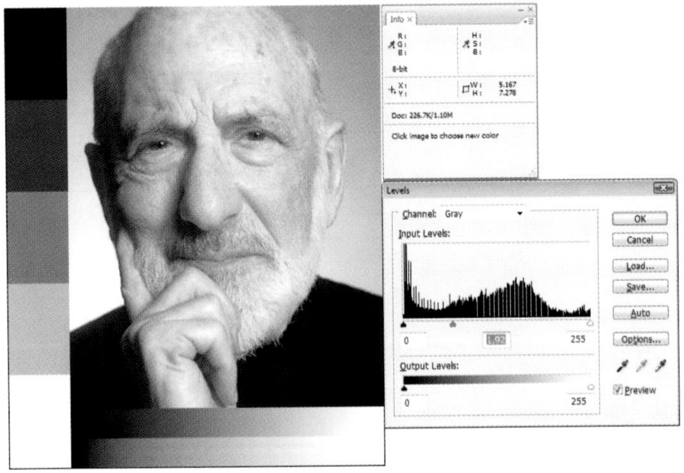

FIGURE 15

Viewing the result of moving the midpoint to the right

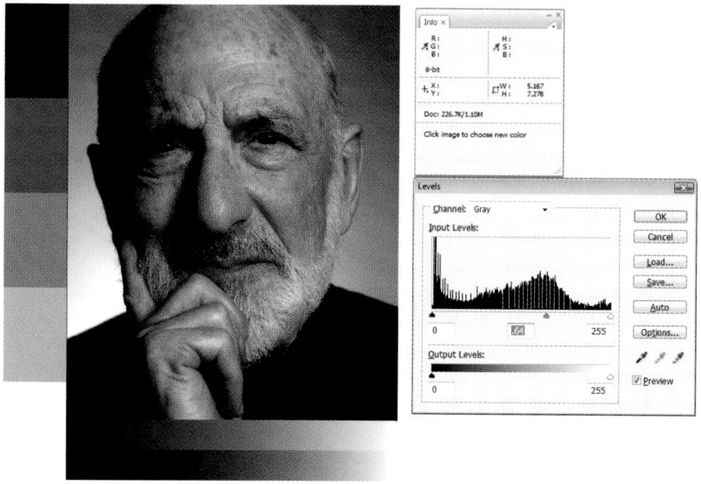

FIGURE 16

Viewing a histogram with "weak" shadow and highlight points

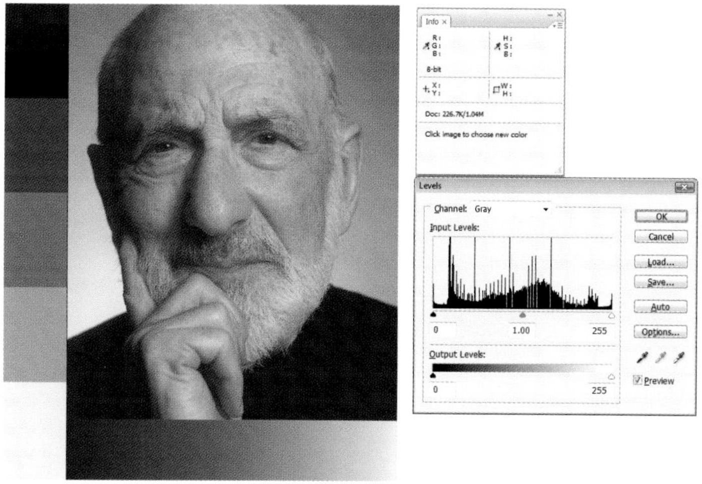

15. Reset the Levels dialog box.
16. Drag the **gray triangle** right until the middle Input text box reads 0.64, then compare your screen to Figure 15.

    Looking at the histogram, note how many more pixels are now positioned between the midpoint value and the black triangle. More of the image now falls in the darker half of the grayscale. Note how the image of the man was substantially darkened. In the gradient, note how long the range is from shadow to midpoint, while the midpoint to highlight point has been shortened.

    TIP Moving the gray midpoint triangle to the right darkens the middle range of a selection.

17. Click **Cancel** to close the Levels dialog box, save your work, then close Levels Intro.

Use levels to set the shadow point and the highlight point

1. Open AP 3-3.psd, then save it as **Shadow & Highlight Points**.
2. Open the Levels dialog box, compare your histogram to Figure 16, then float around the image to sample the darkest and lightest pixels anywhere on the canvas.

   This file has been manipulated to show an example of "weak" shadow and highlight points.

   Weak shadow points occur when dark areas of an image are composed of pixels whose grayscale values aren't dark enough. Conversely, weak highlight points occur when light areas of the image aren't light enough.

(continued)

To create an image with a dynamic range from highlight to shadow, you want the pixels in the image to utilize the entire grayscale. However, as often happens when you scan your own images on relatively less sophisticated equipment, the blacks aren't black enough and the whites aren't white enough.

If you look at the histogram, you can clearly see that although the entire range is being utilized very few pixels are at the low end and the high end of the grayscale. This is reflected in the image as well. If you sample the man's sweater, or the left side of the gradient, or the dark rectangle in the upper-left corner, you would want to find pixels whose grayscale values range from 0–10. However, you'll note that the grayscale values in these areas are much higher.

On the other side of the grayscale, the areas that should be 250 or higher are hovering somewhere in the 230 range. Because of weak highlight and shadow points, the image appears flat and lacks contrast.

3. Float your pointer in the lightest area of the image—over the man's shoulder—as shown in Figure 17.
4. Look for the lightest pixel you can find.

   The lightest pixel you can find is grayscale value 238.
5. In the Levels dialog box, drag the **white triangle** left until the far-right Input text box reads 235, as shown in Figure 18.

(continued)

FIGURE 17
Sampling the lightest areas of the image

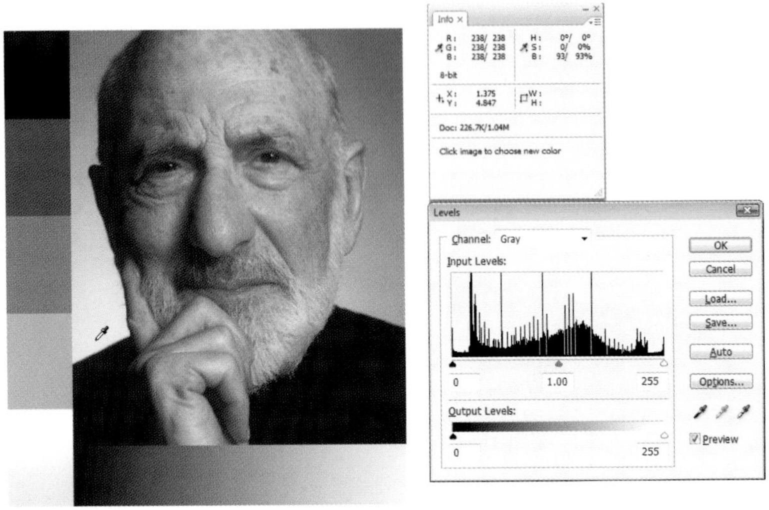

FIGURE 18
Moving the highlight point

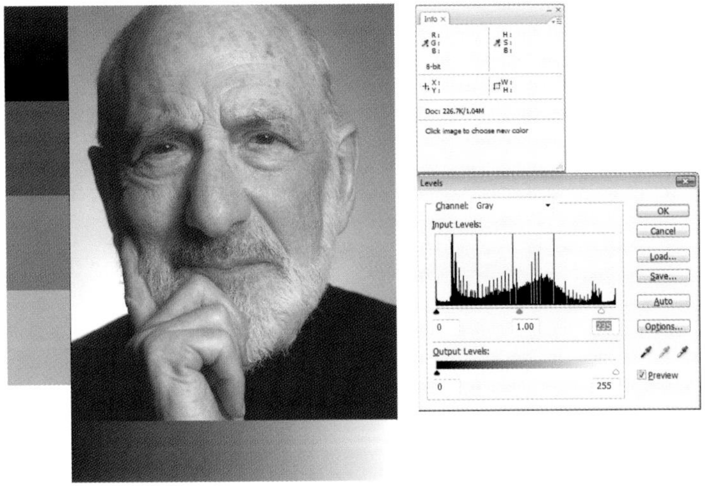

FIGURE 19
Moving the shadow point

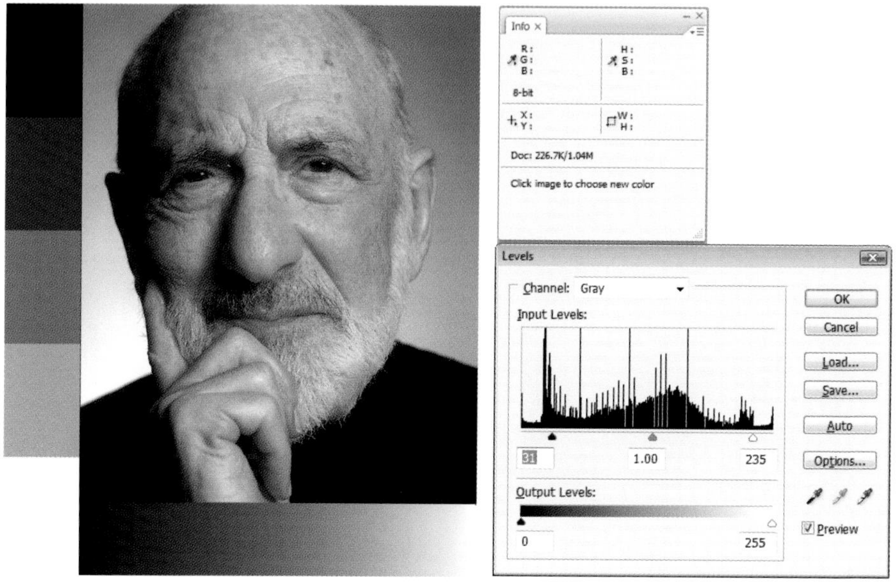

6. Position your pointer over the far-right end of the gradient to verify that the lightest pixel has been brightened to 255.
7. Float your pointer in the darkest area of the image—in the man's sweater—looking for the darkest pixel you can find.

   The darkest pixel to find is grayscale value 31.

   TIP Because you have modified the highlight point, the Info palette now shows before and after values when you sample the image. Note only the before values when you sample.
8. In the Levels dialog box, drag the **black triangle** right until the far-left Input text box reads 31, as shown in Figure 19.

(continued)

9. Click **OK**, then undo and redo the change to see the dramatic change to the image, as shown in Figure 20.

TIP Throughout this book, when you are asked to undo and redo to see a change, always end by redoing the change—in other words, when you are done viewing, be sure that the change has been executed.

10. Save your work.

FIGURE 20

Comparing before and after examples of the image

AUTHOR'S *note*

Educate your eye to look for the kind of improvements that you just applied to this image. The original image was flat: the tonal range from shadow to highlight was limited. The corrected image has "snap"—a certain vitality to it—as though you can almost feel the energy of the transition from the dramatic dark areas to the clean white areas.

Note that, in the original, it's not only the shadows and highlights that are weak. The middle range also suffers from a lack of contrast, say from the three-quarter tones to the quarter tones. In the corrected image, note how the man's face suddenly takes shape. His nose becomes more prominent, the lines in his face show greater detail, and overall the face becomes much more three-dimensional. It's as though you were looking at the image through a dirty glass pane, and the adjustment allowed the true image to show through.

FIGURE 21
"Opening" the midtones

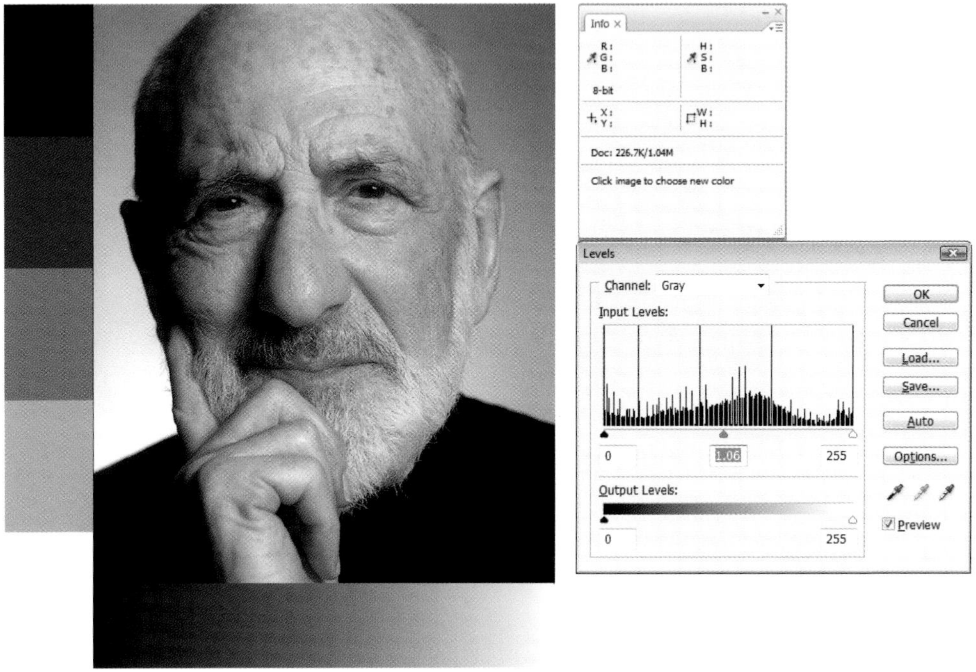

AUTHOR'S *note*

Whereas setting shadow and highlight points is often based on pixel data in the image, lightening or darkening midtones is usually a very subjective choice. An image that looks just fine to one designer may need brightening in the eyes of another designer, whereas a third designer might find the image too light already. In the case of this image, where the overall tone of the face fell on the darker side, a slight brightening was arguably the right move.

Adjust midtones and specific areas of an image

1. Open the Levels dialog box, drag the **midpoint triangle** left until the middle Input Levels text box reads 1.06, as shown in Figure 21.
2. Undo your last step, then redo to see the change.
3. Float your pointer over the man's face and beard, and try to find the brightest pixels that you can find.

   The brightest pixel you can find is 240, which is in the man's beard.
4. Float your pointer in the white background area over the man's shoulder to sample that area.

   The pixels in the white background area do not need to be lightened—they are all in the high range of the grayscale. Despite setting the shadow and highlight points and opening the midtones, the man's face still fails to reach its potential. The white area over the man's shoulder is the brightest area in the image. In other words, most of the highlights aren't even in the man's face, they're in the background.

(continued)

5. Show the Layers palette, then add a Levels adjustment layer over the Background layer.
6. In the Levels dialog box, drag the **white triangle** left until the third Input text box reads 236, as shown in Figure 22.
7. Click **OK**, then hide and show the adjustment layer to see the change.

   The choice was a good one. The tonal range of the face was increased, making the transition from shadow to highlight—in the face—more dramatic. The white beard is now the highlight area on the face, and it provides contrast to the dark areas on the shadowed side of the face. However, notice that the highlights on the hands are getting hot and starting to pop. Because they are in the foreground of the image and because they are close to being white patches, they are stealing focus from the main interest of the image—the man's face and eyes.
8. In the layer mask on the adjustment layer, mask the entire hand so that your Layers palette resembles Figure 23.

   The move was subtle but nevertheless important. Note how the highlights in the hands do not compete with the highlights in the man's beard. This is an excellent example of how you can use layer masks in conjunction with the Levels dialog box to adjust color only in specific areas of an image.

(continued)

FIGURE 22
Moving the highlight point

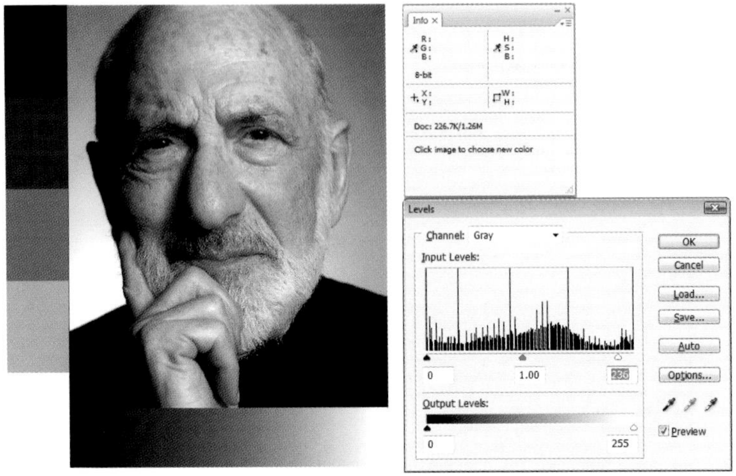

FIGURE 23
Masking the brightened hand

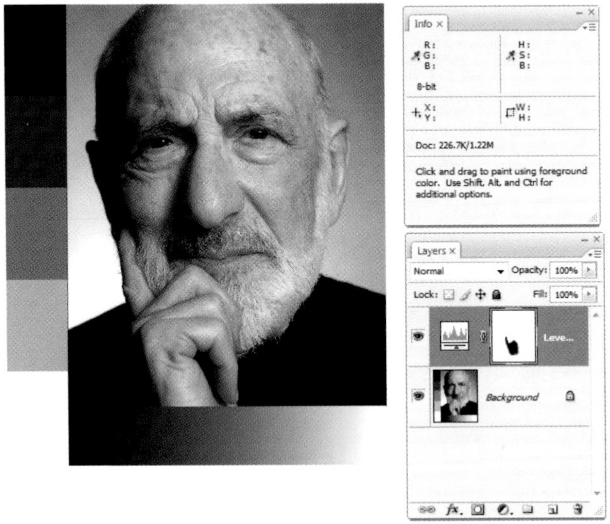

FIGURE 24
Viewing the final adjusted image

9. Load the selection named Man Alone, click **Image** on the menu bar, click **Crop**, deselect, then compare your work to Figure 24.
10. Save your work, then close Shadow & Highlight Points.

LESSON 3

EXPLORE THE Hue/Saturation Dialog Box

What You'll Do

The Hue/Saturation dialog box is a powerful Photoshop utility, one that you'll use over and over again. With it, you can saturate or desaturate an image, convert an image to black and white, and dramatically alter the hue of selected pixels. That's what you'll do in this lesson. You'll make a number of saturation and hue manipulations, and study the effect they have on an image.

FIGURE 25
Viewing modified hues

FIGURE 26
Comparing before/after for all hues

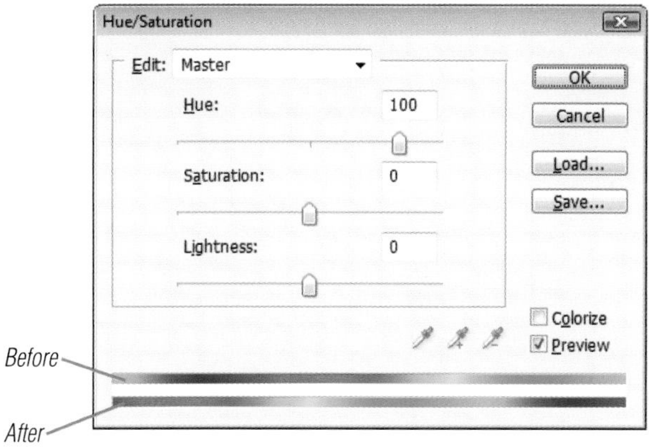

Manipulate hue

1. Open AP 3-4.psd, then save it as **Crayons**.
2. Verify that the Info palette is visible.
3. Target the **Right layer**.
4. Press **[Ctrl][U]** (Win) or **[⌘][U]** (Mac) to open the Hue/Saturation dialog box.

   TIP This is an easy quick key to memorize if you think of the *U* as *hue.*

5. Drag the **Hue slider** to the right so that its value reads 100, or simply type **100** in the Hue text box, then compare your artwork to Figure 25.

   The hue value—for every pixel in the image—has been moved 100 degrees on the color wheel.

6. Sample different pixels in the image, and note the before-and-after change in the hue value.

   For every pixel you click, the new value will be exactly the old value plus 100.

7. Note the two rainbow gradients at the bottom of the dialog box, as shown in Figure 26.

   The top rainbow gradient represents the original color wheel, and the bottom gradient represents the color wheel as it is being modified.

(continued)

8. Compare the red area at the center of the top gradient to the same location in the bottom gradient.

   With the shift in hue, the areas of the image that were originally red are now green. The two gradients in the Hue/Saturation dialog box are useful for predicting the results of modifying the Hue slider.

9. Turn the Preview off and on to compare the red crayon in the original image to its modified version.

   As shown in Figure 27, the red crayon is now green.

10. Compare different areas of the before-and-after rectangles to the before-and-after views of the image.

11. Drag the **Hue slider** to -100.

    Though the hues in the Color Picker are shown from 0 to 359, in the Hue/Saturation dialog box, the slider moves in two directions, positive and negative. Starting with 0 degrees, 0 thru 180 represents a counterclockwise movement on the color wheel. 0 thru -180 represents a clockwise movement on the wheel.

12. Click **Cancel**.

FIGURE 27
Comparing before/after hues

FIGURE 28

Viewing the colorized image

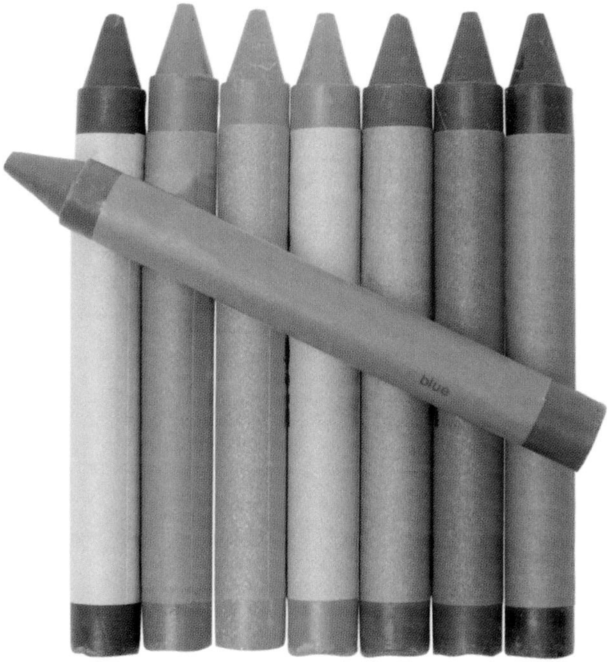

Colorize an image

1. Display the Swatches palette, then click the **RGB Green swatch** near the upper-left corner of the Swatches palette.
2. Click the **Set foreground color button** on the toolbox.
3. Jot down the hue, saturation, and brightness values of the color.

   The values of this color are 120H/100S/100B.
4. Click **Cancel**.
5. Open the Hue/Saturation dialog box, click the **Colorize check box**, then compare your screen to Figure 28.

   When you click the Colorize check box, all of the pixels in the image take on the hue value of the foreground color.
6. Move your pointer over the modified pixels and note the before-and-after H values in the Info palette.

   The hue value for every pixel in the modified image is 120. The only thing that differentiates the pixels is their saturation and lightness values.
7. Note the change to the bottom rainbow gradient in the dialog box.

   Once colorized, every hue on the color wheel becomes the same hue—in this case hue 120. This is identical to what has happened to every pixel in the modified image.

(continued)

8. Drag the **Hue slider** back and forth from left to right.

   By moving the Hue slider, you can colorize the image with any of the 360 hues in the color wheel.

   > **TIP** Note that, once colorized, the Hue slider specifies hues from 0 thru 360 rather than 0 thru 180 and 0 thru -180. This is a bit misleading, because 0–360 is actually a total of 361 hues. However, 0 and 360 represent the same location on the color wheel, and therefore the same hue.

9. Drag the **Hue slider** to 120.

Manipulate saturation

1. Drag the **Saturation slider** to 50, then compare your artwork to Figure 29.

   The green hue is intensified.

2. Drag the **Saturation slider** to 75.

   The green hue is further intensified.

3. Drag the **Hue slider** left and right to see the other hues at this saturation.

   > **TIP** By definition, modifying hue and saturation will always have some impact on the lightness value.

4. Press and hold **[Alt]** (Win) or **[option]** (Mac) so that the Cancel button becomes the Reset button, then click **Reset**.
5. Click the **Colorize check box** to remove the check mark.
6. Drag the **Saturation slider** to 50, then compare your image to Figure 30.

(continued)

FIGURE 29
Increasing the saturation of the colorized image

FIGURE 30
Increasing saturation

AUTHOR'S *note*

Note that, regardless of how you drag the Hue and Saturation sliders, the crayons always look like crayons. The darker crayons always stay darker than the lighter crayons. This is because you are not modifying the lightness values of the pixels. The lightness value defines the image—from shadow to highlight. So long as the overall lightness is maintained, the "reality" of the image will not change.

FIGURE 31
Reducing saturation

original *desaturated*

FIGURE 32
Desaturating the image completely

original *completely desaturated*

All the various hues are intensified. Note, however, that the gray crayon on the right hardly changes. This is because it originally had a low saturation value and the Saturation slider therefore has minimal impact. In other words, it's hard to increase saturation in a pixel that has little or no saturation to begin with.

7. Move your pointer over the modified image, and note the before-and-after values in the Info palette.

   Modifying saturation also affects the H and L values. The impact on the H values is minimal. However, an increase in saturation by definition requires an increase in lightness.

8. Drag the **Saturation slider** to -50, then compare your image to Figure 31.

   This decrease in saturation results in an image that clearly retains color, but that color is muted and not vibrant.

9. Drag the **Saturation slider** to –100, then compare your image to Figure 32.

   With no saturation, every pixel is and can only be a shade of gray.

10. Click **OK**, save your work, then close the Crayons document.

LESSON 4

ADJUST HUE, SATURATION, and Lightness

What You'll Do

In many projects, you will adjust and manipulate HSL to produce a variety of color effects. In other projects, you will adjust and manipulate HSL to achieve effects that are realistic. For example, if you were designing a catalog for a clothing company, they may supply you with a photograph of a green sweater then tell you that they want you to use the photo to also show a red and a blue sweater. Achieving a realistic result when modifying HSL is always interesting and often tricky. Lesson 4 focuses on that challenge. You will be given the task of modifying the color of articles of clothing, and your goal will be to manipulate HSL so that the modification is so realistic that nobody would notice that you've been up to your tricks.

FIGURE 33
Colorizing the yellow suit

Adjust HSL in selected areas

1. Open AP 3-5.psd, save it as **Bathing Suits**, then verify that you are viewing the image at 100%.
2. Target the **Left Suit layer**, make it visible, then create a clipped Hue/Saturation adjustment layer named Red Left.

   In this lesson, you will create a series of Hue/Saturation adjustment layers. For each one, choose the Use Previous Layer to Create Clipping Mask option.
3. Click the **Colorize check box**, drag the **Hue slider** to +355, drag the **Saturation slider** to +82, then compare your artwork to Figure 33.

   In terms of being realistic, the modification works—to a degree. The choice to colorize the image, however, was not a good one. The original (yellow) artwork contained a variety of hues—which is to be expected from a photograph taken in a real-world setting. Choosing to colorize the artwork converts all the hues to the same hue, which by definition is a movement away from reality.

   TIP When modifying HSL to achieve a realistic effect, colorizing the image is not a good choice for most cases.
4. Reset the Hue/Saturation dialog box, then remove the check mark in the Colorize check box.
5. Change the Hue value to -60, then modify the Saturation and Lightness values as you think best to achieve the brightest and most realistic red bathing suit.

   TIP Just preview, don't click OK.

(continued)

6. Compare your artwork to Figure 34.
7. Set the Saturation value to +5 and the Lightness value to 0.
8. Click **OK**, target the **Right Suit layer**, make it visible, then create a clipped Hue/Saturation layer named **Red Right**.
9. Modify the orange suit so that it is the exact same red as the first suit.
10. Compare your artwork to Figure 35.

    I changed the HSL value to –5/+19/–15. What's interesting about those values is that the hue didn't change much, but it was necessary to both darken and saturate the image to achieve the red.

    TIP When modifying HSL to achieve a realistic effect, increasing the lightness usually makes the image less realistic but decreasing the lightness seldom detracts from the illusion of realism.

11. Click **OK**, target the **Red Left adjustment layer**, then hide it.
12. Create a new clipped Hue/Saturation adjustment layer named **Turquoise**.

(continued)

FIGURE 34
Making the yellow suit red

FIGURE 35
Making the orange suit red

FIGURE 36
Making the yellow suit turquoise

FIGURE 37
Making the yellow suit royal blue

13. Modify HSL as you think best to achieve turquoise, then compare your artwork to Figure 36.

    Surprisingly, I found that I needed only to modify the hue. I set the hue value to 90, then found that the result was already so saturated that it required no further saturation. In fact, I found that increasing the saturation had almost no visible effect on the color.

14. Click **OK**, hide the Turquoise adjustment layer, then create a new clipped adjustment layer named **Royal Blue**.

15. Modify HSL to achieve your idea of a royal blue bathing suit, then compare your artwork to Figure 37.

    This is a fine example of how subjective color modifications can be. Your choice will almost certainly vary from the figures, because everybody has their own idea of what royal blue looks like, especially in a sunny beach setting with shiny bathing suit fabric. All of those factors come into play. Note that I both desaturated and darkened when I chose +153/-15/-13.

16. Click **OK**, target the **Red Right adjustment layer,** hide it, then create a new clipped adjustment layer named **Brown**.

(continued)

17. Modify HSL as you think best to achieve chocolate brown.

This one will probably be a challenge. Here are a couple of hints if you want them: Clearly, brown is a dark color, so creating it will involve reducing lightness. On the other hand, brown is indeed a color; it's not gray. Therefore the color will require some saturation, especially since chocolate brown connotes a warm brown. But more than S and L, choosing the right H to begin with will be the key to achieving the brown.

18. Compare your artwork to Figure 38.

I identify a basic brown hue as being somewhere between a dark maroon and a dark mustard. Therefore, I moved the hue to +18, which gave me a reddish yellow to start with, as shown in Figure 39. I then darkened the hue by reducing the lightness to -67. This achieved a brown. I then experimented with increasing the saturation to create a warmer, more vibrant brown. This move was by far the most subjective. I chose a saturation value of +40.

(continued)

FIGURE 38

Making the orange suit chocolate brown

FIGURE 39

Choosing the starting hue for brown

FIGURE 40
Comparing the yellow suit to the chocolate brown suit

19. Type **18**, **40**, and **-67** in the H, S, and L text boxes; click **OK**, hide the Royal Blue adjustment layer, then compare your artwork to Figure 40.

    Compare the bright areas of the chocolate brown suit to the bright areas of the yellow suit. Even though both have minimal shadow areas and almost no detail in the bright areas, the yellow suit appears more realistic than does the chocolate brown suit, which is just barely passing for real.

20. Target the hidden **Royal Blue adjustment layer**, then add a new clipped adjustment layer named **Navy**.

    TIP Note the shadow under the woman's arm and the shadow her hand casts on the yellow suit.

(continued)

21. Set the hue to +170, then experiment with reducing the lightness value to create a dark navy blue.

22. Reduce the Lightness value to -80, click **OK**, then compare your artwork to Figure 41.

    Because the original artwork was so bright and light, it is difficult if not impossible to achieve a realistic color as dark as navy blue. At -80 lightness, the color is dark enough to resemble a dark navy blue, but the suit no longer looks realistic—it looks like a selection filled with a single color. If you compare it to the brown bathing suit, you can see that the navy blue suit is flat. This is because the new hue is darker than the original shadows in the image. Note that the shadow under the arm and even the shadow from the hand are nearly indistinguishable from the rest of the suit. Because there are no shadows, there's no range from dark to light, and therefore no shape. When there's no shape, there's no realism.

23. Open the Navy adjustment layer, change the Lightness value to -45, change the Saturation value to -15, click **OK**, then compare your artwork to Figure 42.

    This is the darkest blue I could achieve while maintaining distinct shadows for shape—and realism—in the image.

24. Undo and redo to see the difference between the unrealistic and the realistic modification.

25. Save your work, then close the file.

FIGURE 41
Losing shadow detail

FIGURE 42
Retaining shadow detail

FIGURE 43
Making the sweater navy blue

FIGURE 44
Making the sweater black

Adjust HSL in dark areas

1. Open AP 3-6.psd, then save it as **Sweater**.
2. Show the Navy Blue adjustment layer, then double-click the **Layer thumbnail** to open the dialog box.
3. Drag the **Hue slider** back and forth to see the sweater as different hues.

   Regardless of what hue you set, the color of the sweater looks realistic.
4. Drag the **Hue slider** to -180, drag the **Saturation slider** to +30, then compare your artwork to Figure 43.

   When you are working with darker images, it's easier to modify the hue and keep the image looking real. This is because, by definition, a darker image has broad shadow areas that clearly define the shape of the image.
5. Click **OK**, press and hold **[Alt]** (Win) or **[option]** (Mac), drag the **layer mask thumbnail** from the Navy Blue adjustment layer on top of the layer mask thumbnail on the Black layer, then click **Yes** when asked if you want to replace it.
6. Hide the Navy Blue adjustment layer, show the Black adjustment layer, then double-click it to open the dialog box.
7. Modify HSL to achieve the effect that the woman is wearing a black (not just dark gray) sweater, as shown in Figure 44.
8. Set the Saturation value to -100, set the Lightness value to -40, then click **OK**.

(continued)

9. Open the Black adjustment layer dialog box again, drag the **Lightness slider** all the way to the left, then click **OK**.

   Compare your screen to Figure 45.

   Undo and redo to see the difference between the two blacks. In our first black sweater, we maintained a range of tone, with areas that were darker than others, such as the folds in the sleeves and under the arm. Note too that you can see a dark black line where the turtleneck folds over and meets the sweater. Compare this to the all-black sweater. This is a great example of how you always want to maintain detail and a range of tone in the dark areas of a realistic image, even an image that is supposed to register as black.

10. Replace the layer mask on the Red adjustment layer with the layer mask from the Black adjustment layer.

11. Hide the Black adjustment layer, show the Red adjustment layer, then double-click it to open the dialog box.

12. Modifying only the Hue and Saturation sliders, experiment with different values and try to make the sweater the most vivid red that you can while maintaining realism.

13. Drag the **Hue slider** to -98, drag the Saturation slider to +80, then compare your result to Figure 46.

    This is as bright and vivid a red sweater as you'll be able to create while maintaining realism. If you push the saturation value past 80, the highlights on the shoulders get hot and start to pop, creating an unrealistic effect.

(continued)

FIGURE 45
Filling the sweater with black

FIGURE 46
Making the sweater red

FIGURE 47
Increasing lightness in the Hue/Saturation dialog box

FIGURE 48
A brighter and more vivid red created using other Photoshop utilities

14. Drag the **Lightness slider** to +20, then compare your result to Figure 47.

    The increase in lightness detracts from the color of the image and makes it look unrealistic. See the Author's note below.

15. Drag the **Lightness slider** to 0, click **OK**, then compare your image to Figure 48.

    The image on your screen will not resemble Figure 48. The red sweater in the figure was achieved by brightening the image using the Curves dialog box. In Photoshop, there are many ways to brighten an image, with the Curves dialog box being the most sophisticated.

16. Save your work, then close the Sweater document.

AUTHOR'S *note*

This is an important footnote to this entire chapter. The Lightness slider in the Hue/Saturation dialog box is not intended to be used to brighten or darken an image. It was not designed for that purpose. Photoshop has a number of other dialog boxes that brighten and darken an image using far more sophisticated algorithms. As you saw in this lesson, the Lightness slider was not at all a good choice for brightening the image. On the other hand, you can use it to darken an image; for example, it did a good job modifying the sweater to black.

Adjust HSL in hard-to-select areas

1. Open AP 3-7.psd, then save it as **Replace Color**.

   Imagine for a moment that your client supplies you with this photo and says, "I want you to use this photo, but I need you to make all the purple elements blue so they work better with the head scarf." How in the world would you select just the purple parts of the costume? Cutting a path around all that embroidered detail wouldn't work. A layer mask might work, but it too would be terribly time consuming.

2. Show the Go Blue layer, target the **Go Blue layer**, then press **[D]** to access default foreground and background colors.

3. Click **Image** on the menu bar, point to **Adjustments**, then click **Replace Color**.

   The Replace Color dialog box, shown in Figure 49, is one of the coolest features in Photoshop and is extremely powerful for manipulating Hue/Saturation in hard-to-select areas. What's even better—it's something of a well-kept secret. Generally speaking, it's not one of the most commonly used features in Photoshop.

4. Verify that the Fuzziness slider is set to 40.

5. Click the **Eyedropper Tool** in the light purple area shown in Figure 50, then note the result in the Replace Color dialog box.

   A mask is being created.

(continued)

FIGURE 49
Replace Color dialog box

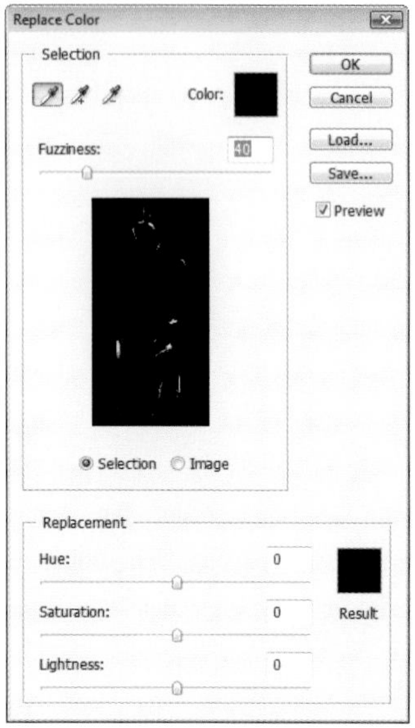

FIGURE 50
Sampling the light purple area

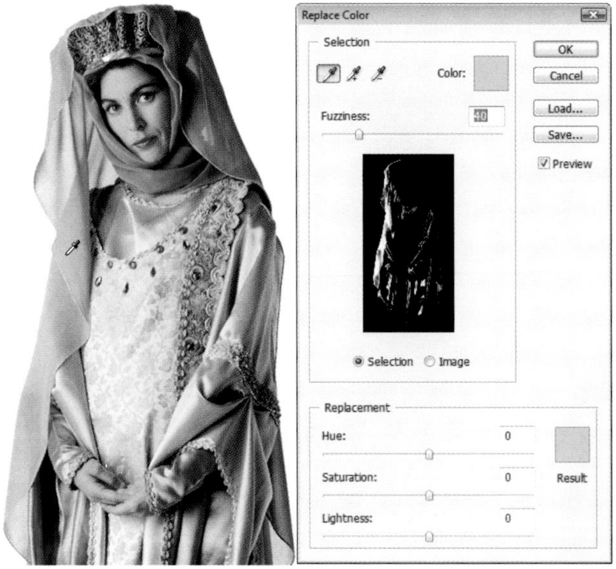

FIGURE 51
Increasing fuzziness increases area to be modified

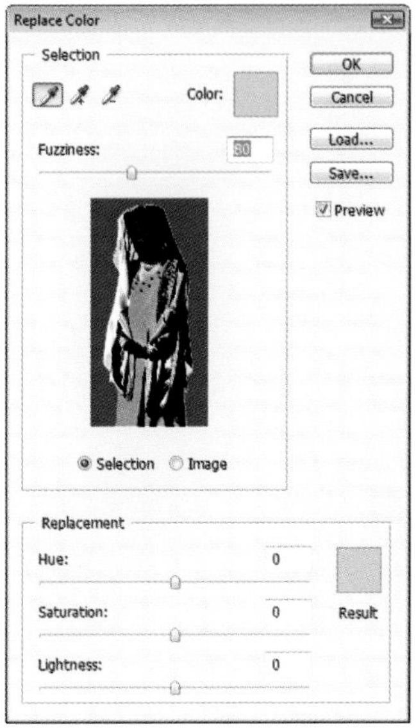

FIGURE 52
Adding a dark purple area to the sample

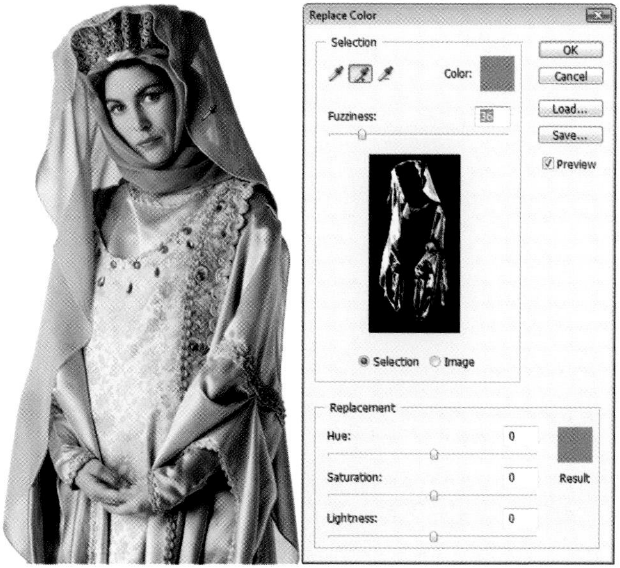

6. Drag the **Fuzziness slider** to 80, then compare your dialog box to Figure 51.

   The increased Fuzziness value greatly expands the white areas of the mask. Note, however that some areas in the face are beginning to show in the mask.

   > **TIP** Feel free to think of *fuzziness* as being the same thing as *tolerance*. With the Magic Wand Tool, tolerance determines how far from where you click the selection will be created. In the Replace Color dialog box, fuzziness determines how far from where you click the Eyedropper Tool the selected areas of the mask will be created.

7. Drag the **Fuzziness slider** to 36, then click the **Add to Sample Tool** .

8. Click in the dark purple area shown in Figure 52.

   The white areas of the mask are expanded by the new sample and the current fuzziness value.

   I prefer to maintain a relatively low fuzziness value and enter multiple samples with the Add to Sample Tool. For example, with these two clicks, we have sampled both a light purple, and a dark purple, and the fuzziness extends from both, creating a layer mask that targets a broad range or purple tones.

(continued)

9. Drag the **Hue slider** to +180, drag the **Saturation slider** to +50, then compare your screen to Figure 53.

   Although our goal is to convert these areas to blue, we changed them to a saturated green for the time being so they will be easy to differentiate from the purple areas that have so far escaped our sampling.

10. Position over the right sleeve in the location shown in Figure 54, then click to add that range of tone to the sample.

   The Replace Color dialog box is dynamic. When you click the Add to Sample Tool in the image, the mask is updated and the modification is applied immediately.

(continued)

FIGURE 53

Modifying the hue and saturation

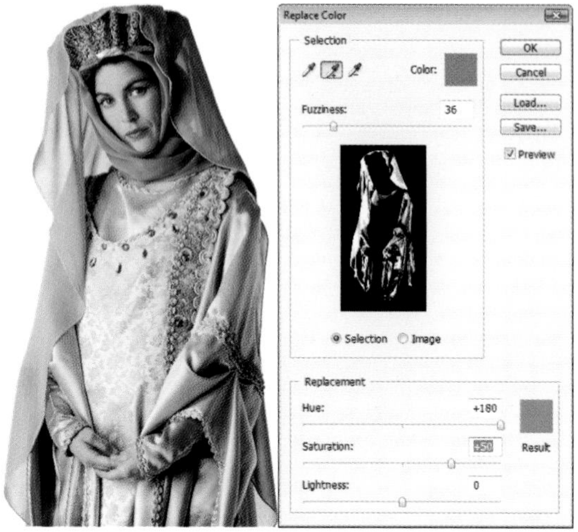

FIGURE 54

Adding more purple areas to the sample

FIGURE 55
Replacing all the purple areas

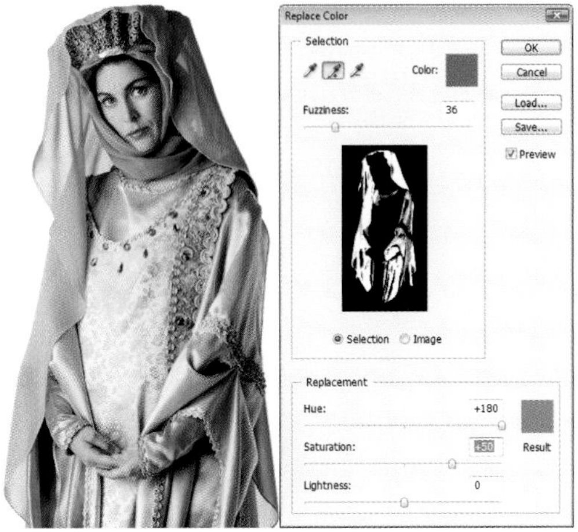

FIGURE 56
The image before and after

11. Click in other purple areas to add them to the sample so that your screen resembles Figure 55.

    TIP Be judicious when you click. Don't overlook the darker purple areas in the shadowy parts of the image. However, be careful not to click neutral shadows. The neutral shadows in the purple areas are not the only neutral shadows in the image. If you add neutral shadows to the sample, the woman's hair and eyebrows will become green!

    TIP You can always undo if you don't like the result of a sample. The Subtract from Sample Tool also allows you to remove areas from the sample.

12. Drag the **Hue slider** slowly to the left to see all the other hues available to you.
13. Set the Hue to -87, set the Saturation to +19, then click **OK**.
14. Hide and show the Go Blue layer to see the change, then compare your results to Figure 56.

    How amazing is that? A global color change in nonspecific areas made without a selection in a matter of minutes if not seconds. What's really stunning is how seamless the modification is—nobody would ever guess. Of course, this image was perfect for this modification, because the purple areas in the costume were the only purple areas in the image.

15. Save your work, then close all open files.

PROJECT BUILDER 1

1. Open AP 3-8.psd, then save it as **Color Woman**.
2. Posterize the image to six levels.
3. Select all the black areas, then fill them with a different color.
4. Select all the white areas, then fill them with a different color.
5. Fill each of the other four levels with four different colors so that each level is all one color.
6. Use the Paint Bucket Tool to add other colors to the artwork.
7. Compare your artwork to Figure 57.
8. Save your work, then close the Color Woman document.

FIGURE 57
Completed Project Builder 1

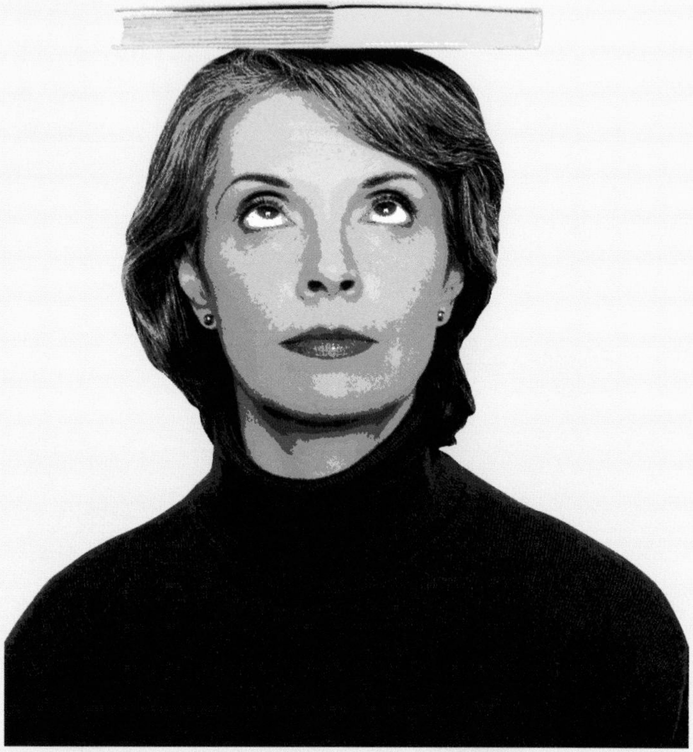

PROJECT BUILDER 2

1. Open AP 3-9.psd, then save it as **Seeing Red**. (*Hint*: The goal in this exercise is to use the Replace Color dialog box to make both the purple areas of the dress and the head scarf red.)
2. Target the Go Red layer.
3. Open the Replace Color dialog box, then sample a light area in the blue head scarf.
4. Click the Add to Sample Tool, then sample a darker area of the blue head scarf.
5. Drag the Hue slider to 151.
6. Add additional samples until the scarf and the blue jewels are red.
7. Increase the Saturation to +10.
8. Click OK, then open the Replace Color dialog box again.
9. Click the Eyedropper Tool, then sample a light area of the purple veil.
10. Convert all the purple areas to red, then compare your screen to Figure 58.
11. Save your work, then close the Seeing Red document.

FIGURE 58
Completed Project Builder 2

chapter

4

WORKING WITH CURVES and Adjusting Color

1. Explore the Curves dialog box.
2. Adjust curves in a grayscale image.
3. Analyze color channels.
4. Adjust color with curves.

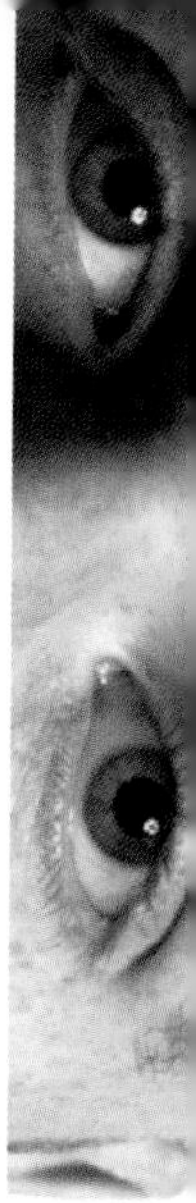

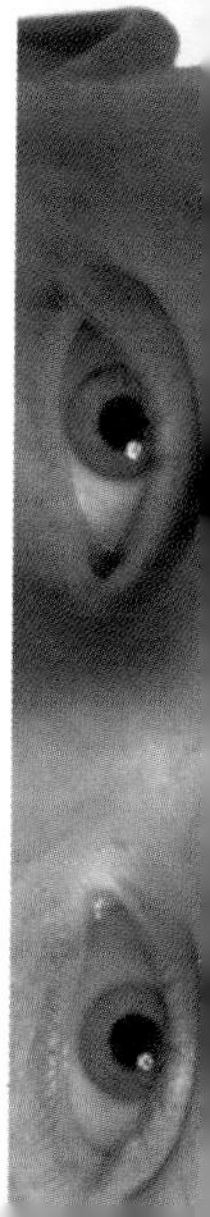

LESSON 1

EXPLORE THE CURVES Dialog Box

What You'll Do

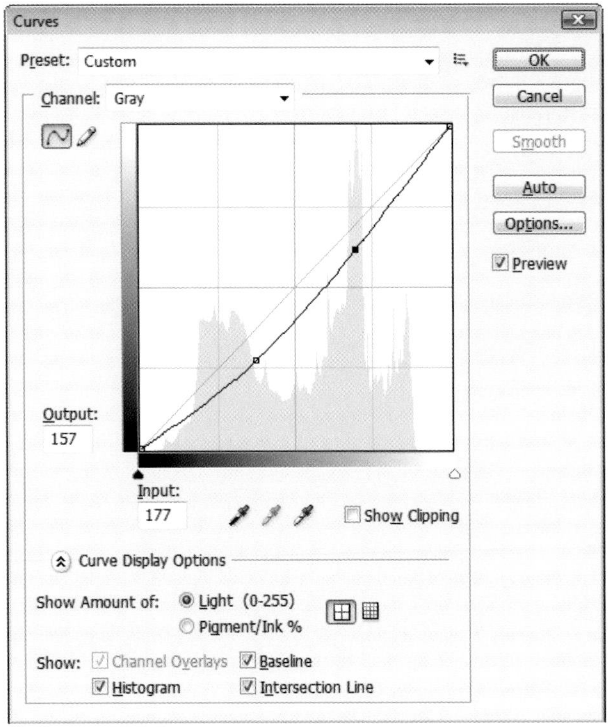

The Curves dialog box is a color manipulation utility in Photoshop, like the Levels dialog box or the Brightness/Contrast slider. What makes the Curves dialog box different is that it is the most comprehensive and most powerful option for manipulating color, and that power is based on the precision that it offers. For example, with the Levels dialog box, you have three sliders to adjust color: the shadow point, the midpoint, and the highlight point. With Curves, you have up to 14 different points throughout an image's tonal range to adjust, and you can quite literally target a specific grayscale value. You can also make very precise adjustments to specific color channels.

Curves are most associated with color manipulation, but it's better to think of them as manipulating the **tonal range** of an image—the range from shadow to highlight. Most often, the result of this manipulation is an adjustment of color, but curves are not only about color. You can—and will—use curves to manipulate the tonal range of a grayscale image, to improve black points, white points, contrast, etc.

When you get to the point that you're working with curves and the Curves dialog box, you're working with some of the central and most powerful concepts in Photoshop. As with most skills, it's all about experience. With time, practice and experience, you'll develop a reliable sense of how to work with curves to achieve a desired effect. Sometimes that desired effect will be a basic adjustment: improving contrast, brightening or darkening an image, or tweaking the overall color. For those adjustments, you'll find that you can rely on standard curve adjustments to do the trick.

At other times, you'll be using curves to achieve unique and less specific challenges, and that's when curves will really test you. Simply put, there will be some color changes you'll want to make that won't be achieved with a standard curve. For these, you'll need to experiment to work your way toward the look you're going for. This is a challenge, because there's never any "right answer." Two designers might achieve the same effect with two very different approaches, two very different sets of curve adjustments.

Again, experience will do wonders for your understanding of curves. But before experience, a solid understanding of the essential concepts and basic functions of the Curves dialog box is of paramount importance for your ability to grow and evolve and improve your work.

That's where this first lesson begins—with the essential concepts and basic functions of the Curves dialog box. The goal is to establish a solid foundation to build on, and that foundation is a thorough understanding of what the Curves dialog box is, what options it offers, and how it does what it does.

Explore the Curves dialog box

1. Open AP 4-1.psd, then save it as **Sunset Swans**.

   We're beginning with a grayscale image for an important reason: a grayscale image has a single channel. Pixels in a grayscale image can be one, and only one, of 256 shades of gray. Using a basic grayscale image allows you to make adjustments with curves and really understand what's happening to the image.
2. Open the Levels dialog box, take a mental picture of the histogram, then close the Levels dialog box.
3. Verify that Tools, Info, and Layers are the only open palettes and verify that the Info palette has at least one color readout set to RGB.
4. Create a Curves adjustment layer, then compare your Curves dialog box to Figure 1.
5. Click the **Curve Display Options button**  to expand the dialog box, then verify that the Histogram, Baseline, and Intersection Line check boxes are all checked.

(continued)

FIGURE 1
The Curves dialog box

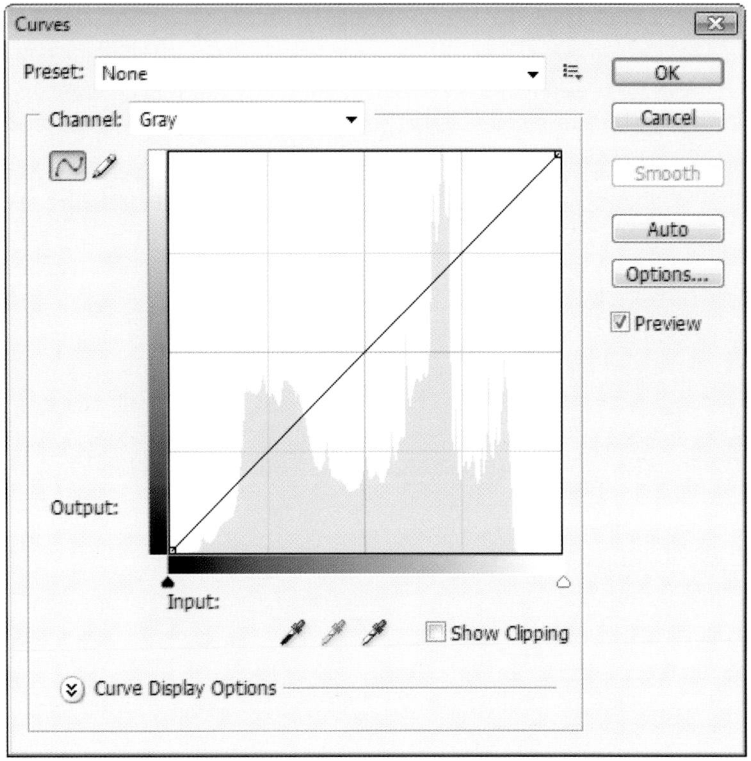

AUTHOR'S *note*

The Light (0-255) vs Pigment/Ink % option determines how the Curves dialog box presents its information.

If you choose the Light (0 -255) option, the dialog box presents its information in terms of grayscale, with pixels and the curve being identified from 0 (black point) to 255 (white point). This is true for color or black and white images.

With the Pigment/Ink % option, the dialog box provides tonal information for actual printing, as though it were evaluating what percentages of ink on paper are represented by the tonal areas in the image.

Obviously, there's a lot going on with these options, but don't worry about it. This book does not focus on offset printing and how to use Photoshop to prep images for offset printing. Therefore, the Pigment/Ink % option does not apply to anything we're doing in the Curves dialog box.

Instead, this book is designed and written as an approach to using Photoshop as software on your computer and images displayed on your computer screen. Everything displayed on your computer screen is displayed as light, and light is represented in Photoshop as grayscale (0 -255). Therefore, for all the exercises in this chapter, you should choose the Light (0 -255) option in the Curves dialog box.

6. In the Show Amount of section, click the **Light (0–255) option button**. See the Author's note on this page.
7. To the right of the Show Amount of section, toggle the two grid options on and off, then verify that the left option, "Display simple grid with quarter-tone increments," is activated.

(continued)

8. Note the histogram.

The histogram in the Curves dialog box is identical to the histogram you saw in the Levels dialog box; both are derived from the same information.

> **TIP** The histogram is explained in detail in Chapter 3.

9. Note the black and white triangle sliders beneath the histogram.

The triangle sliders—and how they relate to the histogram—are the component of the Curves dialog box that functions most like the Levels dialog box. The concept is the same: moving the black slider adjusts the black point and moving the white slider adjusts the white point.

10. Note the black-to-white blend along the bottom and along the left side of the grid, as identified in Figure 2.

The blends (or 'ramps') have no practical function in the dialog box and don't change as a result of any changes you make to the curve. Their function in the dialog box is simply to represent the movement of shadow to highlight. In other words, the bottom blend shows you that the tonal range moves from shadow to highlight (black to white) as you move from left to right in the grid. The side vertical blend shows that the tonal range moves from black to white as you move from bottom to top in the grid.

(continued)

FIGURE 2
The Curves dialog box

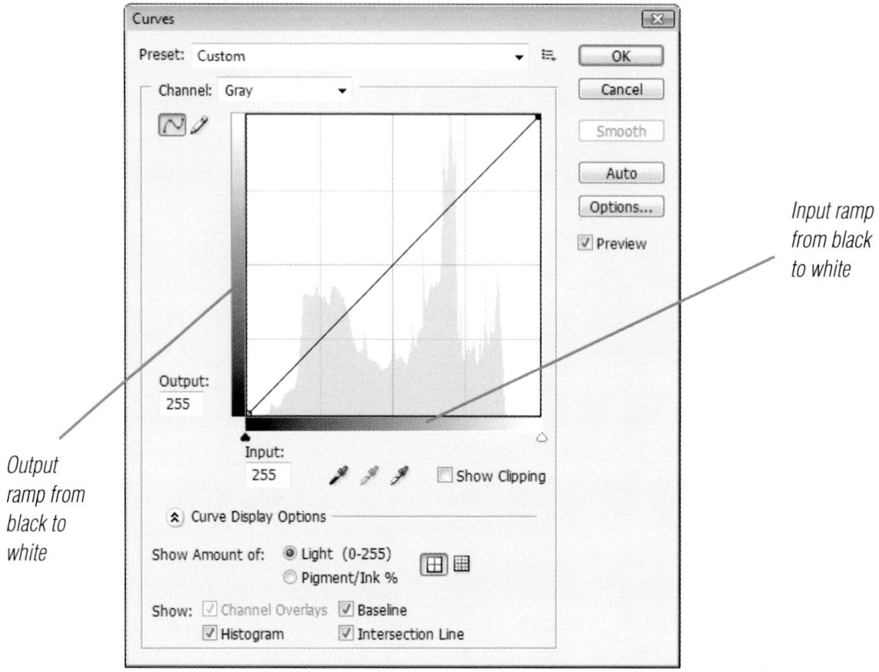

FIGURE 3
Adding a point to the curve

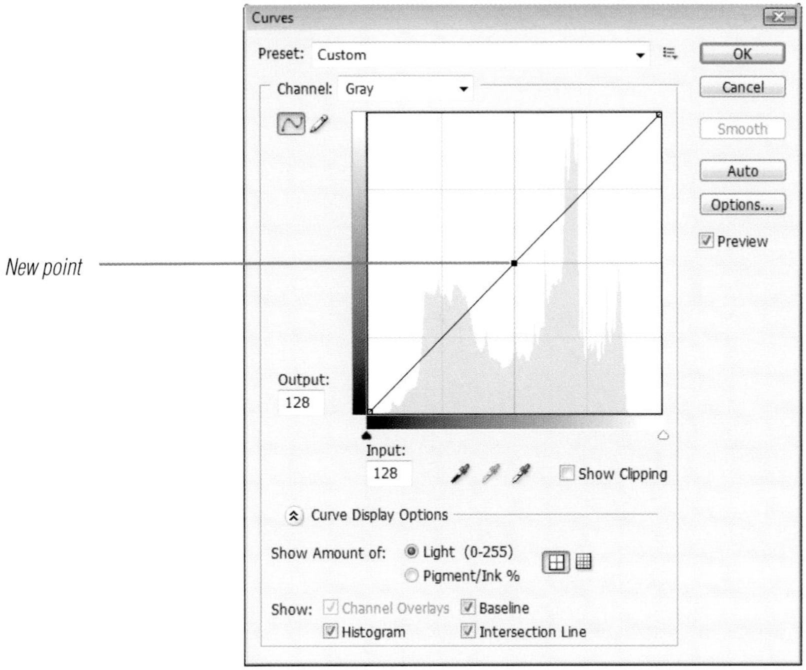

11. Move the mouse pointer over the grid so that your cursor turns into a crosshair, position the crosshair in the center of the grid so that the Input and Output text boxes both read 128, then click to add a point.
12. Compare your dialog box to Figure 3.

    Think of the Input and Output text boxes as being the Before and After representation of any changes you make to the curve. Because you've made no changes to the curve up to this point, the Input/Output values for the point you clicked—and every other point on the curve—are the same.

(continued)

13. Drag the point straight up so that the Input/Output text boxes match Figure 4.

This move and its result convey—in a simple and basic way—what the Curves dialog box is all about. We've altered the tonal range of the image. Pixels that had a grayscale value of 128 now have a value of 160. Therefore, those pixels are lighter by 32 shades of gray. But it's not only those specific pixels that have changed, the entire image has been brightened, and the curve is a visual representation of that change. Note how it deviates from the light gray intersection line. Pixels in the middle range of the grayscale are most affected by the move, with the adjustment tapering off in equal measure at the brightest highlights and darkest shadows.

14. Move the mouse pointer over the curve and note the changes to the Input/Output text boxes.

Figure 5 shows a sample of what's happened to the pixels roughly between the midpoint and the black point. They have been brightened—their Output value is higher than the Input value—but the increase is not as dramatic as it is in the midrange of the curve.

15. Drag the point on the curve to different areas of the grid and note the effect on the image.

When you drag the curve below the intersection line, the image is darkened.

16. Type **95** in the Input text box, then type **70** in the Output text box.

(continued)

FIGURE 4
Changing the curve

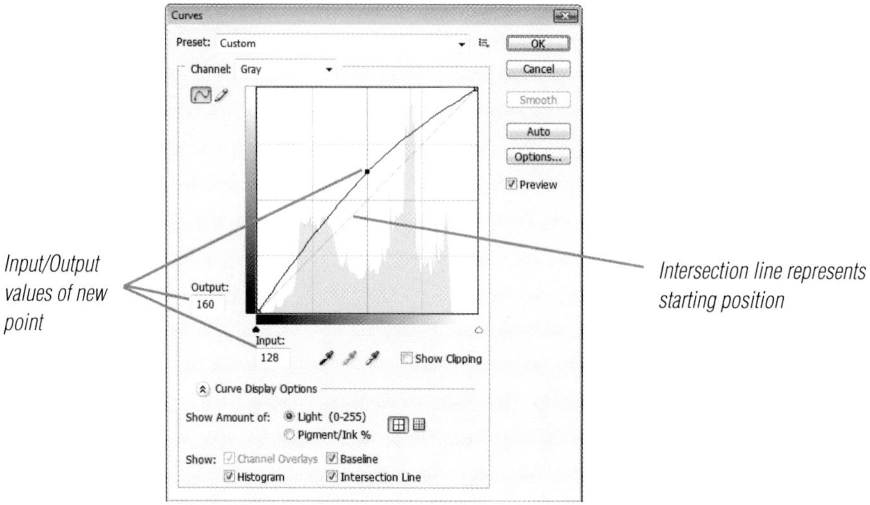

FIGURE 5
Sampling an area of the curve

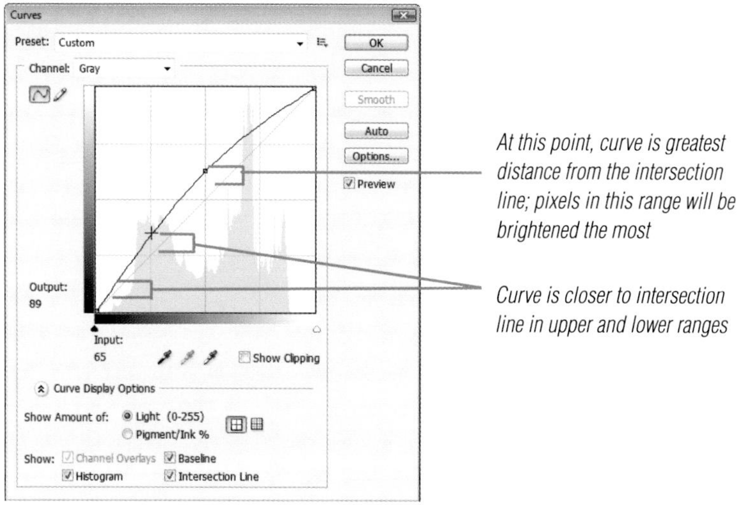

FIGURE 6
Sampling the image against the curve

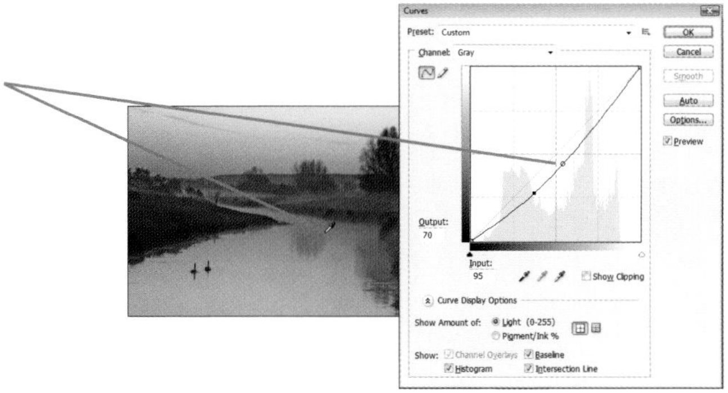

FIGURE 7
Viewing the added point on the curve

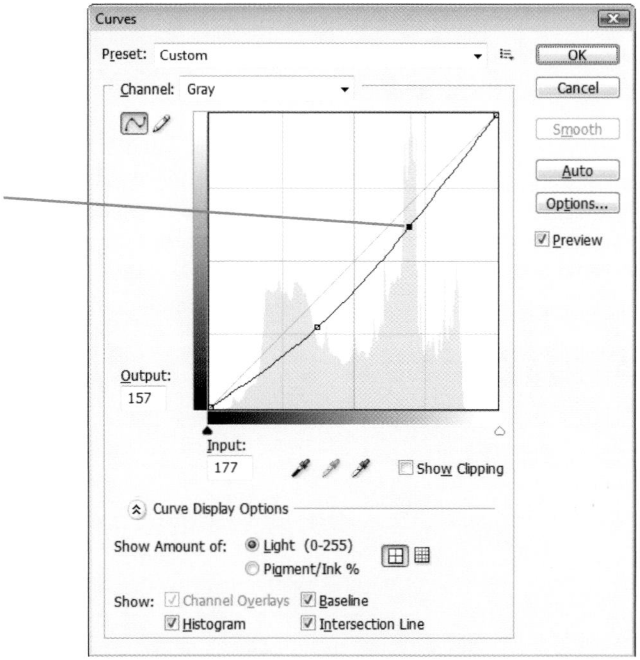

17. Position your Curves dialog box so that you can see as much of the image as possible.
18. Move the mouse pointer over the image so that your cursor changes to the Eyedropper pointer, then click and drag the Eyedropper pointer to different areas of the image.

    As shown in Figure 6, a small circle appears on the curve showing where the sampled pixels in the image appear on the curve.
19. Press and hold **[Ctrl]**(Win) or [⌘] (Mac), then click anywhere in the water in the foreground of the image.

    As shown in Figure 7, a new point appears on the curve. Its location on the curve is that of the grayscale value of the pixel that you clicked.
20. Click and drag the **second point** straight up to remove it from the curve.
21. Click **OK**, save your work, then close Sunset Swans.psd.

LESSON 2

ADJUST CURVES IN A Grayscale Image

What You'll Do

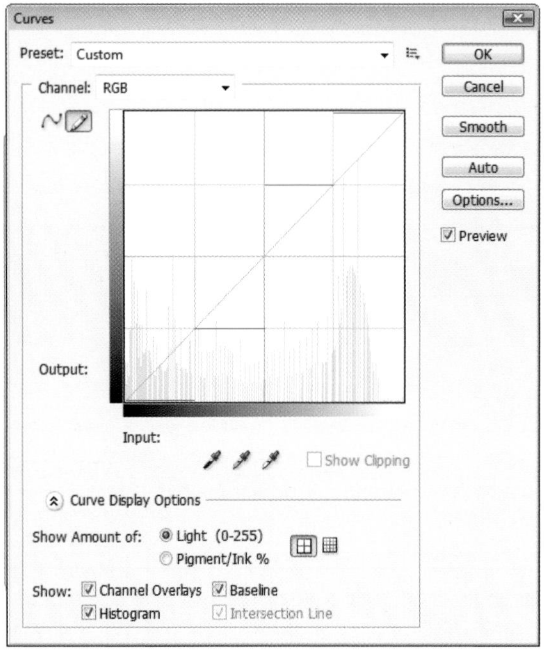

When it comes to adjusting color, the Curves dialog box is the most sophisticated utility that Photoshop has to offer. Quite literally, you can use a curve to manipulate a specific level of gray in an image—it's that precise.

Mastering the Curves dialog box is one of the great challenges in Photoshop. It's an art, it's a craft, and it's a technical challenge as well.

As a designer, you don't need to be a color technician, and you don't need to master curves and color retouching. But you most certainly do need to work with curves and to understand the central concepts of how they control the color and the tonal range of the image.

AUTHOR'S *note*

If you've walked through the color department of a design firm, advertising agency, or offset printer, you've probably seen men and women in a dark room staring intently at images on their monitors.

These are the people who are responsible for the color quality of a job; these are the people who make sure that the client's million-dollar print campaign looks great when it's printed. These people—scanners, retouchers, and color specialists—spend much of their well-paid days working with curves.

You could spend years learning about curves and still not know everything there is to know. You're not going to learn everything in the next five lessons. However, you are going to learn basic curve adjustments, and it's important to understand that you can use these skills in the real world, when you're designing and creating artwork.

Professional designers use these same skills every day. However, designing something that looks great on your monitor is completely different from getting that something to look as great when it's printed. So understand that the skills you are about to learn are only the tip of the proverbial iceberg, and they don't factor in the exacting standards and tough realities of the offset printing world. For that, you'll need a professional to help you translate your artwork to the printed page.

Should you worry about this? The answer is an emphatic No. As a designer, it's your job to create great artwork, and if you use curves to create that artwork, good for you. It's not your job to worry about making the image print-ready. In most professional settings, designers are free to create artwork to the best of their skills, and it is the job of the retoucher or the color specialist to translate that artwork into something that can be reproduced.

So in a professional setting, you're usually covered. In a freelance setting, however, or if you're in charge of the whole project, be sure to factor in a color professional somewhere in the process.

Invert an image using curves

1. Open AP 4-2.psd, then save it as **Analyze Curves**.
2. Verify that the **Original layer** in the Layers palette is targeted and is the only visible layer.
3. Click **Image** on the menu bar, point to **Adjustments**, then click **Invert**.

   How does the Invert command work? Before moving forward, take a few moments to imagine creating this effect with curves. What would the curve look like?
4. Undo your last step.
5. Click **Layer** on the menu bar, point to **New Adjustment Layer**, then click **Curves**.
6. Drag the **black point** up to the upper-left corner so that your image and your Curves dialog box resemble Figure 8.

   > **TIP** Verify that the Preview check box is checked, and position the Curves dialog box so that you can see the image.

   The 0 Input value of the black point changes to an Output value of 255. Because the entire curve now sits at the very top of the grid, every pixel now has an Output value of 255. Thus, the entire image is white.

(continued)

FIGURE 8
Relocating the black point

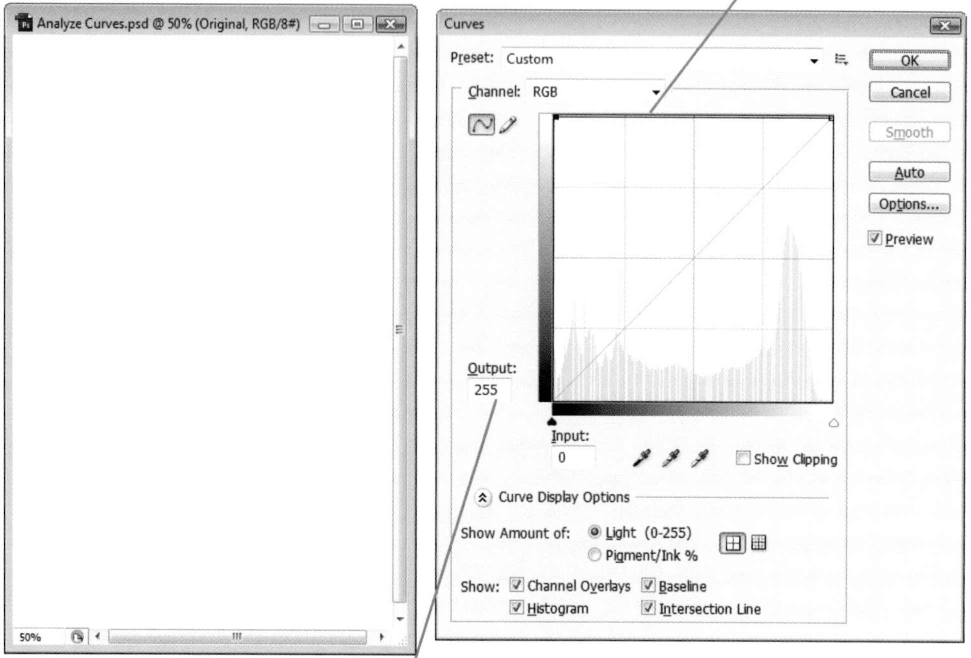

FIGURE 9
Relocating the white point

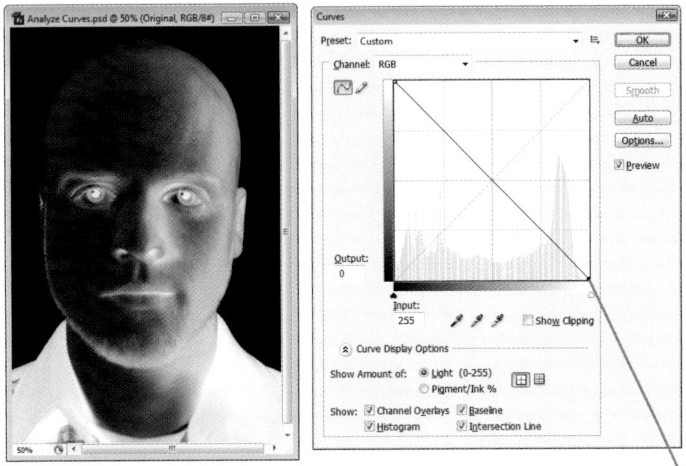

White point output at grayscale 0

FIGURE 10
Viewing the change to pixel 191

Original location of pixel 191

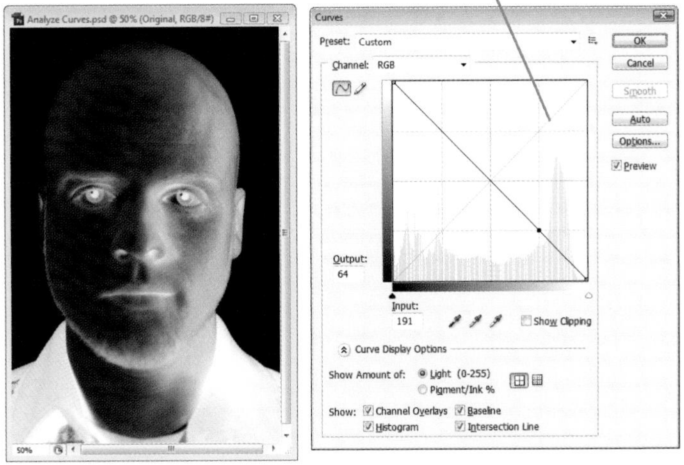

7. Drag the **white point** to the lower-right corner so that your image and your Curves dialog box resemble Figure 9.

   The curve is now inverted. The black point has changed from 0 to 255 and is now white. The white point has changed from 255 to 0 and is now black. All the points in between are also inverted. In other words, pixels that were in the bottom half are now in the top half and vice-versa.

8. Position your pointer over the curve, then click to add a point in the location shown in Figure 10.

   Nothing changes—we added a point only for the sake of sampling the change to the curve. Pixel 191—originally the mid-point between 128 and 255—will be output as 64, its inverse on the grayscale and the mid-point between 0 and 128. In other words, a light-gray pixel is inverted and becomes a dark gray pixel.

(continued)

9. Position your pointer over the curve, then click to add a point in the location shown in Figure 11.

   Pixels with an Input value of 64 will be output as their inverse: 191.

   Stop for a moment and ask yourself this question about Figure 11: If you were to click to add a point in the exact middle of the curve, what would the Input value be, and what would the Output value be? Take the time to figure it out before moving ahead.

10. Add a point at the very center of the curve.

    Pixel 128 is the middle gray pixel—128 is the median point between 0 and 255. The curve has not changed location at the 128 point on the grid. All the other pixels have swapped values with their counterparts on the other side of the midpoint. 129 is 127. 130 is 126. 131 is 125, and so on.

11. Click **OK**, hide the new adjustment layer, then save your work.

FIGURE 11

Viewing the change to pixel 64

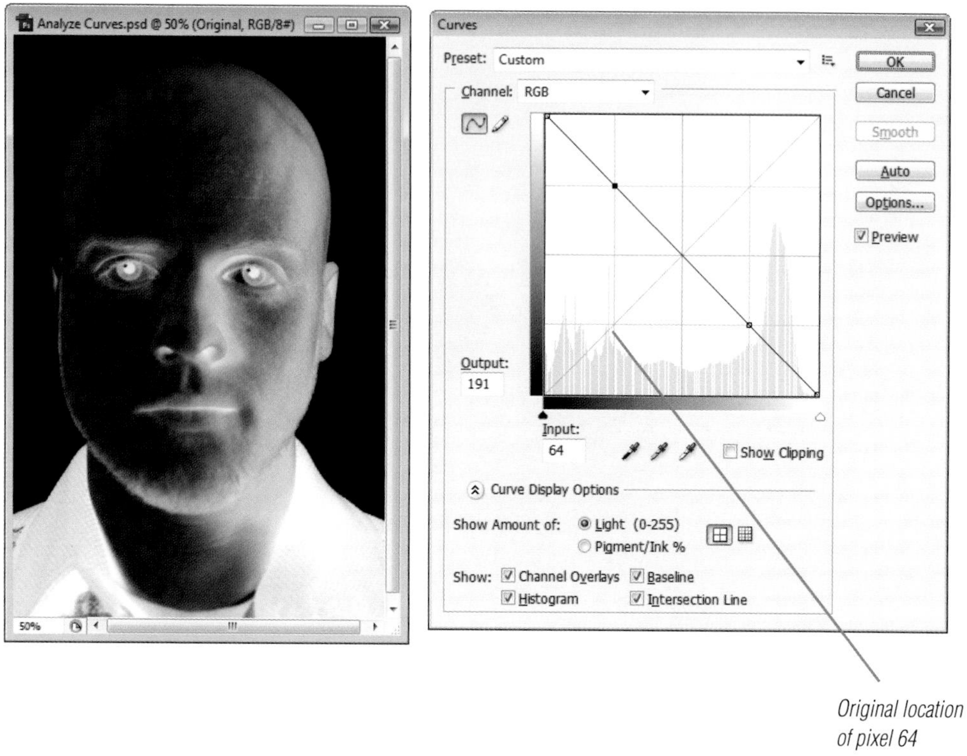

FIGURE 12

Assessing the tonal range of the image

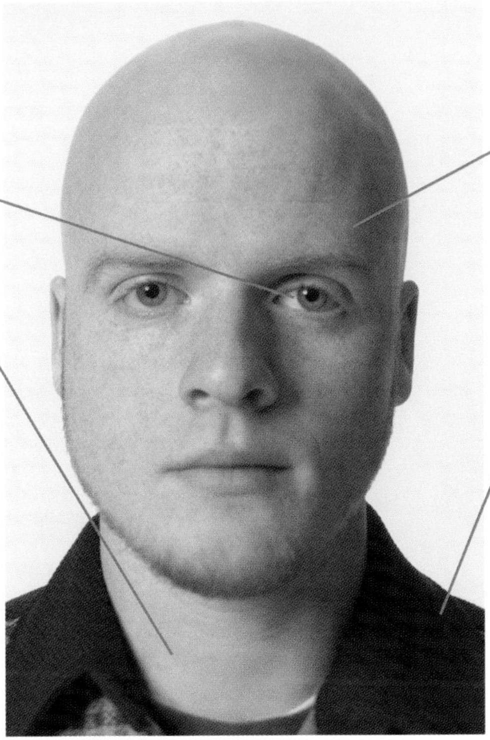

> **AUTHOR'S** *note*
>
> When sampling for highlights, don't sample the white circles that usually appear in the center of a subject's eyes, as they do in this image. These highlights are created from a reflection of the camera's flash. In other words, they are artificial, and therefore shouldn't be used as part of your sample when adjusting highlights. Printers and retouchers refer to these highlights as *spectral* highlights.

Relocate the black point, the white point, and the midpoint

1. Hide every layer except for the Weak Highlights and Shadows layer, then target the **Weak Highlights and Shadows**.

   As shown in Figure 12, the image on this layer has been manipulated to show an example of weak shadow and highlight points—the darkest pixels need to be darker, and the lightest pixels need to be lighter.

2. Move the mouse pointer around over the image and use the Info palette to find the lightest grayscale value that you can.

   The light background contains the lightest pixels to be found—those with a grayscale value of 235. This means that there are 20 lighter pixels available on the grayscale that this image is not using.

3. Move the mouse pointer over the image and try to find the darkest grayscale value that you can.

   The darkest pixels to be found are in the shadows underneath the man's collar—those with a grayscale value of 26. This means that there are 26 darker pixels available on the grayscale that this image is not using.

4. Create a clipped Curves adjustment layer named **Improve Highlight/Shadow Points**.

5. Click and drag the **Eyedropper pointer** around the image to see where different areas are positioned on the curve.

(continued)

6. Drag the **highlight point** straight to the left, so that your Input/Output values read 235/255, respectively.

   With this move, the lightest pixels in the original image—235—will be output as the lightest value on the grayscale—255. But remember the big point with curves: wherever the curve moves, all of the pixels on the curve change. Look carefully at the curve—at no point is it in the same location as it was originally. At every point, it is slightly above its original location. Note that the black point is the only point on the curve that didn't change. You cannot change the black point by moving the white point.

7. Drag the **black point** to the right, so that your Input/Output values are the same as those in Figure 13.

   With this move, the pixels that were originally 26 are now 0. Note the change to the curve. In the lower-left quadrant, the curve is below its original location—the dark half got darker. In the upper-right quadrant, the curve is above its original location—the lighter half got lighter. This, by definition is an increase in contrast.

8. Click to add a point anywhere on the curve, then move the point to the center so that your Input/Output is 128/128.

   TIP If you like, you may enter numbers directly into the Input and Output text boxes.

   (continued)

FIGURE 13
Relocating the black point

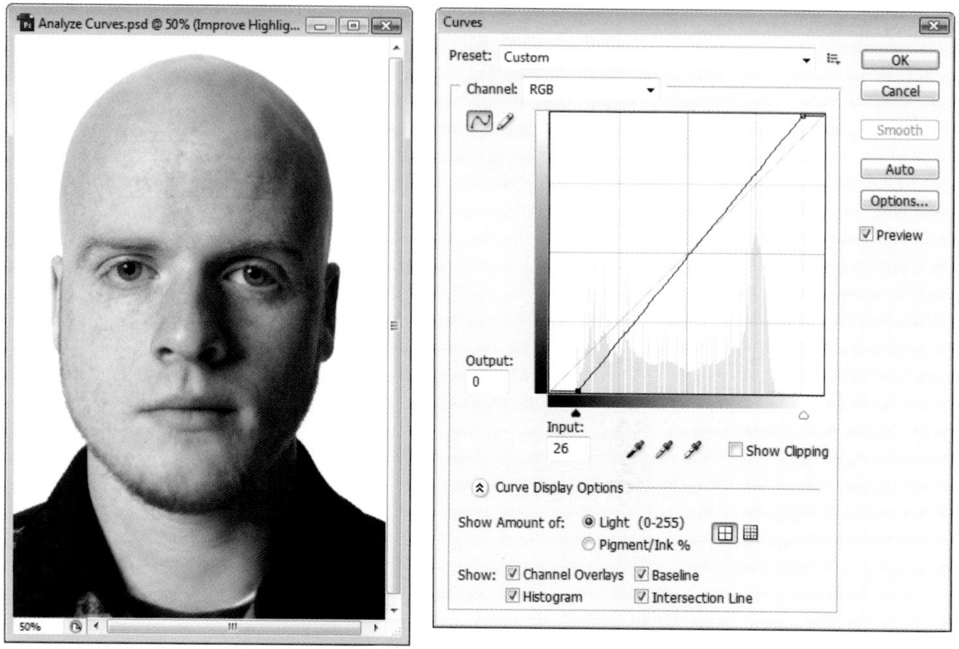

FIGURE 14
Brightening the midtones

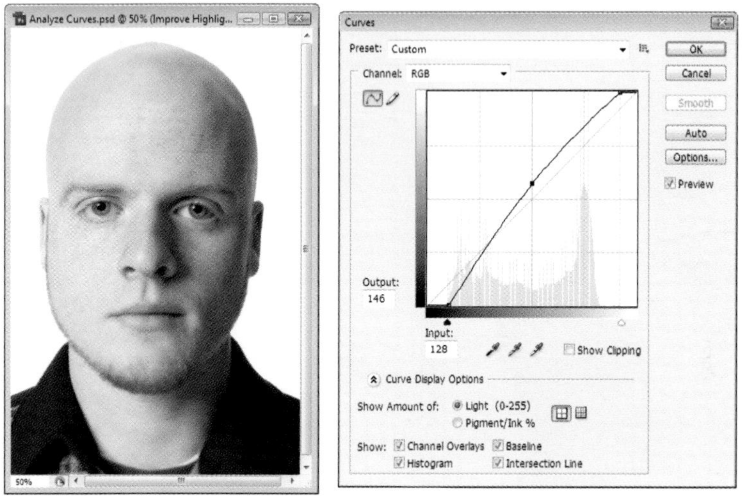

FIGURE 15
Darkening the midtones

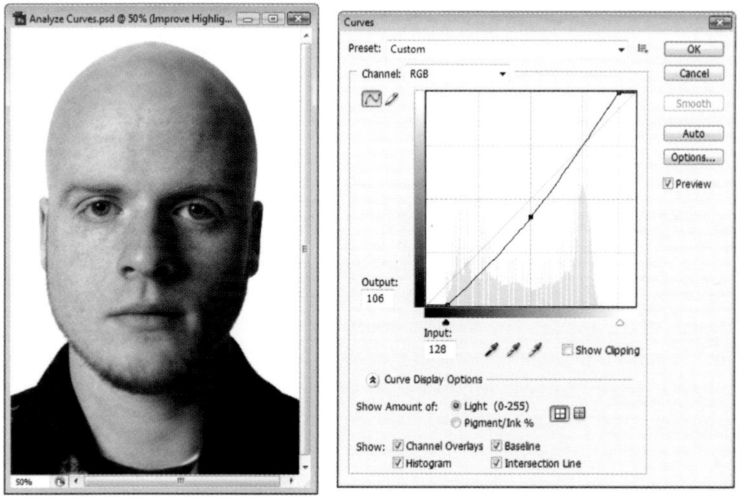

9. Drag the **midpoint** straight up so that your dialog box resembles Figure 14.

   The middle tones of the image are brightened overall.

10. Drag the **midpoint** straight down so that your dialog box resembles Figure 15.

    The middle tones of the image are darkened overall.

11. Remove the midpoint by dragging it out of the Curves dialog box.

12. Click **OK**, then save your work.

Improve contrast with curves

1. Hide every layer except for the Poor Contrast layer, then target the **Poor Contrast layer**.

2. Move the mouse pointer over the image and try to find the lightest grayscale value and the darkest grayscale value that you can.

   The image on this layer has been manipulated to show an example of poor contrast in the dark gray to light gray range. Don't confuse this with the black point and the white point. In this image, the black and white points are set properly. The darkest pixels are in the single-digit area of the grayscale, and the lightest pixels are 250 or over. The poor contrast is in the range from the dark grays (grayscale value 64) and the light grays (grayscale value 191).

(continued)

3. Use the Eyedropper Tool and the Info palette to sample the pixels on the man's cheek, screen left.

   The pixels on the light side of the face are in the 165–195 range.

4. Create a new clipped Curves adjustment layer named **Improve Contrast**.

   Note that the histogram in the far right quadrant of the grid—the highlights—shows that almost no pixels in the image have those values. The white pixels in the background are all 255 and therefore represented at the white point. But the light grays in the image—on the screen-left side of the man's face and neck, for example—all fall in the middle right quadrant. This makes sense, because our sampling of the screen-left side of the man's face showed pixels in the range of 165–195. Those pixels should be in the highlight range: 191–255. In other words, what should be the highlights in the image are instead middle range grays.

5. Click the curve to add a point at 128/128.

6. Click the curve to add a point at 191/191.

   Grayscale 191 is commonly recognized as the central area of the highlights in an image, because 191 is exactly between 128 and 255. For this image though, the pixels that are 191 in the image need to be much brighter highlights.

7. Drag the **191 point** straight up so that your Input/Output values are 191/220, then compare your screen to Figure 16.

(continued)

FIGURE 16
Brightening the highlights

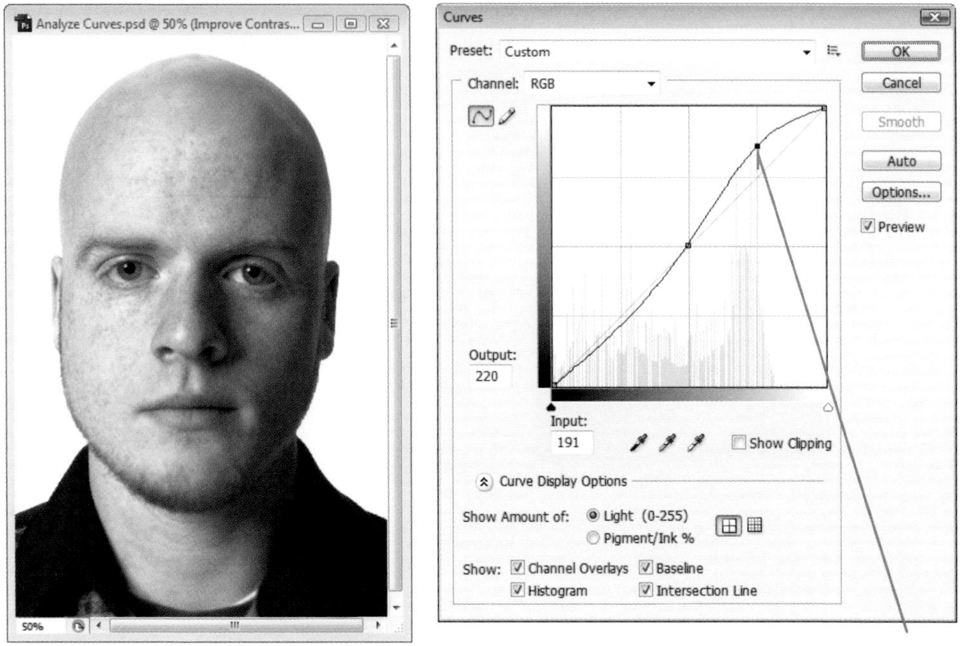

Brightening in highlight areas

AUTHOR'S *note*

Don't get your terms mixed up. *Highlights* are light gray areas of the image. The *highlight point*—or *white point*—is the whitest area of the image. *Shadows* are the dark gray areas of the image. The *shadow point*—or *black point*—is the blackest area of the image. This is all lingo, and none of it is official. The design and print worlds are replete with lingo, jargon, and catchphrases. It's important that you develop your own set of terminology that you can use to clearly identify specific areas of an image. Consider using the following five terms: *black point*, *shadows*, *midtones*, *highlights*, *white point*.

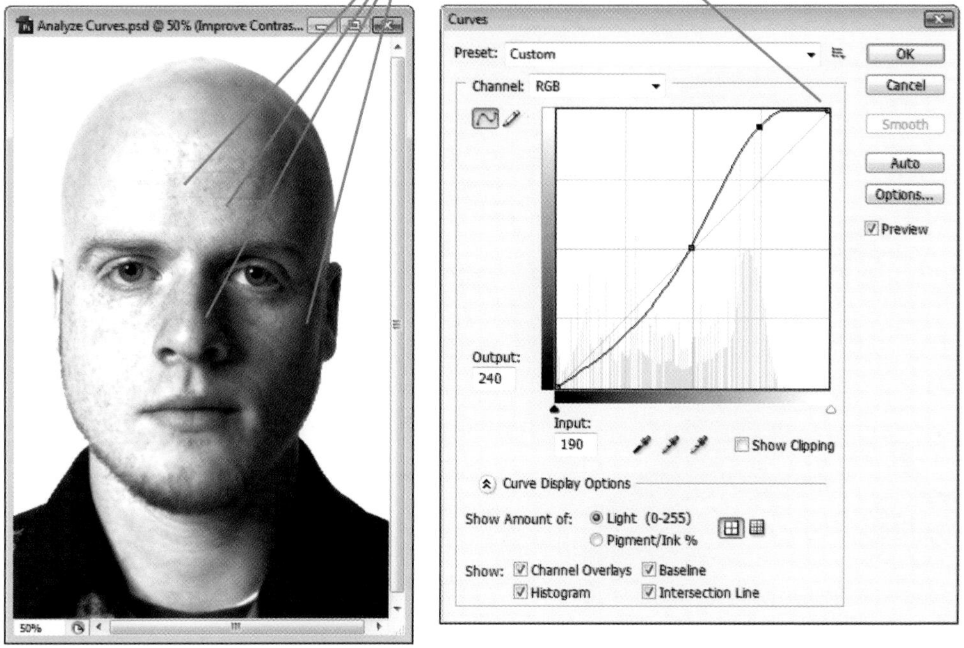

FIGURE 17
Brightening the highlights too much

Note the curve from the midpoint of the grid to the white point. With this move, every pixel in the "upper half" of the grayscale has been brightened, and the curve is furthest away from the intersection line at the top end of the curve. Note too that the bottom half of the curve has darkened slightly.

8. Click the **Preview check box** on and off to see the change to the image.

   Try to relate the changes in the image to the changes in the curve. Note that light areas on the face screen-left have been changed dramatically, while the face screen-right and the dark shirt collar change only slightly. Note too that the face screen-left is lightened, but those pixels are not white.

9. Verify that the Preview check box is checked.

10. Change the Output value to 240, then compare your screen to Figure 17.

    Figure 17 shows an example of "blown out" highlights. Note that patches of the face screen-left are all white and no longer show any detail. This is reflected at the very top of the curve, where it has flattened out at the top. A whole range of pixels have been "blown out" to white.

11. Undo the move.

12. Use the **Eyedropper Tool** to sample the shadows on the collar.

    The pixels in the collar are where they should be on the curve: at the low end, but not at the black point. However, the shadow areas on the face screen-right still seem weak and could be darkened to increase the tonal range of the face from highlight to shadow.

(continued)

13. Click **OK** to close the Curves dialog box, then double-click the thumbnail in the Layers palette to reopen the same Curves dialog box.

This is a good tip for working with Curves. If you like the progress you're making with a curve, click OK to save the changes. When you reopen the curve, you can always click Cancel to discard any subsequent changes you might make if you don't like them, but your original changes will still be preserved.

14. Add a new point to the curve at Input 105 and Output 88, then compare your screen to Figure 18.

15. Toggle the Preview on and off to see the change to the shadow areas.

This was a dramatic move in the right direction. The face is the most important part of the image, and it now has "shape" and a satisfying range from highlight to shadow. Note the "S" shape of the curve and remember it. An "S" curve always represents an increase in contrast.

16. Click **OK**, then hide and show the Improve Contrast adjustment layer to see the sum total of all the changes we made.

The improvement is dramatic and the face has so much more dimension with the increase in contrast. Make a note of the layer mask that comes automatically with the adjustment. Remember, if by darkening the face we made the collar too dark, we could always use the layer mask to decrease the effect of the adjustment layer in those dark areas.

17. Save your work.

Substantial darkening of shadow areas

FIGURE 18
Darkening the shadows

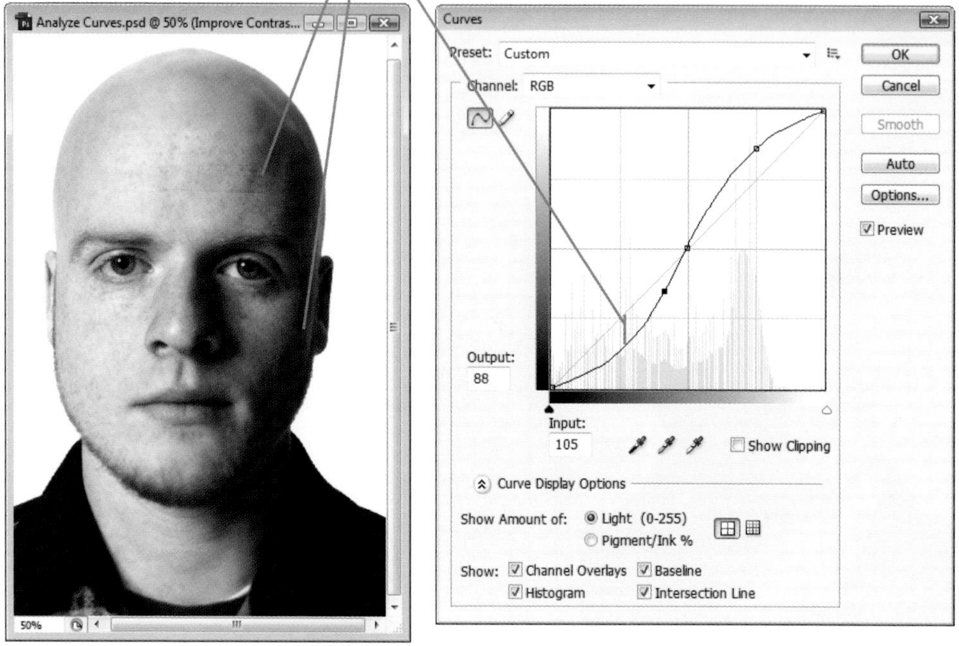

FIGURE 19
Posterize effect made with the Posterize command

Draw a Posterize curve

1. Hide all layers except for the Posterize Command layer, then target the **Posterize Command layer**.

   First, you will posterize the image using the menu command.

2. Click **Image** on the menu bar, point to **Adjustments**, then click **Posterize**.
3. Type **4** in the Levels text box, if necessary, then click **OK**.

   Your screen should reemble Figure 19. Why does the posterized image appear the way it does? Because all the pixels from 0–63 are now black. The pixels from 64–127 are now dark gray. The pixels from 128–190 are light gray, and the pixels from 191–255 are now white. So here's the question: If you were to duplicate this effect using a curve, what would you do? What would the curve look like? Take some time to think about it before moving on. Sketch it out on a piece of paper. Apply everything you've learned about grayscale and how the Curves dialog box functions. Test yourself. How would you do it?

(continued)

4. Show and target the **Posterize Curve layer**.
5. Create a new clipped Curves adjustment layer named **Posterize**.

   Before we begin, a quick disclaimer: it's extremely unlikely that you would ever use curves to posterize an image. Why would you when the Posterize command does such a quick and effective job? We're creating a posterize curve 1) to drive home the central concepts of manipulating curves, 2) to show you a new function in the Curves dialog box (the pencil), and 3) because this is a great illustration of how what you might think of as only a menu command is actually related to curves and can be duplicated with curves. Keep these three points in mind as you proceed.
6. Click the **pencil icon** in the upper-left section of the dialog box, then click where the black point normally would be. This would be the 0 Output and 0 Input point.
7. Press and hold **[Shift]**, then click the **Input 63/Output 0 point** on the grid.

   See Figure 20. All pixels input from 0–63 are now 0.

(continued)

FIGURE 20
Using the pencil

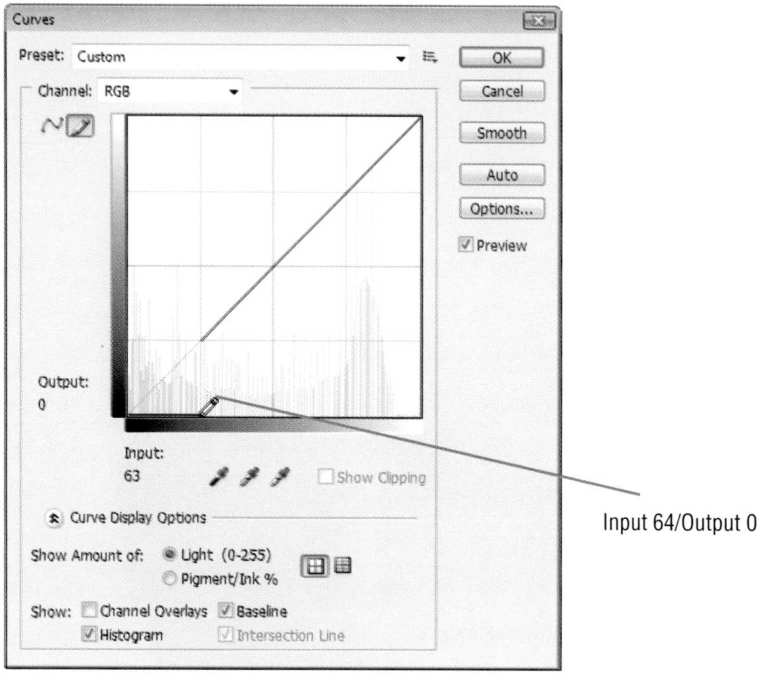

FIGURE 21

Posterize effect created in the Curves dialog box

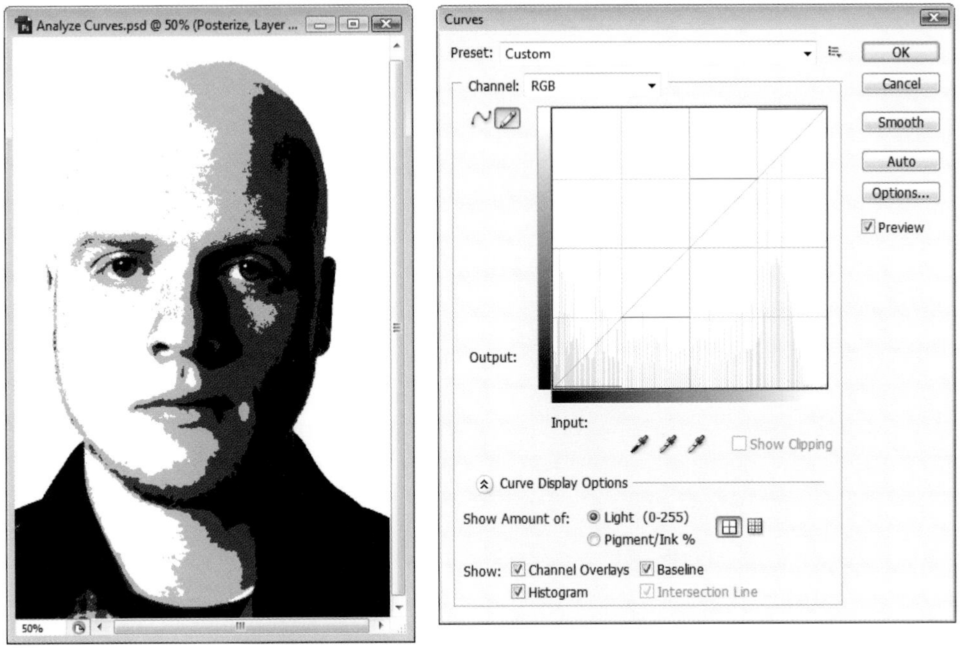

8. Release [Shift] then click the **64/64 point** on the grid.
9. Press and hold **[Shift]**, then click the **128/64 point** on the grid.

   All pixels from 64–128 are now 64.
10. Release [Shift] then click the **129/191 point** on the grid.
11. Press and hold **[Shift]**, then click the **191/191 point** on the grid.

    All the pixels from 129–191 are now 191.
12. Release [Shift] then click the **192/255 point** on the grid.
13. Press and hold **[Shift]**, then click the **white point (255/255)**.
14. Compare your screen to Figure 21.
15. Hide and show the Posterize Curve layer to compare it to the Posterize Command layer.

    The result will be nearly identical, with the possible difference that the grays may be darker or lighter.
16. Save your work, then close Analyze Curves.

LESSON 3

ANALYZE Color Channels

What You'll Do

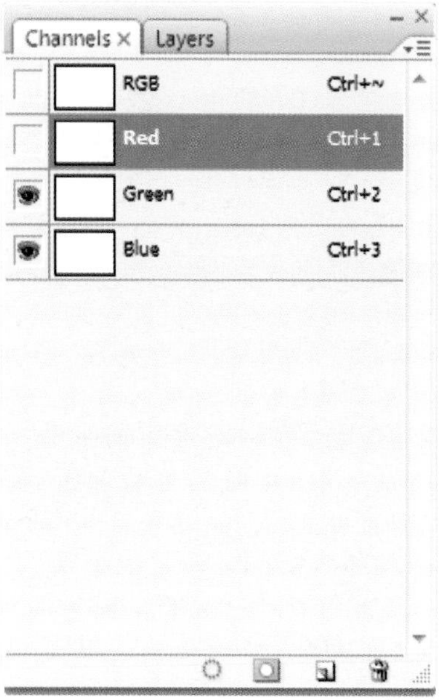

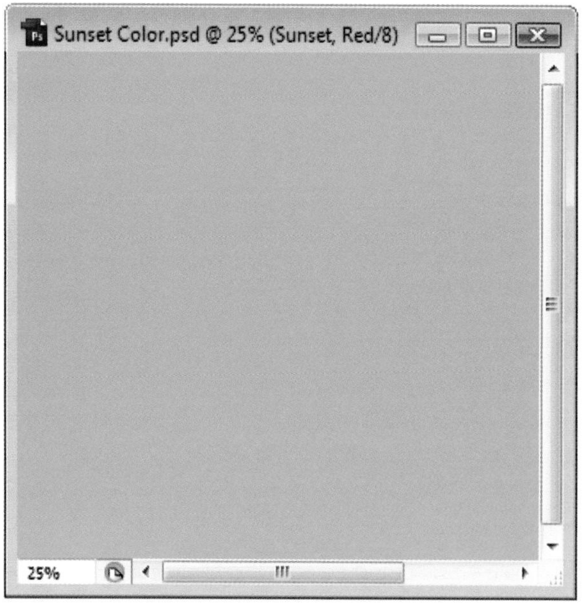

One very important connection to make is that between RGB and grayscale. Earlier in the lesson—and in the previous chapter—we analyzed and adjusted a grayscale image, which had a single channel. Thus, every pixel could be one and only one of 256 shades of gray. The concept is the same for RGB color files with one very big difference: an RGB file has three channels, and each of those channels has a grayscale range of 0–255. Thus, every pixel in an RGB file can be one of 256 shades of red and one of 256 shades of green and one of 256 shades of blue. For example, a pixel's color might be 50R/220G/145B.

With 256 shades available per pixel and per channel, the number of colors available is 256 x 256 x 256. This means that, in an RGB file, each pixel can be one of over more than 16 million colors. But remember, even though it has three color components, R G & B, each pixel is only one color, and that one color is the result of the combination of the three primary colors.

One of the best methods for building color adjustment skills is to first develop a solid understanding of the basic concept of each color channel. All color images on your monitor are composed of the three primary colors of light: red, green, and blue. Thus, for a color image, Photoshop provides you three color channels: red, green, and blue. Working together, the three channels produce all of the color you see in the image.

FIGURE 22
The Red channel in black and red

Brightest areas represent pixels in the image with highest red component

Darkest areas represent pixels in the image with lowest red component

FIGURE 23
The Red channel in black and white

Darkest pixels brightened; red component increased

Understand grayscale in a channel

1. Open AP 4-3.psd, then save it as **Analyze Channels**.
2. Click **Edit** (Win) or **Photoshop** (Mac) on the menu bar, point to **Preferences**, then click **Interface**.
3. Click the **Show Channels in Color check box**, if necessary, then click **OK**.
4. Verify that the Sunset layer is targeted, then open the Channels palette.
5. Click the **Red channel thumbnail** to see only the red channel, then compare it to Figure 22.

   Channels are often called "channel masks," and it's helpful to think of them that way. In a channel, dark areas represent less color and light areas represent more color. In Figure 22, there's a lot of red in the pixels that make up the sky, but very little red in the dark foliage along the river.
6. Return to the Preferences/Interface dialog box, remove the check mark in the Show Channels in Color check box, then click **OK**.
7. Compare your Red channel to Figure 23.

   Nothing changed. Photoshop is now displaying the channel as 256 shades of gray (black to white) as opposed to 256 shades of red (black to red). Now, the white areas represent the areas of the image where red will be most prevalent.
8. Click the **RGB thumbnail**, then verify that the Info palette is showing and that at least one of the color readouts is set to RGB.

(continued)

9. Move the mouse pointer over the sky and note the readout in the Info palette.

   In an RGB file, every pixel has one red value (from 0–255), one green value (from 0–255), and one blue value (from 0–255). Because the sky area of the image was white in the Red channel, you can expect that the pixels that make up the sky all have a Red readout that is high on the grayscale: over 240.

10. Move the mouse pointer over the dark foliage on the left side of image, and note the readout information for the Red channel in the Info palette.

    The Red readouts will be low, some of them under 30, because these are the darkest areas of the image.

11. Click the **Red channel thumbnail**, then open the Curves dialog box.

    When you open the Curves dialog box in a targeted channel, that channel is automatically targeted in the Curves dialog box.

12. Drag the black point to the location shown in Figure 24, click **OK**, then compare the change in your Red channel to Figure 25.

    The entire channel is brightened considerably and the shadow areas are now a mid-range gray.

(continued)

FIGURE 24
Increasing the red component in all pixels

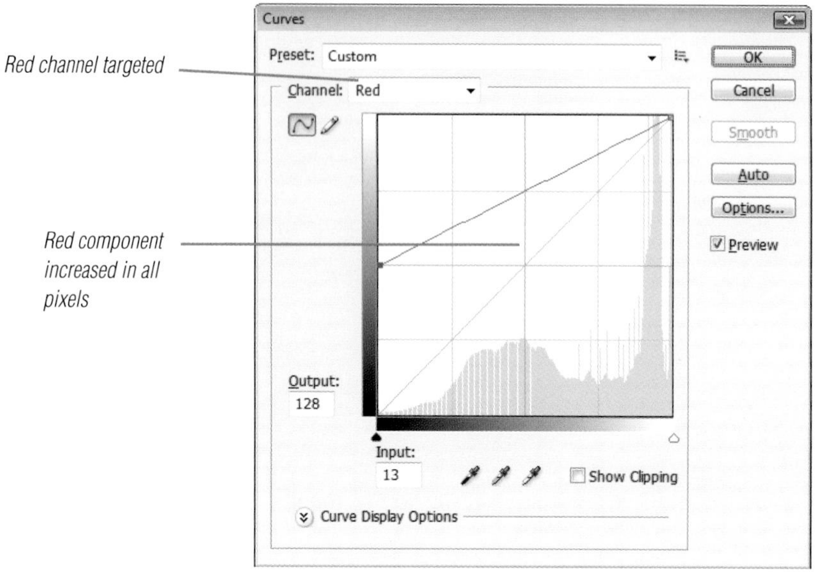

FIGURE 25
Results of increasing the Red component

FIGURE 26

Color change in the composite image

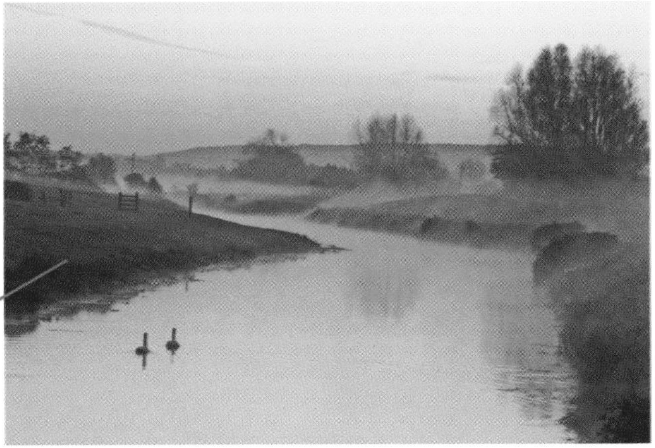

Red component increased in all pixels

FIGURE 27

The composite of the Red and Green channels

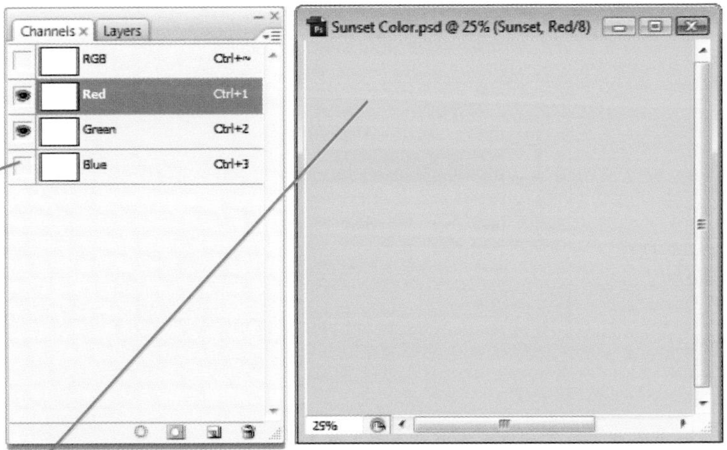

Blue channel hidden

255 Red + 255 Green = yellow pixels/yellow = minus Blue

13. Click the **RGB thumbnail,** then compare your image to Figure 26.

    The image now has a red color cast because the Red channel has been brightened dramatically.

    TIP The RGB channel is called the **composite channel** because it is the presentation of all three color channels combined.

14. Undo and redo the curves adjustment to see the change.
15. Revert the file.

Viewing two of three channels

1. Verify that only the Background layer is visible.

   All of the pixels on the canvas are white.

2. In the Channels palette, click the **Blue channel thumbnail**, the **Green channel thumbnail**, then the **Red channel thumbnail**.

   All three of the channels are white. A white pixel in an RGB image has an RGB value of 255R/255G/255B.

3. Verify that the Red channel is targeted and that it is the only visible channel, then make just the Green channel visible.

   As shown in Figure 27, 255R/255G/0B produces yellow pixels. To put it in other words, Red + Green = Yellow. Or, you can also say Yellow = "Minus Blue." These two equations provide a good basic principle when adjusting color. If you want an image to be more yellow, or to be "warmer," you know that those pixels will have higher grayscale values in the red and green components relative to the blue component.

(continued)

One basic color adjustment principle is that if you want an image to be more yellow, reduce the blue component. If that's not enough, increase the red and green components.

4. Show just the Red and Blue channels.

   As shown in Figure 28, 255R/0G/255B produces magenta pixels. Red + Blue = Magenta, or Magenta = "Minus Green." Like yellow, magenta is one of the process ink colors. When you're adjusting color in an RGB image, if you want the image to be more red, increase the red, but if you want it to be more magenta, reduce the green component.

5. Show just the Green and Blue channels.

   As shown in Figure 29, 0R/255G/255B produces cyan pixels. Green + Blue = Cyan, or Cyan = "Minus Red."

6. Click the **RGB channel thumbnail**, make the Sunset layer visible, and target the **Sunset layer**.

(continued)

FIGURE 28
The composite of the Red and Blue channels

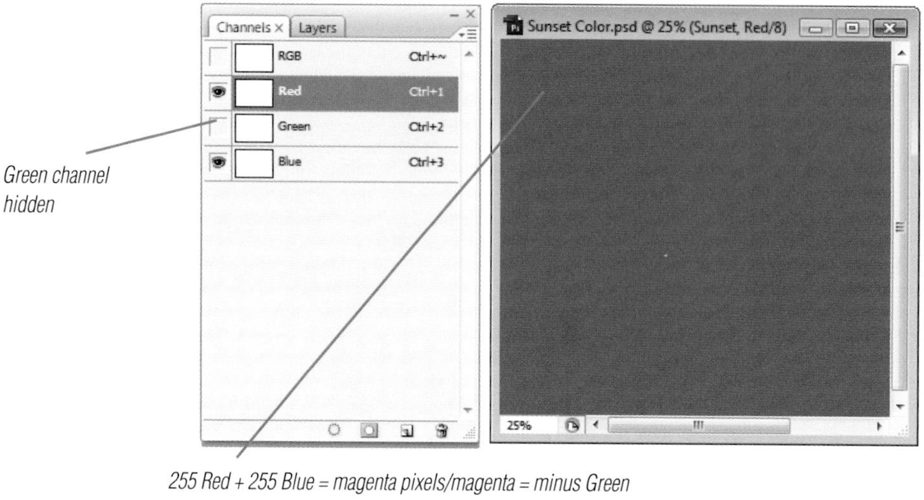

FIGURE 29
The composite of the Green and Blue channels

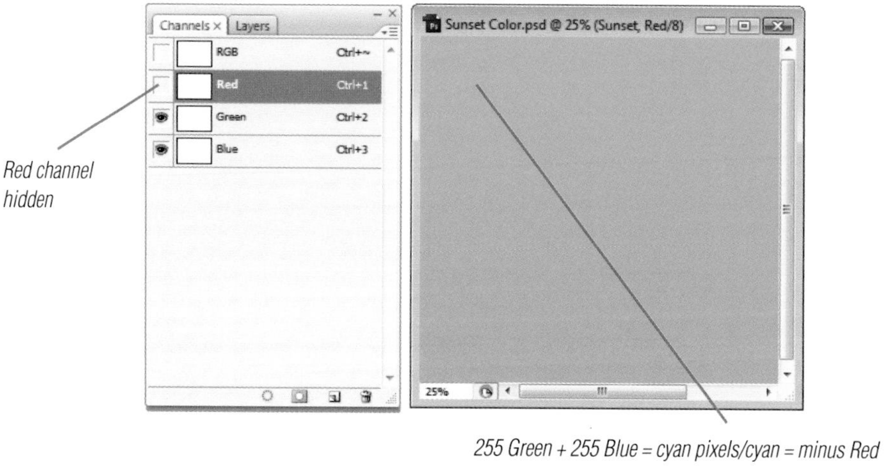

FIGURE 30

Positioning elements in the workspace

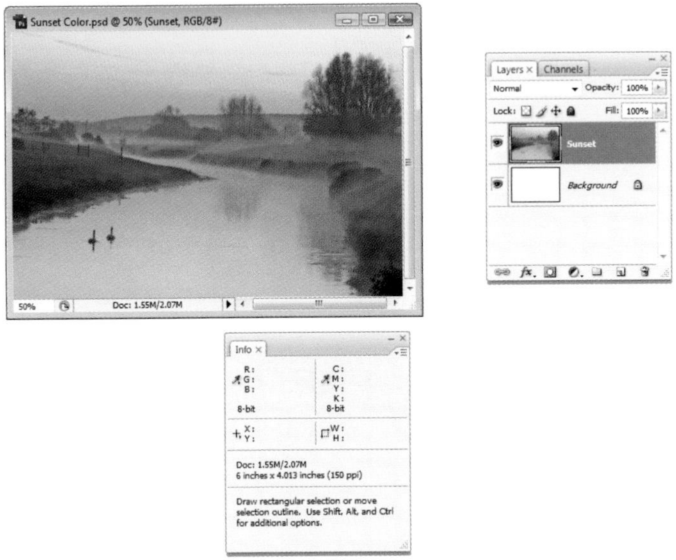

FIGURE 31

Increasing the Red component

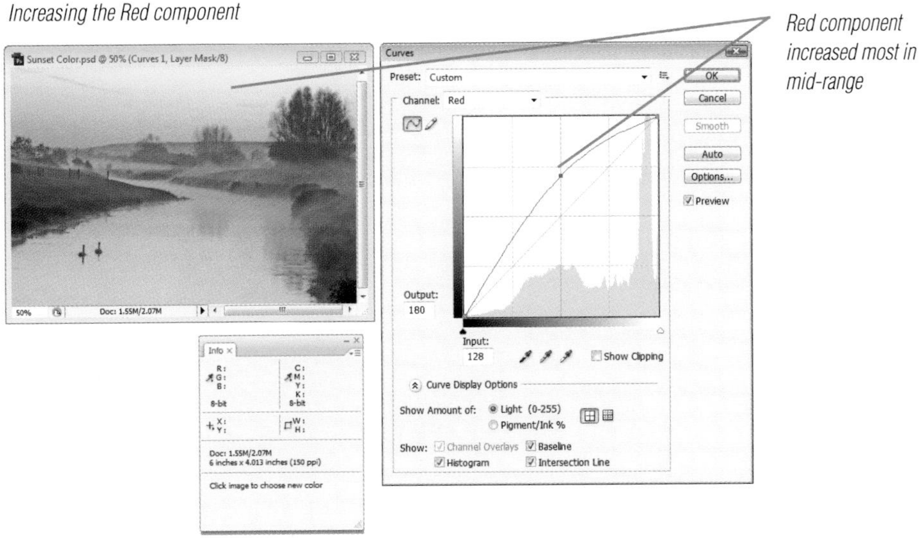

7. Position the image, the Layers palette, and the Info palette as shown in Figure 30.
8. Create a new clipped Curves adjustment layer and position the dialog box so that you can see the image.

   The Sunset image is one that is not color specific. Compared to an image of someone's face, in which the fleshtone color is either correct or incorrect, the color in this image could work with many different variations. Presently, the overall tone is a warm orange.
9. Click the **Channel list arrow**, click **Blue**, then add a point to the curve at Input 128/Output 180.

   The image overall becomes more blue. Note that the Blue histogram shows no pixels in the far right quadrant of the grid. That's because the lightest pixels in the image—those in the sky—have blue components that are lower than grayscale 191.
10. Remove the point from the Blue curve, then repeat the same steps to add a point at Input 128/Output 180 to the Green curve.

    The image becomes more green.
11. Remove the point from the Green curve, then repeat the same steps for the Red curve.

    As shown in Figure 31, the image becomes more red.
12. Remove the point from the Red curve, click the **Channel list arrow**, then click **Green**.

(continued)

13. Reduce the Green overall as shown in Figure 32, then position the Eyedropper Tool over the image as shown in the figure.

The image becomes noticeably more magenta—more purplish—with the reduction of green. It's more reddish, but not in the same way as Figure 31. The Info palette shows a before and after readout. Note that in the RGB readout, only the Green value has changed.

> **TIP** The CMYK readout in the Info palette shows that the Magenta ink component would be increased by nearly 20% if this image were printed with the 4-Color printing process.

14. Remove the point from the Green curve, apply the same move to the Blue curve, then position the Eyedropper Tool over the image to see the before/after readouts.

The image becomes noticeably more yellow with the reduction of blue.

> **TIP** The CMYK readout in the Info palette shows that the Yellow ink component would be increased if this image were printed with the 4-Color printing process.

15. Remove the point from the Blue curve, apply the same move to the Red curve, then move the Eyedropper Tool over the image to see the before and after readouts.

The image becomes noticeably more cyan with the reduction of red.

> **TIP** The CMYK readout in the Info palette shows that the Magenta ink component would be increased if this image were printed with the 4-Color printing process.

16. Click **Cancel**.

(continued)

FIGURE 32
Decreasing the Green component

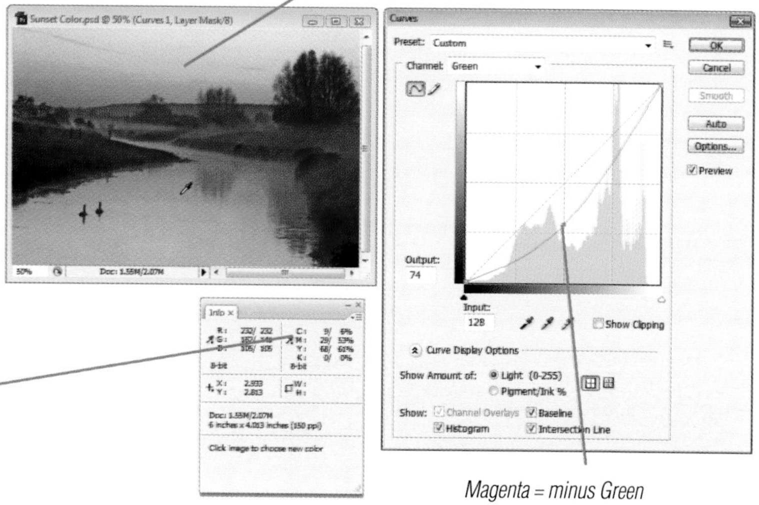

FIGURE 33
Color Balance dialog box

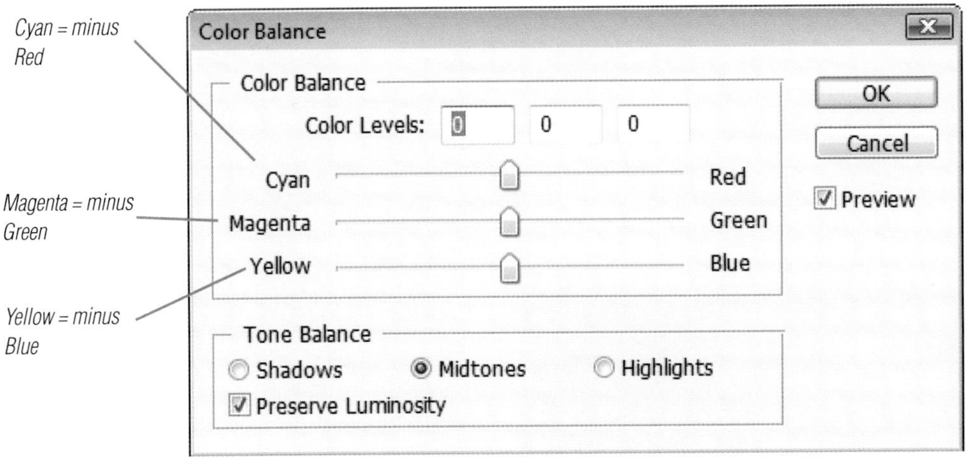

FIGURE 34
Moving the color balance away from Green and towards Magenta

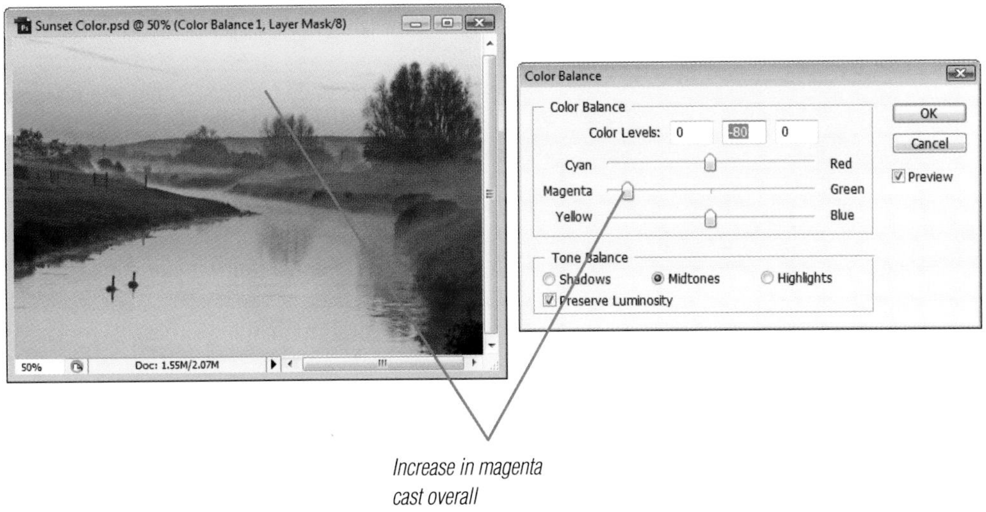

17. Click **Layer** on the menu bar, point to **New Adjustment Layer**, click **Color Balance**, then click **OK**.

    The Color Balance dialog box opens as shown in Figure 33. Color Balance is another color manipulation utility, like Levels, Curves, or HSB.

18. Note the two ends of each of the three sliders.

    This dialog box is a visual reiteration of this entire discussion. The more you move away from Red, you move closer to Cyan. Magenta is opposite Green. Yellow is opposite blue.

19. Drag the **middle slider** left so that the middle text box reads -80.

    The result, shown in Figure 34, is the same as the move you made in Step 13 when you reduced the green component. In fact, it should be clear to you exactly how this dialog box works: each slider manipulates one of the three color channels. This is a great illustration of why curves are the most sophisticated color manipulation utility. The Color Balance dialog box allows you to adjust midtones (the middle of the curve), shadows (the lower end of the curve), and highlights (the upper end of the curve). Compare that to curves, where you can manipulate any point on the entire curve and add multiple points to the curve for a far more complex adjustment.

20. Experiment with moving the other sliders in the dialog box.

21. Click **OK**, save your work, then close the Analyze Channels document.

LESSON 4

Adjust
Color with Curves

What You'll Do

When it comes to adjusting color, one of the first moves you should make isn't about adjusting color, at least not specifically. Before you even begin to consider the overall color balance, you first need to analyze the overal tonal range of the image. Think of it this way: if there's poor contrast, if the shadows are weak, if the white point is too dark, or if the midrange of the image is too dark or too light, trying to make color adjustments is futile. You must address the tonal range first, verify that the shadows and highlights are strong, verify that there's good contrast—that the image has "snap." Once this has been achieved, you're ready to make smart and effective color adjustments.

Don't confuse the two, but keep in mind that adjusting the tonal range is adjusting color. When an image has poor contrast or weak shadows or dim highlights, those factors have a direct influence over the the color throughout the image. When you correct those problems, you'll be amazed at how those moves alone can dramatically improve color.

Dull, muddy color suddenly becomes vivid and vibrant.

Generally speaking, adjusting color means changing the relationship between the Red, Green, and Blue channels, whether that adjustment is overall or "local." You might decrease the Red component in a fleshtone, for example, or increase the Blue component for a more vivid sky.

Still speaking in general terms, adjusting the tonal range of an image is something you do in the RGB composite channel. The RGB channel shows one curve that is the composite—or the combination—of the three color channels. Changes that you make to the RGB curve affect all the channels equally. For example, if you adjust the RGB curve to brighten the mid-range of the image, that adjustment brightens the Red, Green, and Blue channels by the same measure.

Finally, it helps to consider some useful terminology. When working in the RGB composite channel, the adjustments you make fall into the categories of brightening the image, darkening the image, increasing or "bumping" the contrast, "opening" shadows for more detail, improving the black and white points, and maintaining highlights so that they don't "pop" or get "blown out" to pure white. Note that none of these terms refers to a specific color channel. These are changes that you make to the composite image.

You can make all of these changes to individual channels, but it helps if you don't think of adjustments to individual color channels as "brightening" or "darkening." It's much clearer to think in terms of "increasing" or "decreasing" the specific color. So, rather than think, "I need to brighten the reds in the sky," I'd say, "I need to increase the red component of the pixels in the sky." Maybe not quite so formal, but the distinction helps. In another case, rather than say, "The blues are too dark in the shadows," which, if you think about it, is really confusing, it's much clearer to say, "There's not enough blue in the shadows; I need to increase blue."

These are not hard and fast rules, and you'll find all kinds of jargon when it comes to correcting curves. The takeaway point is this: The lighter the pixels in a color channel—the closer they are to grayscale 255—the greater the component of that color in the pixel. The darker the pixels in a color channel—the closer they are to grayscale 0—the lesser the component of that color in the pixel.

Remove a color cast in a landscape image

1. Open AP 4-4.psd, then save it as **Outback**.
2. In the Info palette, verify that the first readout is set to RGB and the second readout is set to CMYK.
3. Assess the overall appearance of the image in terms of color.

   With landscapes, it's seldom the case that the color is "wrong," as it might be with a flesh-tone or a commercial product. As shown in Figure 35, this image clearly has a yellow cast overall and the foliage that would naturally be green is closer to yellow and orange. However, the image is set at sunset, which would justify that palette.
4. Sample different areas of the image with the Eyedropper Tool .

   Though I never color adjust an image in terms of CMYK, I do use the CMYK readout in the Info palette as an indication of the color balance of the image. In the case of this image, the yellow readout in the Info palette is substantially higher than the other readouts, and that's an indication of a direction to follow.
5. Create a new Curves adjustment layer.

(continued)

FIGURE 35
Assessing the image

FIGURE 36

The original image and the image after the adjustment

6. Add a point to the Blue curve at Input 128/Output 150.

   I decided to counter the overall yellow cast by increasing the blue. It is now clear that there's an overall red cast to the image. This makes sense, because yellow is made with the Red and Green channels. The yellow cast appears to have been the result of too little blue and too much red.

7. Add a point to the Red curve, then experiment by moving the point to various locations beneath the intersection line.

   Experimenting this way is a smart solution for adjusting color. Different reductions of red will result in different qualities of green for the foliage in the image.

8. Drag the new point on the Red curve to Input 147/Output 100.

9. Click **OK**, make the image as large as possible on your screen, then hide and show the Curves adjustment layer to see the change.

   As shown in Figure 36, the change is dramatic and the original image did indeed have a heavy red/yellow cast throughout. One measure of why this move was an improvement is the increase in detail overall. Note how the mountains in the background are more differentiated from the midground. Note how the fencepost is more prominent, and how the red patches of sunlight on the ground in the foreground are so much more pronounced against the green foliage. Finally, note how the plants in the foreground now show so much more color variation and detail.

(continued)

10. Assess the overall appearance of the image in terms of color.

    When you make a color adjustment that improves an image dramatically, it's easy to jump to the conclusion that your work is done, because the image looks so much better. Instead, after every move, stop and assess the image. In this case, the improvement is dramatic, but the overall color tone of the image is cold. The greens are cold—like the color of evergreen trees. This makes me think that I might have gone too far with the increase of the blue component overall.

11. Double-click that **Curves adjustment layer**, then compare your dialog box to Figure 37.

    The grid shows the adjustment that you made to the red channel and the blue channel. This is a great feature that you can turn on and off by clicking Channel Overlays at the bottom of the dialog box.

12. Experiment with reducing the Blue channel by various degrees.

13. Decrease the Blue channel to Input 128/Output 139, then click **OK**.

    Though it was a small move, it improved the greens and warmed up the image overall.

14. Double-click that **Curves adjustment layer**.

    Whenever I adjust color and am satisfied, I always take a moment to experiment with adjusting the contrast.

15. Remove the check mark in the Channel Overlays check box so that you can see the RGB composite curve better, then recreate the curve shown in Figure 38.

(continued)

FIGURE 37
The RGB composite grid showing adjustments made to Red and Blue channel

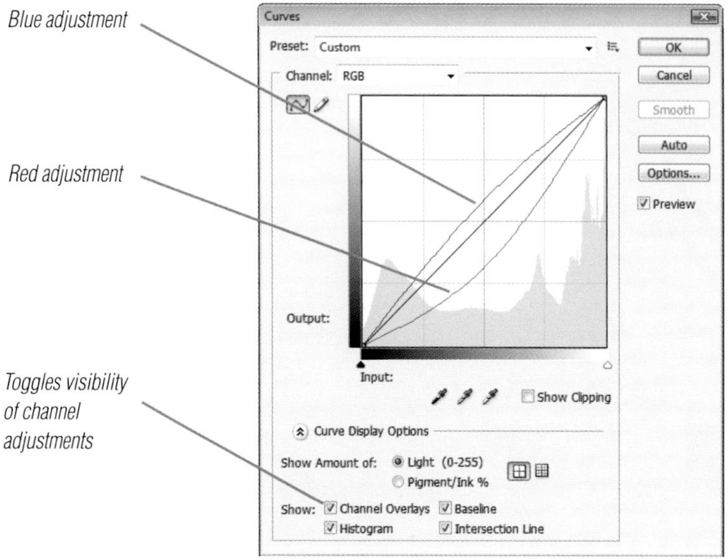

FIGURE 38
Increasing contrast overall

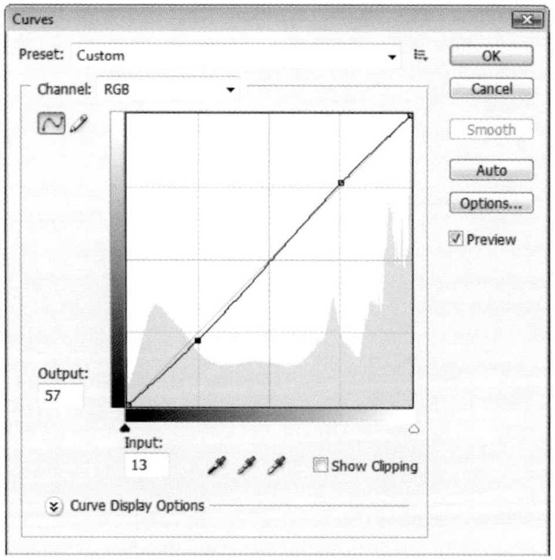

FIGURE 39

A before and after view of the original and all the adjustments

16. Click **OK**, then Undo and Redo to evaluate the increase in contrast.

    The "contrast bump" shows that the shadows were weak and the increase in contrast improves the image.

17. Hide and show the adjustment layer to see all the changes, then compare your final image to Figure 39.

18. Save your work, then close Outback.

Adjust color in a fleshtone and make local color adjustments

1. Open AP 4-5.psd, then save it as **Red Scarf**.
2. Assess the appearance of the image.

   There's a white hot spot over the woman's shoulder where the pixels are all white, but it's not too distracting. At first glance, the image looks good in terms of color balance, but the colors are all very cold. There's a sense of drabness; the red scarf is not vibrant and the face seems a bit lifeless.
3. Click the **Eyedropper Tool**, then sample the shadow areas in the scarf and neck area.

   The shadow areas have grayscale readings in the 20s, which indicates weak shadows and offers some explanation for the overall drabness.
4. Create a new Curves adjustment layer.

   The histogram shows no pixels at the far left edge, which confirms that the shadows in the image are weak.
5. Drag the **black point** to the right so that its Input/Output values are 14/0.
6. Click to add a point to the curve, then set its Input/Output values to 195/205.
7. Click to add another point to the curve, set its Input/Output values to 77/64, then compare your curve to Figure 40.

   This curve represents significant change. The black point has been darkened—which darkened the entire image—and the "S" curve increased contrast by brightning the highlights and darkening the shadow areas further.

(continued)

FIGURE 40
Darkening the shadow point and increasing contrast

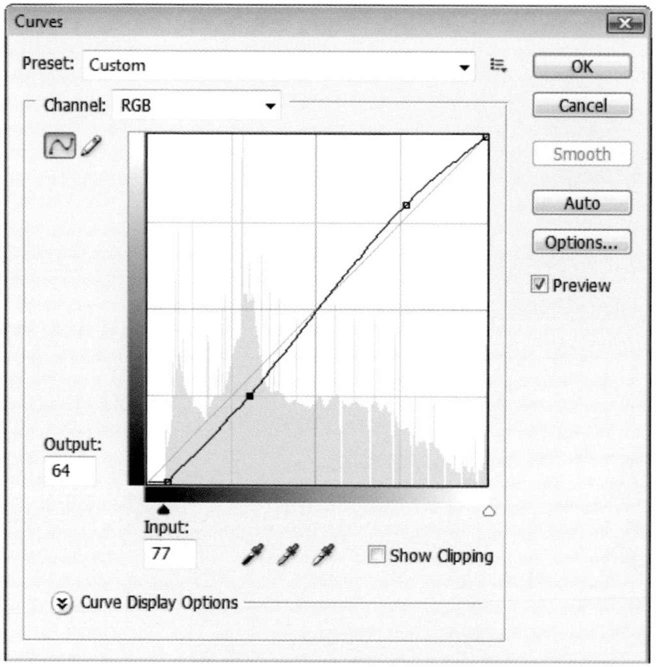

FIGURE 41
Before and after view of the adjustment

8. Click **OK**, then hide and show the Curves adjustment layer to see the changes.

   This is a good illustration of how adjusting black and white points and adjusting contrast is also a color adjustment. As shown in Figure 41, along with the dramatically improved contrast, the adjusted image shows a palette of colors that is far more vibrant. However, note too that the bump in contrast has increased the hot spot at screen left and, more troubling, has blown out the highlights on the jacket, screen-right.

9. Click the Brush Tool, then mask the adjustment layer completely over the jacket screen-right.

   As you can see in the before image in Figure 41, the highlights in this area of the jacket were already blown out. This is a problem with the photography, something a professional photographer would have controlled. Photoshop can't "fix" blown out highlights—you can't adjust detail in an area that has no detail to begin with—but of course you don't want to increase the problem when adjusting other areas of the image. The contrast bump also made the hot spot on screen left larger and brighter, but interestingly, it works better this way. Brighter and larger, it seems more intentional, like an intended effect.

(continued)

10. Create a new Curves adjustment layer above the first adjustment layer.

    The fleshtone still looks cold and "ruddy," so I want to experiment with some color shifts. Rather than go back to the first adjustment layer, I'd prefer to leave it alone and use a new curve for this adjustment.

11. Target the **Blue channel,** add a point to the Blue curve, then set the Input/Output values to 166/150.

12. Click **OK**, then hide and show the second adjustment layer to see the changes.

13. Mask the adjustment layer so that it doesn't affect the eyes, the jacket, or the hair at the top and screen right.

    As shown in Figure 42, the decrease in blue adds a sense of warmth to the fleshtone, the scarf, and the background. I masked the adjustment from the eyes to preserve the ice-blue color and the cold whites. I masked the adjustment from the jacket to maintain the neutral gray and not create a color bias by making the jacket yellowish.

14. Create a third Curves adjustment layer, add a new point to each channel, then adjust the curves so that the Input/Output values are as follows: Red 126/137; Green 128/120; Blue 133/113.

15. Click **OK,** then press **[Ctrl][I]**(Win) or [⌘] **[I]** (Mac).

    The layer mask on the new adjustment layer is inverted from default white to black. The entire adjustment is entirely masked.

(continued)

FIGURE 42
"Warming" the flesh tone

FIGURE 43
Before and after view of all the adjustments

16. Use a soft brush and paint 100% white over the scarf so that the adjustment affects only the scarf.

    The red of the scarf becomes more vivid.

    TIP When you make adjustments to just specific areas of an image, those are called "local" adjustments, as opposed to "global"—overall—adjustments.

17. Set the opacity on the Brush Tool to 30%, then gradually "paint in" red highlights to brighten the hair and make its color more vivid.

18. Select the three adjustment layers in the Layers palette, then press **[Ctrl][G]**(Win) or [⌘] **[G]** (Mac).

    The three adjustments are grouped into a single group folder.

19. Hide and show the group folder to see the sum total of adjustments to the image.

    Compare your result to Figure 43.

20. Save your work, then close Red Scarf.

Adjust color in a water image

1. Open AP 4-6.psd, then save it as **Sailboat**.
2. Click the **Eyedropper Tool** , then sample the white sail of the boat.

   From a photography standpoint, this isn't a great photo because the entire white canopy has been blown out to white. As shown in Figure 44, there's no detail in the canopy to work with. It's just a field of white.
3. Sample the back end of the boat.

   The pixels at the back of the boat are 0/0/0—pure black. These two samples tell us that we don't want to move the white point or black point. There's already too much pure white in the image, and the overall contrast looks good.
4. Sample other areas of the image.

   This image is a good example of a common occurrence with a water image: an overall blue cast. Think of how much blue there is in the image. There's a big blue sky over an expanse of blue water. The boat itself is blue, and there's a bright blue sail cover to boot. In addition, there's a substantial amount of green grass, and blue is a big component of that green. It's often the case with a sunny water image that the photographer or the camera or both will overcompensate to capture all that blue, and that will result in an overall blue cast to the image. As you sample the image, you'll see in the CMYK readout in the Info palette that Cyan dominates almost every pixel in the image. The clouds are also a big hint: they're not white—they're pale blue.

(continued)

FIGURE 44
Assessing the image

Clouds have blue cast
White canopy is "blown out" and has no detail

FIGURE 45
Moving the white point in the Red channel

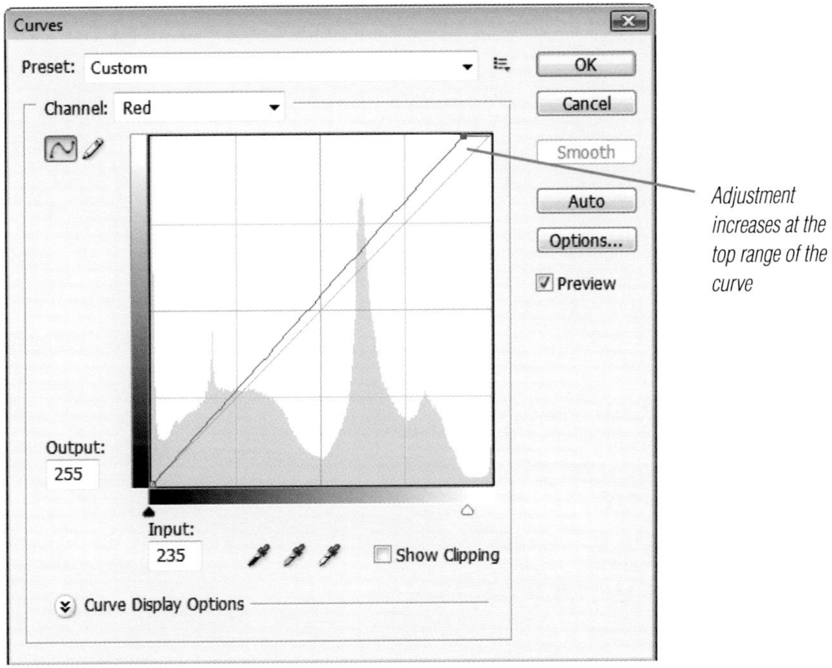

5. Create a new Curves adjustment layer, then experiment with reducing the Blue component to various degrees.

   Reducing the blue a little bit improves the image, but doesn't completely remove the color cast. Reducing the blue significantly is no help at all—it just creates a weird green/yellow cast. When adjusting one channel isn't enough, that's usually a good hint that an adjustment of another channel is needed.

6. Change the Blue channel curve's Input/Output values to 130/107, click **OK**, then sample different areas of the image.

   The blue reduction made a subtle improvement, but the clouds alone show that the blue cast remains strong overall. Where to go from here? The hint is in the CMYK readout in the Info palette, which shows that Cyan continues to dominate the entire image. Since you know that Cyan is created from subtracting Red, that tells you that adding Red will decrease the Cyan cast.

7. Double-click the adjustment layer thumbnail to open the Curves dialog box, then move the Red channel's white point as shown in Figure 45, so that its Input/Output values are 235/255.

(continued)

8. Click **OK**.

   Figure 46 shows the original image and the image with this Red adjustment. The Red adjustment was a big move, and clearly a move in the right direction. The Red move needed to be dramatic, because Cyan was so dominant in the original image it required a big Red move as a counter. We moved the white point because we wanted the adjustment to have a major impact on the upper half of the curve. With this method, Red is increased in the midtones and increased even more dramatically in the highlights. Had we increased Red from the midpoint, the effect would taper off in the highlight range, and the Cyan cast would have remained in the clouds.

9. Hide/show the adjustment layer to see the before/after result.

   As shown in the figure, the adjusted image corrected the original. In the adjusted image, the green of the grass, the gold/tan of the reeds, and the pink and white glow of the clouds shows how far off the original image was. The important take-away point from this lesson is that what we read initially as a Blue cast was actually a Cyan cast. Thus, reducing the Blue channel wasn't enough to fix the problem. The key was increasing the Red channel substantially to counter the Cyan cast.

10. Save your work, then close Sailboat.

FIGURE 46
The original and final images

FIGURE 47
Assessing the image

Adjust color in a poor quality image

1. Open AP 4-7.psd, then save it as **Old Car**.
2. Assess the photographic quality of the image.

   As shown in Figure 47, this image clearly has big problems. Before we even address the color problems, note that the photo itself is poorly shot. The buildings in the background are overlit and pretty much blown out. The subject of the image—the car—is in the foreground, and the entire foreground is in shadow. This means that no matter what adjustments we make, the background and the buildings will be the brightest and most prominent components of this image.
3. Assess the color quality of the image.

   This image clearly has big color problems. Now that's what you call a color cast. The whole thing is clearly purple. Based on what we learned in the previous set of steps, we want to now check to see if that purple is too much red, too much magenta, too much blue, or too much cyan.
4. Position the Eyedropper Tool over the street pavement in the foreground.

   Keep in mind the Sailboat from the previous set of steps when you sample this image. Unlike with the Sailboat, the Info palette shows that Cyan is not dominant in the CMYK readout. Instead, Yellow is weak. That's a clear hint that there's too much Blue, because Yellow is created in RGB by subtracting Blue. In the RGB readout, note that Blue is dominant almost throughout the image. This image has a Blue cast, not a Cyan cast.

(continued)

5. Move the pointer over the deep shadow under the side of the car, as shown in Figure 48.

   Dark shadows are always reliable areas of an image to sample, because they should be neutral. A neutral dark shadow should show the three RGB channels as lower numbers with all of them close in value. 12R/12G/12B would be a very satisfactory neutral dark shadow. In this case, the readout on the shadow is 1R/0G/20B!

6. Create a new Curves adjustment layer.

   First we must address the overall brightness of the image. The blown out background means that the highlights can't be brightened. However, the foreground and most important part of the image is in shadow, so it is best to keep the shadow areas as bright as possible to show detail in the car.

7. Add a point to the curve, then set its Input/Output values to 57/68.

   The shadow areas of the image are brightened.

8. Add another point to the curve, then set its Input/Output values to 215/215.

   Adding this point insures that no pixels higher than 215 will be brightened.

9. Switch to the Blue channel, add a point to the Blue curve, then set its Input/Output values to 101/63.

(continued)

FIGURE 48
Sampling the shadows

FIGURE 49

Before and after view of the blue reduction

FIGURE 50

Darkening the black point in the Blue channel

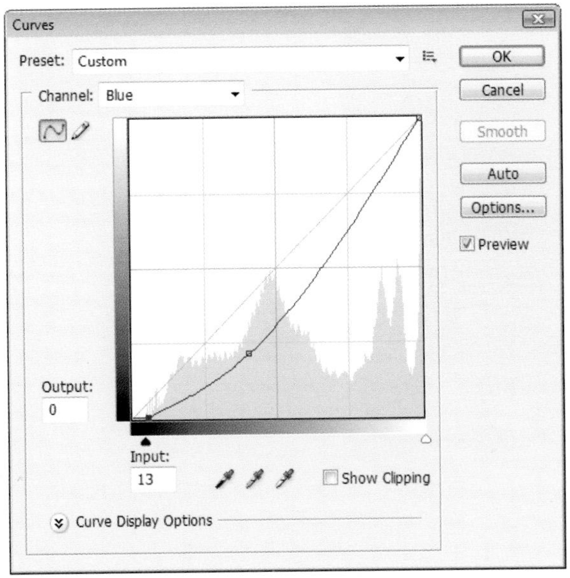

10. Click **OK**, then hide and show the new adjustment layer to see the change.

    As shown in Figure 49, the foreground is brightened slightly and the image appears far more balanced in color. However, the grass in the foreground has become an unreaslistically bright lime green.

11. Use the layer mask to reduce the impact of the adjustment layer on the grass in the foreground to a point that you think looks best.

12. Sample the dark shadow at the side of the car.

    Blue is still very dominant in the dark shadow, which tells you that the reduction of blue didn't have enough impact on the lower end of the Blue curve.

13. Open the adjustment layer dialog box, then move the black point on the Blue curve to the right so that its Input/Output values are 13/0, as shown in Figure 50.

14. Sample the change in the same shadow areas.

    The Blue value has been reduced.

15. Click **OK** then evaluate the image.

    At this point, there aren't any more global changes you can make with curves to make the red of the car more vivid. Increasing Red and reducing Green would do the trick but would create a color cast everywhere else in the image. In that case, you'd need to create a complex layer mask to affect only the red of the car.

16. Create a new Hue/Saturation adjustment layer.

17. Click the **Edit list arrow**, then click **Reds**.

(continued)

18. Increase the Saturation to +35, then click **OK**.

This is a good alternative to creating a complex layer mask. The Hue/Saturation dialog box has algorithms that allow you to target and manipulate specific colors in the image. How does this work? The algorithm uses a lookup table with predefined RGB combinations identified as producing red. It then finds those combinations in the image—red pixels, in this case—and affects only those pixels.

19. Hide and show the Hue/Saturation adjustment layer.

The improvement is noticeable. Given that the car is in shadows, this red is reasonably bright and vivid; a hot, vivid red would not be realistic in these lighting conditions. In the sunshine, yes. In the shade, no.

20. Create a layer group for the two adjustment layers, then hide and show the layer group to see the overall changes.

As shown in Figure 51, the image is dramatically improved from the original.

21. Save your work, then close Old Car.

FIGURE 51

Before and after view all the adjustments

Part 1

1. Open AP 4-8.psd, then save it as **Curves Review**.
2. Show the Top Right layer, target it, then zoom in so that you are viewing the image at 50%.
3. Use the Eyedropper Tool to find the brightest pixels in the image, then write down that grayscale value on a piece of paper.
4. Use the Eyedropper Tool to find the darkest pixel, then write down that number.
5. Click Layer on the menu bar, point to New Adjustment Layer, then click Curves.
6. Name the new adjustment layer **White/Black Point**, and be sure to use the previous layer as a clipping mask. (*Hint*: Be sure to click the Use Previous Layer as Clipping Mask check box whenever you create a new adjustment layer in the remainder of this Project Builder.)
7. In the Curves dialog box, improve the image by resetting the white point and the black point.
8. Click OK when you are done.

Part 2

1. Show the Bottom Left layer, target it, then zoom in so that you are viewing the image at 50%.
2. Find the brightest pixel in the image.
3. Find the darkest pixel.
4. Create a new Curves adjustment layer named **Midtone Adjustment**.
5. Improve the image by correcting the white point and the black point.
6. Lighten or darken the midtones to a level that you think looks best.
7. Click OK when you are done.

Part 3

1. Show the Bottom Right layer, target it, then zoom in so that you are viewing the image at 50%.
2. Use the Magic Wand Tool to select only the white background of the image.
3. Click Select on the menu bar, click Inverse, then hide the selection marquee.
4. Create a new Curves adjustment layer named **Head Selection**.
5. Make the image look the best you think it can look.
6. Compare your artwork to Figure 52.
7. Save and close Curves Review.

Part 4

1. Make only the Top Left layer visible, target it in the Layers palette, then zoom in so that you are viewing the image at 50%.
2. Create a new Curves adjustment layer.
3. Click the Pencil button (Draw to Modify the Curve).
4. Draw four horizontal lines of any length anywhere on the grid to create a posterized effect.
5. Click OK when you are done.
6. Save your work, then close Curves Review.

FIGURE 52
Completed Project Builder 1

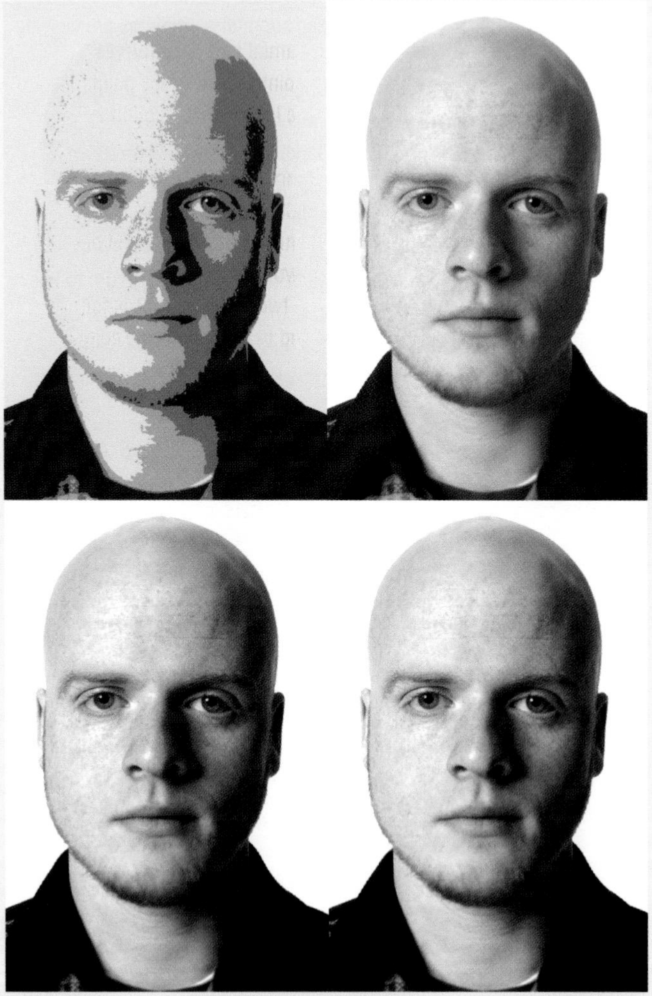

PROJECT BUILDER 2

Part 1

1. Open AP 4-9.psd, then save it as **Half and Half**.
2. Target the layer named Left Side.
3. Create a new Curves adjustment layer named **Left Side Curves**.
4. In the Curves dialog box, fix the white point and the black point, and brighten the midtones until you think the left side looks good.
5. Target the layer named Right Side.
6. Create a new Curves adjustment layer named **Right Side Curves**, and be sure to click the Use Previous Layer as Clipping Mask check box.
7. Use the curve to improve the contrast only until you think the right side looks good. Don't yet try to match the two sides.
8. Adjust either side or both sides until the two halves can pass for one image, as shown in Figure 53. You'll need to adjust specific color channels to make them match.
9. Save and close Half and Half.

FIGURE 53
Completed Project Builder 2

LAURA KENT
ANTHONY BURTON
BLACK KNIGHT
THEATRUM MUNDI PICTURES PRESENTS
MIRIBILE VISU AND THEATRUM MUNDI PRESENT IN ASSOCIATION WITH AD ASTRA AND AD CROMENUM A ALEA IACTA EST PRODUCTION "IPSISSIMA VERBA"
DUX FEMINA FACTI PLACENS UXOR AND DRAMATIS PERSONAE CASTING DIRECTOR INTER PARES MAKE-UP ARTIST SIMPLEX MUNDITISS COSTUME DESIGNER VESTITUS AMPLUS PRODUCTION DESIGNER IGNIS FATUUS
EDITOR TOTIDEM VERBIS DIRECTOR OF PHOTOGRAPHY FIAT LUX MUSIC BY SCHOLA CANTORUM LINE PRODUCER DATA ET ACCEPTA BASED ON THE NOVEL "IPSISSIMA VERBA" BY EDITO PRINCEPS EXECUTIVE PRODUCER FATA VIAM INVENIENT
SCREENPLAY BY OPUS ARTIFICEM PROBAT PRODUCED BY NIHIL QUOD TETIGIT NON ORNAVIT DIRECTED BY LAPSUS CALAM
HOLLYWOOD STUDIO

chapter 5

DESIGNING WITH Multiple Images

1. Create a concept for a poster.
2. Assess supplied images.
3. Position images for a background setting.
4. Integrate multiple images into a single background image.
5. Position foreground images.
6. Merge two images.
7. Integrate foreground images.
8. Finish artwork.

LESSON 1

CREATE A CONCEPT for a Poster

What You'll Do

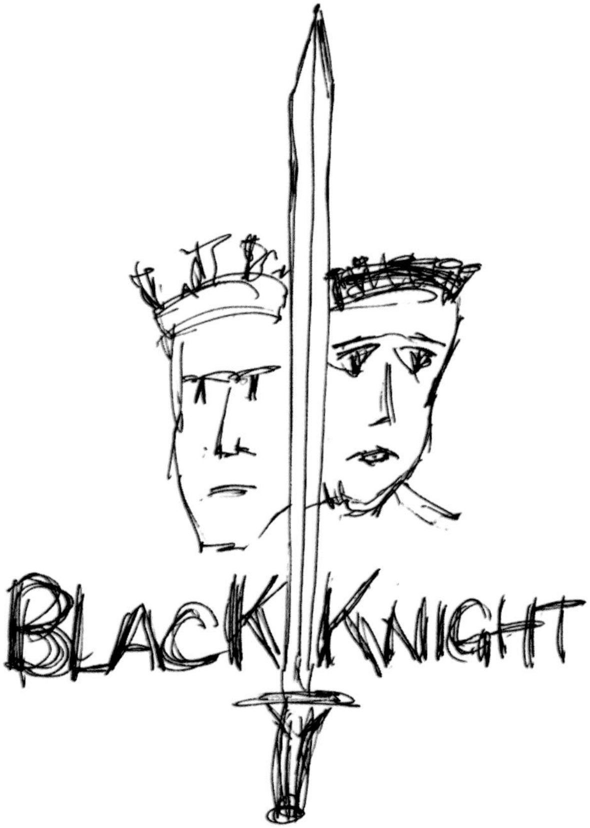

Fasten your seatbelts; you're in for a great ride. Throughout the eight lessons in this chapter, you're going to build a movie poster—from scratch. Actually, you're going to build the movie poster that I built when I first wrote this chapter. The design dialog that runs throughout the chapter will be first-person commentary from me, sharing with you the decisions I made—and why I made them—as I created this poster.

Step by step, you'll build the poster with me, just as I did the first time around. You'll even make the mistakes that I made and take the same wrong turns that I took. And then you'll backtrack and fix your mistakes just like I did. My goal here was to create as much of a real-world project as I could, and then strap you in beside me—my designer copilot—as I retrace my steps.

Real-world is the key here. The images you'll use are stock images that I researched myself—having no idea if they'd actually work together for the concept I had in mind. About the only thing that I created in advance was the concept.

The concept is this: We are art directors working for a Hollywood agency that designs and produces first-run movie posters. We've just been brought in on a new project: *Black Knight*. Here's what the client has told us about *Black Knight*.

- It's an American-produced film, but it was shot in England.
- It stars two respected actors.
- The actress has the leading role. She is played by a very popular American actress (doing a solid English accent).
- The actor is British, well-respected for both his stage and film work.
- The plot, in a nutshell, is as follows: The king has been away at battle for months. The queen falls in love with another man—a knight, believing that her jealous king is far away and may never return. Unknown to her, he has actually returned and is masquerading as a servant in the castle. The queen's handmaiden alerts the queen to the King's ruse. Before the king can confront the queen about her admirer, she has him jailed as a thief who has invaded the castle. A battle of wills develops between the royals—she knows that he knows, and he knows that she knows that he knows. Trying to test her, he sentences the man to death, believing the queen will have no choice but to confess her infidelity. To his surprise, the defiant queen accepts his gambit. Vowing vengeance, the "thief" is suited in armor and burned at the stake. His silver armor is blackened. After his death, stories begin circulating that a mysterious black knight has been seen in the dark of

night. The royals dismiss this as mere hysteria— until the queen's handmaiden is found dead.

- The marketing team has positioned this film in two important ways: first, as an historical thriller, with lots of action, suspense, and sword battles between mounted knights and kings; however, it's also positioned as a costume-drama-romance. The client's marketing team wants your agency to design a poster expressing both these approaches.

After coming up with this concept, I sketched out the thumbnails shown in Figures 1, 2, and 3. Based on the marketing strategy, I determined that I wanted the following five elements in the poster: the queen, the king, the black knight, a sword, and a castle. The king and queen are the "star sell"—the famous people that everybody likes and wants to pay money to see. The black knight is the title character.

FIGURE 1
Poster thumbnail

A black knight is so visually interesting that I knew it alone would define the mysterious, menacing quality that I wanted the poster to have. Working in concert with the beautiful queen, it would also generate the romantic aspect that I needed to convey: a dangerous story of forbidden love, passion, and revenge.

I knew immediately that I wanted to use a castle somewhere in the poster. I need it to establish a sense of place and time—nothing says medieval England like a castle. Finally, the sword plays a central role in the poster. As a visual cue, it signals both the action/battle and the history/romance that the client desires.

FIGURE 2
Thumbnail of castle and knight

FIGURE 3
Thumbnail of sword

ASSESS SUPPLIED Images

What You'll Do

Before I even think about starting to design a poster, I prepare myself for at least a few hours of assessing, retouching, and preparing my supplied images to be used as artwork.

You've probably heard thousands of times that "those beautiful people in the ads don't really look like that." Well guess what…it's true. In every case, posters, advertisements, magazine covers, you name it, the final images you see have gone through substantial amounts of preparation and retouching.

As a designer, this stage for you has two components. First you must assess the images to get a sense of how they can be positioned and combined to achieve the look that you are working toward. It's one thing to sketch out a concept, but it's another thing to utilize actual photography that will work within that concept. Second, you must clean up the raw materials.

Whenever you're working with photographs that show people, some amount of retouching will be involved. It may be minor, or it may be extensive, but it will always be necessary.

When retouching, I approach an image from three perspectives: cosmetic, enhancement, and practical. From the cosmetic perspective, I work to hide flaws. Those flaws might be problems with the photograph such as dust or hairs in the image, or they might be problems with the subject, such as skin imperfections.

From the enhancement perspective, I work to improve the overall effect of the image. Especially when you are working on a project like this, which is romantic and atmospheric, it's important that your artwork be effective. This type of retouching would include making the color of the image more vivid, the eyes more entrancing, and so on.

Finally, from the practical perspective, I try to identify problems with the originals that won't work realistically within my concept. These could include any number of problems, and they're not always easy to identify before you start working.

One example would be lighting. If I'm planning to combine two headshots of two different actors, it will be a practical problem if one is lit from the right and the other from the left. Or if one has a blue highlight and the other has a red highlight.

In this lesson, you will examine three photographs to see the changes and retouching that I applied. You won't actually do the retouching—that's something you'll do in an upcoming chapter—but you will be able to see the work that I did to the images long before I began designing the poster. I timed myself, and in total, I spent about 2.5 hours working on the images you're about to assess.

Assess the image of the big knight

1. Open Big Knight.psd, shown in Figure 4.
2. Hide and show the Adjust Levels layer.

   This was a simple move in which I darkened the shadow point to increase contrast and to improve the depth of the shadows. When you are done examining the change, verify that the Adjust Levels layer is showing.

   > **TIP** Throughout this chapter, you will be asked to hide and show layers to see a before and after effect. In every case, verify that the layer is showing when you are done.

3. Hide and show the Remove Sword layer.

   As shown in Figure 5, I removed the sword entirely using the Clone Stamp Tool. Where the sword overlapped the armor was difficult and time consuming. If you look closely, however, you'll see that I wasn't overly concerned with making the armor "perfect." This is because I knew in advance that the knight will be very dark against a very dark background and that not too much detail would be visible.

(continued)

FIGURE 4
Big Knight.psd original

FIGURE 5
Removing the sword

FIGURE 6
The silhouette

FIGURE 7
Actress.psd original

4. Target and show only the Silo layer.

   Because the background was basically one color, I was able to use the Magic Wand Tool to quickly select the background. I refined the selection in Quick Mask mode, then created the silhouette in Figure 6.

5. Verify that all layers are showing, save your work, then close Big Knight.psd.

Assess the image of the actress

1. Open Actress.psd, shown in Figure 7.
2. Verify that the Background layer is the only layer visible and that it is targeted.

   The very first problem I noticed was a big one—my lead actress was not in costume. Often, actors and actresses are photographed in their street clothes simply for a face shot. Another model is then photographed in the costume for the movie. As the poster designer, you're expected to merge the face of the actor into the costume. Head swaps, costume swaps, hair swaps etc: these are all very common with entertainment advertising projects.

(continued)

3. Open Damsel.psd, shown in Figure 8.

   I chose this image for the costume. Eventually, I'll need to replace the damsel's face with the actress's face. I must keep this in mind as I assess the photo of the actress.

4. Return to the Actress.psd file, then click the **Zoom Tool** on her nose until you are viewing the entire head at 100%.

   The blue highlight and the very soft edge on the right side of her face will present a problem when she's copied into the damsel's costume. There will be no reason for the actress to have a blue highlight on her face. In fact, because of the scarf that will be "put on" her head, her face will be shadowed rather than highlighted. Also, the soft, out-of-focus edge will simply make no sense.

5. Show the No Highlight layer.

   As shown in Figure 9, this change involved replacing the soft, highlighted edge of her face. I created a path to define the edge of her face, then spent about 30 minutes cloning with the Clone Stamp Tool and the Healing Brush Tool to create a flesh tone that was continuous with the rest of her face. I didn't worry about the hard edge because I knew that it would be in the shadow when I merged it with the damsel's costume.

6. Show the Remove Scar layer.

   There's a faint but noticeable horizontal scar on the bridge of the woman's nose, between her eyes—an excellent example that nobody's perfect.

(continued)

FIGURE 8
Damsel.psd original

FIGURE 9
Removing a highlight from the face

FIGURE 10
Enhancing the eyes

7. Show the Smooth Eyeshadow layer.

   Conceptually, this one was trickier than it seems. A woman in medieval times wouldn't have had such dramatic eyeshadow, if any at all. However, this is a romantic Hollywood movie and she's a glamorous actress—not a plain Jane. My choice was to keep her beautiful and glamorous, but to reduce the extreme touches.

8. Show the Reduce Lip Gloss layer.
9. Show the Shadow right side layer.

   Nobody's face exists on a flat plane, so I added shadow to convey a sense of dimension. Also, I knew in advance that her face would be shadowed on the sides when she's pasted into the damsel's costume.

10. Show the Whiten Eyes, Outline Iris, and Eye Power layers.

    As shown in Figure 10, these standard moves can make the eyes far more interesting and entrancing. Again, since this is a romantic movie about kings, queens, and knights, these changes are that much more useful for the overall effect.

11. Show the Darken Eyebrows layer.

    From reading the script, I know that the character of the queen is both the heroine and the villain. Darkening the brows adds intensity and an edge to her features.

(continued)

12. Target the **No Highlight layer**, press and hold **[Shift]**, then select all the layers above it.

TIP Only the Background layer should not be selected.

13. Press **[Ctrl][G]** (Win) or **[⌘][G]** (Mac).

The selected layers are collected into a single folder named Group 1.

14. Hide and show the Group 1 layer to see a before-and-after comparison of all the retouching changes applied to the image.

15. Keep the Actress file open, but do not save changes at this point.

16. Close the Damsel.psd document.

Assess the image of the king

1. Open King.psd, then zoom in so that you are viewing his face at 100%.

2. Target the **Background layer**, then verify that the Background layer is the only layer visible.

3. Arrange the King.psd and the Actress.psd documents side by side, if possible.

The focus and the lighting on the king image is very different from that of the actress image. Since they will be positioned side by side in the final poster, I needed to make the two images as similar in tonal range as possible.

(continued)

FIGURE 11
Lightening the king to match the actress

FIGURE 12
Smoothing the king's face

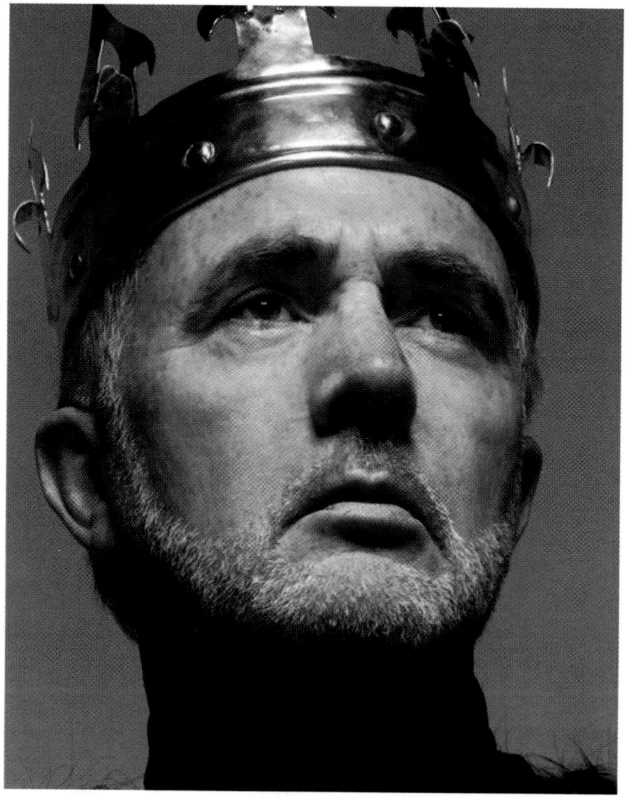

4. Show the No Sword layer.
5. Show the Match Actress layer.

   As shown in Figure 11, I lightened the highlights and midtones dramatically to improve contrast and to mimic the overall lightness of the actress image.
6. Show the Lighten eyes layer.
7. Show the Smooth skin layer.

   As shown in Figure 12, the face is smoothed out overall.
8. Show the next three layers to see the same standard eye retouches as you saw in the actress file.
9. Show the Add Grain layer.

   The Actress.psd document has a distinct grainy quality that the King.psd document lacks.
10. Create a new layer group with all the retouched layers, then hide and show the new group for a before-and-after view of all the changes.
11. Close King.psd and Actress.psd, without saving changes to either.

AUTHOR'S *note*

Nobody's perfect, but alas some are closer to perfect than others. Our older actor lacks the near-flawless complexion of our youthful actress. That's not such a big deal, as he is indeed older and, as a king, he's rugged and manly. However, 20 minutes with the Clone Stamp Tool and the Healing Brush Tool softened the harsh texture overall and helped to make our leading man just a bit more Hollywood handsome.

LESSON 3

POSITION IMAGES FOR a Background Setting

What You'll Do

The great thing about designing movie posters is that you need to tell a story. Sometimes, when there's a really big star in the movie, all you need to do is run a picture of the star and the title. Any poster for a movie with Jim Carrey would be a good example of this. For most titles, however, the poster needs to convey some aspect of the story. For a designer, this is an opportunity to get creative and to design some interesting, evocative artwork.

But make no mistake, in today's Hollywood the movie poster is usually a "star sell." Not always, of course, but if there's a recognizable star in the movie, the studio usually wants that star in the poster. For the designer, this means that telling the story will happen in the background, usually behind a big headshot of the big movie star.

With this type of poster, the challenge for you is to design the poster as a world unto itself. It's almost as if the poster is a glimpse into the world of the movie. This means that much of your work will be focused on the background imagery of the poster—and that's usually the place you start to work.

FIGURE 13
Stars.psd image in the poster file

Position images

1. Open AP 5-1.psd, then save it as **Black Knight Poster**.
2. If necessary, resize the window so that you can see the entire canvas.
3. Open Stars.psd, select all, copy, then close the file.
4. Paste the selection into the poster, then name the new layer **Stars**.

   TIP If the Paste Profile Mismatch dialog box appears, click the Don't show again check box, then click OK.
5. Compare your canvas to Figure 13.
6. Sample the blacks in the Stars image to verify that they are truly black.

   This is an example of how you need to be conscious of grayscale values while you work. In our concept, this is a deep, dark black night's sky. Take the time to sample the image to verify that it is as black as can be, which in this case, it is.
7. Open Billing.psd, select all, copy, then close the file.

(continued)

8. Paste the selection into the poster, then name the new layer **Billing**.

   In the final version of this poster, I would recreate this layer as an editable live type layer. Photoshop is very good with type creation and typography. Generally speaking, it's a good idea always to save a live type version of the typography in your designs.

   TIP Be sure to name layers with descriptive names. By the end of this chapter, this file will have about 50 layers, and you'll be so thankful when you're scrolling through the Layers palette that you took the time to name each individual layer.

9. In the Layers palette, change the blending mode for the Billing layer to Screen, then compare your canvas to Figure 14.

   The Screen blending mode makes black pixels completely transparent.

10. Save your work.

FIGURE 14
Result of the Screen blending mode

AUTHOR'S *note*

When I design posters, one of the first things I do is position the important text elements. The type elements do a lot to define the look of the piece. Already, this looks like a movie poster, and that helps me to visualize the final poster while I'm working. Also, I place the type elements in the beginning of the project simply to reserve space for them while I'm working. Otherwise, I might create a great piece of artwork then realize I've not left enough room for the billing block!

FIGURE 15
The Big Knight artwork pasted on the Big Knight layer

Position an image precisely

1. Target the **Stars layer**.
2. Open Big Knight.psd, target the **Silo layer**, select all, copy, then close the file.
3. Paste the selection, then name the new layer **Big Knight**.

   Your canvas should resemble Figure 15.
4. Hide the Billing layer.
5. Verify that the Options bar is visible or click **Window** on the menu bar, then click **Options**.
6. Press **[Ctrl][T]** (Win) or **[⌘][T]** (Mac) to scale the image.

   Once you press **[Ctrl][T]** (Win) or **[⌘][T]** (Mac), the Options bar displays the physical attributes of the image within the bounding box, such as its X and Y locations, and its horizontal and vertical scale.
7. Verify that the center point is selected in the Reference point location in the Options bar.
8. Moving left to right, type **555.7** in the X text box, press **[Tab]**, type **514.7** in the Y text box, press **[Tab]**, type **80** in the W text box, press **[Tab]**, type **80** in the H text box, then press **[Tab]**.

(continued)

AUTHOR'S *note*

Throughout this chapter you will scale and position images exactly as I did when I designed the poster. Not only will this help us to avoid potential problems with your images being a slightly different size or a slightly different location than mine, it offers the opportunity for you to learn to use the Options bar to position the images in a specific location.

9. Click the **Move Tool** , click **Apply** to execute the transformation, then compare your screen to Figure 16.

   The Big Knight image was scaled 80%; the location of its center point is 555.7 pixels from the left edge of the canvas and 514.7 pixels from the top.

10. Save your work.

FIGURE 16
Positioning the big knight

AUTHOR'S *note*

At this point, an alert is sounding in my head. I'm thinking that the knight is looking a lot like Darth Vader, especially against that black starry sky that looks so much like outer space. This is not a big shock—Darth Vader really does look a lot like a knight. From my design perspective, this is first a bad thing, but also a good thing. It's bad because I don't want the final image to look silly or like a cheap knock-off of *Star Wars*. It's a good thing because I remember the great *Star Wars* posters and how Darth Vader was used so effectively as a background image.

FIGURE 17
Hard Light blending mode

Use the Hard Light blending mode

1. Verify that the Big Knight layer is targeted.
2. Experiment with all of the blending modes in the Layers palette.

   So much of working in modern day Photoshop involves blending modes, and so much of working with blending modes involves experimentation. Through experimentation, you can become familiar with the basic functions of the major blending modes. Be sure to take note of how they are grouped in the palette menu. Modes that lighten an image are grouped together, as are modes that darken an image.
3. Choose the Hard Light blending mode, then compare your screen to Figure 17.
4. Click **Layer** on the menu bar, point to **New Adjustment Layer**, then click **Hue/Saturation**.
5. Type **Desaturate** in the Name text box, click the **Use Previous Layer to Create Clipping Mask check box**, then click **OK**.

   TIP Whenever you are asked to create an adjustment layer, always click the Use Previous Layer to Create Clipping Mask check box unless you are instructed not to.
6. Drag the **Saturation slider** to –50, then click **OK**.

   Because the Hard Light blending mode made the knight artwork transparent, we can see the stars artwork through the knight artwork, which is not an effect I want.

(continued)

7. Press and hold **[Ctrl]** (Win) or [⌘] (Mac), then click the **Layer thumbnail** on the Big Knight layer to load its selection.
8. Click the **Rectangular Marquee Tool**, press and hold **[Shift]**, then add the bottom of the canvas to the selection so that your screen resembles Figure 18.
9. Target the **Stars layer**.
10. Press and hold **[Alt]** (Win) or **[option]** (Mac) then click the **Add layer mask button** on the Layers palette.

    As shown in Figure 19, a layer mask is added with the selected area automatically filled with black. Everything is automatically deselected.

    TIP When any selection is loaded, pressing and holding [Alt] (Win) or [option] (Mac), then clicking the Add layer mask button creates a layer mask in which the selected pixels are filled with black. If you are not holding [Alt] (Win) or [option] (Mac) when you click the Add layer mask button, the selected pixels will be filled with white in the layer mask and the inverse will be black.
11. Target the **Big Knight layer**, press and hold **[Shift]**, then click to select the adjustment layer above it.
12. Press **[Ctrl] [G]** (Win) or [⌘] **[G]** (Mac).
13. Rename the new group **Black Knight Group**.
14. Show the Billing layer to see how things are looking, hide it again, then save your work.

FIGURE 18
Selecting areas for a mask

FIGURE 19
Masking out the stars where they overlap the big knight

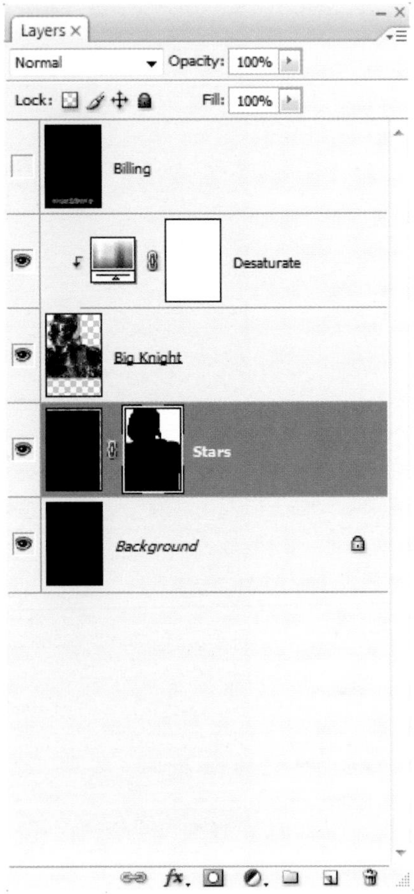

FIGURE 20
Reducing the opacity of the White layer

Control the effect of the Hard Light blending mode

1. Sample the image, then note in the Info palette that the black areas of the image are pure black.

   The knight is too black, so much so that he's mostly invisible against the black background and difficult to identify as a knight. Since there's no way to control the degree to which the Hard Light blending mode affects the artwork, I'm going to use a work-around technique.

2. Click the **gray triangle** to expand the Black Knight Group, then target the **Big Knight layer**.
3. Press and hold **[Ctrl]** (Win) or [⌘] (Mac), then click the **Create a new layer button** on the Layers palette.

   A new empty layer is added *below* the Big Knight layer.

4. Name the new layer **White**.
5. Press and hold **[Ctrl]** (Win) or [⌘] (Mac), then click the **Layer thumbnail** on the Big Knight layer to load its selection.
6. Fill the selection with white, then deselect.
7. Reduce the opacity of the White layer to 30%, then compare your screen to Figure 20.

   With this method, we can use the White layer as an artificial way to control the effect that the Hard Light blending mode has on the relationship between the knight and the background.

(continued)

8. Add a layer mask to the White layer.

9. Click the **Brush Tool**, type **[X]** to switch to a black foreground color, verify that the Opacity is set to 100%, then choose a medium-sized hard brush.

10. Mask out every area of the White layer except the head.

    Your artwork should resemble Figure 21.

11. **[Alt]** (Win) or **[option]** (Mac)-drag the **layer mask** from the White layer to the Big Knight layer, so that only the knight's head is visible.

12. Reduce the opacity of the White layer to 10%, then compare your screen to Figure 22.

13. Collapse the Black Knight Group layer.

14. Save your work.

FIGURE 21
Masking the white copy

FIGURE 22
The final effect

FIGURE 23
Positioning the castle

Position three background images

1. Verify that the **Black Knight Group layer** is targeted.
2. Open Castle.psd, target the **Silo layer**, select all, copy, then close the file.
3. Paste the selection, then name the new layer **Castle**.

   TIP The new layer should be immediately above the Black Knight Group layer.

4. Press **[Ctrl][T]** (Win) or [⌘]**[T]** (Mac) to scale the image.
5. Type **692** in the X text box, press **[Tab]**, type **1283** in the Y text box, press **[Tab]**, type **63** in the W text box, press **[Tab]**, type **63** in the H text box, then press **[Tab]**.
6. Click the **Move Tool** to execute the transformation, click **Apply**, then compare your screen to Figure 23.
7. Target the **Black Knight Group layer**.
8. Open Moon.psd, target the **Silo layer**, select all, copy, then close the file.

(continued)

AUTHOR'S *note*

The castle plays such an important role. First, it identifies a recognizable place. Second, it provides depth to the background. The black grass provides a much-needed foreground object, which also adds to the sense of depth.

9. Paste the selection into the poster, then name the new layer **Moon**.

10. Press **[Ctrl][T]** (Win) or ⌘**[T]** (Mac) to scale the image.

11. Type **881** in the X text box, press **[Tab]**, type **843** in the Y text box, press **[Tab]**, type **52** in the W text box, press **[Tab]**, type **52** in the H text box, then press **[Tab]**.

12. Click  to execute the transformation, click **Apply**, then compare your screen to Figure 24.

13. Open Small Knight.psd, target the **Silo layer**, select all, copy, then close the file.

14. Verify that the **Moon layer** is targeted, paste the selection, then name the new layer **Small Knight**.

15. Press **[Ctrl][T]** (Win) or ⌘**[T]** (Mac) to scale the image.

16. Type **824** in the X text box, press **[Tab]**, type **731.5** in the Y text box, press **[Tab]**, type **40** in the W text box, press **[Tab]**, type **40** in the H text box, then press **[Tab]**.

17. Click  to execute the transformation, click **Apply**, then compare your screen to Figure 25.

18. Save your work.

(continued)

FIGURE 24
Positioning the moon

FIGURE 25
Positioning the small knight

INTEGRATE MULTIPLE IMAGES INTO A Single Background Image

What You'll Do

Once you've positioned the images that you want to use in a poster, there always comes a critical point where the hodgepodge needs to be integrated into one piece of art. This is often a strange, exciting, and nerve-wracking transition. Positioning the images is a challenge for a designer's layout skills. Integrating the images challenges a whole different set of skills. This is where your individuality as a designer really comes into play. Given the layout in this chapter, 10 different designers would create 10 different pieces of artwork—even though they're all working with the same base imagery. And that's great—because design is all about individuality, and there's never a right solution. However, the challenge itself is always that same one: How do you use a bunch of photos to make one piece of art?

Create depth between placed images

1. Assess the relationship between the castle and the small knight behind it.

   Together, these two images are a great example of one of the toughest challenges you'll face when working with multiple images: the need to create a sense of depth. First, look at the castle. Clearly, the knight is behind the castle, but how far behind it? They appear to be on the same plane.

2. Click the **Brush Tool** , then specify black as the foreground color.
3. Choose the Soft Round 200 pixels brush, then target the **Small Knight layer**.
4. Paint a black streak across the bottom half of the small knight, below his belt, as shown in Figure 26.

   The simple black streak creates the illusion that the knight is farther back behind the castle. This is a standard technique: put some color between two overlapping images to create depth. It's just an illusion, but the eye registers it instantly as depth.

(continued)

FIGURE 26
Painting black to convey depth and distance

FIGURE 27
Scaling and aligning the second small knight

5. Undo and redo to see the effect.
6. Click **Edit** on the menu bar, then click **Undo Brush Tool**.
7. Open Small Knight.psd.
8. Target the **Knight and Trees layer**, select all, copy, then close the document.
9. Paste the selection into the poster, then name the new layer **Knight and Trees**.

> **TIP** The new layer should be immediately above the Small Knight layer in the Layers palette.

10. Scale the small knight in the Knight and Trees layer 40%, then align him to the previous copy of the small knight.

    Because the Knight and Trees layer has different content than the Small Knight layer, the X/Y coordinates you entered when you placed the small knight will not align the two knights.

    Your screen should resemble Figure 27.

11. Change the blending mode on the Knight and Trees layer to Multiply.

    Multiply is one of the most commonly used blending modes. Pixels retain their color, but they become completely transparent.

> **TIP** Because Multiply makes pixels transparent, you can use it as a quick way to align two overlapping images. It's not the best way—you'll learn that in a later chapter—but it is quick.

12. Zoom in and verify that the two knights are perfectly aligned.

> **TIP** Use the arrow keys to move the top image one pixel at a time. When the details are in focus, the images are aligned.

(continued)

13. Zoom out so that you can see the entire canvas.
14. In the Layers palette, drag the **Knight and Trees layer** below the Small Knight layer, then compare your screen to Figure 28.
15. Target the **Small Knight layer**, click the **Create a new layer button** on the Layers palette, then name the new layer **Darken Small Knight**.
16. Click the **Brush Tool**, then paint with black to create a shadow below the knight's belt, as shown in Figure 29.
17. Clip the Darken Small Knight layer into the Small Knight layer beneath it.
18. Select the three Small Knight layers, make a new layer group, then name the new group **Small Knight Group**.
19. Save your work.

FIGURE 28
Moving the layer

FIGURE 29
Shadowing the small knight

FIGURE 30
Desaturating the castle

Use adjustment layers to integrate artwork

1. Target the **Castle layer**.
2. Click **Layer** on the menu bar, point to **New Adjustment Layer**, then click **Hue/Saturation**.
3. Type **Desaturate Background** in the Name text box, do not check the Use Previous layer to Create Clipping Mask check box, then click **OK**.
4. Drag the **Saturation slider** to –80, click **OK**, then compare your canvas to Figure 30.
5. Undo and redo to examine how this simple move does so much to integrate the artwork.

   Desaturated, the images all share a common look. Also, the setting is more realistic. With the desaturation, it is reasonable to believe that both the castle and the knight are illuminated by the moon.

(continued)

6. Display the Info palette, then sample the shadow areas on the small knight.

   The small knight suffers from weak shadows. Note how the streak of black paint is so much darker than the shadow areas of the small knight.

7. Expand the Small Knight Group layer, then target the **Darken Small Knight layer**.

8. Create a Curves adjustment layer and verify that it's not clipped.

9. Drag the **black triangle** to the right so that it's Input value is 22, then click **OK**.

   Because the Curves adjustment layer is not clipped, it is affecting all the layers beneath it, but we want it to affect just the Small Knight group.

10. Select the Small Knight Group folder, change its blending mode from Pass Through to Normal, then compare your artwork to Figure 31.

    When a group folder is set to Normal, adjustment layers in the group affect only artwork on layers within the group.

(continued)

FIGURE 31
Darkened shadows in small knight artwork

FIGURE 32
Adjusting levels

FIGURE 33
Brightening the moon

11. Collapse the Small Knight Group layer, then target the **Castle layer**.

    As a foreground image, both the castle and the water in front of it should be brighter, sharper, and more distinct than the shadowy knight.

12. Apply a Levels adjustment layer named **Brighten Castle**.

    TIP Be sure to click the Use Previous Layer to Create Clipping Mask check box.

13. Type **20** in the left Input text box, type **1.3** in the middle text box, type **240** in the right text box, click **OK**, then compare your artwork to Figure 32.
14. Make a new layer group named **Castle Group** for the Castle layer and its adjustment layer.
15. Target the **Moon layer**.
16. Create a Curves adjustment layer.

    TIP Be sure to click the Use Previous Layer to Create Clipping Mask check box.

17. Click to add a point to the curve, set its Input value to 58, set its Output value to 96, click **OK**, then compare your artwork to Figure 33.
18. Make a new layer group named **Moon Group** for the Moon layer and its adjustment layer.
19. Save your work.

Use a fill adjustment layer to integrate artwork

1. Target the **Desaturate Background layer**.
2. Click **Layer** on the menu bar, point to **New Fill Layer**, then click **Solid Color**.
3. Type **Colorize Background** in the Name text box, do not click the Use Previous Layer to Create Clipping Mask check box, then click **OK**.
4. Type **84** in the R text box, type **110** in the G text box, type **179** in the B text box, then click **OK**.
5. Change the blending mode to Multiply so that the blue fill layer becomes transparent.
6. Reduce the opacity to 70%.
7. Show the Billing layer, then compare your screen to Figure 34.
8. Save your work.

FIGURE 34
The background

POSITION FOREGROUND Images

What You'll Do

Transitioning from background to foreground is always an interesting step when building a composite image. In many ways, it's like shifting gears.

When working on the background, the focus of your work usually involves pushing things back, making them less distinct, blurring the line between one image and another, muting colors, and so on. The opposite is usually true when working with the foreground. With this type of poster—a lush, romantic thriller—I think of the foreground as the "eye candy." The foreground sells the poster, it sells the story, and it sells the movie.

This lesson is about positioning the foreground elements. Note how you'll use bright colors and central locations to make these elements the focus of the poster.

Position the sword

1. Hide the Billing layer.
2. Open Sword.psd, then show the White and Silo layers to see the retouching that was done.

   The original sword had a rounded edge. For this poster, a sharp point for the sword will be a subtle but necessary component to the concept as a whole.
3. Target the **Silo layer**, select all, copy, then close the file.
4. Target the **Colorize Background layer**, paste, then name the new layer **Sword**.
5. Click **Edit** on the menu bar, point to **Transform**, then click **Rotate 180°**.
6. Press **[Ctrl][T]** (Win) or [⌘]**[T]** (Mac) to scale the image.
7. Type **506** in the X text box, press **[Tab]**, type **833** in the Y text box, press **[Tab]**, type **37** in the W text box, press **[Tab]**, type **37** in the H text box, then press **[Tab]**.
8. Click the **Move Tool**, click **Apply**, then compare your screen to Figure 35.
9. Save your work.

FIGURE 35
Positioning the sword

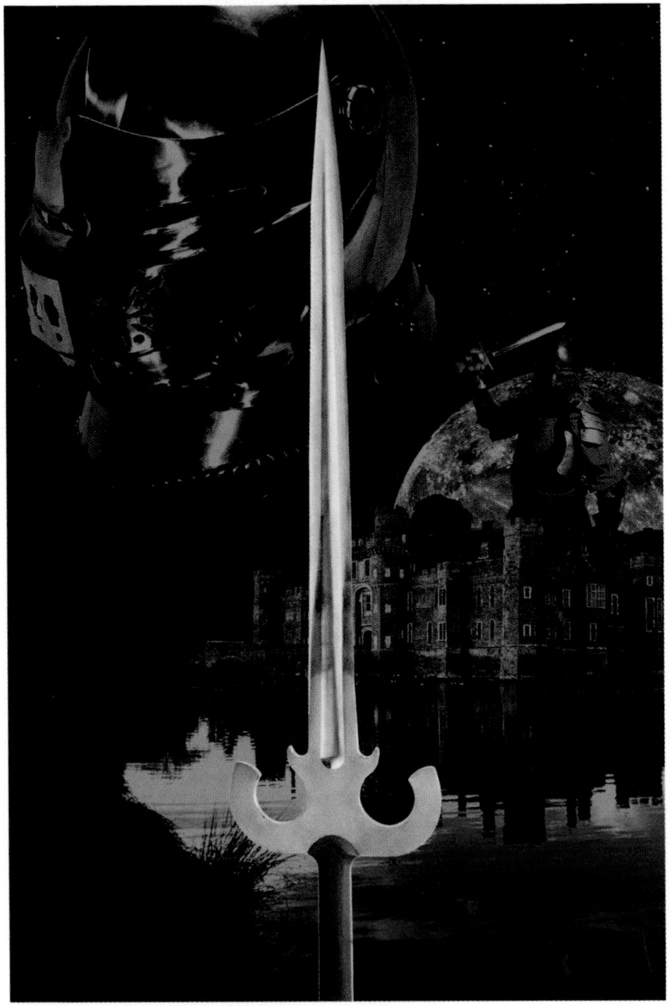

FIGURE 36
The sword enhanced with a layer style

Enhance the sword

1. Click **Layer** on the menu bar, point to **Layer Style**, click **Bevel and Emboss**, then verify that the Preview check box is checked.
2. Verify that the Style is set to Inner Bevel and that Technique is set to Smooth.
3. Set the depth to 750%.
4. Set the Size to 11 px.
5. Set the Opacity of the Highlight Mode and Shadow Mode to 90%.
6. Click the **Gloss Contour list arrow**, double-click the eighth contour named **Ring**, then click the **Anti-aliased check box**.
7. Click **OK**, then compare your artwork to Figure 36.
8. Click **Layer** on the menu bar, point to **New Adjustment Layer**, then click **Levels**.
9. Type **Brighten Sword** in the Name text box, click the **Use Previous Layer to Create Clipping Mask check box**, then click **OK**.

(continued)

10. Drag the **black triangle** in the Input Levels section to the right until the far-left Input text box reads 18, drag the **white triangle** left until the far-right Input text box reads 235.
11. Click **OK**, then target the **Sword layer**.
12. Drag a rectangular selection marquee around the sword but not the handle, as shown in Figure 37.
13. Apply a 6-pixel feather to the selection, click **Filter** on the menu bar, point to **Sharpen**, then click **Unsharp Mask**.
14. Type **100** in the Amount text box, then click **OK**.

    The tones in the sword become much more distinct and hard edged. You will study sharpening techniques in more detail in upcoming chapters.
15. Deselect, then create a new layer group for the Sword and its adjustment layer, then name the new group **Sword Group**.
16. Save your work.

Place the king

1. Target the **Colorize Background layer**.
2. Open King.psd, make all layers visible except for the top layer named Silo, then target the **Background layer**.

(continued)

FIGURE 37
Selecting the sword

FIGURE 38
Positioning the king

3. Press and hold **[Ctrl]** (Win) or [⌘] (Mac), then click the **Layer thumbnail** on the Silo layer to load its selection.

   The selection is loaded but the Silo layer remains hidden.

4. Click **Edit** on the menu bar, then click **Copy Merged**.

   The Copy Merged command is very useful if you want to copy an image on your screen that is being created from multiple layers. The Copy Merged command copies all the visible layers as though they were a single, merged layer.

5. Close King.psd, switch to the Black Knight Poster document, paste, then name the new layer **King**.

   This is a good method for file management. Rather than bring all the layers from the King file into the Black Knight document, we're working with a single merged image of the king. Our layers still exist in the King file if we need them, so there's no need to increase the complexity and file size of the Black Knight Poster document with all those layers.

6. Click **Edit** on the menu bar, point to **Transform**, then click **Flip Horizontal**.

7. Press **[Ctrl][T]** (Win) or [⌘]**[T]** (Mac) to scale the image.

8. Type **426** in the X text box, press **[Tab]**, type **947** in the Y text box, then press **[Tab]**.

9. Click the **Move Tool**, click **Apply**, then compare your screen to Figure 38.

(continued)

It's difficult to see, but a horizontal white line above the king's head was inadvertently copied from the King.psd file. If you zoom in or move the image of the king around, you'll see it more clearly. There's no reason for this to have happened; we loaded the silo selection and applied the Copy Merged command. These inexplicable glitches happen often, and you must keep an eye out for them.

10. Add a layer mask to the King layer, make the selection shown in Figure 39, then fill the selection in the layer mask with black.
11. Deselect, then save your work.

Mask the king

1. Select the entire right half of the canvas, then mask out all elements of the king image that are on the right side of the sword.
2. Deselect all, then compare your screen to Figure 40.
3. Click the **Brush Tool**, choose the Soft Round 100 pixels brush, then mask out only the hand, the gold handle and white areas of the costume.
4. Moving upward slowly and making small moves, mask the king's black costume so that it merges with the shadows that surround the blue water.

(continued)

FIGURE 39
Masking an unintended white line

FIGURE 40
Masking the king to the right of the sword

FIGURE 41
Final mask effect for the king

5. Show the Billing layer so that your artwork resembles Figure 41. As shown in Figure 41, the king's costume merges seamlessly with the shadows in the water. Rather than a floating head, we now recognize the king's shoulder, his collar, and the shiny detail on his chest and sleeve. However, those elements transition into the shadows in a way that you really can't tell where the king ends and the shadows on the water begin.
6. Hide the Billing layer, then save your work.

LESSON 6

MERGE TWO Images

What You'll Do

Merging two images to create a third image is perhaps the most delicate surgery you can do in Photoshop, especially when it involves somebody's face. It's one thing to paste a tree into a field; it's a whole different thing to take the eyes from one photo and paste them onto the face in another photo—with nobody catching on. You might be surprised at how often it's done. I do a lot of work with movie posters, and in most cases, the actor's head and the actor's body are from two different original photos. This happens because, when choosing from originals, the face in one photo might be perfect for the concept, but the body might be in the wrong position. But in another photo, the body is in a great position, but the actor won't approve the face shot. So a merge is necessary—put this head on that body.

If you're really good and you do it well, the best compliment is no compliment at all—because nobody realizes the tricks you've been playing.

FIGURE 42
Retouching applied to Damsel.psd

Prepare the base image for merging

1. Open Actress.psd.
2. Open Damsel.psd, then position it beside Actress.psd so that you can see both images.

   The angles in the two photographs aren't compatible. In the Actress photo, the model's head tilts slightly right. In the Damsel photo, the model's head tilts left.
3. Click the **Damsel.psd window**, click **Image** on the menu bar, point to **Rotate Canvas**, then click **Flip Canvas Horizontal**.
4. Show the Final layer to see the retouching that was done.

   As shown in Figure 42, the veil was removed from the side of the face and the cloth on her chest was brought up so that it meets the scarf around her head.
5. Click **Select** on the menu bar, then load the selection named **Head and Shoulders**.

(continued)

AUTHOR'S *note*

When merging photos, it's very important that you think ahead. It would be very easy to jump in and paste the actress into the damsel image. If you did so, you'd need to scale down the actress's head, and you'd need to rotate her head counterclockwise. But here's the problem: Damsel.psd is not the final image. The poster is the final image. At this point, you have no idea how Damsel.psd will fit into the poster image. In fact, it is too small for the poster and will need to be scaled up. Therefore, this means you would have scaled the actress down only to scale her back up again in the poster file. Not a good idea.

6. Target the **Final layer**, click **Edit** on the menu bar, then click **Copy**.
7. Switch to the Black Knight Poster document, then target the **Sword Group layer**.
8. Paste, then move the damsel image to the right.

   As shown in Figure 43, the damsel's head is too small and tilts too far to the right in comparison to the king.
9. Press **[Ctrl][T]** (Win) or ⌘ **[T]** (Mac) to scale the image.
10. Type **150** in the W text box, press **[Tab]**, type **150** in the H text box, press **[Tab]**, type **–11.5** in the Rotate text box, then press **[Tab]**.
11. Click the **Move Tool** to execute the transformation, click **Apply**, then compare your screen to Figure 44.

    These scale and rotation values work for the damsel image in relation to the image of the king.
12. Delete the new layer, then return to Damsel.psd.
13. Deselect.
14. Click **Image** on the menu bar, then click **Image Size**.
15. Verify that the Constrain Proportions and Resample Image check boxes are both checked.

(continued)

FIGURE 43
Assessing the size of the damsel image

FIGURE 44
Transforming the image

FIGURE 45
Scaling the file

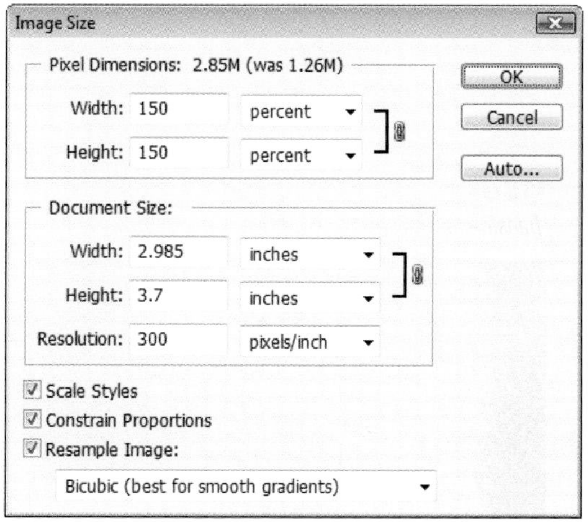

FIGURE 46
Rotating the canvas

16. In the Pixel Dimensions section, change the Width and Height list arrows to **percent**.
17. Type **150** in the Width text box so that your dialog box resembles Figure 45.
18. Click **OK**.

    The file is scaled 150%.
19. Press **[D]** to access a white background color.
20. Click **Image** on the menu bar, point to **Rotate Canvas**, then click **Arbitrary**.
21. Type **11.5** in the Angle text box, click the **°CCW option button**, then click **OK**.

    As shown in Figure 46, the image is rotated –11.5 degrees.
22. Save the file as **Actress Damsel Merge**.

(continued)

Remove the face in the base image

1. Show the Green Screen layer, then add a layer mask to the Final layer.
2. Zoom in on the face, click the **Brush Tool** , then choose the **Hard Round 19 pixels brush**.
3. Mask out the entire face, using Figure 47 as a guide.

   Try to paint as close to the blue scarf as possible so that you don't leave a black line around the perimeter. Don't worry about the hair in the upper-right corner—we will address that later.
4. Save your work.

Place the paste image behind the base image

1. Switch to the Actress.psd file, then make every layer visible.
2. Display the Paths palette, press and hold **[Ctrl]** (Win) or ⌘ (Mac), then click **Path 1**.

   Path 1 is loaded as a selection.
3. Click **Edit** on the menu bar, then click **Copy Merged**.*Positioning the scaled artwork*
4. Switch to the Actress Damsel Merge file, then target the **Green Screen layer**.
5. Paste.
6. Name the new layer **Actress**.
7. Click the **Move Tool** , then position the actress artwork as shown in Figure 48.

(continued)

FIGURE 47
Masking the face

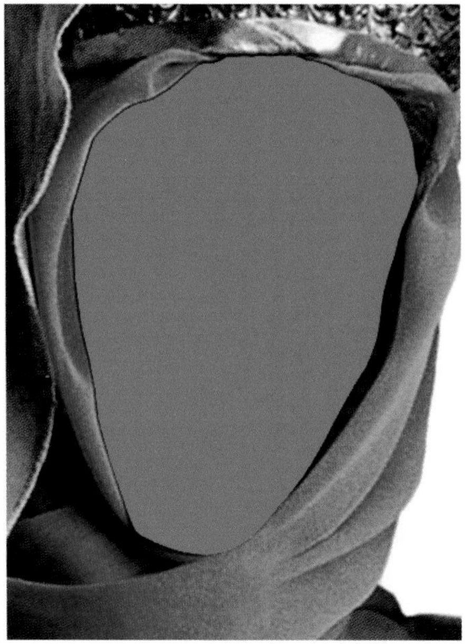

FIGURE 48
Positioning the artwork before scaling

FIGURE 49
Positioning the scaled artwork

FIGURE 50
Hiding a bare spot

8. Press **[Ctrl][T]** (Win) or **[⌘][T]** (Mac) to scale the image.
9. Type **588** in the X text box, press **[Tab]**, type **469** in the Y text box, press **[Tab]**, type **77** in the W text box, press **[Tab]**, type **77** in the H text box, then press **[Tab]**.
10. Click , click **Apply**, then compare your screen to Figure 49.
11. Target the **layer mask** in the Final layer, choose a small soft paint brush and a white foreground color, then smooth the transition between the damsel's dark hair and the actress's blond hair.
12. Hide the Green Screen layer.
13. Target the **Background layer**, click the **Layers palette list arrow**, then click **Duplicate Layer**.
14. Accept the default layer name, then click **OK**.
15. Click , then click ← four times so that it "patches" the hole at the right side of the actress's face, as shown in Figure 50.
16. Save your work.

(continued)

Create a shadow for the paste image

1. Delete the Green Screen layer.
2. Duplicate the Actress layer, name it **Shadow**, then move it to the top of the Layers palette.
3. Click **Image** on the menu bar, point to **Adjustments**, then click **Levels**.
4. Drag the **middle triangle** to the right until the middle Input value reads 0.65.
5. Click **OK**.
6. Click **Image** on the menu bar, point to **Adjustments**, then click **Hue/Saturation**.
7. Reduce the saturation to –30, then click **OK**.

   Your artwork should resemble Figure 51.
8. Press and hold **[Ctrl]** (Win) or [⌘] (Mac), then click the **layer mask** in the Final layer.

   When you load the selection of a layer mask, all of the white areas of the layer mask are selected. In this case, this means that the center of the actress's face, her eyes, nose, mouth, and so on, are not selected.

(continued)

FIGURE 51
Darkening and desaturating the image

FIGURE 52
Removing areas that will not be shadowed

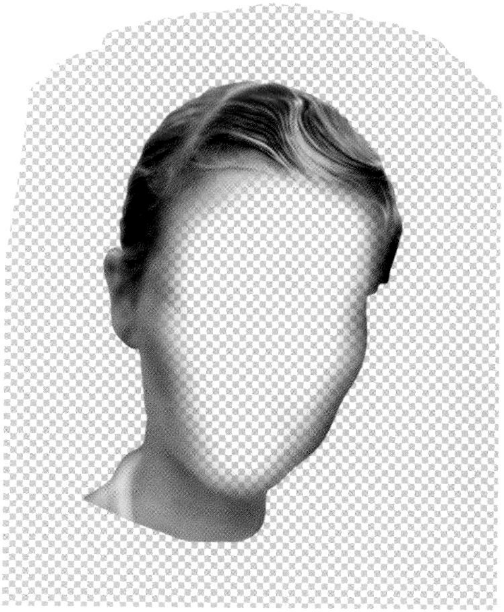

FIGURE 53
Final shadow effect

9. Click **Select** on the menu bar, then click **Inverse**.

   The actress's face is now selected.
10. Click **Select** on the menu bar, point to **Modify**, then click **Contract**.
11. Type **12** in the Contract By text box, then click **OK**.
12. Click **Select** on the menu bar, then click **Refine Edge**.
13. Type **12** in the Feather text box, then click **OK**.
14. Show only the Shadow layer.
15. Click **Edit** on the menu bar, then click **Cut**.

    Compare your screen to Figure 52.
16. Show all layers.
17. Drag the **Shadow layer** beneath the Final layer, then compare your artwork to Figure 53.
18. Hide and show the Shadow layer to see the impact of your work.
19. Save your work.

LESSON 7

INTEGRATE FOREGROUND Images

What You'll Do

When finishing the background art, we responded to a central challenge: How do you use a bunch of photos to make one piece of art? For the background, that meant creating a night world of stars and a black sky, a shadowy castle and menacing knights, barely visible. This night world is dark, and we used the concept of darkness to integrate the artwork. Now, with the foreground, we need to switch gears. The challenge is the same: use the photos of the sword, the king, and the queen to make one piece of art. But in this case, the art is foreground art. It needs to be bright and eye-catching. It needs to sell the concept. Darkening, desaturating, muting, blurring—none of these useful techniques are the answer for the foreground images—at least not in the way they were used for the background art. In this lesson, you will utilize the power of blending modes to integrate the foreground artwork while maintaining brightness and color.

FIGURE 54
Positioning the queen

FIGURE 55
Masking the queen

Position the queen

1. Verify that the top layer is targeted in Actress Damsel Merge.psd. and that all the layers are showing.
2. Click **Select** on the menu bar, click **Load Selection**, then load the Head and Shoulders selection.
3. Click **Edit** on the menu bar, then click **Copy Merged**.
4. Switch to the Black Knight Poster file, make the Billing layer visible, then target the **King layer**.
5. Paste, then name the new layer **Queen**.
6. Press **[Ctrl][T]** (Win) or ⌘**[T]** (Mac).
7. Type **640** in the X text box, press **[Tab]**, type **747** in the Y text box, then press **[Tab]**.
8. Click the **Move Tool**, click **Apply**, compare your screen to Figure 54, then save.

Mask the queen

1. Add a layer mask to the Queen layer.
2. Select the entire left half of the canvas, then mask out all elements of the queen image that are on the left side of the sword.
3. Deselect all.
4. Click the **Brush Tool**, choose the Soft Round 100 pixels brush, mask the queen's dress so that your artwork resembles Figure 55, then save.

Use adjustment layers to apply blending modes

1. Target the **King layer**, press **[Shift]** and click the **Queen layer**, then create a new layer group named **Royals**.
2. Set the blending mode on the Royals layer group to Normal.
3. Expand the Royals layer group, target the **Queen layer**, click the **Create new fill or adjustment layer button** , then click **Hue/Saturation**.
4. Without making any modifications in the Hue/Saturation dialog box, click **OK**.
5. Name the new adjustment layer **Hard Light Desat**.
6. Change the blending mode on the Hard Light Desat adjustment layer to Hard Light, then compare your result to Figure 56.

   This is an example of one of the more complex concepts when working with adjustment layers. An adjustment layer is like a virtual copy of the layers beneath it. In this case, it's like a copy of the king and the queen on top of the original king and queen artwork. When you set the adjustment layer to Hard Light, it's the same thing as if you'd duplicated the King and the Queen layers, merged them, then set the merged layer to Hard Light. What's better about this method is that you can now modify the adjustment layer to manipulate the Hard Light effect.

(continued)

FIGURE 56
Hard lighting the king and queen

FIGURE 57
Final color effect

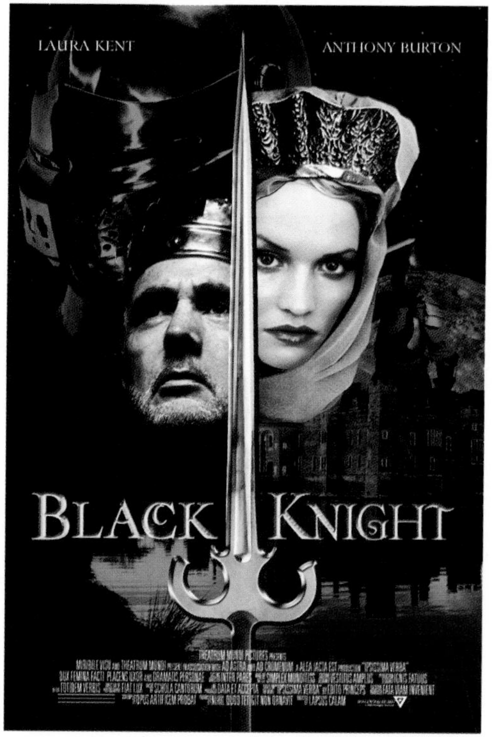

FIGURE 58
Positioning the title

7. Double-click to open the Hard Light Desat adjustment layer, drag the **Saturation slider** to −90, then click **OK**.
8. Create an un-clipped Curves adjustment layer, drag the **white triangle** left until its Input value reads 128, then click **OK**.
9. Set the blending mode to Multiply, set the opacity to 50%, then compare your artwork to Figure 57.

Position the title

1. Open Title.psd.
2. Target the **Title layer**, select all, copy, then close the file.
3. In the Black Knight Poster file, show and target the **Billing layer**.
4. Paste, then name the new layer **Title**.
5. Press **[Ctrl][T]** (Win) or [⌘]**[T]** (Mac) to scale the image.
6. Type **503** in the X text box, press **[Tab]**, type **1056** in the Y text box, then press **[Tab]**.
7. Click the **Move Tool**, click **Apply**, compare your screen to Figure 58, then save.

LESSON 8

FINISH Artwork

What You'll Do

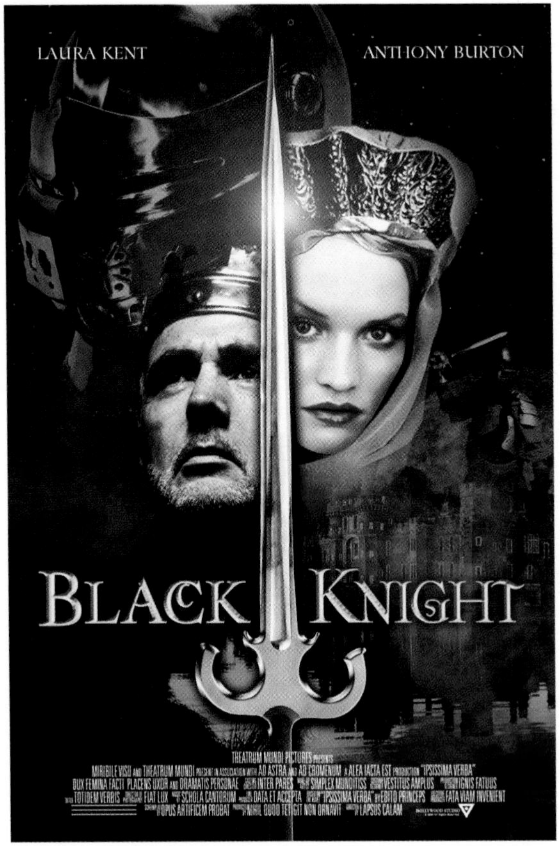

Finish artwork may sound like, *Get it done.* But in the design world, *finish* is used the way a carpenter would apply a finish to a table. Finishing artwork is the final design stage of a project.

In a way, finishing is everything, and everything leads up to finishing. It is the point at which you must distill your work into one cohesive piece of art in which all components are fully integrated and working together.

FIGURE 59
Scaling and repositioning the castle, small knight, and moon

Reposition elements

1. Assess the poster in terms of layout—the position of elements and how they relate to each other.

   Overall, the poster is working well. However, there are issues that need to be addressed. First and foremost, the queen is covering the castle and is in conflict with the small knight. Overall, the poster is a bit top-heavy. I don't like the moon—I'm feeling that it makes the top half of the poster crowded and congested.

2. Target the **Castle Group layer**, press and hold [⌘] **[Shift]**, then click the **Small Knight Group** and **Moon Group layer groups**.

   The three groups should all be targeted.

3. Press **[Ctrl][T]** (Win) or [⌘]**[T]** (Mac).
4. Type **766** in the X text box, press **[Tab]**, type **1197** in the Y text box, press **[Tab]**, type **92** in the W text box, press **[Tab]**, type **92** in the H text box, then press **[Tab]**.
5. Click the **Move Tool**, click **Apply**, then compare your screen to Figure 59.

(continued)

6. Target the **Royals layer group**, press and hold **[Shift]**, then press ↓ three times.

   The royals are moved down 30 pixels.

7. Compare your artwork to Figure 60.

   The last two steps shifts the focus more toward the vertical center of the poster. It also creates a much-needed relationship between the king and the title. However, I feel like the moon is still making the right side feel very crowded

8. Target the **Moon Group layer**, reduce its opacity to 60%, then compare your canvas to Figure 61.

   With the moon's opacity reduced, the entire top half of the poster feels less crowded. The royals are now the only bright characters in the piece, which seems right, and the small knight is so much more creepy now that he appears to be emerging from the shadows.

9. Save your work.

FIGURE 60
Repositioning the royals

FIGURE 61
Reducing the opacity of the moon

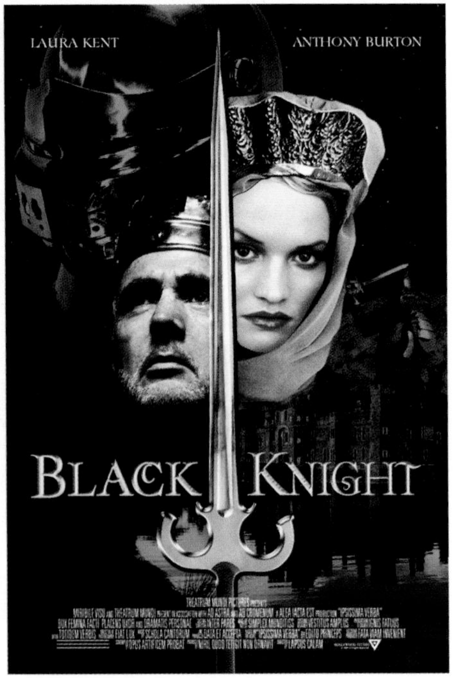

FIGURE 62
Applying an outer glow effect to the sword

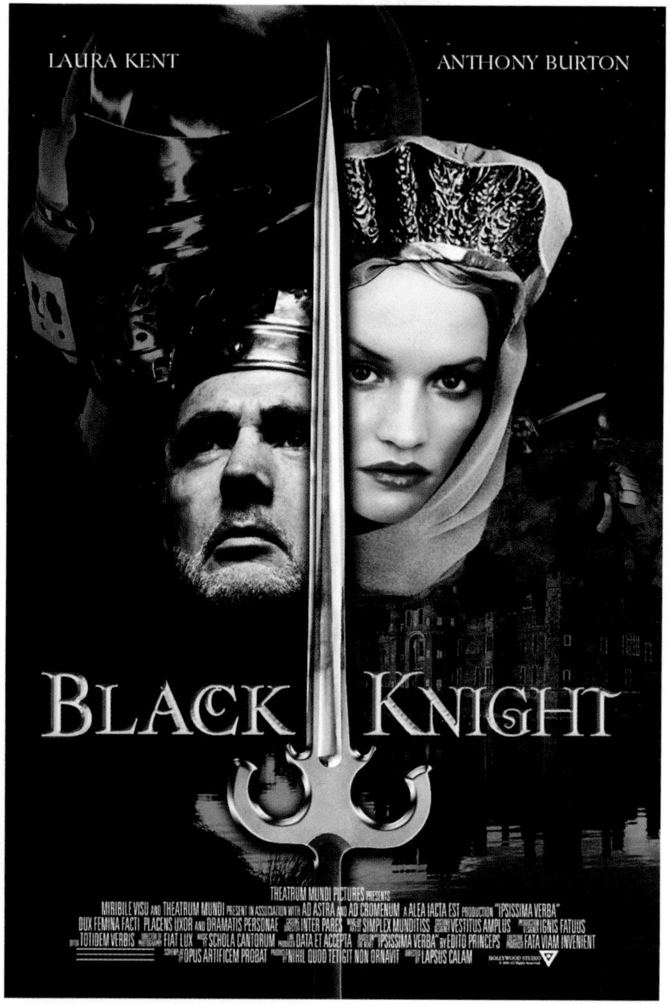

Use shadows to increase depth

1. Expand the Sword Group layer.
2. Double-click the **Bevel and Emboss effect** to open the Layer Style dialog box.
3. In the Styles list on the left, click **Outer Glow**.
4. Click the **Set color of glow button** to open the Color Picker.
5. Type **0** in the R, G, and B text boxes, then click **OK**.
6. Change the blending mode to Multiply.
7. Change the Spread value to 8, change the Size value to 24, click **OK**, then compare your artwork to Figure 62.
8. Press and hold **[Alt]** (Win) or **[option]** (Mac), then drag the **Outer Glow effect** up to the Title layer so that the title has the same effect.

(continued)

9. Compare your artwork to Figure 63.

10. Save your work.

Mask a layer group

1. Assess the relationship between the queen's head scarf and the background.

   The queen's head scarf and crown both have a hard edge. Also, the queen could still be moved down a bit to integrate better with the king and the castle.

2. Target the **Queen layer**, move it down 20 pixels, target the **Royals layer group**, then add a layer mask.

3. Paint with a large soft brush and a low opacity to fade the queen's blue scarf, so that your artwork resembles Figure 64.

   Applying the mask to the Royals layer group rather than to the mask on the Queen layer is a strategic move: with this method, the change to the scarf could be easily removed or modified and it is separate from the mask on the Queen layer.

   > **TIP** Feel free to mask the queen's pink scarf so that it too fades into the background. Be sure that none of your moves accidentally fade the king's face.

4. Save your work.

(continued)

FIGURE 63
Applying an outer glow effect to the title

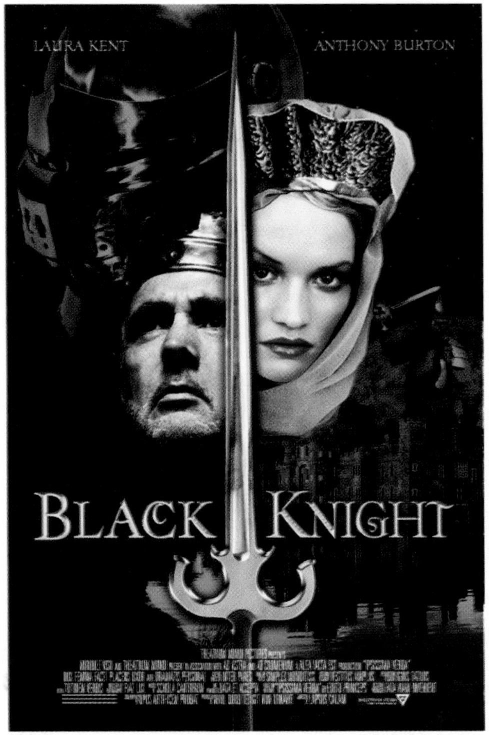

FIGURE 64
Masking the scarf by masking the layer group

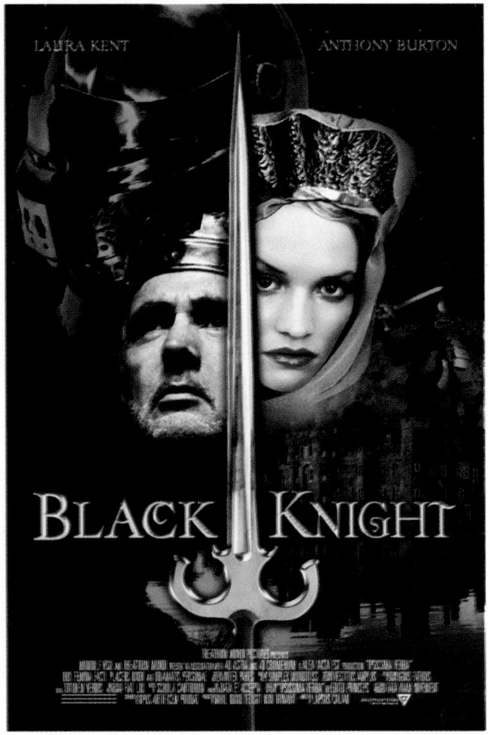

FIGURE 65
Lens Flare dialog box

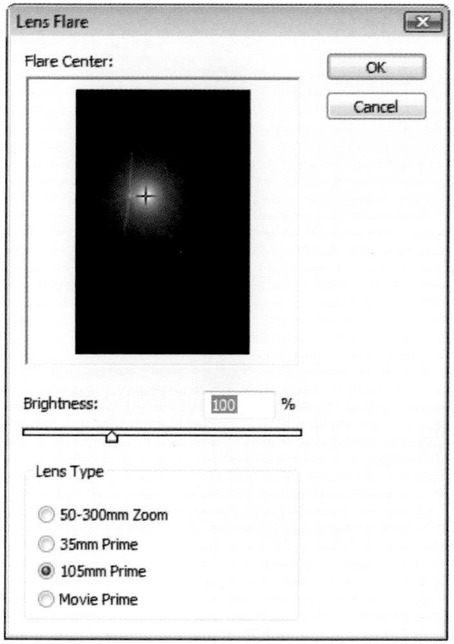

FIGURE 66
Positioning the lens flare

Add a lens flare effect

1. Hide the Billing and Title layers.
2. Target the **Sword Group layer**, verify that it is compressed, then click the **Create a new layer button** on the Layers palette.
3. Name the new layer **Lens Flare**, then fill the layer with the black foreground color.
4. Click **Filter** on the menu bar, point to **Render**, then click **Lens Flare**.
5. Click **105mm Prime**, as shown in Figure 65.
6. Click **OK**.
7. Click **Layer** on the menu bar, point to **New Adjustment Layer**, then click **Levels**.
8. Type **Screen Flare** in the Name text box, click the **Use Previous Layer to Create Clipping Mask check box**, then click **OK**.
9. Drag the **black triangle** to the right until the first input value reads 100, then click **OK**.
10. Change the blending mode to Screen, then change the Opacity of the layer to 90.
11. Click the **Move Tool**, then position the flare as shown in Figure 66.

Integrate the entire concept

1. Show the Billing layer and the Title layer.
2. Open Smoke.psd.

   Smoke.psd is a photograph that I shot with my own camera. I lit a cigar and positioned it against a large piece of black foam core. I then shined a bright spotlight on the setting to illuminate the smoke.
3. Select all, copy, then close Smoke.psd.
4. Target the **Title layer**.
5. Paste, then name the new layer **Smoke**.
6. Press **[Ctrl][T]** (Win) or ⌘**[T]** (Mac).
7. Type **600** in the X text box, press **[Tab]**, type **752** in the Y text box, press **[Tab]**, type **53** in the W text box, press **[Tab]**, type **53** in the H text box, then press **[Tab]**.
8. Click the **Move Tool**, then click **Apply**.
9. Change the blending mode to Screen, then compare your artwork to Figure 67.

   With the Screen blending mode, the black areas become invisible. This is why I shot the smoke against the black background: I knew I could remove the black background and show only the smoke.

(continued)

FIGURE 67
Screening the smoke

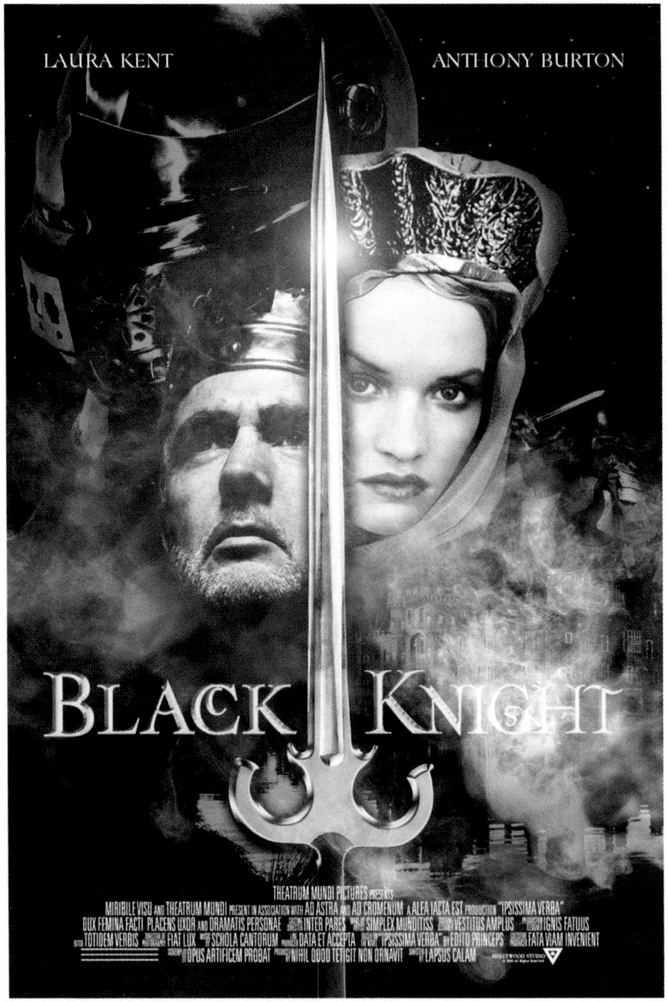

FIGURE 68
The final poster

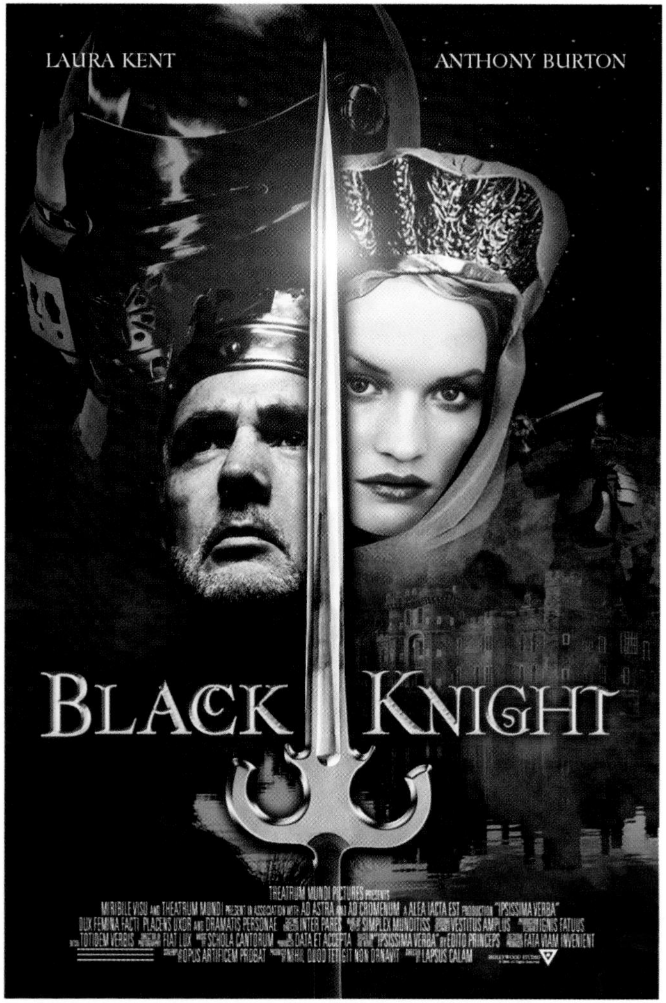

10. Drag the **Smoke layer** down below the Colorize Background layer in the Layers palette.
11. Change the opacity to 60%.
12. Reduce the opacity of the Outer Glow on the Title layer to 50%
13. Use a layer mask to mask out the Lens Flare layer anywhere that it overlaps the moon and the small knight.
14. Compare your screen to Figure 68.
15. Save your work.
16. Close the Black Knight Poster document.

PROJECT BUILDER 1

1. Open AP 5-2.psd, then save it as **Project Builder 1**.
2. Hide the All Type group.
3. Duplicate the Background layer, then rename it **High Pass 3**.
4. Click Filter on the menu bar, point to Other, then click High Pass.
5. Drag the Radius slider to 3, then note the preview. (*Hint*: The High Pass filter converts all the pixels to a neutral gray, then finds high-contrast areas of the image—"edges" where dark and light pixels meet.)
6. Drag the Radius slider to 10, then note the Preview. (*Hint*: The greater the amount, the more the high-contrast edges show through the gray.)
7. Drag the slider back to 3, then click OK.
8. Change the blending mode on the High Pass 3 layer to Overlay.
9. Toggle the layer on and off to see the effect. (*Hint*: The image is sharpened overall.)
10. Change the blending mode to Soft Light.
11. Change the blending mode to Linear Light.
12. Change the blending mode back to Overlay, then add a layer mask.
13. Use the layer mask to reduce the effect in areas where it might be a bit harsh, such as the king's crown, the queen's headpiece, and the king's face.
14. Show the All Type layer group.
15. Compare your results to Figure 69.
16. Save your work, then close Project Builder 1.

FIGURE 69
Completed Project Builder 1

PROJECT BUILDER 2

1. Open AP 5-3.psd, then save it as **Project Builder 2**.
2. Target the High Pass 3 layer.
3. Press and hold [Alt] (Win) or [option] (Mac), then click the Create a new layer button on the Layers palette.
4. Type **Noise 7** in the Name text box.
5. Click the Mode list arrow, then click Overlay.
6. Click to activate Fill with Overlay-neutral color (50% gray), then click OK.
7. Click the Filter menu, point to Noise, then click Add Noise.
8. Set the Amount to 7, the Distribution to Gaussian, then click to activate Monochromatic.
9. Click OK.
10. Toggle the Noise 7 layer off and on to see the noise effect.
11. Compare your screen to Figure 70.
12. Save your work, the close Project Builder 2.

FIGURE 70
Completed Project Builder 2

LAURA KENT
ANTHONY BURTON
BLACK KNIGHT

chapter

6

INVESTIGATING PRODUCTION

Tricks and Techniques

1. Explore issues with resolution.
2. Create a high-resolution mechanical for a billboard.
3. Create black and white from color.
4. Use the Unsharp Mask filter to sharpen edges.
5. Apply grain effects.
6. Automate workflow.

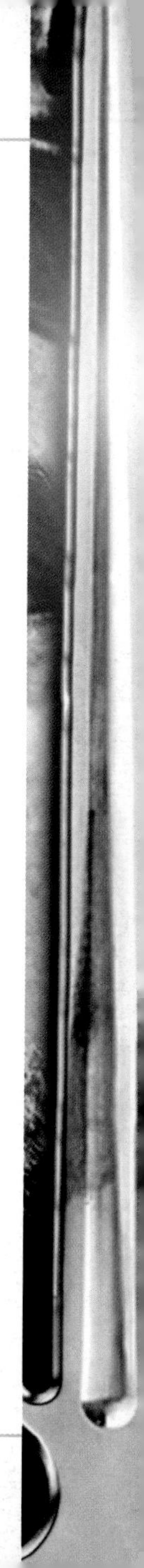

LESSON 1

EXPLORE ISSUES with Resolution

What You'll Do

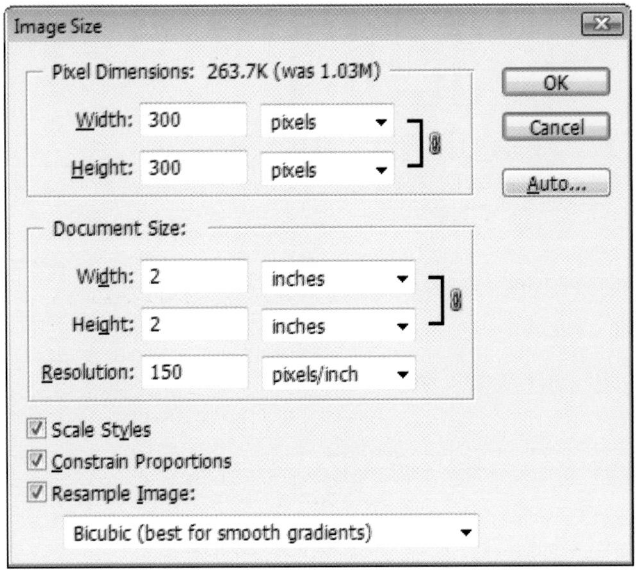

All digital images are bitmap images. All bitmap graphics are composed of pixels. The word **pixel** is derived from the words picture and element—pixel. You can think of a **bitmap image** as being a grid of pixels—thousands of them.

Resolution is a term that refers to the number of pixels per inch (ppi) in a digital image. For example, if you had a 1" × 1" Photoshop file with a resolution of 100 pixels per inch, that file would contain a total of 10,000 pixels (100 pixels width × 100 pixels height = 10,000 pixels).

High-resolution files have more pixels. Pixels must be small to create the representation of a photographic image—you want to see the image, not the pixels. 300 ppi is considered a high resolution for any file that will be professionally printed. For your home desktop printer, 150 ppi is generally enough resolution for a good-looking print. For Web and other "on screen" graphics, the standard resolution is low—just 72 ppi. Think about how much smaller the pixels are in a 300 ppi file than in a 72 ppi file: they're less than 1/4 the size!

Image size refers to the dimensions of the Photoshop file. Image size is not dependent on resolution; in other words, you could create two 3" × 5" files, one at 72 ppi and the other at 300 ppi. They'd have the same image size, but different resolutions.

Image size is, however, related to resolution, because anytime you modify a file's image size, that will have a direct affect on its resolution. And because resolution is so closely associated with image quality, resizing an image can affect quality.

This lesson is a quick refresher course in image resolution and the many issues and considerations involved when specifying resolution and resizing an image.

FIGURE 1
Decreasing resolution without resampling

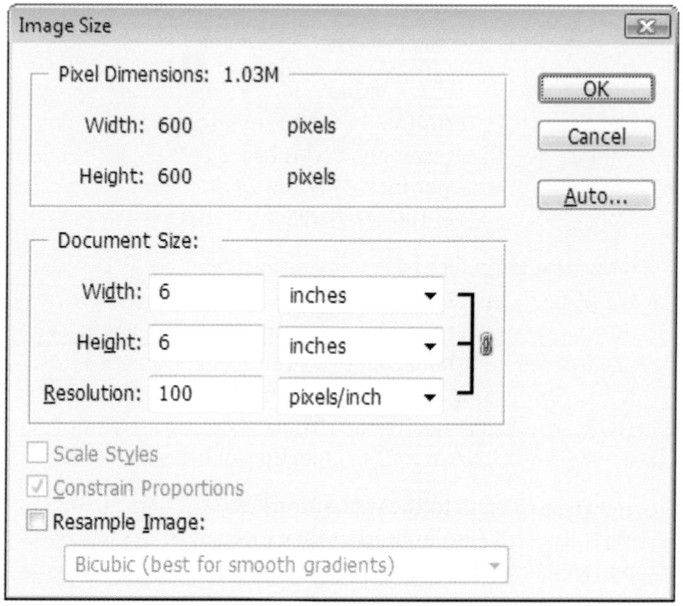

Understand and manipulate resolution

1. Open AP 6-1.psd, then save it as **Freckles Resize**.
2. Click **Image** on the menu bar, then click **Image Size**.

   The Document Size section specifies that this is a 2" x 2" file with a resolution of 300 ppi—thus making this a high-resolution file. The Pixel Dimensions section specifies that the full width of the file is 600 pixels (300 ppi x 2") and the height is 600 pixels. Thus, this image is composed of exactly 360,000 pixels.
3. Click the **Resample Image check box** to remove the check mark.

   The Resample Image check box is perhaps the most important option in this dialog box. When Resample Image is not checked, the total number of pixels in the image must remain the same. In other words, no matter how you resize the image or change the resolution, no pixels can be added or discarded.
4. Double-click the **Resolution text box**, type **100**, press **[Tab]**, then note the changes in the Width and Height values.

   As shown in Figure 1, the width and height of the file changes to 6". Because the total number of pixels cannot change, when the number of pixels per inch is reduced to 100, the file must enlarge to six inches width and height to accommodate all the pixels. In other words, no pixels were added or discarded with the change in resolution—they were simply redistributed.

(continued)

5. Press and hold **[Alt]** (Win) or **[option]** (Mac) so that the Cancel button changes to the Reset button, then click the **Reset button**.

   The Image Size dialog box returns to its original values and the Resample Image check box is once again checked.

6. Change the resolution from 300 to 150, press **[Tab]**, then note the changes to the Width and Height values and to the pixel dimensions.

   As shown in Figure 2, the resolution is reduced to 150 ppi, but the width and height remain at 2". The pixel dimensions show that the full width of the file is 300 pixels (150 ppi x 2") and the full height is 300 pixels. This means that, if you click OK, the total number of pixels will be 90,000. Think about this: 75% of the original 360,000 pixels will be discarded because of the reduction in resolution from 300 to 150 ppi.

7. Click **OK**.

   Though the image doesn't look much different on your screen, 75% of its original data has been discarded.

8. Click **File** on the menu bar, then click **Revert**.

   TIP The Revert command returns a file to the condition it was in when opened or last saved.

FIGURE 2
Decreasing resolution with resampling

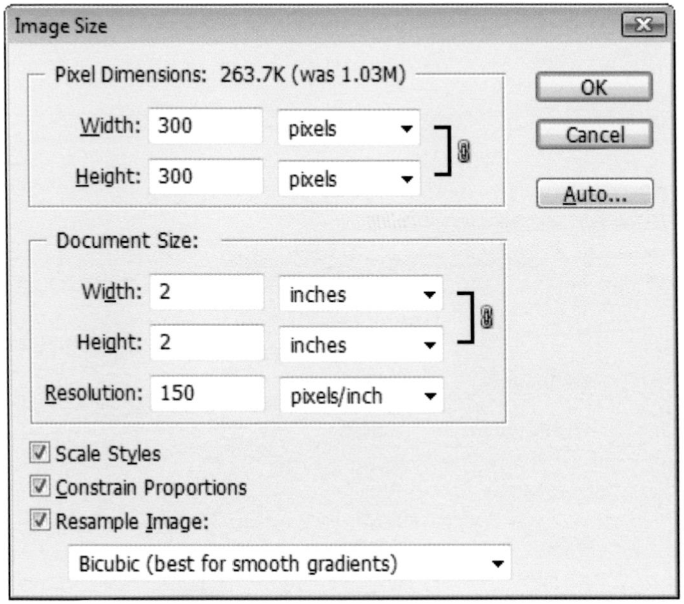

AUTHOR'S *note*

Don't confuse the terms image size and file size. Image size refers to the physical dimensions of the image—its width and height. So if you say an image is 8" × 10", that's its image size. File size refers to how big the file is in computer memory—how much memory it takes up on your computer. If an image is 42 MB (megabytes), that's its file size. Remember that every pixel in an image increases the file size of the image. To put it differently, the greater the number of pixels, the greater the file size. Therefore, resolution and image size both affect file size. The greater the resolution—the more pixels per inch—the greater the file size. The greater the image size—the more inches of pixels—the greater the file size. If you were printing an 8" × 10" color poster, your file would contain more than 7 million pixels and your file size would be somewhere close to 27 MB!

FIGURE 3

Increasing image size and resampling pixels

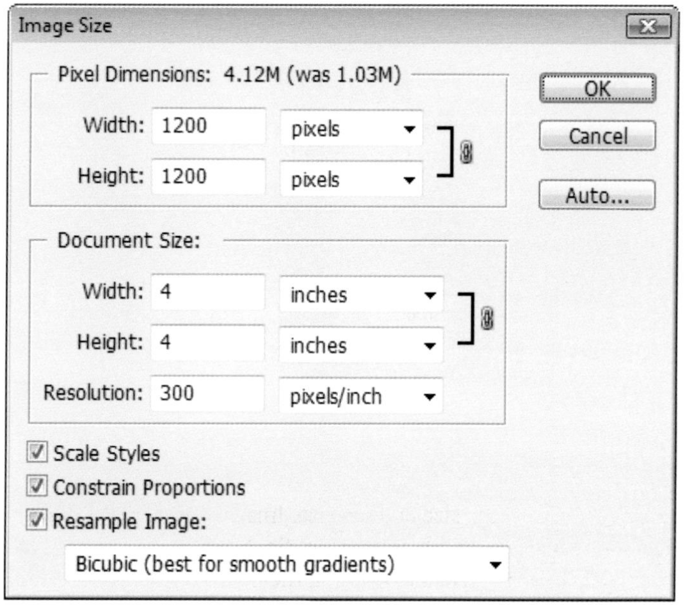

Manipulate image size

1. Open the Image Size dialog box.
2. Note that the Resample Image check box is checked by default.

   When the Resample Image check box is checked, pixels can be added or discarded when you resize an image. This file is 2" x 2" and we need it to be 4" x 4".
3. Type **4** in the Width text box, then compare your dialog box to Figure 3.

   TIP The Height value changes automatically because the Constrain Proportions check box is checked.

   In order to be used in a color magazine at the specified size of 4" x 4", the file must be 300 ppi at that size. Photoshop is able to scale the image to that size and resolution. However, note the pixel dimensions. Because we've doubled the size of the original, the new size now must contain 1,440,000 pixels to maintain a resolution of 300 pixels per inch. The supplied image was scanned at 360,000 total pixels. Where did all the new pixels come from? If you click OK, Photoshop will create them from the existing pixels using a process called interpolation.
4. Click **OK**, double-click the **Zoom Tool** to view the image at 100%, then evaluate the enlargement in terms of image quality.

   TIP When inspecting an image for quality, you must be viewing at 100% or larger.

(continued)

Photoshop has done a good job enlarging the image and overall it still looks good. However, as a high-resolution image for quality print reproduction, this image is unacceptable because it is composed of 75% interpolated data. In other words, 75% percent of the pixels are not "real" samples scanned from the original photo or captured in a digital camera. In a real world situation, you would contact the client to let them know that the image size and resolution of the file delivered was too small to be used at 4" x 4". They might tell you to go ahead and "res it up"—use the enlarged file with interpolated data—but that's a choice for which they should be responsible.

5. Revert the file, then open the Image Size dialog box, and ensure that Resample Image is checked.

   Next we will resize the file so that it could be used on a Web site.

6. Change the Width and Height values to **4**, change the resolution to **72**, then compare your dialog box to Figure 4.

   All you need to do is look at the before-and-after file sizes above the Pixel Dimensions section to see that the new size requires fewer pixels than the original size. At the new specifications, the file size will be reduced from 1.03MB to 243K. Even though we doubled the image size from 2" x 2" to 4" x 4", the reduction in resolution from 300 ppi to 72 ppi resulted in the need for fewer than 25% of the number of original pixels.

(continued)

FIGURE 4
Decreasing image size and resampling pixels

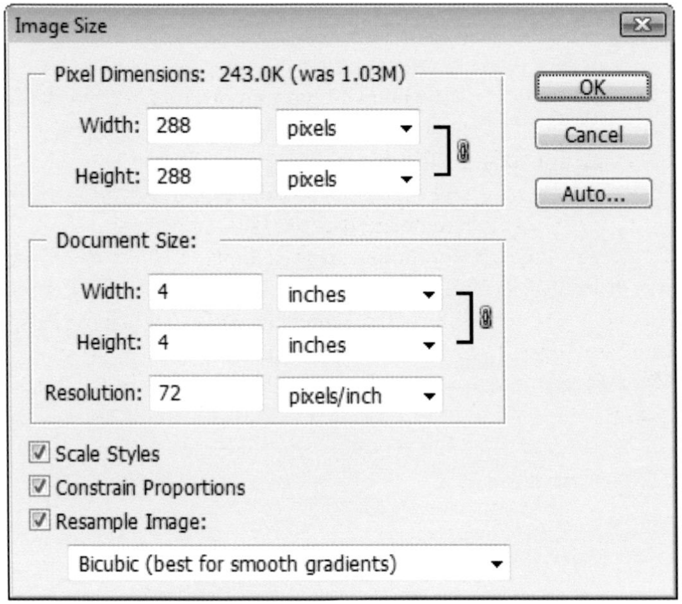

AUTHOR'S *note*

What is a "high-res" file? Generally speaking, a "high-res," or high-resolution, file pertains only to the world of printing. Web graphics and any other graphics for on-screen display are generally 72 ppi. So when you think of "high-res," think of images—color or black and white—printing at a high quality, like in a magazine or a poster. This type of reproduction requires the industry standard of 300 pixels per inch.

AUTHOR'S *note*

Inevitably, there will come a time when you have no other choice but to increase the resolution or the image size of a file and live with the results. When this happens, it's best to use the default "Bicubic (best for smooth gradients)" Resize Sample method in the Image Size dialog box. Also, remember that since Photoshop is running complex algorithms to create the new data, don't make it more complicated by enlarging by odd numbers. For example, if you had a 3" square image that needs to print at 5.75" square, double the image size to 6" square. It's much easier for Photoshop to interpolate data with such a simple doubling of the existing image size; this will result in a higher-quality interpolation and a better result for your enlarged image. Remember though, it's always better to avoid using interpolated data.

7. Click **OK**, then evaluate the enlargement in terms of image quality.

   Viewed at 100%, the image looks great on screen, which is our goal, given that it will be used on a Web site. Even though Photoshop has discarded more than 75% of the original number of pixels, the reduced image contains only original data and no interpolated data.

   TIP Reducing an image's image size or resolution does not involve the creation of interpolated data and is therefore acceptable in terms of image quality.

8. Save your work, then close the document.

LESSON 2

CREATE A HIGH-RESOLUTION
Mechanical for a Billboard

What You'll Do

Sizing a file and determining resolution can become very challenging very quickly when you are working with large scale output like posters, billboards, bus wraps, and wallscapes. A simple movie poster, for example, is 27" × 40". If you were creating artwork for a movie poster in Photoshop, at what physical size would you build the file, and at what resolution? If you built it at 27" × 40" at 300 ppi, the file size would be 278 megabytes—without layers!

This lesson is based on a hardcore production project: building the mechanical for a 14' × 48' billboard. Use this exercise as an opportunity to learn industry-standard rules for determining resolution for large-scale output and for building a file with that all-important production element: a bleed. Finally, don't miss Project Builder 2, where you'll learn how to create an extension for the billboard.

FIGURE 5

Dimensions and resolution of the composite

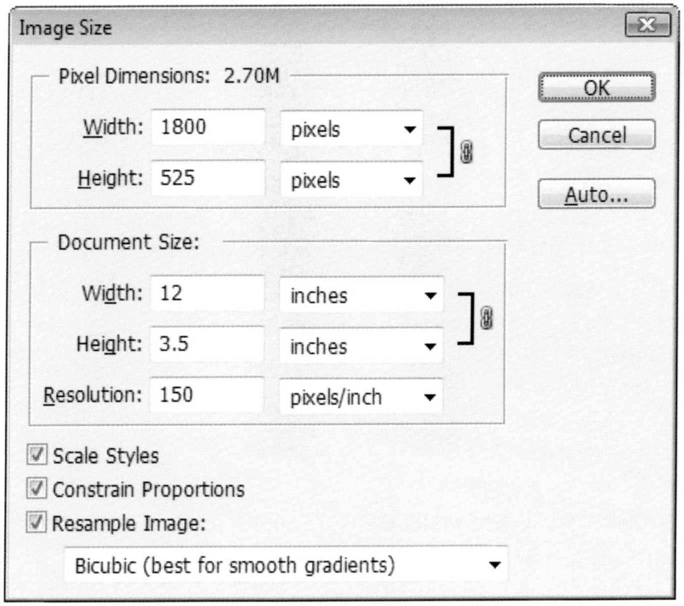

Resize a comp for a high-resolution billboard mechanical

1. Open AP 6-2.psd, then save it as **48x14 Billboard**.

   The file is a designer's low-res comp file for a 48' x 14' billboard based on an original poster.

   TIP When naming files for outdoor media—billboards, wallscapes, etc.—the dimensions of the file precede the file name. 48' x 14' is a standard and common billboard size: 48-feet width by 14-feet height.

2. Click **Image** on the menu bar, click **Image Size**, then compare your Image Size dialog box to Figure 5.

   This file is not built to the full size of the output. A 48-foot by 14-foot billboard would be 576 inches by 168 inches. This file is 12 inches by 3.5 inches. It must be resized to be output as a high-resolution file for a 48' x 14' billboard.

3. Verify that the Scale Styles, Constrain Proportions, and Resample Image check boxes are all checked and that Bicubic (best for smooth gradients) is chosen for the interpolation method.

   The Scale Styles option is critical. Think of all the styles applied in this artwork—drop shadows, outer glows, bevels and embosses, etc. If you were to double the image size, you would want the settings for those styles to double as well so that they would have the same relationship to the resized artwork. The Scale Styles option scales all styles in proportion to the artwork.

(continued)

4. Change the Width value to **48**, change the resolution value to **300**, then compare your Image Size dialog box to Figure 6.

   The first basic rule for determining resolution for large-scale media is the 1 foot = 1 inch at 300 ppi rule. As shown in Figure 6, the Image Size dialog box now shows just that: A 48" x 14" document at 300 ppi for a 48' x 14' output.

5. Note the Pixel Dimensions value at the top of the dialog box.

   At this new size, the file would be 173 megabytes—with just one layer! Given that this file has nearly fifty layers—all of which increase the file size—if we were to click OK, the layered file would be approximately 1.5 gigabytes. That is a very large file size for most computers to work with effectively. Also, that would mean that the images—the king and queen, for example—would be 14 feet tall. The high-res image of the king certainly would not have been captured at 14 feet tall and would need to be scaled up to be used at this size. Therefore, it's pointless to build the file at such a large size.

6. Note the number of pixels in the Width text box of the Pixel Dimensions section.

   The second rule for determining resolution for large-scale files is the 6000-pixels rule. This means that for all large-scale sizes—48-foot wide billboards or 100-foot tall wallscapes—6000 pixels is the target for the number of pixels in the mechanical, either width or height. In other words, anything over 6000 pixels is overkill. At its present dimensions and resolution, the billboard file would have 14,400 pixels in its width, more than double the 6000 pixel target.

(continued)

FIGURE 6

Dimensions and resolution using the 1-foot = 1-inch @ 300 ppi rule

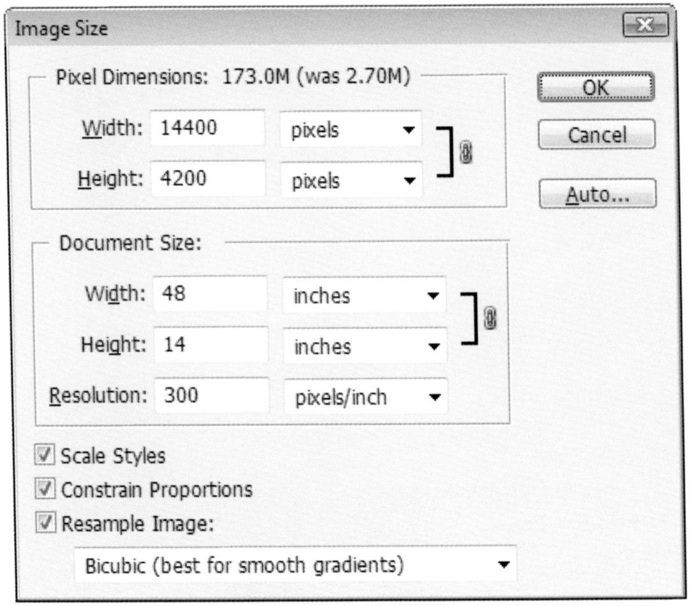

FIGURE 7
Dimensions and resolution using the 6000 pixels rule

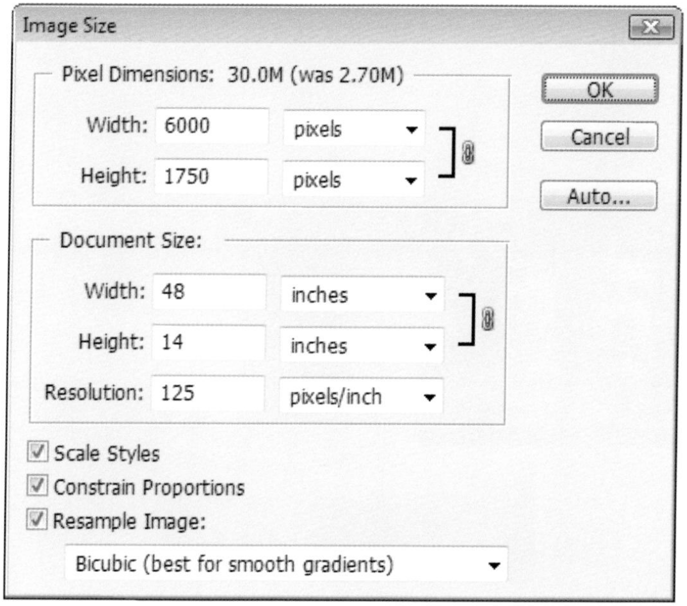

FIGURE 8
Viewing the entire canvas

7. Reduce the resolution to **125**, then compare your dialog box to Figure 7.

   At 125 pixels per inch, the 48-inch wide document is 6000 pixels wide. This is high-resolution for the 48' x 14' billboard mechanical.

8. Click **OK**.

   The new layered file is approximately 322 megabytes.

9. Save your work.

Use the Reveal All command

1. Zoom down so that you can see the entire canvas, as shown in Figure 8.

   The comp file was built at 12" x 3.5", which we scaled up to the trim size of 48" x 14". This is a big problem, because the comp file at 12" x 3.5" was built without a bleed. All four sides of the image should extend the trim by .25". It's important to understand that whatever images are in the file are visible only where they intersect the canvas. In other words, there are often image components outside of the canvas that you cannot see.

2. Open the file named 20x3.tif, select all, copy, then close the file.

   The file is 20 inches tall, which is 6 inches taller than the height of the billboard mechanical.

3. Target the **Names layer** in the Layers palette, then paste.

   The file is pasted at the center of the billboard file.

(continued)

4. Click **Image** on the menu bar, click **Reveal All**, then compare your screen to Figure 9.

   The Reveal All command reveals the areas of the 20x3.tif artwork that were pasted off of the canvas. It also reveals all of the other artwork in the comp that was pasted outside of the canvas dimensions. It's important to understand that all of this artwork—even though not visible—nevertheless is taking up memory. The file size of the image is based on the reveal all dimensions necessary to show all of the artwork.

   TIP It's our hope that some of this "extra" artwork will be usable for the bleed for the mechanical.

5. Undo, delete the new layer with the 20x3.tif artwork, then save your work.

Create a bleed for a high-resolution mechanical

1. Verify that the Paths palette is visible.
2. Select all on the canvas, click the **Paths palette list arrow**, then click **Make Work Path**.
3. Type **.5** in the Make Work Path dialog box, then click **OK**.

   A new path named *Work Path* is added to the Paths palette.
4. Double-click ***Work Path***, then name it **TRIM 48" x 14"**.

   The new path is the size of the trim of the document.
5. Target the **Background layer** in the Layers palette.

(continued)

FIGURE 9
Viewing all of the artwork in the file with the Reveal All command

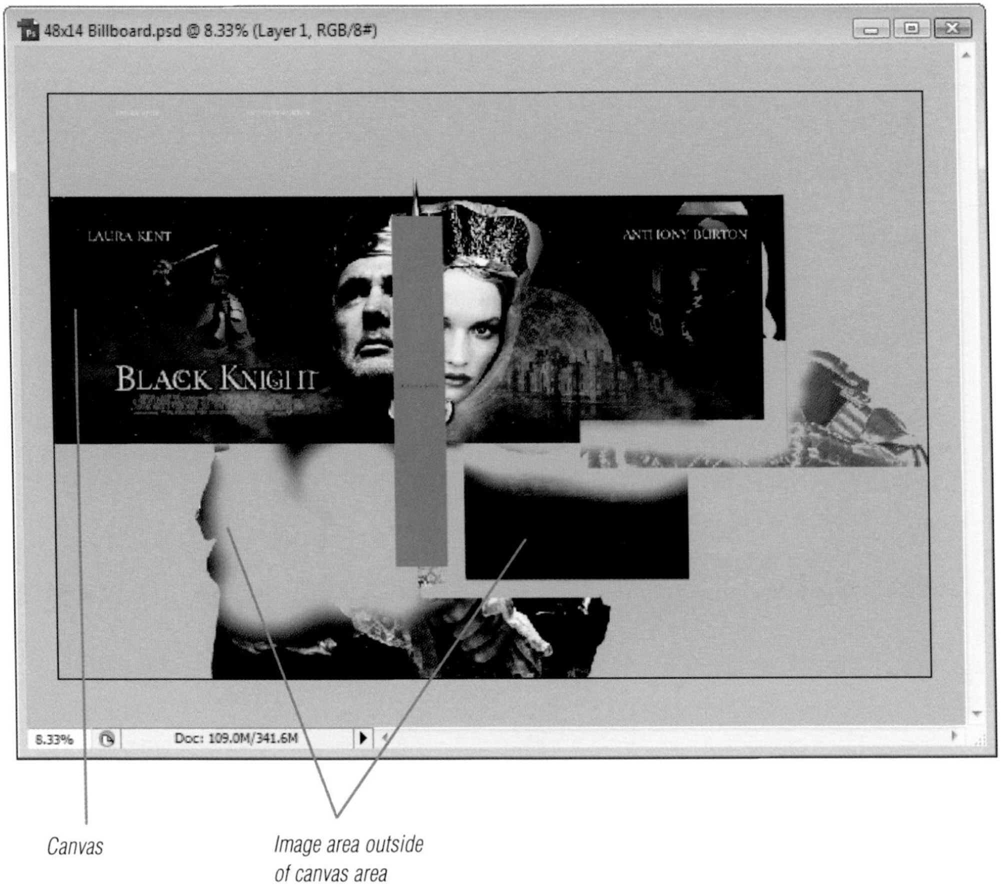

FIGURE 10
Canvas Size dialog box

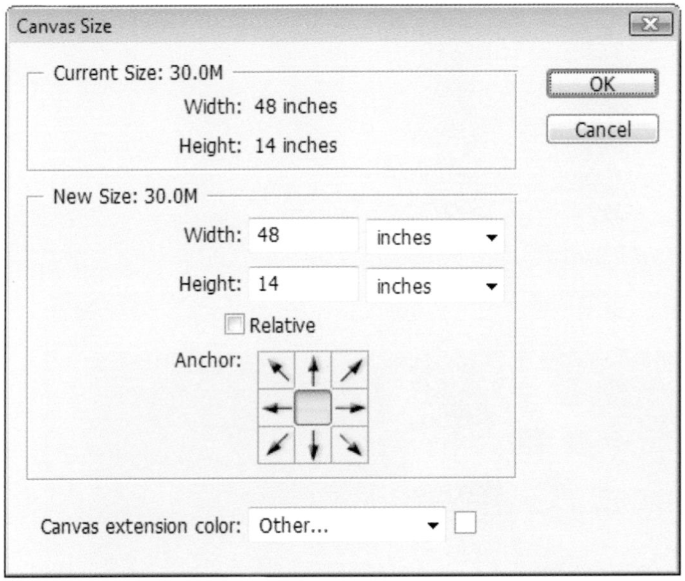

FIGURE 11
Billboard mechanical with the increased canvas size

6. Click **Image** on the menu bar, click **Canvas Size**, then compare your dialog box to Figure 10.

   A .25" bleed needs to be added to all four sides of the canvas.

7. Click the **Canvas extension color list arrow**, then click **Black**.
8. Type **48.5** in the Width text box, type **14.5** in the Height text box, click **OK**, then compare your canvas to Figure 11.

   The path identifies the trim and the area outside of the path as the bleed area. We got very lucky in that there was enough image outside of the canvas to fill the bleed area. Had there not been, we would be facing the major challenge of rebuilding the entire document with imagery in the bleed area. The solution to this potential problem should have been implemented at the beginning of the process: The designer should have created the comp at a larger size to include the necessary bleed elements.

9. Target the **Names layer** in the Layers palette.
10. Click the **Path Selection Tool**, then click the path on the canvas to select it.
11. Click **Layer** on the menu bar, point to **New Fill Layer**, then click **Solid Color**.
12. Type **Bleed** in the Name text box, then click **OK**.
13. Type **128** in the R, G, and B text boxes, then click **OK**.

(continued)

14. Click the **path** with the Path Selection Tool to select it.

15. Click the **Subtract from shape area (–) button** on the Options bar.

16. In the Paths palette, click below the listed paths to deactivate the path, then compare your canvas to Figure 12.

    The bleed area is masked with a shape layer, defined by the path. Masking out the bleed area allows you to view the artwork at the trim size—the way it will appear on the real billboard—without the bleed elements.

17. Select all, click **Image** on the menu bar, click **Crop**, then deselect.

    The image is cropped to the bleed size. All of the unnecessary artwork that we viewed with the Reveal All command is discarded, and the file size is reduced accordingly.

18. Save your work.

Replace low-resolution images with high-resolution images

1. Identify which images need to be replaced with high-resolution images.

   The comp was built at a very low resolution. We enlarged that comp 400% to be a high-resolution sized mechanical. The images that need to be replaced include:

   - King
   - Queen
   - Sword

(continued)

FIGURE 12
Billboard mechanical with the bleed area masked

FIGURE 13
Viewing the result of the Invert/Align

- Big Knight
- Small Knight
- Title Treatment
- Castle
- Moon

Because the image will be used on a billboard, it's not necessary to replace the stars background with a high resolution version—the change wouldn't be noticeable. For the same reason, it's not necessary to replace the smoke artwork. It's not necessary to replace the billing block or the stars' names, as those will be replaced by actual type in the final mechanical.

2. Open AP 6-3.psd, then save it as **Invert Align**.
3. Verify that your Info palette is showing, then duplicate the Background layer.
4. Target the **Background layer**, then press **[Ctrl][I]**(Win) or ⌘ **[I]**(Mac) to invert the layer.
5. Target the **Background copy layer**, set its opacity to 50%, then compare your result to Figure 13.

   As shown in the figure, the entire image becomes gray. If you sample anywhere in the image, you'll see that the RGB values in the Info palette are all the same—either all 127 or all 128.
6. Save your work, then close Invert Align.psd.

(continued)

That's the end of this exercise. Its purpose was only for you to see the Invert/Align procedure performed on a simple image. You will now apply the same procedure to the complex billboard file.

7. Expand the Royals layer group, then target the **King layer** in the 48x14 Billboard.psd file.
8. Open King Hi-Res.psd, then view the two documents side by side.

   TIP You can tile the two documents vertically by clicking Window on the menu bar, pointing to Arrange, and then clicking Tile Vertically.

9. Verify that the King Hi-Res layer is targeted, click the **Move Tool**, then drag and drop the artwork into the 48x14 Billboard.psd file.

   The artwork is positioned on a new layer, named King High-Res, above the King layer.

10. Close the King Hi-Res.psd file.
11. Move the King Hi-Res artwork so that it is positioned over the King artwork.

    The King Hi-Res artwork is smaller than the scaled-up King artwork. This is often the case when working on large-scale projects: Even high-res files aren't large enough for the high-res mechanical.

12. Target the **King layer**, click the **Create new fill or adjustment layer button** on the Layers palette, then click **Invert**.

    A new Invert adjustment layer appears above the King layer and the King artwork is inverted. Because the Royals layer group is set to Normal, the Invert adjustment layer doesn't affect any other artwork.

(continued)

AUTHOR'S *note*

Whenever you duplicate a layer, then invert the bottom layer and set the opacity of the top layer to 50%, the composite result of the two layers will be an entirely gray image. If you run the numbers, it makes sense. To keep things simple, let's say you're working with a single-channel grayscale image. Let's say a pixel in the original image on the Background layer had a grayscale value of 150. When you duplicate the layer, you now have two identical pixels with the grayscale value of 150 on top of one another. When you invert the bottom of the two layers, the grayscale value of the pixel changes to 106 (256 – 150 = 106). You now have two overlapping pixels that, if added together, must equal 256. However, you can't see the inverted image because it is beneath the duplicated image above it. Then you set the opacity on the duplicated layer to 50%. Now ask yourself: How much of each of the two layers is visible? The answer is 50% of each. The top layer is set to 50% opacity, so by definition, only 50% of it is visible. Therefore, it only makes sense that the artwork on the layer beneath it is 50% visible. With that in mind, ask yourself: What do the two overlapping pixels now add up to? The answer is explained with the following equation:

$$(150 + 106) / 2 = 128.$$

The grayscale values of the two overlapping pixels add up to 256. Then, when divided by two, the result of their overlapping must be a grayscale value of 128, which is gray. This will be the result for all the overlapping pixels in an image. Thus, when you overlap duplicate images in this manner, the result must be a completely gray image.

FIGURE 14
Aligning the high-res king with the low-res king

13. Target the **King Hi-Res layer**, then reduce its opacity to 50%.
14. Click **Edit** on the menu bar, point to **Transform**, then click **Scale**.
15. Verify that the center point on the Reference point location icon on the Options bar is selected.
16. Type **125** in the Width and Height text boxes.
17. Type **2830** in the X text box, type **1641** in the Y text box, press **[Enter]**(Win) or **[return]**(Mac), click the **Move Tool**, click **Apply**, then compare your screen to Figure 14.
18. Set the opacity on the King Hi-Res layer to 100%, then delete the Invert adjustment layer.
19. Press and hold **[Alt]**(Win) or **[option]**(Mac), then drag the **layer mask** from the King layer to the King Hi-Res layer.

    An identical layer mask is added to the King Hi-Res layer.
20. Delete the King layer.

    In a real-world project, we would need to repeat this procedure on all the other photographic images in the layout.
21. Be sure to save your work at this point.

Convert a layered file from RGB to CMYK

1. Click **Image** on the menu bar, point to **Mode**, then click **CMYK Color**.

   A warning dialog box appears.

2. Click **OK**, then compare your artwork to Figure 15.

   As shown in the figure, converting a file from RGB to CMYK when it contains adjustment layers and layers with blending modes can't be done. The adjustment layers and blending modes cannot be translated correctly from one mode to another. In most cases, designers build their files in RGB Color mode. There are many more benefits of working in RGB Color mode, not the least of which is that more filters and third-party programs only work in RGB Color mode. However, this requires that, when the file is converted to CMYK Color, all adjustment layers and any layers with blending modes must be merged.

3. Undo your last step.

4. Target the **Colorize Background layer**.

   This layer is set to Multiply over all of the images beneath it. Therefore, it must be merged with all the layers beneath it.

5. Press **[Shift]**, then click the **Background layer** so that all the layers between the two are selected, as shown in Figure 16.

6. Click the **Layers palette list arrow**, then click **Merge Layers**.

(continued)

FIGURE 15
Viewing a bad CMYK conversion

Hard lines

FIGURE 16
Targeting layers to be merged

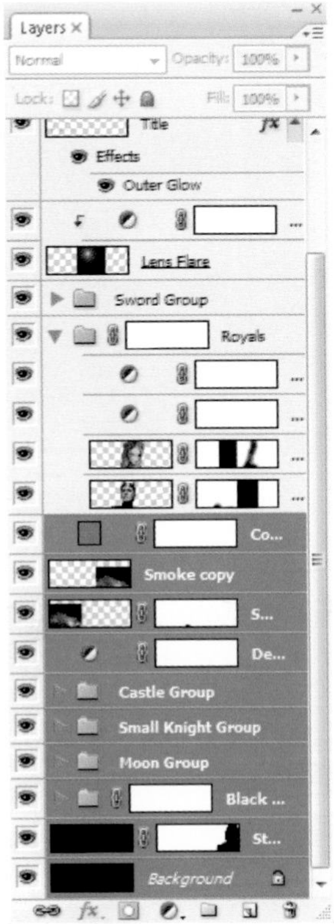

FIGURE 17
Targeting layers to be merged

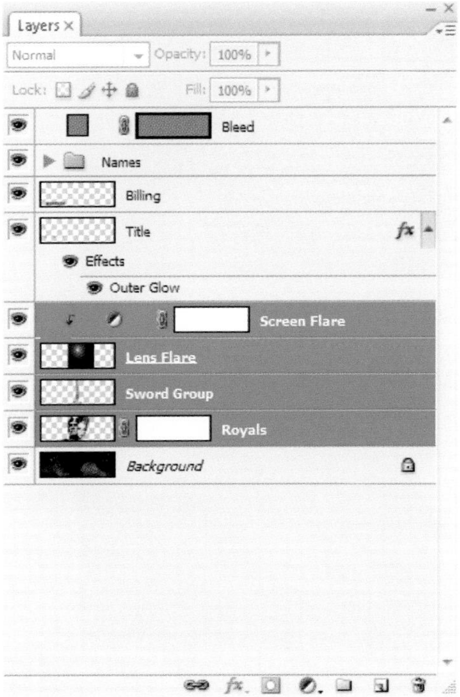

FIGURE 18
Identifying problems with the merged artwork

7. Target the **Royals layer group**.

   The Royals layer group is set to Normal, which means it doesn't need to be merged with the background. However, the group contains two adjustment layers and each has a blending mode applied to it.

8. Click the **Layers palette list arrow**, then click **Merge Group**.

   The two adjustment layers are merged with the two layers of artwork (the king and queen), but the resulting merged artwork is set to Normal.

9. Examine the contents of the Sword Group layer group.

   It contains a single adjustment layer which is clipped into a layer with effects applied. Effects are often applied with built-in blending modes.

10. Merge the **Sword Group layer group**.

11. Target the **Lens Flare layer**.

    The Lens Flare layer is set to Screen. Because the screened lens flare artwork affects the sword and the king and queen artwork, they all must be merged.

12. Target the layers shown in Figure 17.

13. Merge the targeted layers, then compare your result to Figure 18.

(continued)

As shown in the figure, because of the built-in relationships between the layers, the merge doesn't work. At this point, one solution would be to discard the Lens Flare layer, convert the file, then recreate the lens flare in CMYK Color mode. However, the Lens Flare filter is not available in CMYK Color mode. Rather than flatten all the artwork, we will convert the lens flare and see what we get.

14. Undo the merge.

    See the Author's note on this page.

15. Convert the file to CMYK Color mode, then compare your result to Figure 19.

    Everything worked well except the billing block and the lens flare. We don't care about the billing block, because it's "for position only" (FPO) and will be replaced in the output stage. However, the lens flare needs work.

16. Delete the Billing layer.

17. Add a clipped Levels adjustment layer to the Lens Flare layer, drag the **black triangle** in the Levels dialog box to **86**, then click **OK**.

    Compare your result to Figure 20. We have succeeded in converting the artwork to CMYK while maintaining the segregation of various art elements to separate layers.

18. Save your work.

FIGURE 19
Converting the file—with problems

FIGURE 20
Fixing the Lens Flare artwork

AUTHOR'S *note*

At this point, you might be wondering, why not just flatten the whole thing, save a CMYK copy, and keep the RGB file layered. That works, but the key is that you want to deliver a CMYK file to the printer or output service as editable as possible. When they output the file, they will want to tweak the color in the file based on the calibration of their output device. At that point, you would much prefer that they make those tweaks in a simplified, layered CMYK file rather than go back to your highly complex RGB file with all of its blending modes and adjustment layers. And once they'd made their tweaks, they'd need to convert the RGB file all over again. So in the case of this billboard, it's our goal to deliver a file with the background artwork all on one layer, the king and queen on their own layer, the sword on its own layer, and the lens flare above them all.

FIGURE 21

Viewing the artwork after applying the High Pass filter

Only "edges" are visible

Use the High Pass filter to sharpen artwork

1. Hide the Bleed layer, then target the **Names layer group**.
2. Select all, click **Edit** on the menu bar, then click **Copy Merged**.
3. Paste, then name the new layer **High Pass 3.0**.
4. Click **Filter** on the menu bar, point to **Other**, then click **High Pass**.
5. Type **3.0** in the Radius text box, click **OK**, then compare your canvas to Figure 21.

   The High Pass filter first grays out the entire image—it changes all pixels to 128. Then, as you increase the Radius value, it reveals edges in the image. **Edges** are defined as any place in the image where high contrast pixels abut. For example, the line where the queen's bright face meets the dark background would be an edge. At a radius of 3.0, that edge becomes visible within the grayed-out image.
6. Change the blending mode of the High Pass 3.0 layer to **Overlay**.
7. Zoom-in on the king's face, then hide and show the High Pass 3.0 layer.

   In Overlay mode, all gray pixels become invisible. Thus, the non-edge areas of the image that remained gray are not visible. The edges that were revealed are now being overlayed over the artwork. The result is that the edge areas of the image are exaggerated and the overall effect is that of a sharper image with greater detail.

(continued)

TIP You must view an image at a minimum of 100% to get a reliable representation of the sharpening effect.

8. Change the blending mode to **Soft Light**.

   All of the blending modes in the Overlay section make grays invisible, so all of them will work with the High Pass filter. The Soft Light blending mode produces a sharpening effect that is less intense than the Overlay blending mode.

9. Change the blending mode to **Linear Light**.

   Linear Light produces the most intense sharpening effect with high pass artwork. It is seldom used.

10. Change the blending mode back to **Overlay**, then save your work.

Add noise to high resolution artwork

1. Verify that the High Pass 3.0 layer is targeted.
2. Press and hold **[Alt]**(Win) or **[option]**(Mac), then click the **Create a new layer button** on the Layers palette.
3. Type **Noise 3.0** in the Name text box.
4. Click the **Mode list arrow**, then click **Overlay**.
5. Click the **Fill with Overlay-neutral color (50% gray) check box**.

   Your dialog box should resemble Figure 22.

(continued)

FIGURE 22
New Layer dialog box set to Overlay with a neutral gray fill

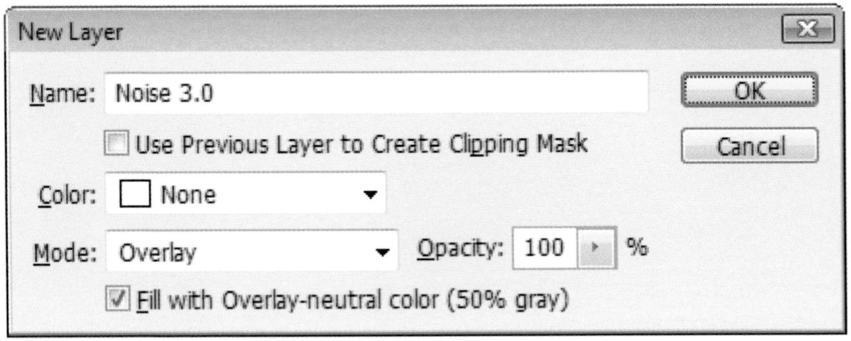

FIGURE 23
Add Noise dialog box

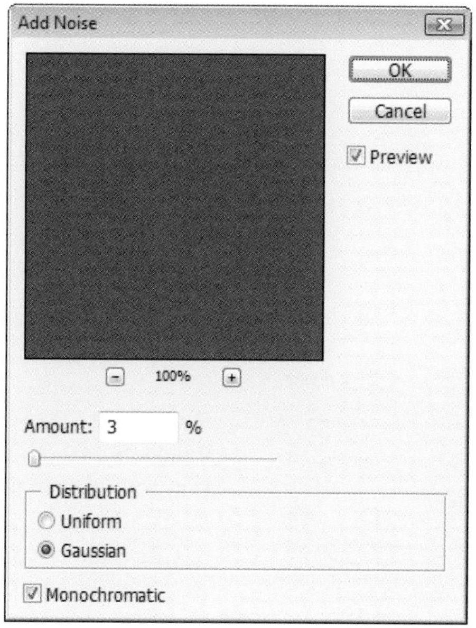

FIGURE 24
The final high-resolution billboard mechanical

6. Click **OK**.

   The canvas registers no change. The new layer is created with a gray fill and is set to Overlay, so the pixels in the layer are not visible.

7. Click **Filter** on the menu bar, point to **Noise**, then click **Add Noise**.
8. Enter the settings shown in Figure 23, then click **OK**.
9. Zoom-in on the queen's face, then hide and show the Noise 3.0 layer.

   The graininess of the noise produces a subtle sharpening effect overall. Noise is also useful for creating a consistent texture across an entire image. This can be very useful for artwork like the billboard, which is composed of multiple images. The consistent texture has a unifying effect.

   TIP You must view an image at a minimum of 100% to get a reliable representation of a noise effect.

10. Change the blending mode to **Soft Light**.

    The Soft Light blending mode produces a noise effect that is less intense than the Overlay blending mode.

11. Change the blending mode to **Linear Light**.

    Linear Light produces the most intense noise effect. It is seldom used, except in cases when noise is meant to be a noticeable effect.

12. Change the blending mode back to **Overlay**, then make the Bleed layer visible.
13. Compare your canvas to Figure 24.
14. Save your work, then close 48x14.psd.

LESSON 3

CREATE BLACK AND WHITE from Color

What You'll Do

It's always smart to question single-method solutions. Take creating a black-and-white image, for example. If you have a color image that you want to use as a black-and-white image, the most basic solution is to convert it to Grayscale or completely desaturate it in the Hue/Saturation dialog box.

Those are solutions, true. To some, they're the only solution. That's false. Photoshop offers many alternative methods for creating a black-and-white version of a color image; you aren't stuck with only the image in Grayscale mode.

In this lesson, you'll use the Lab Color mode to create a variety of grayscale images, and you'll also use powerful Black and White adjustment layer, new to Photoshop CS3. The techniques you learn here will provide you with alternative methods for creating grayscale images and, perhaps more importantly, prompt you to experiment with different methods until you find the best grayscale effect for a given image.

FIGURE 25
Result of converting to Grayscale mode

FIGURE 26
Image from the Blue channel

Use the Lab Color mode to create a grayscale image

1. Open AP 6-4.psd, then save it as **Simple Grayscale**.
2. Click **Image** on the menu bar, point to **Mode**, click **Grayscale**, click **Don't Flatten**,then click **Discard** in the Message dialog box that follows.
3. Compare your canvas to Figure 25.
4. Open AP 6-5.psd, then save it as **LAB Grayscale**.
5. Display the Channels palette, click the **Channel thumbnail** on the Blue channel, then compare your canvas to Figure 26.

   TIP If your channel appears blue as opposed to gray as shown in the figure, you need to change your preferences. Go to the Interface Preferences dialog box, then verify that the Show Channels in Color check box is not checked.

(continued)

The Channel thumbnails in the Channels palette often provide interesting versions of grayscale images. In this case, the image on the Blue channel is darker and very interesting. If you were designing for an unconventional look, this image would probably be a better choice. Remember, too, that you can always modify the image. Figure 27 shows the image from the Blue channel with a simple levels correction, and the result is a stunning black and white.

> **TIP** If you want to use an image in a channel as a file, click the Channel thumbnail, select all and copy, click File on the menu bar, click New to create a new document, then paste the copied channel.

6. Click the **RGB Channel thumbnail** in the Channels palette.
7. Click **Image** on the menu bar, point to **Mode**, then click **Lab Color**.
8. Note the channels in the Channels palette, as shown in Figure 28.

   In Lab Color mode, the image is created by three channels: Lightness, a, and b.

(continued)

FIGURE 27
Image from the Blue channel after Levels correction

FIGURE 28
Channels palette in Lab Color mode

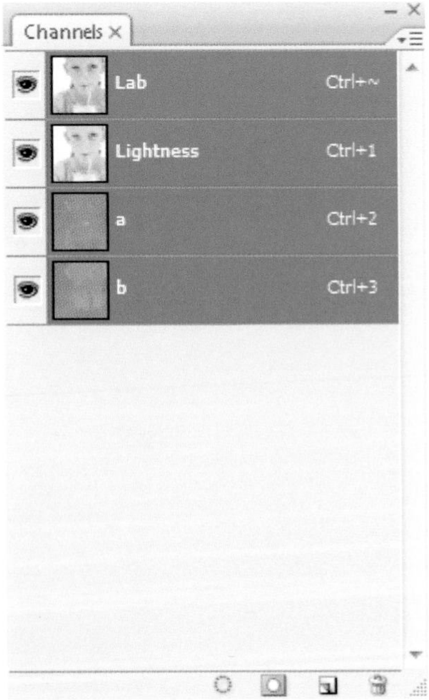

FIGURE 29
Image from Lightness channel

9. Click the **Channel thumbnail** on the Lightness channel, then compare your canvas to Figure 29.

   To paraphrase a well-known saying, Lab Color is like a box of chocolates—you never know what you're gonna get. The Lightness channel is always a black-and-white image, and sometimes it produces an interesting alternative. In this case, the image from the Lightness channel is quite beautiful in the smoothness of its light gray tones. What this image lacks, however, is detail and definition in the eyes. As you know, there are a number of methods to correct this. When working in Lab Color mode, don't forget that the a and b channels are also there for your use.

10. Duplicate the Lightness channel, select all, copy, then click the **Channel thumbnail** on the Lab channel.
11. Return to the Layers palette, then paste the copy as a new layer.
12. Name the new layer **Lightness Art**, then hide it.
13. Duplicate the b channel in the Channels palette, select all, copy, then click the **Channel thumbnail** on the Lab channel.

(continued)

14. Return to the Layers palette, then paste the copy as a new layer so that your canvas resembles Figure 30.

TIP It was critical that you hid the Lightness Art layer in Step 12. Remember, art in the Channels palette is dynamic; whatever is visible on the canvas is represented in the channels. Had you kept the Lightness Art layer visible, the a and b channels would have been completely gray with no art.

15. Name the new layer **b Art**, then show the Lightness Art layer.

From this point, there are a number of directions you can experiment with. However, whenever you have a predominantly gray image on a layer, the first move you should try is the Overlay mode, because gray becomes invisible in Overlay mode.

16. Set the blending mode on the b Art layer to Overlay, then compare your canvas to Figure 31.

TIP Hide and show the b Art layer to see the change.

The result is not very satisfactory; the eyes are still too light, and the image as a whole is too light. This is an important hint of what to try next. The image as a whole was lightened in Overlay mode—the opposite of what we wanted. This tells us that the image on the b Art layer is too light; we want its opposite.

(continued)

FIGURE 30
Image from b channel pasted as the top layer

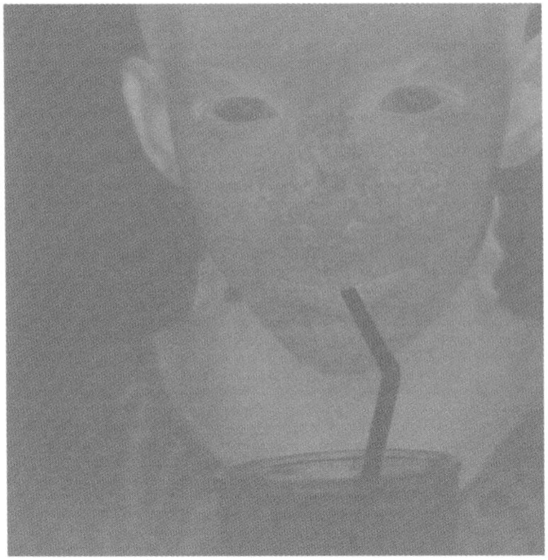

FIGURE 31
Image from b channel in Overlay mode

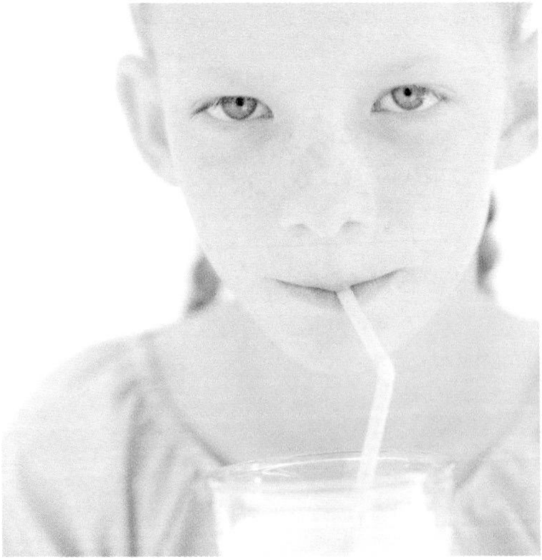

FIGURE 32
Inverted b channel image in Overlay mode

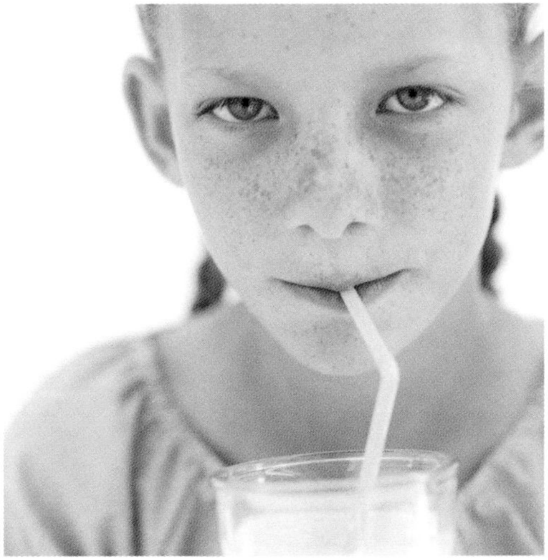

FIGURE 33
Multiplying the b channel image

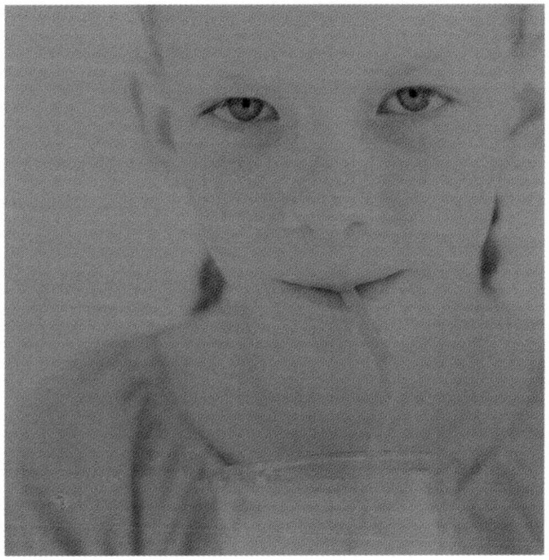

17. Invert the b Art layer, then compare your canvas to Figure 32.

    Now we're moving in the right direction. Inverted, the Channel thumbnail on the b channel is darker in the areas of detail, like the eyes, eyebrows, lips, and so on. The detail has definitely improved, but the image has darkened over all. This means that we've lost those airy, light gray flesh tones from the Lightness channel. We could, of course, use a layer mask and allow only the eyes, lips, and so on from the b Art layer to show, but we're going to go with another method.

18. Undo your last step.

    The image on the b Art layer is no longer inverted.

19. Change the blending mode of the b Art layer to Multiply, then compare your artwork to Figure 33.

    The darkest areas of the b channel art were in the eyes. It follows logically that, if multiplied, the b channel artwork must darken the eyes.

20. Select all, click **Edit** on the menu bar, then click **Copy Merged**.

21. Paste a new layer, name it **Merged**, then hide the b Art layer.

(continued)

22. Change the blending mode on the Merged layer to Overlay, then compare your canvas to Figure 34.

The result is stunning. Overlayed, the merged art has dramatically darker eyes. However, because the other areas of the merged art are close to a neutral gray, they have very little impact when the Overlay mode is applied.

(continued)

FIGURE 34
Overlaying the merged art

FIGURE 35
Comparing the simple grayscale to the LAB grayscale

23. Compare this black-and-white image to the black-and-white image in the Simple Grayscale file.

    As shown in Figure 35, the two images are dramatically different. The important point to remember is that there is no standard color correction—curves, levels, and so on—that you could apply to the simple grayscale black and white that would mimic the nuance and depth of the Lab Color black and white.

24. Close the LAB Grayscale and Simple Grayscale documents, saving your work in both of them.

Use a Black and White adjustment layer

1. Open AP 6-6.psd, then save it as **BW Adjustment**.
2. Click the **Create new fill or adjustment layer button** on the Layers palette, then click **Black & White**.

   The Black and White dialog box, shown in Figure 36, opens and the image changes to black and white.
3. Drag the **Greens slider** left and right and note the effect on the image.

   Because there are really no green areas in the artwork, moving the Greens slider has very little effect.
4. Drag the **Greens slider** all the way to the left.
5. Drag the **Cyans slider** left and right, then position it at 40.

   Because there's so much blue throughout the image, the Cyans slider has a broad effect, but the effect is strongest on the queen's scarf. With the ability to manipulate the scarf from light gray to dark gray, you can differentiate the scarf from the dark background and the lightness of the queen's face. At 40, it's exactly between the two.

(continued)

FIGURE 36
Black and White dialog box

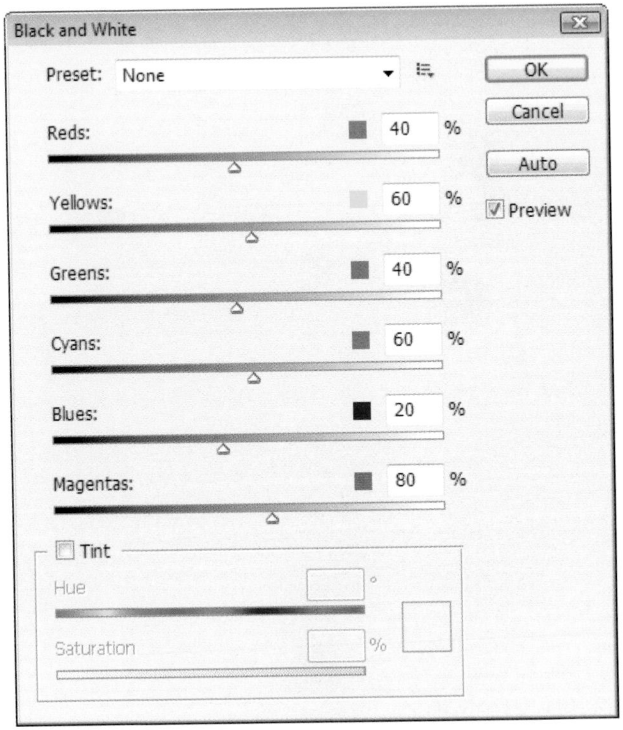

FIGURE 37

A color image with a Black and White adjustment

6. Position your cursor over the queen's forehead so that the eyedropper icon appears, then click and drag your cursor over the queen's forehead and face.

   Because red is the dominant color in the queen's face, the Reds slider moves as you drag over the image. This is a good technique for identifying which slider to move to adjust a specific area of the image.

7. Drag the **Reds slider** to 79 so that the faces are the brightest elements of the image.

   At this relatively high setting, the faces seem to glow against the background.

8. Experiment with various settings of the Blues slider.

   Blue is by far the most dominant color in the image overall, so the Blues slider will affect almost all areas of the background.

9. Drag the **Blues slider** to 25, click **OK**, then compare your artwork to Figure 37.

   The controls in the Black and White adjustment layer allowed you to create a customized black and white image with a bright foreground, a dark background, and detailed grays in the midground.

10. Save your work, then close BW Adjustment.psd.

LESSON 4

USE THE UNSHARP MASK FILTER
to Sharpen Edges

What You'll Do

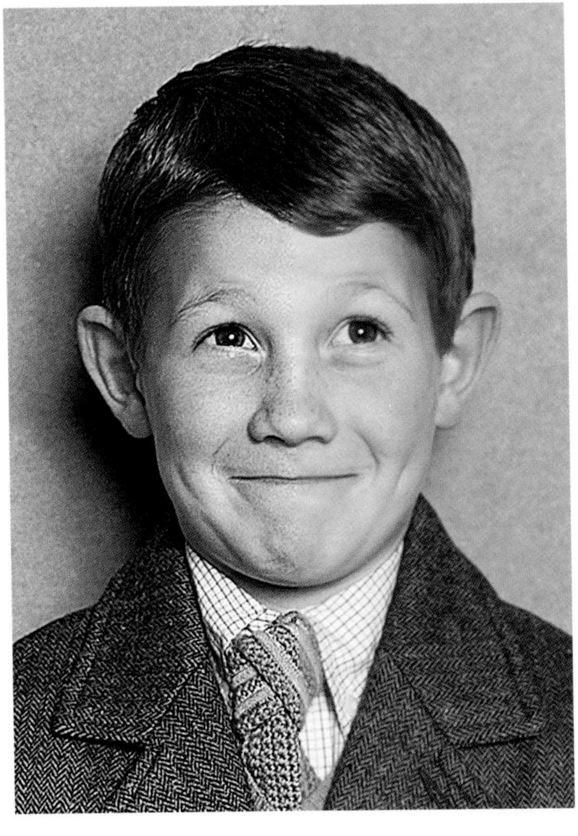

When you scan an image, the resulting scan is, by definition, of lesser quality than the original. That's because it's a second-generation reproduction, and a reproduction is always inferior to an original. When you scale an image—especially when you enlarge an image—you will suffer a loss of quality as well. In both of these examples, the loss of quality will be a blurring of the image—a loss of fine detail.

Unsharp Mask is an important filter that addresses this issue. It's a sophisticated algorithm that creates the effect of sharpening an image. It's only an effect, of course. The filter works by shifting color to create contrast, which the eye perceives as sharpness—an increase in focus and detail.

Because Unsharp Mask is so useful, it's a smart idea for you to take some time to investigate it, to understand its settings, and to get a sense of how it does what it does.

Your ability to apply unsharp masking in a way that is best for a given image can really make the difference in attaining excellent results.

FIGURE 38
Image Size dialog box

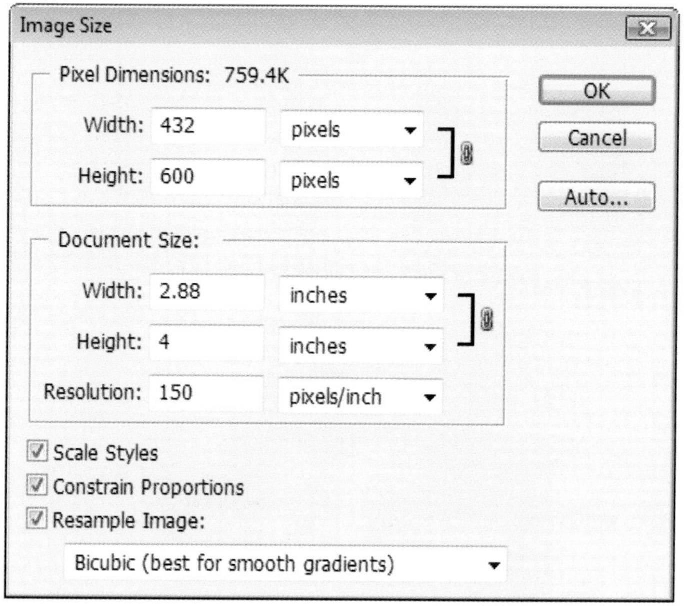

Use the Unsharp Mask filter to sharpen edges

1. Open AP 6-7.psd, then save it as **Unsharp Mask**.
2. Assess the image for contrast.

   The Unsharp Mask filter creates the illusion of sharpness by increasing the contrast at the image's "edges." In Photoshop, *edges* refer to areas of an image where pixels differ noticeably from surrounding pixels. It would be a mistake to use the Unsharp Mask filter to improve contrast overall. That's why it's always a good idea to, when you are about to use the Unsharp Mask filter, first verify that the image's contrast is where you want it to be.
3. Make the Contrast layer visible.

   With the Contrast layer visible, it is clear that the image needs a bit of a contrast bump. Curves are designed to do just that, not the Unsharp Mask filter.
4. Target the **Background layer**, click **Image** on the menu bar, then click **Image Size**.

   As shown in Figure 38, the image is 4" tall at 150 pixels per inch. In other words, if you were to count one column of pixels from bottom to top, you would count a total of 600 pixels, which is what is shown in the top section of the dialog box.

(continued)

5. Type **7** in the Height text box in the Document Size section so that your Image Size dialog box matches Figure 39.

   By making this move, you are saying you want this image to be resized to the height of 7 inches. Note that the Resample Image check box is checked. This means that at 7 inches tall you still want 150 pixels per inch. From top to bottom, that's a total of 1050 pixels per column. Where will you get 450 extra pixels per column?

6. Click **OK**, then compare your image to Figure 40.
7. Click the **Rectangular Marquee Tool**, select the left half of the image, then hide the selection marquee.
8. Zoom in so that you are viewing the boy's face at 100%, if necessary.

(continued)

FIGURE 39
Image Size dialog box

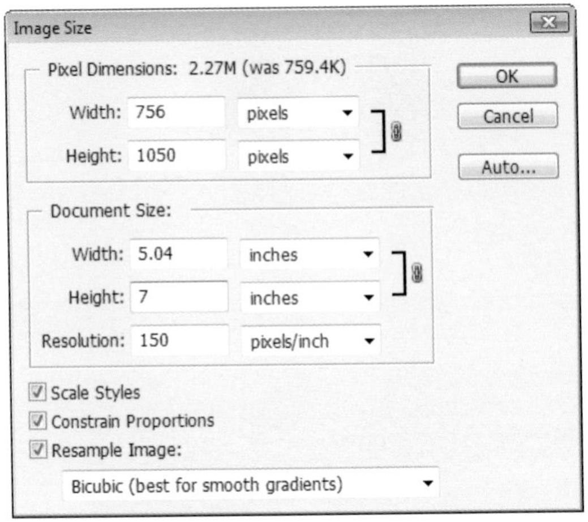

FIGURE 40
Image enlarged with interpolated pixel data

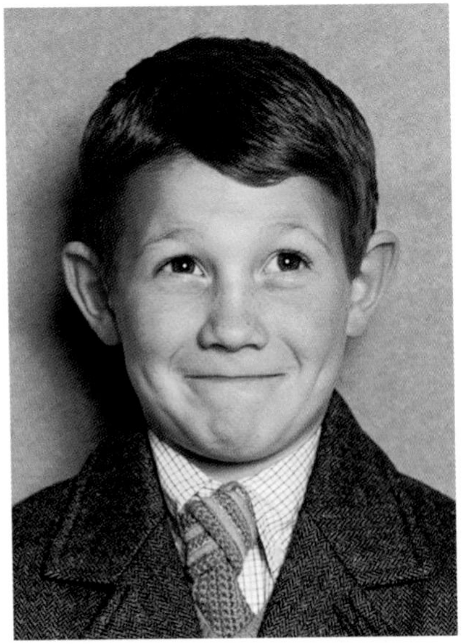

FIGURE 41
Filter applied with a high Amount value

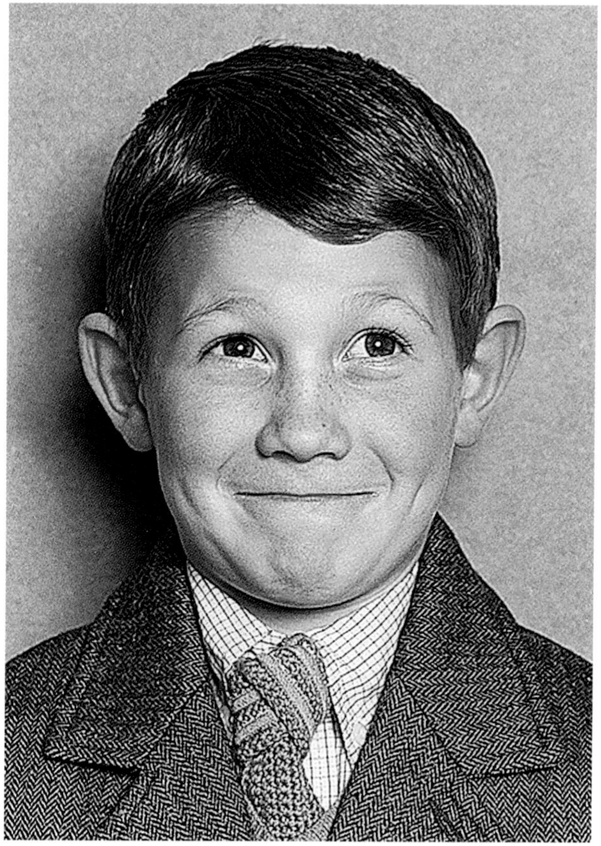

AUTHOR'S *note*

Though the Unsharp Mask dialog box has a preview window, you are much better off moving the box to the side and viewing the effect on the image at 100%. The result of the Unsharp Mask filter is much more noticeable on screen than when printed because of the many factors in play during the offset printing process that blend and blur fine detail.

9. Click **Filter** on the menu bar, point to **Sharpen**, then click **Unsharp Mask**.

   The Unsharp Mask filter works by identifying the edges of the image. Remember that edges refer to areas of an image where pixels differ noticeably from surrounding pixels. For example, in this image, the line where the boy's white shirt collar meets the coat's brown collar would be an edge, as would the point where his dark hairline meets his pale forehead. The Unsharp Mask filter increases the contrast in these areas—it makes the light edges lighter and the darker edges darker—to create the effect of focus and sharpness.

10. Type **150** in the Amount text box.

    For high-resolution images—images that are 300 pixels per inch or more—an amount of 150–200% is typically recommended. Though this image is not high resolution, we have entered a high Amount value so that the effect will be dramatic and noticeable. The higher the Amount value, the more pronounced the effect. For example, Figure 41 shows the image sharpened drastically with a high Amount value. Note the sharpness especially in the hair and the tweed coat. The effect is most visible in these areas because they include so many dark pixels that abut light pixels.

(continued)

11. Drag the **Radius slider** to 2.0 pixels.

The Radius value determines the number of pixels surrounding the edge pixels that are included in the calculation that produces the sharpening. That's not a calculation that you need to keep in your head. Instead, remember that the higher the Radius value, the wider and more visible the sharpened edges will be. For high-resolution images, set the Radius value to 1 or 2. Figure 42 shows an example of the Radius value set at 24.

12. Set the Threshold value to 0, if necessary.

The Threshold value offers significant control of how this filter is applied—it determines what Photoshop defines as an edge. For example, if the Threshold were set to 10 pixels, that would mean that pixels surrounding a given pixel would need to be at least 10 grayscale values higher or lower than that given pixel to be considered an edge and therefore sharpened. When the Threshold value is higher, fewer areas of the image are sharpened. Zero is the default Threshold value meaning that, by default, all areas of the image will be sharpened to some degree.

(continued)

FIGURE 42
Filter applied with a high Radius value

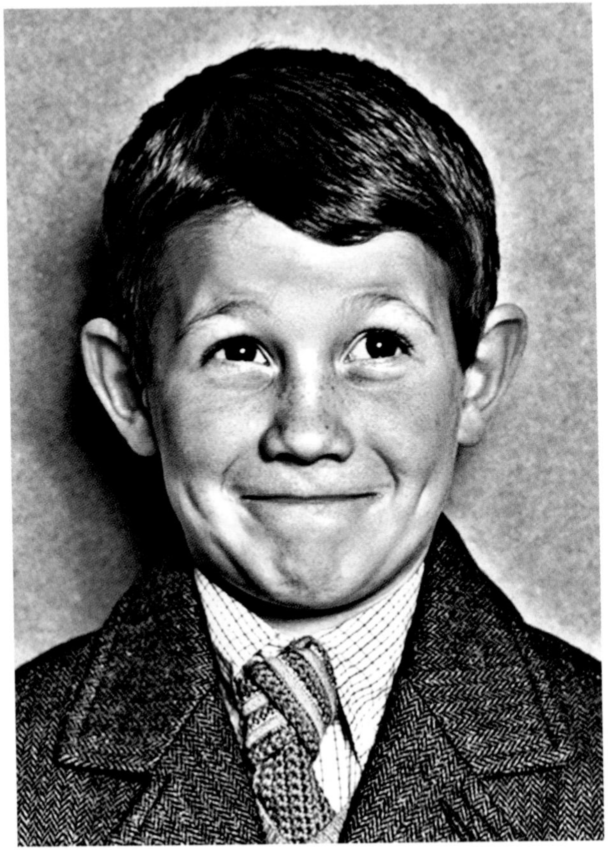

FIGURE 43
Image with left side sharpened

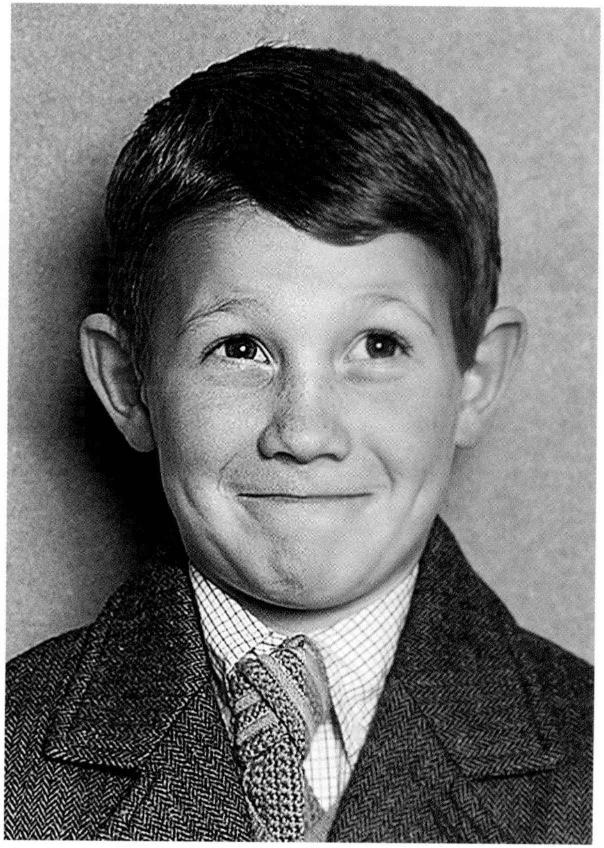

13. Click **OK**, then compare your result to Figure 43.

    On screen especially, the effect is substantial. If you undo and redo your last step, you'll see that it is most noticeable in the hair, the tie, and the tweed coat. If you zoom in on the tweed coat, then undo and redo again, you'll get a vivid example of how the filter lightens the lights and darkens the darks. Viewed at 100%, note the more subtle sharpening in the areas with less contrast, such as on the boy's cheeks and even in the texture on the wall behind him.

14. Save and then close the file.

AUTHOR'S *note*

The Unsharp Mask filter doesn't necessarily need to be used for practical, realistic image improvement. When applied at high values, it also produces an interesting special effect, one that can be used especially when you want to exaggerate the lines within an image, such as for cartooning purposes.

LESSON 5

APPLY GRAIN
Effects

What You'll Do

Adding grain to an image is a very popular design technique, one that most designers use very often. Grain adds texture and nuance to an image. Applying grain across multiple images from different sources is useful for making them all appear to be more consistent in tone and texture. Photoshop offers a number of options for creating and simulating grain. The techniques you'll learn in this lesson offer the ability to apply grain and the flexibility to determine where and how the grain affects the image.

FIGURE 44
Grain dialog box

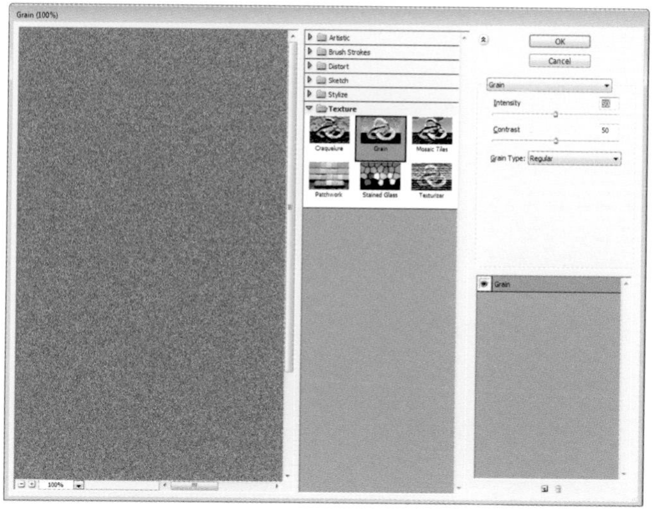

FIGURE 45
Multicolored grain

Apply a basic grain effect

1. Open AP 6-8.psd, then save it as **Grain**.
2. Zoom in so that you are viewing the image at 100%, then center the girl's face in the window.

   TIP When working with fine detail such as grain, you must view the image at 100% to get a realistic representation of the effect.

3. Create a new layer, name it **Regular Grain**, then fill it with 128R/128G/128B.
4. Click **Filter** on the menu bar, point to **Texture**, then click **Grain**.
5. Click the **Grain Type list arrow**, view the list of grain types, then click **Regular**.
6. Set the Intensity and Contrast values to 50 so that your Grain dialog box resembles Figure 44, then click **OK**.
7. Change the blending mode on the Regular Grain layer to Overlay, then compare your artwork to Figure 45.

(continued)

8. Use the Hue/Saturation dialog box to completely desaturate the Regular Grain layer, then compare your results to Figure 46.

   Undo and redo your last step to see the change between the colored grain effect and the desaturated grain.

9. Duplicate the Regular Grain layer, name the new layer **Black Grain**, then compare your artwork to Figure 47.

10. Save your work.

FIGURE 46
Desaturated grain

FIGURE 47
Grain effect doubled

FIGURE 48
Image with black grain effect

FIGURE 49
Overlaying the Black Grain layer

Apply black grain and white grain

1. Hide the Regular Grain layer.
2. Set the blending mode of the Black Grain layer to **Normal**, then fill it with **White**.
3. Click **Filter** on the menu bar, point to **Noise**, then click **Add Noise**.
4. Type **30** in the Amount text box, click the **Gaussian option button**, then click the **Monochromatic check box** to select it.
5. Click **OK**.
6. Set the layer's blending mode to **Multiply**, then compare your artwork to Figure 48.

   TIP When multiplied, white pixels become transparent.

7. Change the blending mode to Overlay, set the opacity to 50%, then compare your screen to Figure 49.

   This effect is a nice alternate to a basic grain overlay. It's not for every image, and not for every type of project, but as an effect, it's an interesting and rather unusual method for adding grain.

(continued)

8. Hide the Black Grain layer, create a new layer named **White Grain**, then fill it with Black.
9. Click **Filter** on the menu bar, point to **Noise**, then click **Add Noise**.
10. Set the Amount value to 40%, then click **OK**.
11. Set the layer's blending mode to Screen, then compare your artwork to Figure 50.

    TIP When screened, black pixels become transparent.

12. Click **Filter** on the menu bar, point to **Blur**, then click **Motion Blur**.
13. Set the Angle to –45°, set the Distance to 5 pixels, then click **OK**.

(continued)

FIGURE 50
Image with white grain effect

FIGURE 51
White grain artwork in Color Dodge mode

FIGURE 52
Using two grain layers and two grain effects

14. Set the blending mode to Color Dodge, then compare your result to Figure 51.

    Dodge is synonymous with light; the Color Dodge blending mode lightens the image using information on the blended layer as brightening information for the layers beneath. With the Color Dodge blending mode, black has no effect, which makes sense as this mode is all about lightening. Light pixels lighten areas of the image, with white pixels having the most extreme brightening effect.

15. Set the blending mode back to Screen, make the Black Grain layer visible, then compare your canvas to Figure 52.
16. Save your work, then close the file.

LESSON 6

AUTOMATE Workflow

What You'll Do

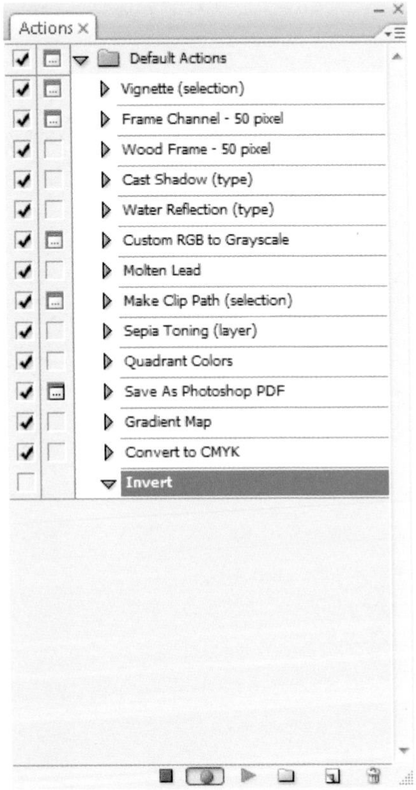

The title says it all: Automate workflow. As designers, we like to focus on the big projects: the magazine covers, the posters, the billboards, the CD covers. But in the real world, it's not only the big projects that come across the desk. No, it's often the small stuff that you've got to handle as well. And often, the small stuff requires repetition. For example, here are 25 RGB files. Please convert them to CMYK, and resize them so that they're all seven inches wide. Or, here's a folder full of PSD files. Please open them all, convert to Grayscale, then save them as 72-dpi JPEG files that we can use on our Web site. Sound like fun?

Fortunately, Adobe has made an enormous commitment to automation, especially since the advent of the Internet and the enormous amount of image processing that creating and maintaining a Web site demands.

You might have played with the Actions palette before, but in this lesson, you're going to take a more rigorous and in-depth tour, and you're going to play with more advanced features like batch processing and modal controls. Also, you're going to use Photoshop's Image Processor, which is a file conversion dream come true. Then, you can move on to that billboard. And that magazine cover. And that poster . . .

FIGURE 53
Image Processor dialog box

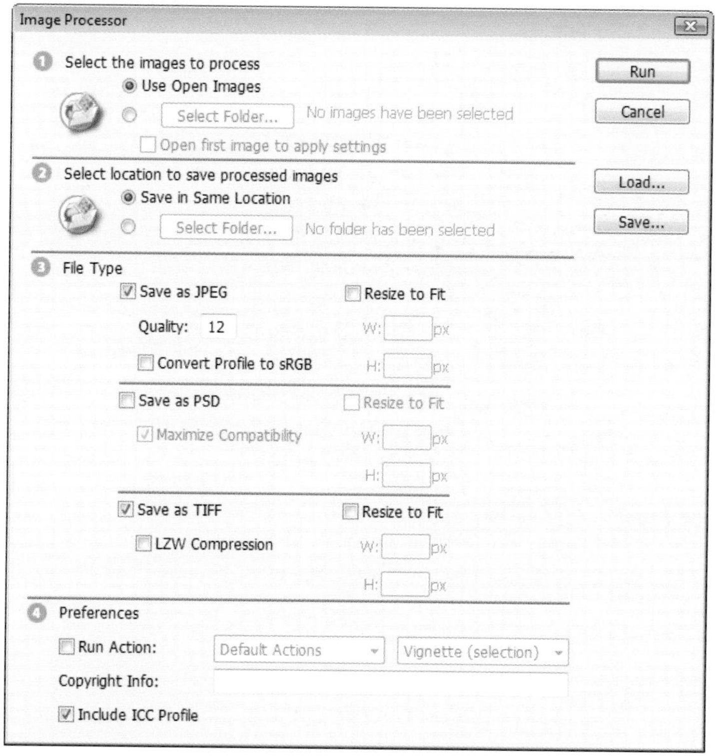

Use the Image Processor

1. Open the seven files in the Automation folder located in the Chapter 6 Data Files folder.

   The files are all Photoshop.psd files. The goal of this lesson is to create one TIFF and one JPEG copy of each of the seven files.

2. Click **File** on the menu bar, point to **Scripts**, then click **Image Processor**.
3. In Section 1, click the **Use Open Images option button**.
4. In Section 2, click the **Save in Same Location option button**.
5. In Section 3, click the **Save as JPEG check box**, then type **12** in the Quality text box.
6. In Section 3, check the **Save as TIFF check box**.
7. Verify that nothing is checked in Section 4, then compare your Image Processor dialog box to Figure 53.
8. Click **Run**.

   The seven PSD files remain open after the Image Processor is done.

9. Navigate to the Automation folder, then open the Automation folder.

   The Automation folder contains the seven original PSD files. It also contains a folder named JPEG and a folder named TIFF. These two folders contain the JPEG and TIFF copies generated by the Image Processor.

10. Return to Photoshop.

Create and run an action in the Actions palette

1. Click **Window** on the menu bar, then click **Flowers.psd**.
2. Click **Window** on the menu bar, then click **Actions**.
3. Click the **Actions palette list arrow**, then remove the check mark next to Button Mode to deactivate Button Mode, if necessary.
4. Click the **Actions palette list arrow**, then click **New Action**.
5. Type **Invert** in the Name text box, click **Record**, then compare your Actions palette to Figure 54.

   A new action named Invert appears in the list and is highlighted. The red Begin recording button is activated on the Actions palette.

   TIP The other actions listed in your Actions palette may vary.
6. Click **Image** on the menu bar, point to **Adjustments**, then click **Invert**.

   The Flowers.psd image is inverted.
7. Click **File** on the menu bar, then click **Save**.
8. Click **File** on the menu bar, then click **Close**.
9. Compare your Actions palette to Figure 55.

   The three commands that you executed—Invert, Save, and Close—are listed as commands under the Invert action.
10. Click the **Stop playing/recording button** on the Actions palette.

(continued)

FIGURE 54
Actions palette

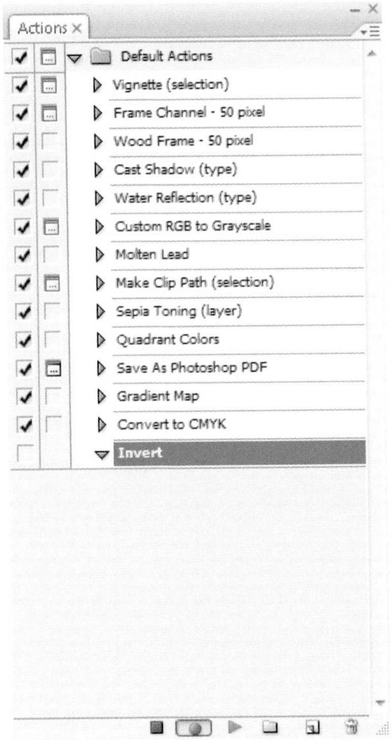

FIGURE 55
Invert action with three commands

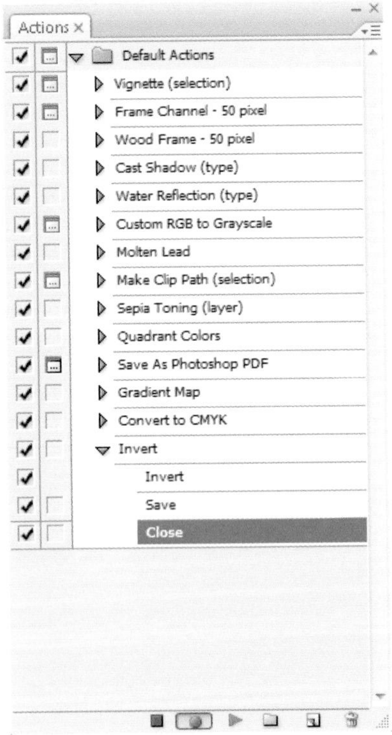

FIGURE 56

Invert action targeted in Actions palette

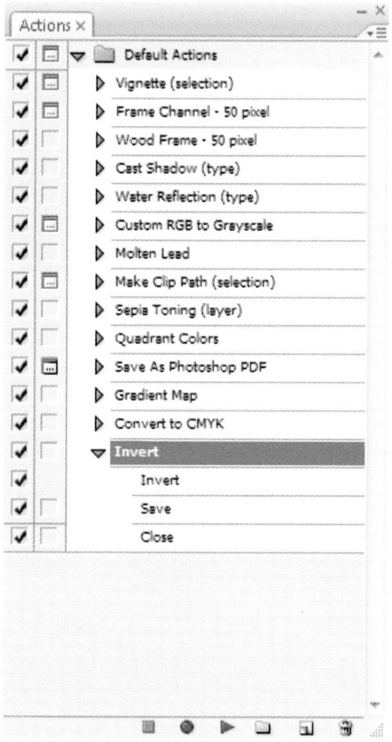

11. Click **Window** on the menu bar, then click **Marble.psd**.
12. Click **Invert** in the Actions palette list so that it is highlighted as shown in Figure 56.

    TIP When running actions, this is an easy step to miss—you must target the action itself before you can apply it.

13. Click the **Play selection button** in the Actions palette.

    You will see nothing happen other than the image closing. This is because Close is the final command of the action.

14. Repeat the Invert action for the remaining open images.
15. Open all seven PSD files in the Automation folder.

    All seven images have been inverted.

Batch process an action

1. Click **File** on the menu bar, point to **Automate**, then click **Batch**.
2. In the Play section, click the **Action list arrow** to see all the actions available, then click **Invert**.

   All of the actions in the Actions palette are listed.

3. In the Source section, verify that Folder is chosen, then click **Choose**.
4. Navigate to and select the Automation folder, then click **OK** (Win) or **Choose** (Mac).

(continued)

5. Verify that none of the four check boxes in the Source section is checked.

   Remember, because of the work we did with the Image Processor in the first lesson of this chapter, the Automation folder now contains two subfolders—JPEG and TIFF. We do not want to apply the action to the contents of those folders.

6. In the Destination section, verify that None is chosen.

   No destination means that we want to affect the targeted images in the folder and for those images to be saved with the change. If we wanted to affect them and save the affected images as *copies*, then we'd need to specify a destination for the copies.

7. In the Errors section, verify that Stop for Errors is chosen, then compare your Batch dialog box to Figure 57.

8. Click **OK**.

   The seven images open, are affected by the action, then closed.

9. Open all seven PSD files from the Automation folder.

   All seven have been inverted and now appear as they did originally.

Create a complex action

1. Click **Window** on the menu bar, then click **Bricks.psd**.

2. Click the **Actions palette list arrow**, then click **New Action**.

(continued)

FIGURE 57
Batch dialog box

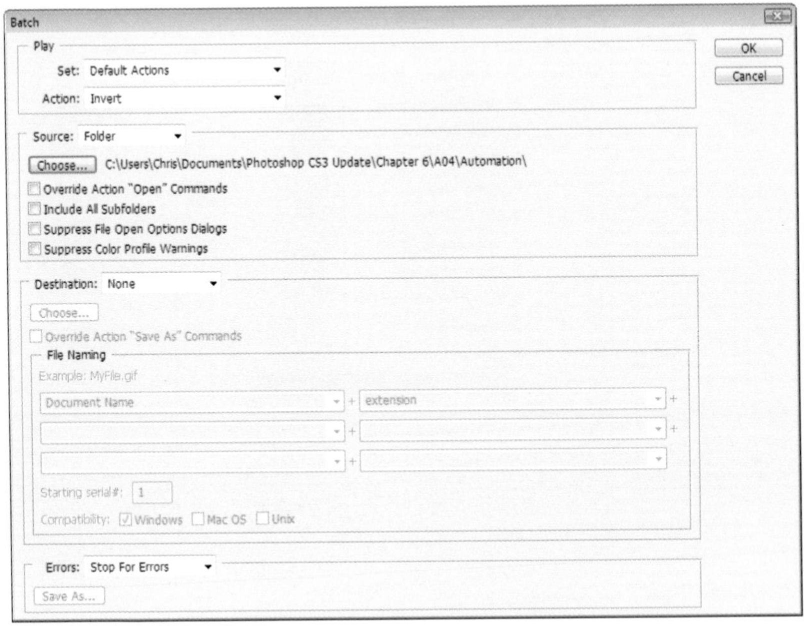

FIGURE 58
Image Size dialog box

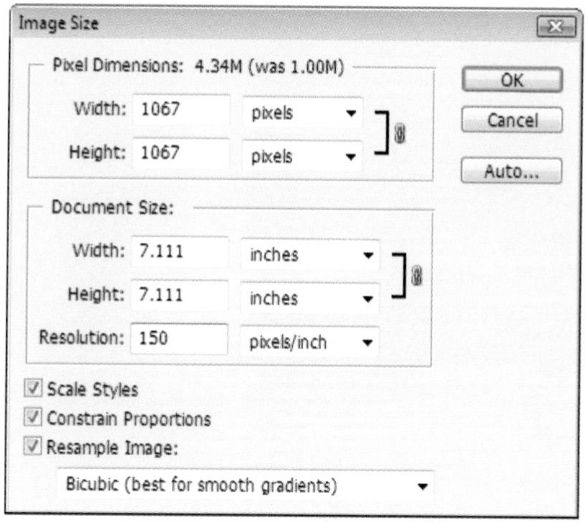

FIGURE 60
Curves bump

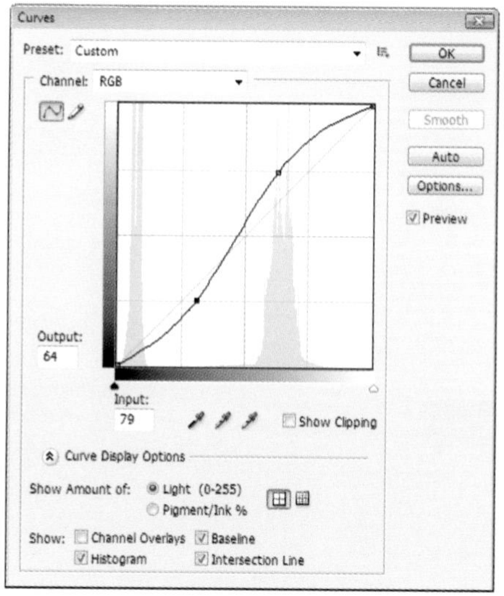

FIGURE 59
Unsharp Mask dialog box

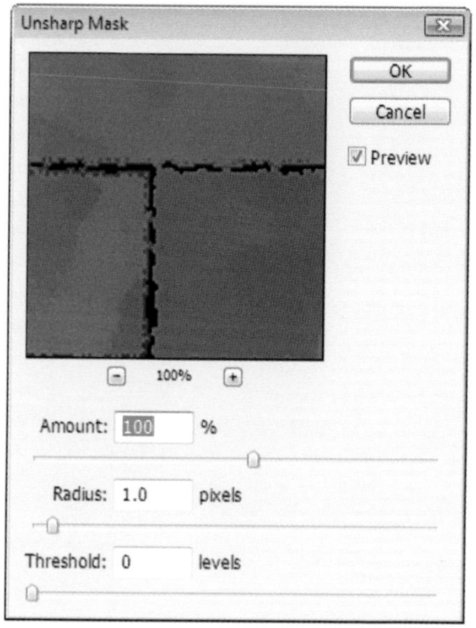

3. Type **Processed Textures**, then click **Record**.
4. Click **Image** on the menu bar, point to **Mode**, then click **CMYK Color**.
5. Click **Image** on the menu bar, then click **Image Size**.
6. Type **150** in the Resolution text box, then verify that all three check boxes in the Image Size dialog box are checked so that your dialog box resembles Figure 58.
7. Click **OK**.
8. Click **Filter** on the menu bar, point to **Sharpen**, then click **Unsharp Mask**.
9. Enter the settings shown in Figure 59, then click **OK**.
10. Click the **Create new fill or adjustment layer button** on the Layers palette, then click **Curves**.
11. Create a contrast bump similar to the one shown in Figure 60, then click **OK**.
12. Click **File** on the menu bar, then click **Save As**.
13. Navigate to the Automation folder, then create a new folder named **Processed Textures**.
14. Save the file as a .PSD in the Processed Textures folder.

    Note that we did not enter a new name for the file.
15. Click the **Stop playing/recording button** in the Actions palette.

(continued)

16. Click the triangle next to Make adjustment layer in the Actions palette to expand the action, then compare your palette to Figure 61.

The specific settings that you used when creating the contrast bump in the curves adjustment layer are recorded with the command. (Your settings will differ slightly based on the specific curve that you made.)

17. Expand the Save action in the Actions palette.

The file format and the destination folder are recorded with the command.

18. Collapse the Make adjustment layer and Save commands.

19. Click **Window** on the menu bar, click **Wood.psd**, then target the **Processed Textures action** in the Actions palette.

20. Click the **Play selection button** in the Actions palette.

All of the commands are applied to the Wood.psd file and it is saved to the new folder as a .PSD file. It is important that you understand that all of the commands were applied with the exact settings that you entered when creating the action.

Apply modal controls to an action

1. Click **Window** on the menu bar, then click **Water.psd**.

(continued)

FIGURE 61
Expanding an action to see its settings

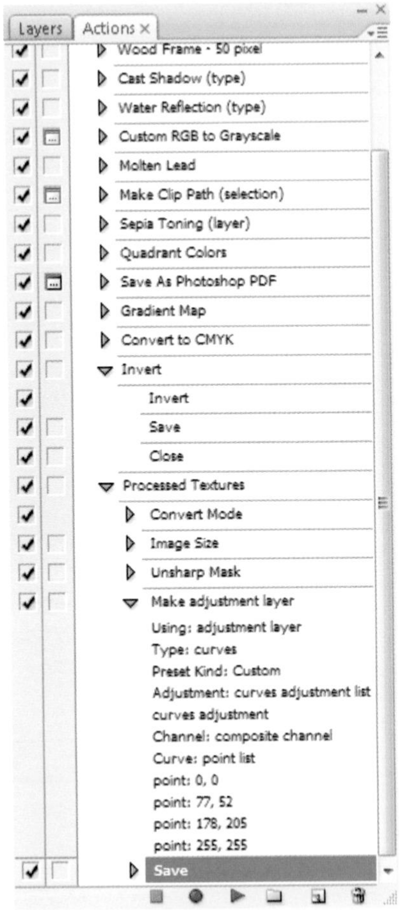

FIGURE 62
Modal controls activated for two actions

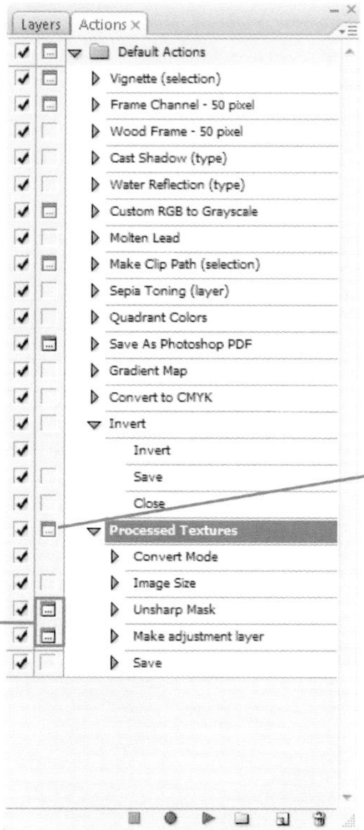

The two boxes you clicked are named Toggle dialog on/off. When running an action, they do exactly that: toggle a dialog box on or off. When showing, they are set to toggle on the dialog boxes for these two commands. These two icons are also called modal controls.

The red modal control icon beside the Processed Textures action indicates that the action contains some commands that are modal.

2. Click the **Toggle dialog on/off button** next to the Unsharp Mask command and the Make adjustment layer command so that your Actions palette resembles Figure 62.

   TIP The Toggle dialog on/off button is the empty gray square to the left of the command.

3. Target the **Processed Textures action** in the Actions palette.
4. Click the **Play selection button** ▶.

   The Processed Textures action is run as before; however, this time, when it comes to the Unsharp Mask command, it opens the dialog box and awaits your input.

5. Change the Amount value to 75%, then click **OK**.

   The command is executed, then the New Layer dialog box is opened to create the Curves adjustment layer.

6. Type **Water Curve** in the Name text box, then click **OK**.

   The Curves dialog box opens showing the exact curve that was originally created for this command.

7. Tweak the contrast bump to increase the contrast even more, then click **OK**.

   The remaining commands run through to completion.

8. Apply the Processed Textures action to the remaining four PSD files, entering whatever settings you like in the dialog boxes.
9. Close all open files.

PROJECT BUILDER 1

1. Open AP 6-9.psd, then save it as **Project Builder 1**.
2. Click Image on the menu bar, point to Mode, then click Lab Color.
3. In the Channels palette, click the Channel thumbnail on the Lightness channel.
4. Duplicate the Lightness channel, select all, copy, then click the Lab Channel thumbnail in the Channels palette.
5. Return to the Layers palette, then paste the copy as a new layer.
6. Name the new layer **Lightness Art**, then be sure to hide it.
7. Duplicate the b channel, select all, copy, then click the Lab Channel thumbnail in the Channels palette.
8. Return to the Layers palette, then paste the copy as a new layer named **B**.
9. Show the Lightness Art layer.
10. Set the blending mode of the B layer to Multiply.
11. Select all, click Edit on the menu bar, then click Copy Merged.
12. Paste a new layer, name it **Merged**, then hide the B layer.
13. Change the blending mode on the Merged layer to Overlay.
14. Set the opacity of the Merged layer to 40%, then compare your result to Figure 63.
15. Save your work, then close Project Builder 1.

FIGURE 63
Completed Project Builder 1

PROJECT BUILDER 2

1. Open AP 6-10.psd, then save it as **Extension Billboard**.

   The client for this project has requested that the mechanical for this billboard be recreated into an extension billboard where the sword artwork extends the actual artwork above the rectangular billboard. The client informs you that the specifications for the billboard allow for artwork to exceed the billboard area by five feet at the top.
2. Target the Background layer, then open the Canvas Size dialog box.

   The mechanical is built at 48 inches by 14 inches (with an additional .25 inches on all sides for bleed). At 48 inches x 14 inches, the mechanical is 1/12 the size of the actual output of 48 feet by 14 feet.
3. Click the bottom-center square of the anchor, then change the height value to 19.25.

   We know from the client that the extension at the top can be five feet maximum, or 60 inches. Since the mechanical is 1/12 the size of the actual output, that means we can add 5 inches to the top of the mechanical—from the trim line—for the extension. That brings the new height of the file to 19.25 inches: .25 inches for the bottom bleed, 14 inches for the actual artwork, and 5 inches for the extension at the top.
4. Click OK.

   Because the Bleed layer was created as a shape layer, the gray fill is extended with the increase in canvas size. This is a great example of why it's useful to create a bleed layer as a shape layer.
5. Target the Sword Group layer group, the Lens Flare layer, and the Levels adjustment layer above the Lens Flare layer, then drag all three to the top of the Layers palette, so that all are above the Bleed layer.
6. Expand the Sword Group layer group, then add a layer mask to the Sword Shadow layer.
7. Mask the shadow where it extends the billboard, then compare your work to Figure 64.
8. Save your work, then close Extension Billboard.psd.

FIGURE 64
The final extension billboard mechanical

PLASTIC

chapter 7

WORKING WITH TYPE, Shape Layers, and Filters

1. Design chiseled type.
2. Design plastic type.
3. Design recessed type.
4. Design eroded type.
5. Mask images with type.

LESSON 1

DESIGN CHISELED Type

What You'll Do

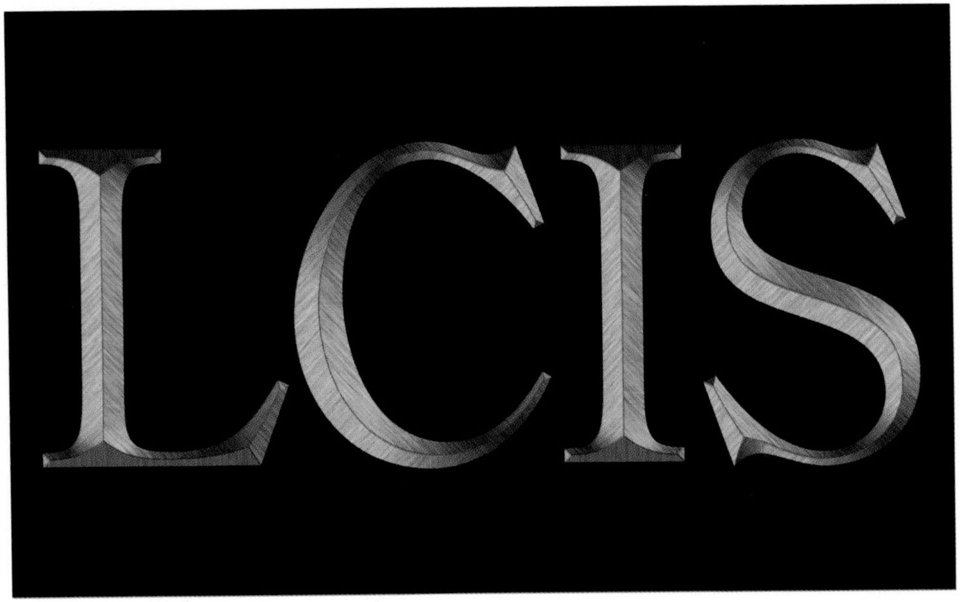

Photoshop has a number of settings and styles that allow you to make gorgeous chiseled type, which is a good thing because chiseled type works well with a number of different design concepts. Chiseling type has many applications: it can be used for metallic textures, stone textures, and wood textures. It can be shiny or dull, dark or bright. Chiseled text is timeless. Of course, it's the first thing you think of when you think of ancient writing, Roman numerals, and mythology. Yet it is just as appropriate to use it in modern contexts. It connotes hardness, yet it also connotes elegance. In this lesson, you'll explore the many options Photoshop makes available for working with this essential and versatile style.

FIGURE 1
Filling the text with gray

AUTHOR'S *note*

When creating chiseled text, I like to use a serif type face because it has interesting lines and arcs. This typeface is Century Old Style, 160 pt.

Chisel text

1. Open AP 7-1.psd, then save it as **Chisel Text**.
2. Set the foreground color to **128R/128G/128B**, fill the text on the Text layer with the foreground color, then compare your canvas to Figure 1.

   When designing text, it's usually a good idea to start with gray text using 128R/128G/128B, because this gives you the full upper half of the grayscale to create highlights and the full lower half of the grayscale to create shadows.
3. Click **Layer** on the menu bar, point to **Layer Style**, then click **Bevel and Emboss**.

   TIP Position the dialog box so that you can see the changes to the image as you work.
4. Verify that the Style is set to Inner Bevel, click the **Technique list arrow**, then click **Chisel Hard**.
5. Drag the **Depth slider** back and forth to see its effect.

   All bevel and emboss effects are created by making one side of a graphic darker and the other side brighter. The Depth slider controls the darkness of the shadows and brightness of the highlights. Increasing the Depth value increases the contrast between the shadows and highlights.

(continued)

6. Drag the **Depth slider** to 150.
7. Slowly drag the **Size slider** to the right to increase the chisel effect.
8. Drag the **Size slider** to 42, then compare your canvas to Figure 2.
9. Click the **Gloss Contour list arrow**, click through each setting in the list, then click **Cone – Inverted**, the third contour in the top row.
10. Verify that the Anti-aliased check box is not checked, click **OK**, then compare your result to Figure 3.

FIGURE 2
Setting the Chisel Hard technique in the Layer Style dialog box

FIGURE 3
Chisel effect

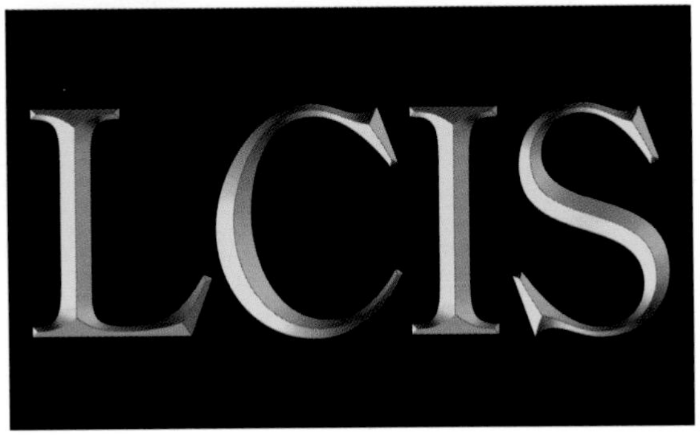

AUTHOR'S *note*

Of the many looks available in the Bevel and Emboss layer style category, the chisel effect in Figure 3 is one of my favorites. I really like the way it raises the center of the letterform to a sharp point that is defined by the dark gray line. However, from a design perspective, this is in no way original art. Though the artwork is pleasing, it's a "canned solution," meaning anybody could recreate it simply by dragging the same sliders and inputting the same values. The challenge when working with layer styles is to create a unique effect. Therefore, it's a good idea to think of the art at this stage as the base effect to which you can add your own techniques and create an original piece of artwork.

FIGURE 4
Overlaying the fill color layer

Apply a fill layer

1. Click **Layer** on the menu bar, point to **New Fill Layer**, then click **Solid Color**.
2. Type **Orange** in the Name text box, click the **Use Previous Layer to Create Clipping Mask check box**, then click **OK**.
3. Type **205R/111G/0B** in the Color Picker, click **OK**, then compare your screen to Figure 4.

   This solid color layer is simply that, a solid fill of color. Its blending mode is set to Normal. However, it appears transparent because it is clipped into the Text layer, and it therefore takes on the Bevel and Emboss layer style applied to the Text layer. If you were to unclip it, it would appear as a simple solid color.

Create selection masks from artwork

1. Press and hold **[Shift][Ctrl][Alt]** (Win) or **[Shift] [option]** [⌘] (Mac), press **[N]**, then press **[E]**.

   For the remainder of this chapter, I will refer to this move as "Create a new stamp visible layer."

   Name the new layer **Stamp Visible**.
2. Click the **Magic Wand Tool**, set the Tolerance value to **4**, then verify that the Anti-alias and Contiguous check boxes are both checked.
3. Select the tops and bottoms of the letters *L* and *I* so that your canvas resembles Figure 5.
4. Click **Select** on the menu bar, point to **Modify**, then click **Expand**.
5. Type **1** in the Expand By text box, then click **OK**.
6. Save the selection as **Tops/Bottoms**, then deselect.
7. In the Channels palette, click the **Channel thumbnail** for the Tops/Bottoms channel to see the selection mask.
8. Click the **Channel thumbnails** for the **Red, Green**, and **Blue channels** to see what's on each of them.

(continued)

FIGURE 5
Selecting the tops and bottoms

FIGURE 6
Blue channel loaded as a selection

FIGURE 7
Half Round gloss contour

9. Click the **Channel thumbnail** on the RGB channel, press and hold **[Ctrl]** (Win) or [⌘] (Mac), then click the **Channel thumbnail** on the Blue channel.

   TIP Pressing and holding [Ctrl] (Win) or [⌘] (Mac) when clicking a Channel thumbnail loads the channel as a selection mask.

   Our goal is to create a selection mask for the left side of each letter. As shown in Figure 6, the Blue channel gets us the closest to that goal—but not close enough.

10. Deselect, return to the Layers palette, then delete the Stamp Visible layer.

    We needed the Stamp Visible layer only to create the Tops/Bottoms selection.

11. Double-click the **Bevel and Emboss effects layer**, click the **Gloss Contour list arrow**, click **Half Round**, then click **OK**.

    As shown in Figure 7, with the Half Round gloss contour, the chisel effect has very light highlights.

(continued)

12. In the Channels palette, duplicate the Blue channel, rename it as **Right Side**, then compare the new channel, as shown in Figure 8.

13. Open the Levels dialog box, drag the **white triangle** left until the third Input text box reads 182, then click **OK**.

    The right side of the letterforms are now white in the selection mask. However, the tops of the letters are also white, which means they too would be part of any selection made from this mask.

    TIP You can open the Levels dialog box by pressing [Ctrl] [L] (Win) or [⌘] [L] (Mac)

14. Press and hold **[Ctrl]** (Win) or [⌘] (Mac), then click the **Channel thumbnail** for the Tops/Bottoms channel.

    The Tops/Bottoms channel is loaded as a selection in the Right Side channel.

15. Fill the selection with black, deselect, then compare your selection mask to Figure 9.

    We have now successfully isolated the right side of the letterforms from the left side and from the tops and bottoms of the letterforms. The tops of the C and S letters are white or light gray; they will be selected or partially selected when this mask is loaded. As you'll see, this won't be a problem; keep an eye on these areas as we move forward.

16. Duplicate the Right Side channel, then name the new channel **Left Side**.

(continued)

FIGURE 8
Duplicated Blue channel

FIGURE 9
Masking out the tops and bottoms

FIGURE 10
Inverted channel

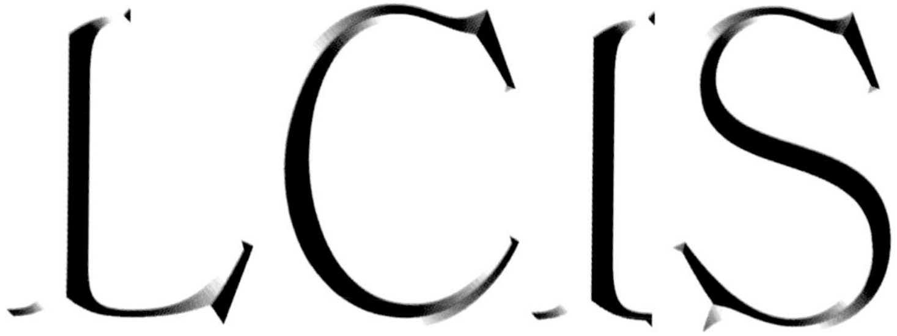

FIGURE 11
Masking out the tops and bottoms

17. Press **[Ctrl][I]** (Win) or ⌘ **[I]** (Mac) to invert the channel.
18. Open the Levels dialog box, drag the **black triangle** right until the first Input text box reads 40, then click **OK**.

    Compare your screen to Figure 10.
19. Load the Tops/Bottoms channel as a selection, expand the selection by 1 pixel, fill the selection with black, then deselect so that your Left Side channel resembles Figure 11.
20. Click the **RGB channel**, then return to the Layers palette.
21. Double-click the **Bevel and Emboss effects layer**, click the **Gloss Contour list arrow**, click **Cone – Inverted**, then click **OK**.
22. Save your work.

Create a texture

1. Click **Image** on the menu bar, click **Duplicate**, type **Texture** in the As text box, then click **OK**.
2. Flatten the duplicate file, then fill the canvas with the gray foreground color.
3. Save the file as **Texture.psd**.
4. Click **Filter** on the menu bar, point to **Noise**, then click **Add Noise**.
5. Type **124** in the Amount text box, verify that the Uniform option button is selected, then verify that the Monochromatic check box is checked.
6. Click **OK**, duplicate the Background layer, then name the new layer **Left Angle**.

(continued)

7. Duplicate the Left Angle layer, name the new layer **Top**, then hide the Top layer.
8. Target the **Left Angle layer**, click **Filter** on the menu bar, point to **Blur**, then click **Motion Blur**.
9. Drag the **Distance slider** to 32, set the Angle to 45, compare your Motion Blur dialog box to Figure 12, then click **OK**.
10. Show and target the **Top layer**, click **Filter** on the menu bar, point to **Blur**, then click **Motion Blur**.
11. Verify that the Distance slider is set to 32, set the Angle to 90, then click **OK** to close the dialog box.
12. Hide the Top layer, target the **Left Angle layer**, select all, then copy.
13. Return to the Chisel Text document, then target the **Orange layer**.

(continued)

FIGURE 12
Motion Blur dialog box

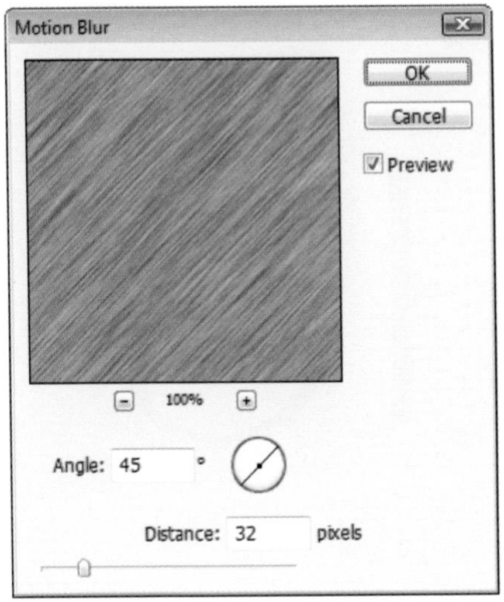

AUTHOR'S *note*

When applying filters, it's a good idea to write down the specifications you use because, unlike layer styles or adjustment layers, filters cannot be modified once they are applied. The next time you return to the filter's dialog box—in this case, the Add Noise dialog box—it will show the previous settings that you used. However, that's the only record you have of the move you made. It's best that you write the information down somewhere because if you come back to this illustration three weeks or three years from now, you'll have no idea which settings you used.

FIGURE 13
Pasting the left-side texture

FIGURE 14
Flipping the artwork

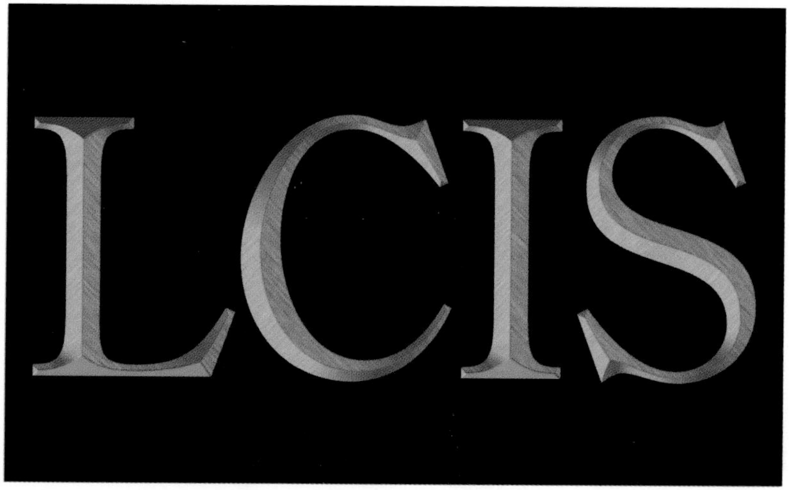

Apply textures

1. Verify that the Orange layer is targeted, then load the **Left Side** selection.
2. Click **Edit** on the menu bar, click **Paste Into**, then compare your canvas to Figure 13.

   The texture has been pasted everywhere on the canvas except the right sides and the tops and bottoms, which are masked in the Left Side selection that you loaded.
3. Name the new layer **Left**, set its blending mode to Multiply, then set its Opacity to 40%.
4. Load the **Right Side** selection, click **Edit** on the menu bar, then click **Paste Into**.

   The same Left Angle artwork is pasted into the Right Side selection.
5. Click **Edit** on the menu bar, point to **Transform**, then click **Flip Horizontal**.

   As shown in Figure 14, the texture on the right side of the letterforms is now angled in the opposite direction.

(continued)

6. Name the new layer **Right**, then change its blending mode to Overlay.
7. Load the **Tops/Bottoms** selection.
8. Switch to the Texture document, show and target the **Top layer**, select all, (if necessary), copy, then return to the Chisel Text document.
9. Click **Edit** on the menu bar, then click **Paste Into**.
10. Name the new layer **Top/Bottom**, set the blending mode to Overlay, then compare your artwork to Figure 15.
11. Save your work.

FIGURE 15
Tops and bottoms with texture

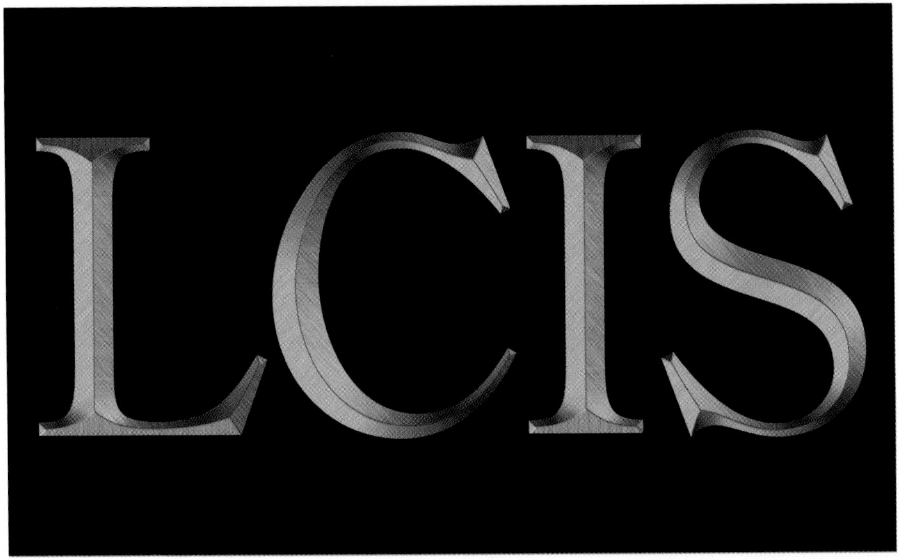

FIGURE 16
Duplicating the left side

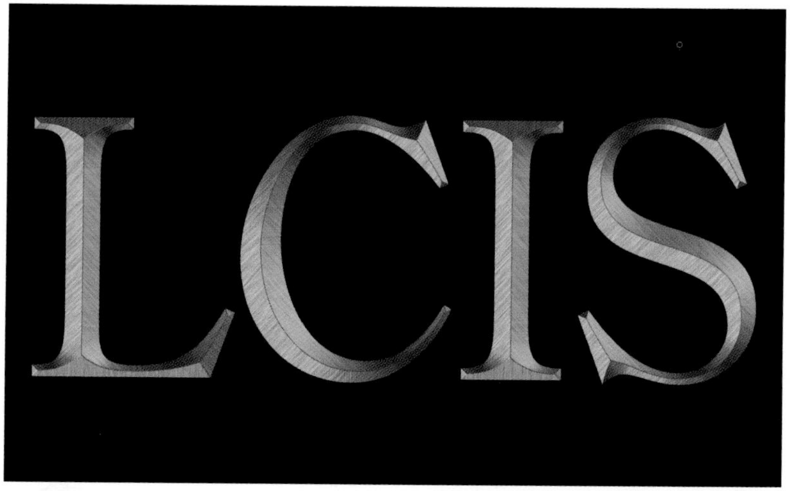

FIGURE 17
Final artwork

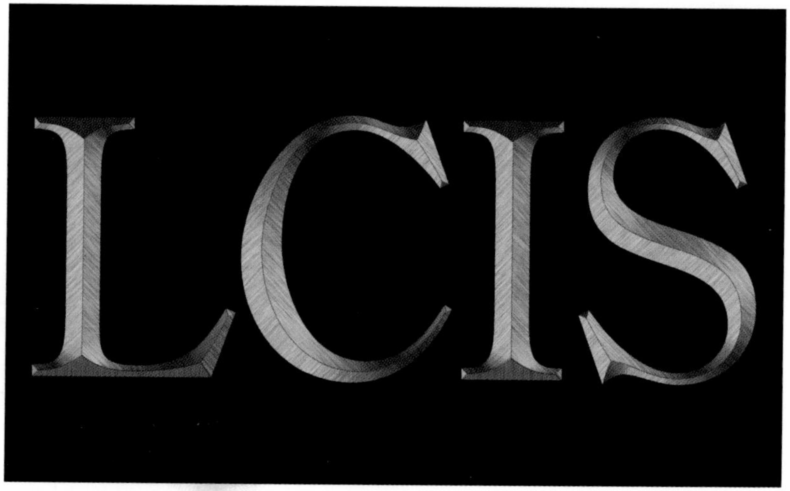

Modify blending modes to modify effects

1. Target the **Left layer,** then press **[Ctrl][J]** (Win) or [⌘] (Mac) to duplicate the layer.
2. Change the blending mode to Overlay, then change the opacity to 100%.

   As shown in Figure 16, the move made the texture more distinct and detailed without darkening highlights.
3. Duplicate the Right layer.

   Duplicating the Right layer intensifies the color and texture on the right side of the letterforms.
4. Target the **Top/Bottom layer**, then change its blending mode to Multiply.

   As shown in Figure 17, the Multiply blending mode darkens both the tops and bottoms of the letterforms, allowing the right sides of the letterforms to be the brightest and most saturated areas of the illustration. The effect is that a gold light source is shining on the letters from the right.
5. Save your work, close Chisel Text, then save and close Texture.

LESSON 2

DESIGN PLASTIC Type

What You'll Do

Plastic type, unlike chiseled text, is unusual and not regularly seen, which makes it a great technique for you to have in your skills set. One of the great things about working with type is that it allows you to use some of the more extreme filters—ones that would have little or no application for a realistic image. The Plastic Wrap filter is one of those filters—a very cool effect, but one that is rarely used with images, except maybe for dramatic special effects. When you learn how to use it with text, it opens the door for a number of practical applications: it's fun, it's playful, and it is an eye-catcher.

FIGURE 18

Applying the Round Corners filter to Illustrator text

FIGURE 19

Pasting text as a shape layer

Create text with rounded corners

1. Open AP 7-2.ai in Adobe Illustrator, then save it as **Round Corners**.
2. Select all, click **View** on the menu bar, then click **Hide Edges**.
3. Click **Filter** on the menu bar, point to the first **Stylize** command, then click **Round Corners**.
4. Type **.1"** in the Radius text box, click **OK**, then compare your artwork to Figure 18.
5. Click **Edit** on the menu bar, click **Copy**, then save your work.
6. Switch to Photoshop, open AP 7-3.psd, then save it as **Plastic**.
7. Set the foreground color to **128R/128G/128B**, then paste.
8. In the Paste dialog box, click **Shape Layer**, click **OK**, then compare your canvas to Figure 19.

   The artwork is pasted on its own layer as a vector graphic and uses the current foreground color as its fill. The path that defines the letterforms is a vector graphic, like any path in Photoshop or Illustrator. As a vector graphic, the path—and therefore the letterforms—can be scaled, rotated, and otherwise transformed without any loss in quality.

(continued)

9. Show the Paths palette.

   When you create a shape layer, the path on the layer is automatically listed in the Paths palette as a vector mask. The vector graphic on the shape layer is no different than creating a path in Photoshop using the Pen Tool.

10. Double-click **Shape 1 Vector Mask** in the Paths palette.

11. Type **Text Path** in the Name text box of the Save Path dialog box, then click **OK**.

    The path on the shape layer is added to the Paths palette as a path.

12. Switch to the Layers palette, click the **Vector mask thumbnail** on the Shape 1 layer to make the path invisible, then compare your canvas to Figure 20.

13. Save your work.

FIGURE 20
"Base text" in Photoshop

FIGURE 21
Applying the Pillow Emboss

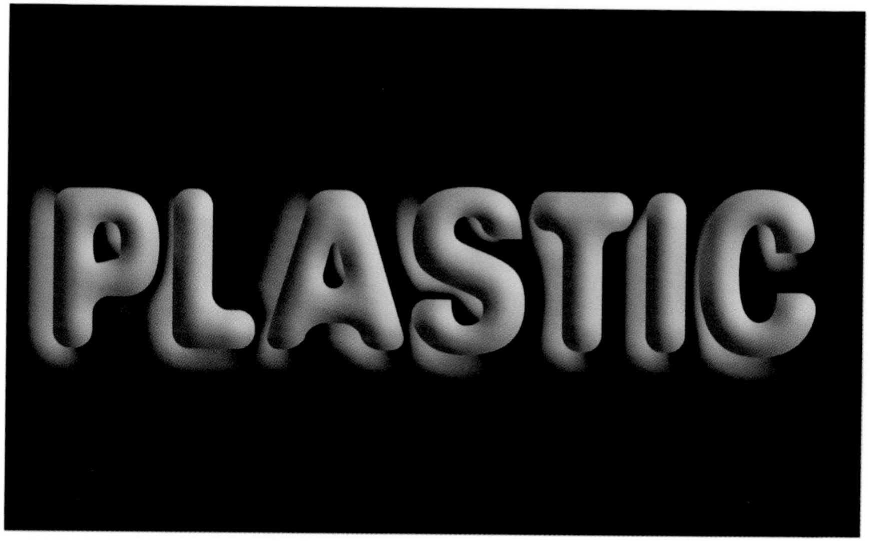

Emboss for a plastic effect

1. Click **Layer** on the menu bar, point to **Layer Style**, then click **Bevel and Emboss**.
2. Set the Style to **Pillow Emboss**, then verify that the Technique is set to Smooth.
3. Drag the **Depth slider** to 100, drag the **Size slider** to 98, then drag the **Soften slider** to 7.
4. Click **OK**, then compare your canvas to Figure 21.

   The pillow emboss gave us the texture we want for the letterforms; it also gave us the white shadows behind the letterforms, which we don't want.
5. Press and hold **[Ctrl]** (Win) or ⌘ (Mac), then click the **Layer thumbnail** on the Shape 1 layer to load it as a selection.
6. Click **Edit** on the menu bar, then click **Copy Merged**.

   Copy Merged is an important and extremely useful command. When you apply the Copy Merged command to layered artwork, it copies the selected artwork as though all the layers were merged and the image was flattened. To put it in other terms, the Copy Merged command copies selected artwork as it *appears*, regardless of how many different layers are involved in creating the artwork.

(continued)

7. Click **Edit** on the menu bar, click **Paste**, then name the new layer **Plastic Text**.
8. Hide the Shape 1 layer, then compare your canvas to Figure 22.
9. Save your work.

Apply color for a plastic effect

1. Click **Layer** on the menu bar, point to **New Fill Layer**, then click **Solid Color**.
2. Type **Gold** in the Name text box, click the **Use Previous Layer to Create Clipping Mask check box**, then click **OK**.
3. Type **255R/234G/94B** in the Color Picker, then click **OK**.

(continued)

FIGURE 22
Letterforms alone

AUTHOR'S *note*

Plastic objects are created by pouring a liquid into a mold and then allowing it to solidify. My goal with the pillow emboss was to make the text appear rounded, with soft shadows and soft highlights as though it were created from a mold. The round corners were created in Illustrator with the Round Corners filter.

FIGURE 23

Increasing saturation

4. Set the blending mode on the Gold layer to Soft Light.
5. Press and hold **[Alt]** (Win) or **[option]** (Mac), click the **Create new fill or adjustment layer button** on the Layers palette, then click **Hue/Saturation**.

   TIP When you use this method to create an adjustment layer, the New Layer dialog box opens.

6. Click the **Use Previous Layer to Create Clipping Mask check box**, then click **OK**.
7. Drag the **Saturation slider** to +50, click **OK**, then compare your result to Figure 23.

   The combination of the Soft Light blending mode and the increased saturation creates an effect that mimics the vibrant color and muted sheen of plastic. Note that the overall texture is smooth and round because the shadows are not too deep. Though the highlights are distinct, they are not harsh or glaring.

8. Save your work.

Apply the Plastic Wrap filter

1. Verify that the Hue/Saturation adjustment layer is targeted, select all, click **Edit** on the menu bar, then click **Copy Merged**.
2. Click **Edit** on the menu bar, click **Paste**, then name the new layer **Plastic Wrap**.

   TIP The Select All – Copy Merged – Paste sequence yields the same result as the Stamp Visible sequence.
3. Click the **Rectangular Marquee Tool**, then select the left side of the canvas as shown in Figure 24.
4. Press **[Ctrl][H]** (Win) or ⌘ **[H]** (Mac) to hide the selection edges, click **Filter** on the menu bar, point to **Artistic**, then click **Plastic Wrap**.
5. Drag the **Highlight Strength slider** to 15, drag the **Detail slider** to 8, then drag the **Smoothness slider** to 9.
6. Click **OK**, then compare your result to Figure 25.

   The Plastic Wrap filter has different effects on different selections. For example, if we had selected the entire image, the filter would have yielded a different result. We selected only the first four letters because, after experimenting, this was my favorite result for the *P*, the *L*, the *A*, and the *S*.
7. Click **Edit** on the menu bar, then click **Fade Plastic Wrap**.

(continued)

FIGURE 24
Selecting the first four letters

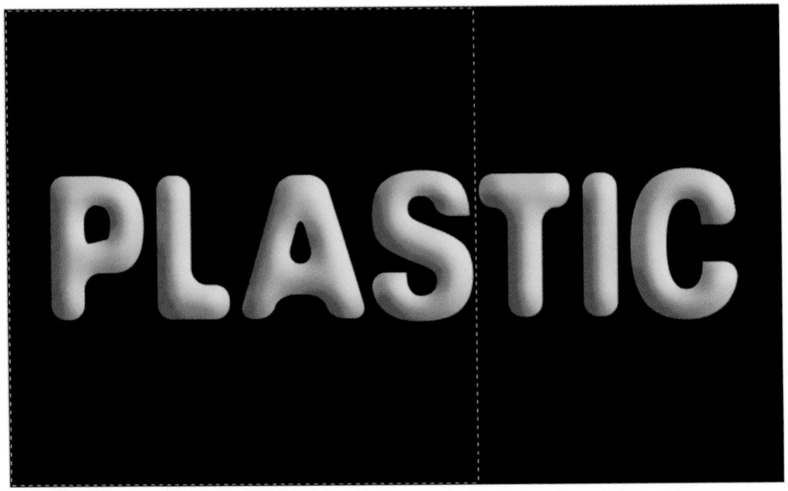

FIGURE 25
Applying the Plastic Wrap filter to the selection

FIGURE 26
Applying the Plastic Wrap filter to the remainder

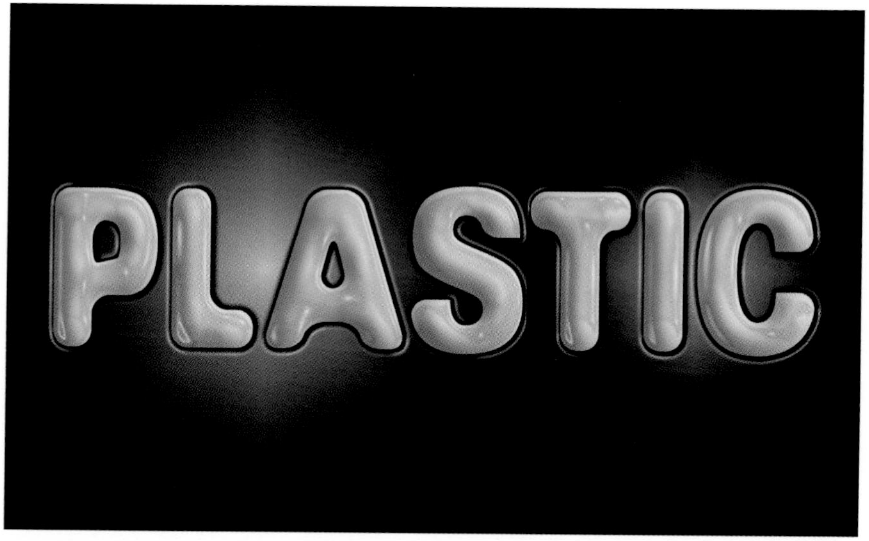

8. Verify that Preview is checked, drag the **Opacity slider** to 75%, click the Mode list arrow, click **Hard Light**, and keep the Fade dialog box open.

   The Fade dialog box is something of a secret when it comes to working with filters. It offers a "one-time" chance to apply an opacity setting and/or a blending mode to a filter. I think of it as a secret because who would think to check the Edit menu to modify a filter? We're not going to execute this Fade Plastic Wrap command. Because we are applying the filter to a merged layer, we can apply an opacity setting and/or a blending mode to the layer itself. This way, we'll be able to modify the opacity and/or blending mode whenever we want to.

9. Click **Cancel**.
10. Click **Select** on the menu bar, then click **Inverse**.
11. Hide the selection, click **Filter** on the menu bar, click **Plastic Wrap** at the very top of the Filter menu, then compare your result to Figure 26.

    TIP The Filter menu lists the last filter used (with the settings last used) at the top of the menu.

12. Save your work.

Using blending modes to modify a filter effect

1. Verify that the Plastic Wrap layer is targeted, press and hold **[Ctrl]** (Win) or [⌘] (Mac), then click the **Layer thumbnail** on the hidden Shape 1 layer to load a selection of the shape.
2. Click the **Add layer mask button** on the Layers palette, then compare your result to Figure 27.

   On its own, with no blending mode, this effect could be used for a number of real-world applications, especially for graphic projects like a comic book, a graphic novel, or as cover art for a video game. In terms of looking like plastic, however, without a blending mode, the result looks a bit more like wax than it does plastic.
3. Change the blending mode to Hard Light.

   The Hard Light blending mode saturates the yellow overall. It removes the midrange effects from the filter while maintaining the extreme highlights. The result is a very dramatic effect that does indeed look like plastic.

(continued)

FIGURE 27
Plastic Wrap filter applied

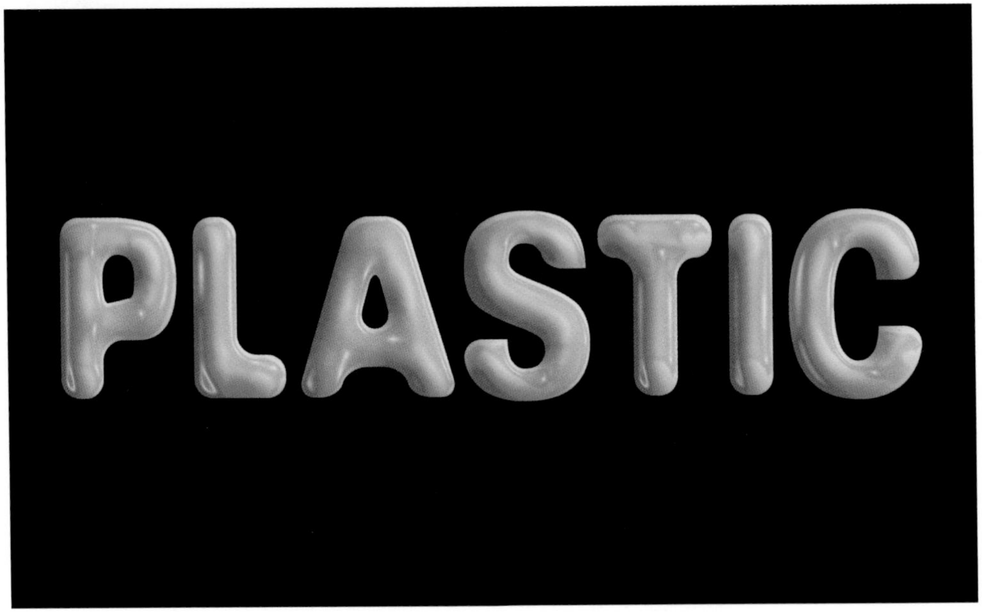

FIGURE 28
Applying the Luminosity blending mode

4. Change the blending mode to Lighten.

   With the Lighten blending mode, only the areas of the top layer that are lighter than those of the image below it remain visible. With this artwork, this means that the grayish, midrange "plastic" from the filter becomes invisible, because it is darker than the image below. Only the white highlights from the filter remain visible, because they are so much lighter than the image below.

5. Change the blending mode to Luminosity, then compare your result to Figure 28.

   Luminosity is just another word for brightness. The Luminosity blending mode applies the brightness information of the image on the targeted layer to the image below. It doesn't alter the hue or the saturation of the pixels below, only the brightness. For this artwork, I found Luminosity to be the most interesting choice. As with the Hard Light and Lighten blending modes, it maintains the highlights from the filter. Unlike the Hard Light and Lighten blending modes, Luminosity allows the midrange plastic wrap effects from the filter to show through.

6. Save your work, then close the Plastic document.

LESSON 3

DESIGN RECESSED Type

What You'll Do

Recessed type is one of those effects that always looks good. As a designer, I often find myself working to *build up*—to make my artwork three-dimensional, to make it jump off of the canvas. Let's just say that I use the Bevel and Emboss layer style quite often. This lesson is designed to remind you to look the other way and to remember that dimensionality can also be created by pushing things back, pushing them in, and pushing them away. This is a complex, in-depth exploration into one of my favorite techniques for creating dramatic recessed type effects. It's also a great example of a great challenge—how to make multiple layer styles work together to produce a single effect.

FIGURE 29

Inner Shadow settings in the Layer Style dialog box

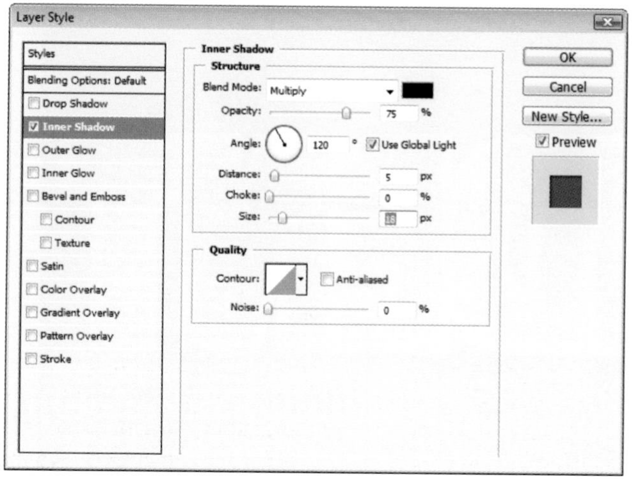

FIGURE 30

Inner Shadow effect

Use the Inner Shadow layer style

1. Open AP 7-4.psd, then save it as **Inner Shadow**.
2. Target **Layer 1**, click the **Add a layer style button** fx on the Layers palette, then click **Inner Shadow**.
3. Set the **Angle** to 120, then drag the **Size slider** to 18 so that your dialog box resembles Figure 29.
4. Click **OK**, then compare your artwork to Figure 30.

   This is the most basic effect from the Inner Shadow layer style.
5. Save your work, then close Inner Shadow.

Use the Inner Shadow layer style in conjunction with a drop shadow

1. Open AP 7-5.ai in Adobe Illustrator.

   In this Illustrator file, I used the Offset Path command to create the larger black type behind the red type.

2. Close AP 7-5.ai, switch to Photoshop, open AP 7-6.psd, then save it as **Indent**.

   I exported the Illustrator file with its layers as a .psd document, then added the hidden gradient layer when I opened it in Photoshop.

   TIP For an in-depth explanation of exporting layered artwork from Illustrator to Photoshop, see Chapter 1.

3. Target the **Background layer**, then fill it with black.
4. Target the **Offset layer**, fill the black type with white, then compare your result to Figure 31.
5. Click the **Add a layer style button** *fx* on the Layers palette, then click **Inner Shadow**.
6. Set the **Angle** to 135, verify that the Use Global Light check box is checked, then set the **Opacity** to 85%.
7. Drag the **Distance slider** to 9, drag the **Size slider** to 8, then click **OK**.

   The black area is now a foreground element, and it is casting a shadow on the white and red type, which are both on one plane behind the black area.

(continued)

FIGURE 31
Modifying the artwork

FIGURE 32
Applying a drop shadow to the red type

FIGURE 33
Sample letterforms with interesting negative spaces

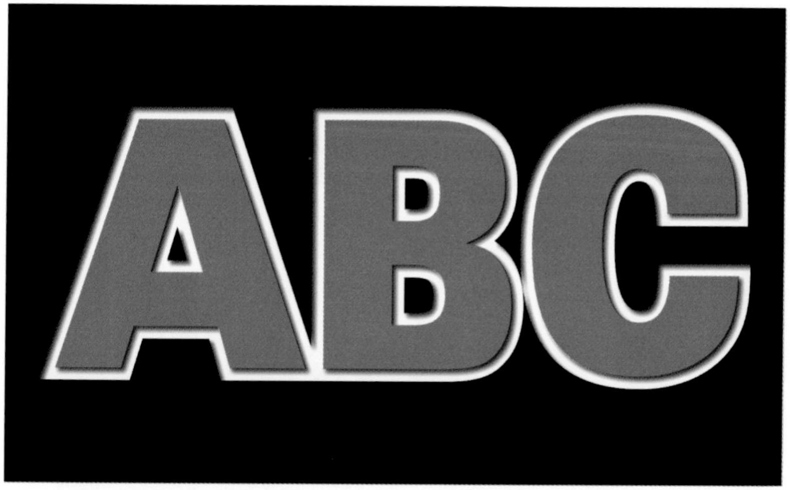

8. Target the **Red Type layer**, click *fx* on the Layers palette, then click **Drop Shadow**.
9. Verify that the Angle is set to 135 and that the Use Global Light check box is checked, then set the **Opacity** to 85%.
10. Drag the **Distance slider** to 9, then drag the **Size slider** to 8.

    Since we want the red text and the black areas to appear to be on the same plane, they must cast the same shadow. Therefore, we are inputting the same specifications for the drop shadow as we did for the inner shadow.
11. Click **OK**, then compare your artwork to Figure 32.
12. Note the black at the center of the letter *D* and between the lines of the *E*.

    When working with type, you're always at the mercy of the letters that make up the word. In this case, the word *INDENT* is a bit boring—all straight lines except for the letter *D*.
13. Compare your artwork to Figure 33.

    The letters in Figure 33 are a bit more interesting for this effect—the triangle in the letter *A*, the two half circles in the letter *B*, and the black negative space that defines the letter *C*. For these letters, the black negative spaces add an interesting component to the overall effect. For the word *INDENT*, the black negative spaces are awkward, especially in the letter *E*.

(continued)

14. Target the **Offset layer**, then unlock the transparent pixels.
15. Drag a **rectangular marquee** around the two black rectangles in the letter *E*.
16. Fill the selection with white, deselect, then compare your artwork to Figure 34.
17. Using the same method, remove the negative space from the center of the letter *D*, then deselect.
18. Target the **Red Type layer**, click **Filter** on the menu bar, point to **Noise**, then click **Add Noise**.
19. Type **15** in the Amount text box, verify that the Uniform option button is selected and that the Monochromatic check box is checked, then click **OK**.
20. Click **Edit** on the menu bar, click **Fade Add Noise**, set the blending mode to Multiply, then click **OK**.

    When working with type only, say for a logo or a headline, adding noise is a favorite technique of mine for adding texture to the type and making the artwork more interesting. I think it adds richness to the text and the suggestion of sparkle.
21. Make the Gradient layer visible, set its blending mode to Multiply, then clip it into the Red Type layer.
22. Compare your artwork to Figure 35.
23. Save your work, then close the Indent document.

FIGURE 34
Removing the black rectangles

FIGURE 35
Multiplying the gradient layer

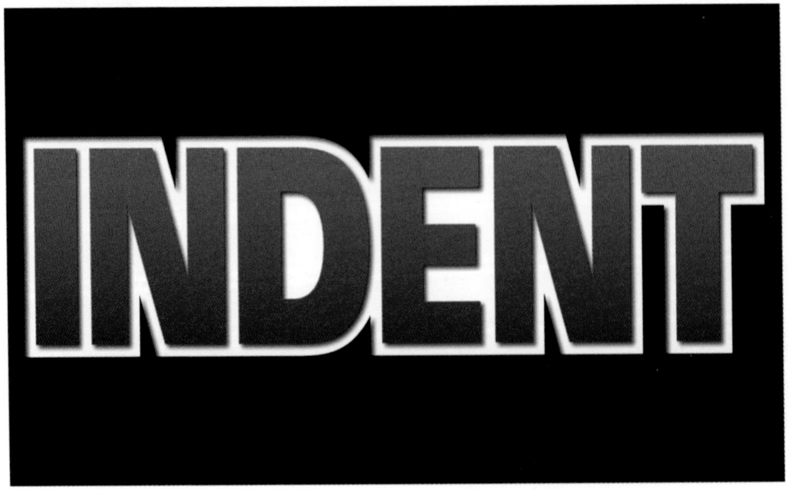

FIGURE 36
Original artwork

FIGURE 37
Applying the Bevel and Emboss layer style

Use the Inner Shadow layer style in conjunction with the Bevel and Emboss layer style

1. Open AP 7-7.psd, save it as **Jazz 2006**, then compare your screen to Figure 36.

   This is artwork that I created in Illustrator. The red type was the original artwork that I set in a Universe bold typeface. I used the Offset Path command to create the three offset outlines, then exported the artwork to Photoshop. Note that this illustration could not have been created in Photoshop, because Photoshop doesn't offer an Offset Path command.

2. Change the foreground color to **128R/128G/128B**.

   TIP From this point on this lesson, we'll refer to this color as "neutral gray."

3. Hide the Red and Orange layers.
4. Fill the Blue layer with neutral gray.

   TIP The Lock transparent pixels option is activated on all four layers.

5. Click the **Add a layer style button** *fx* on the Layers palette, then click **Bevel and Emboss**.
6. Verify that the Style is set to Inner Bevel, click the **Technique list arrow**, then click **Chisel Hard**.
7. Slowly drag the **Size slider** to 16, and watch the effect on the artwork as you drag.

   As shown in Figure 37, at a 16-pixel size the chiseled edge butts up against the edge of the green artwork.

(continued)

8. In the Shading section, set the **Angle** to 45.
9. Click **OK**, then fill the Green layer with neutral gray.
10. Click *fx* on the Layers palette, then click **Inner Shadow**.
11. Verify that the Blend Mode is set to Multiply, the Opacity is set to 75%, the Angle is set to 45, and that the Use Global Light check box is checked.

    The Use Global Light option allows you to set one "master" lighting angle that you can then apply quickly to any other layer styles that use shading. This is a great option for quickly applying a consistent light source to all of your layer styles.

12. Drag the **Distance slider** to 11, drag the **Choke slider** to 14, drag the **Size slider** to 16, then compare your artwork to Figure 38.

    The illustration at this point is composed of two pieces of artwork on two different layers. However, it's important that you note that the two layer styles are working in conjunction so that the artwork appears as one object. The bevel and emboss creates the outer edge of the "object." The inner shadow creates indentations to the interior of the "object." Take a moment to analyze the overall effect, because it's a fine example of an important concept: Don't get caught up in trying to make one layer style carry the whole load. More often than not, it's *many* layer styles working together that create a *single* effect.

(continued)

FIGURE 38
Applying the Inner Shadow layer style

FIGURE 39
Applying the Pattern Overlay

13. Click the words **Pattern Overlay** on the left side of the dialog box.

    TIP If you clicked the Pattern Overlay check box instead of the words, the pattern overlay would be activated with the current texture. Because you clicked the words, the Pattern Overlay style is activated and its dialog box is visible.

14. Click the **Pattern list arrow**, then click the third pattern in the top row (Woven).
15. Click the **Blend Mode list arrow**, click **Soft Light**, click **OK**, then compare your artwork to Figure 39.
16. Make the Orange layer visible, then fill it with neutral gray.
17. Click the **Add a layer style button** *fx* on the Layers palette, then click **Bevel and Emboss**.
18. Verify that the Style is set to Inner Bevel, click the **Technique list arrow**, then click **Chisel Hard**.
19. Drag the **Size slider** to 9.
20. Click the **Gloss Contour list arrow**, click **Ring**, then click the **Anti-aliased check box** to activate it.

(continued)

21. Click **OK**, then compare your artwork to Figure 40.

22. Make the Red layer visible, then fill it with neutral gray.

23. Click *fx* on the Layers palette, then click **Inner Shadow**.

24. Type the settings shown in Figure 41, then click **OK**.

(continued)

FIGURE 40

The second bevel and emboss effect

FIGURE 41

Inner Shadow settings in the Layer Style dialog box

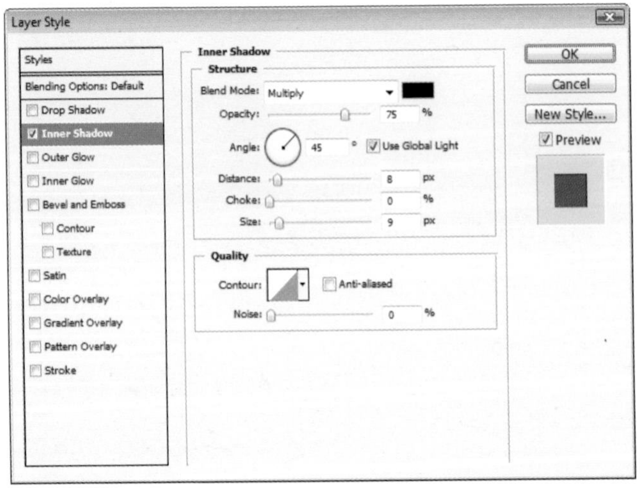

FIGURE 42
The second inner shadow effect

FIGURE 43
Applying a fill layer to the artwork

25. Compare your artwork to Figure 42.
26. Click the **Create new fill or adjustment layer button** on the Layers palette, then click **Solid Color**.
27. Create a color that is **147R/55G/144B**, then click **OK**.
28. Clip the new fill layer into the Red layer, then compare your artwork to Figure 43.

    Now that the text has been filled with purple, the pattern overlay looks too light; there's no contrast between it and the letters above it.

(continued)

29. Double-click the **Pattern Overlay effects layer style** (in the Green layer), change the blending mode to Multiply, change the **Opacity** to 65%, click **OK**, then compare your artwork to Figure 44.

When designing this illustration, at this point, the effect was not working for me. My goal with this illustration was to create the effect of recessed type; I wanted the purple letters to be *indented* into the layer beneath it. I wasn't sure of what was wrong, but I knew the effect wasn't right.

The essential problem for me was that the most notable effect of the illustration was the embossing, which is exactly the opposite of the recessed effect that I was going for. Also, the Inner Shadow effect on the purple letters was not doing the trick.

If you look at the purple letters, you can see the Inner Shadow effect, and they appear to be recessed. But you can look at them another way in which the inner shadow looks like an emboss! This is especially noticeable in the two zeros in 2006. They look embossed, as though they were *above* the silver artwork behind them rather than indented.

Since the word *embossed* kept coming up as the problem for me, I decided that I would make the embossing less shiny and eye-catching, with the hopes that it would no longer dominate the inner shadow effect.

(continued)

FIGURE 44
Changing the blending mode on the Pattern Overlay

FIGURE 45
Removing the gloss contour from the beveled edge

AUTHOR'S *note*

Take a moment to think back to the original artwork. The purple text was taken from the original text that I set in Illustrator. Knowing what I was trying to achieve, I made some specific design decisions when setting the type. The first was the letter *J*. I made it extra large so that it would integrate the two lines of text into one piece of artwork: the *J* is the bridge, so to speak. But even more importantly, I used the hook of the big *J* to get that interesting shape on the left side of the artwork. I knew that it would show off the embossing and the inner shadow effects quite dramatically. I did the same thing with the number *6*. Note how the point at the top extends farther to the right than the *Z* above it. I knew that the *6*, with its point and its round base, would be very interesting once the layer styles were applied.

30. Double-click the **Bevel and Emboss effects layer** on the Orange layer.

    We used the Bevel and Emboss layer style on two layers: the Blue layer and the Orange layer. However, only on the Orange layer did we apply a gloss contour.

31. Click the **Gloss Contour list arrow**, click **Linear**, click **OK**, then compare your result to Figure 45.

    This one step solved the entire problem! If you undo and redo the last step, you'll see what a dramatic difference it made. With the gloss contour removed, the embossed artwork is no longer the dominant effect. Instead, the eye goes immediately to the purple letters.

    The purple letters themselves are unmistakably recessed—they are inset into the embossed artwork. Even if you try, you can't make your eye see them as embossed, not even the two zeros. The only problem is that, without the gloss contour, the artwork is now a bit boring; it's gray overall and lacks contrast. The solution for that is very straightforward: if the art works, but it lacks contrast, don't change the art, just increase the contrast.

(continued)

32. Target the **Color Fill 1 layer**, click [icon] on the Layers palette, then click **Curves**.

33. Add a point to the curve, then set its Input value to **80** and its Output value to **47**.

34. Add a second point to the curve, set its Input value to **155**, set its Output value to **185**, then click **OK**.

35. Compare your artwork to Figure 46.

    Again, one step solved the entire problem. Note that although the increase in contrast is substantial, we did not go too far. The shadows on the embossed artwork are dark gray, not black. The highlights are light gray, not white.

    There's an interesting design lesson to be learned here. My initial instinct was to use the gloss contour to add contrast and snap to the artwork. But the gloss contour ended up working against the effect. As it turns out, all I needed to do was add contrast to get contrast.

36. Save your work, then close Jazz 2006.

FIGURE 46

Final artwork with increased contrast

LESSON 4

DESIGN ERODED
Type

What You'll Do

The need for type with rough edges comes up regularly, and the ability to create it is an essential skill every designer must have. It's ironic, really, when you consider that in the early days of desktop publishing the great goal and the great achievement was to produce smooth lines and curves, both for type and for line art. And yet, you will find that smooth lines and curves are exactly what you don't want for a number of types of artwork.

The technique you'll use in this lesson is very versatile; it can be used to create many different rough, very rough, and not-so-rough edges that you can use for all kinds of type or line art designs. Don't get so caught up in the details though that you miss the big picture. You're going to manipulate a layer mask in conjunction with a vector mask to achieve the effect. This technique is essential, very powerful, and one that has applications far beyond just making rough edges.

Experiment with shape layers

1. Open AP 7-8.psd, save it as **Eroded Text**, then compare your screen to Figure 47.

   The gray artwork was designed in Illustrator and then copied into Photoshop as a shape layer, as shown by the Vector mask thumbnail on the Original Paste layer.

   TIP By default, shape layers appear as gray in the Layers palette so that they are easy to distinguish from layer masks.

2. Press and hold **[Shift]**, then click the **Vector mask thumbnail** in the Original Paste layer to deactivate the shape layer.

   TIP [Shift]-clicking the Vector mask thumbnail in a shape layer toggles it between active and inactive.

(continued)

FIGURE 47
Artwork on the shape layer

FIGURE 48
Deactivating the shape layer

FIGURE 49
Moving a path with the Path Selection Tool

3. Release **[Shift]**, click the **Vector Mask thumbnail** again to activate its path, then compare your screen to Figure 48.

   The Original Paste layer is filled with the gray foreground color. It's important that you understand that the *entire* layer is filled with the gray foreground color. The shape layer uses paths—vector graphics, just like you would create with the Pen Tool—to define what is visible on the layer and what is not visible. With shape layers, anything within the path is visible; anything outside is not.

   TIP Single-clicking a Vector mask thumbnail toggles the path between visible and not visible.

4. [Shift]-click the **Layer mask thumbnail** to reactivate it.
5. Click the **Path Selection Tool**  .
6. Click the center of the letter *c*, then drag it to another location on the canvas.

   Your screen should resemble Figure 49. The paths in a shape layer are all editable. They can be moved. The gray color is visible wherever the path is moved to.

7. Undo your last move, then click anywhere on the black iron background to deactivate the path on the letter *c*.

(continued)

8. Click **Edit** on the menu bar, point to **Transform Path**, click **Rotate 180°**, then compare your artwork to Figure 50.

   Paths used in a shape layer can be transformed just like any other path or any other artwork in Photoshop.

9. Undo your last move.

10. Click the **Direct Selection Tool** , which is located behind the Path Selection Tool.

11. Position your cursor at the edge of the letter *w* in works, then click the path.

    The anchor points on the path become visible. The anchor points all have a hollow center, which indicates that they can be selected individually. That is the difference between the Path Selection Tool and the Direct Selection Tool—with the Direct Selection Tool, you can select individual anchor points on a path.

12. Click and drag any anchor point on the letter *w* to a different location, then compare your result to Figure 51.

    The path is redrawn. More of the layer's gray fill is visible.

13. Delete the Original Paste layer.

(continued)

FIGURE 50
Transforming the path

FIGURE 51
Moving a single anchor point with the Direct Selection Tool

FIGURE 52
The Machine layer

FIGURE 53
The M layer

14. Target the **M layer**, then make it visible.

The first design move we are going to make is to add a Bevel and Emboss layer style to the artwork. However, because the letter *M* is so much bigger than the surrounding letters, we need different settings for the two components. Therefore, we will isolate the letter *M* on its own layer.

15. Duplicate the M layer, then name the new layer **Machine**.

16. Hide the M layer, then target the **Machine layer**.

17. Click [tool icon], then select and delete the letter *M* and the circle around it.

Your screen should resemble Figure 52.

18. Hide the Machine layer, target the **M layer**, then show the M layer.

19. Delete the surrounding text and lines so that your artwork resembles Figure 53.

20. Save your work.

Use shape layers as masks

1. Verify that the M layer is targeted and the Machine layer is hidden.
2. If the path on the M layer is showing, click the **Vector mask thumbnail** to hide the path.
3. Make the Rust layer visible, then drag it down so it is immediately above the M layer.
4. Clip the Rust layer into the M layer, then compare your artwork to Figure 54.

   The shape layer defines the perimeter for the clipped artwork.

   TIP The paths will be hidden in the remaining figures in this lesson unless there is a reason for them to be visible.
5. Click the **Move Tool**, then move the Rust image around in the layer mask to find interesting textures and colors.

   The rust artwork contains some bright yellow areas that you can use as interesting highlights on the letter M. Choose an area that appeals to you.
6. Duplicate the Rust layer, then name the new layer **New Rust**.
7. Drag the **New Rust layer** above the Machine layer, show the Machine layer, then clip New Rust into the Machine layer.

   Your artwork should resemble Figure 55.

(continued)

FIGURE 54
Clipping the Rust layer

FIGURE 55
Clipping the New Rust layer

FIGURE 56
Bevel and Emboss settings

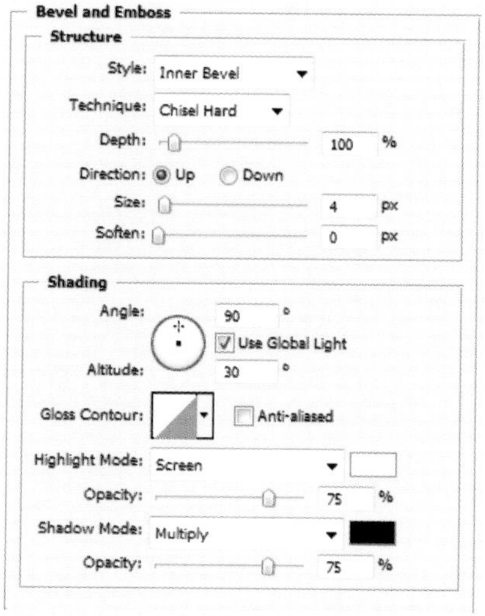

FIGURE 57
Drop Shadow settings

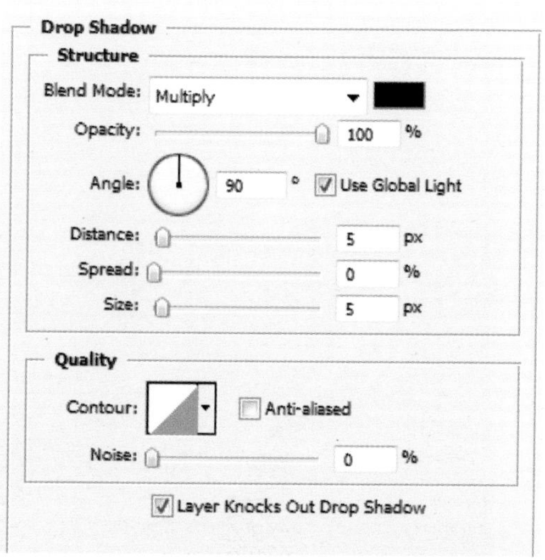

8. Hide the Black Iron layer.

   The Black Iron layer is so dark that it would be difficult to see the subtle changes we're about to make.

9. Target the **M layer**, click the **Add a layer style button** fx on the Layers palette, then click **Bevel and Emboss**.

10. Using Figure 56 as a guide, apply the settings shown in the Structure section, apply the same settings for Angle and Altitude, and leave the Layer Style dialog box open when finished.

    The Chisel Hard edge is an important component to this effect. We want to "erode" the type along its edges, so the visual qualities of the edges play an important role in the final effect. The Chisel Hard style creates a clean, sharp edge that readily shows the pits and dents that create the erosion effect.

11. Click the **Set color for highlight box** (next to Highlight Mode), type **250R/250G/150B**, then click **OK**.

    The yellow highlight works better with the orange rust.

12. In the Styles section on the left, click the words **Drop Shadow**, then enter the settings shown in Figure 57.

(continued)

13. Click **OK**, then compare your artwork to Figure 58.
14. Copy the layer styles from the M layer to the Machine layer.
15. Double-click the **Bevel and Emboss effect** on the Machine layer, change the Size setting to 3, then click **OK**.
16. Make the Black Iron layer visible, then compare your artwork to Figure 59.

    Ultimately, this lesson is about creating eroded text, so take a moment at this stage of the work to look at the logo. The shadow and the bevel and emboss contribute greatly to the illusion of this logo being raised from an iron background. It's a cool effect, but notice how the clean straight lines and smooth curves work against the concept of rusted iron. Smooth is the last word you would think of when you think of rust.
17. Save your work.

Use the Spatter filter

1. Hide the two rust layers so that you can better see the base artwork and how smooth the edges are.
2. Hide the Machine layer, then target the **M layer**.
3. Press and hold **[Ctrl]** (Win) or [⌘] (Mac), then click the **Vector mask thumbnail** on the M layer to load it as a selection.

(continued)

FIGURE 58
Layer styles applied to the M layer

FIGURE 59
Layer styles applied to the Machine layer

FIGURE 60
A layer with a layer mask and a shape mask

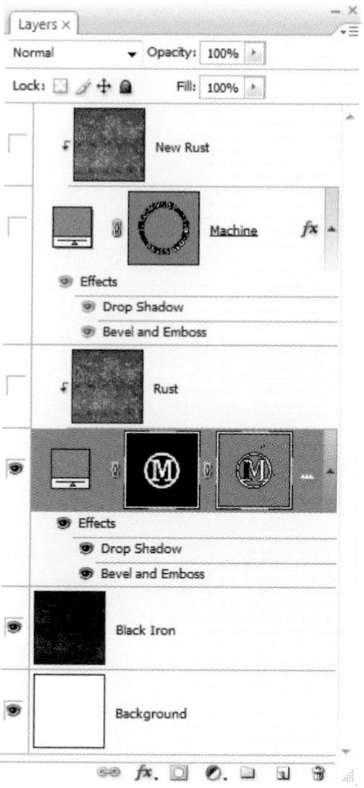

FIGURE 61
Moving the path but not the mask

4. Click the **Add layer mask button** on the Layers palette, then compare your Layers palette to Figure 60.

   A layer mask is added to the layer. Don't be confused when a layer has both a layer mask and a shape layer, because all of the basic rules still apply. The layer mask works like a layer mask, and the shape layer works like a shape layer; nothing changes in terms of how they function.

5. Click the **Path Selection Tool**, select the path, then move the path straight up to the top of the canvas.

   As shown in Figure 61, the artwork is visible *only* where the path overlaps the white areas of the layer mask. The black areas of the layer mask continue to mask the art.

6. Undo your last move.
7. Press and hold **[Alt]** (Win) or **[option]** (Mac), then click the **Layer mask thumbnail** on the M layer.

   The canvas changes to show the contents of the layer mask.

8. Verify that the shape layer's path is not visible.

(continued)

9. Click **Filter** on the menu bar, point to **Brush Strokes**, then click **Spatter**.
10. Drag the **Spray Radius slider** to 14, then drag the **Smoothness slider** to 15.
11. Click **OK**, click the **Vector mask thumbnail** to make the path visible, then compare your screen to Figure 62.

    The path shows the outline of the original artwork. The Spatter filter modified the layer mask in such a way that some of the white areas now extend outside of the original outline, and some of the black areas now extend into the outline, thus creating the rough edge. However, this layer mask does not show the true result of how the filter will affect the artwork, because all of the white areas outside the path will *not* be transparent. The white areas of the layer mask only function as white where they overlap the path. In other words, when a layer has both a layer mask and a shape layer, white areas of the layer mask don't function and are not transparent if they are outside of the path.
12. With the layer mask still visible and targeted, click **Image** on the menu bar, point to **Adjustments**, click **Threshold**, drag the slider all the way to the right, then click **OK**.

    The Threshold adjustment removes the gray pixels and roughens the mask.

(continued)

FIGURE 62
Modified layer mask and the path

FIGURE 63
Eroded edge with the path visible

13. Press and hold **[Alt]** (Win) or **[option]** (Mac), click the **Layer thumbnail**, then compare your screen to Figure 63.

    No part of the layer is visible outside of the path, which is *perfect* for this illustration. Our goal is to create eroded type—in this case, rusted type. When metal rusts, its edges chip and fall away, leaving indentations *into* the edge. It doesn't corrode *outside* of its original shape; it doesn't get bigger when it corrodes. So the path masking out the white areas of the layer mask allows the spatter filter to only cut *into* the original artwork.

14. Hide the path.
15. Show the Machine layer, load the selection from the shape layer, then create a new layer mask.

(continued)

16. Press and hold **[Alt]** (Win) or **[option]** (Mac), click the **Layer mask thumbnail** to view it, click **Filter** on the menu bar, point to **Brush Strokes**, then click **Spatter**.

17. Drag the **Spray Radius slider** to 12, then click **OK**.

18. With the layer mask still visible and targeted, click **Image** on the menu bar, point to **Adjustments**, click **Threshold**, drag the slider all the way to the right, then click **OK**.

19. Press and hold **[Alt]** (Win) or **[option]** (Mac), click the **Layer thumbnail**, then compare your screen to Figure 64.

   TIP Hide the path if necessary.

20. Show the two Rust layers, then compare your artwork to Figure 65.

21. Save your work, then close the Eroded Text document.

FIGURE 64
Eroded edge with clipped imagery

FIGURE 65
Final artwork

LESSON 5

MASK IMAGES with Type

What You'll Do

In this lesson, you're going to create lots of different effects using type to mask images. The lesson is not designed to show you how to do it—it's designed more to show you how to *think* it: how to choose images that work well with a given style of typography, how to combine blending modes to create an effect, how to duplicate and invert layers to branch off into unexpected directions.

When I created this lesson, I really had no final artwork in mind. Instead, I just wrote the steps as I went along. Now you get to take that trip with me. Where you end up is where I ended up. This lesson is designed to show you how I got there, and then you're free to keep going in any direction your imagination leads you.

Use chiseled type to mask images

1. Open AP 7-9.psd, then save it as **Chisel Type Images**.
2. Hide the Orange layer, then show and target the **Wave layer**.
3. Clip the Wave layer into the Text layer, then compare your artwork to Figure 66.

   The image adds an interesting color dynamic that works very well with the silver layer style and texture overlay.
4. Invert the Wave layer, then compare your artwork to Figure 67.

   Another simple move that yields a dramatic effect. Inverted, the whites of the Wave image overlaying the chiseled text creates a sheen that fades into steel blues—perfect for this illustration.

(continued)

FIGURE 66
Clipping the Wave image

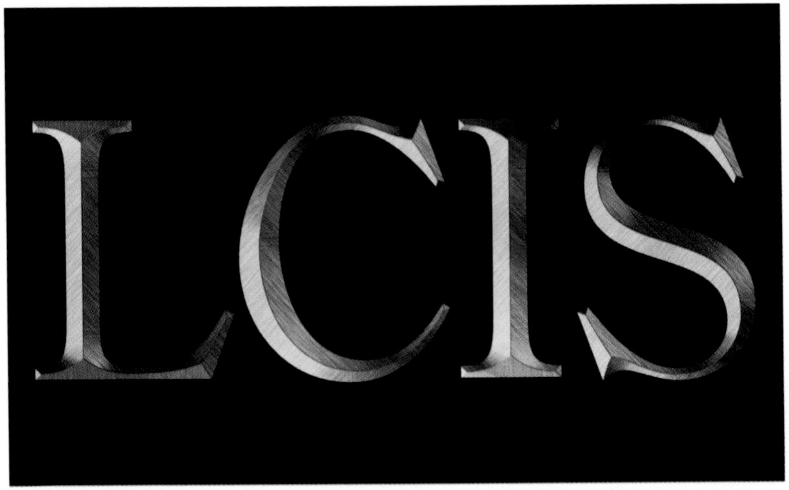

FIGURE 67
Inverting the Wave image

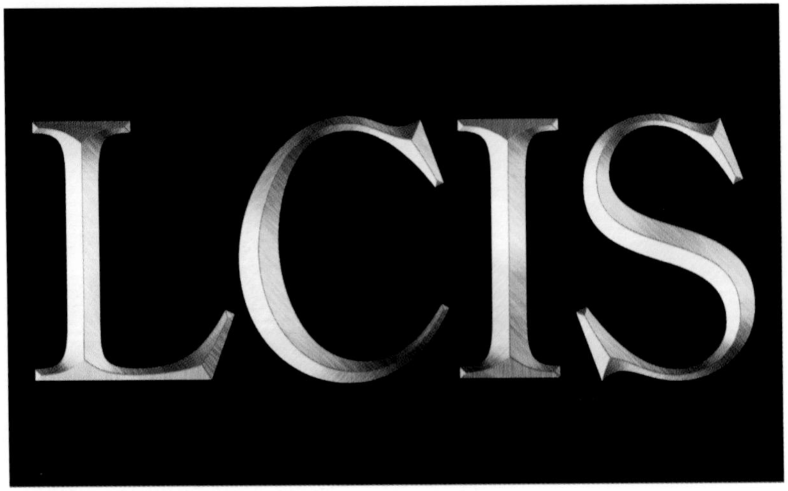

FIGURE 68
Color Burn mode

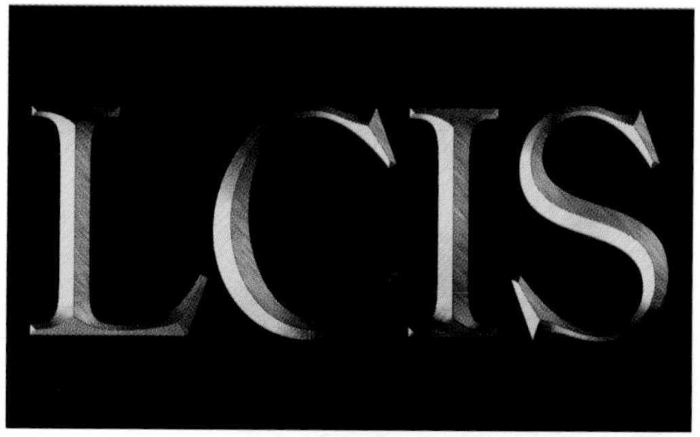

FIGURE 69
Duplicating the Wood layer to achieve a richer image

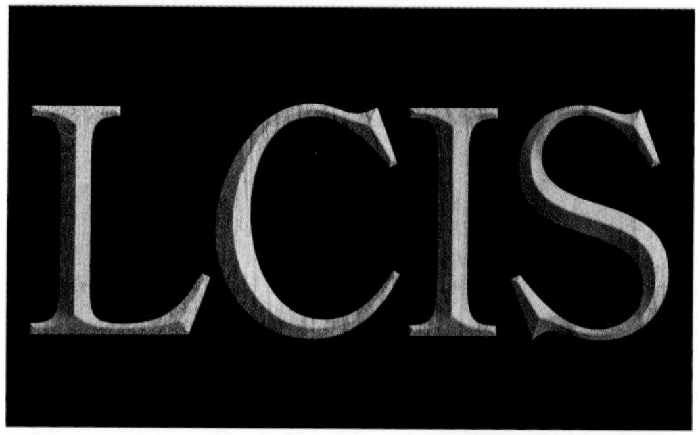

FIGURE 70
Inverting and multiplying the Wood layer

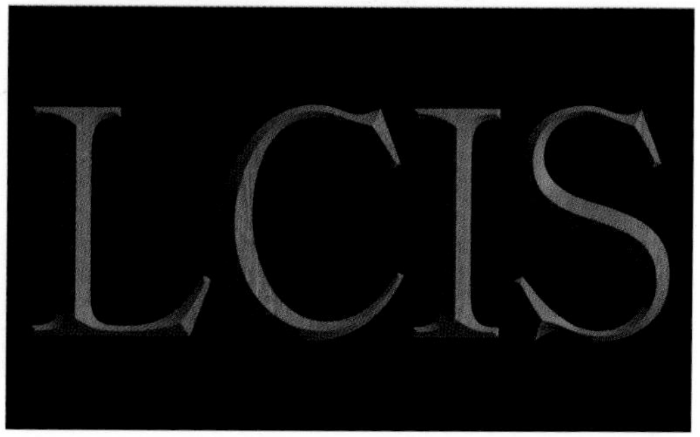

5. Change the blending mode to Color Burn, then compare your result to Figure 68.
6. Hide the Wave layer, show and target the **Wood layer**, click the **Blending mode list arrow**, then click **Overlay**.

   Though the effect is visually interesting, the shine on the text has too much sheen and is too shiny to appear realistically as a wooden texture. Also, the overlayed texture looks too much like brushed steel to work with the wood artwork.
7. Hide the Texture layer.
8. Double-click the **Bevel and Emboss** layer style, change the Gloss Contour to **Linear**, then click **OK**.
9. Duplicate the Wood layer, then compare your artwork to Figure 69.
10. Invert the Wood copy layer to create a wood effect that is much smoother.
11. Change the blending mode to Multiply, then compare your artwork to Figure 70.

(continued)

12. Change the blending mode to Color, change the Gloss Contour on the **Bevel and Emboss** layer style back to Cone-Inverted, then compare your artwork to Figure 71.

13. Hide the two wood layers, show and target the **Granite layer**, change its blending mode to Overlay, then compare your artwork to Figure 72.

    Unlike the Wood image, the Granite image can overlay the shiny gloss contour and maintain a realistic appearance.

(continued)

FIGURE 71
Color mode

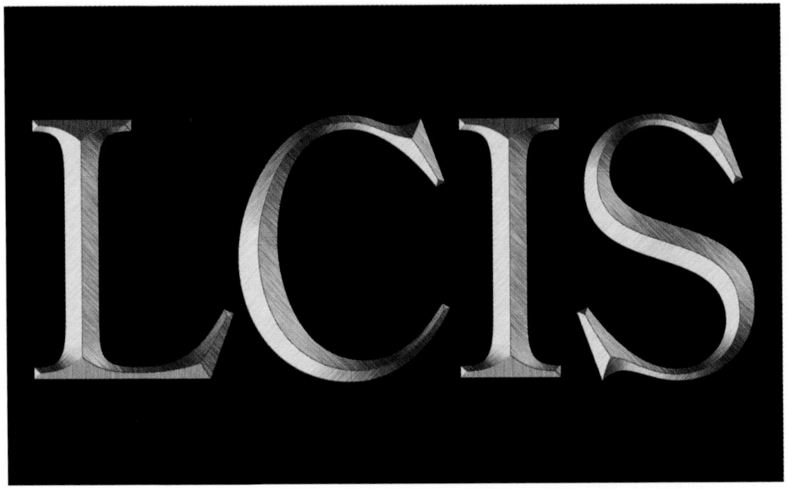

FIGURE 72
Granite image overlayed

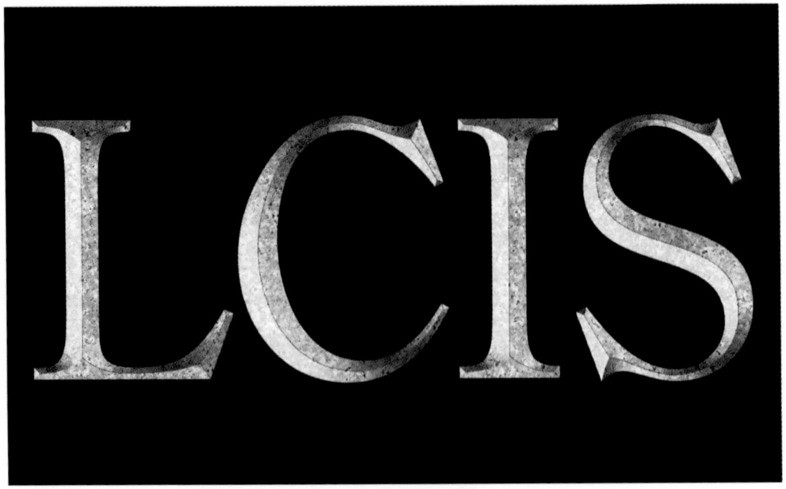

FIGURE 73
Granite image multiplied

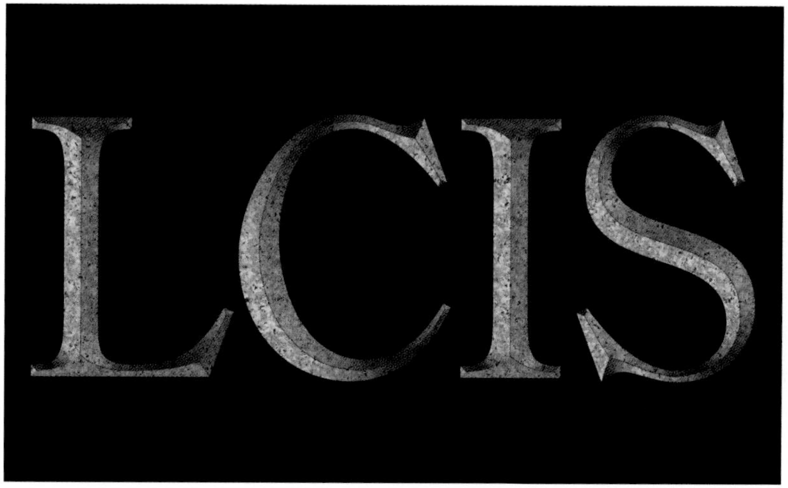

FIGURE 74
Final artwork

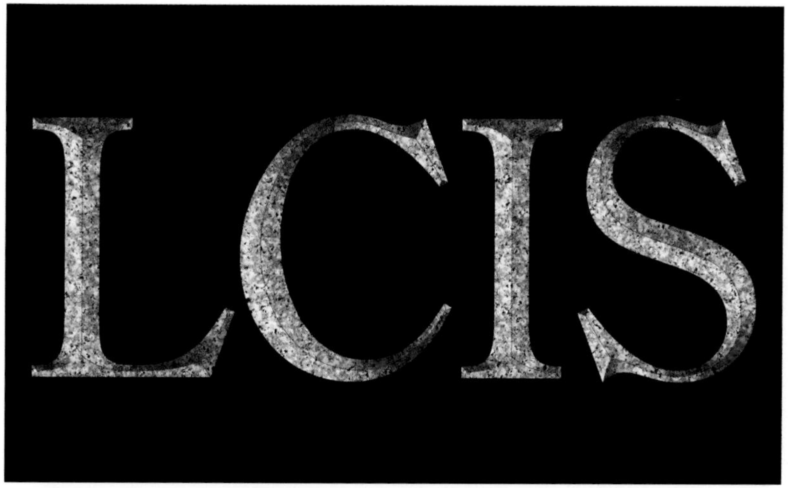

14. Change the blending mode to Multiply, then compare your artwork to Figure 73.
15. Duplicate the Granite layer, then change the blending mode on the copy to Overlay.
16. Make the Wood copy layer visible, then compare your artwork to Figure 74.

    We now have two images and three different blending modes working together to create the final effect.
17. Save your work, then close the file.

Use plastic type to mask images

1. Open AP 7-10.psd, then save it as **Plastic Type Images**.
2. Show and target the **Abstract blue layer**, then change its blending mode to Overlay.
3. Hide the Abstract blue layer, show and target the **Mountains layer**, change its blending mode to Overlay, then compare your artwork to Figure 75.
4. Hide the Mountains layer, show and target the **Geometry layer**, then change its blending mode to Overlay.
5. Hide the Geometry layer, show and target the **Flowers layer**, change its blending mode to Overlay, then compare your artwork to Figure 76.
6. Save your work, then close the file.

Use inset type to mask images

1. Open AP 7-11.psd, then save it as **Inset Type Images**.
2. Open AP 7-12.psd, select all, copy, then close the file.
3. Hide the Red, Orange, and Green layers, then target the **Blue layer**.

(continued)

FIGURE 75
Mountains artwork overlayed

FIGURE 76
Flowers artwork overlayed

FIGURE 77
Clipping the image into the Blue layer

FIGURE 78
Final artwork

4. Paste, clip the image into the Blue layer, then compare your artwork to Figure 77.
5. Show and target the **Green layer**, paste, then clip the image into the Green layer.
6. Show and target the **Orange layer**, paste, then clip the image into the Orange layer.
7. Change the blending mode on the image to Multiply.
8. Show and target the **Red layer**, paste, then clip the image into the Red layer.
9. Compare your artwork to Figure 78.
10. Save your work, then close the file.

PROJECT BUILDER 1

1. Open AP 7-13.psd, then save it as **Carved Wood**.
2. Target the Logo layer, add an Inner Shadow layer style using the settings shown in Figure 79, then keep the Layer Style dialog box open.
3. In the Styles column on the left, click the words Inner Glow.
4. Click Center as the source, then enter the settings shown in Figure 80.
5. Click OK, then set the Logo layer to Multiply.
6. Duplicate the Outer layer, then name the new layer **Inner**.
7. Drag the Inner layer below the Outer layer.
8. Load the selection of the Logo layer.
9. Target the Outer layer, then click the Add layer mask button on the Layers palette.
10. Invert the layer mask.
11. Add a Bevel and Emboss layer style to the Outer layer, enter the settings shown in Figure 81, then keep the Layer Style dialog box open.
12. Change the color on both the Highlight and Shadow modes to 250R/250G/140B.
13. Set the Opacity on the Highlight mode to 100%.
14. Change the blending mode on the Shadow mode to Screen, change its Opacity setting to 45%, then click OK.
15. Target the Inner layer, then move it 3 pixels to the left.
16. Target the Outer layer, then lock the transparent pixels.
17. Click Edit on the menu bar, then click Fill.
18. Fill the layer with 15% White, click OK, then compare your result to Figure 82.
19. Save your work, then close Carved Wood.

FIGURE 79
Applying the Inner Shadow

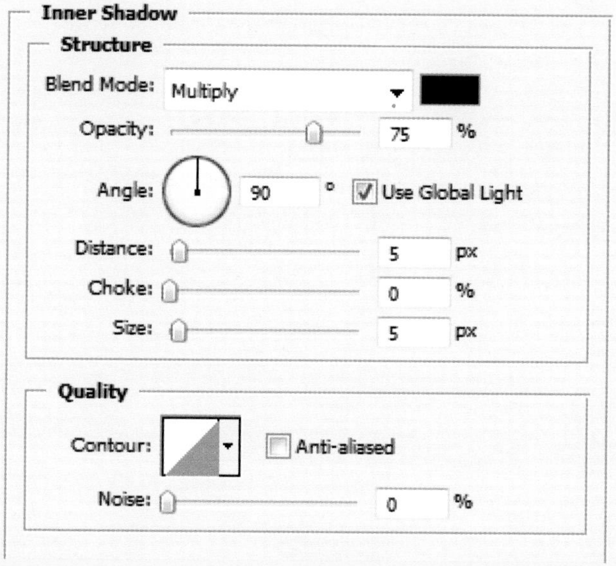

FIGURE 80
Applying the Inner Glow

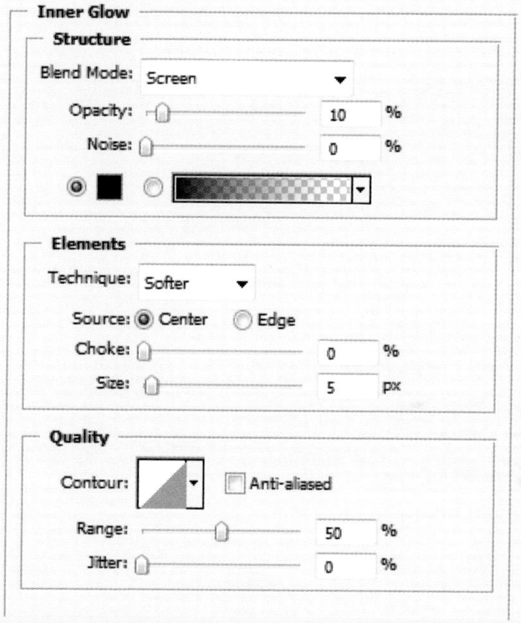

FIGURE 81
Applying the Bevel and Emboss

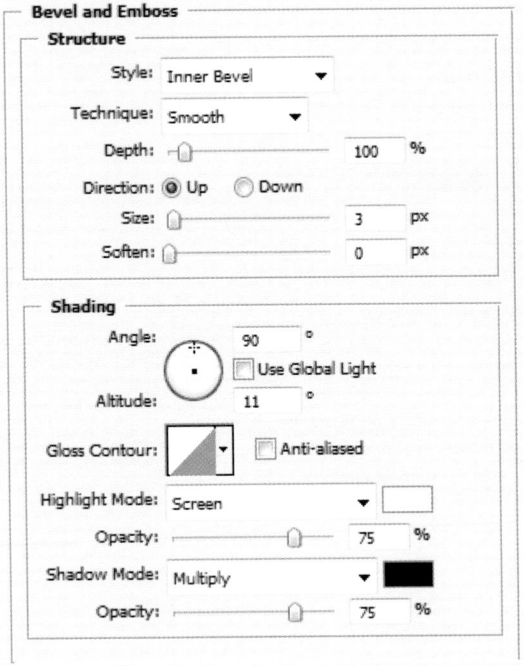

FIGURE 82
Completed Project Builder 1

PROJECT BUILDER 2

1. Open AP 7-14.psd, then save it as **White Mischief**. (*Hint*: What you see is a well-known effect, created with a Drop Shadow layer style. This exercise will show you a neat variation that is less common.)
2. Change the foreground color to **235R/235G/235B**.
3. Fill the Background layer with the new foreground color, then fill the text with the new foreground color.
4. Double-click the Drop Shadow effect, then change its size to 6 pixels.
5. Click Bevel and Emboss, then drag the Depth slider all the way to the right.
6. Set the Opacity slider on the Highlight mode to 100%.
7. Drag the Opacity slider on the Shadow mode to 0, then click OK.
8. Compare your artwork to Figure 83. (*Hint*: The effect is similar, but improved by the subtle and elegant white highlight at the top right of the letterforms. You can manipulate the size and distance settings on both the Drop Shadow and Bevel and Emboss layer styles to create many effective variations.)
9. Save your work, then close White Mischief.

FIGURE 83
Completed Project Builder 2

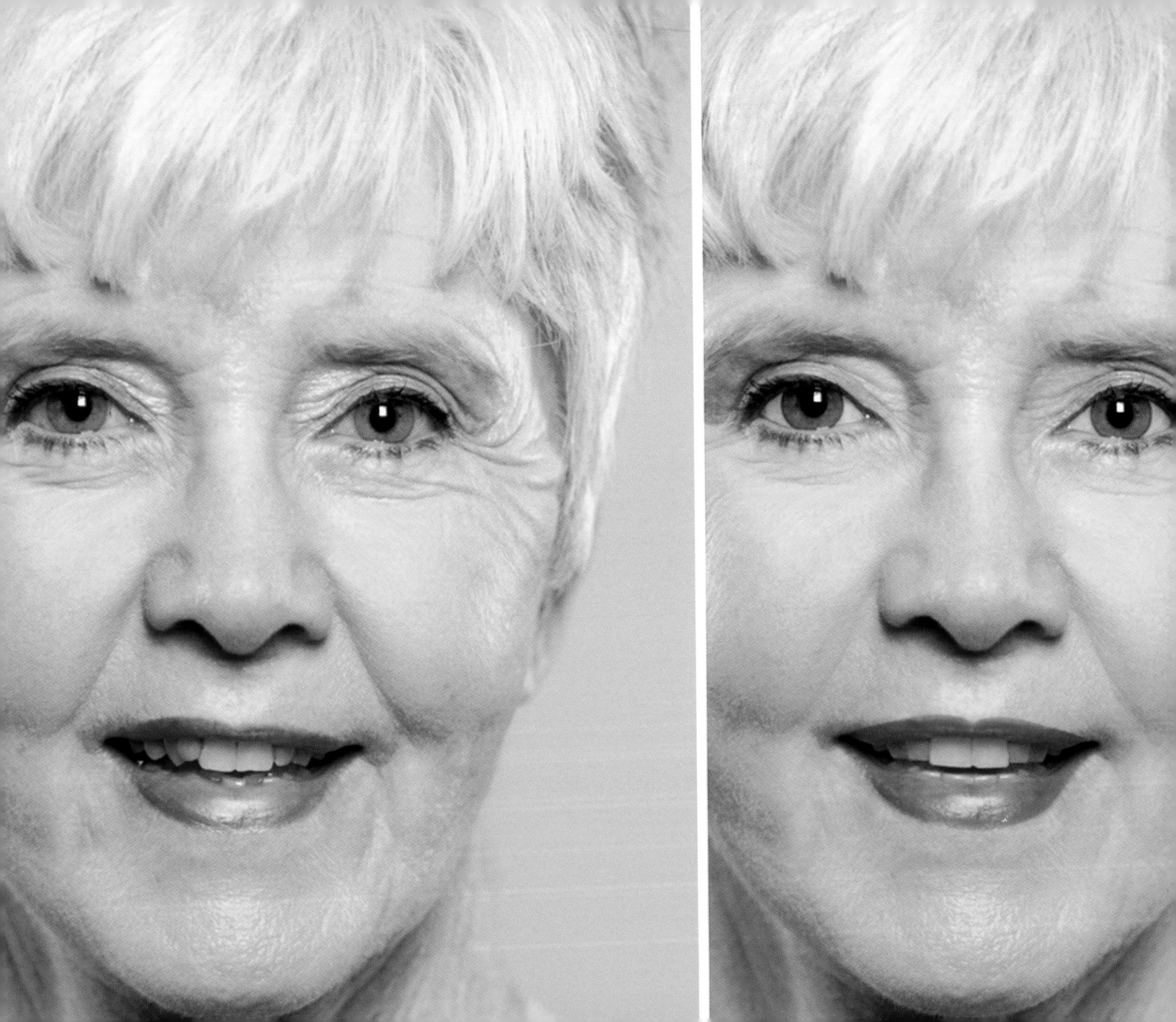

chapter 8

RETOUCHING AND Enhancing Images

1. Whiten eyes.
2. Investigate the Overlay blending mode.
3. Overlay detail.
4. Use a channel as a mask.
5. Use the cloning tools.
6. Retouch teeth.
7. Clone strategically within adjustment layers.

LESSON 1

WHITEN Eyes

What You'll Do

Whitening eyes is a standard move in almost every retouching project that involves a person's face.

People's eyes are seldom perfect. Even the "perfect" models in the magazines get blood-shot eyes. However, it's not only for cosmetic reasons that eyes usually require retouching. In actuality, it's difficult to photograph a subject in a way that the whites of eyes are white, as opposed to a dull bluish gray. Because of eyelids and eyebrows, eyes are usually in shadow, and it usually requires professional lighting techniques to capture a vivid bright, white eye for a portrait.

There are many techniques for whitening eyes, and it seems like every retoucher has his or her own tricks. The technique we're going to execute in this lesson is a standard approach that retouchers use as a baseline—meaning that this technique gets you to a point that the eyes are white enough that they can be cloned or further retouched.

FIGURE 1
Assessing the histogram

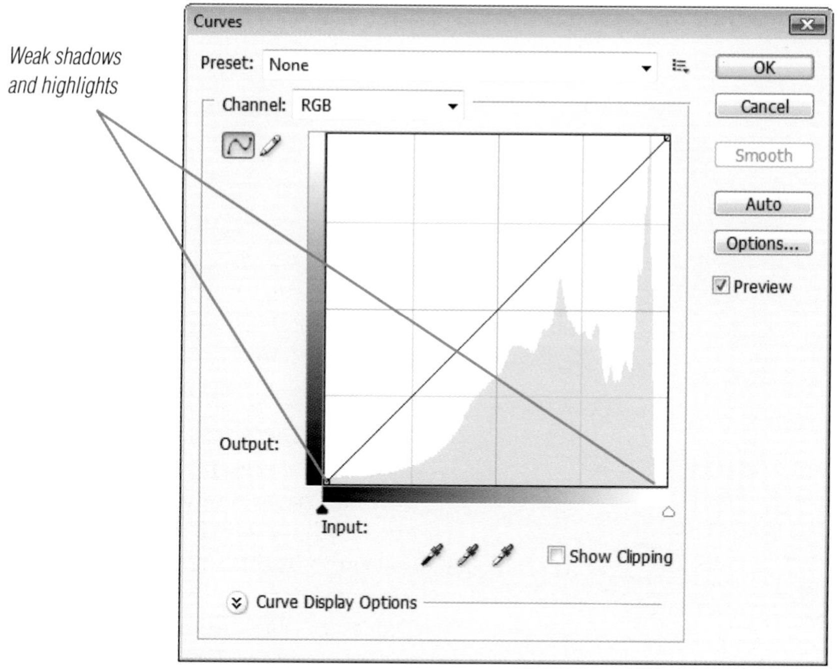

Whiten eyes

1. Open AP 8-1.psd, then save it as **Bright Eyes**.
2. Assess the image.

   This is an image that has very few obvious problems. The model is young; he has clear skin, no wrinkles, and no age spots. His mouth is closed, so if he has chipped yellow teeth, it's not our problem. If you were asked to retouch this image, what is the first thing your eye would go to? Perhaps the most obvious retouching issue would be his red cheeks. Is that the first thing you noticed, or did your eye find other problems with the image?
3. Verify that the Background layer is targeted, add a new Curves adjustment layer named **Basic**, then compare your histogram to Figure 1.

(continued)

AUTHOR'S *note*

Before you do any retouching, it is critical that you know the context in which an image is to be used. This is the major determining factor of the artistic goal that you set for the retouching. For example, if this image were to be used to profile a new young author in the Sunday section of the *New York Times Book Review*, that fact would have enormous impact on how I want the final image to appear. I would retouch only obvious flaws in the image, with the goal of keeping the image very realistic and not stylized. When an author—even a hip young author—is being profiled in the *New York Times*, that author wants to be taken seriously. For this project, the image is being used to profile a rap star in a music magazine, like *Rolling Stone*. With that in mind, we're going to use techniques that exaggerate and define elements of the image so that the photo is vivid and eye-catching, but we're not going to overdo it—we do not want the final image to be obviously retouched or to look like a computer-generated special effect.

The first step in retouching is adjusting levels or curves to create the best image to start with. Most images, whether they come from a stock house or from a photographer that you work with, require some degree of adjustment. In the case of this photograph, a stock photo that has not been modified, the histogram shows that there is minimal detail in the shadow areas, which explains why the image is flat and has weak shadows.

4. Drag the **black triangle** to Input 33/Output 0, drag the **white triangle** to Input 243/Output 255, click **OK**, then compare your screen to Figure 2.
5. Undo and redo to see the change.
6. Create a new layer above the Basic layer, then name the new layer **Whiten Eyes**.

(continued)

FIGURE 2
Adjusted curves

FIGURE 3
Painting the whites white

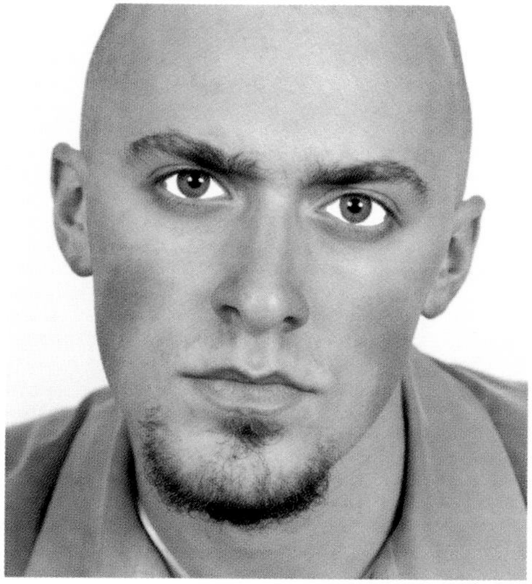

FIGURE 4
Reducing opacity for realism

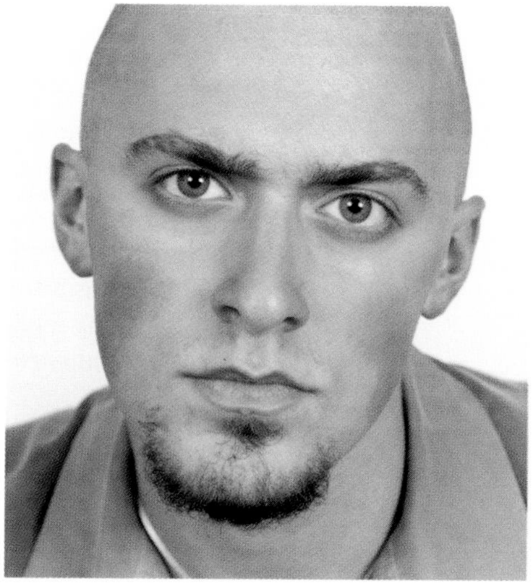

7. Zoom in to 200% and position the eyes in the document window so that you have a good view of them.

   Both eyes are noticeably bloodshot, especially at the outer sides. Note too the red line in the left eye, just below and left of the iris.

8. Click the **Brush Tool**, select a small soft brush, then using Figure 3 as an example, paint the white areas of the eyes white.

   In Figure 3, the Soft Round 5 pixels brush was used. For the corner areas, I reduced it to 2 pixels.

   TIP Be sure to paint up to but not over the iris. Note too that the pink corners of the eye were not painted.

9. Zoom out so that you are viewing the image at 50%, reduce the opacity of the Whiten Eyes layer to what you think is the best whitening you can achieve while still maintaining realism, then compare your artwork to Figure 4.

10. Set the opacity of your Whiten Eyes layer to 30%.

11. Add a layer mask, then paint with black to soften any edges on the white that need softening.

    The Whiten Eyes layer is serving two purposes. It is whitening the eyes, and it is also hiding the red bloodshot lines. The opacity of the Whiten Eyes layer in Figure 4 is 30%—the eyes are whitened dramatically, yet they still look realistic. I also used a layer mask to reduce the whites on the outside of the eyes and to soften the edge where the white paint meets the irises.

12. Save your work.

LESSON 2

INVESTIGATE THE OVERLAY
Blending Mode

What You'll Do

If you get a chance to observe a professional retoucher working, you'll see that the Overlay blending mode plays an important role for enhancing detail. "High-end" retouchers refer to overlay techniques as *overlay detail*. These techniques produce remarkable effects, but it's difficult to appreciate how they are achieved until you understand the basics of how the Overlay blending mode works.

Overlay is one of the most practical and powerful of the blending modes, one you use for retouching, for enhancing an image, and for producing special effects. Although most designers use it and are familiar with the effects it produces, many do not understand—on a technical level—how it works.

Use this chapter as an opportunity to investigate this blending mode. Understanding how a blending mode works increases your Photoshop skills set exponentially.

FIGURE 5

Darkening the image by moving the shadow point

FIGURE 6

Lightening the image by moving the highlight point

Investigate the Overlay blending mode

1. Make the Highlight/Shadow layer visible, target it, select the entire right half of the image, then hide the selection.
2. Open the Levels dialog box.
3. Drag the **black triangle** to 128, click **OK**, then compare your artwork to Figure 5.

   The pixels in the selection are darkened dramatically. The pixels that were 128–255 are now 0–255. Any pixel that was 127 or lower is now 0, black.
4. Select the inverse, then open the Levels dialog box.
5. Drag the **white triangle** to 128, click **OK**, then compare your artwork to Figure 6.

   The pixels in the selection are lightened dramatically. The pixels that were 0–128 are now 0–255. Any pixel that was 129 or higher is now 255.

(continued)

6. Deselect all.
7. Hide the Highlight/Shadow layer, then make the Overlay White Black layer visible.
8. Change the blending mode on the Overlay White Black layer to Overlay, then compare your screen to Figure 7.

   The effect is identical to the levels moves. Overlaying black is the same as moving the shadow point to 128. Overlaying white is the same as moving the highlight point to 128.
9. Hide the Overlay White Black layer, then make the Overlay White Gray Black layer visible.
10. Change the blending mode on the Overlay White Gray Black layer to Overlay, then compare your screen to Figure 8.

    With the Overlay blending mode, neutral gray (grayscale value 128) becomes transparent. The fact that gray becomes transparent is one of the key components of the Overlay blending mode.

(continued)

FIGURE 7
Overlaying white and black

FIGURE 8
Overlaying gray

FIGURE 9
Overlaying a gradient

11. Hide the Overlay White Gray Black layer, then make the Overlay Gradient layer visible.
12. Change the blending mode on the Overlay Gradient layer to Overlay, then compare your screen to Figure 9.

    Overlaying the gradient showcases the true nature (and power) of the Overlay blending mode. It's not just black, white, and gray. Black and white are the extremes—black overlayed produces the darkest effect; white overlayed produces the lightest effect. Gray is neutral. The range between gray and black gradually darkens the image, while conversely, the range between gray and white gradually lightens the image.
13. Hide and show the Overlay Gradient layer to see the effect before and after.
14. Hide the Overlay Gradient layer, then save your work.

AUTHOR'S *note*

Note that black overlay has a more dramatic effect on darker areas. For example, on the right cheek, note that the redness has become much darker, while the effect on the adjacent flesh tones is not so dramatic. Note too—this is very important—that the black areas of the gradient have only a minimal effect on the white background. On the opposite side of the gradient, note that the light areas under the right eye become almost white with the white overlay. However, the effect on the dark areas in the beard and eyebrows is minimal.

LESSON 3

OVERLAY Detail

What You'll Do

Overlay detail is a term retouchers use for a technique that enhances detail in an image. When you paint on a layer set to the Overlay blending mode, painting with white or black either lightens or darkens the pixels below, respectively.

This is very different from painting with white or black in Normal mode, and it's important that you understand the distinction. When you paint with white or black in Normal mode, you change the targeted pixels to white or black. Even with reduced opacity, the ultimate expression of the move is to push the pixels toward white or black.

In Overlay mode, you use white and black "paint" to lighten or darken the original pixel information. The ultimate expression of the move is not a white or black pixel. Instead, it is a much lighter or much darker version of the original, but never all white or all black.

With the Overlay blending mode, you are quite literally painting with light.

FIGURE 10
Darkening the edge of the left iris

Overlay detail

1. Click the **Brush Tool**, select a small soft brush, then set the opacity of the tool to 10%.
2. Press **[D]**, then press **[X]** to access a white foreground color.
3. Target the **Whiten Eyes layer**, then create a new layer above it.
4. Name the new layer **Overlay Detail**, then set the blending mode to Overlay.
5. Zoom in on the eyes, then paint over both eyes, lightening the hazel parts of the iris to a point that you think looks good but is still realistic.

   TIP Paint *inside* the iris—don't lighten the edge of the iris, where it meets the whites of the eyes.

6. Press **[X]** to access a black foreground color, then reduce your brush size to 2 pixels.
7. Darken the edge of the left iris—literally paint a dark line around it—then compare your result to Figure 10.

   The effect is stunning yet remarkably realistic. This is a standard retouching technique: lighten the iris, darken the edge of the iris.

   TIP You don't necessarily need to paint the edge in one move. Your paint brush is at only 10% opacity and it does not flow, so the change will be subtle. You will need to paint over the edge a few times to achieve the effect shown in the figure.

(continued)

8. Darken the edge of the right iris, hide and show the Overlay Detail layer to see a before-and-after view of the effect, then compare your result to Figure 11.
9. Note the areas of the eye identified in Figure 12.

   These are the edges of the eyelids. Note that, even without retouching, they already have a highlight.
10. Switch your foreground color to white, then lighten these areas to a point that you feel enhances the eyes but maintains realism.
11. Compare your result to Figure 13.

    We human beings like to see distinct features, even exaggerated. In the movies, we like our leading men and women with square jaws (think Jim Carrey), prominent cheekbones (think Tom Cruise), long necks (think Gwyneth Paltrow), and defined lips (think Angelina Jolie). We look for this detail especially in the eyes. This move exaggerates that definition, and it makes the eyes more interesting. However, this move needs to be very slight and subtle; if you lighten too much, it is noticeably retouched and looks bizarre.
12. Lighten the highlight on the top lip slightly.

(continued)

FIGURE 11
Darkening the edge of the right iris

FIGURE 12
Identifying areas to be enhanced

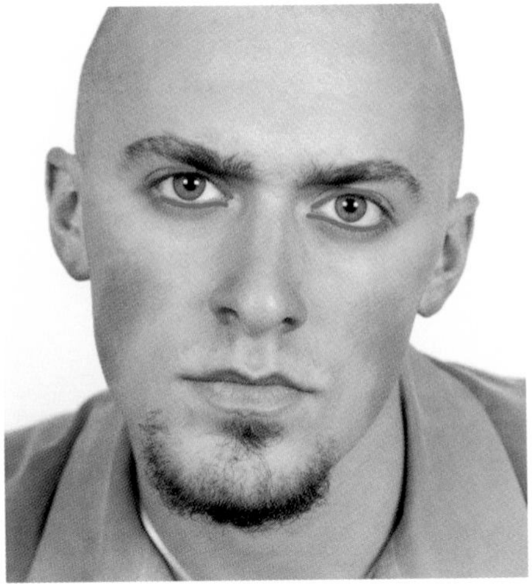

FIGURE 13
Enhancing eye areas

FIGURE 14
Identifying an area to be darkened

FIGURE 15
Darkening and adding eyelashes

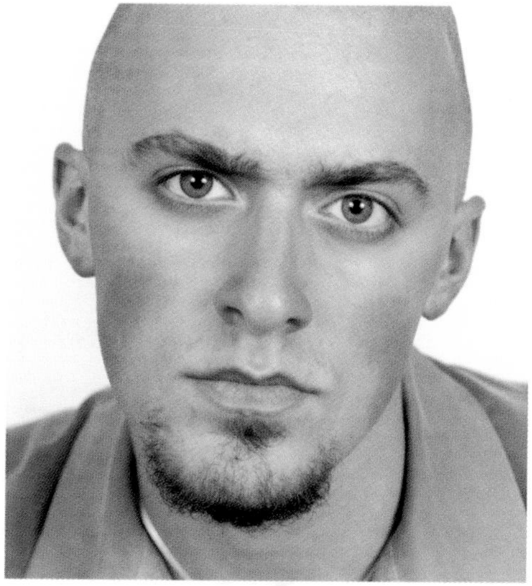

13. Switch your foreground color to black, then darken the dark area of the top lip beneath the ridge, identified in Figure 14.
14. Zoom in on the eyes, then darken the top eyelashes on each eye.
15. Change your brush to Hard Round 1 pixel, increase the brush opacity to 18%, darken each of the eyelashes, one at a time, at the bottom of both eyes, and add eyelashes where they're missing.

    This is easier than it sounds. Remember, you are not painting with black, you're painting with dark. Therefore, you can't paint "out of the lines." If you miss an eyelash, all you'll do is darken the skin behind it, and it will be almost unnoticeable.
16. Compare your results to Figure 15.

(continued)

17. Choose a larger soft brush, then darken the eyebrows.

18. Compare your results to Figure 16.

19. Choose a big soft brush (I used Soft Round 100 pixels), then darken the jacket, the neck, and the line where the jaw meets the neck.

20. Compare your results to Figure 17.

    Darkening the jacket and neck serves two important purposes. First, it brings the entire head forward in the image: that which is lighter we interpret as closer; that which is darker we interpret as recessed. Second, darkening the neck but not the jaw makes the jaw line appear stronger and more distinct.

21. Hide and show the Overlay Detail layer to see the image with and without the detail, then save your work.

FIGURE 16
Darkening eyebrows

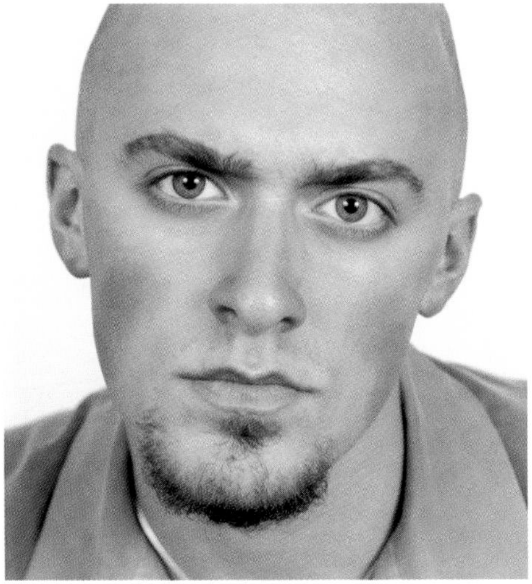

FIGURE 17
Darkening the neck and jacket

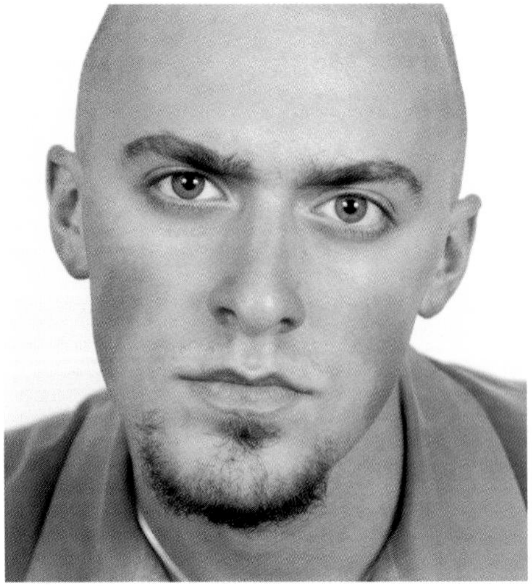

LESSON 4

USE A CHANNEL as a Mask

What You'll Do

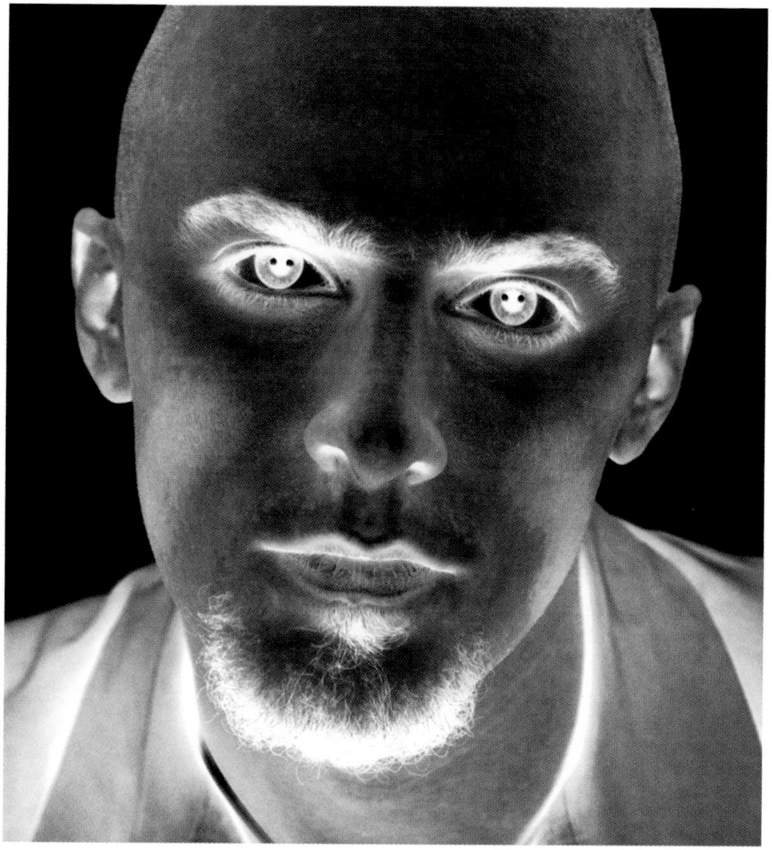

Manipulating channels offers many useful and powerful options for manipulating an image and for creating special effects, but you'll find that it's usually the advanced users who work with channels, who have an understanding of what they are, and toward what end they can be manipulated. This is so much the case that the ability to work with channels is often the line that separates intermediate users from advanced users or "power" users.

In this chapter, we are going to use a channel to perform a delicate color move on a nonspecific area of an image. This exercise is a great example of how powerful and useful channels can be, and, practically speaking, it's a great techinique to learn for targeting and manipulating hard-to-select areas of an image.

Reduce reds in flesh tones

1. Verify that the Overlay Detail layer is targeted, create a new Hue/Saturation adjustment layer, then click **OK** without making any adjustments.

   The goal of this lesson is to reduce the distinct red flesh tones in the cheeks, the ears, and the nostrils. The question is, how would you select those areas to reduce the reds? Instead of using the selection tools or creating a layer mask, we're going to use one of the RGB channels as a ready-made layer mask.

2. View the Red, Green, and Blue channels one at a time.

   We're looking for the channel in which the red cheeks are most distinct from the adjacent flesh tones. As shown in Figure 18, the Green channel best meets this criterion.

3. Drag the **Green channel** to the Create new channel button in the Channels palette.

   The Green channel is duplicated and the canvas now shows only the image in the new channel.

4. Name the new channel **First Selection**, then assess it as a selection mask for the red flesh tones.

   As a selection mask, the cheeks are darker than the adjacent flesh tones. If you loaded this channel as a selection, the cheeks would be less selected than the adjacent flesh tones.

(continued)

FIGURE 18
Green channel

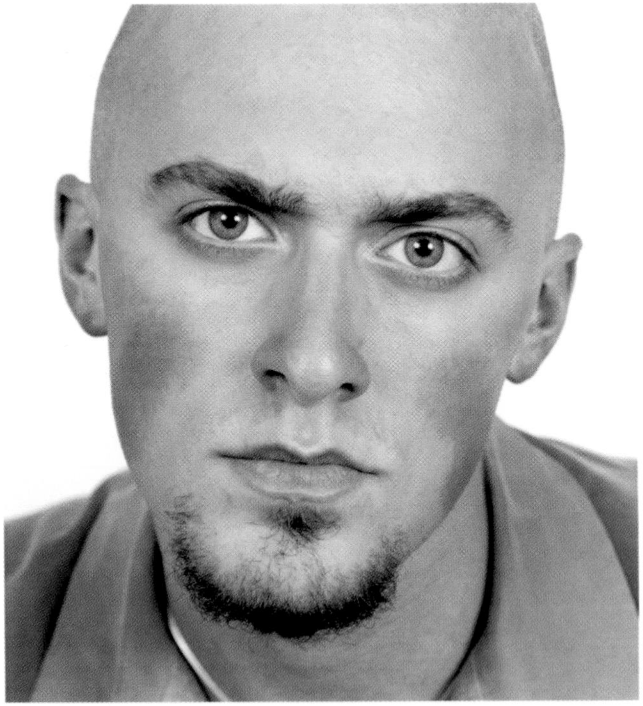

FIGURE 19
Selection mask inversed

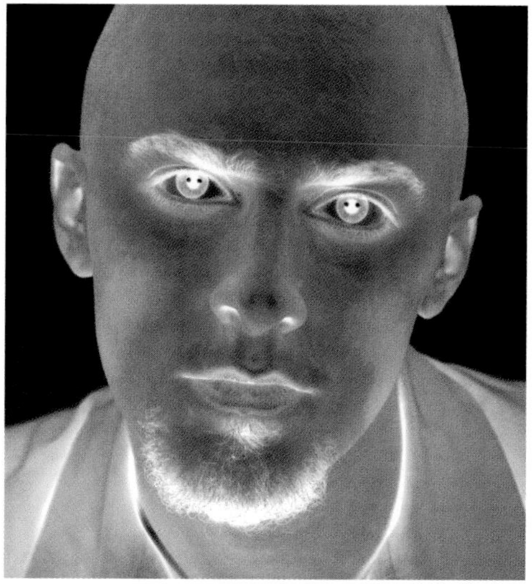

FIGURE 20
Overlaying an image over itself

5. Click **Image** on the menu bar, point to **Adjustments**, click **Invert**, then compare your channel to Figure 19.

   With the channel inverted, the cheeks are now lighter than the surrounding areas, meaning they will be more selected. However, they are very close in tone to those surrounding areas—not very distinct at all.

6. Click the **RGB channel thumbnail** to return to the composite image.

7. Change the blending mode of the Hue/Saturation adjustment layer to Overlay, then compare your screen to Figure 20.

   Overlaying the Hue/Saturation adjustment layer is the same as overlaying a duplicate of the image over itself. The result is what you should expect, based on our investigation of the Overlay mode earlier in this chapter: The dark areas get darker and the light areas get lighter. With this image, the dark red cheeks get darker while the adjacent flesh tones, which were lighter to begin with, get even lighter.

(continued)

8. Return to the Channels palette, duplicate the Green channel, name it **Second Selection**, then compare it to Figure 21.

   The channels always reflect the image in its current state. Therefore, the cheeks are dramatically darker than the adjacent flesh tones.

9. Invert the channel, then compare it to Figure 22.

   TIP Use quick keys to invert the channel: [Ctrl][I] (Win) or [⌘][I] (Mac).

(continued)

FIGURE 21
New selection mask

FIGURE 22
Selection mask inverted

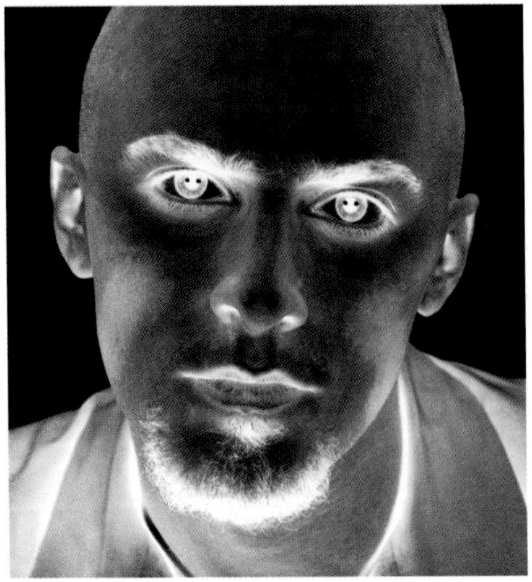

FIGURE 23
Selection mask adjusted

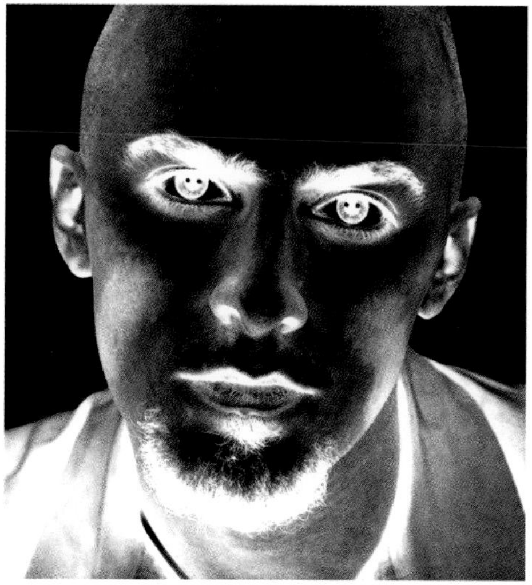

FIGURE 24
"Masking out" areas of the mask

FIGURE 25
Whitening the cheeks

10. Open the Levels dialog box, type **24** in the first Input text box, type **.90** in the second Input text box, type **199** in the third Input text box, click **OK**, then compare your result to Figure 23.

    Our goal is to make the cheek area as light as possible and the areas of normal flesh tone surrounding the cheeks as dark as possible.

11. Click the **Brush Tool**, set the opacity to 100%, choose a big soft brush, then paint black so that your selection mask resembles Figure 24.

    We've blackened out the eyes, mouth, facial hair, and jacket so that they won't be affected by the following steps.

12. Switch the foreground color to white, change the opacity to 50%, then paint the right cheek and the left cheek to lighten them so that your mask resembles Figure 25.

    TIP Use a soft brush and choose the right size brush for the job, one that's big enough to paint the area of each cheek with just one click.

(continued)

13. Click the **RGB channel thumbnail**, return to the Layers palette, then delete the Hue/Saturation adjustment layer.

14. Click **Select** on the menu bar, click **Load Selection**, click the **Channel list arrow**, click **Second Selection**, click **OK**, then compare your selection marquee to Figure 26.

TIP A faster way to load a selection is to [Ctrl] (Win) or [⌘]-click the channel.

15. Apply a 4-pixel feather to the selection, then hide the selection marquee.

16. Create a new unclipped Hue/Saturation adjustment layer, drag the **Hue slider** to +14, drag the **Lightness slider** to +12, click **OK**, then compare your result to Figure 27.

17. Deselect all.

18. Select the Whiten Eyes layer, the Overlay Detail layer and the Hue/Saturation adjustment layer, then make them into a new layer group named **Retouched**.

(continued)

FIGURE 26
Loading the selection mask

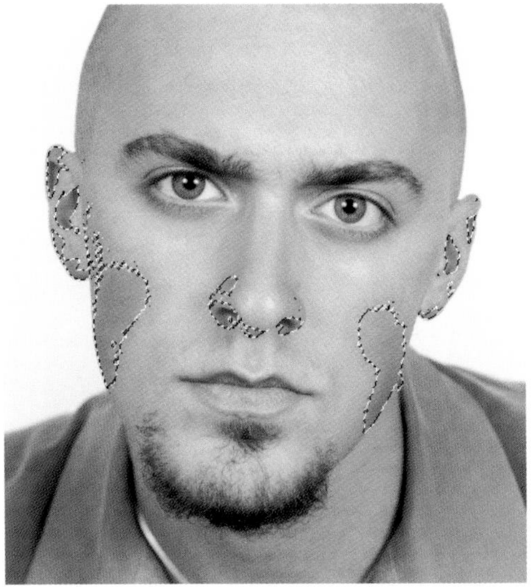

FIGURE 27
Adjusting hue and lightness

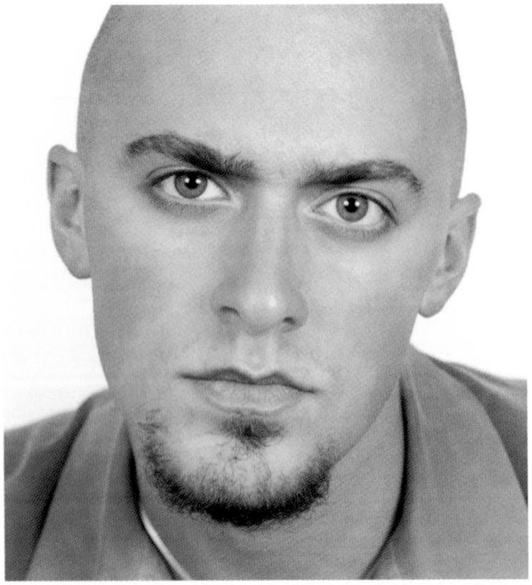

FIGURE 28
Image before and after retouching

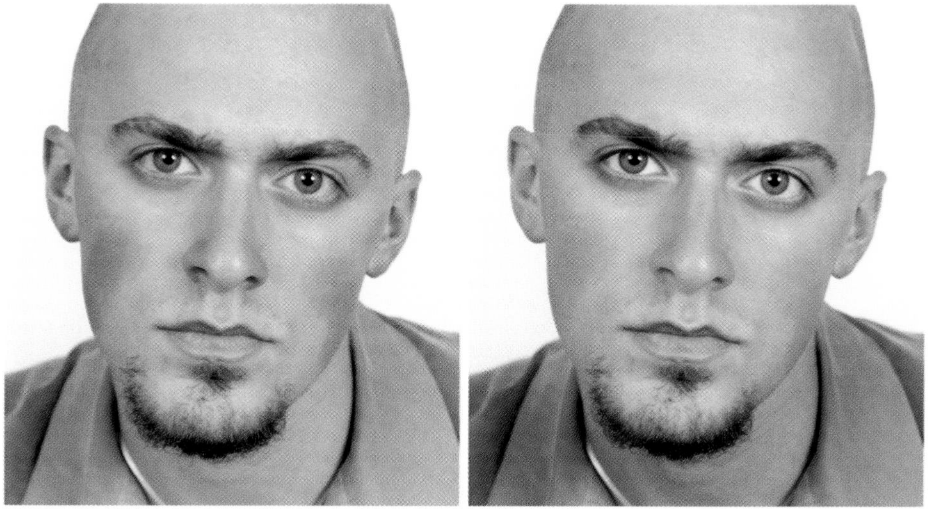

FIGURE 29
Final image

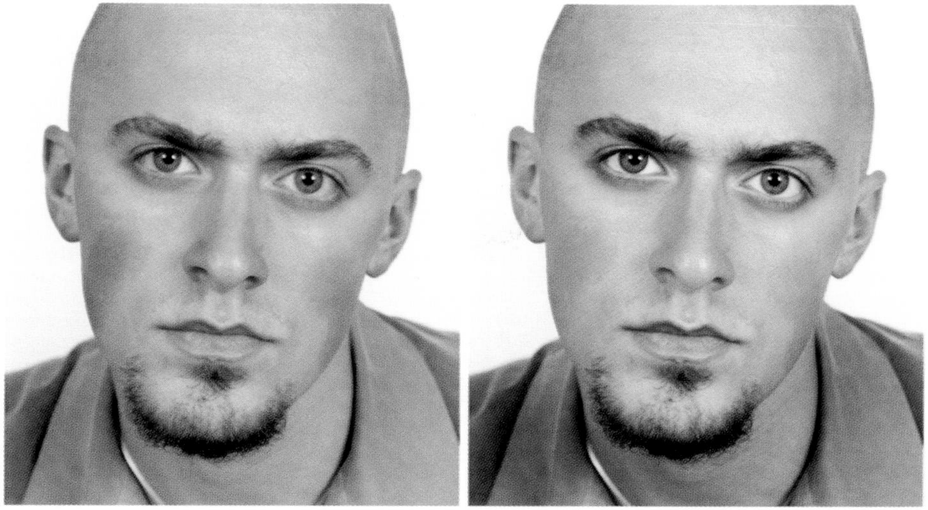

19. Hide and show the Retouched layer group to see the image with and without the retouching, then compare your artwork to Figure 28.

    Though all of the adjustments we made were subtle, the overall improvement of the image is stunning, especially the reduction of red in the cheeks, ears, and nostrils and the enhancement of the eyes. Take a moment to appreciate that the image does not look doctored or fake—it just looks like a good photograph.

20. Expand the Retouched layer group, target the **Hue/Saturation adjustment layer**, then add a new Curves adjustment layer named **Contrast Bump.**
21. Add a point anywhere on the curve, change its Input value to 75, then change its Output value to 65.
22. Add a second point, change its Input value to 188, change its Output value to 198, then click **OK**.
23. Hide and show the Retouched layer group, then compare your artwork to Figure 29.
24. Save your work, then close Bright Eyes.

LESSON 5

USE THE Cloning Tools

What You'll Do

Everybody loves the cloning tools. Whenever Photoshop is being demonstrated, you can be sure that a substantial amount of time will be given to wowing the crowd with cloning tricks: Creating an extra eye, replacing the head of a dog with the head of a horse, cloning the picture of a cat onto the surface of the planet Mars—you know the routine. The cloning tools are a blast, and it doesn't take long for any novice user to find them and start playing. Mastering the cloning tools is a whole different game because they're some of the trickiest tools to use effectively. *Effectively* means achieving the goal you want to achieve. Using the Clone Stamp Tool effectively means choosing the right brush, sampling from the right area, and cloning with the best technique to make your work look realistic. That's the challenge. For many versions, the Clone Stamp Tool was the only cloning tool in Photoshop. Then the Patch Tool and the Healing Brush Tool were introduced to provide options that the Clone Stamp Tool just couldn't. In this lesson, you'll work with all three.

FIGURE 30
First area to retouch

FIGURE 31
Positioning the brush

> **AUTHOR'S** *note*
>
> Let's agree that the goal of this exercise is to retouch this image so that it can be used in a medical advertisement in a magazine targeted toward senior citizens. The client has instructed you that the model should represent a vibrant older woman—a portrait of healthy aging.

Use the Clone Stamp Tool

1. Open AP 8-2.psd, then save it as **Smooth Lines**.
2. Hide and show the Eyes Retouched layer group to see the retouching work that I've already done on the eyes.

   TIP I also adjusted the curves of the image.
3. Verify that the Eyes Retouched layer group is showing and targeted, then create a new layer above it named **Smooth**.
4. Figure 30 identifies the first area that we want to retouch.
5. Click the **Clone Stamp Tool** , verify that its Mode is set to Normal, that Sample is set to All Layers, and that its Opacity and Flow are both set to 100%.
6. Create a Soft Round 70 pixels brush, then position it over the area shown in Figure 31.

   We will use this area as the sample. It is very close in color and tone to the area we want to fix, and it is also smooth, with no wrinkles or indents.

(continued)

7. Press and hold **[Alt]** (Win) or **[option]** (Mac) then click to sample the area.

   For this lesson, I will presume that you know the basics of how to use the Clone Stamp Tool to clone areas of an image. From this point on, I will simply tell you to sample an area.

8. Position the pointer over the area to be fixed (Figure 30), click once, then compare your result to Figure 32.
9. Using the same method, but with a smaller brush size, clone out the blemish shown in Figure 33.

(continued)

FIGURE 32
Result of clicking Clone Stamp Tool

FIGURE 33
Cloning out the blemish

FIGURE 34
Next area to be fixed

FIGURE 35
Result of cloning using smooth area of cheek

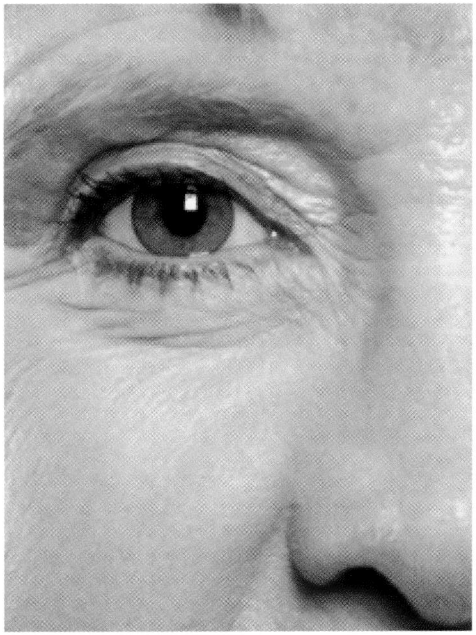

10. See Figure 34 for the next area to be fixed.

    This area is usually problematic, whether the model is younger or older. In this image, the area is dotted with small highlights. Possibly, the model's makeup was clumpy or flaky in this area, or maybe the skin itself had large pores or small pock marks. In any case, it's distracting and can be fixed easily.

11. Change the brush size back to 70 pixels, sample a smooth area from the left cheek, then clone out the area completely, so that your image resembles Figure 35.

    TIP I clicked two times to completely cover the area.

(continued)

12. Reduce your brush size to 27 pixels, then see Figure 36.
13. Sample the area indicated by the black circle, then clone out the entire cheek line by clicking in the area indicated by the green circle and dragging to the area indicated by the red circle.
14. Compare your result to Figure 37.

    Yes, this looks fake. Reality is not our goal at this stage of retouching. Our goal is to cover lines with similar flesh tones. Later, we will bring back some of the detail using opacity.

(continued)

FIGURE 36
Third area to be fixed

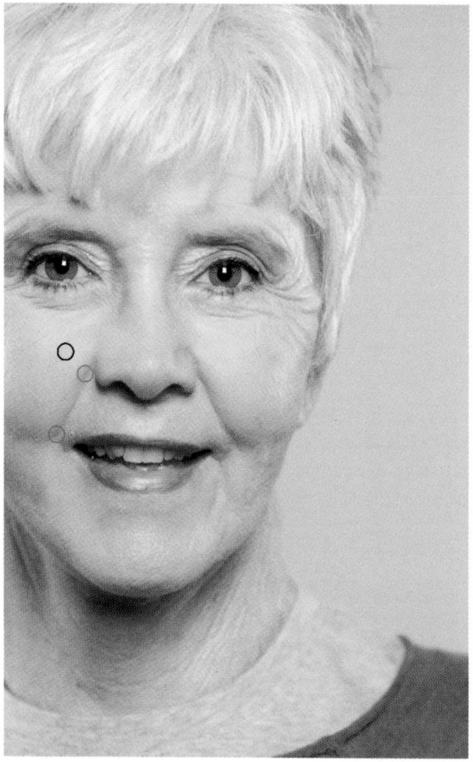

FIGURE 37
Result of cloning out the cheek line

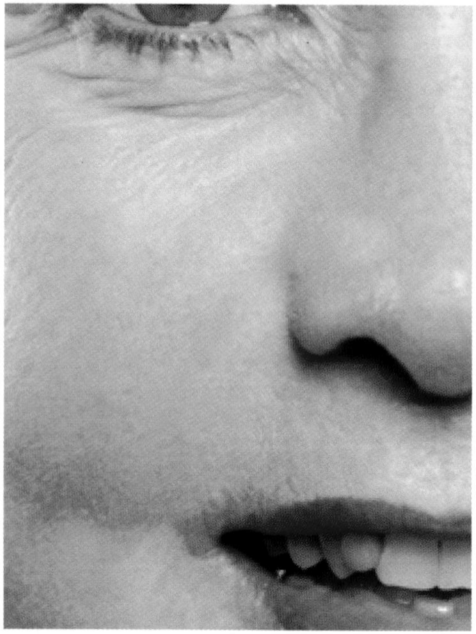

FIGURE 38
Smooth light area

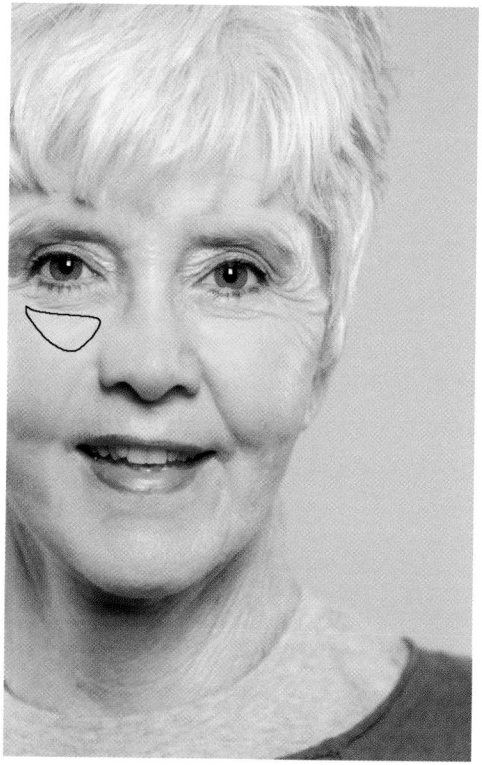

FIGURE 39
Result of cloning out wrinkles

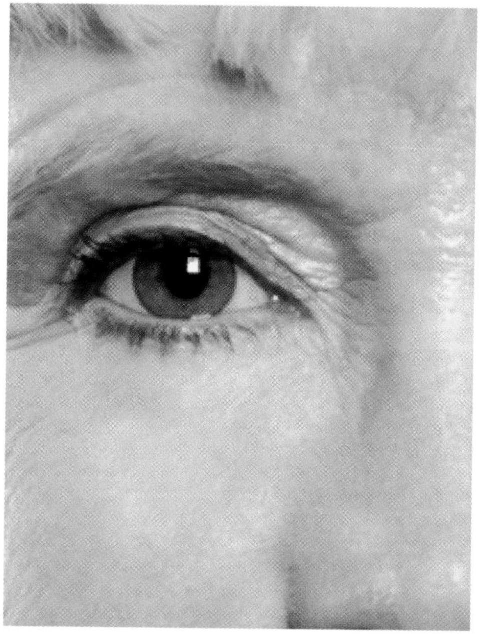

15. Sampling from the smooth light area at the top of the left cheek, identified in Figure 38, clone out all of the wrinkles under the left eye, then compare your results to Figure 39.

(continued)

16. Sampling from the same area, but with a smaller brush, clone out the line in the forehead to the upper left of the left eyebrow, then compare your result to Figure 40.

17. See Figure 41.

    This area is perhaps the most problematic in the image. The flesh tone is bright, making the wrinkles that much more noticeable. The eyes are the first thing everybody looks at, so improving this area is important. The problem with fixing this area is that there's very little area to sample. We have no choice but to clone from another area of the image.

(continued)

FIGURE 40
Cloning out line in the forehead

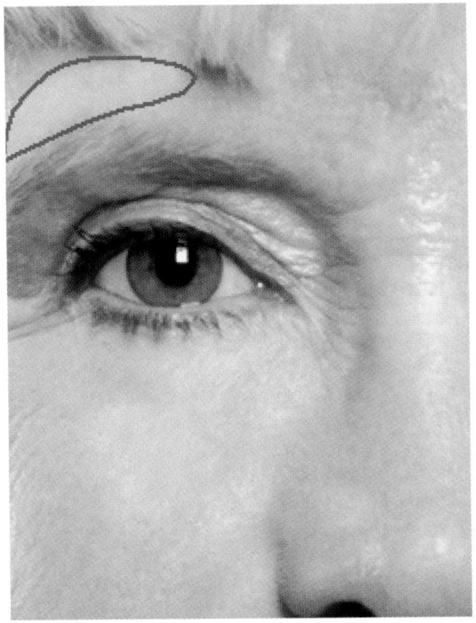

FIGURE 41
Assessing a problematic area

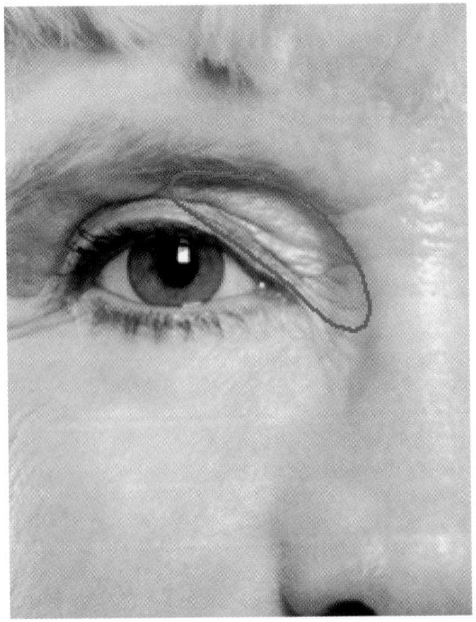

FIGURE 42
Cloning over the eye

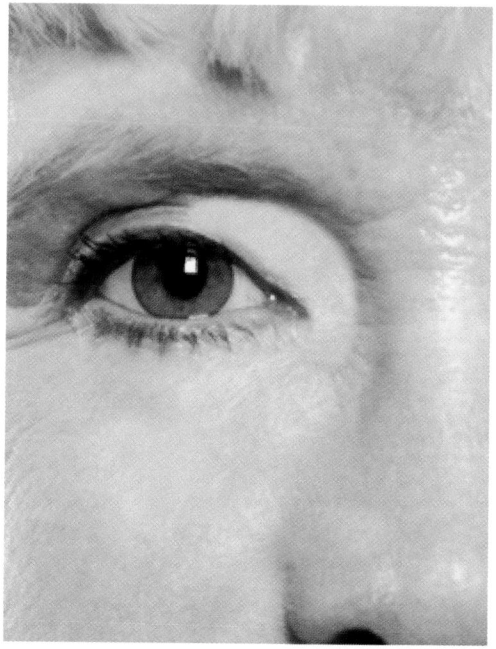

FIGURE 43
Identifying lines on the neck

18. Sample from the middle of the left cheek, then clone over the eye as shown in Figure 42.
19. Save your work.

Use the Healing Brush Tool

1. Note the lines on the neck identified in Figure 43.

   The Clone Stamp Tool is not very effective for cloning out these lines simply because there's no place to sample—there's no other area of the image that has a smooth flesh tone that is as dark as this area.

(continued)

2. Set your brush size to 27 pixels, then sample the area shown in Figure 44.
3. Clone out the lower heavy wrinkle so that your artwork resembles Figure 45.

   The sample area is too light for the area being replaced.
4. Undo the last step.
5. Click the **Healing Brush Tool**, then verify that the Mode is set to Normal, that the Sampled option button is selected, and that the Sample option is set to Current & Below.

   Make sure you are using the Healing Brush Tool and not the Spot Healing Brush Tool.

(continued)

FIGURE 44
Area to be sampled

FIGURE 45
Result is too light

FIGURE 46
Result using the Healing Brush Tool

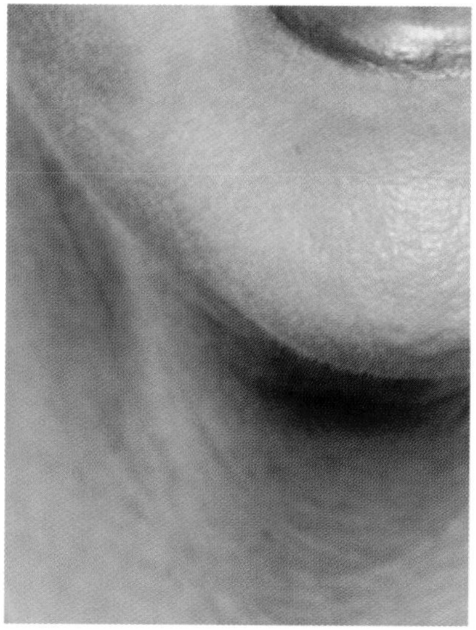

FIGURE 47
Cloning upper wrinkle

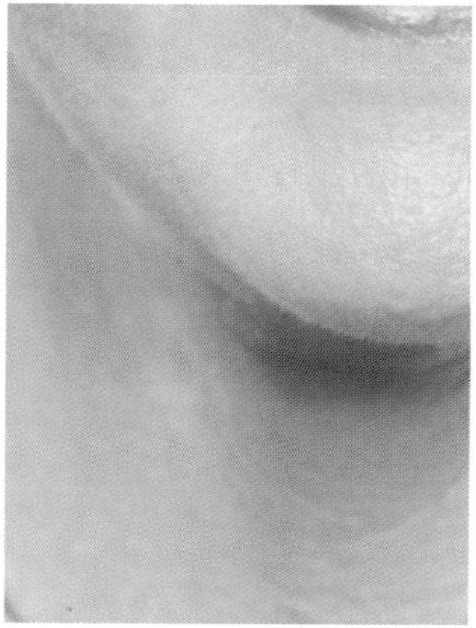

6. Repeat Steps 2 and 3, then compare your result to Figure 46.

   The Healing Brush Tool clones just like the Clone Stamp Tool. The big difference is that the Healing Brush Tool automatically adjusts the color of the clone to match its new surroundings as closely as possible.

7. Using the same method and sampling from the same location, smooth out the entire area, then compare your screen to Figure 47.

(continued)

8. Increase the brush size to 32 pixels, then see Figure 48.

9. Sample the area indicated by the black circle, click the area indicated by the green circle, **[Shift]**-click the area indicated by the red circle, then compare your result to Figure 49.

   The result is odd. This is the type of clone that the Healing Brush Tool doesn't do as well as the Clone Stamp Tool. Compare this result to the same area on the left cheek that we cloned out with the Clone Stamp Tool. We will investigate this further in the next lesson.

10. Undo the last move, click the **Clone Stamp Tool**, then completely clone out the entire area indicated in Figure 48.

(continued)

FIGURE 48
Sampling an area

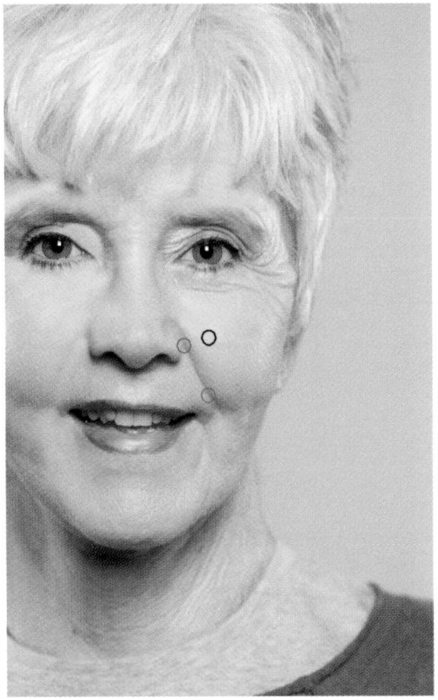

FIGURE 49
Results of Healing Brush Tool

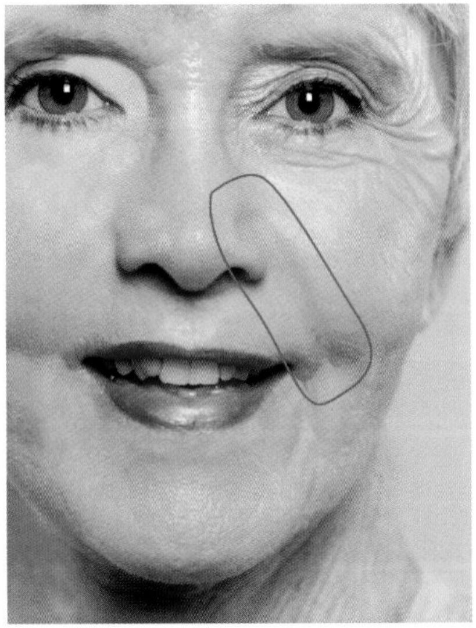

FIGURE 50
Using the Healing Brush Tool on the neck

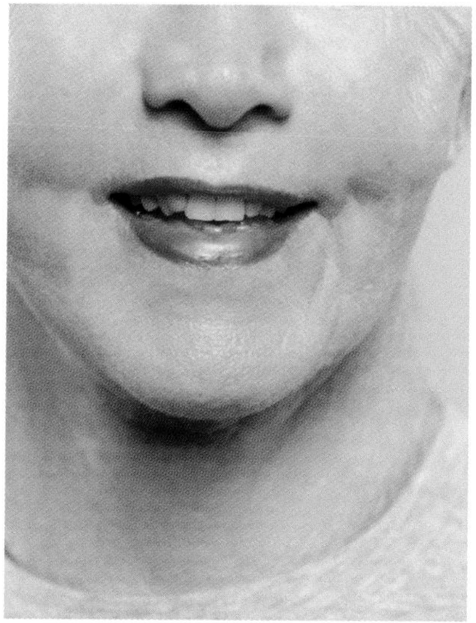

FIGURE 51
Selecting an area

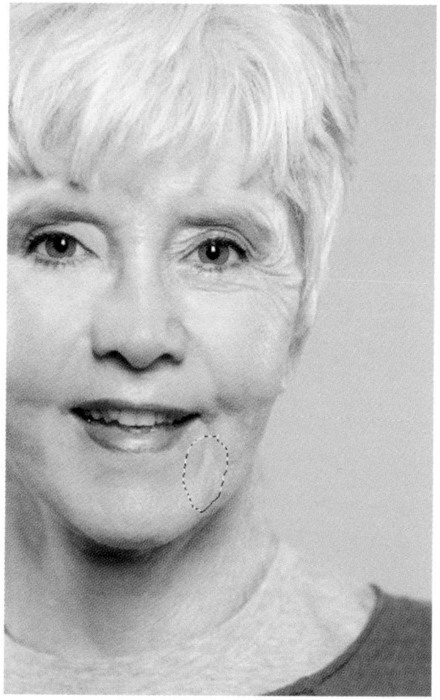

11. Practice with the Healing Brush Tool on the entire neck so that your work resembles Figure 50.

    The Healing Brush Tool will work on all areas of the neck except if you get too close to the jaw line.

12. Save your work.

Use the Patch Tool

1. Verify that the Smooth layer is targeted, select all, click **Edit** on the menu bar, then click **Copy Merged**.
2. Paste, then name the new layer **Patch**.

   The new layer is a copy of the original image with all of the retouching we've done so far.

3. Click the **Patch Tool**, then select the area shown in Figure 51.

(continued)

4. Drag the selection up to a smooth area of the left cheek, as shown in Figure 52, then release the mouse button.
5. Deselect, then compare your result to Figure 53.

   The Patch Tool works like the Healing Brush Tool, but with the added benefit of a visual preview. First, you select the area that you want to replace. Then, you drag the selection to an area that has a texture that you want to use. As you drag, you get a dynamic preview of the clone before the color adjustment. When you release the mouse button, the Patch Tool clones the area where you deselect, "patches" it into the original selection, then color corrects it to match the tonal range of the original selection. The Patch Tool is often very successful in matching the clone to the tonal range of the original, and because you can work with large selections, the Patch Tool is very effective for getting a lot of retouching done quickly.

   TIP The Patch Tool won't work on a transparent layer, like the cloning we did on the Smooth layer. This is why we needed to create the copy merged Patch layer to use the Patch Tool.

(continued)

FIGURE 52
Dragging selection to smooth area of left cheek

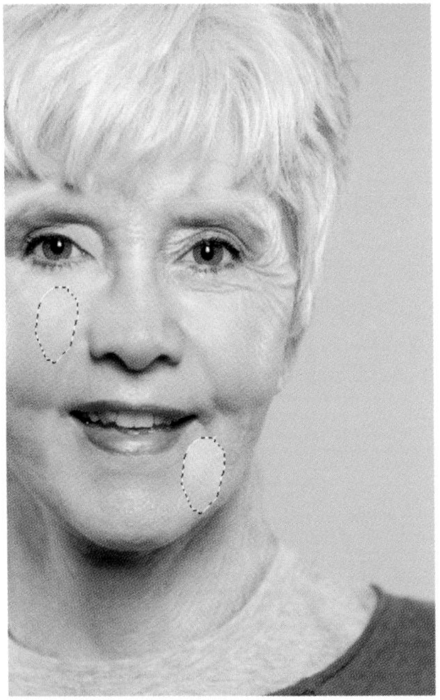

FIGURE 53
Result of using the Patch Tool

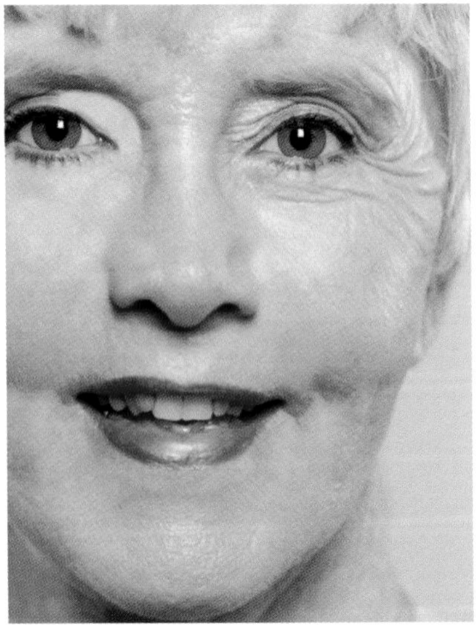

FIGURE 54
Selecting an area to patch

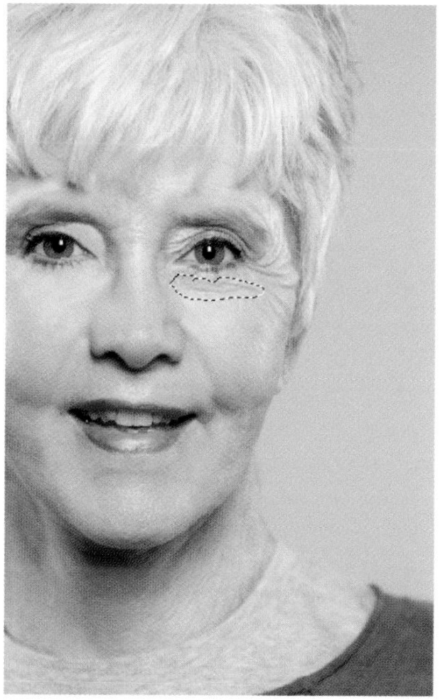

FIGURE 55
Result of using the Patch Tool

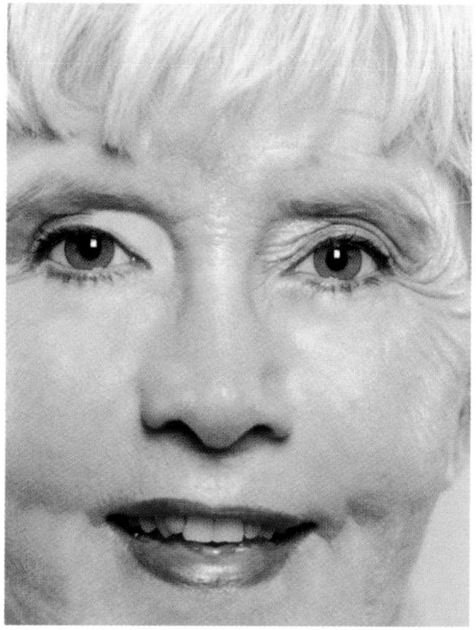

6. Select the area shown in Figure 54, hide the selection edges, drag the selection to the smooth area under the left eye, release the mouse button, then deselect.
7. Compare your result to Figure 55.

(continued)

8. Select the area shown in Figure 56, clone from the smooth cheek above it, deselect, then compare your result to Figure 57.

(continued)

FIGURE 56
Selecting an area to patch

FIGURE 57
Result of using the Patch Tool

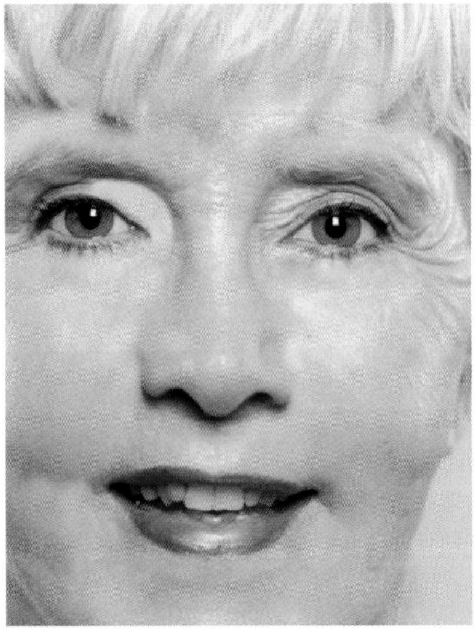

FIGURE 58
Selecting the eyelid

FIGURE 59
Result of using the Patch Tool on eyelid

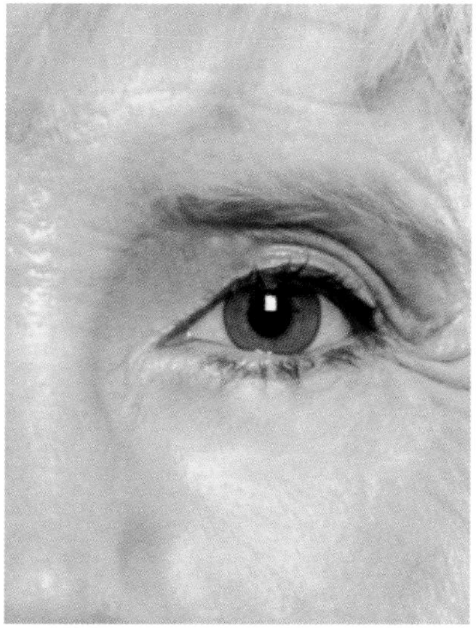

9. Select the area shown in Figure 58, then clone from the smooth area under the left eye.
10. Compare your result to Figure 59.

    Note how much better (and faster and easier) the Patch Tool worked on this eye than the Clone Stamp Tool did on the left eye.

(continued)

11. Use the Healing Brush Tool to remove the deep wrinkles to the right of the right eye and the scar on the lower right cheek.

TIP If you get unwanted results, feel free to switch to the Clone Stamp Tool or the Patch Tool.

12. Smooth out any other areas of the image that you think need retouching, then compare your work to Figure 60.

13. Group the Smooth and the Patch layers into a new layer group named **Cloning**.

(continued)

FIGURE 60
Result of removing wrinkles and scar

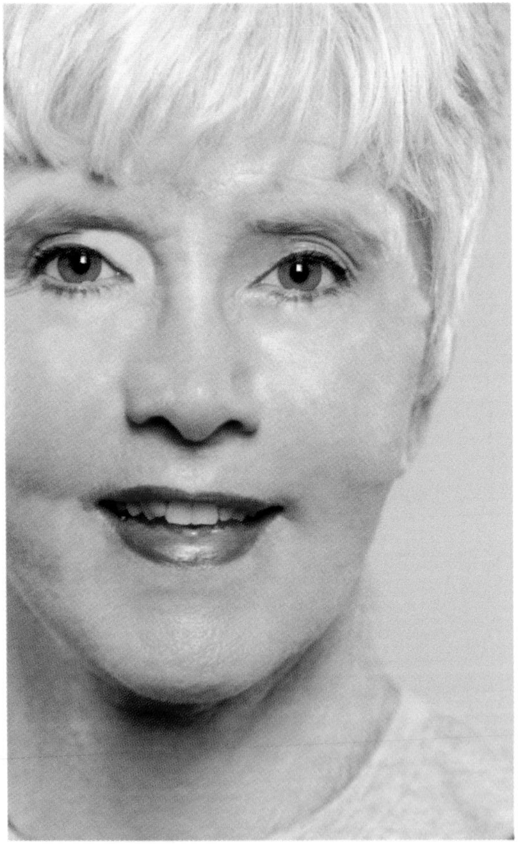

FIGURE 61
Before and after results

14. Add a layer mask to the Cloning layer group, click **Edit** on the menu bar, then click **Fill**.
15. Click the **Use list arrow**, choose 50% gray, verify that the blending mode is set to Normal and the opacity is set to 100%, then click **OK**.

    Rather than set the Cloning layer group to 50% opacity, we have used a mask with 50% gray to achieve the effect. This leaves us the option of painting in the layer mask to intensify or lessen the retouching in local areas. Remember this trick; it's always best to leave yourself with options.
16. Select both the Cloning layer group and the Eyes Retouched layer group, then make a new layer group named **Retouching**.
17. Hide and show the Retouching layer group to see the before-and-after results, then compare your screen to Figure 61.

    In my experience, this is the most effective method for retouching wrinkles. We have not removed a single wrinkle. We've only reduced them. Allowing 50% of the original image to show through grounds the image in reality; there's no visible blurring, cloning, or awkward textures. The retouching is invisible. And with the 50% gray layer mask, we can paint to subtly increase or decrease the cloning where necessary.
18. Save your work, then close Smooth Lines.

LESSON 6

RETOUCH
Teeth

What You'll Do

If you liked whitening eyes and reducing wrinkles, you're going to love working with teeth. Teeth are usually the greatest challenge to the retoucher. They almost always need work—a little whitening here, a little straightening there. What's really tough about retouching teeth is that it usually requires making precise selections and many small moves with the retouching and paint tools. And the margin of error is small—make that, the margin of reality is small. It's very tricky to retouch teeth in a way that is not noticeable, to fool the eye into believing that the retouched teeth—the color, the shape, and the texture—are the real thing.

In this lesson, instead of retouching the teeth yourselves, you're going to click through the layers to see the retouching that I applied. As I was working, I didn't know if the techniques I was using would ultimately work. They did, and the goal of this chapter is to have you retrace my steps to see the objectives that I identified, the techniques I used to achieve them, and the choices I made along the way.

FIGURE 62
Assessing the model's teeth

Fix teeth

1. Open AP 8-3.psd, then save it as **Fix Teeth**.
2. Look at Figure 62 to assess the model's teeth.

   Teeth almost always need retouching. Sometimes, it's light retouching, such as a slight whitening. Other times . . . let's just say it's extensive.

   The subject of this photo does not have perfect teeth. On the left side, one yellow tooth overlaps another, her lip is hooked on one of the bottom teeth, and a silver or gold filling is visible. On the right side, the teeth are a bit chipped, and one bottom tooth is bent behind the others. Other than that, the right side isn't so bad, and we're going to use that to our advantage. One more note: Did you notice that whoever did the makeup for this model didn't do a very good job? The application of the lipstick is uneven—note her bottom lip. The edges are very soft and the line of her lips is indistinct and unflattering.
3. Zoom in so that you are viewing the teeth at 100%, then expand the Teeth layer group to view the layers within.

(continued)

4. Make the Square Off Teeth layer visible.

   As shown in Figure 63, I squared off the three teeth on the right side of the mouth. To do so, I made a clipping path in the shape that I wanted the teeth to be, used the path as a selection, then cloned to make the teeth larger and more square.

5. Make the Fix Bottom Row layer visible.

   The bottom row was more of a challenge because one tooth is bent all the way back. As shown in Figure 64, I cloned out the bent tooth. I then cloned the tooth to the right to replace the old tooth. Then came the challenge: The teeth weren't lining up. The line between the two top front teeth was still to the left of the left edge of the clone. I enlarged the clone slightly, then stretched it to the left.

(continued)

FIGURE 63
Three teeth squared off

FIGURE 64
Lining up the teeth in the bottom row

FIGURE 65
Darkened lipstick

FIGURE 66
Sharper lipstick line

6. Make the Darken Lipstick layer visible.

   As shown in Figure 65, I darkened the lips to make the lipstick darker, more distinct, and more consistent in tone throughout. I used the overlay detail technique, which worked well, but it was not without its challenges. With red, the color shifts quickly and dramatically. Parts of the lips had lipstick, and parts were bare, and I wanted everything darker. Trying to match the two areas was tricky.

7. Make the Improve Edge layer visible.

   As shown in Figure 66, I created a sharper line for the lipstick to cover the indistinct line beneath it. First, I created a path to use as a selection. When I made the path, I drew the path above the top lip a bit to increase its size, then cloned red into the new area. I did the same to strengthen the edge of the bottom lip.

(continued)

8. See Figure 67.

   I selected the right half of the mouth as shown, copied it, then pasted it on its own layer. Note the left edge of the selection marquee. I positioned that left edge very carefully. I zoomed in to be sure that the pixels that made up the left edge of my selection were the pixels that drew the line between the top two teeth.

9. Make the Flip Horizontal layer visible.

   As shown in Figure 68, I flipped the "good side" of the mouth, then positioned it over the "bad" left side. Up to this point, I wasn't certain that my idea would work. The flipped artwork looked pretty good, but pretty good doesn't cut it when retouching. It needed to be unnoticeable. It needed to hide in plain sight.

(continued)

FIGURE 67
Selecting right side of the mouth

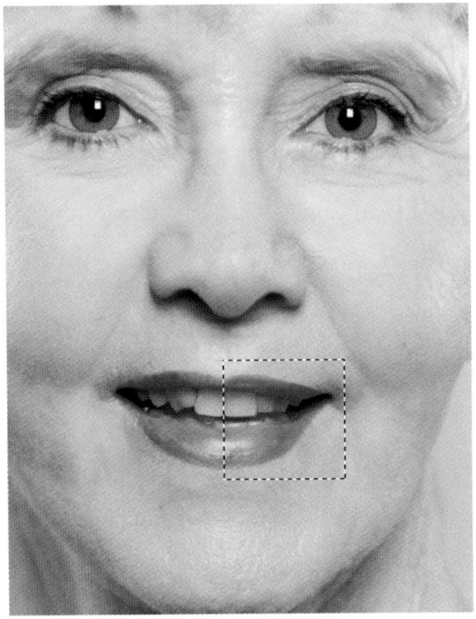

FIGURE 68
Right side of mouth flipped to left side

FIGURE 69
Distorting mouth to create natural look

10. Make the Distort layer visible.

As shown in Figure 69, I distorted the mouth so that the two sides weren't perfect mirror images of one another. The mouth is stretched wider on the left side and is rotated clockwise. It is a subtle move, but it needs to be there. The two sides can't be perfect mirrors. However, the adjustment is too subtle to completely solve the problem, and the horizontal flip is still evident.

11. Hide the Flip Horizontal layer.

The Distort layer artwork replaces the Flip Horizontal artwork, so we no longer want the Flip Horizontal artwork to be visible.

(continued)

12. Press and hold **[Shift]**, then click the **Layer mask thumbnail** on the Distort layer to activate it.

As shown in Figure 70, the layer mask sells it. Hide and show the layer mask to see the change. I used the mask to allow some of the original left sides of the lips to show through. That small but important move solved the problem.

The eye is quick to pick up a mirror image. However, it's just as quick to stop scanning when it picks up asymmetrical detail. It doesn't take much: note the bump on the upper lip, the darker edge at the left side of the bottom lip, and the softer highlight on the bottom lip. They are enough to convince the eye to move on without questioning it.

13. Collapse the Teeth layer, create a new layer group using the Teeth and Retouching layers, then name it **Final Retouch**.

14. Hide and show the Final Retouch layer group to assess the final effect.

15. Save your work, then close Fix Teeth.

AUTHOR'S *note*

Overall, the retouching achieved its objective. The improvement in the eyes and the reduced wrinkles dramatically decrease the model's age. However, if you hide the retouching, take a moment to note how much of the model's character and personality is lost in the retouching.

The final question I always ask myself when retouching is "Did I leave enough personality?" If this were a photo that the model was going to give to her family, I would say I removed too much of her character, especially in her eyes. And I would have not cloned out an entire half of her mouth and changed her smile!

But that wasn't the job. The retouched photo could legitimately be used as part of a medical advertisement in a magazine for seniors. The reduction in wrinkles is just right for the age we want the model to appear to be. The clear eyes and perfect smile make her an appealing example of healthy aging, and the slight vacantness in those same eyes and smile actually work to our advantage: they make her a bit of a generic everywoman, and that's exactly who the client wants to sell medicine to—every woman.

FIGURE 70
Results of layer mask

LESSON 7

CLONE STRATEGICALLY WITHIN Adjustment Layers

What You'll Do

When working with the cloning tools, often you will find that you need to do some retouching after you've applied adjustment layers, like Curves adjustments or Hue/Saturation adjustments. In these cases, where you position your retouching layer in the Layers palette relative to the adjustment layers becomes a critical decision. Also critical is how you sample the adjusted artwork.

The issues that must be navigated in this situation involve the adjustment layers. The big thing about adjustment layers is that they can be adjusted—over and over again. This big benefit can become a big problem when you clone adjusted artwork, because if you modify an adjustment layer *after* you clone, your cloning can become visible with the modification. In other words, when you clone adjusted artwork, you want to sample in a way that allows you the option to modify the adjustment layers without exposing your retouching.

FIGURE 71
White scratch in hood

1. Open AP 8-4.psd, then save it as **Smart Sampling**.
2. Note the two adjustment layers in the Layers palette.

   The original image has been modified with a Curves and a Hue/Saturation adjustment layer.
3. Note the white scratch in the hood, as shown in Figure 71, that needs to be removed.

   The scratch can be removed easily with the Clone Stamp Tool or the Healing Brush Tool. The question though, is where do you position the layer to do your retouching in relation to the adjustment layers.
4. Target the **Hue/Saturation adjustment layer**, then create a new layer above it.
5. Click the **Clone Stamp Tool**, click the **Sample list arrow**, then click **All Layers**.
6. Use the Clone Stamp Tool to remove the white scratch.

   Be sure that you understand that when you sample, you are sampling the composite of all three of the layers beneath the new layer. In other words, when you click to sample, you're sampling the image as it appears as the result of the three layers—the original image with the Curves adjustment and the Hue/Saturation adjustment.

(continued)

7. Hide the Hue/Saturation adjustment layer, then compare your image to Figure 72.

   As shown in the figure, the way you sampled when you cloned has resulted in the problem that you can no longer adjust either of the two adjustment layers. This is because both were involved in the sample when you cloned, and now any adjustment to the adjustment will differ from the original sample and become visible.

8. Delete the new layer, then make the Hue/Saturation adjustment layer visible again.

9. Target the **Background layer**, create a new layer, click the **Clone Stamp Tool**, click the **Sample list arrow**, then click **Current & Below**.

   TIP These same sampling options are also available for the Healing Brush Tool.

10. Use the Clone Stamp Tool to remove the white scratch on the hood.

    Because the Current & Below option is selected, when you sample with the Clone Stamp Tool, you are sampling only the current (empty) layer and the layer beneath it. You are not sampling either of the two adjustment layers above.

(continued)

FIGURE 72
Retouching layer in the wrong location in the Layers palette

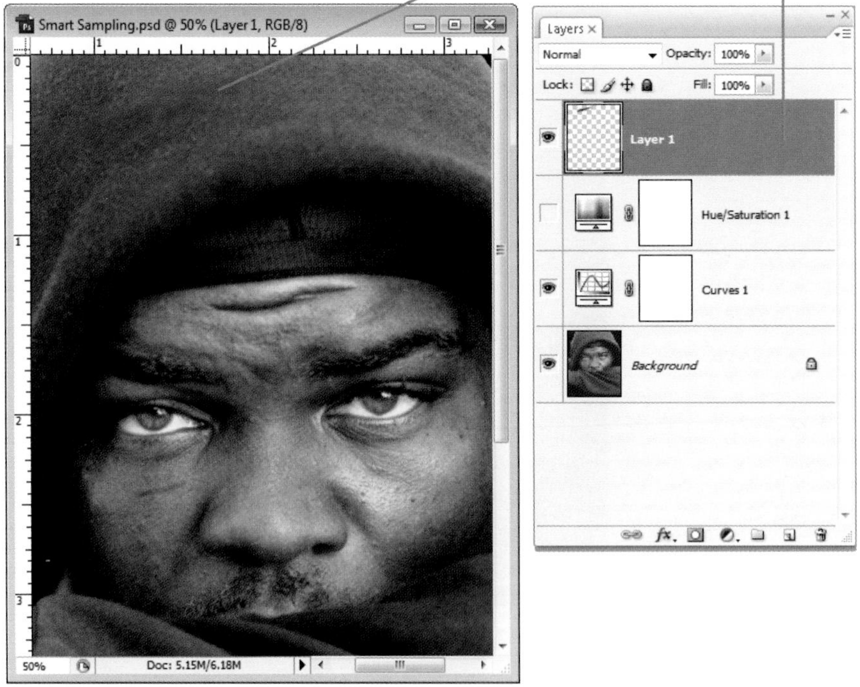

FIGURE 73

Retouching layer in the correct position in the Layers palette

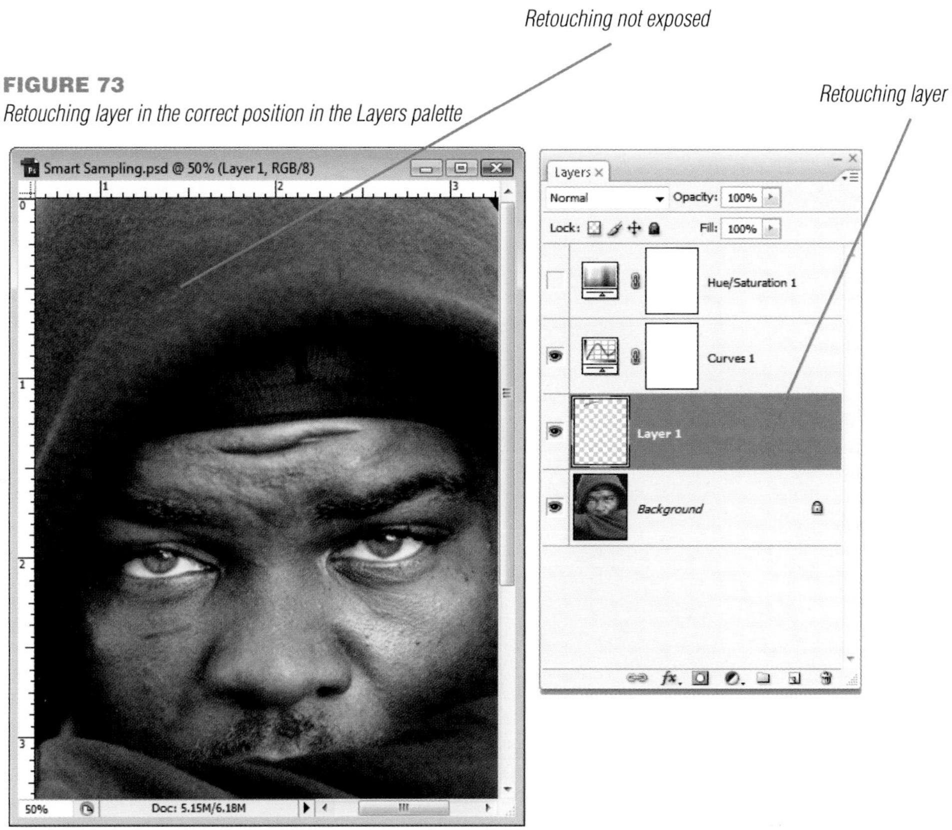

11. Hide the Hue/Saturation adjustment layer, then compare your image to Figure 73.

    Hiding the Hue/Saturation layer has no adverse effect on the image. The Hue/Saturation layer wasn't involved in the cloning.

12. Note once again the position of the new layer in the Layers palette and the Current & Below option in the Options bar.

    Remember this setup. Whenever you need to retouch an image and adjustment layers are involved, position your retouching layer immediately above the artwork that needs retouching. Retouch the artwork with the Current & Below sampling option and any adjustment layers above the retouching layer will not be sampled.

13. Save your work, then close Smart Sampling.psd.

PROJECT BUILDER 1

1. Open AP 8-5.psd, then save it as **Red Boy**.
2. Whiten the eyes and increase the saturation on the irises.
3. Use the overlay detail method to add detail to the irises.
4. Reduce the harsh lines and bluish tones under the boy's eyes.
5. Create a new, unclipped Hue/Saturation adjustment layer, then click OK without making any changes.
6. Overlay the new adjustment layer so that the red cheeks, ears, and chin get darker and redder.
7. Duplicate the Green channel, then name it **Hot Spots**.
8. Invert the channel.
9. Open the Levels dialog box, then make the whites whiter, the blacks blacker, and the midtones darker.
10. Blacken out the areas that you don't want to be affected. (*Hint*: Figure 74 shows one example of the selection mask.)
11. Click the RGB layer thumbnail, then delete the Hue/Saturation adjustment layer.
12. Load the Hot Spots selection, apply a 4-pixel feather, then hide the selection.
13. Open the Hue/Saturation dialog box, click the Edit list arrow, then choose Reds. (*Hint*: For this image, we are going to modify specifically the red hues in the selection.)
14. Drag the Hue slider to +14, then click OK.
15. Open the Curves dialog box, increase the contrast to a degree that you feel improves the image, then click OK.
16. Compare your results to Figure 75.
17. Save your work, then close Red Boy.

FIGURE 74
Selection mask

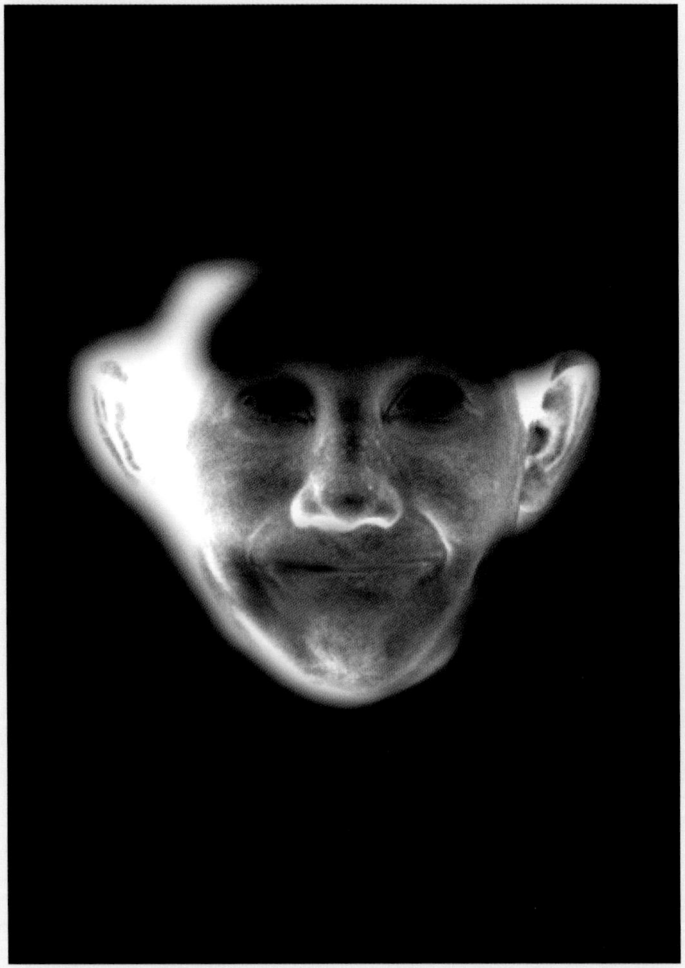

FIGURE 75
Completed Project Builder 1

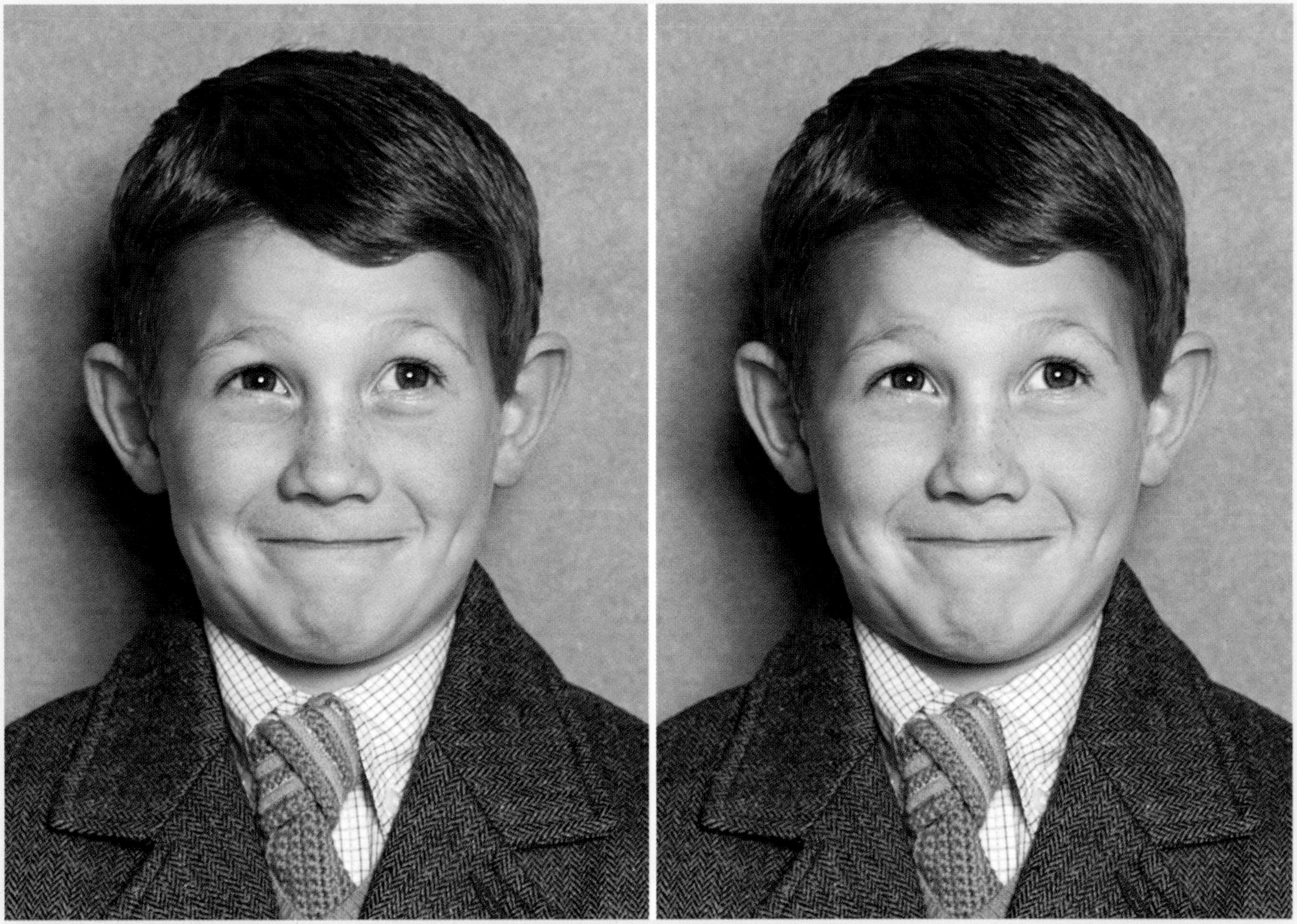

PROJECT BUILDER 2

1. Open AP 8-6.psd, then save it as **Teeth Project**.
2. Click the Rectangular Marquee Tool then make a square marquee that selects the entire mouth.
3. Click Edit on the menu bar, then click Copy Merged.
4. Paste, then name the new layer **Square Off Teeth**.
5. Zoom in, click the Pen Tool, then draw a path that represents the shape of the top right row of teeth as you would want them to be. (*Hint*: Figure 76 shows one example of the path.)
6. Convert the path to a selection with no feather, then use the Clone Stamp Tool to clone the original teeth into the new shape.
7. Use the Clone Stamp Tool, the Pencil Tool, the Sponge Tool (set to Desaturate) or a combination of the three to remove the yellow stains between the teeth. (*Hint*: Be sure you don't remove the lines between the teeth.)
8. Paint out or clone out the bent bottom tooth where it breaks the line between the top row of teeth and the bottom row of teeth.
9. Click the Pen Tool, then draw a path around the tooth to the right of the original bent tooth. (*Hint*: Figure 77 shows an example of the path.)
10. Convert the path to a selection with no feather, copy, paste a new layer, then name the new layer **Fix Bottom Row**.
11. Scale the new tooth slightly, then stretch it horizontally so that its left edge aligns with the line between the top two front teeth.
12. Use a layer mask, if necessary, to hide any of the unwanted areas of the copy.
13. Create a new layer, name it **Darken Lipstick**, then set the layer to the Overlay blending mode.
14. Paint with the overlay detail technique to darken the lipstick over the entire mouth and to make it all more consistent in color.
15. Click the Pen Tool, then draw a path around the lips.
16. Tweak the path to improve the shape of the top lip. (*Hint*: Figure 78 shows an example of the path.)
17. Convert the path to a selection with no feather, copy, then paste a new layer named **Improve Edge**.
18. Use the Clone Stamp Tool, the Paint Brush Tool, or a combination of both to increase the lips to fill the new selection.
19. Click the Rectangular Marquee Tool, then select the right half of the mouth.
20. Click Edit on the menu bar, then click Copy Merged.
21. Paste the selection, then name the new layer **Flip Horizontal**.
22. Click Edit on the menu bar, point to Transform, then click Flip Horizontal.
23. Reposition the artwork to create the left side of the mouth.
24. Duplicate the Flip Horizontal layer, name the new layer **Distort**, then hide the Flip Horizontal layer.
25. Target the Distort layer, then distort or rotate or scale (or any combination of the three transformations) the artwork so that it is no longer a perfect mirror image of the right side of the mouth.
26. Add a layer mask, then mask out the lipstick on the Distort layer to show as much of the original lipstick as you can while maintaining realism.
27. Compare your results to Figure 79.
28. Save your work, then close Teeth Project.

FIGURE 76
Clipping path for top row

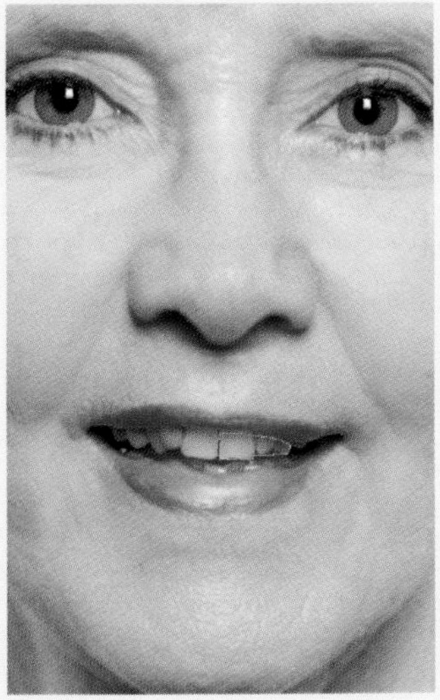

FIGURE 77
Clipping path for bottom tooth

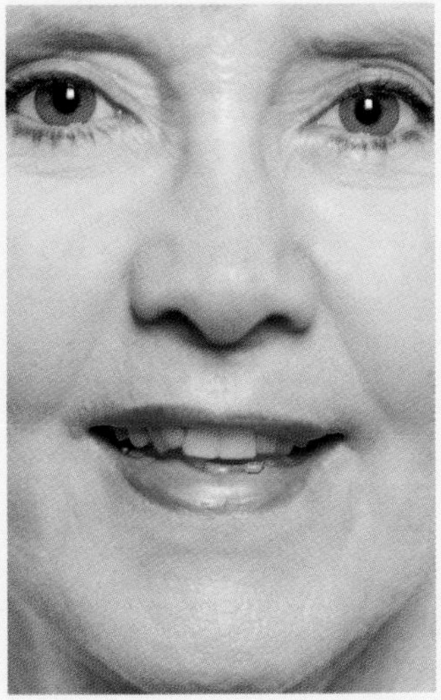

FIGURE 78
Clipping path for lips

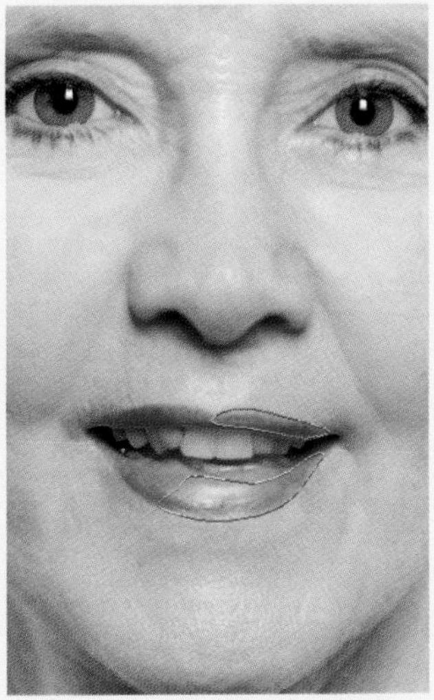

FIGURE 79
Completed Project Builder 2

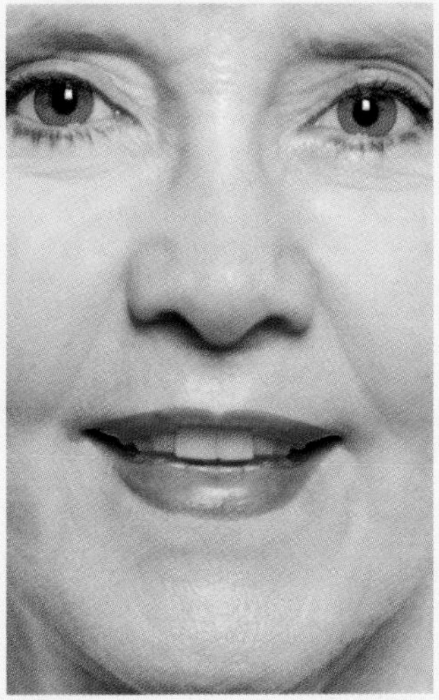

(banned)

chapter 9
CREATING SPECIAL Effects

1. Work with smart filters.
2. Create a solarize effect.
3. Create mezzotint and halftone effects.
4. Create neon effects.
5. Create a ripped effect.
6. Create monotones and duotones.

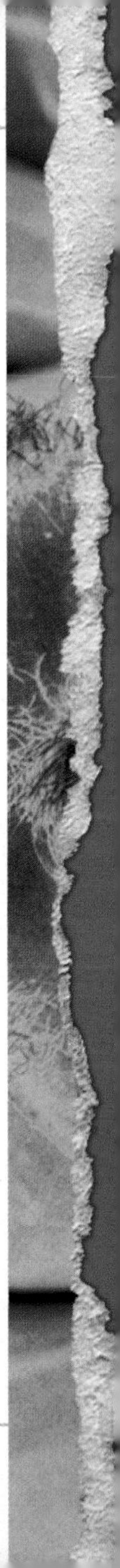

LESSON 1

WORK WITH Smart Filters

What You'll Do

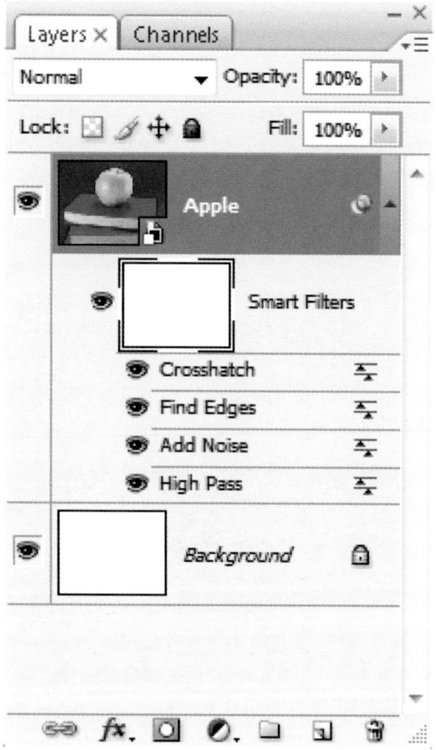

This lesson is all about an exciting new feature in Photoshop CS3: Smart Filters. For a long time now, Photoshop users have been asking for the ability to apply filters in a non-destructive manner, and in CS3, Adobe has finally delivered.

Photoshop has long offered non-destructive adjustment layers, allowing you to apply curves, hue/saturation, and levels adjustments, among many others, without permanently affecting the artwork beneath. Another big key with adjustment layers is that the adjustment is editable: You can go back at any time, reopen the adjustment dialog box, and modify the adjustment.

The Smart Filters feature applies this same concept to filters. You can apply filters without permanently altering the original image. Just as with adjustment layers, you can go back and modify the filter at any time. And an important added bonus with Smart Filters is the default layer mask, which allows you to show or mask the filter to control how it affects the artwork beneath.

FIGURE 1

Converting a layer to a Smart Object

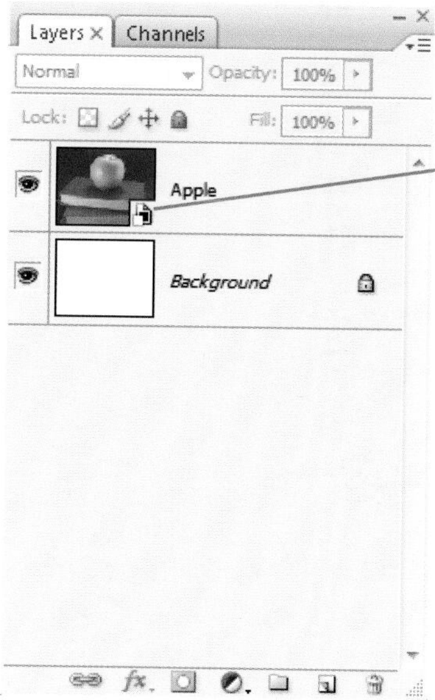

FIGURE 2

Viewing the High Pass smart filter

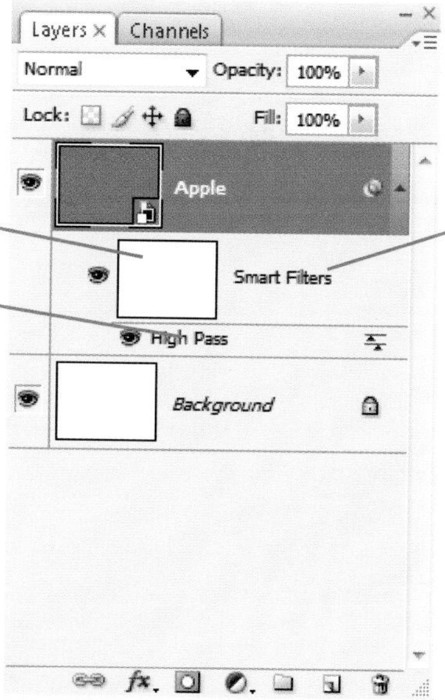

Create and apply smart filters

1. Open AP 9-1.psd, then save it as **Smart Filters**.
2. Target the **Apple layer**, click **Filter** on the menu bar, then click **Convert for Smart Filters**.

   In order to apply smart filters, a layer must first be converted to a smart object. The Background layer now includes an icon called Smart Object thumbnail, as shown in Figure 1.
3. Click **Filter** on the menu bar, point to **Other**, then click **High Pass**.
4. Type **2.0** in the Radius text box, then click **OK**.

   As shown in Figure 2, a new Smart Filters layer appears beneath the Apple layer. The High Pass smart filter is listed under the Smart Filters layer.
5. Double-click the **icon** to the right of High Pass in the Layers palette.

   The Blending Options (High Pass) dialog box opens.
6. Click the **Mode list arrow**, click **Overlay**, then click **OK**.

   Applying the High Pass filter with the Overlay blending mode is a standard sharpening technique that we explored in Chapter 5 without using smart filters.
7. Click the **Toggle individual smart filter visibility** icon repeatedly to hide and show the High Pass smart filter.

(continued)

The artwork on the Apple layer exists independently from the High Pass filter. The smart filter can be shown or hidden.

TIP Be sure that the High Pass filter is showing when you complete this step.

8. Click **Filter** on the menu bar, point to **Noise**, then click **Add Noise**.
9. Enter the settings shown in Figure 3, then click **OK**.
10. Compare your Layers palette to Figure 4.

    The Add Noise smart filter is listed above the High Pass smart filter. Photoshop applies smart filters from the bottom up. In this case, that means that the High Pass filter is applied to the apple artwork first, then the Add Noise filter is applied.
11. Save your work.

Modify smart filters

1. Double-click **High Pass** in the Layers palette.
2. Click **OK** in the warning dialog box.

   The High Pass filter dialog box opens showing the setting – Radius 2.0 – previously applied.
3. Type **4** in the Radius text box, then click **OK**.
4. Double-click the **Add Noise filter** to open the dialog box.
5. Type **4** in the Amount text box, then click **OK**.

   As shown in Figure 5, the artwork reflects the increase in both filters.
6. Save your work.

FIGURE 3
Add Noise dialog box

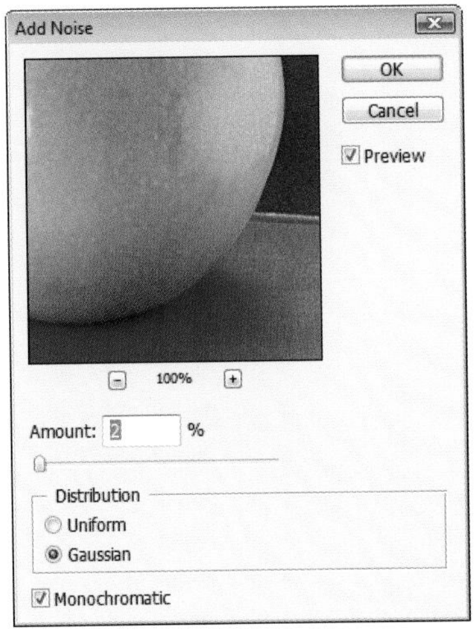

FIGURE 4
Viewing the Add Noise smart filter

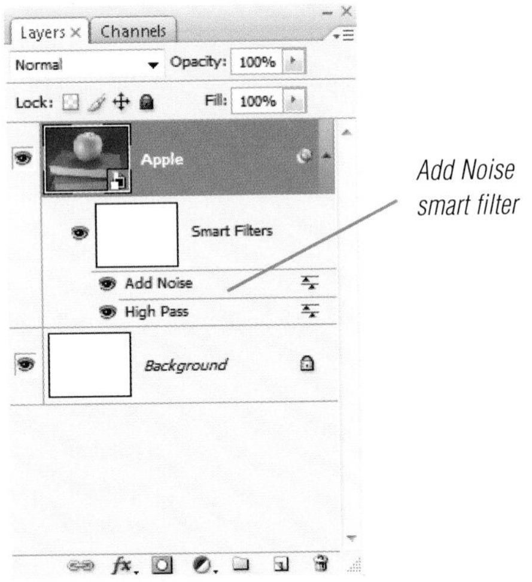

FIGURE 5
Viewing the result of increasing both smart filters

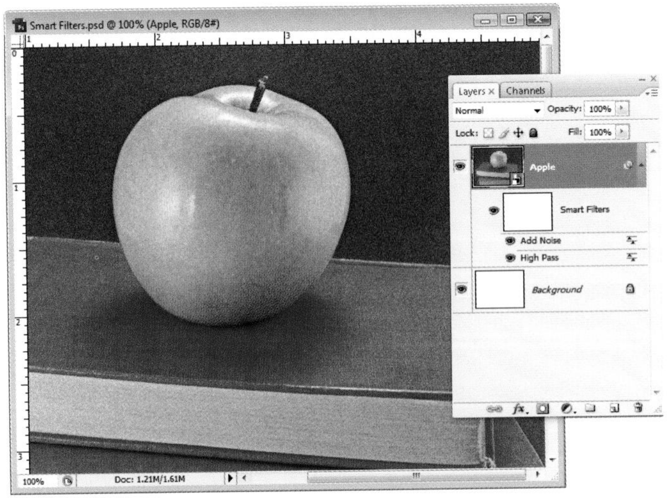

FIGURE 6
Crosshatch filter dialog box

FIGURE 7
Viewing the Crosshatch smart filter applied

Reorder smart filters

1. Verify that the Apple layer is targeted in the Layers palette.
2. Click **Filter** on the menu bar, point to **Brush Strokes**, then click **Crosshatch**.
3. Enter the settings shown in Figure 6, then click **OK**.

   The Crosshatch smart filter is listed in the Layers palette, above Add Noise and High Pass.
4. Double-click the **icon** to the right of Crosshatch in the Layers palette.

   The Blending Options (Crosshatch) dialog box opens.
5. Click the **Mode list arrow**, then click **Color Burn**.
6. Set the Opacity value to 50%, click **OK**, then compare your screen to Figure 7.

   The Crosshatch smart filter is applied at 50% opacity with the Color Burn blending mode.
7. Click **Filter** on the menu bar, point to **Stylize**, then click **Find Edges**.

   The Find Edges smart filter is listed in the Layers palette, above Crosshatch, Add Noise, and High Pass.

(continued)

8. Double-click the **icon** to the right of Find Edges in the Layers palette.
9. Click the **Mode list arrow**, click **Overlay**, type **75** in the Opacity dialog box, then click **OK**.

   Figure 8 shows the results of applying the four smart filters to the artwork in the order shown in the Layers palette.
10. Drag the **Find Edges smart filter** below the Crosshatch smart filter, then compare your result to Figure 9.

    The artwork reflects the change in order of the smart filters. The Crosshatch smart filter is now being applied to the artwork after the Find Edges smart filter is applied.
11. Save your work.

FIGURE 8

Viewing the image with the Find Edges smart filter applied

FIGURE 9

Viewing the image with the Find Edges smart filter relocated

FIGURE 10
Targeting the filter effects mask on the Smart Filters layer

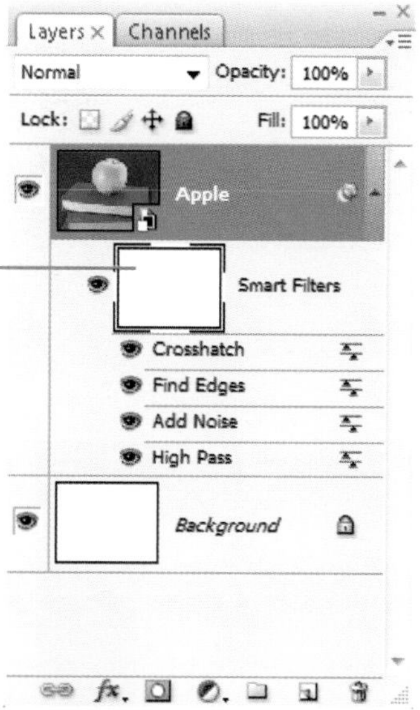

Filter effects mask thumbnail targeted

FIGURE 11
Viewing all smart filters being applied through the layer mask

Black-to-white blend added to filter effects layer mask

Use a layer mask with smart filters

1. Click the **Filter effects mask thumbnail** on the Smart Filters layer so that it is framed, as shown in Figure 10.
2. Click the **Default Foreground and Background Colors button** in the Tools palette.
3. Create a black to white blend from the left edge of the image to the right edge of the image.

   A black to white blend is added to the filter effects mask in the Layers palette.
4. Compare your results to Figure 11.

   As shown in the figure, all of the four filters are masked on the left edge and gradually become visible from left to right.
5. Hide and show the Smart Filters layer in the Layers palette.

   The original artwork is not permanently affected by the smart filters.
6. Save your work, then close Smart Filters.

LESSON 2

CREATE A Solarize Effect

What You'll Do

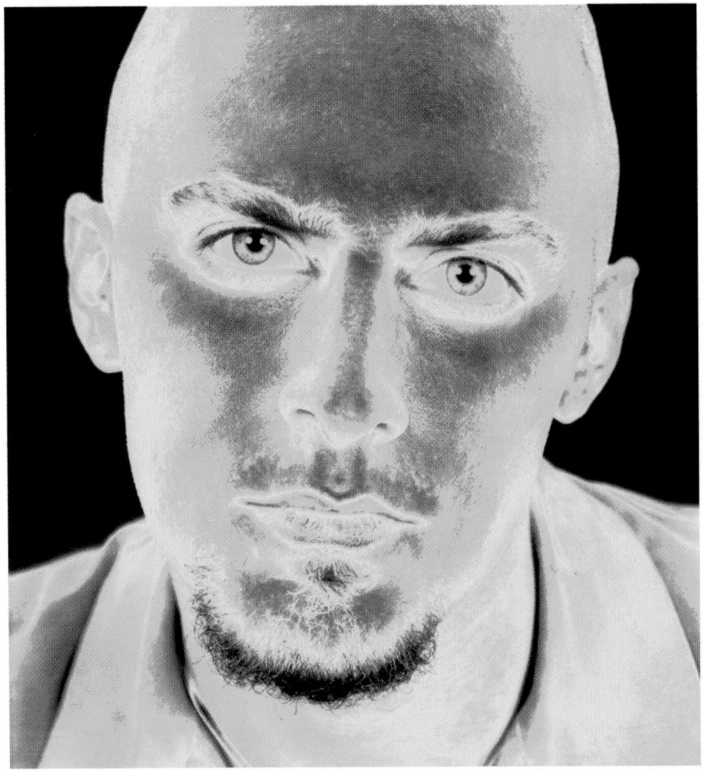

Solarize is a filter that has been available since the first release of Photoshop. It mimics a long-established effect in photography: mixing both the positive areas with negative areas. What's really interesting is that you can use the Curves dialog box to reproduce the Solarize filter's effect or to create your own version of the effect. The Solarize filter does not offer a dialog box with settings that you can adjust. It simply executes an algorithm and you are stuck with the results. However, because the solarize effect can be created and manipulated with curves, this gives you the power to create a customized solarize effect that is just right for a given image.

FIGURE 12
Image inverted

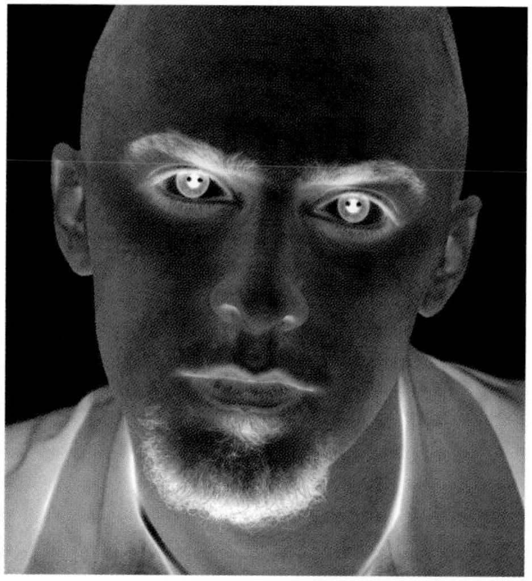

FIGURE 13
Image with the Solarize filter applied

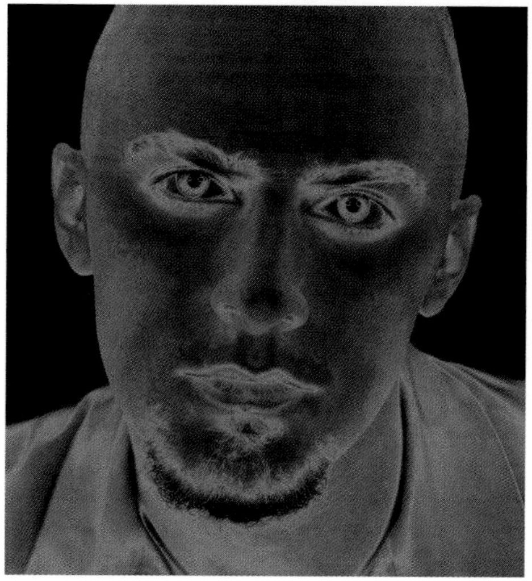

Solarize an image

1. Open AP 9-2.psd, then save it as **Solarize**.
2. Convert to Grayscale mode, then convert back to RGB Color mode.

   This is a standard method for working with a black-and-white image in a color mode.
3. Invert the image, then compare your result to Figure 12.

   Note especially the dark areas that have become white, such as his beard and eyebrows.
4. Undo your last step.
5. Click **Filter** on the menu bar, point to **Stylize**, click **Solarize**, then compare your result to Figure 13.

   With the Solarize filter, the light areas of the image are inverted, while the dark areas are not affected. If you compare this to the fully inverted image in Figure 12, you can see the difference. Note how the dark areas of the beard and the black pupils in his eyes remained black.
6. Undo your last step to remove the filter.

(continued)

7. Click the **Create new fill or adjustment layer button** on the Layers palette, then click **Curves**.
8. Click the **pencil icon** in the Curves dialog box, then click the lower-left corner of the grid.
9. [Shift]-click the center point of the grid, then [Shift]-click the lower-right corner of the grid so that your Curves dialog box resembles Figure 14.

   This curve is easy to "read." From 0–128, nothing has changed. From 129–255, everything has been inverted—the curve moves downward instead of upward, meaning the pixels move back toward black rather than toward white.
10. Click **OK**, then compare your canvas to Figure 15.

    The result is identical to Figure 13, because this is the exact curve used when the Solarize filter is applied. Using the Curves dialog box to solarize opens up many options for manipulating the effect.

(continued)

FIGURE 14
Standard solarize curve

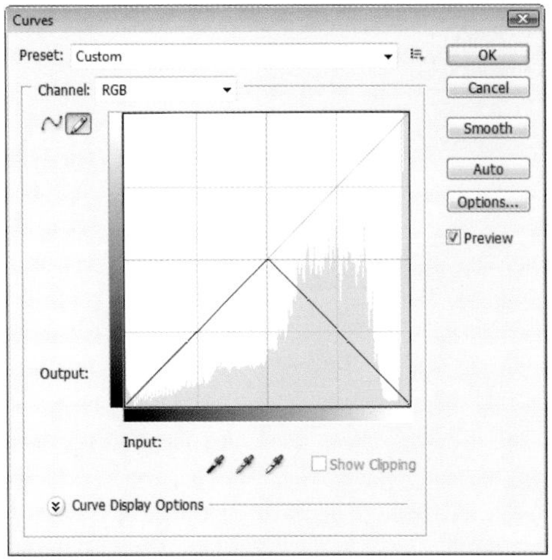

FIGURE 15
Image solarized

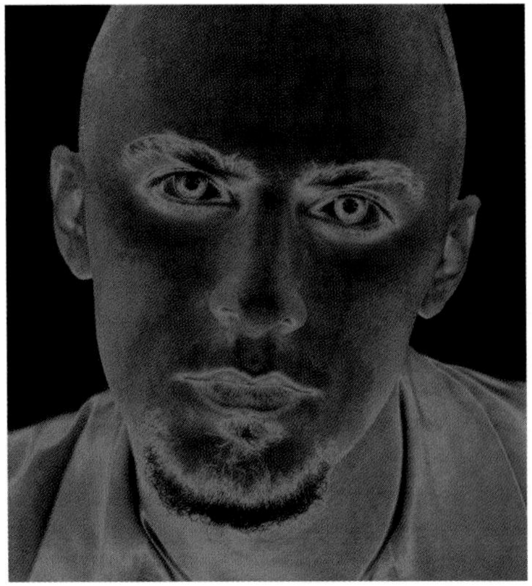

FIGURE 16
Darkening the solarize effect

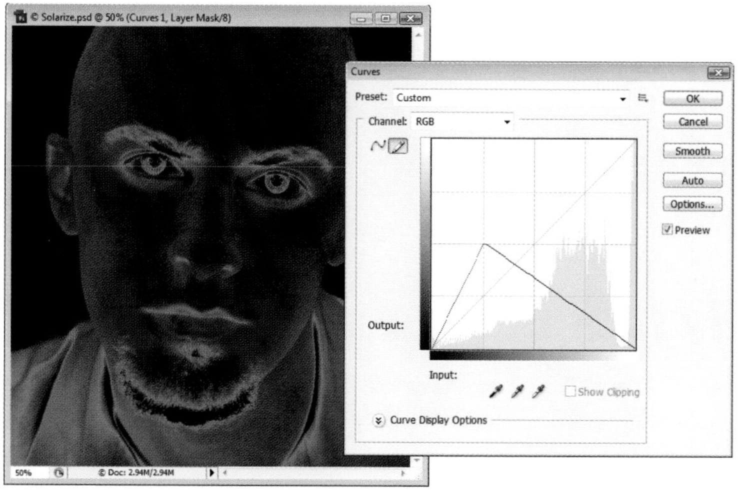

FIGURE 17
Lightening the solarize effect

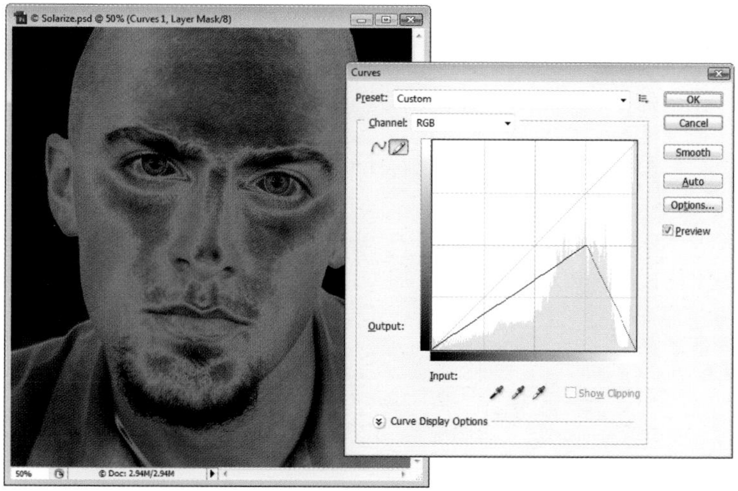

11. Reopen the Curves adjustment layer then, starting at the lower-left corner, redraw the curve so that it resembles Figure 16.

    The shadow half of the curve is shortened by this move, and the dark areas of the image are therefore darkened. With a solarize effect, the goal is usually to create a "silver" person or image, which involves brightening, not darkening the image. This is not a curve that is typically used to solarize.

12. Using the same method, redraw the curve so that it resembles Figure 17.

    This move is more in the right direction to achieve the silver effect.

(continued)

13. Redraw the curve to match Figure 18, then click **OK**.
14. Click the **Create new fill or adjustment layer button** on the Layers palette, then click **Solid Color**.
15. Type **255R/216G/0B**, click **OK**, set the new layer's blending mode to Overlay, then compare your artwork to Figure 19.
16. Click the **Brush Tool**, set the Opacity to 50%, then set the foreground color to black.

(continued)

FIGURE 18
Lightening the effect substantially

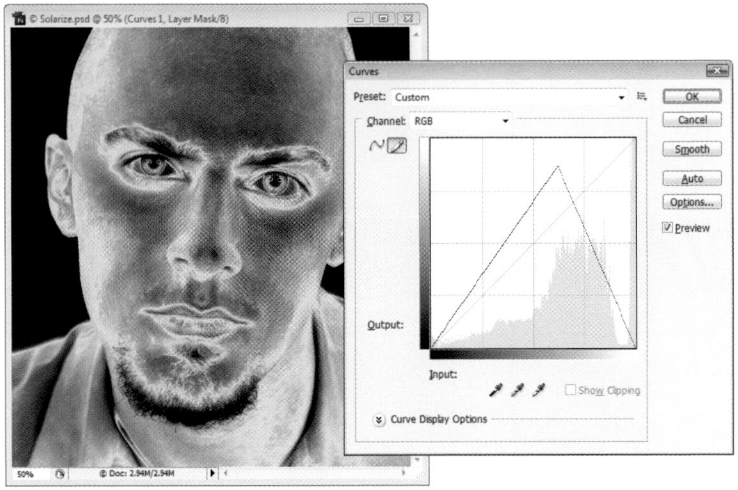

FIGURE 19
Applying a color fill

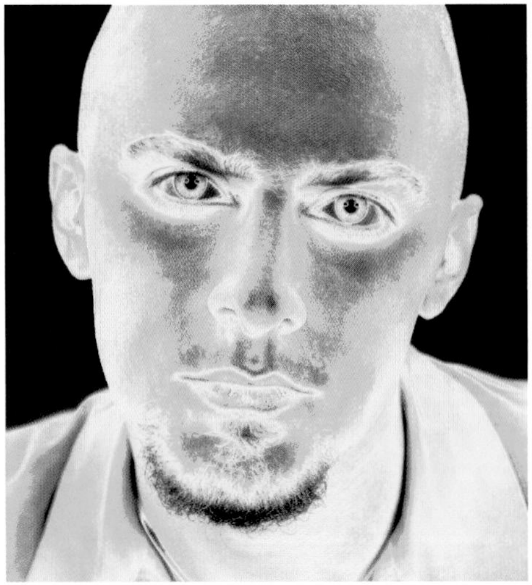

FIGURE 20
Masking the effect from the eyes

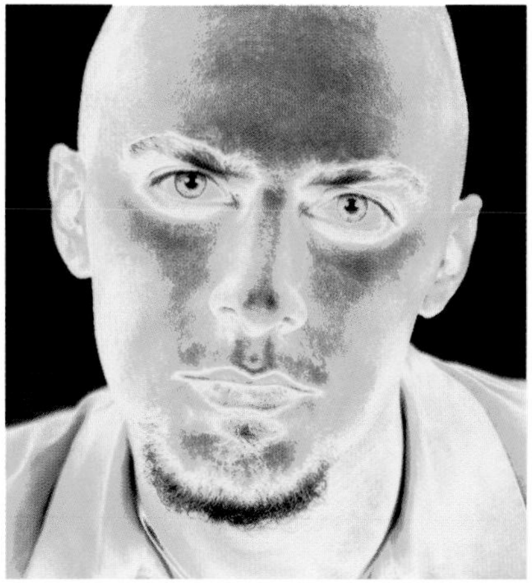

FIGURE 21
Reducing the effect in the highlights

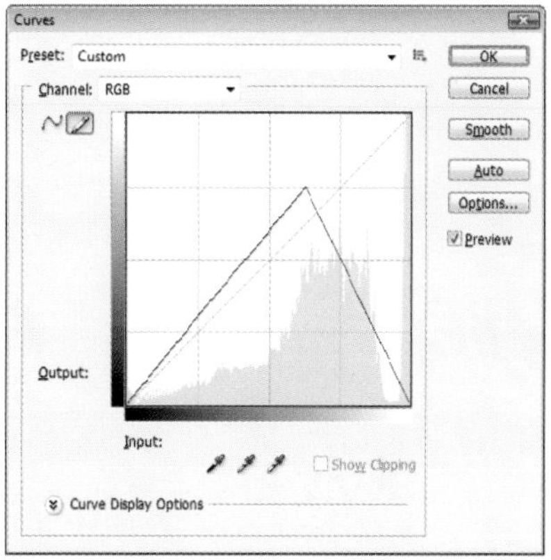

FIGURE 22
Final effect

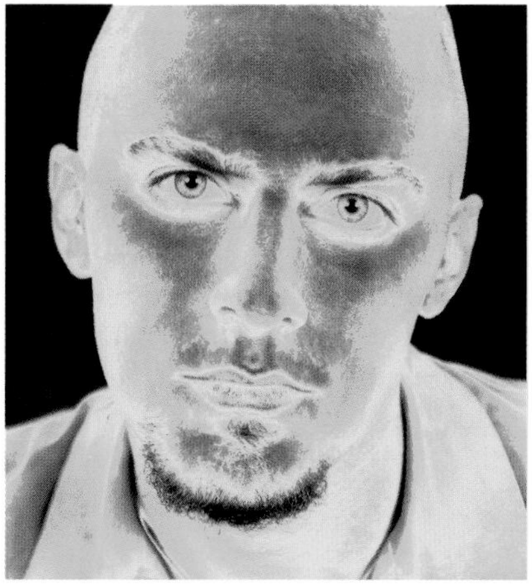

17. Using the layer mask beside the curves adjustment layer, reduce the solarization effect over the eyes so that your artwork resembles Figure 20.

    Since the solarize effect at this point is very extreme, we can always reduce the contrast by adjusting the curve.

18. Double-click the **Curves adjustment layer thumbnail**, then redraw the curve as shown in Figure 21.
19. Click **OK**, then compare your result to Figure 22.
20. Save your work, then close the file.

LESSON 3

CREATE MEZZOTINT AND Halftone Effects

What You'll Do

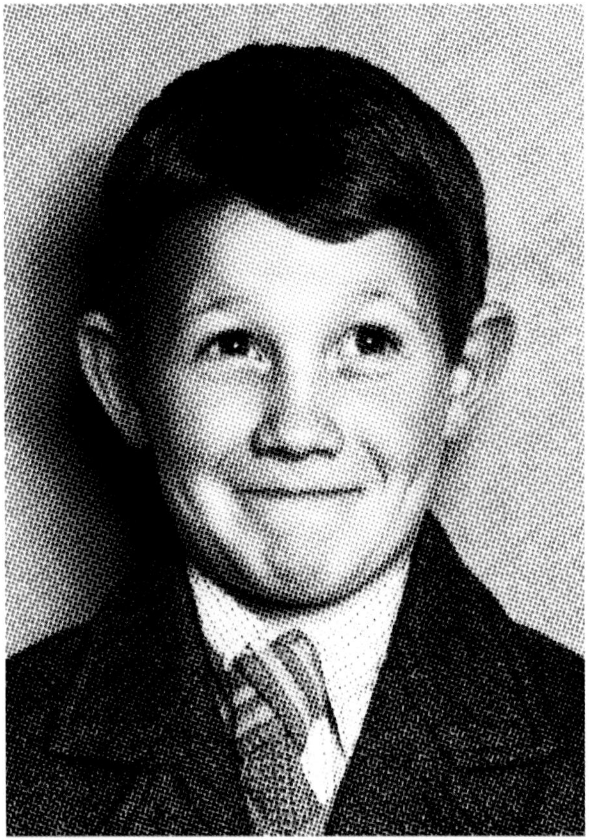

Mezzotints and halftoning are long-established procedures in the world of printing and prepress. In one sense, they're practical: They're used as part of the process to reproduce an image on a printing press. In another sense, they're a special effect, because they make an image look pretty cool. Of the two, you are certainly most familiar with halftoning. A continuous-tone image is reproduced with dots of ink that are various sizes. In prepress and printing, a mezzotint is a screening technique that you can use as an alternative to a conventional halftone. As an effect, it's a sweet alternative to applying a conventional grain overlay. Speaking of *overlay*, it's good for you to know that in the early versions of Photoshop, it required more complex procedures to apply the halftone and mezzotint filters as components in an overall effect. Photoshop's relatively new blending modes—like Overlay and Soft Light—have made it much quicker and easier to apply these filters in a way that *integrates* the effect with the base image.

FIGURE 23
Mezzotint filter

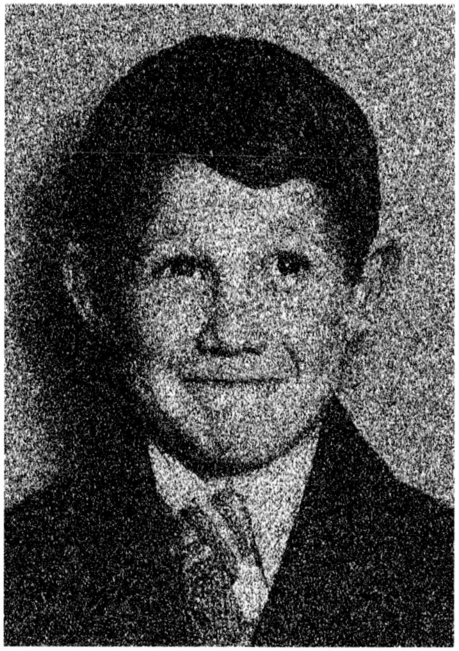

FIGURE 24
Mezzotint filter in Overlay mode

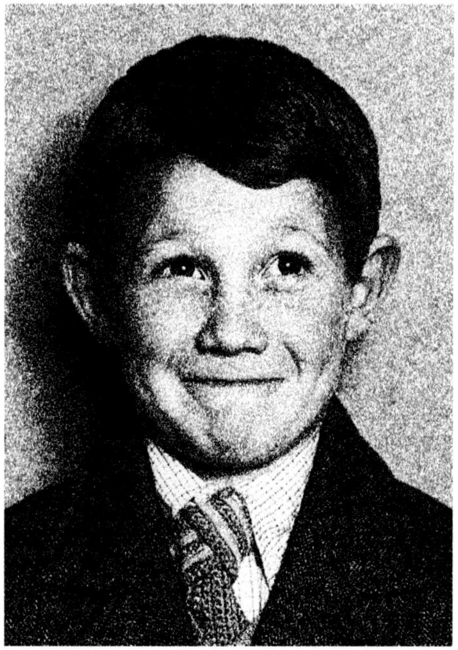

Create a mezzotint effect

1. Open AP 9-3.psd, then save it as **Mezzotint**.
2. Duplicate the Background layer, then name the new layer **Mezzotint**.

   TIP If you like, feel free to execute the following steps with smart filters.

3. Click **Filter** on the menu, point to **Pixelate**, then click **Mezzotint**.
4. Verify that the Type is set to Fine dots, click **OK**, then compare your result to Figure 23.
5. Zoom in on the effect so that you can see the pixels.

   The effect produced by the Mezzotint filter is often called a "bitmap effect" because it renders the image with only black or white pixels. Though this file is in Grayscale mode—256 shades of gray available per pixel—there are no gray pixels that make up the filtered image.

6. Zoom out so that you are viewing the image at 50%.
7. Set the blending mode on the Mezzotint layer to Overlay, then compare your result to Figure 24.

   Overlayed, the mezzotint effect produces a grainy, high-contrast image with white whites, dark blacks, and very few midtones.

(continued)

8. Change the blending mode to Soft Light, then compare your result to Figure 25.

   The Soft Light blending mode produces a much softer grain effect with less contrast and more detail in the midtones.

9. Save your work, then close Mezzotint.

Create a halftone effect

1. Open AP 9-4.psd, then save it as **Halftone**.
2. Duplicate the Background layer, then name the new layer **Halftone**.

   TIP If you like, feel free to execute the following steps with smart filters.

3. Click **Filter** on the menu bar, point to **Pixelate**, then click **Color Halftone**.
4. Type **4** in the Max. Radius text box, click **OK**, then compare your result to Figure 26.
5. Convert the file to RGB Color mode, then click **Don't Flatten** in the dialog box that follows.

   TIP Throughout this chapter, always click Don't Flatten when prompted.

6. Zoom in on the image so that you can see the pixels.

   Unlike with the Mezzotint filter, the Color Halftone filter produces both black and gray pixels to create the effect.

(continued)

FIGURE 25
Mezzotint filter in Soft Light mode

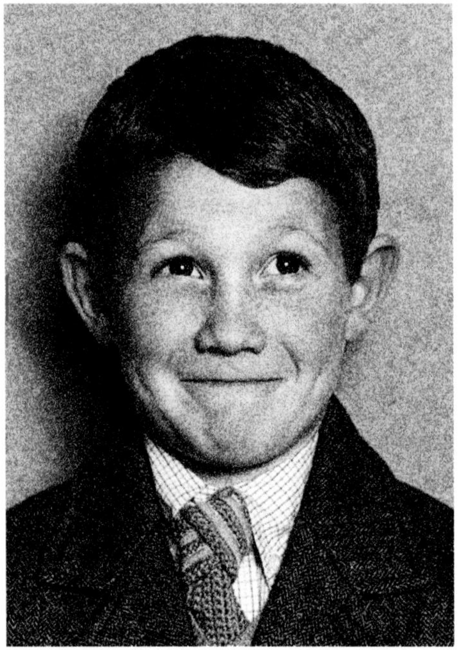

FIGURE 26
Color Halftone filter

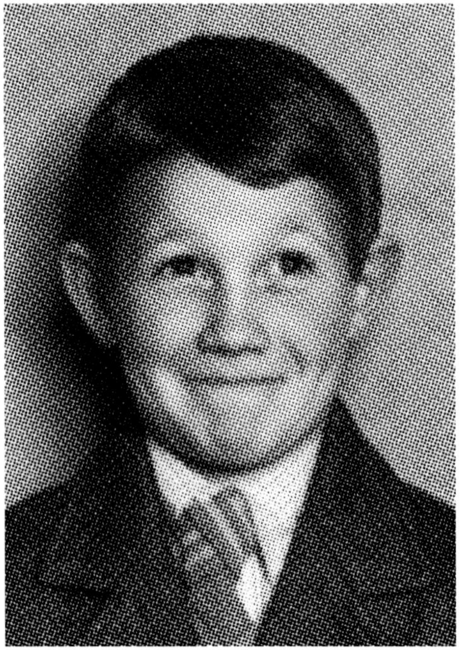

FIGURE 27
The Blue, Red, Yellow gradient

7. Click the **Magic Wand Tool**, type **8** in the Tolerance text box, then verify that the Anti-alias and Contiguous check boxes are not checked.
8. Click a white pixel.

   All of the white pixels in the image are selected.
9. Click **Select** on the menu bar, then click **Inverse**.

   All of the non-white pixels that make up the filtered image are selected.
10. Zoom out so that you are viewing the image at 50%.
11. Copy, paste a new layer, then name the new layer **Halftone Transparent**.

    With this step, you have isolated the filtered image on a transparent layer—the pixels that were originally white are now transparent.
12. Delete the Halftone layer, then create a new layer named **BRY Gradient** above the Halftone Transparent layer.
13. Click the **Gradient Tool**, click the **Gradient picker list arrow** on the Options bar, then click the **Blue, Red, Yellow gradient**.
14. Drag the **Gradient Tool pointer** from the upper-left corner to the bottom-right corner of the canvas so that your result resembles Figure 27.

(continued)

15. Clip the BRY Gradient layer into the Halftone Transparent layer so that your canvas resembles Figure 28.
16. Select both the Halftone Transparent and the BRY Gradient layers in the Layers palette, click the **Layers palette list arrow**, then click **Merge Layers**.
17. Change the blending mode on the new merged layer to Overlay.
18. Compare your result to Figure 29.
19. Save your work, then close the Halftone document.

FIGURE 28
Clipping the gradient into the filtered artwork

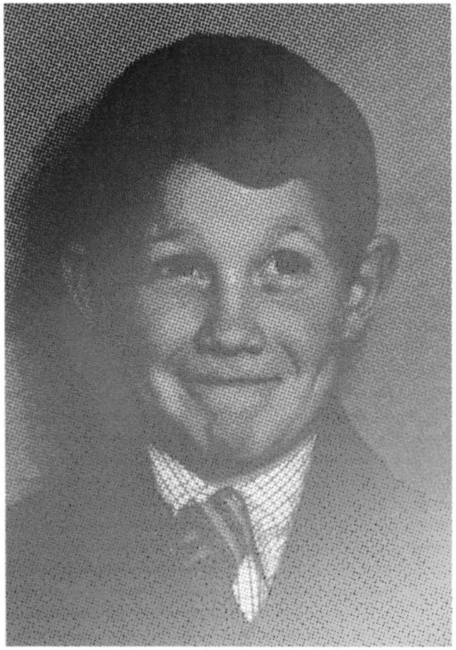

FIGURE 29
Overlaying the merged artwork

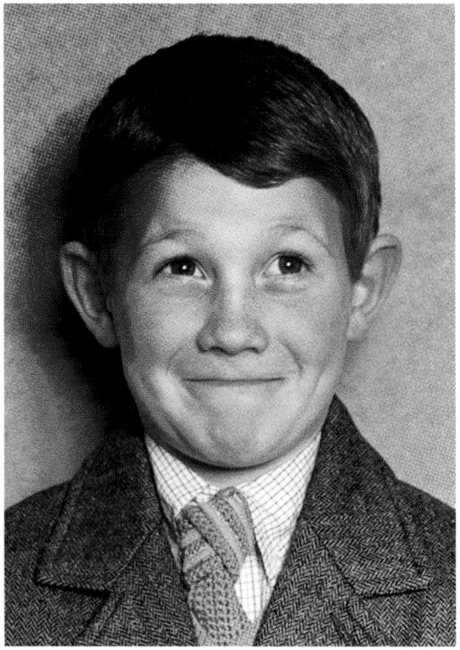

FIGURE 30

Final variation

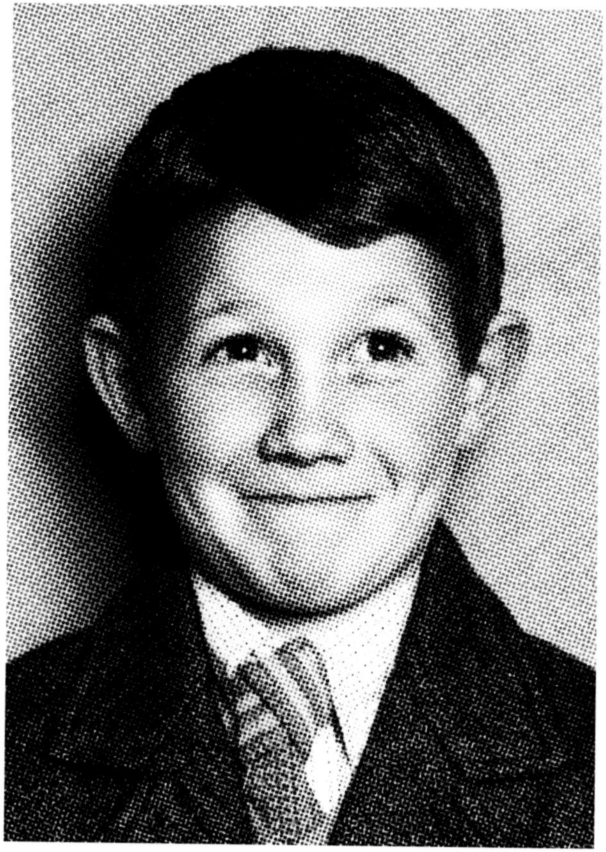

Create a variation of a halftone effect

1. Open AP 9-4.psd, then save it as **Halftone Variation**.
2. Duplicate the Background layer, then name the new layer **Halftone**.
3. Click **Filter** on the menu bar, point to **Pixelate**, then click **Color Halftone**.
4. Type **4** in the Max. Radius text box, then click **OK**.
5. Convert the file to RGB Color mode.
6. Create a new layer named **BRY Gradient** above the Halftone layer.
7. Click the **Gradient Tool**, click the **Gradient picker list arrow** in the Options bar, then click the **Blue, Red, Yellow gradient**.
8. Drag the **Gradient Tool pointer** from the upper-left corner to the bottom-right corner of the canvas.
9. Change the blending mode on the BRY Gradient layer to Overlay.
10. Merge the BRY Gradient and the Halftone layers, then set the blending mode on the merged layer to Overlay.
11. Compare your result to Figure 30.
12. Save your work, then close the Halftone Variation document.

LESSON 4

CREATE NEON Effects

What You'll Do

Neon effects are another Photoshop staple, one that you've been able to do one way or another since the first release. They make for stunning special effects, and they're practical because they work so well with type. Neon is effective and it's classic: it can be used as a title treatment for many different types of projects.

Many books and manuals supply tips and tricks for creating simple neon effects—and that's the problem. They stop at the simple, which usually involves stroking a path or using the Inner Glow or Outer Glow layer styles. But if you spend some time driving around and noticing the many types of neon effects just sitting out there in the real world, you'll see soon enough that you can get a lot more creative than simply stroking a path.

That's what this lesson is about—creating a complex neon effect. You'll do it the old-fashioned way, with paths rather than layer styles. You'll learn some great techniques for reproducing a neon effect, but you'll also explore more complex design concepts that will lead you to a multilayered effect that shines and fades and glows hot.

FIGURE 31
Path 2 stroked with Top Blue

Create a neon effect

1. Open AP 9-5.psd, then save it as **Neon**.
2. Display the Paths palette, then click **Path 2** to activate it.
3. Create a new foreground color that is **0R/127G/254B**, then save it in the Swatches palette as **Top Blue**.

   TIP To add a color to the Swatches palette, click the Swatches palette list arrow, then click New Swatch, enter a name in the Color Swatch Name dialog box, then click OK, or click the Paint Bucket Tool and then click an empty section in the Swatches palette. The foreground color on the toolbox is the color that will be added to the Swatches palette.
4. Click the **Brush Tool**, then set its size to Soft Round 28 pixels.

   Throughout this chapter, verify that your Brush Tool is set to 100% Opacity and 100% Flow.
5. Create a new layer named **Top Blue 28px**.
6. Click the **Paths palette list arrow**, then click **Stroke Path**.
7. Click the **Tool list arrow** in the Stroke Path dialog box, click **Brush**, then click **OK**.
8. Deactivate Path 2, then compare your result to Figure 31.

   The Stroke Path command strokes the path with the tool you select. It uses the tool's current settings for size, hardness, opacity, and so on, when creating the stroke.

(continued)

TIP For all the figures in this lesson, the path is deactivated so that you can better see the artwork. To avoid repetition, we won't continue to instruct you to deactivate your path when comparing it to a figure, though you can feel free to.

9. Create a new layer named **Top Border**.
10. Click **Path 1** to activate it, then click the **Stroke path with brush button** ○ on the Paths palette.

    Like the Stroke Path command in the palette menu, the **Stroke path with brush button** strokes the path with the Brush Tool using its current settings.
11. Compare your canvas to Figure 32.

    Had the two paths been combined as one path, we could have created this artwork with one stroke instead of two. However, it is necessary for the final artwork that we are able to access these two paths independently from one another.
12. Create a Hue/Saturation adjustment layer named **Colorize** for the Top Border layer only.
13. Click the **Use Previous Layer to Create Clipping Mask check box**, then click **OK**.
14. In the Hue/Saturation dialog box, click the **Colorize check box**.
15. Set the Hue value to 0, the Saturation value to 25, the Lightness value to 0, click **OK**, then compare your result to Figure 33.

(continued)

FIGURE 32
Path 1 stroked with Top Blue

FIGURE 33
Path 1 colorized

FIGURE 34
Paths 1 and 2 stroked with White 19 pixels

16. Change the diameter on the Brush Tool to 19 pixels, then change the foreground color to white.
17. Create a new layer named **White 19px**.
18. Click **Path 1**, then click the **Stroke path with brush button** ○ in the Paths palette.
19. Click **Path 2**, click the **Stroke path with brush button** ○, then compare your artwork to Figure 34.
20. Create a new layer group of the artwork named **Tubes**.

    TIP Don't include the Background layer in the group.

21. Save your work.

AUTHOR'S *note*

This is the point at which most books on Photoshop stop, with the neon "tubes" against a black background. It's a cool effect, but there's so much more you can do to enhance the effect by creating a reflection of the neon graphics, which is what we'll do in the next lesson.

Design a drop shadow for neon effects

1. Create a new foreground color that is 129R/156G/182B, then save it in the Swatches palette as **Drop Blue**.
2. Increase the Brush Tool diameter to 50 pixels.
3. Hide the Tubes layer group.
4. Target the **Background layer**, then create a new layer named **Drop Blue 1 (50px)**.
5. Verify that Path 2 is active, click the **Path Selection Tool**, click the letter **O**, then [Shift]-click the letter **P** so that your selection resembles Figure 35.
6. Click the **Paths palette list arrow**, then click **Stroke Subpaths**.
7. Click **OK**, then compare your result to Figure 36.

(continued)

FIGURE 35
Selecting only the O *and* P *paths*

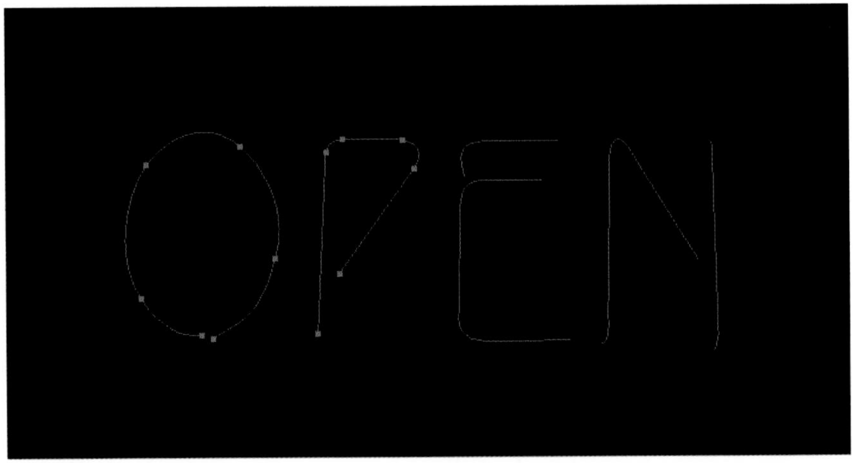

FIGURE 36
Stroking the subpaths

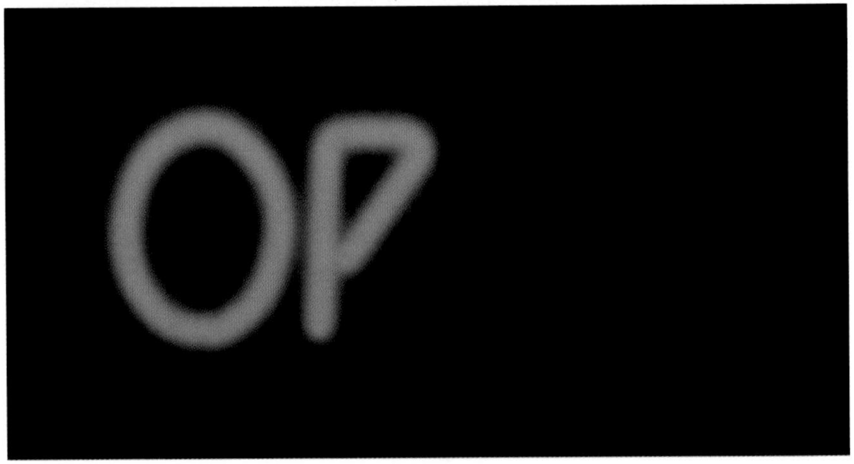

FIGURE 37
Selecting only the E and N paths

FIGURE 38
Stroking the subpaths

8. Select the paths for the letter **E** and **N** so that your selection resembles Figure 37.
9. Create a new layer in the Layers palette, then name it **Drop Blue 2**.
10. Stroke the subpaths, then compare your results to Figure 38.

    The first two and the last two letters are on different layers.
11. Show the Tubes layer group, then target the **Drop Blue 1 (50px) layer**.
12. Click **Filter** on the menu bar, point to **Other**, then click **Offset**.
13. Type **13** in the Horizontal text box, type **8** in the Vertical text box, then click **OK**.
14. Target the **Drop Blue 2 layer**, then return to the Offset dialog box.
15. Type **-13** in the Horizontal text box, type **8** in the Vertical text box, then click **OK**.

(continued)

16. Change the opacity for both the Drop Blue layers to 50%, then compare your artwork to Figure 39.
17. Target the **Background layer**, then create a new layer named **Drop Red 64px**.
18. Create a new foreground color that is 178R/39G/27B, then save it in the Swatches palette as **Drop Red**.
19. Increase the Brush Tool diameter to 64 pixels, click **Path 1**, then stroke the path.
20. Set the layer's opacity to 50%, then compare your results to Figure 40.
21. Save your work.

FIGURE 39
Final drop shadow effect

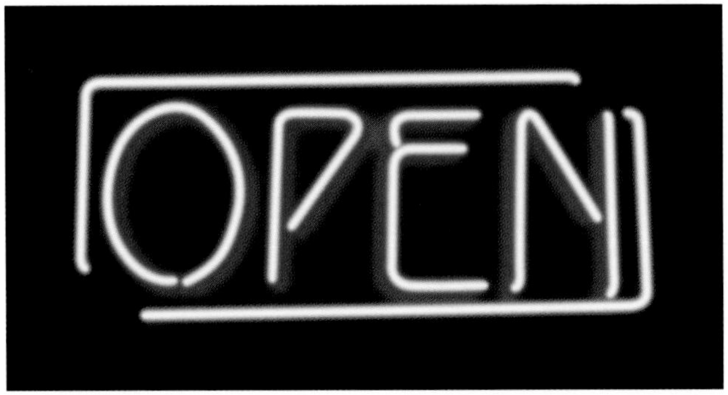

FIGURE 40
Adding the red drop shadow

AUTHOR'S *note*

If you compare Figure 40 to Figure 34, you'll see that the drop shadow behind the text and the glow behind the border goes a long way in enhancing the effect, mostly by creating a sense of depth. However, you must ask yourself, what is the neon shining against? What is the background that is reflecting that drop shadow? It's a key question when creating a neon effect, because you can use a background as a reflective surface to really make the neon glow.

FIGURE 41
Fill Path dialog box

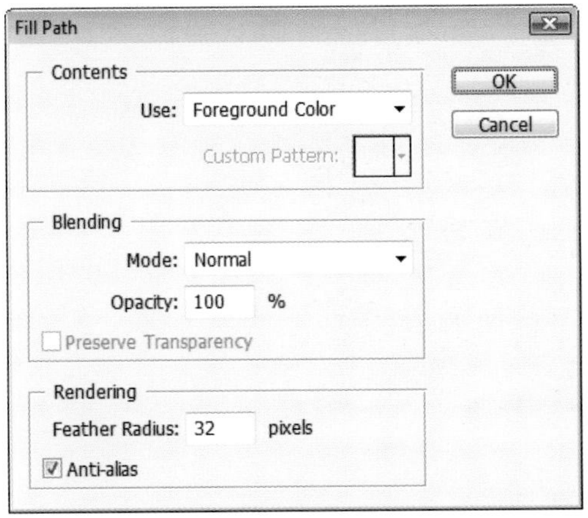

FIGURE 42
Adding the reflective background surface

Design a reflective background surface for a neon effect

1. Target the **Background layer**, then create a new layer named **Top Blue Fill**.
2. Change the foreground color to Top Blue, then click **Path 4** to activate it.
3. Click the **Paths palette list arrow**, then click **Fill Path**.
4. Enter the settings shown in Figure 41, then click **OK**.
5. Deactivate the path, change the opacity on the layer to 25%, then compare your artwork to Figure 42.

   Some neon signs are set within a metal box, and the neon light reflects off that surface. The fill that we added in Figure 42 represents that surface, and it is very effective in creating context for the drop shadow behind the neon text. The drop shadow now has a background to reflect off, and that gives us the opportunity to reflect even more dramatic colors off that surface.

(continued)

6. Create a new layer above the Top Blue Fill layer, then name the new layer **Drop Red 150px**.
7. Change the foreground color to Drop Red, then increase the Brush Tool's diameter to 150 pixels.
8. Stroke Path 1, change the layer's opacity to 33%, then compare your result to Figure 43.
9. Create a new layer above Drop Red 150px, then name the new layer **Top Blue 150px**.
10. Change the foreground color to Top Blue, click **Path 2** to activate it, then stroke the path.

(continued)

FIGURE 43
Adding the large glow behind the neon border

AUTHOR'S *note*

The deep blue artwork on the Top Blue 150px layer has enormous impact on the illustration, and there are many interesting insights to be gained by analyzing its role. If you turn the layer on and off, you see that the deep blue artwork actually makes the neon tubes appear to glow more intensely. That's because your eye reads the glow as the reflection of the neon tubes against the background surface, and any light that creates such a large and intense reflection must itself be very intense. The deep blue glow also enhances the role of the drop shadow behind the letters; it now appears to reflect *through* the blue glow. Toggle the blending mode between Normal and Hard Light; this effect is a great example of how Hard Light is one of the few blending modes that works well against a dark or even black background, which is important to remember. In Normal mode, the glow still works, but in Hard Light mode it takes on the quality of a deep, dark midnight blue that contrasts so well with the pale, "hot" blue of the neon tubes.

FIGURE 44
Adding the large glow behind the neon text

11. Set the opacity on the layer to 55%, change the blending mode to Hard Light, then compare your results to Figure 44.
12. Save your work.

Finish the illustration

1. Merge the Drop Blue 1 (50px) and Drop Blue 2 layers.
2. Rename the merged layer **Drop Blue (50px)**, then click the **Add layer mask button** on the Layers palette.
3. Set the foreground color to black.
4. Expand the Tubes layer group, then load the selection of the Top Blue 28px layer (the blue neon type).
5. Click **Select** on the menu bar, point to **Modify**, then click **Expand**.
6. Type **2** in the Expand By text box, then click **OK**.

(continued)

7. Feather the selection 4 pixels.

   Your canvas should resemble Figure 45.

8. Click the **Layer mask thumbnail** on the Drop Blue (50px) layer, then fill the selection with black.

9. Deselect, then compare your artwork to Figure 46.

   If you undo, redo the move, you'll see that this move is both subtle and important. Prior to this move, the shadow appeared to be emanating from the tubes themselves. With the move, the drop shadow no longer abuts the neon tubes, and by creating this separation, the neon tubes are now clearly *in front* of the drop shadow, and the drop shadow itself is now a reflection *against the back surface.*

10. Collapse the Tubes layer group, target the **Tubes layer**, then create a new layer named **Black Tubes**.

11. Change the diameter on the Brush Tool to 18 pixels, then change the Hardness value to 80%.

(continued)

FIGURE 45
Selecting the neon text

FIGURE 46
Masking pixels behind the tubes

FIGURE 47
Stroking the path to create the "black" tubes

FIGURE 48
Adding a highlight

12. Display the Color palette, click the **Color palette list arrow**, click **Grayscale Slider**, then specify a foreground color that is 94% Black.
13. Click **Path 3** to activate it, stroke the path, then compare your canvas to Figure 47.
14. Change the foreground color to 88% Black.
15. Change the diameter on the Brush Tool to 10 pixels, then change the Hardness value to 0%.
16. Stroke Path 3 again, deactivate the path, then compare your artwork to Figure 48.

    The second stroke plays the role of a subtle highlight; we used a 0% Hardness value so that its edge would be soft, like a highlight. Note that when we created the first black stroke, we used a high hardness value. The neon effect is created by using very soft edges of color; the soft edges create the effect that they glow. Because we want these black tubes to *not* glow, we used a harder edge.
17. Drag the **Black Tubes layer** below the Tubes layer group in the Layers palette.

(continued)

18. Reduce the opacity on the Black Tubes layer to 35%, then compare your artwork to Figure 49.

The black tubes add what I call a "recognizable reality" to the artwork. I especially like the tubes above the letter N, *behind* the N, and between the P and E. However, there's a problem that I saw immediately when I first designed this. Note the relationship between the black tubes and the type's drop shadow. Because the black tubes artwork is at 35% opacity, we see the drop shadow behind it. The effect is that there's a highlight on the black tubes, as though the drop shadow is emanating from the neon text and shining on the black tubes. That's the problem. As noted above, we want the drop shadow to be a reflection off the back surface. This means that the drop shadow must be behind the neon tubes. I call this a "visual logic" problem. Visually, it doesn't make sense. Don't make the mistake of thinking that it's so subtle it's not important or that I'm just being overly picky. Visual logic problems, even when subtle, can do great damage to an illustration. We've discussed this in earlier chapters: if the eye says "No, something's wrong," it can ruin an illustration.

(continued)

FIGURE 49
Viewing the black tubes art

19. Undo your last move so that the Black Tubes artwork is at 100% opacity, then [Ctrl]-click (Win) or [⌘]-click (Mac) the **Layer thumbnail** to load a selection.

20. Click the **Layer mask thumbnail** on the Drop Blue (50px) layer, fill the selection with black, then deselect.

21. Change the opacity on the Black Tubes layer back to 35%, then compare your final artwork to Figure 50.

    If you look at the black tube between the *O* and the *P*, you can really see how important it is to the overall effect that the black tube is in front of the neon drop shadow.

22. Save your work, then close the Neon document.

FIGURE 50
Final artwork

AUTHOR'S *note*

From a design perspective, the black tubes really pay off. They add complexity to the illustration because their texture is completely different from every other element in the illustration. By contrast, the black tubes' dullness and hardness only serve to make the neon that much more vibrant and glowing. As a designer, I always keep an eye out for these extra elements or extra details that I can use to enrich an illustration.

LESSON 5

CREATE A Ripped Effect

What You'll Do

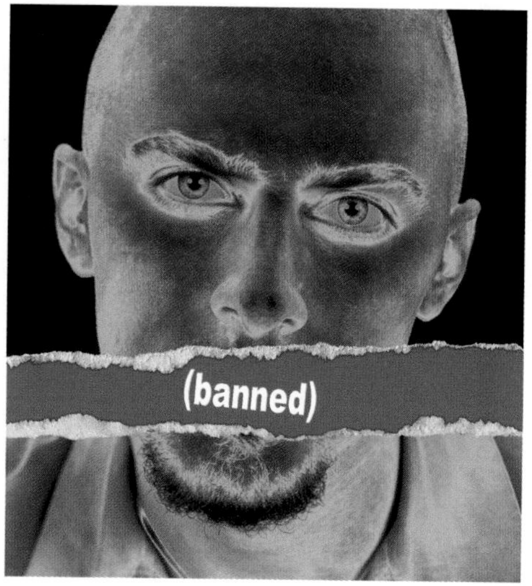

Rips are your friend; rips are your buddy. Rip effects—as though an image has been torn, leaving a rough edge—are an old standby when creating a concept. That's because they are so versatile. For any kind of conflict—war, homicide, law and order, love triangle—a ripped effect gets the message across. But rips can also be fun. They can be used for a cool before-and-after effect. For example, if you had a picture of your house in summer and another in winter when the house is covered with snow, you could put the two together side by side, then mask around the ripped edge so that the summer view on the left half "rips" to show the winter view on the right.

In this lesson, we're going to design the most complex type of ripped edge: one with texture in the ripped edge. It involves some foresight when scanning the original, and some tricky layer mask moves. One last word on ripped effects though: they're a bit overused, and because of that, they can be a bit cliché. Just be aware of that, but don't be put off. For the right concept and with the right artwork, a ripped effect can be just the right trick to make the whole thing work.

FIGURE 51

Isolating the ripped edges

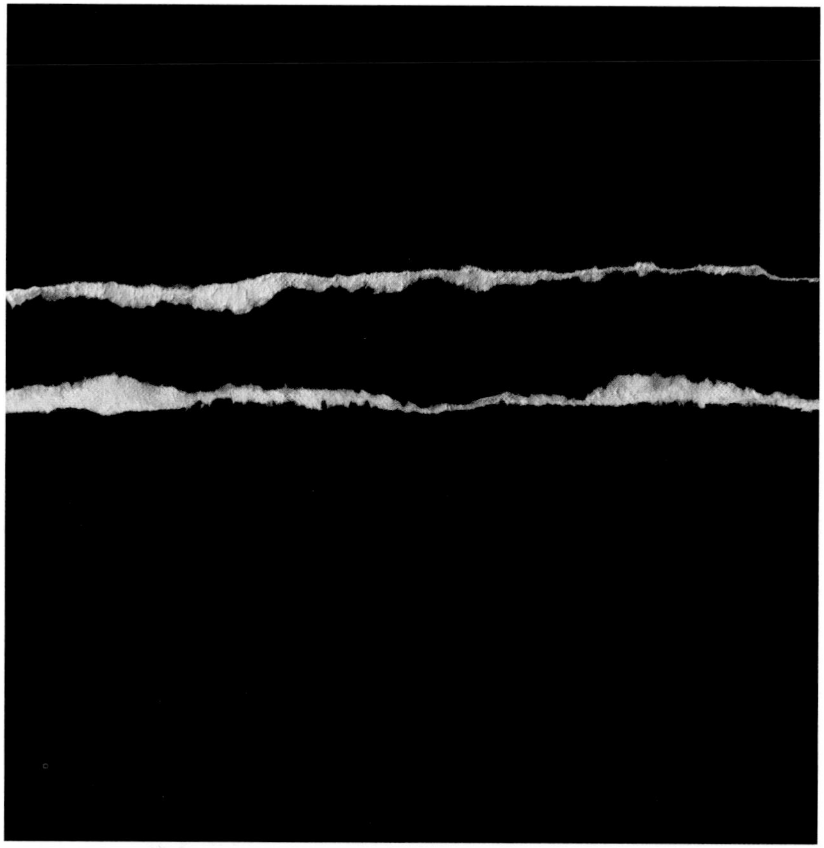

Prepare a layer mask for a ripped effect

1. Open AP 9-6.psd, then save it as **Ripped Original**.

   This file is a scan of a manila folder that has been torn in half. Using a magic marker, I first filled in the length of the folder with black ink. I then tore the folder down the middle of the black ink, creating two torn edges. I then scanned each half against a black background, which produced the file at hand.

2. Open the Levels dialog box, drag the **black triangle** to the right until the first Input Value text box reads 60, then click **OK**.

3. Paint the manila folder surface with black isolating the ripped edges, so that your artwork resembles Figure 51.

   TIP Paint carefully when you get close to the ripped edges. You want to maintain as much of the original rip detail from the scan as possible.

4. Open the Levels dialog box, drag the **black triangle** to the right until the first Input Value text box reads 16, drag the **gray midtone triangle** left until the middle Input text box reads 1.40, then click **OK**.

(continued)

5. Click **Filter** on the menu bar, point to **Sharpen**, then click **Smart Sharpen**.

   The Smart Sharpen dialog box is an upgrade of the Unsharp Mask dialog box. In addition to providing a large preview window, it offers the ability to control how specific areas of the image (such as highlights, shadows, and so on) are sharpened and the ability to choose different algorithms for sharpening the image.

6. Note that the Remove setting is set to Gaussian Blur.

   The Remove option determines which algorithm will be used to sharpen the image. You can choose among three: Gaussian Blur is the same algorithm that the Unsharp Mask filter uses; Lens Blur is designed to sharpen fine detail; Motion Blur is designed to sharpen areas of an image that are blurry because the subject moved or was moving when the image was captured.

7. Click the **Remove list arrow**, then click **Lens Blur**.

   We want to sharpen the fine detail in the grains of paper in the ripped edge.

8. Set the Amount value to 120, then verify that the Radius value is set to 1.0.

9. Click the **More Accurate check box**, if necessary, so that your Smart Sharpen dialog box resembles Figure 52.

10. Click **OK**.

(continued)

FIGURE 52
Smart Sharpen dialog box

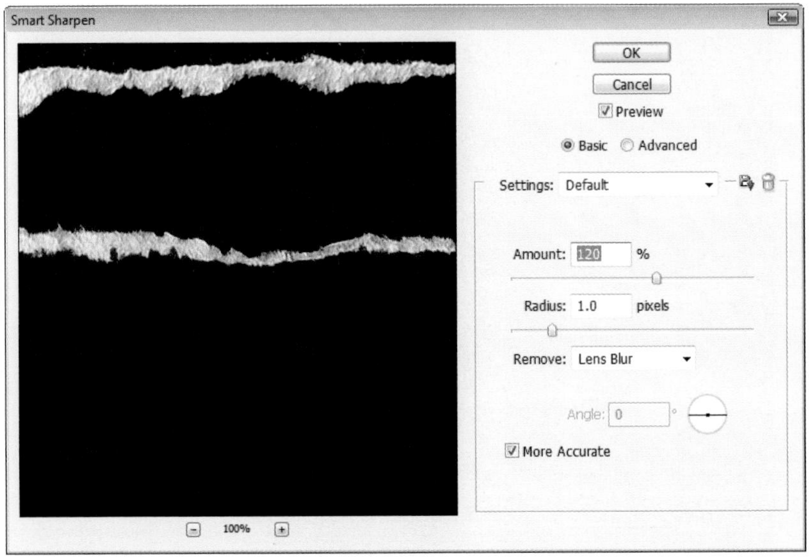

FIGURE 53
Applying a Hue/Saturation adjustment layer

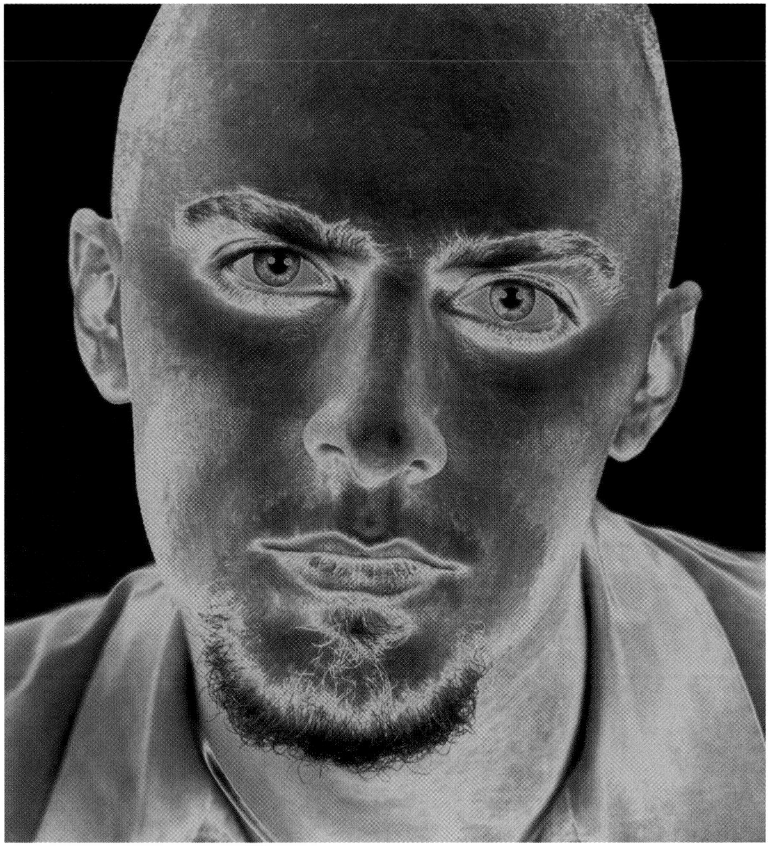

11. Click **Select** on the menu bar, click **Load Selection**, click the **Channel list arrow**, click **Top Rip**, then click **OK**.

    Top Rip is a selection that I made with the Magic Wand Tool by clicking the black areas then inverting the selection. I then spent about 10 minutes tweaking the selection to exclude stray black pixels.

12. Click **Edit** on the menu bar, then click **Copy**.
13. Open AP 9-7.psd, then save it as **Ripped**.
14. Duplicate the Background layer, rename it **Solarize**, then drag it to the top of the Layers palette.
15. Click **Layer** on the menu bar, point to **New Adjustment Layer**, then click **Hue/Saturation**.
16. Type **Blue** in the Name text box, click the **Use Previous Layer to Create Clipping Mask check box**, then click **OK**.
17. Click the **Colorize check box**, drag the **Hue slider** to 200, drag the **Saturation slider** to 35, click **OK**, then compare your artwork to Figure 53.

    On the comedy circuit, if an act is risque or uses foul language, the comic is said to "work blue" or to use "blue material." Sometime, the act itself is called "a blue act." Because this illustration is about an artist whose work is controversial, the Hue/Saturation move is a nice metaphor.

(continued)

18. Click **Edit** on the menu bar, click **Paste**, then position the top rip as shown in Figure 54.

19. Return to the Ripped Original document, load the selection called Bottom Rip, copy it, then paste it in the Ripped document as shown in Figure 55.

20. Merge the two ripped layers, then name the new layer **Rips**.

21. Click the **Magic Wand Tool**, set the Tolerance value to 4, then verify that the Anti-alias check box is not checked and that the Contiguous check box is checked.

22. Click the canvas in the area above the top rip, then [Shift]-click the area below the bottom rip.

(continued)

FIGURE 54
Positioning the top rip

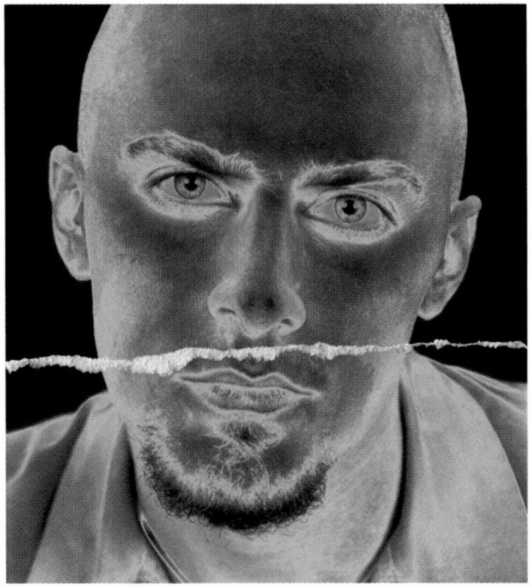

FIGURE 55
Positioning the bottom rip

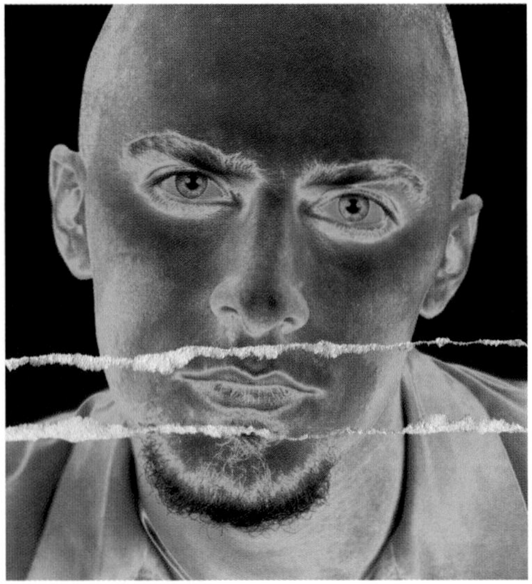

FIGURE 56
Selecting with the Magic Wand Tool

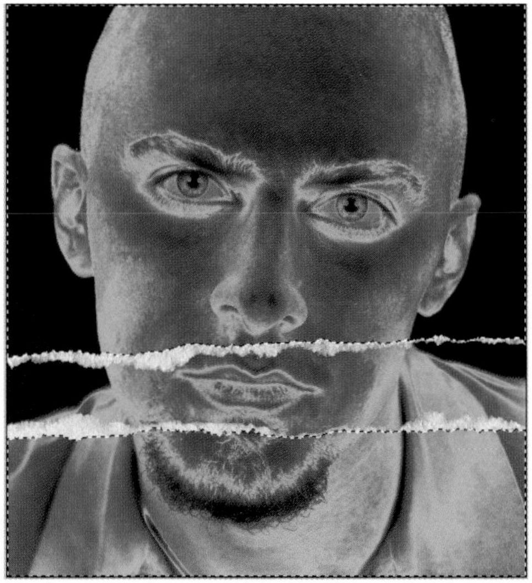

FIGURE 57
Adding a layer mask to the Solarize layer

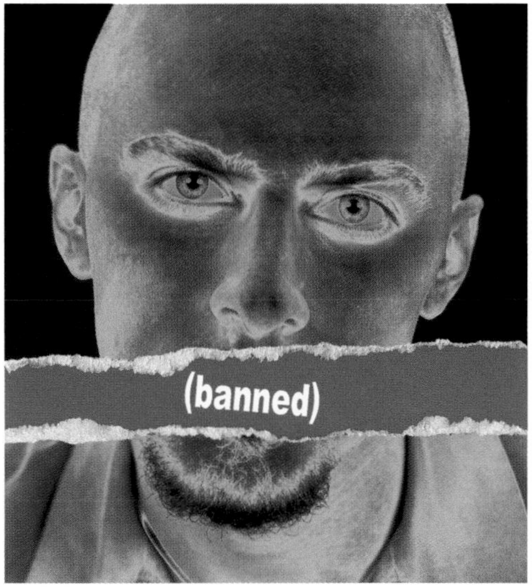

23. Expand the selection by 1 pixel, then compare your selection to Figure 56.

24. Target the **Solarize layer**, click the **Add layer mask button** on the Layers palette, then compare your result to Figure 57.

25. Paint white in the Solarize layer mask to hide any red pixels that are showing through the ripped texture.

26. Target the **Rips layer**, open the Hue/Saturation dialog box, drag the **Saturation slider** to 0, then click **OK**.

    Photos are printed on white paper. We don't want the yellowish cast to suggest that we used a manila folder to create the rip.

27. [Ctrl]-click (Win) or [⌘]-click (Mac) the **Rips Layer thumbnail** to load it as a selection.

(continued)

28. Expand the selection by 1 pixel, then feather the selection by 1 pixel.

29. [Ctrl]-click (Win) or [⌘]-click (Mac) the **Create new layer button** on the Layers palette.

    A new layer is added *below* the Rips layer.

30. Name the new layer **Rips Shadow**, fill the selection with black, then deselect all.

31. Add a layer mask to the Rips Shadow layer, then completely mask out the shadow along the top edge of the top rip and along the bottom edge of the bottom rip.

32. Reduce the opacity of the Rips Shadow layer to 50%, then compare your results to Figure 58.

33. Save your work, close the Ripped document, save the Ripped Original document, then close it as well.

FIGURE 58
Completed artwork

AUTHOR'S *note*

A key factor in this artwork is the texture of the rip. You will often see this effect done with the quickie method of having a hard edge with no texture or with a white-filled ripped edge. The paper texture within the ripped edge is very satisfying and a fine example of how some effects just demand scanned artwork. The Smart Sharpen filter played an important role in exaggerating the ripped paper detail. Remember that a sharpening filter is always more noticeable on your monitor screen than it is when printed. Our use of hard-edged selections (not anti-aliased) was important for maintaining the hard edge of the rip. Of course, you see this where the rip meets the red, but take a moment to notice the effect where the rip meets the image—it's very realistic. Remember to keep a copy of these two rips in your collection of artwork—you can use them over and over again. Finally—and this has nothing to do with rips—think back to when you retouched this artwork. You've done so many extreme modifications to the artwork with the high-contrast solarize effect and the blue hue move, but don't make the mistake of thinking that the retouching was all for naught. Note the clarity in the whites of the eyes, the dark rim around the irises, the white highlights surrounding the eyes, and the dark intensity of the eyebrows and beard. Those are just some of the payoffs from the retouching, and they are important to the final image.

LESSON 6

CREATE MONOTONES and Duotones

What You'll Do

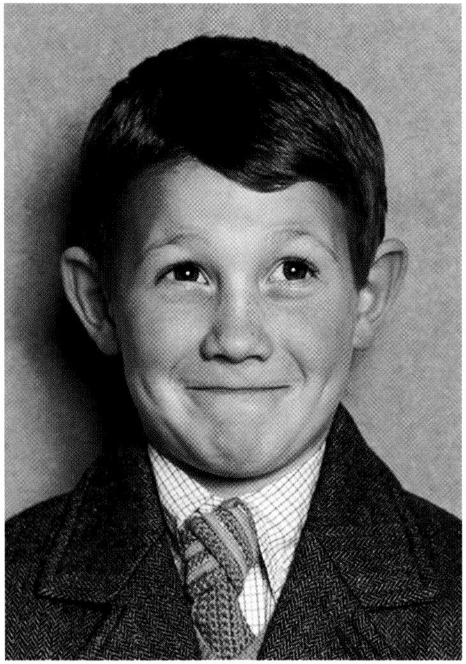

With blending modes and color overlays, the Layers palette offers a number of options for creating effects that look like colorized black-and-white images. As a result, over the last decade or so, many designers have steadily moved away from creating monotones and duotones. It's not so much that they've fallen out of fashion as that everybody's sort of forgotten about them.

Don't let that be you. Monotones, duotones (and tritones) are very practical and important components in a designer's bag of tricks. From a design point of view, if you are laying out a page that has a number of color images, you can use duotones to "push back" or "mute" some images—which allows you to emphasize the full-color images.

When you are working on a two-color job, usually Black and a PMS color, that's when duotones really come into play. In Duotone mode, you can apply the PMS color to the images in the piece, which can be very effective. I can't tell you how many times I see two-color jobs in which the designer uses the PMS color only in the type elements and runs black-and-white images. That's a designer that has forgotten about Duotone mode. One more thing: if you get a chance to do a three-color job (Black and 2 PMS inks), then take some time to experiment with tritones (in Duotone mode). With three colors, you can create some really cool color effects.

FIGURE 59
Duotone Options dialog box

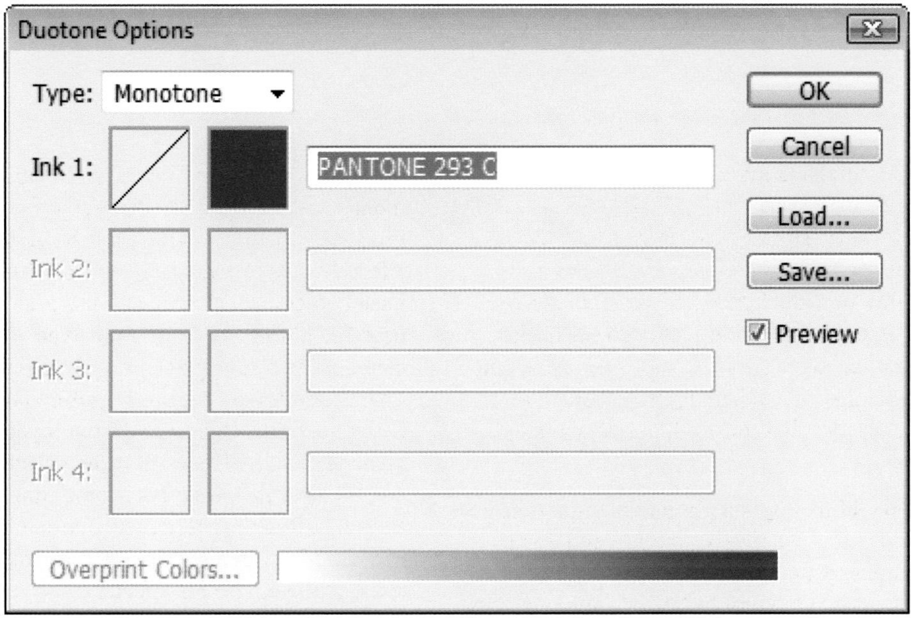

Create a monotone

1. Open AP 9-8.psd, then save it as **Monotone**.

   To access the Monotone, Duotone, or Tritone modes, you must first convert an image to Grayscale mode.
2. Click **Image** on the menu bar, point to **Mode**, then click **Duotone**.
3. Click the **Type list arrow**, then click **Monotone**.
4. Click the **black square** next to Ink 1 in the Duotone dialog box, then click **Color Libraries** in the Color Picker dialog box.
5. Click the **Book list arrow**, then click **PANTONE® solid coated**.
6. Use the triangles to scroll to Pantone 293 C, click **Pantone 293 C**, then click **OK**.

   Your Duotone Options dialog box should resemble Figure 59. Photoshop automatically names the ink with the standard PANTONE naming convention.

(continued)

7. Click **OK**, then compare your canvas to Figure 60.

   A monotone image is the same thing as a grayscale image. Both refer to a single-channel image that will be printed with a single ink, and both have 256 colors available per pixel. The term *monotone* is used to distinguish an image that prints with an ink other than black, usually a PANTONE ink.

8. Save and then close the file.

Create a duotone

1. Open AP 9-9.psd, then save it as **Duotone**.
2. Click **Image** on the menu bar, point to **Mode**, then click **Duotone**.
3. In the Duotone Options dialog box, click the **Type list arrow**, then click **Duotone**.

   PANTONE 293 C is automatically set as the first color if you did the previous lesson before doing this lesson.

4. Click the white square next to Ink 2, then click **Picker** in the Color Libraries dialog box.

(continued)

FIGURE 60
Monotone image

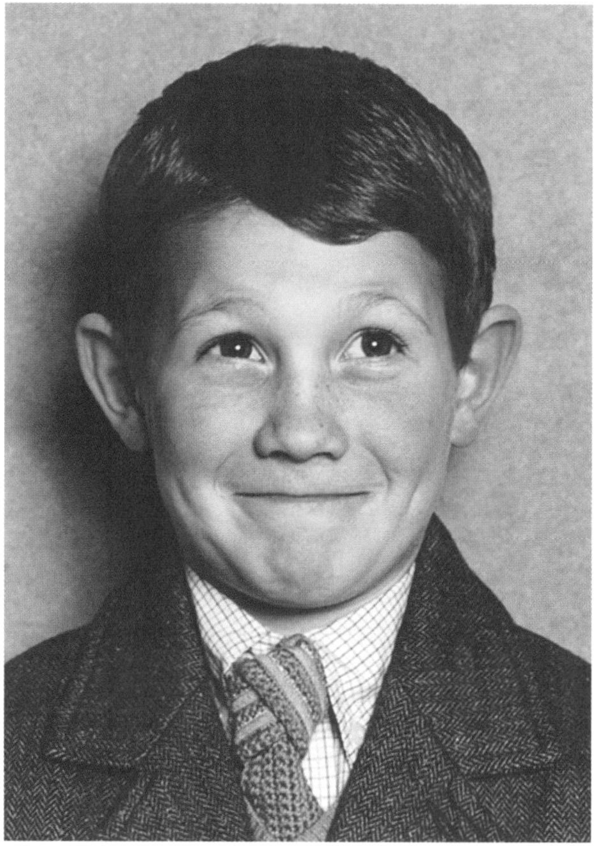

FIGURE 61
Duotone Options dialog box

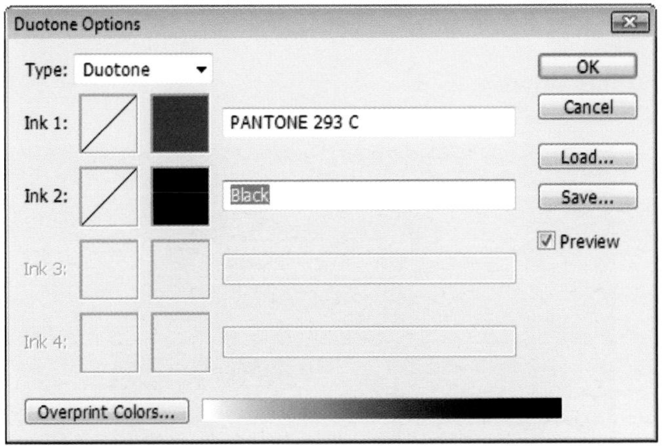

FIGURE 62
Duotone image, Black and PANTONE 293 C

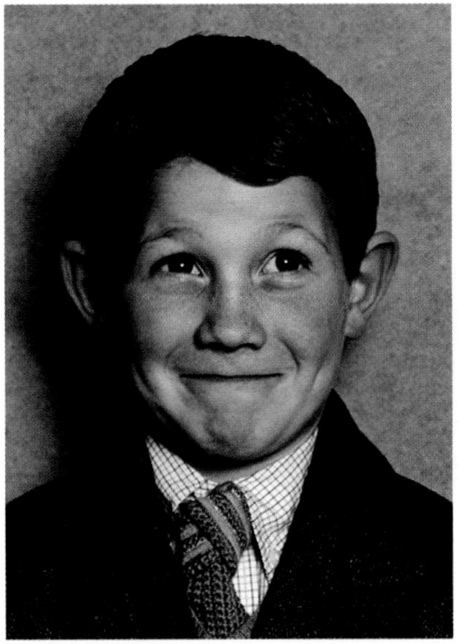

5. Choose Black—0R/0G/0B—then click **OK**.

   Notice that "Black" is automatically supplied next to Ink 2. Your Duotone Options dialog box should resemble Figure 61.

   TIP When typing the name of an ink, it is standard to capitalize the first letter of the four process inks.

6. Click **OK**, then compare your duotone to Figure 62.

   In a layout application such as InDesign, this image would be separated onto two inking "plates"—the Black process ink plate and a plate for PANTONE 293 C. When printed, the image is printed using those two inks only. This is why duotones are often referred to as *two-color images*.

7. Save your work.

Edit a duotone

1. Click **Image** on the menu bar, point to **Mode**, then click **Duotone**.

   To edit a duotone, you must do so in the Duotone Options dialog box.
2. Click the blue PANTONE 293 C color box.
3. Scroll to and click **PANTONE 485 C**, then click **OK**.
4. Click **OK** again, then compare your canvas to Figure 63.

   In addition to changing the colors in a duotone, you can also manipulate the relationships between the two inks and control how each is distributed across the grayscale.
5. Click **Image** on the menu bar, point to **Mode**, then click **Duotone**.
6. Click the diagonal line in the box next to the PANTONE 485 C ink to open the Duotone Curve dialog box.

   At this point, the distribution of the two inks across the grayscale is identical. Wherever you would find a certain value of black ink, you'd also find the same value of PANTONE 485 C ink.

(continued)

FIGURE 63
Duotone, Black and PANTONE 485 C

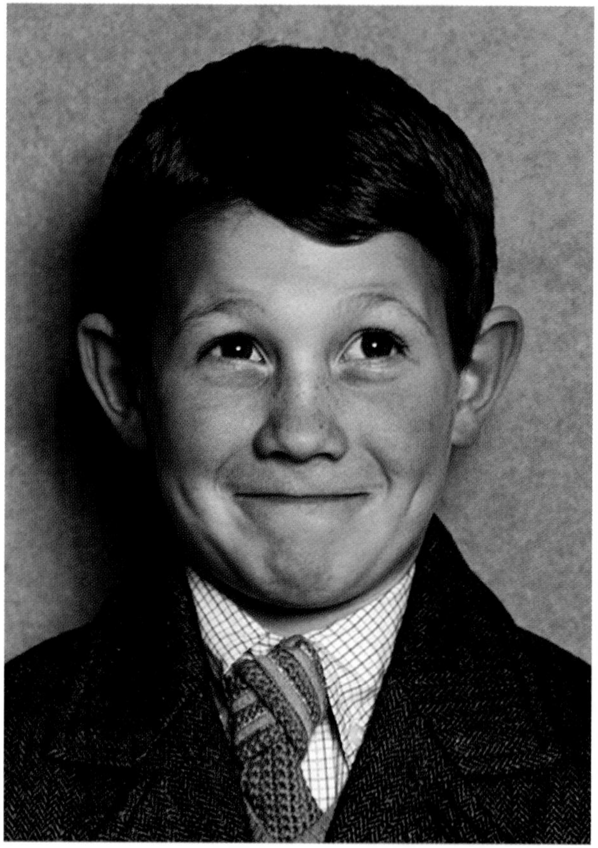

FIGURE 64
Duotone Curve dialog box

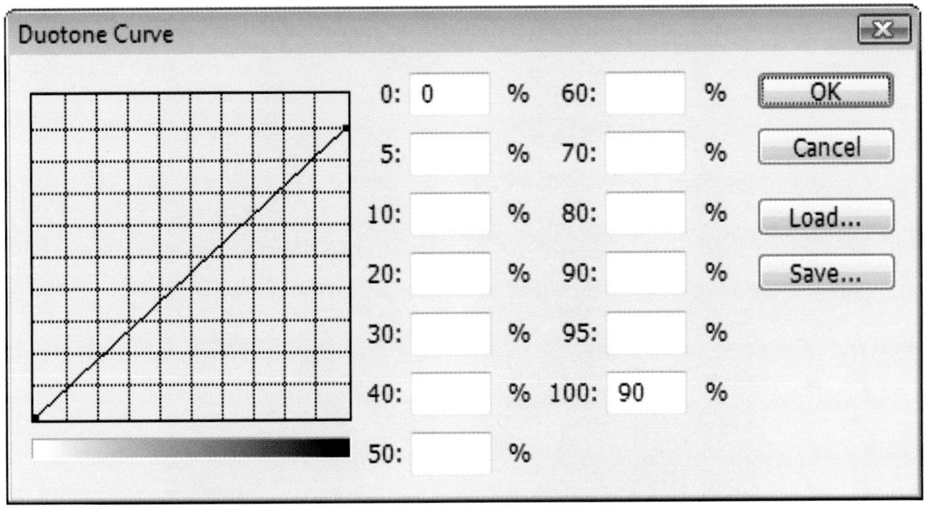

7. Type **90** in the 100% text box, then compare your Duotone Curve dialog box to Figure 64.

   The Duotone Curve dialog box is specified in ink printing percentages. 0% ink is no ink and represents the highlight areas of an image. 100% ink is full ink coverage and represents the shadow areas of an image.

   Note the gradient at the bottom of the grid; it moves from highlight to shadow, left to right. This means that the lower-left corner represents the highlight areas of the image, and the upper-right corner represents the shadows. Lowering the value for any point on the curve means the point prints with less ink.

   For example, because we typed 90 in the 100% text box, this means that a 90% dot of PANTONE 485 C will be used to print in the shadow areas. Because we haven't changed the curve on the Black ink, a 100% dot of black will print in this same area.

(continued)

8. Type **20** in the 50% text box, click **OK**, click **OK** to close the Duotone Options dialog box, then compare your artwork to Figure 65.
9. Display the Info palette, click the **Tracks actual color values button** (eyedropper) in the Info palette, then click **Actual Color**.
10. Sample different areas of the image to see the distribution of PANTONE 485 C throughout the image and in relation to Black.

    At these settings, PANTONE 485 C will print heavily in the shadow areas only. If you sample the shadow areas, such as the boy's hair or coat, you will see a high percentage of PANTONE 485 C (identified as *1* in the Info palette) along with Black (*2*). If you sample light areas, such as the face, you will see that the PANTONE 485 C values are drastically lower than the Black values in the same area.
11. Click **Image** on the menu bar, point to **Mode**, then click **Duotone**.
12. Click the **duotone curve** beside PANTONE 485 C.

(continued)

FIGURE 65
Duotone, Black and PANTONE 485 C

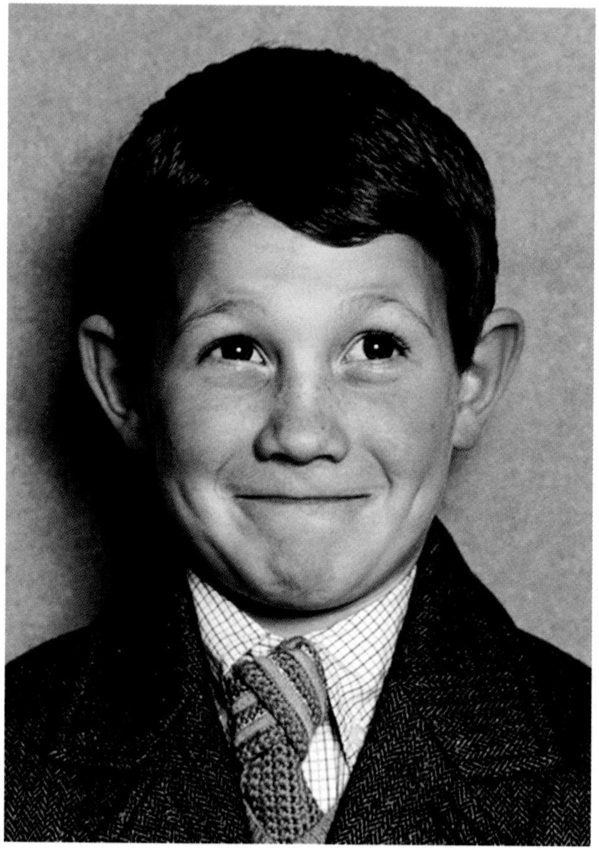

FIGURE 66
Duotone, Black and PANTONE 485 C

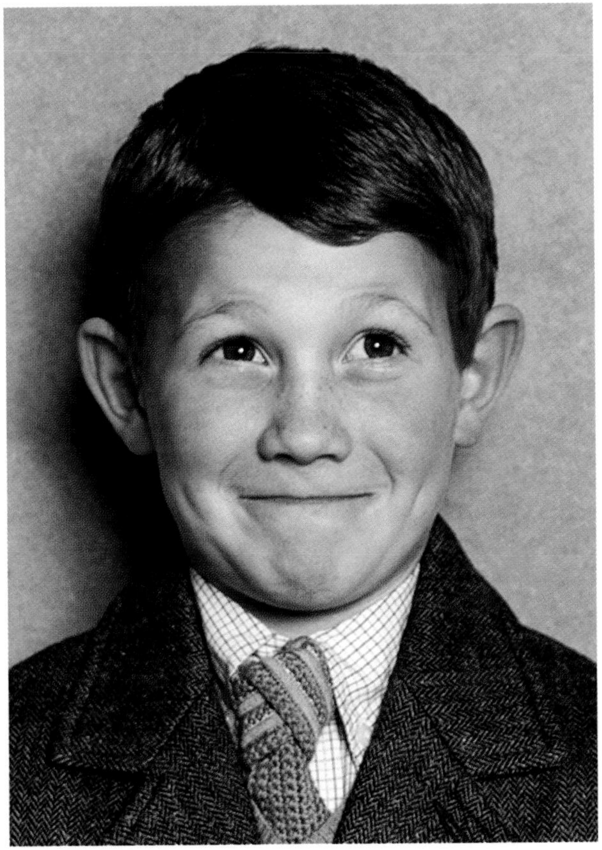

13. Type **50** in the 50% text box, then click **OK**.
14. Click the **duotone curve** beside the Black ink.
15. Type **20** in the 40% text box, type **60** in the 80% text box, then click **OK**.
16. Click **OK** to close the Duotone Options dialog box, then compare your artwork to Figure 66.

    If you sample the image, you will see that the Black ink values in the face are reduced and the PANTONE 485 C inks are increased.
17. Save the file, then close Duotone.

PROJECT BUILDER 1

1. Open AP 9-10.psd, then save it as **Color Mezzotint**.
2. Target the Silo Layer, then apply the Mezzotint filter with fine dots.
3. Zoom in on an area of the silo so that you can see white pixels easily.
4. Click the Magic Wand Tool, set its Tolerance value to 4, verify that neither the Anti-alias nor the Contiguous check boxes are checked, then click a white area to select all the white pixels on the layer.
5. Inverse the selection to select all the black pixels on the layer, copy then paste.
6. Name the new layer **Black Only**, then zoom out to view the entire face.
7. Set the Silo layer's blending mode to Overlay.
8. Show the Gradient layer at the top of the Layers palette, then target it.
9. Clip the Gradient layer into the Black Only layer.
10. With the Gradient layer still targeted, click the Layers palette list arrow then click Merge Down.
11. Zoom in so that you are viewing the face at 100%
12. Change the blending mode to Overlay.
13. Change the blending mode to Soft Light.
14. Change the blending mode to Hard Light.
15. Change the blending mode to Vivid Light.
16. Change the blending mode to Linear Light.
17. Change the blending mode to Pin Light.
18. Change the blending mode to Hard Mix, change the zoom level to 50% to see the entire face then compare your result to Figure 67.

FIGURE 67
Completed Project Builder 1

PROJECT BUILDER 2

1. Open AP 9-11.psd, then save it as **Single Rip**.
   (*Hint*: A single rip effect is very different from the rip effect created in Lesson 4 of this chapter. In that project, the photo had two ripped edges, as though a strip had been torn from the image. With a single rip, the image is ripped along a single edge.)
2. Load the Rip layer as a selection, then save the selection as **Rip Right**.
3. Deselect, then click the Rip Right channel to view it.
4. Make everything to the right of the rip white, so that the entire right half of the channel is completely white.
5. Click the RGB channel, then click the Background layer.
6. Click Image on the menu bar, then click Canvas Size.
7. Change the width measurement to 7.52 inches, click the square to the left of the center square, then click OK.
8. Target the Rip layer, load the Rip Right selection, click Edit on the menu bar, then click Copy Merged.
9. Click Paste, then name the new merged layer **Right Half**.
10. Load the Rip Right selection again, target the Solarize layer, then click the Add layer mask button on the Layers palette.
11. Invert the layer mask.
12. Drag the Rip layer below the Solarize layer, then hide the Rip layer.
13. Click the Move Tool, then drag the artwork on the Right Half layer all the way to the right edge of the canvas.
14. Target the Rip layer, make it visible, then load it as a selection.
15. Contract the selection by 2 pixels.
16. Press and hold [Alt] (Win) or [option] (Mac), then click the Add layer mask button.
    (*Hint*: With this keyboard command, the layer mask is added with the selected pixels being masked.)
17. Click the Brush Tool, then use a hard brush to mask out the remaining right edge of the rip.
18. Click the Pencil Tool, then set the diameter to 3 pixels.
19. Painting in the layer mask, hide additional areas of the white edge and also show more of the white edge so that it is not so even down the left half.
20. Add a Drop Shadow layer style to the Right Half layer, then compare your artwork to Figure 68.
21. Save your work, then close the Single Rip document.

FIGURE 68
Completed Project Builder 2

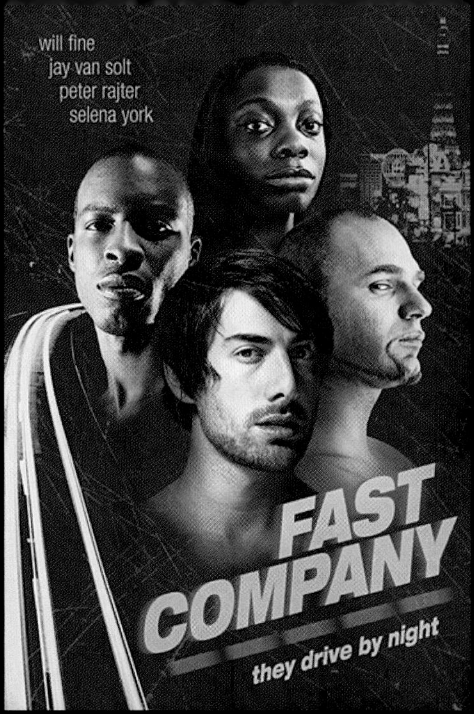
will fine
jay van solt
peter rajter
selena york
FAST
COMPANY
they drive by night

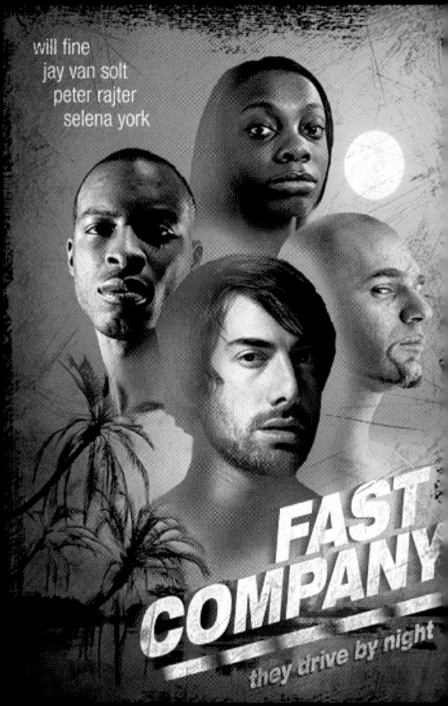
will fine
jay van solt
peter rajter
selena york
FAST
COMPANY
they drive by night

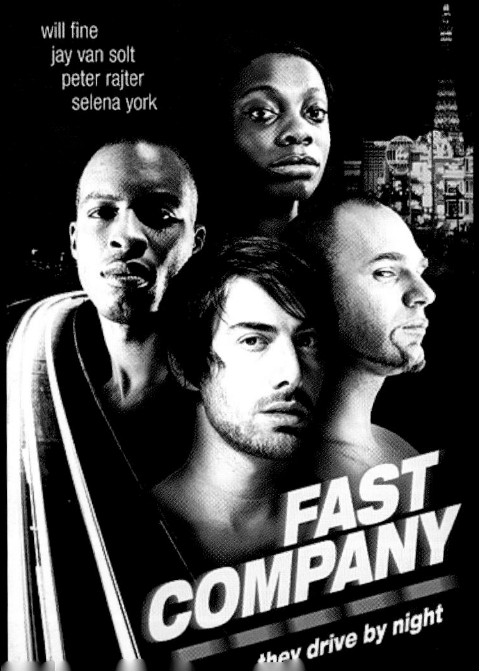
will fine
jay van solt
peter rajter
selena york
FAST
COMPANY
they drive by night

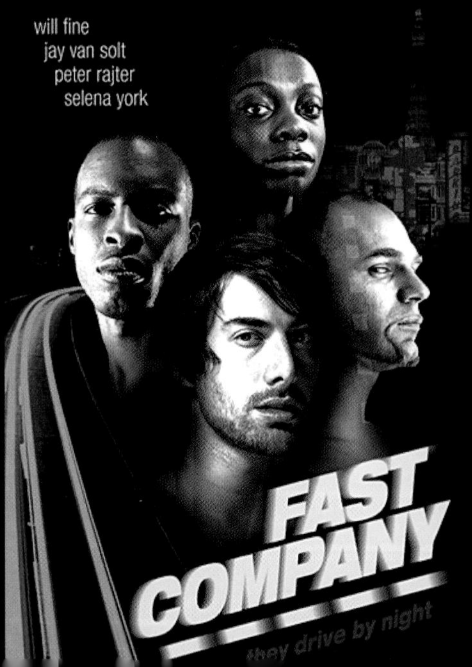
will fine
jay van solt
peter rajter
selena york
FAST
COMPANY
they drive by night

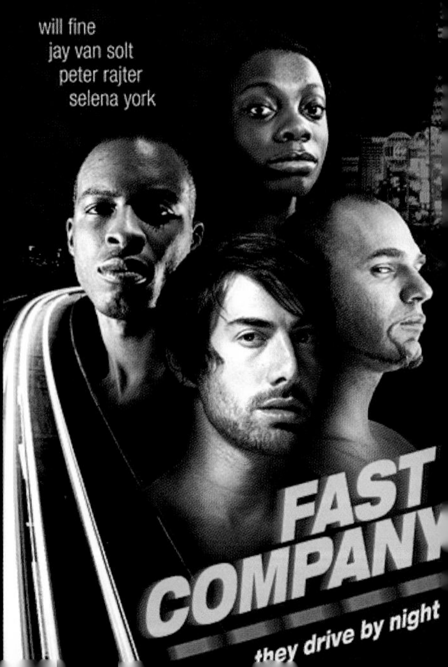
will fine
jay van solt
peter rajter
selena york
FAST
COMPANY
they drive by night

chapter 10

WORKING WITH Blending Modes

1. Color balance a photo montage.
2. Add depth and dimension to a photo montage.
3. Use the Luminosity and Hard Light blending modes.
4. Use blending modes in calculations.
5. Use the Overlay and Screen blending modes.
6. Use the Multiply, Color, and Soft Light blending modes.
7. Combine blending modes with color fills.
8. Work with textures.

LESSON 1

COLOR BALANCE A Photo Montage

What You'll Do

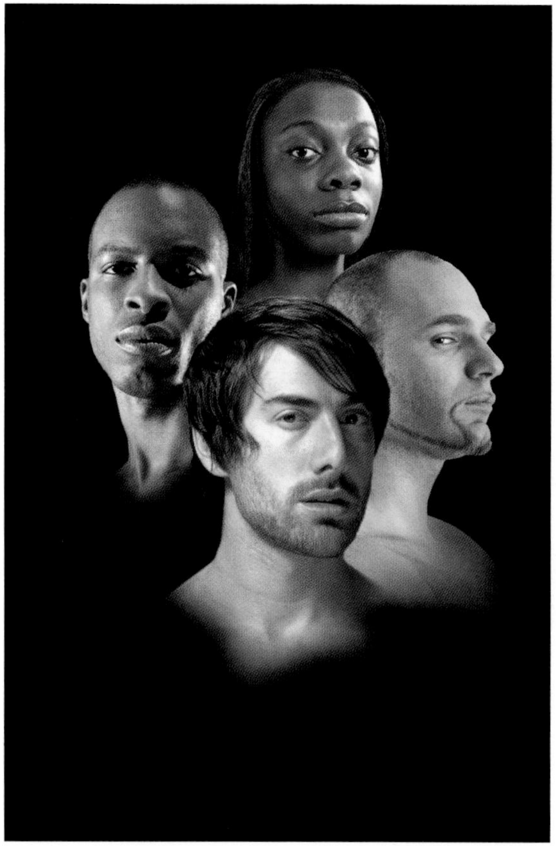

Whenever you are creating a montage with different images, color becomes an important consideration, especially if the images are from different sources and different photographers. Even if all the component images are themselves color balanced and color corrected, when juxtaposed in a montage, variations in tonal range and color cast are evident immediately. If your goal is to create a montage with all the images having consistent color, then you'll need to adjust levels and color balance to achieve that goal.

In this lesson, you'll do just that. You'll be supplied with four images from an online stock photography service. Each is from a different studio and a different photographer. You'll be surprised at how very different they are in terms of color and tone, and you'll be pleasantly surprised at how effective you can be in making that color and tone consistent between the four.

FIGURE 1
Comparing four component images

Compare images in a montage for lighting and color

1. Open the following four files: North.psd, South.psd, East.psd and West.psd.

   The four images will be used together as a composite image. Each was found on an online stock photography Web site, and each was taken by a different photographer. I did some minor retouching on all four (removed blemishes, whitened eyes, and so on), but I did not manipulate levels, curves, or color balance in any way.

2. Close the four images.
3. Open AP 10-1.psd, then save it as **Fast Company Composite**.

   Throughout this chapter, I will refer to each image as North, South, East, and West.

4. Compare your screen to Figure 1.

   When the images are juxtaposed, it becomes clear immediately how different they are on so many visual levels. The goal of this lesson is to manipulate the images so that they can be used together as composite art for a poster. We want the four images to appear consistent, as though the four models were photographed together.

(continued)

5. Identify the direction of the light source on each of the four images.

   In terms of light source, this montage isn't perfect, but it's not so bad either. North and West share the same source, from the right. East is well lit from the right, but you can see an intense highlight coming from the left and shining above where his ear would be if it were visible. This makes East consistent with South, as the light source for South clearly comes from a left angle. Overall, the composite works well with its two light sources, one from the left, the other from the right.

6. Compare the four images in terms of color.

   This is where all four diverge from one another. If you compare North and West, North's flesh shows warm reds, and yellows, whereas West's is cold, dark, and blue. South is cold too, but in a different way. South is bright—but not warm. He looks like he's in a hospital under fluorescent light. And then there's East, whose color is warm and peachy, completely different from the other three.

AUTHOR'S *note*

Light source is a critical component when creating a montage. If the models in a montage were in the same room, then they'd be subject to the same lighting conditions. As a designer, however, when compositing with "found imagery" consider yourself lucky if all the images share a consistent light source. It's not usually the case. This is why most professional studios will schedule a special photo shoot with all the models literally in the same room to be photographed. If you can begin a project with all the photography having the same light source and the same color tones, you are really starting off on the proverbial right foot.

FIGURE 2

Changing the background to black

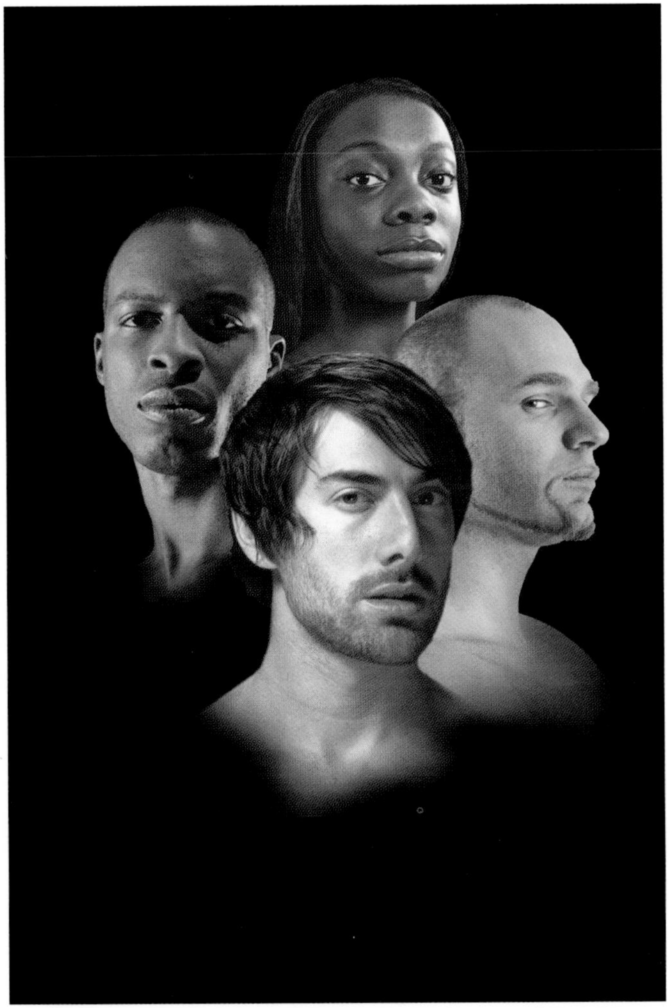

Adjust levels in a montage

1. Press **[Ctrl][I]** (Win) or **[⌘][I]** (Mac) to invert the Background layer so that it is black, then compare your screen to Figure 2.

   Before addressing color, you first need to address the shadow-to-highlight range for each of the component images in a montage. Consistent shadow qualities will be critical. Positioning the images against a black background is very useful to see if the shadows are weak or strong.

2. Show the History palette and click the **Create new snapshot button** on the palette.
3. Assess the images in terms of shadow quality and contrast.

   Of the four, only East appears to have satisfactory contrast. West is so flat that it was noticeable against the white background. The black background reveals that North and South both need a contrast bump and that North has weak shadows. This is especially evident where her hair meets the black background. The shadow behind her neck is weak also.

4. Make the North Curves layer visible, then double-click the **Layer thumbnail** to see the adjustments made in the Curves dialog box.

(continued)

The histogram shows that the shadows in the original were weak. I darkened those shadows, but not so much that I lost the highlight and the detail in her hair. I did not move the highlights much at all, because I'd already assessed that the light on her face was the most intense of the four images. I tweaked it for contrast only.

5. Click **Cancel**.
6. Make the West Curves layer visible, then double-click the **Layer thumbnail** to see the adjustments.

   West required a dramatic adjustment, which was expected given that the original was so flat. Note how little pixel detail was available in the original's upper highlight range, and note how far I moved the black triangle to darken the shadows.
7. Drag the **black triangle** all the way to the left and note the effect on West.

   The image is flat because the shadows in the original were weak. This is especially evident in his forehead and in his hair, which is bluish gray rather than black. Even his forehead is grayish.
8. Click **Cancel**.

(continued)

FIGURE 3
Adjusted levels on West and North

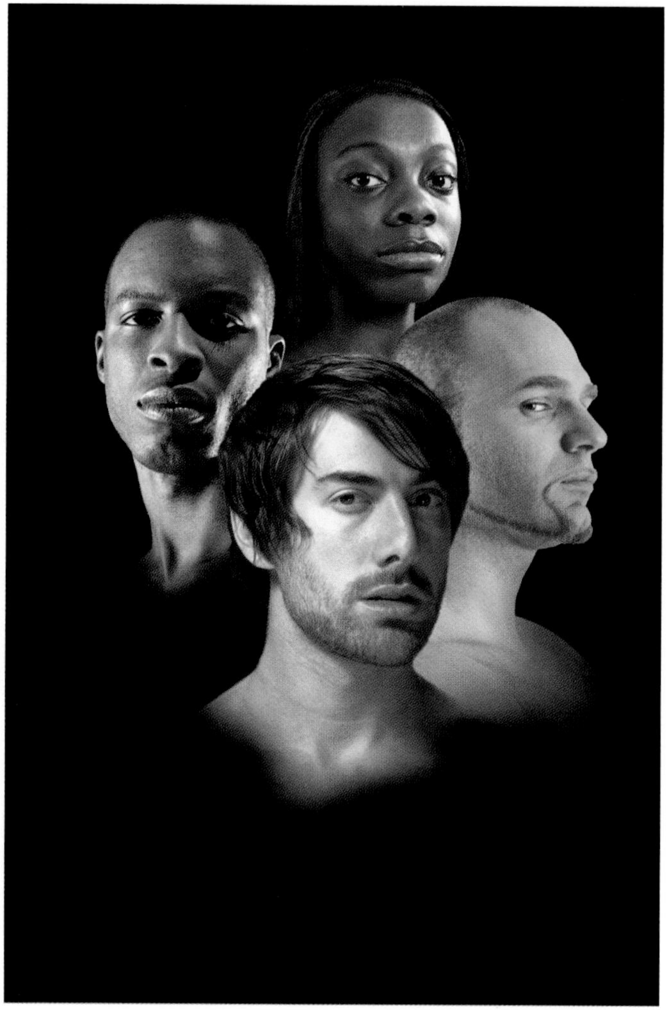

FIGURE 4
Adjusted levels overall

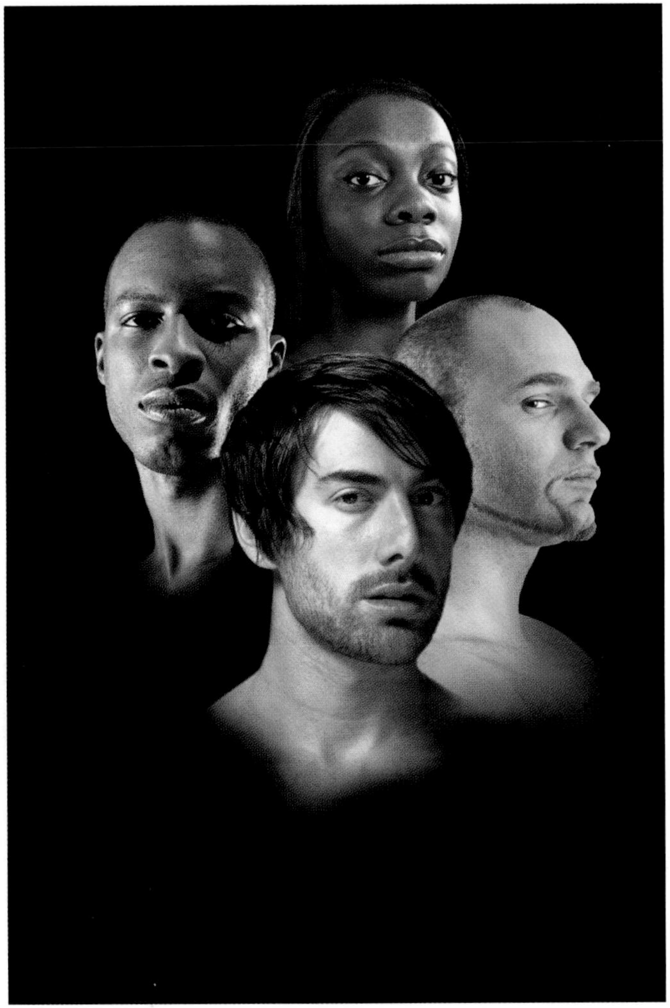

9. Compare your artwork to Figure 3, then toggle the West Curves layer on and off to see the dramatic change.

   Note how much more *shape* his face has with the contrast bump, how much more prominent his cheekbones become, for example. The hair at the top of his head is black, not gray. Note too how the contrast move "warmed up" his flesh tone. Finally, note how flat South now appears compared to West and North.

   TIP Throughout this chapter, when you are instructed to toggle a layer on and off to see a change, be sure to toggle the layer on when you are done viewing.

10. Make the East Curves layer visible.

    As good as East looked at the beginning, the contrast bump removed a dull gray cast overall and brightened him even more.

11. Make the South Curves layer visible, compare your screen to Figure 4, then toggle the South Curves layer on and off to see the change.

    With the adjustment, it becomes apparent that the right side of his face and the shadow on his shoulder were especially weak.

12. Save your work.
13. Click **Snapshot 1** in the History palette to see the canvas before the layer adjustments.
14. Click **Edit** on the menu bar, then click **Undo State Change**.
15. Click the **Create new snapshot button**  on the History palette.

Work with Color Balance adjustment layers

1. Target the **West Curves layer**, press and hold **[Alt]** (Win) or **[option]** (Mac), click the **Create new fill or adjustment layer button** on the Layers palette, then click **Color Balance**.
2. Type **West Color Balance** in the Name text box, click the **Use Previous Layer to Create Clipping Mask check box** to activate it, if necessary, then click **OK**.

   TIP Use these steps when making color balance adjustment layers for the remainder of this chapter.

   We want to move the color in West so it is more like North—warm and appealing. When adjusting color, "warm" always signifies yellow, magenta, and red, while "cold" signifies blue, cyan, and green.
3. Drag the **top slider** to +15 and note the effect on West.

   Don't rush through these moves. Take time to experiment with the slider—push it to the extremes, see what happens. After you've experimented, be sure to input the specified value.
4. Drag the **middle slider** to –5, drag the **bottom slider** to –20, click **OK**, then compare your result to Figure 5.
5. Using the default layer mask on the West Color Balance layer, mask out the color adjustment so that it doesn't affect his eyes.

   We don't want the whites of his eyes to turn yellow.

(continued)

FIGURE 5
Warming up West

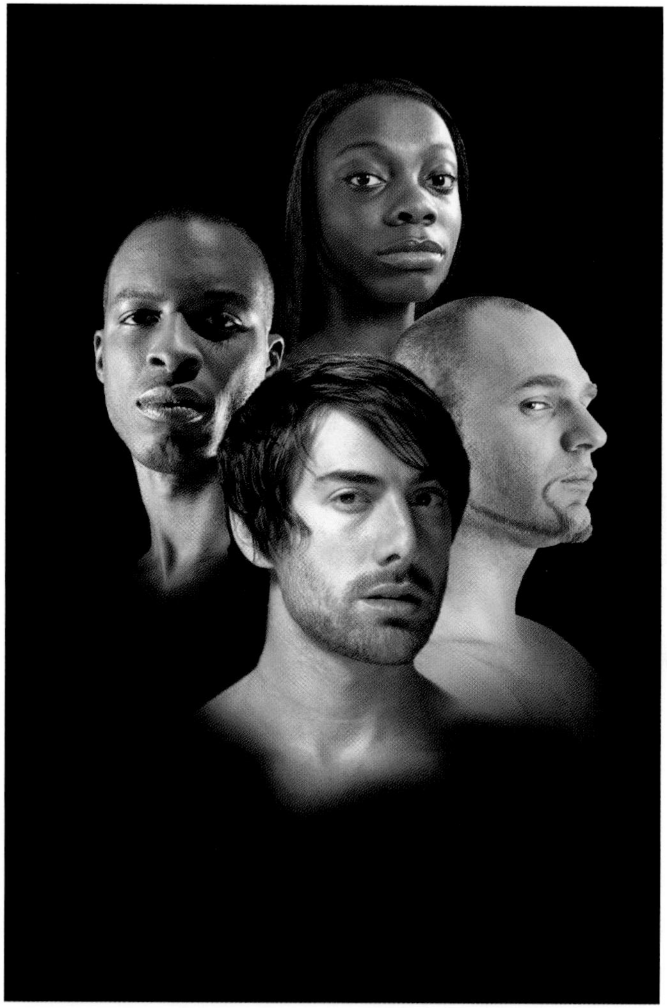

FIGURE 6
Cooling off North

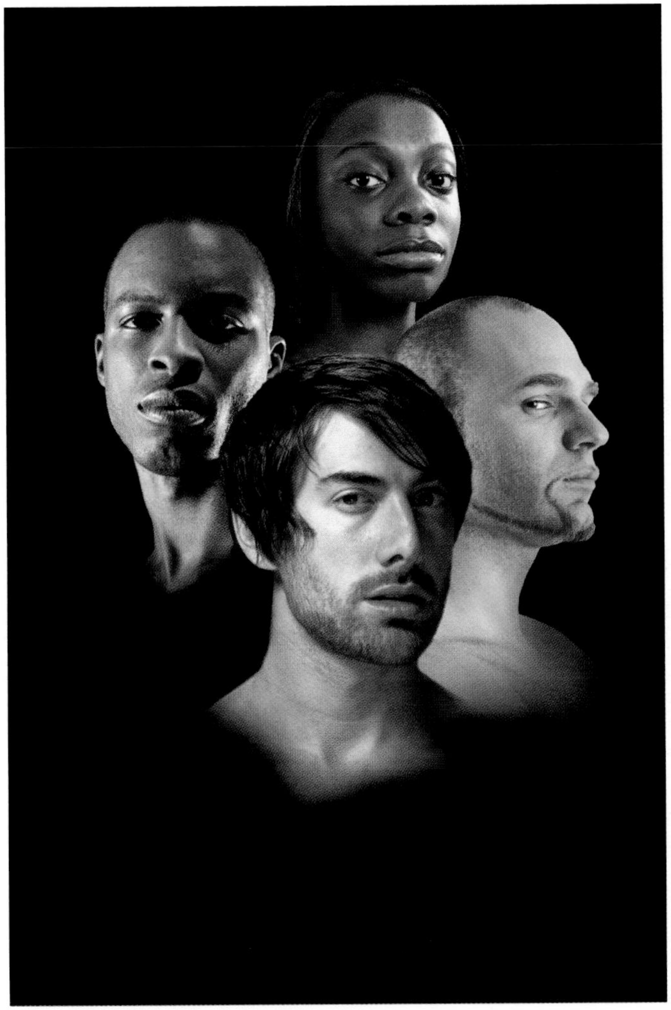

6. Target the **North Curves layer**, then create a color balance adjustment layer named **North Color Balance**.

   North needs to cool off a bit to fall more into line with West and eventually with South, so we want to remove the warm red and yellow tone from the face.

7. Drag the **top slider** to –10, drag the **bottom slider** to +5, click **OK**, then compare your result to Figure 6.

   TIP Feel free to toggle the adjustment layer on and off to see the change.

   With this simple move, note how similar the color is between North and West—it's as though they were photographed together under the same lighting conditions.

8. Target the **South Curves layer**, then add a color balance adjustment layer named **South Color Balance**.

(continued)

9. Drag the **top slider** to +15, then drag the **bottom slider** to –20.

   To move this away from the cold blue, we've made these two dramatic moves—one toward red, the other toward yellow.

10. Click **OK**, then compare your result to Figure 7.

   If you toggle the adjustment layer on and off you can really see how blue—actually, how purple—South was originally.

11. Target the **East Curves layer**.

   East is going to need more than just a color balance adjustment. East's tonal range is entirely different from the other three—where they are moderately lit with a full range from shadow to highlight, East is lit very brightly—so much so that there are no shadows on him. To be more consistent with the others, East's brightness must be reduced.

(continued)

FIGURE 7
Warming up South

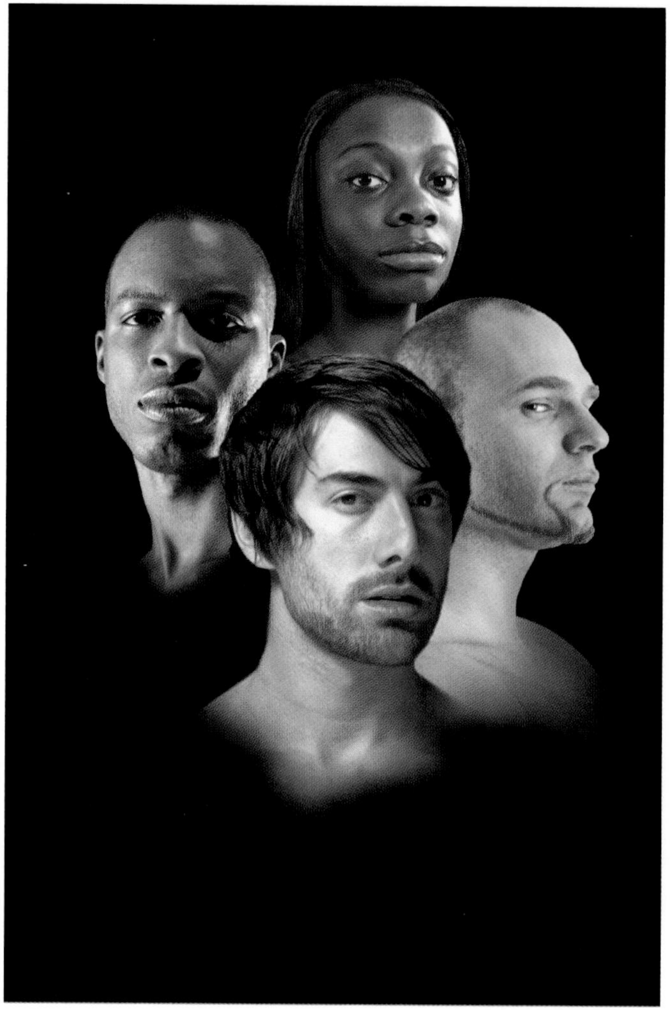

FIGURE 8
Reducing the saturation on East

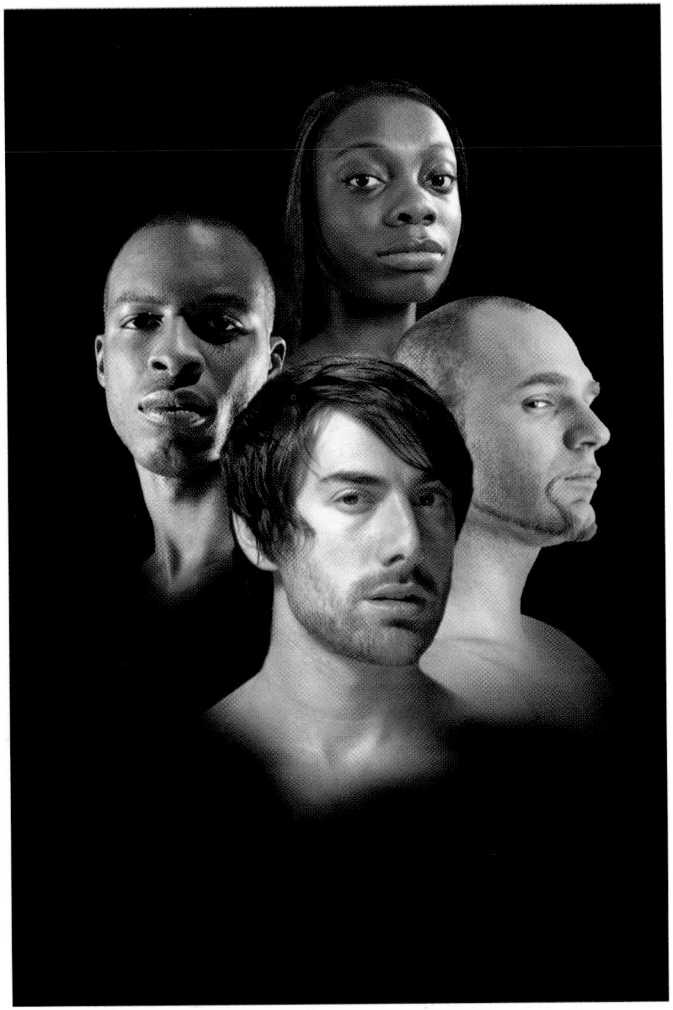

12. Add a new curves adjustment layer named **Darken East**.
13. Add a point to the curve, type **76** in the Input text box, then type **66** in the Output text box.

    The image is darkened. However, we don't want it to go too flat, so we'll return the highlights to where they were originally.
14. Add a second point to the upper half of the curve, type **191** in the Input text box, type **191** in the Output text box, then click **OK**.

    This was a move in the right direction, but the tricky thing about East is that when you darken the artwork, it gets more intensely red. Therefore, this move needed to be slight. However, the intense red is a tip-off for the next move. If an image's color is in the right range but is too intense, that tells you to reduce saturation.
15. Add a new Hue/Saturation adjustment layer.
16. Drag the **Saturation slider** to –15, click **OK**, then compare your result to Figure 8.
17. Add a new color balance adjustment layer named **East Color Balance**.

    We're still fighting the red cast, so we'll use the color balance adjustment to cool him down.

(continued)

18. Drag the **top slider** to –10, drag the **middle slider** to +5, drag the **bottom slider** to +5, then click **OK**.

    This was a good move, but after all this, he's *still* too bright.

19. Add a new curves adjustment layer named **Darken East More.**

20. Click to add a point to the curve, type **128** in the Input text box, type **111** in the Output text box, move the shadow point so that its Input value is 12, click **OK**, then compare your result to Figure 9.

    This is the first time that we've used dual curves adjustment layers, but this is a very common technique. Could we have gone back to adjust the first curves adjustment? Sure. But this type of work is all about building and moving *forward*, and not so much about going back. The first curves adjustment was one of the steps that got us to where we were when we realized we wanted to darken the image again. So we moved forward; we added another curves adjustment layer and made the move.

21. Save your work.

22. Click **Snapshot 2** in the History palette to see the artwork before all of the color adjustments you made.

23. Toggle between Snapshot 2 and the artwork in its most current state.

24. Verify that the artwork is at the state when you saved, then click the **Create new snapshot button** .

FIGURE 9
Reducing East's brightness again

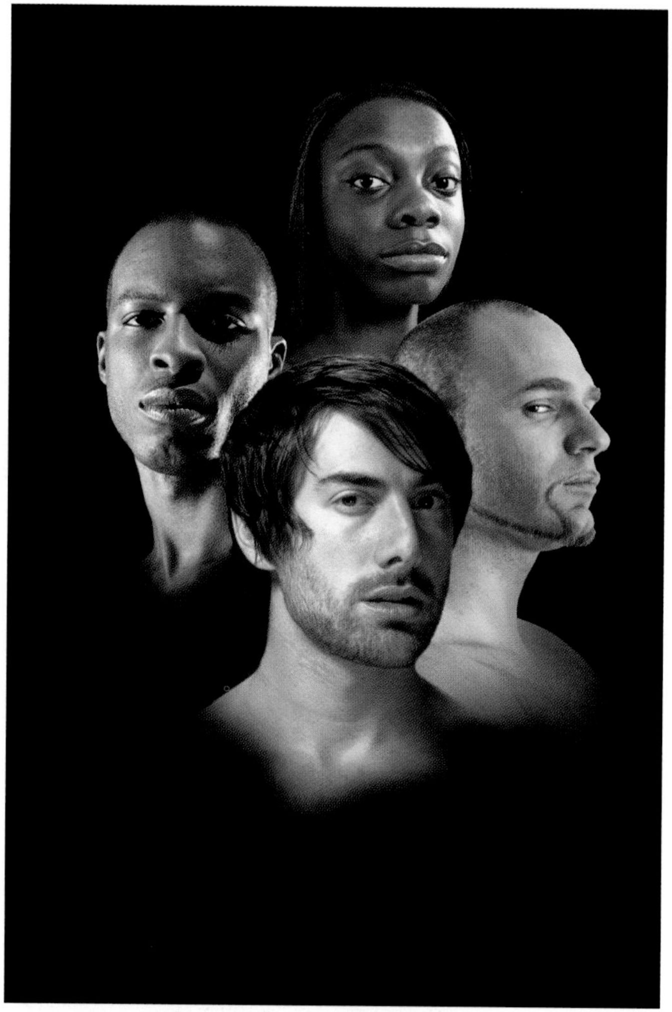

LESSON 2

ADD DEPTH AND DIMENSION to a Photo Montage

What You'll Do

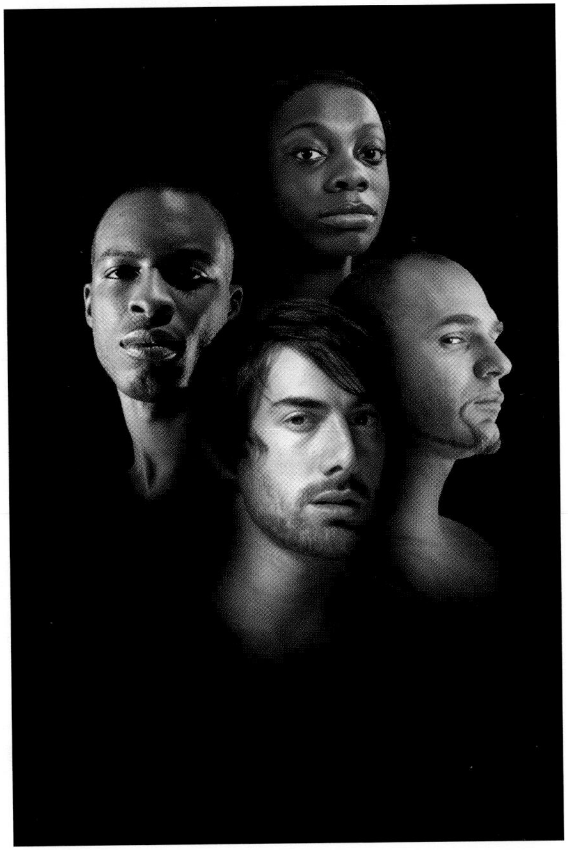

In this lesson, you'll focus on another important challenge: creating the *spatial relationship* between the individual images. In this challenge, you face head on the one word that haunts every photo montage: *flat*. When you layer individual pieces of art, that's what they are: flat. The challenge is to create depth and dimension, to bring some components forward and push others back. In doing so, you create the all-important spatial relationship between the components, you fight the flat, you make the artwork feel *real*. And the big irony is, with photo montage, the techniques you use to make it "real" are dramatic shadows, artistic touches, and wild effects that never have and never will exist in the real world.

"Paint depth between layered artwork"

1. Target the **South layer**, then [Shift]-click its **Layer mask thumbnail** to toggle the layer mask off and on.

   This layer mask defines the relationship between South and the background, but it really has no effect on the relationship between South and East whatsoever.

2. Target the **West layer**, then toggle its layer mask off and on.

   With the layer mask activated, the black background becomes visible between South's shoulder and West's neck. And that black space creates *distance* between South and West. Why? Because your eye interprets that black space as some sort of negative space that exists *between* them.

3. Toggle East's layer mask on and off, and note that the layer mask makes it appear as though East's chest is darkened as it fades into the background.

4. Target the **Background layer**, invert it, then compare your canvas to Figure 10.

   With the black background inverted to white, East's chest is now lightened as it fades into the background. It's important that you understand that East's chest was *neither* darkened nor lightened. It was made semitransparent in its layer mask, and the background was showing through. The illusion that it was darkened was dependent on the black background.

(continued)

FIGURE 10
Artwork against a white background

FIGURE 11
Shadow on East

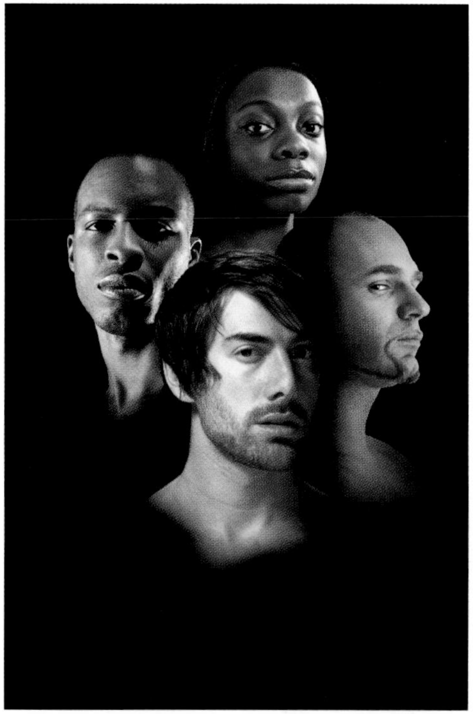

FIGURE 12
Shadow on South

5. Note the relationship between South and West.

   Though the background is now white, the suggestion of space between them continues to exist. White or black, the eye continues to perceive the negative space between them as distance.

6. Undo the invert so that the background is black once again.

7. Note the relationship between South and East.

   As with the relationship between South and West, we must create the suggestion of distance between South and East, and to do that, we must create negative space.

8. Make the East Shadow layer visible, then compare your canvas to Figure 11.

   The darkening of the East artwork creates the distance between South and East. To achieve that darkening, I created an empty layer, painted black in the layer, then clipped the layer into the East layer so that the black paint didn't affect any of the other artwork. I did not darken East by painting in the layer mask. That would not really be darkening the artwork, it would be making it transparent. I wanted it darkened, not transparent.

9. Make the South Shadow layer visible, then compare your artwork to Figure 12.

   Just like with a light source, shadows in a montage must also have a visual logic. The shadow over the left ear of South is from the same direction as the shadow cast over East.

(continued)

10. Make the North Shadow layer visible, then compare your artwork to Figure 13.

    The North Shadow is important to create distance between the two front images and the North artwork. However, if North is shadowed under her chin, then the strong light shining on West's cheek no longer makes sense, because it would also be shining on North's neck.

11. Make the West Shadow layer visible, then compare your artwork to Figure 14.
12. Click **Snapshot 3** to see the artwork before the masking and shadowing.
13. Toggle between Snapshot 3 and the artwork in its current state.
14. Save your work, then close Fast Company Composite.

FIGURE 13
Shadow on North

FIGURE 14
Shadow on West

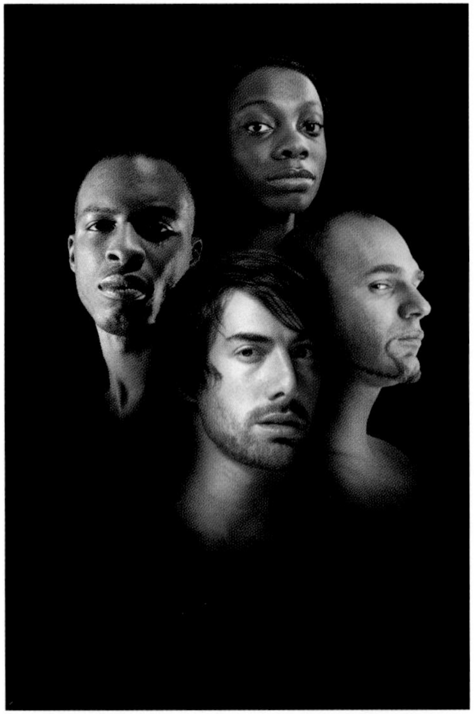

LESSON 3

USE THE LUMINOSITY AND HARD LIGHT Blending Modes

What You'll Do

Hard Light is a popular blending mode, one that you'll use often and to great effect. Whenever you apply the Hard Light mode, the color of artwork on the Hard Light layer is intensified, as though it were shining a "hard light" on the layers beneath. The Hard Light blending mode can be unpredictable because the resulting effect changes dramatically depending on the color of those layers beneath. However, when you use Hard Light against a black background, you can be sure of two things: middle and dark areas will go black, and brighter colors will become more intense. The Luminosity blending mode uses a simpler algorithm to create its effect. When you set a layer to Luminosity, it reads only the brightness values of the layer, then applies those values to the artwork beneath the layer. Simple though it may be, it provides interesting results.

Use the Luminosity blending mode

1. Open AP 10-2.psd, then save it as **Fast Company Overlay**.

   The montage artwork in this file is a copy of the artwork you worked on in Lessons 1 and 2. The only changes that have been made are that North, South, East, and West have been grouped individually, and each has been sharpened slightly with the Unsharp Mask filter.

2. Target the **Background layer**, create a new layer above it, then name the new layer **Clouds**.

   Whenever I'm creating layered artwork, I am leery about working with a flat color background. With this file, I want to create a texture to use with the black background, just to have some sort of detail rather than a flat black.

3. Press **[D]** to access default foreground and background colors, then change your foreground color to **0R/162G/238B**.

4. Switch the foreground and background colors so that white is the foreground color.

5. Click **Filter** on the menu bar, point to **Render**, click **Clouds**, then compare your result to Figure 15.

   The Clouds filter works with any foreground and background color. It uses the foreground to create the clouds and the background to create the "sky" background. Clouds is a random filter—every time you

(continued)

FIGURE 15
Clouds filter

FIGURE 16
Clouds with the Luminosity blending mode against black

apply it, it renders a unique result. Therefore, your clouds will not exactly match Figure 15.

6. Press and hold **[Shift][Alt]** (Win) or **[Shift][option]** (Mac), click **Filter** on the menu bar, point to **Render**, then click **Clouds**.

   This keyboard combination causes the filter to render clouds with higher contrast.

7. Change the blending mode to Luminosity, then compare your canvas to Figure 16.

   To best understand the result—and how the Luminosity blending mode works—think of the black background artwork and the sky artwork as working together to produce this new background image. The Luminosity blending mode takes all the brightness values—and only the brightness values—from the pixels on the Clouds layer and applies those values to the brightness values of the pixels on the black Background layer. To put it another way, the black Background layer is being brightened by the artwork on the Clouds layer.

(continued)

8. Reduce the opacity of the Clouds layer to 8%.

9. Invert the Clouds artwork.

   In its original state, the Clouds layer was bright overall, with the bright blue "sky" and the even brighter clouds. Inverting the layer creates artwork with more contrast. The white clouds are now black, and black will have no effect on the background when set to Luminosity. Therefore, those areas remain black and the Background layer is now brightened only by the "sky" component of the artwork. Thus, the effect has more contrast.

10. Compare your result to Figure 17.

    Not only do the clouds create a more complex background, they also make the layer masks on the models work better. Now, it appears that the models are emerging from clouds of smoke rather than just fading into a flat black background.

(continued)

FIGURE 17
Inverted clouds artwork against black

FIGURE 18

Duplicating a Hard Light effect against a black background

11. Save your work, and keep the Fast Company Overlay document open.

Analyze the Hard Light blending mode

1. Open AP 10-3.psd, then save it as **Hard Light Analysis**.

   When working with blending modes, it's a big plus if you have an intellectual grasp of how they work—an understanding of the mathematical process that makes them create the effect they create. Some modes, like Luminosity and Multiply, are fairly easy to understand. Hard Light is a bit more complex, but we're going to use this quick lesson to give you a better understanding of how Hard Light does what it does.

2. Target the **Bottom Vegas layer**, then change its blending mode to Hard Light.
3. Double-click the **Layer thumbnail** on the Test Levels layer, drag the **black triangle** to 128, click **OK**, then compare your result to Figure 18.

   The result is identical. The move you made in the Levels dialog box yields the same result as applying Hard Light to the same image against a black background.

4. Undo your last step.

(continued)

5. Invert the background, then note the change to the Bottom Vegas artwork now that it is hard lit against the white background.
6. Double-click the **Layer thumbnail** on the Test Levels layer, drag the **white triangle** to 128, click **OK**, then compare your result to Figure 19.

   This move in the Levels dialog box is different from the first. In that step, you moved the black triangle to 128. The move of the white triangle to 128 yields the same result as applying Hard Light to the bottom image against a white background.

(continued)

FIGURE 19
Duplicating a Hard Light effect against a white background

Effect created with a Layers adjustment

Effect created with Hard Light blending mode against a white background

FIGURE 20

Viewing the inability to duplicate a Hard Light effect against a colored background

Effect created with a Layers adjustment unaffected by yellow background

Effect created with Hard Light blending mode changes against a different background

7. Fill the Background layer with yellow, then compare your result to Figure 20.

   Because the layer is set to Normal, the artwork on the Top Vegas layer does not interact with the Background layer, regardless of the color of the background or the moves you make adjusting levels. On the Bottom Vegas layer, the algorithm that defines the Hard Light blending mode causes the artwork to be affected differently by different background colors.

8. Save your work, then close the file.

Apply Hard Light to background images

1. Return to the Fast Company Overlay document.
2. Hide the Clouds layer, then hide the four group layers.
3. Show and target the **Highway layer**, change its blending mode to Hard Light, then compare your result to Figure 21.

   If you toggle the move, note how the midrange tones become black with the Hard Light mode and how only the bright colors are preserved.
4. Activate the Layer mask thumbnail on the Highway layer.
5. Show and target the **Vegas layer**, change its blending mode to Hard Light, activate its layer mask, then compare your results to Figure 22.
6. Reduce the opacity on the Vegas layer to 50%.
7. Save your work.

FIGURE 21
Hard Lighting the Highway art

FIGURE 22
Hard Lighting the Vegas art

LESSON 4

USE BLENDING MODES in Calculations

What You'll Do

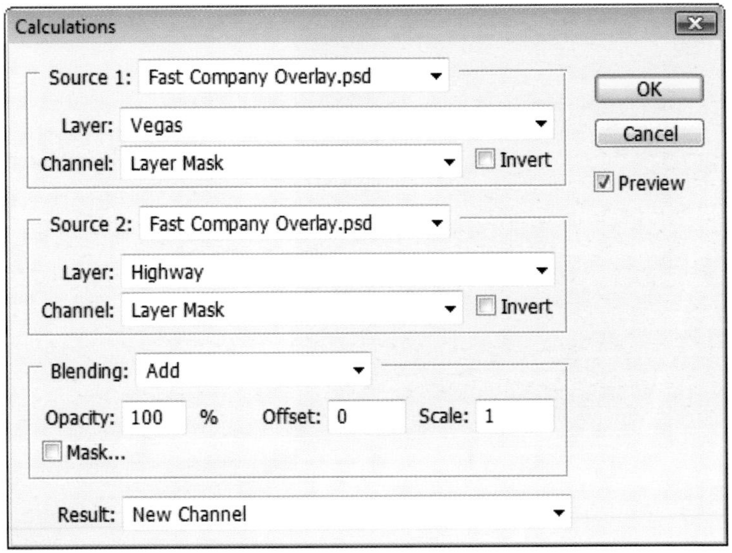

Calculations have long been a feature of Photoshop, and they are the precursor to the blending modes now listed in the Layers palette. In the early days of Photoshop, calculations were *the* advanced feature of the application, the exclusive province of the power user. Like the blending modes, calculations are algorithms that can be applied when blending one or more images to create special effects. Before there was a Layers palette, you used calculations to blend one file with another, with the result being a third file. In that situation, each file was functioning like a layer does in present-day Photoshop, and each calculation was functioning like a blending mode. With the advent of layers and blending modes, calculations have become really obscure. However, they remain a very powerful feature, and learning how to use them can really strengthen your intellectual understanding of layer masks, channels, and blending modes.

Create a layer mask using calculations

1. Make the Clouds layer visible, drag it above the Vegas layer, change its blending mode to Hard Light, then compare your artwork to Figure 23.

   We want to create a layer mask for the Clouds layer so that it doesn't show in the areas occupied by the Highway and Vegas artwork. There are many ways to achieve this, but we're going to use this as an excuse to use the Calculations command.
2. Verify that you can see the Vegas, Highway, and Clouds layers in your Layers palette.
3. Click **Image** on the menu bar, then click **Calculations**.

   TIP Move the Calculations dialog box so that you can see the Layers palette, if necessary.
4. Enter the settings shown in Figure 24.

   Here's how to read the information in this dialog box. It says that the file for Source 1 and Source 2 is the same: Fast Company Overlay.psd. In the Source 1 section, it says that we're going to use the Vegas layer's layer mask as Source 1. For Source 2, we're going to use the Highway layer's layer mask. The Blending section determines the calculation—the blending mode that will be used to apply Source 1 to Source 2. We've specified the Add blending mode, and the result of the calculation will be a new channel in the Fast Company Overlay document.

(continued)

FIGURE 23
Clouds overlapping the Highway and Vegas artwork

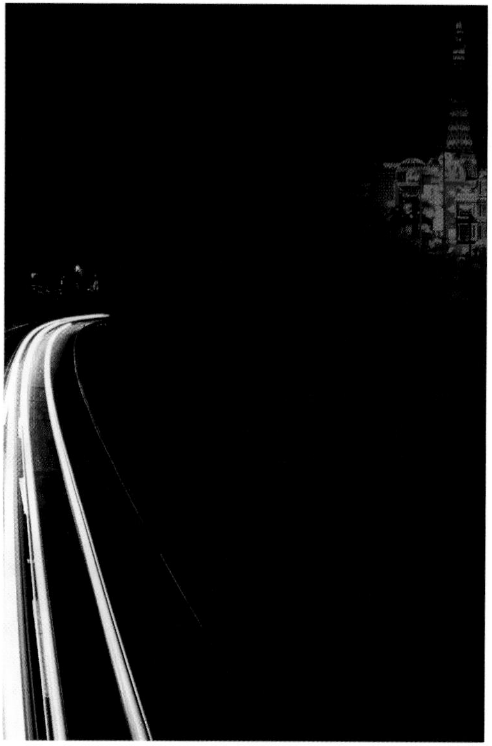

FIGURE 24
Calculations dialog box

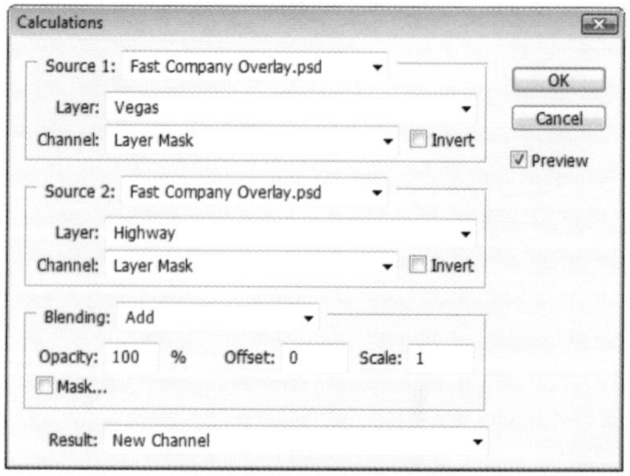

FIGURE 26
Clouds layer with new layer mask

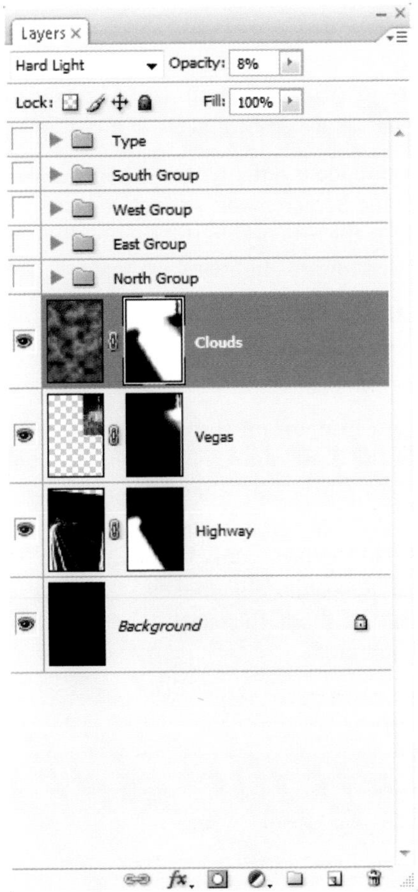

FIGURE 25
New channel resulting from the calculation

5. Click **OK**, open your Channels palette, then compare your canvas to Figure 25.

   TIP Your canvas automatically changes to show the new channel.

   The Add blending mode does exactly that: it takes the two layer mask, then adds the grayscale values of the pixels in the first with those in the second. The result of the calculation is the new channel. Remember that a black pixel's grayscale value is 0, so any lighter pixel that overlaps a black pixel and is added to that pixel is unchanged, because any number + zero isn't changed.

6. Invert the new channel, click the **RGB channel**, then target the **Clouds layer**.
7. **[Ctrl]** (Win) or [⌘] (Mac)-click the **new Alpha 1 channel thumbnail** to load it as a selection.
8. Click the **Add layer mask button** on the Layers palette, compare your Layers palette to Figure 26, then save.

   The Clouds layer now has a layer mask that is black in the areas where it overlaps the Highway and Vegas artwork.

   It's often the case that you'll want to create a layer mask that is the combination of one or more other masks, and this calculation is the quickest method for making it happen.

LESSON 5

USE THE OVERLAY AND SCREEN Blending Modes

What You'll Do

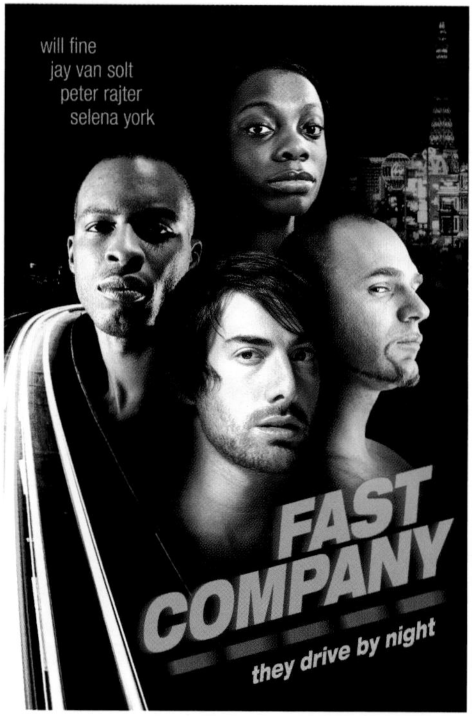

In this chapter, you're going to work with the Overlay mode to overlay images for special effect.

From a practical standpoint, Overlay is important because it makes a neutral gray transparent. Thus, as we've done in earlier lessons, you can add noise to a gray layer, add a lens flare to a gray layer, or add a texture to a gray layer, then make the gray invisible, leaving only the noise, flare, or texture visible against the layers beneath.

Overlay is just as important and useful from the artistic perspective. When you overlay color over an image or when you overlay a copy of an image over itself, the Overlay mode is an intensifier. Shadows get darker, highlights get lighter, and color becomes more intense and vivid. Vivid color—remember that phrase when you think of the Overlay mode.

Screen mode is a lightener—whenever you apply the Screen mode, the active layer lightens the artwork on the canvas. Screen is biased towards light and white.

Highlights play the important role in Screen mode—it's the highlights in the active layer that brighten the artwork.

The most important thing to remember about the Screen mode is that black pixels become transparent when screened. If you had white type on a black layer, then screened the layer, only the white type would be visible. This makes the Screen mode the exact opposite of the Multiply mode.

FIGURE 27
Overlaying the artwork over itself

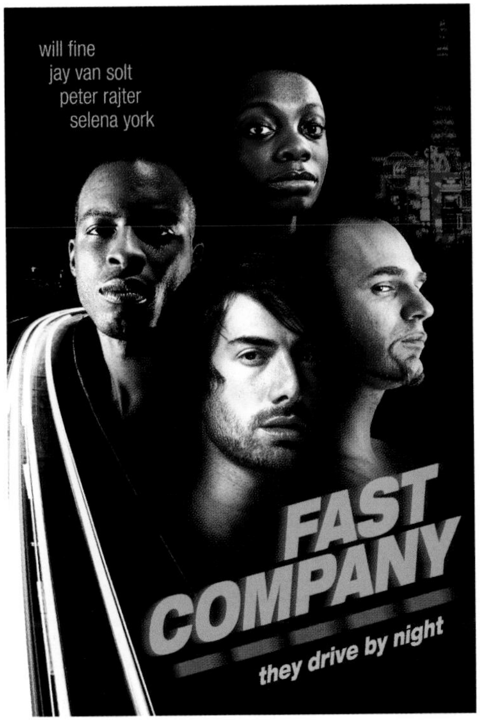

FIGURE 28
Reducing the darkening effect of the Overlay blending mode

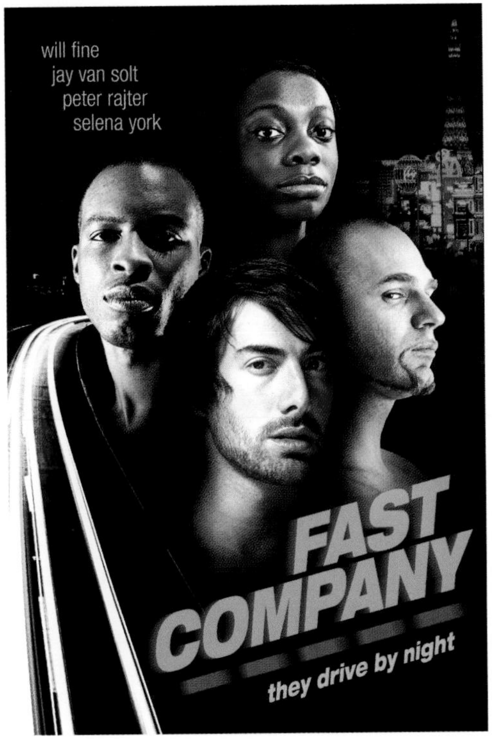

Use the Overlay blending mode with a montage

1. Make the North, South, East, and West groups visible.
2. Make the Type group visible.
3. Target the **South Group**, click the **Create new fill or adjustment layer button**, then click **Hue/Saturation**.
4. In the Hue/Saturation dialog box, click **OK** without making any adjustments.
5. Apply the Overlay blending mode to the Hue/Saturation adjustment layer.

   Note that the Overlay blending mode doesn't affect any of the type elements because they are all above the Hue/Saturation adjustment layer.
6. Compare your artwork to Figure 27.

   The Overlay blending mode has made all the colors more vivid and intense, which works well especially for the models. However, the shadows are now too dark. Rather than mask the Overlay blending mode from the shadows, we can adjust the Overlay blending mode itself.
7. Double-click the **Hue/Saturation adjustment layer thumbnail**, drag the **Lightness slider** to +30, click **OK**, then compare your result to Figure 28.

(continued)

Adjusting the brightness allows you to control the Overlay blending mode. Toggle it on and off and you'll see that the blending mode still makes the colors more vivid, but the effect on the shadows is no longer so overwhelming.

8. Click the **Create new fill or adjustment layer button** , then click **Solid Color.**
9. Type **248, 208**, and **24** in the R, G, and B text boxes, then click **OK**.

   This color is the same yellow used in the title artwork.
10. Name the new layer **Yellow Overlay**, set its blending mode to Overlay, set the opacity to 30%, then compare your result to Figure 29.

Use the Screen blending mode with a montage

1. Hide the Yellow Overlay layer, target the **Hue/Saturation 1 adjustment layer**, click the **Create new fill or adjustment button** , then click **Hue/Saturation**.
2. Making no adjustments, click **OK**, then rename the new adjustment layer **Screen**.
3. Change the Screen adjustment layer's blending mode to Screen.
4. Double-click the **Screen adjustment layer's thumbnail** to open the Hue/Saturation dialog box.

(continued)

FIGURE 29
Overlaying a yellow fill

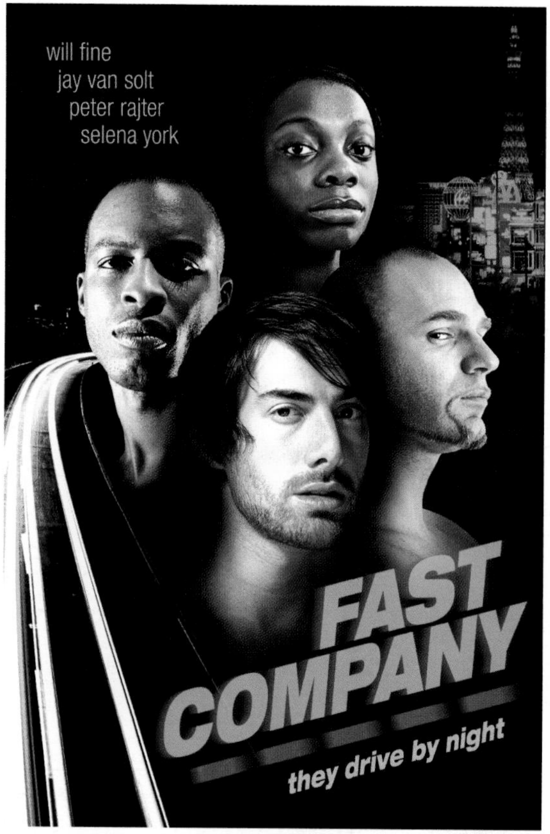

AUTHOR'S *note*

If you toggle the Color Overlay layer on and off, you can see that, even without the yellow overlay, all of the artwork is unified in look and feel, and it all works together as one piece. With that in mind, it's interesting to see how the yellow overlay takes that even further. It pulls it all together, the models *and* the highway *and* the city *and* the title treatment. No one element pulls your focus or stands apart from the rest.

FIGURE 30
Colorizing the screened artwork

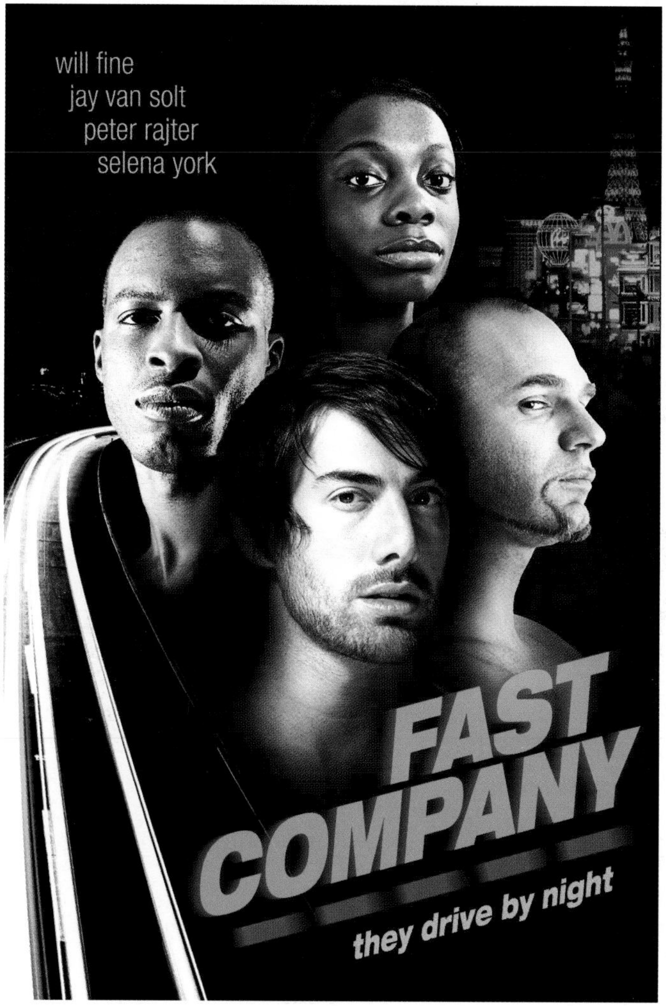

5. Click **Colorize** to activate it, drag the **Hue slider** to 0, drag the **Saturation slider** to 50 and the **Lightness slider** to –50.
6. Click **OK**, then compare your result to Figure 30.
7. Toggle the Screen adjustment layer on and off to see its effect.
8. Save your work, then close Fast Company Overlay.

LESSON 6

USE THE MULTIPLY, COLOR, AND Soft Light Blending Modes

What You'll Do

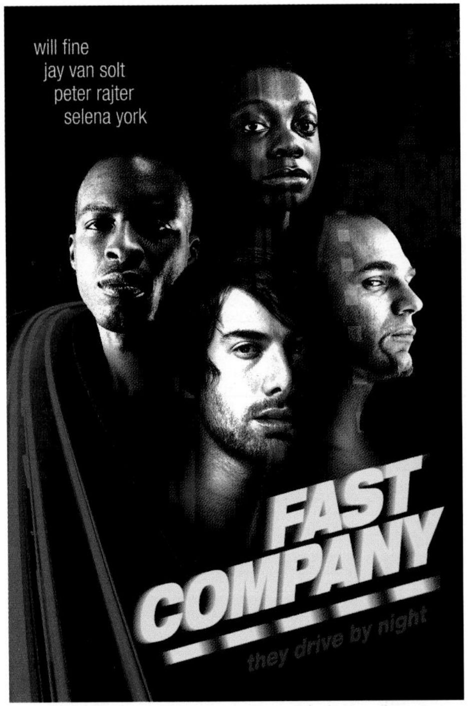

There are two important rules to remember about the Multiply mode: first, anything multiplied with black becomes black; and second, when multiplied, white pixels disappear. Multiply is the opposite of the Screen blending mode. If you had white type on a black layer and you multiplied the layer, the white area of the layer would become completely transparent.

When you multiply color artwork, the artwork retains its color, but it becomes transparent. You can think of multiplying color artwork like working with colored markers. The color is transparent, and it colors the artwork beneath it. Multiplied artwork always darkens the artwork beneath it.

The Color blending mode applies the hue and saturation values of the pixels on the active layer to the pixels on the underlying image. Color mode does not affect the lightness value of underlying pixels; therefore, it doesn't change the shadow-to-highlight range of the underlying artwork.

It only makes sense that the Soft Light mode is a reduced version of the Hard Light mode, right? Strangely enough, that's not the case. Soft Light and Hard Light usually create dramatically different effects, which doesn't make sense, given their names. Actually, Soft Light is much more like the Overlay mode than the Hard Light mode. Like Overlay, Soft Light makes 50% gray pixels disappear and makes brighter areas brighter and darker areas darker. The difference is that Soft Light has a more subtle effect than Overlay.

FIGURE 31
Multiplying the Green channel art

Use the Multiply blending mode

1. Open AP 10-4.psd, then save it as **Fast Company Multiply**.
2. In the Channels palette, duplicate the Green channel, then click the **Green copy channel** to view it.
3. Select all the artwork in the Green copy channel, click **Edit** on the menu bar, then click **Copy**.
4. Click the **RGB thumbnail** in the Channels palette.
5. In the Layers palette, target the **Montage layer group**, paste the copy, then name the new layer **Green Multiply**.
6. Change the blending mode to Multiply.
7. Load the saved selection Montage Only, then click the **Add layer mask button** .
8. Compare your result to Figure 31.
9. Create a new empty layer immediately below the Green Multiply layer, then name it **White Back**.
10. Load the Montage Only selection again, click **Select** on the menu bar, point to **Modify**, then click **Contract**.
11. Type **2**, click **OK**, then fill the selection with white.

    This is a great trick for working with multiplied artwork. If you position a flat fill color behind the artwork, you can manipulate the fill color and the layer to control the color and the opacity of the multiplied effect.

(continued)

12. Deselect, reduce the opacity on the White Back layer to 80%, then hide the Montage layer group.

13. Target the **Green Multiply layer**, then add a levels adjustment layer named **Brighter Whites**.

> **TIP** Be sure to click the Use Previous Layer to Create Clipping Mask check box. We want the Levels move to affect only the montage art.

14. Drag the **black triangle** to 12, drag the **white triangle** to 195, then click **OK**.

15. Click the **Desat adjustment layer**, click the **Create new fill or adjustment layer button**, then click **Solid Color**.

16. Type **17R/26G/93B**, then click **OK**.

17. Change the blending mode to Color, make the Type layer group visible, then compare your result to Figure 32.

The Color blending mode applies the hue and saturation values of the solid fill color to the artwork beneath. The Color blending mode does not affect the artwork's Lightness value.

(continued)

FIGURE 32
Color fill with the Color blending mode

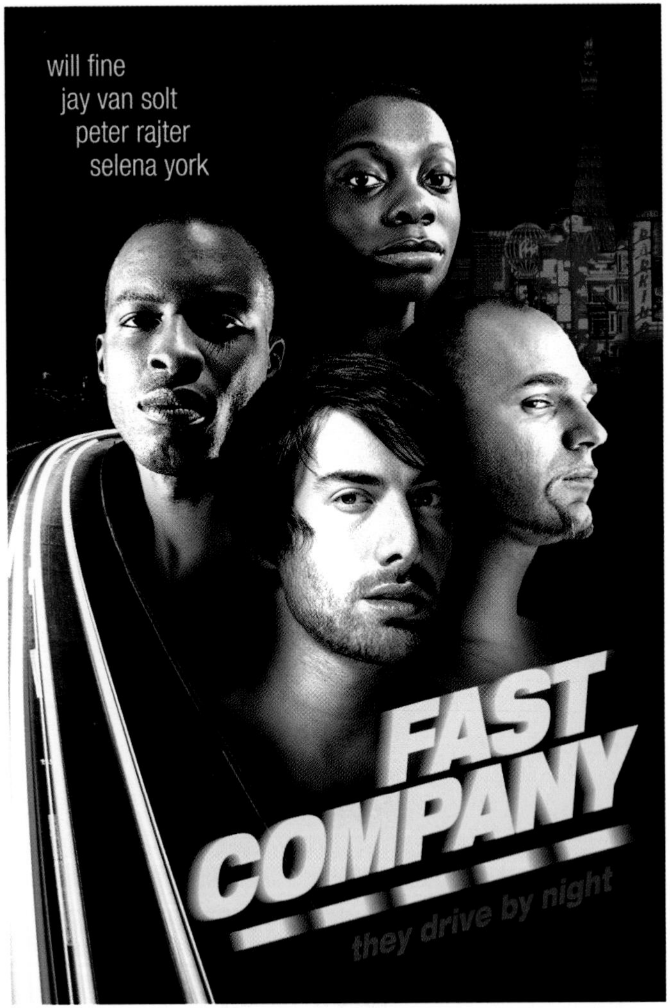

FIGURE 33
Final artwork

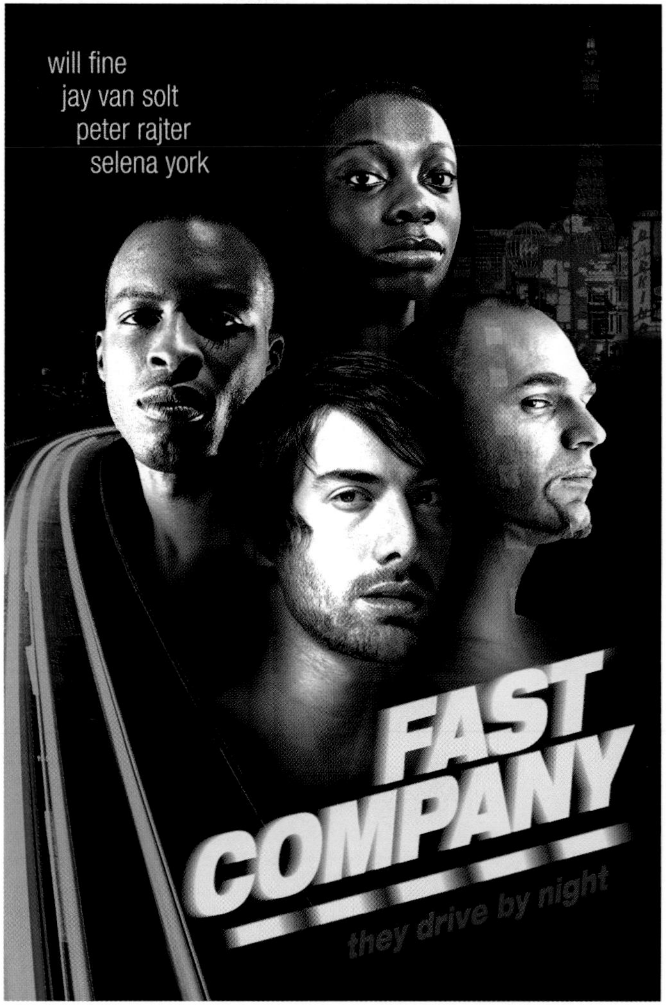

18. Make the Highway Abstract layer visible, reduce its opacity to 70%, then drag it below the Type layer group.
19. Change its blending mode to Soft Light, then activate its layer mask.
20. Expand the Background layer group, reduce the opacity of the Vegas layer to 40%, then reduce the opacity of the Highway layer to 50%.
21. Verify that you are viewing the artwork at 50%.
22. Press **[F]** three times to view the artwork against a black background, then press **[Tab]** to hide all palettes.
23. Compare your results to Figure 33.
24. Zoom in to view the artwork at 100%.
25. Press **[F]** to return to Standard Screen Mode, press **[Tab]** to show your palettes, save your work, then close Fast Company Multiply.

LESSON 7

COMBINE BLENDING MODES with Color Fills

What You'll Do

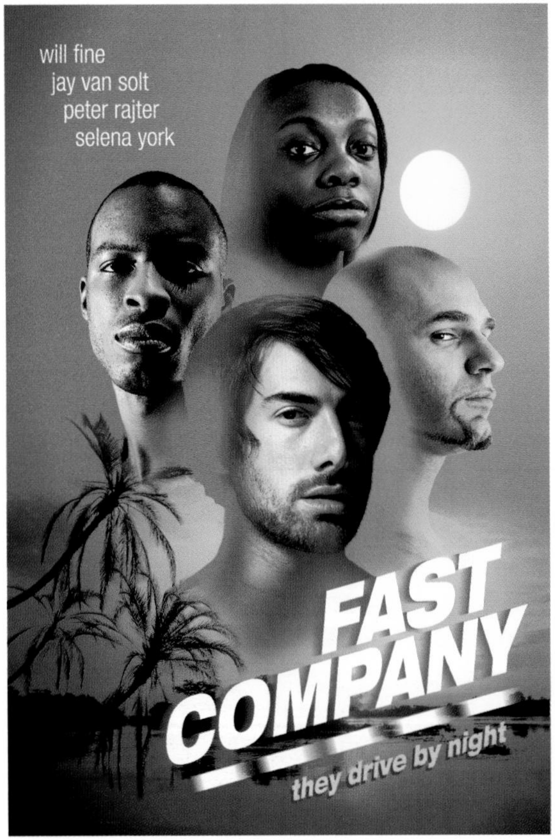

One common way of creating effects with blending modes is to duplicate an image on a layer, then blend the copy over the original. Another common way is to duplicate a black-and-white channel and blend it over RGB artwork. Filling a layer with a solid color and applying a blending mode is a very effective way to unify a piece that contains multiple images, and it's also very effective for creating a mood. For example, if your background image shows a snowy, wintry scene and you want your foreground art to feel cold, overlaying or multiplying a blue fill color can make all the difference in shifting the foreground to integrate with the background.

FIGURE 34
Clipping Sunset into South Shadow

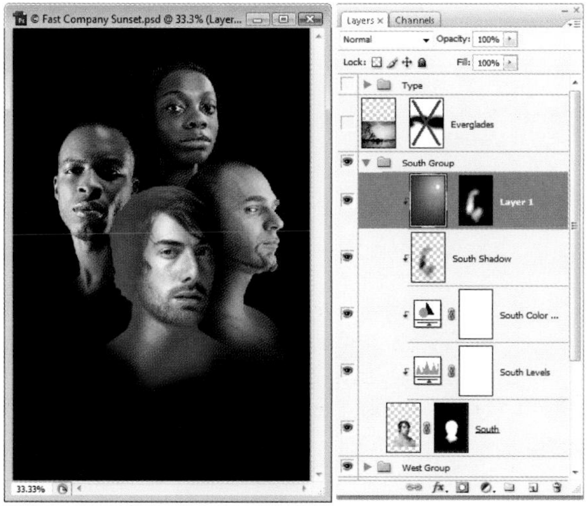

FIGURE 35
Clipping Sunset into all four shadows

Use blending modes with color fills

1. Open AP 10-5.psd, then save it as **Fast Company Sunset**.
2. Target the **Sunset layer**, select all, copy, then hide the Sunset layer.
3. Expand the South layer group.
4. Target the **South Shadow layer**.
5. Press and hold **[Ctrl]** (Win) or [⌘] (Mac), then click its **Layer thumbnail** to load it as a selection.
6. Click **Edit** on the menu bar, then click **Paste Into**.
7. Clip the new layer into the South Shadow layer.
8. Compare your canvas and your Layers palette to Figure 34, then collapse the South layer group.
9. Using the same steps you used in Steps 5, 6, 7, and 8, paste and clip the sunset artwork into the West Shadow, East Shadow, and North Shadow layers so that your canvas resembles Figure 35.

   TIP Be sure that you *target* each shadow layer then load it as a selection before applying the Paste Into command.

(continued)

10. Make the Sunset layer visible, then compare your canvas to Figure 36.
11. In the Channels palette, duplicate the Red channel by dragging it down to the Create a new channel button on the Channels palette, select all, copy the channel artwork, then click the **RGB channel thumbnail**.
12. In the Layers palette, target the **South group,** paste, then name the new layer **Red Channel**.
13. Change the blending mode on the Red Channel layer to Multiply.
14. Create a new empty layer above the Red Channel layer, name it **Overlay**, then fill it with **255R/181G/7B**.
15. Change the blending mode to Overlay.
16. Target the **Red Channel layer**, then create a new Levels adjustment layer.

TIP Be sure to click the Use Previous Layer to Create Clipping Mask check box.

17. Drag the **black triangle** to 53, drag the **white triangle** to 227, then click **OK**.

At this point, the artwork is too hot. Much of that has to do with the way the Overlay layer is interacting with the Red Channel layer.

(continued)

FIGURE 36
Viewing the shadows against the Sunset layer artwork

FIGURE 37
Final artwork

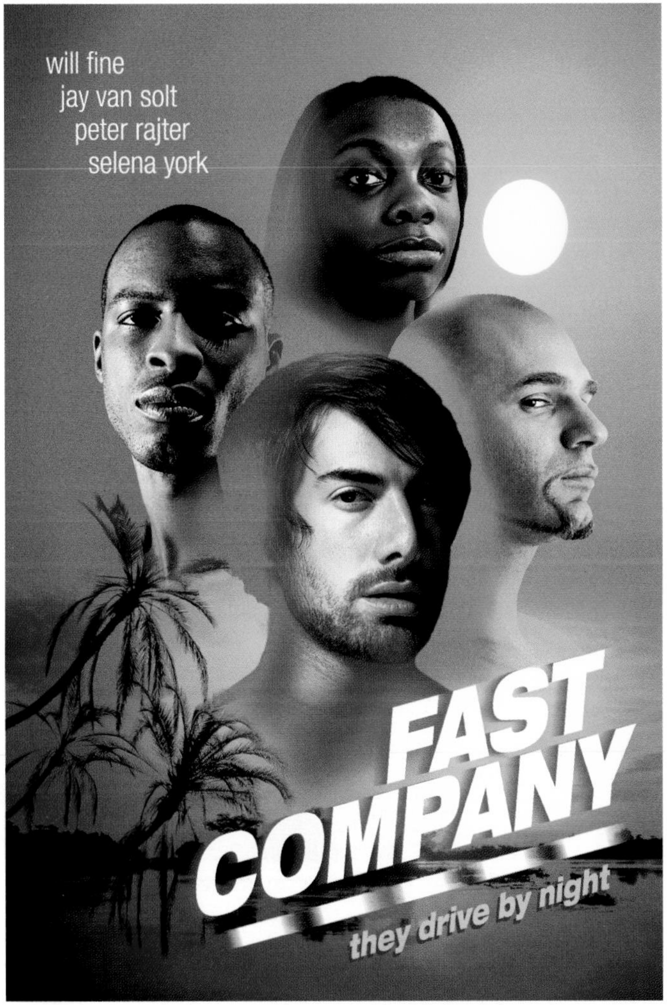

18. Drag the **Overlay layer** below the Red Channel layer.
19. Make the Everglades layer visible, then activate its layer mask.
20. Drag the Everglades layer below the North Group layer.

    The color of the Everglades artwork changes because of the yellow Overlay layer.
21. Change the blending mode of the Everglades layer to Hard Light.
22. Make the Type group layer visible.
23. Verify that you are viewing the artwork at 50%.
24. Press **[F]** three times to view the artwork against a black background, then press **[Tab]** to hide all palettes.
25. Compare your results to Figure 37.
26. Zoom in to view the artwork at 100%.
27. Press **[F]** to return to Standard Screen Mode, then press **[Tab]** to view the palettes.
28. Save your work, then close Fast Company Sunset.

WORK WITH Textures

What You'll Do

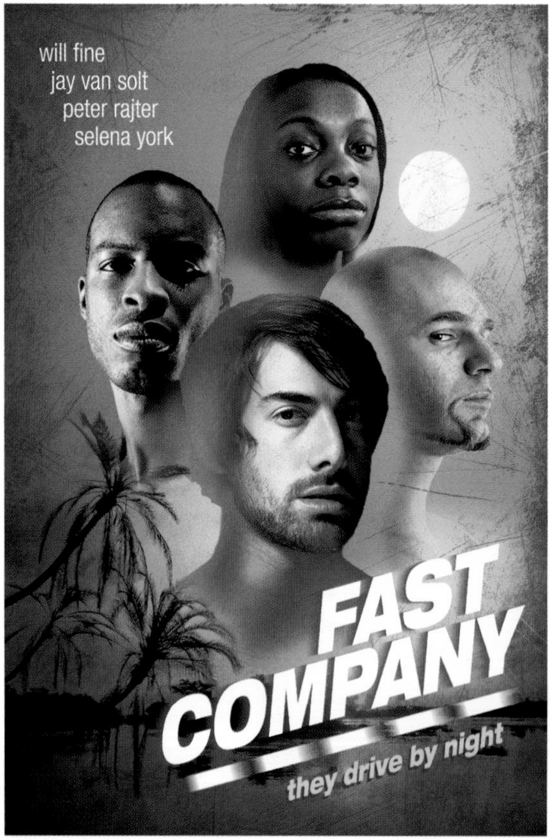

In the quest to unify artwork in a montage, textures can be your secret weapon. When the art allows for it and you can apply a texture—scratches, grain, creases, grit, raindrops, and so on—its remarkable how powerful a force a texture can be in bringing the disparate elements together as a whole, as one complete thought. When designers talk about textures, they're not talking about filters. They're talking about homemade, handmade artwork that is scanned in and incorporated into a piece via a blending mode. You'll find that most designers have their own secret stash of textures, which they often guard like a treasure. In my own work, I've scanned in such unexpected items as a white bath towel, sandpaper, a big piece of tin foil, and a rubber mouse pad. You never know what will work, nor do you know how it will work. The best part is that it's unique. It's your own artwork and a great way of incorporating handmade art into a digital environment.

FIGURE 38
Darkening the raindrops texture file

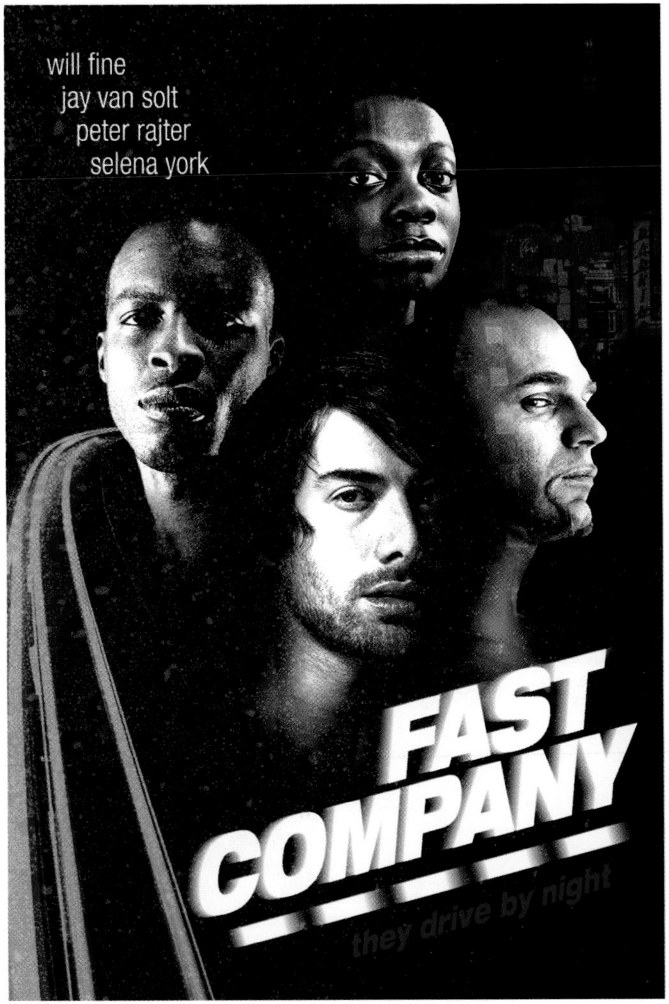

Use raindrops as a texture

1. Open AP 10-6.psd, then save it as **Multiply Raindrops**.
2. Open the file named Raindrops.psd.
3. Select all, copy, then close the file.
4. Target the **Highway Abstract layer**, paste, then name the new layer **Raindrops**.

   TIP If the Paste Profile Mismatch dialog box appears, click the Don't show again check box, then click OK.

5. Change the blending mode to Screen, then reduce the opacity to 30%.

   Overall, the texture file looks like it will create an interesting effect. However, its middle tones are flattening out the artwork. Since we know that with the Screen mode black becomes transparent, darkening the image will make it more transparent.

6. Create a new group folder to hold the Raindrops layer.
7. Name the group folder **Texture**, then change the folder's blending mode to Normal.
8. Create an unclipped Levels adjustment layer above the Raindrops layer, drag the **black triangle** to 128, click **OK**, then compare your result to Figure 38.

   The left side now looks really good. However, the right side no longer looks like raindrops; it looks more like a bunch of white dots.

(continued)

9. Add a layer mask to the Raindrops layer, then fill it with a gradient that goes from white on the left to black on the right.
10. Press **[Ctrl][J]** (Win) or [⌘] **[J]** (Mac) to duplicate the Raindrops layer.
11. Target just the **Raindrops copy layer**, click **Edit** on the menu bar, point to **Transform**, then click **Rotate 180°**.
12. Reduce the opacity of the Raindrops copy layer to 20%.
13. Reduce the opacity of the Texture layer group to 50%.
14. Press **[F]** three times to view the artwork against a black background, then press **[Tab]** to hide all palettes.
15. Compare your results to Figure 39.
16. Zoom in to view the artwork at 100%.
17. Press **[F]** to return to Standard Screen Mode, press **[Tab]**, save your work, then close Multiply Raindrops.

FIGURE 39
Final artwork

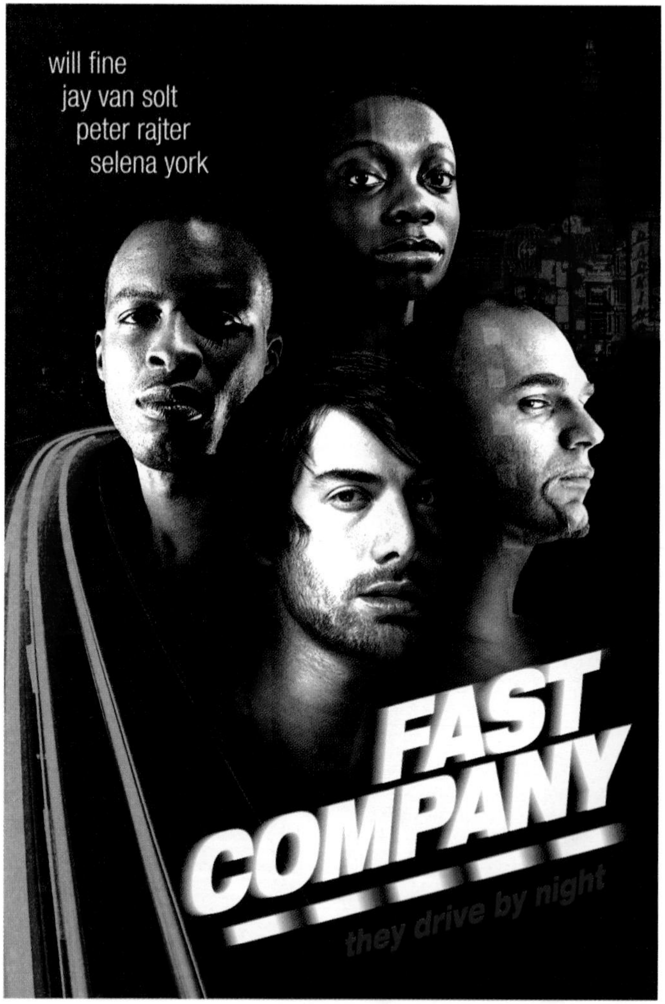

FIGURE 40
Scratch texture multiplied over artwork

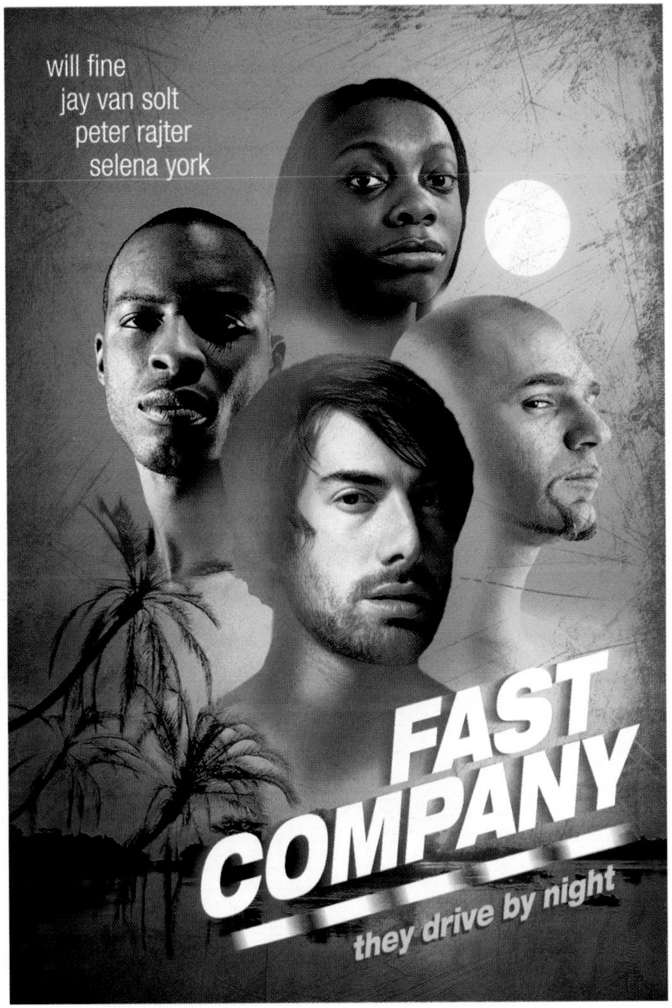

Use scratches as a texture

1. Open AP 10-7.psd, then save it as **Sunset Scratches**.
2. Open Scratches on White.psd.
3. Select all, copy, then close the file.
4. Target the **Overlay group layer**, paste, then name the new layer **Scratches**.
5. Change the blending mode to Multiply, then reduce the opacity to 60%.
6. Verify that you are viewing the artwork at 50%.
7. Press **[F]** two times to view the artwork against a black background, then press **[Tab]** to hide all palettes.
8. Compare your results to Figure 40.
9. Save your work, then close Sunset Scratches.

PROJECT BUILDER 1

1. Open AP 10-8.psd, then save it as **Complex Sepia.**
2. Duplicate the Green channel, select all, copy it, paste it above the Type group, then name it **Green 1**.
3. Open Grit.psd, select all, copy, paste it beneath the Green 1 layer, then name it **Grit**.
4. Reduce the opacity on the Green 1 layer to 30%.
5. Duplicate the Green 1 layer, then rename it **Green 2**.
6. Drag the Green 2 layer above the Color Overlay layer, then increase its opacity to 75%.
7. Change its blending mode to Luminosity.
8. Duplicate the Green 2 layer, then name it **Green 3**.
9. Load the Montage Only channel as a selection, then click the Add layer mask button.
10. Change its blending mode to Soft Light.
11. Make the Creases layer visible, change its blending mode to Screen, reduce its opacity to 50%, then activate its layer mask.
12. Duplicate the Color Overlay layer, then drag the copy to the top of the Layers palette.
13. Reduce its opacity to 10%, then compare your artwork to Figure 41.
14. Save your work, close Grit.psd, then close Complex Sepia.

FIGURE 41
Completed Project Builder 1

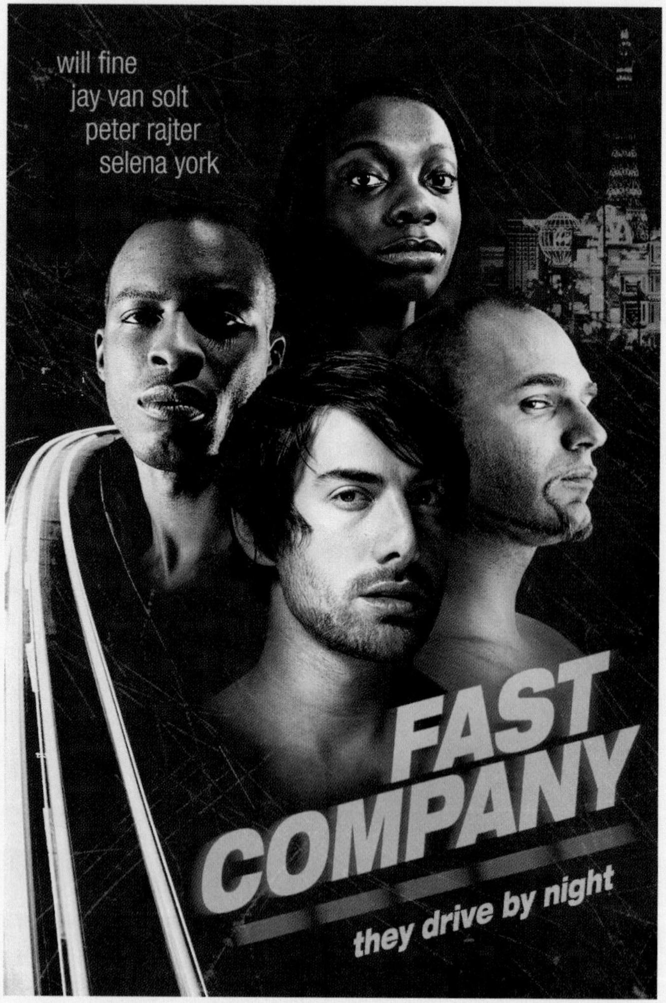

PROJECT BUILDER 2

1. Open AP 10-9.psd, then save it as **Sunset Brushes**.
2. Open Brush Texture.psd.
3. Select all, copy, then close the file.
4. Target the Type group layer, paste, then name the new layer **Brushes**.
5. Add a clipped Levels adjustment layer, drag the black triangle to 46, drag the white triangle to 179, then click OK.
6. Target the Brushes layer, apply the Invert command, then set its blending mode to Multiply.
7. Make the Scratches layer visible.
8. Evaluate how the brushes and scratches textures are interacting with the models' faces, the title treatment, the stars' names, etc.
9. Decide what areas—if any—of the scratches or brushes texture need to be reduced or masked out, then do so.
10. Compare your results to Figure 42.
11. Save your work, then close Sunset Brushes.psd.

FIGURE 42
Completed Project Builder 2

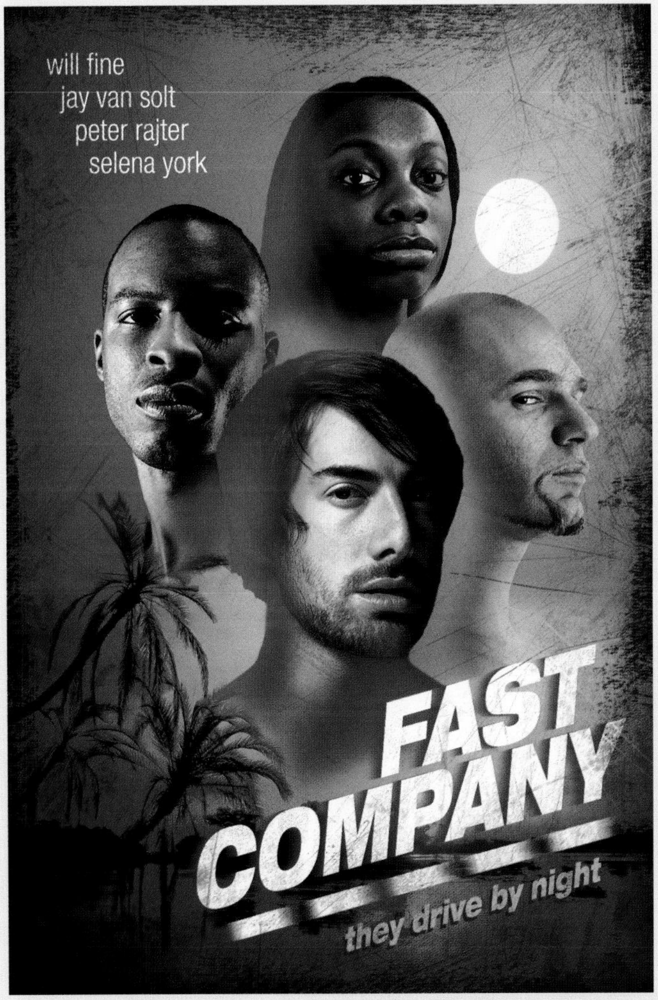

LAURA KENT
ANTHONY BURTON
BLACK KNIGHT
THEATRUM MUNDI PICTURES PRESENTS
MIRIBILE VISU AND THEATRUM MUNDI PRESENT IN ASSOCIATION WITH AD ASTRA AND AD CROMENUM A ALEA IACTA EST PRODUCTION "IPSISSIMA VERBA"
DUX FEMINA FACTI PLACENS UXOR AND DRAMATIS PERSONAE CASTING DIRECTOR INTER PARES MAKE-UP ARTIST SIMPLEX MUNDITISS COSTUME DESIGNER VESTITUS AMPLUS PRODUCTION DESIGNER IGNIS FATUUS
EDITOR TOTIDEM VERBIS DIRECTOR OF PHOTOGRAPHY FIAT LUX MUSIC BY SCHOLA CANTORUM LINE PRODUCER DATA ET ACCEPTA BASED ON THE NOVEL "IPSISSIMA VERBA" BY EDITO PRINCEPS EXECUTIVE PRODUCER FATA VIAM INVENIENT
SCREENPLAY BY OPUS ARTIFICEM PROBAT PRODUCED BY NIHIL QUOD TETIGIT NON ORNAVIT DIRECTED BY LAPSUS CALAM
HOLLYWOOD STUDIO

Read the following information carefully!

Find out from your instructor the location where you will store your files.

- To complete the chapters in this book, you need to use the Data Files provided on the DVD included in the book.
- Your instructor will tell you whether you will be working from the DVD or copying the files to a drive on your computer or a server. Your instructor will also tell you where you will store the files you create and modify.

Copy and organize your Data Files.

- Use the **Data Files List** to organize your files to a USB storage device, a hard drive, or other storage device if you won't be working from the DVD.
- Create a subfolder for each chapter in the location where you are storing your files, and name it according to the chapter title (e.g., Chapter 1).
- For each chapter you are assigned, copy the files listed in the **Data File Supplied** column in that chapter's folder. If you are working from the DVD, you should still store the files you modify or create in each chapter in the chapter folder.

Find and keep track of your Data Files and completed files.

- Use the **Data File Supplied** column to make sure you have the files you need before starting the chapter or exercise indicated in the **Chapter** column.
- Use the **Student Creates File** column to find out the filename you use when saving your new file for the exercise.
- The **Used In** column tells you which lesson or end-of-chapter project uses the file.

Chapter	Data File Supplied	Student Creates File	Used in
1	AP 1-1.psd		L1–L14
	Two Women.psd		L1–L14
	Family.psd		L1–L14
	Beach Girls.psd		L1–L14
	Stretch.psd		L1–L14
	Oar.psd		L1–L14
	Snorkelers.psd		L1–L14
	AP 1-2.psd		Project Builder 1
	Beach Scene.psd		Project Builder 1
	AP 1-3.psd		Project Builder 2
2	AP 2-1.ai		L1
	AP 2-2.psd		L1
	AP 2-3.ai		L2
	AP 2-4.psd		L3–L10
	AP 2-5.psd		Project Builder 1
	AP 2-6.psd		Project Builder 2

Chapter	Data File Supplied	Student Creates File	Used in
3	AP 3-1.psd		L1
	AP 3-2.psd		L2
	AP 3-3.psd		L2
	AP 3-4.psd		L3
	AP 3-5.psd		L4
	AP 3-6.psd		L4
	AP 3-7.psd		L4
	AP 3-8.psd		Project Builder 1
	AP 3-9.psd		Project Builder 2
4	AP 4-1.psd		L1
	AP 4-2.psd		L2
	AP 4-3.psd		L3
	AP 4-4.psd		L4
	AP 4-5.psd		L4
	AP 4-6.psd		L4
	AP 4-7.psd		L4
	AP 4-8.psd		Project Builder 1
	AP 4-9.psd		Project Builder 2
5	Big Knight.psd		L2–L3
	Actress.psd		L2, L6
	Damsel.psd		L2, L6
	King.psd		L2, L5
	AP 5-1.psd		L3–L8
	Stars.psd		L3
	Billing.psd		L3
	Castle.psd		L3
	Moon.psd		L3
	Small Knight.psd		L3–L4
	Sword.psd		L5
		Actress Damsel Merge.psd	L6–L7
	Title.psd		L7
	Smoke.psd		L8

Chapter	Data File Supplied	Student Creates File	Used in
	AP 5-2.psd		Project Builder 1
	AP 5-3.psd		Project Builder 2
6	AP 6-1.psd		L1
	AP 6-2.psd		L2
	20x3.tif		L2
	AP 6-3.psd		L2
	King High-Res.psd		L2
	AP 6-4.psd		L3
	AP 6-5.psd		L3
	AP 6-6.psd		L3
	AP 6-7.psd		L4
	AP 6-8.psd		L5
	Bricks.psd (Automation folder)		L6
	Flowers.psd (Automation folder)		L6
	Marble.psd (Automation folder)		L6
	Rice Paper.psd (Automation folder)		L6
	Water.psd (Automation folder)		L6
	Wood.psd (Automation folder)		L6
	Woodchip Paper.psd (Automation folder)		L6
	AP 6-9.psd		Project Builder 1
	AP 6-10.psd		Project Builder 2
7	AP 7-1.psd		L1
	AP 7-2.ai		L2
	AP 7-3.psd		L2
	AP 7-4.psd		L3
	AP 7-5.ai		L3
	AP 7-6.psd		L3
	AP 7-7.psd		L3
	AP 7-8.psd		L4
	AP 7-9.psd		L5
	AP 7-10.psd		L5

Chapter	Data File Supplied	Student Creates File	Used in
	AP 7-11.psd		L5
	AP 7-12.psd		L5
	AP 7-13.psd		Project Builder 1
	AP 7-14.psd		Project Builder 2
8	AP 8-1.psd		L1–L4
	AP 8-2.psd		L5
	AP 8-3.psd		L6
	AP 8-4.psd		L7
	AP 8-5.psd		Project Builder 1
	AP 8-6.psd		Project Builder 2
9	AP 9-1.psd		L1
	AP 9-2.psd		L2
	AP 9-3.psd		L3
	AP 9-4.psd*		L3
	AP 9-5.psd		L4
	AP 9-6.psd		L5
	AP 9-7.psd		L5
	AP 9-8.psd		L6
	AP 9-9.psd		L6
	AP 9-10.psd		Project Builder 1
	AP 9-11.psd		Project Builder 2
**AP 9-4.psd is opened twice in Lesson 3 and saved as two solution files; Halftone and Halftone Variation.*			
10	East.psd		L1
	West.psd		L1
	North.psd		L1
	South.psd		L1
	AP 10-1.psd		L1–L2
	AP 10-2.psd		L3–L5
	AP 10-3.psd		L3
	AP 10-4.psd		L6

Chapter	Data File Supplied	Student Creates File	Used in
10 (continued)	AP 10-5.psd		L7
	AP 10-6.psd		L8
	Raindrops.psd		L8
	AP 10-7.psd		L8
	Scratches on White.psd		L8
	AP 10-8.psd		Project Builder 1
	Grit.psd		Project Builder 1
	AP 10-9.psd		Project Builder 2
	Brush Texture.psd		Project Builder 2

C

D

INDEX

F

G

L

M

R

Chapter 1
Page 1–2: Image 100/Getty Images
Page 1–12: top left, Comstock Images/Getty Images
Page 1–15: Comstock Images/Getty Images
Page 1–25: Comstock Images/Getty Images
Page 1–25: Digital Vision/Getty Images
Page 1–27: Digital Vision/Getty Images
Page 1–28: Photodisc Red/Getty Images

Chapter 3
Page 3–2: Getty Images
Page 3–22: Stockdisc/Getty Images
Page 3–35: Photodisc/Getty Images

Chapter 4
Page 4–15: Rubberball/Getty Images

Chapter 5
Page 5–6: Burke/Triolo/Getty Images
Page 5–8: Chip Simons/Taxi/Getty Images
Page 5–10: Erik Von Weber/Getty Images
Page 5–12: Erik Von Weber/Stone/Getty Images
Page 5–14: Pete Turner/Imagebank/Getty Images
Page 5–14: Photodisc/Getty Images
Page 5–14: Willie Maldonado/Stone/Getty Images
Page 5–15: Photodisc/Getty Images

Chapter 6
Page 6–24: BaMonica Lau/Getty Images
Page 6–34: Barbara Maurer/Getty Images
Page 6–54: Stockbyte/Getty Images

Chapter 7
Page 7–55: Comstock/Getty Images

Chapter 8
Page 8–2: Ken Weingart/Getty Images
Page 8–22: Steve McAlister/Getty Images

Chapter 9
Page 9–8: Ken Weingart/Getty Images
Page 9–14: Rubberball Productions/Getty Images

Chapter 10
Page 10–2: Eryan McVay/Getty Images
Page 10–2: Eddie Hironaka/Getty Images
Page 10–2: Erin Patrice O'Brien/ Getty Images
Page 10–2: I Vanderharst/Getty Images
Page 10–21: Michael Sharkey/Getty Images
Page 10–24: Neil Emmerson/Getty Images
Page 10–36: Robert Warren/Getty Images
Page 10–36: Shannon Fagan/Getty Images